ALSO BY RICHARD CARWARDINE

Lincoln's Sense of Humor

Lincoln: A Life of Purpose and Power

Evangelicals and Politics in Antebellum America

RIGHTEOUS STRIFE

RIGHTEOUS STRIFE

How Warring Religious Nationalists
Forged Lincoln's Union

RICHARD CARWARDINE

ALFRED A. KNOPF   NEW YORK   2025

THIS IS A BORZOI BOOK
PUBLISHED BY ALFRED A. KNOPF

Copyright © 2025 by Richard Carwardine

Penguin Random House values and supports copyright. Copyright fuels creativity, encourages diverse voices, promotes free speech, and creates a vibrant culture. Thank you for buying an authorized edition of this book and for complying with copyright laws by not reproducing, scanning, or distributing any part of it in any form without permission. You are supporting writers and allowing Penguin Random House to continue to publish books for every reader. Please note that no part of this book may be used or reproduced in any manner for the purpose of training artificial intelligence technologies or systems.

Published in the United States by Alfred A. Knopf, a division of Penguin Random House LLC, New York, and distributed in Canada by Random House of Canada, a division of Penguin Random House Canada Limited, Toronto.

www.aaknopf.com

Knopf, Borzoi Books, and the colophon are registered trademarks of Penguin Random House LLC.

Library of Congress Cataloging-in-Publication Data
Names: Carwardine, Richard, author.
Title: Righteous strife : how warring religious nationalists forged Lincoln's union/ Richard Carwardine.
Description: First edition. | New York : Alfred A. Knopf, 2025. | Includes bibliographical references and index.
Identifiers: LCCN 2023054474 (print) | LCCN 2023054475 (ebook) | ISBN 9781400044573 (hardcover) | ISBN 9780593802625 (ebook)
Subjects: LCSH: United States—History—Civil War, 1861–1865— Religious aspects. | United States—Religion—19th century. | Religion and politics— United States—History—19th century. | Lincoln, Abraham, 1809–1865— Religion. | United States—Politics and government—1861–1865.
Classification: LCC E635 .C37 2025 (print) | LCC E635 (ebook) | DDC 973.7—dc23/eng/20240920
LC record available at https://lccn.loc.gov/2023054474
LC ebook record available at https://lccn.loc.gov/2023054475

Jacket images: (clockwise from upper left, details) Phineas Densmore Gurley, Presbyterian Historical Society, Philadelphia, Pennsylvania; Gilbert Haven, Library of Congress, Washington, D.C.; Clement Vallandigham, Library of Congress, Washington, D.C.; Abraham Lincoln, jjs/Alamy
Jacket design by Jenny Carrow

Manufactured in the United States of America
First Edition

To the History Bees of Corpus

Neutrality in politics is just as impossible as neutrality in religion. There can be but two sides to the present existing troubles of this Union.

—METHODIST MINISTER LEONARD SMITH,
AUGUST 6, 1862

The feeling of antagonism between the two political parties deepened into animosity, . . . and neighbors became enemies. . . . The children of Democrats and Republicans could scarcely sit peaceably together in the same school house, and their parents could scarcely worship together in the same meeting-house.

—*Memoirs of Samuel Rufus Harshman,*
OHIO SCHOOLTEACHER

Contents

INTRODUCTION *xi*

CHAPTER 1 Holding Together: A Righteous Nation *3*

CHAPTER 2 Pulling Apart: A Fracturing Nation *28*

CHAPTER 3 Fast Day, January 1861: Nationalist Riptides *62*

CHAPTER 4 Lincoln, Nationality, and Providence *101*

CHAPTER 5 Lincoln's Fast Day and Antislavery Nationalism, 1861 *124*

CHAPTER 6 Lincoln, Religious Nationalists, and Emancipation, 1862 *154*

CHAPTER 7 Conservative Attack and Lincoln's Rejoinder, 1861–1863 *205*

CHAPTER 8 Lincoln in the Tempest of Religious Nationalisms, 1863–1864 *262*

CHAPTER 9 The Election of 1864 *320*

CHAPTER 10   Emancipation and Providence   *367*

Epilogue   *402*

SELECT GLOSSARY OF TERMS   *413*

ACKNOWLEDGMENTS   *421*

NOTES   *425*

BIBLIOGRAPHY   *515*

INDEX   *561*

INTRODUCTION

On May 17, 1864, the newspaperman Joseph Howard bought a lot of gold. The following morning, before dawn, New York newspapers received for publication a copy of an astounding proclamation from Abraham Lincoln calling for 400,000 volunteers. The text seemed authentic but was in fact Howard's creation, a hoax designed to conjure up an image of a desperate president and so create political panic, depress the stock market, and drive up the price of the gold. Howard's ingenious scheme for self-enrichment failed, though two antiwar newspapers fell for the ruse and printed the bogus document. Lincoln, fearing a wider conspiracy, suppressed the offending publications by a direct order that prompted a nationwide spasm of political acrimony. Instead of paying off his accumulated debts, Howard's reward took the form of three months' military confinement at Fort Lafayette.

This Technicolor political drama is commonly recounted as a lesson in the fiery politics of American Civil War censorship and press freedom. But it merits at least equal attention for what it says about the intimate bond between the wartime Union's religion and politics. Howard decided that his best chance of fooling his victims was to permeate his bogus text with the familiar piety of presidential proclamations. Most of its five paragraphs dwelled on national moral shortcomings, humility before God, the president's personal weakness, and the providential reckoning evident in military disasters. The intended clincher came with Lincoln's purported recommendation of a nationwide day of fasting, humiliation, and prayer, "to approach the Throne of Grace, and meekly to implore forgiveness, wisdom, and guidance."[1]

As Lincoln's mimic, Howard recognized the public effect of the president's formal expressions of religious faith. Like others, he had come to see how, under the weight of wartime leadership, Lincoln's religious voice had become more pronounced and assured. Although not a declared Christian, the president had an unshakable faith that the nation as an instrument of Providence stood at the hinge of American and world history. The prewar experience of fasts and thanksgivings had been mostly limited to the initiative of individual state authorities in New England and its diaspora. Now, during a tumultuous struggle for national existence, the federal government itself took the lead.

In total Lincoln proclaimed three days of fasting and humiliation, and six of thanksgiving, more than any president in the country's history. Each occasion licensed ministers, political leaders, and their audiences to consider how far the nation had fallen short in its historic and current pursuit of righteousness. Responsible citizenship meant reading the Bible as a political record of God's judgments. The Almighty punished some nations for their collective sins and chose others as his agents in the moral progress of humankind. Lincoln's days of religious observance encouraged Americans— meeting together in their churches, sometimes in combined congregations—to reflect on their nation's ethical course and their collective duty as a special people of God. Perhaps because public fasts are today inconceivable as means of bringing public pressure to bear, their wartime significance and flood of nationalist rhetoric have attracted little analysis, though they were freighted with political meaning and stand visible in plain sight. Placed in a wider context, they provide a series of indicative, revelatory landmarks on the course of the competing religious nationalisms in the Civil War Union.

Introduction   xiii

"Religious nationalism" is a plastic concept. It has been used in multiple eras and settings and in diverse, often contradictory ways.[2] I use the term simply to refer to the fusion of religious purpose and nationalist vision, where religious and national identities not only coexist but are mutually reinforcing. Religion in the United States from its founding to the Civil War offered a sacred, even transcendent, framework for defining the nation and prescribing its course. Unlike the sociological concept of American civil religion, which posits a common, unifying, and quasi-religious belief in the nation's political symbols and founding texts, varieties of religious nationalism can foment conflict and political disruption.[3]

This book brings to the fore three key elements of the American Union's religious nationalism of Lincoln's time. It shows, first, that during the decades before the secession crisis of 1860–61 the plural institutions and voices of American religion, despite their unifying potential, helped to drive the political nation apart. That conflict—between the separatist religious nationalists of the pro-slavery South, on one side, and the range of religious nationalist impulses in the North, on the other—exposed the contending value systems inherent in the opposing visions of the republic. It bequeathed a legacy that generated an even more high-stakes political contest within the Civil War Union.

This forms this book's second major theme: the neglected but profound religious clash between antislavery and conservative nationalists in the wartime Union. That chronic conflict powered the beating heart of the war's political narrative, from the shattered optimism of the early months, through the abortive Peninsula campaign, the Emancipation Proclamation, the unprecedented slaughter of 1864, Lincoln's reelection, the congressional passage of the Thirteenth Amendment abolishing slavery, and eventually to Confederate surrender and postwar Reconstruction. In the binary divide between pro-Union nationalists, each side certain of its own righteousness, emancipators slowly gained the advantage, and conservatives railed as they watched their precious world slipping away.

The book's third and primary purpose is to place Abraham Lincoln within the cultural swirl and political milieu of Civil War reli-

xiv   *Introduction*

gion. The crisis reshaped his own religious thinking, just as what he said about faith encouraged others to reflect on the Almighty's purposes. The profound trauma of war gave him a new perception of God, whom he came to see as an active force in history. This "providentialist turn" deepened the antislavery ethic that had animated his political speeches during the 1850s. Then, the beneficiaries of his Republican program to contain the wrong of slavery were to be the white settlers of the free-soil territories; now, a more capacious moral framework led him to embrace emancipation, "a new birth of freedom," and equality of civic opportunity for both black and white.

From the moment he became president-elect in November 1860, Lincoln experienced as never before the turbulence and breadth of the Union's religious opinions. No single category of group petitions and memorials to the president matched those of religious bodies, which arrived by the hundred. The blizzards of incoming correspondence to the Executive Mansion delivered sentiments of religious encouragement and advice, from subtle theologians to eccentric visionaries. The religious significance of the nation's war was never far from his mind, as he intimated to those who won his confidence. His familiarity with the swollen waters of wartime religious faith, and the power of its practice, profoundly shaped his remarkable words on March 4, 1865, delivered at the start of his new presidential term. Just as Edmund Wilson's *To the Finland Station* addresses the currents of revolutionary socialist thought that culminated in Lenin's 1917 arrival in St. Petersburg, so this book could equally be called *To the Second Inaugural Address*.

In the modern United States, the labels "religious nationalist" and "Christian nationalist" are commonly synonymous with the conservative white evangelical Protestants who make up a core strength of the current Republican Party. Most Americans still believe that the country was founded to be a Christian nation, and most white evangelicals think it should be one today. Seeing themselves as the persecuted minority, and taking refuge in biblical and constitutional literalism, many resist connecting white privilege with the historical legacy of slavery. As one respected historian has explained, following the 1960s movement for racial equality evangelicalism "created a safe harbor for white people who wanted to

Introduction   xv

be counted as Christians without having to accept what ecumenical leaders"—channeling Enlightenment perspectives—"said were the social obligations demanded by the gospel, especially the imperative to extend civil equality to nonwhites."[4] Aided by President Richard Nixon's "southern strategy" of exploiting the segregationist sympathies of white southerners to tug them from their traditional Democratic allegiance, the Republican Party secured and tightened a hold on white evangelicals.

This study was conceived well before the term "Christian nationalism" had assumed its current, exclusive usage. It brings into full view the complexity of the religious nationalisms of another era, without joining battle in modern culture wars. Yet, if not its *purpose*, its legitimate *function* is to encourage a reflection on the vital force of religious antislavery discourse in Lincoln's Union. This was a Christian nationalism that sought to put its advocates on the right side of history by embracing an expansive definition of human freedom that squared with their reading of scripture. A recent analysis of its modern-day namesake suggests its power as a cultural identity marker, seized by at least some secularists and nonbelievers, as well as evangelical Protestants and those of other faiths, to claim membership of a political tribe, one that separates "us" from "them."[5] Today's articulation appears to some critics to drain the concept of the theological weight, scriptural complexity, and moral wrestling when compared with the religious nationalisms of Lincoln's less secular age. But, as this book will show, the cultural identification associated with contested religious faith was a feature of that era, too, as each party accused its enemies of debasing Holy Writ.

For anyone wondering how the Civil War story offers lessons for twenty-first-century America, a cautionary word is due. As will become clear, although profound issues of civil and racial equality persist, Lincoln's antislavery Republican Party has little in common with its latter-day namesake; likewise, the white-supremacist Democrats of that earlier time are barely recognizable as the forerunner of today's racially progressive party. American religious culture has changed profoundly, too. Although they had concerns over the growing presence of Catholicism, mid-nineteenth-century evangelical Protestants evinced a striking cultural confidence. They enjoyed a numerical dominance over other strands of Christian faith and other religions. They flourished in a broadly religious and scripturally literate society that was host to secular influences but not characterized by widespread unbelief.

Religion in the early United States, through its national ligaments and institutions, exercised striking cultural power. Its vitality and plural presence in the spiritual marketplace of the new nation extended its reach to encompass most of the people. The new republic inherited from its Puritan forebears, English and colonial, a firm belief in God's overruling Providence. During the Revolution, Continental and state authorities had sanctioned days of fasting and thanksgiving, to acknowledge God's protective role. A providential reading of national fortunes explained the fledgling country's survival during the Napoleonic era and its subsequent flourishing after the War of 1812.

As the United States expanded beyond recognition in geography, material wealth, and size of population between independence and the Civil War, American nationalist sentiment took secular and religious forms, expressed in the cross-fertilizing, interpenetrating worlds of church and politics. The founders prescribed a national framework that separated church and state yet left room for the civic role of Christian ideas and values. As a widening franchise gave a democratic turn to the politics of the early republic, both elite and popular forms of religious faith and identity colored the political parties that sprang up to organize and channel public opinion.

Over time, early political fissures widened into a deep and unbridgeable chasm. One, over the meaning of slavery in God's plan, would split most of the national churches and, eventually, the Union itself. The other line of division, closely related but not identical, ran through the many different expressions of surging evangelical Protestantism, the nation's dominant religious force. On one side clustered the ambitious nationalists of the socially powerful Protestant churches of New England and its Yankee diaspora. Weaving a "Puritan" faith with the political forces that culminated in the Republican Party, zealous reformers afforded the government an essential and providential role in building a righteous nation.

Introduction xvii

They represented an alien cultural force utterly repugnant to those churchgoers who—sometimes from firsthand experience—feared the combined rule of "priest" and politician. The egalitarian doctrines of plain gospel preachers honored localism and popular sensibility as a defense against "religious tyranny" and "pulpit politics." They found a welcoming berth in the successive incarnations of the Democratic Party from Thomas Jefferson through Andrew Jackson to Stephen Douglas—all ambitious nationalists.

A secular and more materialist nationalism flourished alongside and in harmony with this faith-based patriotism. As a purposeful party politician thriving in the world's first mass democracy, Lincoln contributed to the definition of the nation's economic and political purposes shaped by the Whigs and their Republican successors. In material terms, he championed a nation boasting an autonomous and integrated market, secure from British neocolonialism and untroubled by the indigenous inhabitants of the land. More commonly, he celebrated the moral grandeur of the nation's free institutions, shaped by the Revolutionary Patriots and founding fathers. Thanks to their legacies—the Declaration of Independence, celebrating equality, and the federal constitution, guaranteeing freedom—the United States enjoyed a unique liberty, exceeding any other nation. Self-government, religious and civil freedoms, and the exaltation of every citizen's right to an equal chance: these made the American republican experiment a precious historical outlier.

The prepresidential Lincoln engaged hardly at all with the ideologies of religious nationalists. But that would change during his presidency and the national mobilization for four bloody years of war. As leader, Lincoln articulated religious interpretations of the nation's purpose. He acknowledged a God of history who shaped His purposes through the agency of nations. Throughout his presidency the notions of national wrongdoing, penitence, and redemption were regular aspects of his meetings with religious deputations, conversations with the devout, and correspondence from a rich cross section of opinion. Cumulatively, this led many to celebrate— and even revere—him as a moral and even Christian hero; others condemned him as a malign and diabolical influence on the country's ethical course.[6]

Acclaim for Lincoln as a religious leader of the nation (a sort

xviii   *Introduction*

of "half-way clergyman," as one political admirer called him), and the vitriol he attracted for overturning constitutional and scriptural norms, together encourage us to see the Union politics of the era as a clash of opposing religious nationalisms. As antislavery nationalists grew in vigor and reach, so a corresponding force of conservative religious nationalists flexed their ideological muscles. Proponents of each drew on religious sanction, social identities, and political arguments that had been central to prewar cultural conflicts but were now hardened and intensified through the crucible of war. Denominational labels in themselves offered no definitive guide. But powerful religious values and sensibilities shaped these two divergent nationalist imperatives. Many feared that their differences weakened the Union. In practice, they mostly broadened and sustained the nation's wartime determination and persisting sense of invincibility.

During the conflict antislavery religious nationalists extended their reach. Conscientious abolitionists, their ardor forged in the prewar pursuit of racial freedom and equality, cast themselves as radical leaders in the struggle to purify the nation. Others of a more moderate political temperament formed the core of a swelling army of crusaders pressing Lincoln to advance toward and beyond emancipation. Predominantly Protestant in faith, they commonly defined their purposes in biblical terms: a specially chosen people, the citizens of the young country had a duty to apply the prophetic wisdom of the Old Testament and Christ himself by expunging the nation's greatest sin. As Republican Party activists and voters, they urged the administration from the early months of the war to support military leaders' boldness against rebel slaveholders; to bring the benefits of freedom to those slaves escaping into the advancing Federal lines; to cultivate support for emancipation in the loyal border slave states; and to choke slavery in those parts of the Confederacy returning to Union control. Only a distinct minority of white abolitionists shared the goal of complete racial equality that animated African American activists, but common to the mobilizing of all antislavery nationalists was moral outrage over the sinfulness, human injustice, and social evil of enslavement. The fires of Christian conscience and transcendent purpose gave to the Republican Party a missionary dimension that in 1864—under its campaign rebranding—produced an almost complete fusion of Protestant piety and political passion.

Introduction xix

Conservative religious nationalists, no less wedded to the Union, instinctively clung to maintaining unimpaired the rights of the slaveholding states. Their talismanic principles honored the sovereignty of the family, white manliness, localism, the foundational rights and liberties of the states, and resistance to autocratic and theocratic "Puritan" centralism. However, time and events exposed underlying fault lines within conservative Unionism and the Democratic Party that embodied it. Some religious conservatives came to embrace emancipation as the necessary price of national survival; others, equally wedded to a military victory, fixed on retaining the key elements of the antebellum racial order; and yet others pleaded for an armistice and peace negotiations with apparently invincible Confederates. Compared with the broad unity of antislavery nationalists, religious conservatives presented a more diverse and fragmented coalition. Quite apart from the tension between war-supporting Democrats and the growing body of the party's peace-advocating "Copperhead" dissenters, conservative nationalists comprised Catholic and Protestant religious traditions uneasily yoked in common purpose. As the "universal church," Catholics were less invested in the notion of a transcendent American providentialism than their Protestant counterparts. The nationalist amalgam of these conservative faiths lacked the political coherence to achieve more than the sum of its parts. Yet the Democrats in 1864 still took 45 percent of the vote. Foregrounding race, emancipation, and political "despotism," they pressed these issues with a battery of conservative religious and ethical arguments. As furious opponents of the "Puritan fanatics" they held responsible for the bloody course of the war, they cast themselves as moral exemplars utterly mystified that any sound Christian should fall for the unscriptural nonsense spouted by the abolitionists.

Many names stand out as influential representatives of these nationalist tribes, some better known in their own era than today. Typically, Henry Ward Beecher, George Barrell Cheever, Frederick Douglass, William Lloyd Garrison, Stephen Higginson Tyng, Theodore Tilton, Matthew Simpson, and the redoubtable Anna Dickinson gave voice and pen to antislavery religious nationalism in wartime. Conservative defenders of the historic prewar Union included the Protestant tongues of Richard Fuller, Samuel Irenaeus Prime, Nathan Lord, Henry Clay "Dirty" Dean, John Henry Hopkins, and Henry Van Dyke and the deep-dyed reactionary Catholics John Mullaly and James McMaster. Key crossovers to an emancipated Union included the Presbyterians Charles Hodge and Robert J. Breckinridge and the legendary polemicist William Gannaway Brownlow. No name had influence quite like that of the fictional Copperhead pastor and illiterate political commentator Petroleum Vesuvius Nasby—a pro-slavery monstrosity created by the brilliant satirist and newspaperman David Ross Locke. These big fish swam alongside shoals of minnows. Although these lesser public figures lacked countrywide influence, they enjoyed high standing locally and regionally. Many of them are given a platform in the pages that follow, to show the ubiquity, reach, and animating power of the nationalist ideas at the center of this study.

A word about the theological and scriptural language that was so much part of people's experience during the early republic and Civil War era. Some were scrupulously precise in the vocabulary that they used, but others often bandied terms around—like "Calvinist" and "Puritan"—with little or no care for nuance. It is impossible to read the public political and religious discourse of the time without encountering these terms and hard to write about the period without repeating them. To help the general reader pick a way through possibly unfamiliar language and concepts, I have included a Select Glossary of Terms. It comes with a word of encouragement: the meaning will usually be clear from the context. A refined theological palate in the book's readers is neither assumed nor required.

The history of Civil War–era religion once languished, but the field has blossomed over recent decades. Landmark studies of magisterial breadth by Mark Noll, George Rable, and Harry Stout stand out.[7] Writings on multiple related topics have added to a rich story embracing—inter alia—the cultural grip of the Bible, the meaning and management of death, providential thought, religion in the armies, spiritualism, radical Transcendentalism, gendered faith, the factional contests in the upper South borderlands, and the

Introduction   xxi

power of the religious press, as well as case studies of particular faith traditions.[8] Collectively, they have shown how religious faith and institutions molded the lives of the civilian and military populations, North and South, making clear that religious beliefs and devotion did not occupy a discrete cultural silo but influenced ideas and behavior in the round. Despite this, and in evident contrast, overarching studies of Union wartime politics and nationalism have remained largely secular in their focus.[9] In mitigation it could be said that secular republicanism exercised great influence over both Democratic and Republican Parties; that the war's political issues of freedom, rights, and constitutional order stoked the "patriot fires" that warmed American hearts with a new and transcendent attachment to the nation; that many key political figures of the era like Charles Sumner and William Pitt Fessenden were essentially rational and non-churchgoing thinkers.[10] But the neglect of the religious coals on which the iron of the new nation was forged no doubt also reflects the largely secular mind of the modern academy and perhaps an implicit belief that when nineteenth-century politicians spoke with a religious voice, they did little more than decorate basically materialist and secular concerns with the rhetorical idioms of faith. That blind spot is striking. It seriously compromises our view of this period of the American past.

Several recent regional studies of race, religion, and politics, however, when supplemented by both well-established and more recent scholarship on abolitionism, evangelicalism, and radical religion, provide the wherewithal for questioning this take on Civil War–era politics.[11] So, too, does the painstaking statistical research of ethnocultural historians, who some years ago demonstrated to those with eyes to see that ethnic and religious identities were broad indicators of party support.[12] These important works have helped this book break new ground. Mostly, however, it is shaped by a reading of thousands of primary sources, chiefly political and religious newspapers and polemical tracts, sermons, journals, diaries, letters, church reports, and political cartoons. From these I have sought to integrate the nationalist religion of the wartime Union, a polity drenched in faith, into a broad analytical narrative of its politics and electoral mobilization: the political realm became a cockpit where intertwined religious and secular imperatives drove ferocious conflict. Even those citizens who did not share the piety or religiosity of the most devout engaged in an arena whose character reflected the high-octane moral clamor of the "political pulpit." "Religion" bled into "politics," and vice versa. This dynamic characterized the public sphere during the prewar era. It took on even greater force following the outbreak of war. The existential threat to the Union crystallized nationalist thinking. Citizens turned as much to the pulpit as to the political platform in their search for patriotic meaning, instruction, and solidarity. Church congregations were known to clap and cheer ministers' sermons just as they would speakers on the political platform. Religious journals, newspapers, and addresses took political stands; political newspapers and election materials carried sermons and engaged in religious polemics. Many readers subscribed to both secular and religious newspapers. The interpenetration of politics and religion became the wartime norm.

Exploring these issues makes clear that among the opposing religious nationalisms of the Civil War era, the most potent and decisive rendering honored a drive to emancipation nurtured by what Lincoln memorably termed the "better angels" of human nature. The ideology and organizational power of pioneer antislavery nationalists ministered to aspirational American citizens, those confident that the republic's salient Christianity, material well-being, and democratic political system gave it a unique historical role under the direction of Providence. Religious antislavery men and women, both black and white, believed profoundly in the talismanic principles and values of 1776, and that those would prevail over the ideology and practice of enslavement, the legacy of the first African arrivals in the North American colonies in 1619. Their optimistic, millennialist faith—the conviction that the nation was progressing toward the day of Christ's return and His one-thousand-year reign—sustained them through the sacrifices and suffering of war. It promised unprecedented blessings for the post-emancipation republic on the return of peace. As evangelists for righteous politics, they carved out a continuing home in the Republican Party that they had helped to found. The Republicans of the Civil War era energized the world's most progressive mass-based party.

The religious character of Union politics has a bearing on current debates among Civil War historians. Gary Gallagher, James

Introduction xxiii

Oakes, and Adam Smith have led the way in addressing the nature and relative strength of radical and conservative impulses in the North.[13] This book reveals that much of the Union pulpit and religious press almost immediately saw the war as a God-given opportunity to strike against southern slavery. This suggests that Oakes may be right in stressing the fundamental radicalism of Republicans' non-extension policy and that a quasi-abolitionist purpose had already inspired many in the party before the war broke out. But my account also questions the idea that Lincoln was a fully formed radical waiting for the right time to act after the Confederates had fired the first shot; rather, I see the importance of his wartime religious turn in nerving him for dramatic—perhaps even revolutionary—executive action to upend the historic social order.[14] Further, the evidence for the relative conservatism of politico-religious sentiment tallies broadly with Gallagher's argument that the quest to save the Union had the edge over the moral drive to end slavery. But this rigid binary division is unhelpful and misleading: it obscures the broad swath of opinion that thought the Union worth saving *only if* it were a purified Union, cleansed of slavery. As Smith puts it, "A dislike of slavery and a determination to preserve the Union as the last, best hope of Earth were intertwined, indeed mutually interdependent, moral goals."[15] Disliking human bondage and demanding its death as the means of reunification were not, of course, the same as wanting to give African Americans all the rights that white Americans enjoyed. Resistance to this more advanced aim was where instinctive cultural conservatism came into play.

Radicalism and conservatism likewise characterized how Lincoln acted on his newfound understanding of God's Providence. More than any previous president, he turned his political office into an adjunct of faith. He was not the first president to raise the public profile of religion by proclaiming days of national worship. George Washington had set an example. But throughout the early decades of the new American nation that occasional practice had been politically contentious, stirring many to protest that it crossed the constitutional line intended by the First Amendment; moved by similar concern over the separation of church and state, Lincoln's most severe opponents railed at his use of religious proclamations for political ends. Their objections were driven by partisan animus, of course, but they correctly recognized that Lincoln's practice, in its degree, did indeed move the political nation into an unprecedented alignment with public faith.

On the other hand, there were also limits to how far Lincoln's providentialism challenged his thinking and practice. One example above all stands out: his unchanging lifelong commitment to the conquest of Indian country and the extinction of Native Americans' claims to sovereignty. As president he continued, in keeping with the explicit purposes of the Republican Party, to expect Indians to abandon their way of life and make way for white settlers. That he—humane, pragmatic, paternalist—commuted most of the military sentences that in 1862 condemned three hundred Dakota people to be hanged, and that he framed his pardons in moral terms ("I could not afford to hang men for votes"), was the mark of a man of conscience. But this action ought not to divert the eye from the broader picture: the U.S.-Dakota War that threw up this crisis was just one of the inevitable conflicts bred by policies endorsed by Republicans and Democrats alike. Lincoln, conscientious though he was, does not appear to have asked whether the larger process of American colonial expansion enjoyed the smiles of the same Providence that, on his own reckoning, intended the death of slavery.[16]

A final point. My hope is that this book will serve to encourage the opening of minds skeptical that American history offers any evidence of interracial cooperation to achieve radical change. True, the movement for emancipation revealed the complexity of white support, which commonly evinced paternalism and a sense of racial superiority. Yet this should not mask the role of a white minority of out-and-out racial egalitarians inspired to work with an African American vanguard in the service of equal justice for the black race. Theirs was a common, scripturally inspired, Christian nationalism that craved a future in which there was neither black nor white, neither slave nor free.

RIGHTEOUS STRIFE

CHAPTER I

HOLDING TOGETHER: A RIGHTEOUS NATION

The U.S. presidential election of 1860 saw the country pivot on its political axis. For more than seventy years the republic's federal government had propitiated slaveholders. Abraham Lincoln's victory delivered presidential power for the first time to an antislavery party committed to extinguishing human slavery by containing it. This had shattering consequences for national unity. The election, and the secession crisis that it provoked, exposed how much the polarization of North and South owed to irreconcilable nationalist ideologies whose dynamism derived in large part from conflicting religious imperatives. Powerful majority interests in each section inhabited mutually incompatible moral realms shaped by their tailored recourse to biblical precepts and Christian principles.

The riven political nation that Lincoln inherited as president was not, of course, what the founders had intended; indeed, their deliberations had focused on how the new republic could best harness the patriotism and ambition of the Revolutionary struggle in the interests of harmonious national growth. Between 1776 and 1860 the nationalist sentiment to which they and their successors appealed, and which they continued to mold, took both secular and religious form; it achieved multiple expressions in the cross-fertilizing, interpenetrating worlds of church and state. Lincoln, as a party politician in the world's first mass democracy, contributed to the nationalist themes voiced and developed before the Civil War by the Whigs and their Republican successors. As a result, he was in 1860 the chief political beneficiary of one potent form of religious nationalism. But equally, his most severe troubles as president would include challenges from hostile constituencies, North and South, driven by their own powerful religious imperatives.

How American religious institutions and animating faith came to wield such power is a rich story, traced here and in the next chapter. The immediate discussion considers the founders' prescription of a national framework that separated church and state yet left ample space to honor the civic role of Christian values, and it identifies the potential of countrywide churches and religious pluralism for national integration. But, as the next chapter shows, that unifying potential succumbed to twin religious forces pulling the nation apart. We shall see the political standoff between "Puritan" religious culture and popular movements shaped by fear of "theocracy." The other story is the fracture of mainstream churches over human bondage in a political nation constantly striving after righteousness. Taken together, these interlinked subjects explain how the strife between these explosive forces of religious nationalism came to blow the country apart.

FOUNDING A RIGHTEOUS REPUBLIC

The constitutional settlements of the 1780s detached government from religion. Bills of rights and church disestablishment statutes at state level included Jefferson's celebrated Bill for Establishing Religious Freedom in Virginia. The First Amendment to the federal constitution prohibited an establishment of religion by Congress. Together these measures erected a political order unique in Western history. Here was a radical departure from the confessional Christian states of Europe that prized religious uniformity and a legitimacy derived from the Constantinian revolution that had made Christianity the Roman Empire's preferred religion. The Unitarians and deists influential in writing these documents couched them in broadly theistic language, or—like the Philadelphia delegates in

Holding Together: A Righteous Nation 5

1787—chose not to invoke God at all. The founders' modest anti-clericalism and detachment from traditional Calvinism, their prizing human reason alongside (if not above) divine revelation, their faith in human solutions, and their belief that churches established by law would corrupt the polity might appear to have located them, in the sweep of history, closer to modern secular humanism than to the world of the traditional churches. What influential public role could there be for men of God in an officially godless nation?

Yet the nation was not godless, nor did the founders shun religion. The chief framers of the new order held diverse views: Benjamin Franklin and Thomas Jefferson were freethinkers; John Jay and John Witherspoon, orthodox evangelicals; George Washington, a nonsectarian whose personal piety is hard to pin down; Alexander Hamilton, a man of fluctuating Christian convictions; James Wilson, loosely faithful to the Reformed tradition; John Adams, a Trinitarian Congregationalist turned Unitarian; and James Madison, near silent on his religious beliefs. But whatever their differences in faith, they were largely united in the conviction that the morality of reason essentially coincided with the morality of revelation. The First Amendment's guarantee of "the free exercise" of religion was designed to protect religious liberty, not to open the door to the ferocious secularization that French revolutionaries would shortly unleash.[1]

The founders' separation of church and state followed as much from a hardheaded appreciation of religious realities as ideological conviction. The ideal of the confessional state, transplanted to the colonies by Anglicans and Calvinists, could not withstand the religious dynamism of persecuted dissenting churches, notably Baptists and Quakers.[2] The astonishing proliferation of religious groups steadily weakened the standing of established churches and their privileges. Well before the Revolution, through religious revivals and immigration, colonial Christianity came to enjoy an institutional diversity unequaled anywhere in Europe. Baptists, Presbyterians, Quakers, and Anglicans challenged Congregationalist hegemony in New England. The Anglican establishment in Virginia met the defiance of Presbyterians and New Light Baptists (professing God's "new light" through conversion). A striking ethnic mix in the middle and southern colonies nurtured Roman Catholic churches, as well as communities of German Lutherans, Mennonites, Moravians, French Huguenots, Dutch Reformers, Sephardic Jews, and Scottish and Scotch Irish Protestant traditions, including Keithian Quakers.[3] Although Christian churches struggled during war, the 1780s and 1790s saw their diversity further expand, to include Universalists and Unitarians, Shakers and other millennialist groups, and, most significant for the future, New Light Baptists and Methodists.

The fusing of Christian piety with reverence for the new American republic followed naturally from the participation of Patriot clergy in the struggle for independence. Through a torrent of thanksgiving, fast-day, and election sermons, Presbyterians and New England Congregationalists, in particular, turned the events of the Revolution—the forging of intercolonial unity, the emergence of Washington as leader, the crushing of a mighty foe in an unequal contest—into hard evidence that the God who had guided their Puritan forebears toward their City on a Hill was now lavishing his favor on the new nation. The exodus narrative of Hebraic nationalism—Moses leading the people of Israel out of Pharaoh's oppression—offered pertinent lessons about God's judgment, providential victory, and divine purpose for the new nation.[4] "It is abundantly evident, that the Lord hath been on our side, hath fought our battles, and delivered us from the hands of our enemies," a Connecticut pastor declared on the return of peace. "Can the wonders done for our land be ascribed to fortuitous hits and accidents? no . . . they are the effects and productions of the wise and steady counsels of heaven."[5] Moreover, through America's republican institutions—sacred and secular—God had established a model for the world that was designed, the Philadelphia Presbyterian Robert Smith insisted, "to prepare the way for the promised land of the latter days."[6]

THE RELIGIOUS LIGAMENTS OF NATIONAL COHESION: INSTITUTIONS

Patriot ministers of religion during the era of the American War of Independence often cited the prophet Isaiah: "Shall the earth be made to bring forth in one day, or shall a nation be born at once?" They interpreted July 4, 1776, as more than a great historical caesura: it was the sacred day when God fulfilled Isaiah's prophecy.

America—"free, sovereign and independent"—represented that prophecy's literal accomplishment: "a nation born in a day."[7]

Naturally, it would take more than a day to cement a permanent union of states out of the pieces of the fragile republic of 1776. The federal constitution of 1787 established a political structure, but there was not yet a fully developed national consciousness or national culture within the loosely bound elements that made up "America." The colonists' unity was as much a response to an external threat as an expression of a self-conscious attachment to an American nation. Fierce localism, regional and ethnic interest, conflicts between backcountry and Eastern Seaboard, and other jealousies continued into the new nation, imposing limits on how far the inhabitants considered themselves American. In the historian John Murrin's account, the constitutional arrangements provided "a roof without walls" for a fragmented political community whose "national identity was . . . an unexpected, impromptu, artificial, and . . . extremely fragile creation of the Revolution."[8]

Successive generations of political leaders built the walls to support Murrin's roof, pursuing policies shaped by visions of the United States as a potent force in human history, a beacon of republicanism, a model of commercial activity and economic prosperity, and a locus of social opportunity and self-improvement. Political parties, though generally disparaged by the Constitution makers, soon emerged and in presidential elections drew citizens into nationwide contests. Celebrations of the Fourth of July, of George Washington's birthday, and of other national landmarks acted to promote a distinctively American political culture. A sequence of inspirational events encouraged surges of nationalist adrenaline. They included the acquisition of the Louisiana Territory, victory over the British in the War of 1812, and the overpowering of Mexican forces in a war that extended the nation's continental boundaries close to those of today.

Economically, ordinary Americans entered, and mostly embraced, an expanding national market that promised material progress: one linking commercial agriculture to a burgeoning urban and manufacturing sector, held together by credit and a circulating currency stamped with national emblems. It was linked, too, by changes in communications. Canals, navigable waterways, plank roads, railroads, steam presses, and the telegraph collectively "annihilated space" and accommodated a threefold increase in territory and a population that grew by approximately one-third every decade between 1790 and 1860, from under four to over thirty million inhabitants. This was a people as diverse as it was youthful: a potentially unstable chemistry of white and black, of immigrant and native-born, and of plural ethnicities, languages, and religions, whose incorporation into the new nation provided the agenda for patriotic educators. Colleges, professional societies, and businesses, particularly those grounded in New England culture, sought to Americanize a heterogeneous people. And a powerful myth about the birth and meaning of the new country worked to create a shared sense of belonging among those who inherited the Revolution.[9]

Religious agents played a potent role in building this new nation. Through their thousands of pulpits and vast apparatus of print, religious leaders encouraged American national self-consciousness and integration. They delivered nationwide structures and networks at a time when the federal government itself remained remote and relatively weak and anti-statism prevailed. There was, for instance, no federal police force, no public health administration, no federal education framework. The remarkable post office system and the network of army forts were striking but lonely exceptions in the general picture. The most potent national agencies were not agents of the government but the voluntary organizations sustained by private exertions and finance. These included political parties, which every four years harnessed local enthusiasm in the construction of national coalitions. Above all they included the religious denominations and the associated philanthropic agencies of the churches: regional and national networks that served to widen the horizons of individuals and localities.

The churches' program of institutional expansion accommodated the massive increases in general religious adherence between 1790 and 1860. Sacralizing the landscape, almost fifty thousand church buildings sprang up, at a rate exceeding the growth of the general population. In total there were broadly enough meeting-

Holding Together: A Righteous Nation 9

houses in 1860 to accommodate the whole people, should that implausible need arise. Marked by countrywide pulses of revivals from the early nineteenth century—which reached their peak in the early 1840s and have often been described as a Second Great Awakening—the process is more usefully described as a sustained evangelical surge.[10] Churches committed to a Christ-centered theology of the cross dominated the movement, emerging from a position of relative decline during the Revolutionary era, when they enjoyed little standing within the political class, to change the shape of Christianity in America over a few short decades. The potent ecclesiastical forces of the colonial era—Anglican, Congregationalist, Presbyterian, and Quaker—now yielded to the stunning advances of the more demotic evangelicals: the Methodists and Baptists. All sought to construct or reconstruct themselves as American denominations and, dependent now on their own voluntary efforts alone, engaged in ambitious institutional mobilization. Presbyterian synods and General Assemblies, Baptist district and state associations and (from 1814) national General Conventions, Episcopal dioceses and General Conventions: all linked local congregations to a larger arena beyond. None did so more effectively than the humming machinery of Methodism.

Methodists' increasing engagement with ideas of sanctified nationhood was closely related to their evolution into a nationwide church. In 1789, Thomas Coke and Francis Asbury reflected on their challenge as American superintendents. "The difficulty of communication on this extensive continent," they agreed, "obliges us to move on slowly." Yet over the next two decades the Methodist Episcopal Church (MEC) outdid all rivals in building a remarkable nationwide, and easily expandable, system of local societies, quarterly meetings, and annual conferences. A four-yearly General Conference provided central direction, though the more powerful ligaments were the bishops, whose annual preaching tours ranged across the continent. Asbury above all enhanced Methodists' sense of being "a people." During four decades of ministry, he delivered more than ten thousand sermons, traveled well over 100,000 miles on horseback, consecrated thousands of local and traveling preachers, and became the most recognizable person, face-to-face, of his generation.[11] The Methodist system drew its energy from those

Asbury inspired: indefatigable, enterprising, dedicated circuit-riding itinerants who carried the gospel from their heartlands of Virginia, Maryland, and Delaware into the wilderness settlements of the South and West, and into northern New England and Upper and Lower Canada. One early Methodist pamphleteer boasted, with good cause, that Methodism "in a remarkable manner contributes to the cementing of the union," while Nathan Bangs, who completed the first history of the MEC in 1841, pertinently inquired, "What more calculated to soften . . . petty jealousies and animosities, than a Church bound together by one system of doctrine, under the government of the same discipline, accustomed to the same usages, and a ministry possessing a homogeneousness of character, aiming at . . . the salvation of their fellow-men . . . and these ministers continually interchanging from north to south, from east to west, everywhere striving to bring all men under the influence of the same 'bond of perfectness'?" So, he asked, "Did not these things tend to bind the great American family together by producing a sameness of character, feelings, and views?"[12]

Bangs rather overstated Methodist uniformity, but he rightly identified the powerful ethos of union in a movement that drew its adherents into an imagined countrywide community of the pious. Formal structure and a common doctrine played a part, but so, too, did such events as days of fasting or thanksgiving, and especially the proliferation of a celebrated element in the MEC economy, the camp meeting. By 1811, Methodists were organizing four or five hundred a year across the country, drawing average crowds of two or three thousand. Equally important in encouraging Methodists to locate themselves in the wider arena of faith were their church publications. Itinerant ministers carried for sale the experiential religious literature produced by the Methodist Book Concern, though an overdependence on British authors persisted until the 1820s, with the appearance of the instantly successful *Christian Advocate*. Founded in 1826, the New York weekly newspaper soon boasted a circulation of twenty-five thousand, the largest of any American serial. It delivered graphic "scenes in distant places," broadening horizons. "Until after the period in which I became a subscriber for your useful and valuable paper," a presiding elder explained, "my

Holding Together: A Righteous Nation

views were very different from what they now are: then they were entirely local."[13]

The agencies of all Protestant denominations, after the manner of connectional Methodism, spread the word of salvation. News of burgeoning revivals allowed converts to place their own personal journeys of faith into a wider story and to see themselves as inhabitants of a blessed, special, and even national community of the faithful. They learned that in the crucible of revivals their "brethren in Christ" embraced Americans of all stripes—black and white, male and female, young and old, "from every sect and denomination, whether Methodist, Episcopalian, Baptist or Congregationalist." "Great is the joy, great is the glory," exulted the Methodist elder Philip Bruce during a sequence of powerful revivals in Virginia in 1789, foretelling their collective import: "Surely America will become the mart of nations for piety."[14]

THE RELIGIOUS LIGAMENTS OF NATIONAL COHESION: REPUBLICAN FAITH

Suspicion of supernatural religion characterized the civic humanism of historic republican thought. This poses the question: How did the dominant Protestant religious culture of the American founding era, heavily evangelical and conventionally antagonistic toward the humanism of republicanism and commonsense moral reasoning, find shared ground with those secular elements in the process of nation building? The consensual outcome, which gave evangelicals an essential role in fostering the republican nation and its moral well-being, resulted from an "ideological bartering" between secular and religious cultures, with the result that key features of American evangelical Christianity helped make the founding fathers' political ambitions work.[15]

Following independence, most of the political founders embraced the position that George Washington famously expressed in his Farewell Address: "Of all the dispositions and habits which lead to political prosperity, Religion and Morality are indispensable supports. . . . And let us with caution indulge the supposition that morality can be maintained without religion."[16] Christianity would be a welcome, even essential, means of promoting virtue among the people. For their part, American evangelical ministers warmly embraced the founders' reformulation and, by abandoning their own earlier Calvinist understanding of virtue as exclusively dependent upon redemption, removed a key sticking point between the republican and the Reformed Protestant traditions. They no longer insisted on *divine grace* as exclusively necessary for virtue but agreed that ordinary people could by nature and common sense see what was true.[17]

Republican language and reasoning consequently saturated the discourse of American Protestants during the three generations after the Revolution, sacralizing the Constitution as they did so and interweaving a variety of related themes: the role of Christian republics in thwarting proud, despotic ambition; their reliance on ideals of charity; their support of liberty and equality within the larger interests of the commonwealth; the defense of republican freedom during—or even by means of—military conflict; tyranny as the concomitant of vice; republicanism as God given, scriptural, and virtuous. These ideas were ubiquitous in the sermons and writings of evangelicals of the Calvinist or Reformed tradition, expressed well beyond New England and its diaspora.[18]

But what of Methodists? Early on, their idea of the American nation contrasted starkly with the sanctified Puritan nationhood of Patriot Congregationalists and Presbyterians. During and immediately after the War of Independence few Methodist preachers felt a primary loyalty to the idea of America. John Wesley's *Calm Address to Our American Colonies* in 1775 extolled the beneficence of British rule so that while the war raged, as the superintending preacher Francis Asbury put it, "there is not a man in the world so obnoxious to the American politicians as our dear old Daddy."[19] Even Methodist Patriots were tarred with the brush of British "Toryism," a target for whipping, fines, imprisonment, and other forms of persecution. Postwar Methodism continued to be stigmatized as a foreign import. Preachers pushing into the outer settlements of New York and New England faced the charge "that the king of England had sent them to disaffect the people" and stir up another war. James O'Kelly, a radical Revolutionary veteran, anti-Federalist, and Jeffersonian Republican, who damned Coke and Asbury as tyrants and henchmen "on a stretch for power," led a secession of twenty thousand members to form the anti-episcopal "Republican Methodists." As late as the 1820s the smell of British tyranny attached to English-born Methodists.[20]

Despite this, the Methodists had an evangelistic edge over disputatious Calvinists, whose key doctrines included the sinfulness of humankind and God's predetermined choice of an "elect" who would alone secure salvation. By contrast, the Methodists' Arminian doctrine meshed well with the emerging democratic, anti-elitist, and self-empowering culture of the age. It stressed the availability of God's grace to all, through Christ's atonement, and challenged the suffocating notion that anxious sinners should wait inactively for conversion. The early MEC consequently harvested converts by the thousand. As it did so, it showed little interest in championing American nationhood. Defining themselves as primarily citizens of "Zion," the church militant, Methodists differed profoundly from Presbyterian, Congregationalist, and Dutch Reformed churches, whose Calvinism instilled responsibility to the political nation.[21] Asbury and his colleagues worked in the spirit of Wesley's instruction, "that the Methodists are one people in all the world," a transnational movement devoted more to building up "the Redeemer's kingdom" than the country where they labored.[22] Political geography was of secondary concern. Lorenzo Dow, the legendary charismatic, freewheeling, and ubiquitous itinerant, was a self-styled "cosmopolite," blind to political boundaries. Francis Asbury spoke as much of the "empire" of Methodism, and the "continent" of North America, as he did of the American "nation."[23]

Yet forces were at work within Methodism that helped indigenize the movement and give it a role in sacralizing the nation. Admitting into the ministry American-born, Revolutionary Patriot soldiers helped erode the stigma of Methodist Loyalism, as did licensing the sons of Revolutionary militiamen. Methodists' immediate postwar articles of religion in 1784 included a bold statement of loyalty to American rulers. Then, in May 1789, Coke and Asbury stole a march on other denominations by calling on George Washington at home, after his first inaugural, to congratulate him on his appointment to "the presidentship of these States." Asbury, mixing his labor with the country's growth, discovered that a new allegiance had stolen upon him. Traveling across the St. Lawrence River into Canada in 1811, he wrote, "My strong affection for the people of the United States came with strange power upon me when I was crossing the line."[24] When war with Britain broke out in 1812, a minority of grieving pacifist Methodists lamented the calamity of a bloody conflict between two Protestant nations. More remarkable, however, was the response of the Methodist majority in endorsing the war as a holy enterprise. Asbury was much less belligerent than many, but his prayers for President Madison and the U.S. government were consistent with other wartime examples of patriotic Methodist piety: the elder David Lewis's trust in the "God of power," Timothy Merritt's ready identification of the new America with Israel of old, and—on the day of thanksgiving with the coming of peace—the full-blooded nationalism of the westerner William McKendree.[25]

Methodists' sanctifying of the American cause in 1812 marked the drawing together of existing strands of thought. Their 1789 address to Washington acknowledged God's Providence, protection of the country, and "favour on the American people." Their general fast and thanksgiving in 1796 conceived of America as a moral entity, a nation capable of sin and corruption. Independence Day sermons understood God's goodness to operate on humankind as citizens, not mere private sinners. God, John Dow told his New Jersey congregation, had done "great things . . . for us . . . in our national capacity," delivering Americans—as He had the people of Israel—"from the galling yoke of tyranny and oppression." He had blessed the republic with "the sacred privilege of an equal representation . . . [and] of acting for [our]selves." Under autocratic power, he declared, "vital piety . . . has ever groaned and languished, . . . but the equalizing system of republicanism is friendly to the interests of religion, and calculated to promote the cause of truth and virtue." Americans, he warned, must never tolerate "regal power, a form of government which originated with impious heathens." No unreconstructed monarchist merited the privilege of citizenship "in a free and independent country."[26]

With their evolving republican outlook converging with the tenets of Reformed Calvinistic nationalism, with their membership embracing women and men, of all ages, of all social ranks, both black and white, and in all parts of the country, Methodists could plausibly cast themselves as a primary agent of godly nation building. Indeed, in 1812, Methodists posed as the true patriots, since the chief religious opponents of the war, and ministerial sympathizers with the Federalists' threat of secession from the Union, were the Calvinistic clergy of New England. The world had indeed been turned upside down when that year the Methodist Martin Ruter delivered at an Independence Day gathering in Maine what one newspaper called "such a supplication . . . as would have been made by the Whig Clergy in 'the times which tried men's souls.'" During the 1820s and 1830s Methodists—the nation's biggest denomination—would become committed ambassadors of a Christian republic.[27] A young Methodist minister, the well-educated and capable Benjamin Franklin Tefft, offered a shining example of this transformation in a funeral sermon on the death of William Henry Harrison in 1841 (of which more later). Tefft used the occasion not to focus, as an earlier generation of Methodist preachers would commonly have done, on the transient character of human life but to establish at length that "Christianity is the source of the beautiful and glorious conception of that form of national association which we style a republic," and to show that "American civilization" comprised "a union of Christianity with the mental aspirations to liberty." It was "neither merely Christian, nor abstractedly democratic," but "a combination of the two, constituting a civilization purely republican."[28]

THE RELIGIOUS LIGAMENTS OF NATIONAL COHESION: PROVIDENTIAL HISTORY AND PURPOSE

Nineteenth-century American nationalism lacked what its European counterparts had in abundance: a people's sense of ancient territory, of being rooted in lands held by their forefathers over numberless generations. Possibly, too, they felt the absence of a history reaching deep into the mists of time. Yet Protestant leaders did provide an inspiring meta-historical framework that served as a usable past.

The new republic inherited from English and colonial Puritanism a fixed belief in God's overruling Providence. The founding political document of the embryonic American nation, the Declaration of Independence, delivered a moral summons to united action, one that declared God's sanction for colonial separation from Britain. It made no mention of Christianity, but a sprinkling of clues revealed the range and force of the religious faiths that lay behind it. The text emerged from a committee of five that left most of the drafting task to Thomas Jefferson. It took final form after scrutiny by the Second Continental Congress, whose members were a microcosm of the wider religious landscape, with its unique array of spiritual groups.[29]

In its preamble, the declaration asserts that the political independence of the thirteen states—their "separate and equal station" as a power on earth—was sanctioned by "the Laws of Nature and of *Nature's God*." It was a self-evident truth "that all men are created equal, . . . endowed *by their Creator* with certain unalienable Rights," including "Life, Liberty and the pursuit of Happiness."[30] Here, in Jefferson's understanding, was the creator God, a deity consistent with eighteenth-century rationalist ideas, the thought streams of science and philosophy that fed the Enlightenment. The sage of Monticello, in common with other deists of the American founding generation, questioned the divine inspiration of the Bible and dismissed the "demoralizing dogmas of Calvin" as a "counter-religion made up of the *deliria* of crazy imaginations."[31] Two members of the committee offered minor but not material amendments to Jefferson's text: the Unitarian and former Congregationalist John Adams, and the similarly unorthodox Benjamin Franklin, a Freemason devoted to the ideal of human progress. Both shared Jefferson's lifelong interest in religion and esteem for Christianity's ethical principles.[32] Together they ensured the declaration was grounded in righteousness and virtue. Jefferson's original draft began, "We hold these truths to be *sacred & undeniable*." The final text concluded with the signers' pledge to each other, and to their revolutionary project, of "our Lives, our Fortunes and our sacred Honor."

At the same time, however, the declaration in its final form spoke of God in terms consistent with orthodox holy scripture. The signers appealed "to the Supreme Judge of the world for the rectitude of our intentions." They made their pledges "with a firm reliance on the protection of divine Providence." These additions resulted from the intervention of orthodox Christians in Congress. Their standout figure was John Witherspoon, president of the College of

New Jersey, the only minister in Congress, and one of some dozen signers of the declaration whose lives had been shaped by Presbyterianism. A proponent of Scottish Common Sense philosophy, Witherspoon gave unshakable support to the movement for independence, sure that human rights flowed from God's authority, not monarchical power, and that political and religious freedom were inseparably connected.[33] There was nothing in the terms "Nature's God" or "Creator" that would in themselves have troubled Witherspoon and other Trinitarian Christians. God worked through the forces of Nature that He had created. But Witherspoon and his evangelical wing of Protestantism rejected the notion of a prime mover who had withdrawn from the world that He had made to let His clockwork creation run itself. The evangelicals' Almighty was an activist God who judged humankind and intervened in human affairs. He protected or punished His people according to their deserts.[34]

Throughout the Revolutionary struggle both Continental and state authorities sanctioned days of fasting and thanksgiving, to acknowledge, in Witherspoon's words, "the supreme and universal providence" of "the great Governor of the world ... in times of impending danger and publick calamity."[35] The Continental Congress's thanksgiving proclamation of 1777, the handiwork of Richard Henry Lee, asserted "the indispensable duty of all men to adore the superintending providence of almighty God," who had been pleased "to smile upon us in the prosecution of a just and necessary war" for the defense of "our unalienable rights and liberties."[36] William Livingston extolled the value of these government-sanctioned days of public worship. He knew they would be "very agreeable to all pious people, for I never met with a religious Tory in my life."[37]

A providential reading of national fortunes accompanied and explained the United States' survival as a fledgling but independent member of the community of nations during the Napoleonic era. Notwithstanding their divergent readings of God's purposes, both Federalist and Jeffersonian Republican parties understood the country's direction and prospects to be guided by Providence throughout the War of 1812.[38] Deism lost its cultural authority as revivals spread and evangelical churches sacralized the landscape, nurturing popular belief in the direct intervention of a living Trinitarian God. By 1840, the antebellum high point of relative evangelical strength (measured as a percentage of the population), providentialism was deeply embedded in the national psyche.

The grip of providentialist thought tightened when the Whig president, William Henry Harrison, died unexpectedly in April 1841, a month after his inauguration. The new president, John Tyler, called a stunned nation to a day of national fasting. Pulpits and presses explored the meaning of the unprecedented and calamitous loss of a serving president. Democrats who could not see "Old Tip's" death as a calamity wryly suggested that the Almighty had struck the old man down, displeased with the nation's choice; others thought his age (sixty-eight) and onerous duties were explanation enough. Mostly, however, preachers served a keen public appetite to look beyond the "proximate" cause of events. Typically, William C. Crane instructed Alabama Baptists on the power of the "superintending Providence of God." In similar vein, the Massachusetts pastor Joseph Abbott pointed to God's destruction of "the nations of antiquity" for their depravity. "Earth's whole history," he declared, "is but the history of God's providence, unfolding itself in the stern support of righteousness and punishment of sin."[39] Sermon after sermon cataloged the sinful failings of the American nation, notably the volcanic tumult of electoral politics, Sabbath breaking, intemperance, the abuse of racial minorities, and money worship (not to mention the corruption of republican simplicity by "singers and fiddlers and lascivious dancing girls").[40] Yet, all agreed, Harrison himself had been a man of piety, personally undeserving of God's wrath. A Bible-reading Episcopalian, he had used his inaugural address to profess "a profound reverence for the Christian religion," the first president to do that since George Washington.[41] Why, then, had God removed a leader so well equipped to lead by religious example? The Presbyterian Artemas Bullard resolved the paradox. "If it were the design of Jehovah to make this whole people feel their dependence upon him, and the guilt and danger of setting at naught his authority," he surmised, "it is difficult to conceive what [wiser] means he could have employed than the very thing he has now done." David Riddle pointed to the fate of Jesus in the hands of the high priest Caiaphas: "It was expedient for the people that one man die, and the whole nation perish not." Harrison thus became a Christian martyr.[42]

Rays of hope penetrated the gloom. God's dramatic reckoning, preachers told their mourning congregations, told of His benign purposes for the young nation. He had "gigantic greatness" in store for an exceptional people destined to be His agents in regenerating the world and raising humankind to a higher plane of morality, well-being, and achievement. Americans must reset their national compass, to live by the proverbial axiom that only "righteousness exalteth a nation."[43] Good would come from this rebuke to the fevered "hurrah" campaign of 1840. The solemn hush of national mourning revealed "we are at bottom one people." A surge in religious revivals in the spring of 1841 betokened a future when "the nights of earthly calamity lose themselves in the day of unclouded, uninterrupted, universal millennial glory."[44]

By routinely describing the Providence of God as the midwife of the new nation and the active director of its progress, the post-independence press and pulpit gave their audiences a way of imagining their country's character, distinctiveness, and prospects. The understanding that nationalisms originate and are sustained by means of "imagined communities" is well established.[45] The early American republic was arguably held together more by feeling and sentiment than by constitution and law. Through the ministry of their clergy, and the national connections offered by their churches, benevolent associations, and religious periodicals, men and women of the new United States conjured an imagined national Christian community while simultaneously providing the substantial and visible building blocks of nationhood.

At the same time, these agents projected the United States as the historical culmination of the purest form of Christianity. From early- and mid-nineteenth-century pulpits, Protestants learned that their narrative was much more than the slim history since the Pilgrims landed or the even slimmer history since 1776. Rather, they had a leading role in the uneven but ultimately triumphant working out of civil and religious freedom since the days of Christ. That story, as typically told, made the primitive church of the apostles a gathering of proto-republicans—by implication, proto-Americans. Pure apostolic Christianity offered political and eternal salvation.

It championed, in the words of a Cincinnati Congregational minister, "the value of the individual man, . . . the equality of the race, and . . . the only rational idea of civil liberty which the world ever possessed." But the Christian church to which Jesus entrusted his republican system fell into the treacherous and corrupt hands of a despotic papacy. Truth and liberty took refuge in mountain recesses for a thousand years and more, pursued by "the fire-faggot and the sword." Although the Lutheran Reformation raised hopes of a return to the system of early Christianity, Germany and the other European "nations" left it prey to civil despotism. Here the Puritan narrative reached its glorious climax. When England overturned Oliver Cromwell's Commonwealth of gospel truth and republican liberty, God gathered a host of choicest English men and women to lead them forth "like Israel from Egypt." Planting them in the colonial plantations as "the germ of a new nation," the Almighty hand "committed *to them* afresh the solemn trust of Protestant Christianity and human liberty."[46]

This Puritan history spoke particularly to Americans of New England extraction, but its influence was widely felt among Protestants of a broadly Calvinist orientation. Here was a narrative of national exceptionalism that began with the Hebrew commonwealth itself. Through the nation's colonial founding and struggle for independence, God had astonished the world and made His intentions transparently plain. The New York Presbyterian John Krebs declared that "*God . . . has made us to differ*" and could only have done so "to make of us a great nation."[47] The Protestant pulpit routinely contrasted Americans, the providential beneficiaries of Christian republicanism, with the backward, untutored, and oppressed subjects of every other nation under the sun: typically, Russian serfs and other "benighted subjects of despotic power in Asia and Africa," "the vassals of Spanish and Turkish domination," the "convulsive and unintelligent liberty" of the French, and "the unenlightened tenants of Ireland." This cast the United States as the steward of a most holy trust. Americans' moral duty lay in perfecting their Christian republic; their mission, to provide an exemplary pattern of liberty that would enfranchise the world; their destiny, to bring about the political and civil millennium.[48]

THE RELIGIOUS LIGAMENTS OF NATIONAL COHESION: THE PARADOX OF PLURALISM

There is a paradox at the heart of American religious life during the years of the early republic. In stark contrast to the European systems of established churches and confessional states, the new United States, with its free religious marketplace, experienced an extraordinary mushrooming of faiths and identities that, in this respect at least, *did* make the new nation unique. Their chronic and destabilizing conflicts had the capacity to impede national unity and turn the country into a religious battleground of historic ferocity.[49] Yet, incongruously, the United States' proliferation of sects and denominations had integrating, cohesive, and unifying possibilities, too. As well as its centrifugal forces, the American religious marketplace in some ways encouraged convergence and national integration.

On a first reading, then, the defining feature of the new nation was its divisive sectarianism. A plural Christianity meant contending ambitions and sharp doctrinal differences, refracted by region, class, race, and ethnicity. Among the surfeit of examples several lines of division stand out. The orthodox who battled against Unitarianism, deism, and Enlightenment skepticism, as fermented in Tom Paine's *Age of Reason* and the de-Christianizing potions of the French Revolution, were themselves deeply fractured. Predestinarian and biblicist Calvinists contended on the one hand with equally conversionist but staunchly Arminian Methodists and, on the other, with Anglican-style moralists who, denying the need for conversion, stressed the duty of an ethical life. Orthodox Congregationalist clergy continued to hold wherever they could to a standing order, to fashion the future nation in the image of New England. In Massachusetts and Connecticut, Baptists, Methodists, and Quakers battled against the coercive monopoly of a residual establishment while mired in doctrinal and evangelistic confrontation with one another. Episcopalians rebuked Quakers for their social radicalism and Methodists and Baptists for their assault on Anglican authority. Contrasting conservative and radical versions of religious millennialism in the 1780s and 1790s contested the nation's future.[50]

As religious groups multiplied during the early nineteenth century, the profoundest antipathies continued to be those setting orthodox Christians against freethinkers and deists, and Protestant against Catholic, while the emergence of Mormonism in the 1820s alarmed mainstream believers. The bloody landmarks included anti-Catholic riots, arson, and murder in Boston, Philadelphia, and Louisville, and the assassination of the Mormon leader Joseph Smith. However, in a still overwhelmingly Protestant country, the multiplying divisions *within* that tradition also bred strife. Unitarian-Trinitarian controversies were largely confined to the Northeast, especially Massachusetts (Unitarians, it has been said, believed in the fatherhood of God, the brotherhood of man, and the neighborhood of Boston). More widely, the asperities among Protestant Trinitarians poisoned interchurch relations as Calvinist theologians tried to stay the advance of Methodist Arminianism. Conservative Old School Presbyterians and Primitive Baptists likewise resisted the "modern" Calvinism of New School theologians.

Nothing better exemplifies the ferocious warfare between different traditions within Protestantism than the battles between the two giant denominational families, the Baptists and the Methodists, especially in the West and the South, as they competed for souls. Preachers resorted to the metaphors of violent battle; allusions to explosives, firearms, and blowing adversaries "sky-high" confirm Nathan Bangs's description of this conflict as a "sort of warfare."[51] Peter Cartwright's celebrated account of his early career as a Methodist itinerant tells a similar story. Believers in infant baptism appear as predators who would "rush in, and try to take our converts off into the water," and who "made so much ado about baptism by immersion, that the uninformed would suppose that heaven was an island, and there was no way to get there but by *diving* or *swimming*."[52] In this contest, each tradition saw itself as the model of patriotic republicanism and the righteous agent of national construction in contrast to the un-American influences of the other.

At the same time, however, the very diversity of American religion and the competitive pursuit of denominational advantage had the power to integrate the nation. In the tenth Federalist paper, James Madison argued that republics were best protected against the selfishness of their various factional interests, often economically impelled, by their multiplication to the point that no single faction could dominate the state. This was a perspicacious understanding of how a political society might harness selfish interests, through necessary compromise, for the common good. The founders equally understood that a similar sectarian pluralism would help guard against the dominance of an intolerant majority. This was indeed how things developed. The sects and denominations of the early republic tolerated pluralism and embraced (albeit unevenly) the free exercise of religion, as stipulated by the First Amendment, not out of a spirit of ecumenism or a belief in diversity as necessarily a good thing, but because there was no realistic alternative to an expansive provision for dissent. The most that any could aspire to was to become an informal establishment in one region or another.[53]

Surveying American religion at mid-century, the British visitor Robert Baird noted the common, salvationist elements of evangelicals' doctrinal beliefs and practices. The competition between denominations encouraged borrowing and cross-fertilization. Lacking tax support, churches needed members and their voluntary contributions to pay their pastors, maintain meetinghouses, and fund good works. Witnessing the astonishing growth of American Methodism, other evangelical denominations looked on in concern, anxiety, and downright envy at the progress of Wesley's followers. The great hostility to the MEC, an Episcopalian acknowledged, resulted from *"its continued prosperity."*[54] From a few thousand members at the nation's birth, the Church had become the country's biggest by the 1820s. Pondering that stunning success, many Calvinistic evangelicals—Congregationalists, Presbyterians, and Baptists—found it possible to tolerate and even copy Methodists' revival methods and Arminian doctrines. Calvinist ministers, one commentator explained, had no choice but "to bestir themselves or lose their hold upon their people."[55] The era's preeminent revivalist, Charles G. Finney, won fame (and stirred up opposition) by introducing into Presbyterian churches so-called new measures that in fact replicated Methodists' well-established methods. Remarkably, cultural diffusion also prompted forms of evangelical revivalism among Unitarians and Catholics.[56]

Competition encouraged doctrinal convergence, too, evident in the way creative Calvinist theologians adjusted to the era's popular appetite for the democratic, egalitarian, and activist elements of Arminian theology. They saw the powerful attraction of these ideas to ordinary men and women like Deborah Millett, who said she "was a Methodist in sentiment before I knew their doctrines." Notions of human ability helped them make meaningful sense of the world and their place in it. This democratic theological turn influenced Congregationalist and Presbyterian thinkers like Nathaniel W. Taylor and Lyman Beecher, whose "new divinity" accepted that Christ's atonement for the sins of humanity might be universally experienced. Baptists, too, battled against "double-extra Calvinism."[57]

By the 1840s and 1850s much of the earlier denominational hostilities among Protestants had yielded to a recognition of what they held in common. A New York Methodist editor declared in 1852, "One thing is certain, the *evangelical* sects are more harmonious in their feelings towards each other than they were formerly. The Dutch Reformed, Presbyterians, Baptists, and Episcopal Methodists, are now on a very friendly footing with each other."[58] The broad Protestant homogeneity of the population during the era of American independence had by 1860 given way to a more complex reality. Protestant Christians drew defensively together as other faiths swelled in number, including the homegrown Mormon movement and, most strikingly, the Roman Catholic Church.[59] Catholics accounted for more than half of the 4.78 million immigrants who landed in the United States between 1830 and 1860. Forty percent of all arrivals were Irish Catholics; additionally, many of the 1.5 million migrants from Germany belonged to the Roman Church. Many native-born Americans took alarm at this measure of Protestantism's relative decline since its near-total command at the end of the colonial period. Self-identifying heirs of the Protestant Reformation questioned the Catholics' creed, liturgy, and ceremonies, and above all took alarm over Rome's alleged corrosion of republican values. Priests, they charged, condoned the immorality that colored Protestant accounts of Sabbath-breaking, whiskey-swilling, beer-drinking immigrants, the easy prey of vote-rigging political bosses. Equally, they condemned Catholic parochial schools as a fundamental threat to the values of Protestant independent inquiry that characterized public, common school education.

New organizations sprang up to foster Protestant unity. Most influential was the Protestant Reformation Society, founded in 1836, and its successors, the American Protestant Society, which by 1849 was publishing more than two million pages of tract material a year, and the American and Foreign Christian Union, whose agents achieved cross-denominational support. As one commentator observed, anti-Catholicism "becomes the very center of Christian unity."[60] The final great revival of the antebellum period, the most dramatic since the great influx of Catholic immigrants, the so-called awakening of 1857–58, was insistently interdenominational and in many of its aspects marked the high point of Protestant harmony before the Civil War. "Union" prayer meetings were its hallmark. Controversial topics, theological and political, were avoided. A sense that the revival was "a precursor to some great event" encouraged Christians to forget "all past alienations and distractions."[61]

A visiting English Methodist, James Dixon, who toured the United States in 1848, observed that the country was "not convulsed, nor the state put in jeopardy, by religious contentions." Rather, he wrote, there appeared "infinitely less" sectarianism than in England, which he put down to the absence of a religious establishment, so that no ministers, "except popish priests and a few hair-brained [sic] Puseyites, ever dream of saying of other ministers that they are . . . 'usurpers' of the priestly office."[62] He overstated his case—he had his own domestic perspective and political agenda—but he shrewdly understood the function of religious pluralism and the effect of an abundance of faith groups.

All-out religious warfare was checked, too, by the kaleidoscope of sectarian conflict. The country presented no single model of interchurch relations, but multiple local and regional patterns shaped by historic settlement, ethnicity, class, and relative church numbers. For instance, the mutual hostility of Methodists and Baptists ran deep in Appalachia, but in other contexts concern over Catholic arrivals helped draw them closer together. Republican America provided lush acres of cultural space for the churches' individual aspirations, and their corresponding identities and hopes

for America. The new nation gave each group—whether orthodox Protestant, or those like the Mormons, Catholics, and Adventists whom the self-styled mainstream dismissed as outsiders—the
means of self-expression. Churches gave religious meaning to their
members' roles as citizens of the American republic. In addition
to scriptural instruction, they provided social meeting places that
honored believers' ethnic, racial, class, and gendered identities. As
the religious mainstream, evangelical Protestants defined the nation
through the lens of their cultural dominance; Mormons and other
outsiders, by contrast, deliberately differentiated themselves, to feed
on their status as victims and assert a love of American ideals they
could not see in their persecutors.[63]

Equally, the abundance of churches and the founders' rejection
of radical secularism prevented the emergence of an anticlerical
political party. Multitudes of churchgoers made up the constituencies of each of the major parties and helped fashion their programs
and political culture. Jeffersonian Democratic-Republicans and
their Jacksonian successors harbored outspoken freethinkers and
"infidels" but shunned the profound anticlericalism of revolutionary France. "In the United States," observed Alexis de Tocqueville,
"if a politician attacks a sect, this may not prevent the partisans of
that very sect from supporting him; but if he attacks all the sects
together, every one abandons him, and he remains alone."[64] At the
same time, no church could capture the high command of any political party for its own purposes. Rather, American politics offered
something to every religious group. Each had to learn to work in
political harness with others to press their agenda for the nation.

In summary, American religious antagonisms, though strong
and meaningful, were also evolving and multiple. With each faith
finding the space to affirm its own notion of America, plural conflicts
had the potential to function as means of social and national integration. Plainly, however, this was but a single aspect of the larger
canvas, as the next chapter explains. The major feature of American
religion during these years was a developing double fault line that
prevented cohesion around a common unifying religious nationalism. Many of the Methodists, Baptists, and other so-called upstart
churches that gave the movement its dynamism shaped a popular
religion that exploited suspicion of the agents of "theocratic" New

England and their place within the growing Yankee diaspora. The second fault line resulted from the growing economic and social power of southern planters and their increasingly embedded system of racial bondage, which fueled antislavery and pro-slavery ideologies that shattered the nation's most powerful Protestant denominations: Presbyterians, Baptists, and Methodists.

CHAPTER 2

PULLING APART:
A FRACTURING NATION

The bitter clash of conflicting religious cultures, and the incompatible national purposes they represented, played an integral part in the United States' political journey toward Lincoln's presidential victory in 1860. Two profound religious cleavages helped sunder the Union: one, the conflict between imperialist "Puritanism" and "anti-Yankee" piety; the other, earthshaking church schisms over slavery. These were separate battles between partly overlapping sets of antagonists whose interests did not always align. But in time their common ideological elements fused to create a single fault line between antislavery "Puritans" and the pro-slavery enemies of "priestcraft." With the presidential elections of 1856 and 1860, that fault line cracked open to expose an unbridgeable abyss.

PURITANS, PIETISTS, AND PRIESTCRAFT:
THE CLASH OF POLITICAL-RELIGIOUS CULTURES

Robert Baird's *Religion in America*, first published in 1844, offered the first comprehensive scrutiny of American religious thought and practice. He located a fundamental fissure between evangelical and non-evangelical churches: on one side, Congregationalists, Regular

Baptists, Methodists, Low Church Episcopalians, his own denominational family of Presbyterians, and a host of smaller traditions; on the other, such fast-growing churches as Roman Catholics and Mormons. Baird was sure the future lay with evangelical Protestants as the "branches of one great body." After all, he pointed out, they held "a most remarkable coincidence of views on all important points": a Trinitarian God; the depravity, guilt, and condemnation of all humankind; Christ's atonement, sufficient for the sinner's salvation; regeneration by the Holy Ghost; a final judgment of eternal misery for the wicked and blessedness for the righteous; and, to qualify for church communion, evidence of a moral life and a personal experience of salvation.[1]

What Baird and other visiting commentators failed to see, by their focus on the elements of a common Reformation theology, were the deep cultural divisions that ran both through and between evangelical denominations.[2] On one side stood the ambitious nationalizing forces of the socially dominant Protestant churches of New England and the Northeast, salient Patriots of the Revolutionary era. Weaving Puritan faith with political Federalism, they fashioned an American Christian ideal. Theirs was a confident, even bumptious nationalism, but sufficiently self-critical to protest at the jingoism and spread-eagle patriotism that burgeoned after the conclusion of the War of 1812.[3] When the Federalist Party foundered, conservative ministers and ambitious intellectuals abandoned politics to build an empire of missionary and moral improvement societies. Some were transnational in inspiration and scope, taking British voluntary societies as their model, but all aimed to Christianize and enlighten a fast-growing and mobile American population. The American Bible Society labored to ensure every home had a copy of the King James version of scripture; the American Tract Society published morally improving literature; the American Sunday School Union took on the moral nurture of children, "the rising hope of our church and state," in a demographically youthful country.[4] The American Education Society trained ministers; evangelists of the American Home Missionary Society penetrated the West; American Temperance Society agents preached sobriety to a people whose per capita consumption of alcohol had reached levels not seen in America before (or since). Earliest in time, and first in ambition and fame, the American Board of Commissioners for Foreign Missions, founded in 1810, boasted an international purpose and reach. The Reformed Protestant influence of Presbyterians and Congregationalists controlled the first wave of these and other moral reform societies during the second and third decades of the nineteenth century, but soon Methodists, too, had formed their own denominational Bible and Tract Society and Sunday School Union, intent, as one of their ministers, Nathan Bangs, put it, to fashion "*Christian* patriots" out of "thoroughly reformed sinner[s]."[5] Local branches and auxiliaries linked public-minded evangelicals in raising vast sums. In the decade or so between their establishment and 1828, the thirteen leading national benevolent societies spent almost $3 million, an outlay not far short of the $3.6 million that the federal government had spent on internal improvements since its founding.[6]

Inspired by a theology of disinterested benevolence and a profoundly nationalist understanding of progress on earth (it was, they agreed, the destiny of the young republic to shape the whole world for the better), these men and women embraced a confident millennial theology: righteousness and the spread of Christ's gospel would secure the conversion of the world, prior to the Savior's glorious return.[7] Their commitment to immediate change for the better—through evangelical conversions, cascades of religious revival, and a theology of human perfection—disdained the gradualism of Enlightenment thought and practice. Some took alarm at trying to embed a Christian moral order without formal state support. More commonly, however, the assured and buoyant beliefs of enterprising Protestants reflected their faith in the individual's capacity for self-improvement: the self-discipline of Christian citizens, not a coercive established church, would deliver a healthy, moral republic. Lyman Beecher and others showed how pastoral care, revivalist preaching, a modern theology, and imaginative institution building by churches emancipated from the dominion of government could achieve national and republican glory, and secure "the last dispensation of heaven for the relief of this miserable world."[8]

The other side of the cultural fault line comprised the evangelical converts of the versatile and nimble "upstart churches" that ministered to the migrants, some two million and more by 1820,

Pulling Apart: A Fracturing Nation

who streamed over the Appalachians. Methodist and Baptist revivalist preachers, adroit and competitive, were fastest to reach the moving line of frontier settlements in Kentucky, Tennessee, and the Southwest and the northwestern states of Ohio, Indiana, and Illinois.[9] Ambitious but largely uneducated, these religious enthusiasts outpaced the agents of government and the educated ministry of Presbyterians and other less agile eastern churches. They delivered a plain gospel to settlers originating from the southern and middle states, many of whom traced their cultural roots to the backcountry of the pre-Revolutionary South. Their rudimentary meetinghouses served as much a social as a religious need, ministering to isolated communities whose inhabitants endured the hardships, uncertainties, and hazards of a rural environment. Some settlers resented preachers' warnings of eternal perdition since they already suffered—as one remarked—"all those torments of Hell and Damnation to a perfection," but the frontier gospel could be an affirming doctrine, too.[10] This great expansion of evangelical forces amounted to a rebellion against Calvinist authority by a democratic "sovereign audience" who warmed to emotional preaching that honored equality, liberation, and the dispersal of power. Baptists were the quintessential democratizers of American Christianity, anti-elitist and self-confident religious enthusiasts. Their inspirational figure, John Leland, a leading New Light Baptist in Virginia in the 1780s and declared enemy of Federalists, Congregationalists, Episcopalians, clerical hierarchies, missionary agencies, and theological seminaries, fought passionately for religious freedom, exalting "the individual conscience over creedal systems, local control over powerful ecclesiastical structures, and popular sensibility over the instincts of the educated and powerful."[11]

This explosion of Christian power in the West drew special force from what it was not: a replanted, authoritarian, instinctively theocratic New England Standing Order. The preachers and plain folk who populated most trans-Appalachian churches gave voice to a chronic animus against "Yankees" and their moneyed mission machinery. That hostility infused both Arminian and Calvinist churches. It would reach its purest, most extreme expression among those anti-authoritarian Baptists who deplored the centralizing initiatives of easterners in their own church. Taking the name Primitive

Baptists, to assert their lineage from early Christianity and the high Calvinism of eighteenth-century British Strict and Particular Baptists, they championed a fiercely predestinarian doctrine of "eternal and particular election." Sinners could not rescue themselves from damnation through free will or human ability: their only hope came from "effectual calling." Branded by critics as "iron-sided" deviants from orthodoxy, anti-mission Baptists won adherents across the South and West by providing a "hard-shell" defense against the "priestcraft" of the Arminianized, revival-promoting "steam religion" of protracted meetings, anxious benches, and other high-pressure methods of conversion. As pessimistic premillennialists they expected no progress until Christ's Second Coming would inaugurate his thousand-year reign. "Good works" led merely to ruinous sin: pride, self-righteousness, and worldly ostentation. Temperance societies, theological schools, tract societies, Sunday schools, Bible societies, Freemasonry, and other secret brotherhoods—all fatal to religious and civil liberty—were the contrivances by which Yankee "Mammonites" and "money-missionaries" stole the poor man's "last hard-earned fourpence half-penny."[12]

As migrants from New England and the Yankee settlements of upstate New York moved into the northern counties of Ohio, Indiana, and Illinois, they rubbed up against settlers from the middle and southern states. The mutual suspicion and often violent antipathies between these two cultural streams shaped social relations in the trans-Appalachian West. In 1806 the celebrated Methodist itinerant Peter Cartwright encountered a colony of New Englanders in Marietta Circuit, Ohio. "I had never seen a Yankee, and I had heard dismal stories about them," he recalled. "It was said they lived almost entirely on pumpkins, molasses, fat meat, and bohea tea; moreover, that they could not bear loud and zealous sermons, . . . and were always criticising us poor backwoods preachers." Farther west, an old hard-shell Baptist, "Daddy" Briggs, declared—his animus overlaid with disarming humor—that the richness of God's grace "tuck in the isles of the sea and the uttermost parts of the 'yeth.' It embraced the Esquimaux and the Hottentots, and some . . . go so fur as to suppose that it takes in these poor benighted Yankees; but *I* don't go that fur."[13] In the years following the War of 1812, the few Methodists in the Western Reserve, one recalled, "were treated

Pulling Apart: A Fracturing Nation   33

as intruders, and with much contempt" by Yankee Calvinists. The Congregationalists, he complained, had built schoolhouses with the help of other denominations, promising them access for religious worship, but once they were built, "'the standing order' took possession of them . . . to the exclusion of all others," especially the Methodists. Alfred Brunson, born into Connecticut Calvinism, abandoned the Congregational Church in adolescence and became a Methodist traveling minister in the Western Reserve. There he faced a double prejudice: Congregationalist hostility to Methodists, and the contempt of southern Methodist preachers from lower Ohio and Kentucky for Yankees like himself, whom they regarded as "bordering upon the savage state."[14]

This clash of cultures drove political allegiance. The extension of the vote to most white men during the early national period created a vibrant public sphere where political parties contested the character and future course of the nation. Support for the contending Federalists and Democratic-Republicans during the 1790s and early years of the nineteenth century helped shape the political bearings of the developing mass electorate during the heyday of what is known as the second party system of the 1830s and 1840s. Andrew Jackson's Democrats traced a lineage from Jeffersonian Democracy. Federalist ideas fed into, though did not wholly define, the nationalism of the Whig Party, a disparate coalition particularly attractive to reformers and the monitors of public well-being.

The optimistic postmillennialists of the "evangelical united front," mostly Calvinists, deemed the nation a moral agent subject to divine judgment and an instrument of the human progress essential to Christ's return. They trusted the Whig Party to nurture the civic virtue essential to inaugurating God's kingdom on earth. In this spirit Harmon Kingsbury, a Cleveland merchant and reformer, assured the Whig presidential candidate, William Henry Harrison, in 1840 that as God's instrument against "great national sin" he could depend on the votes of "a large portion of the people who regard the oracles of God as of paramount obligation." Harrison's victory gave hope to those like the Ithaca Presbyterian William Wisner dismayed by the country's wrong turning under Jefferson, whose "nakedness of infidelity" had steered his Jacksonian successors into "a constant struggle to cut the nation loose from all religious restraint."[15] Whigs attracted defenders of the Christian Sabbath against the movement of mail on Sundays; humanitarian opponents of Jackson's Indian policies that forcibly expelled the Christian Cherokees and other "civilized tribes" from the South; and evangelicals whose opposition to Freemasonry had previously allied them with the Anti-Masonic Party. The Presbyterian Calvin Wiley and other Whig superintendents of common schools championed free public education as the means of making moral republican citizens. Whig cosmology linked moral and material progress by its faith in the socially transforming power of wealth. Ethical concerns underpinned Whig evangelicals' trust in a national bank and stable currency, antidotes against the speculative fever and blighting panics of the era. Ready to endorse the progressive economic measures offered by Henry Clay's "American System"—protective tariffs, government-financed internal improvements to transportation, and a national bank—evangelical Whigs espoused a conservative approach to social order. The mobs of Jacksonian America alarmed those who knew public discipline underwrote republican liberty. Such precepts spoke especially to those of a residually Federalist mindset, mistrustful of people in the mass, attached to elite rule and deferential politics, and devoted to the ideal of an organic society of harmony, not class conflict. Evangelicals like Charles Hodge, Mark Tucker, and Francis Wayland, who feared "the ascendancy of the rabble" and believed in the primacy of "the mass of intelligence and property of the country," found their natural home in a Whig political community of moral, social, and economic self-improvers.[16]

By contrast, Democrats inherited from Jefferson and the Democratic-Republicans a profound antipathy to any form of political support for religion. The government's role was to protect its citizens from religious tyranny, not smooth the way for the concerted action of priest and politician. With their laissez-faire beliefs and distrust of government intrusion, Democrats appealed to those afraid that "church and state" Whigs would promote a reform agenda by statute. The Jacksonians' egalitarian appeal tapped the culture of lower-class rural folk in the South and West hostile to Yankee missions and alienated by Whiggery's elitist reputation. It attracted the self-conscious democratic Christian "who acknowledges his fellow-man as his equal, and is willing to give to every man the rights which

Pulling Apart: A Fracturing Nation 35

God has given him" and wanted a government that pursued "the permanent good of the whole, unchecked by particular privileges, and unfettered by artificial restrictions."[17] Evangelicals cut from this cloth resisted Sabbatarian enactments as a return to Puritan "blue laws": a state-supported Sabbath would "cleave asunder" America's delicate structure of civil liberty and empower ecclesiastical autocrats. Cries of "priestcraft" accompanied the efforts of temperance advocates to enforce pious sobriety by law. Removal of the Cherokee nation from Georgia likewise polarized Christians, with southern evangelicals generally declaring the question to be beyond the churches' remit. Democrats' defense of religious minorities and dissenters made the party a natural home—as had been the case with the Jeffersonians before them—for deists and freethinkers. Their association with Fanny Wright, Robert Dale Owen, and other notorious secularists gave shameless Whigs scope to paint their opponents as the party of atheists, blasphemers, and "most of the moral dregs, and scurf, and pollution of the land," and so to burnish their own credentials as "the Christian party." Applying a moral lens to economic matters, Jackson's supporters invested his policies with religious force. Sound money, not the "extravagant speculations" of capitalists and the "dangerous power" of the Bank of the United States, spoke to the plain Methodist and Baptist farmers' sense of fairness and of the justice of equal shares, not financial privilege.[18]

In his State of the Union address of 1830 the Democratic president Andrew Jackson used the crisis over Indian removal to impose his own definition of American nationality. He explicitly identified the nation with the white race and justified it theologically. Having defied the missionary philanthropists over Indian dispossession, a president of sporadically Presbyterian mien clad himself in the mantle of a Christian paternalist. The southeastern Indians' removal would, he asserted, protect a race lacking "the intelligence, the industry, the moral habits" of Anglo-Americans and set them on a course to establish their own form of Christian civilization. This tendentious rationalization of racist exclusion dovetailed with western and southern settlers' deep-seated prejudice against the moneyed philanthropy of the national missionary movement.[19]

Jackson needed no convincing that churches must be prevented from following their instincts to suborn the state. In his early days as a Tennessee political officeholder, he had sought the exclusion of religious elites from political office. His anticlericalism squared with the sentiments of the Baptist senator from Kentucky, Richard M. Johnson, who led the fight against Sabbatarians: "Religious zeal . . . when misdirected, excites the worst passions of our nature under the delusive pretext of doing God service." In the summer of 1832, with cholera casting an epidemic shadow over the East Coast cities, some religious bodies looked to the civil authorities to recommend a day of humiliation and prayer to stay the Almighty's hand. The Dutch Reformed Synod of New York asked the president to announce an official fast day. True to his principles, Jackson rebuffed the request. To comply, he wrote, would transcend the Constitution and "in some degree disturb the security which religion now enjoys in this country in its complete separation from the political concerns of the General Government." At a time of heated partisanship over the renewal of the charter of the Second Bank of the United States, the anti-Jackson opposition sensed an opportunity. Henry Clay, in a self-conscious act of civic piety (a welcome surprise to those who knew him as duelist and gambler), presented his own fast-day resolution to Congress. In doing so, he planted a religious standard to rally the anti-Jackson Christian forces that would shortly coalesce into the Whig Party: Anti-Masons, missionary evangelicals, and National Republicans. The resolution was defeated, but a stream of local fast-day initiatives followed. Democrats scoffed at "Priest Clay" and his Puritan maneuver. "A prayer by *State authority!* truly sounds strangely in the public ear," jeered one. "It reminds us of the canting, hypocritical days of Cromwell." But in mobilizing anti-Jackson sentiment over a religious issue, Clay's project worked. Jackson's "anticlericalism bred Christian politics."[20]

Before 1832, days of national fast and thanksgiving had been politically controversial but had not been strict tests of party allegiance.[21] George Washington's first thanksgiving proclamation of 1789 secured congressional approval only after animated debate over its constitutional propriety. John Adams, New England Congregationalist turned Unitarian, twice issued presidential proclamations for thanksgiving and fasting, in 1798 and 1799. These he was sure played a part in his election defeat in 1800, when Jefferson's campaign falsely linked him to the Presbyterian Church. This "secret whisper," he wrote, "allarmed and alienated Quakers, Anabaptists, Mennonists, Moravians, Sweedenborgians, Methodists, Catholicks, Protestant Episcopalians, Arians, Socinians, Arminians & &c.," who suspected Presbyterians aimed at becoming the nation's established church. "Nothing," he told Benjamin Rush, "is more dreaded than the National Government meddling with Religion."[22] Jefferson, who in 1774 had supported a Puritan fast day to galvanize colonial opposition to Britain, refused in office to follow his predecessors' examples. He drew a sharp distinction between the remit of state and federal governments. State authorities might be entitled to recommend days of worship, but, he held, "civil powers alone have been given to the President of the US and no authority to direct the religious exercises of his constituents."[23] His successor and Republican ally, James Madison, felt no similar inhibition during the tumult of war with Britain. Instead of uniting the country, however, the fast day of 1814 aggravated domestic divisions. "The pulpit was made the rostrum of turbulent and rancorous political declamation," the Jacksonian Gulian C. Verplanck sadly recalled. "The language of scripture itself was employed by divines in their sermons, and by magistrates in their proclamations, to point political sarcasms and to enkindle political rage."[24]

Verplanck voted against the proposed fast day in 1832. Religion, he asserted, could not be made "an actor in the halls of human legislation without infinite . . . evil to religion, evil to the State. You inflame the rancor of party politics by adding to it the fervor of . . . sectarian fanaticism, or else you . . . degrade religion by making her the handmaid of human power, or the partisan of personal ambition." But for good or ill, that is how the heated arguments over American national character and purpose developed during the antebellum decades, with the fusing of political and religious imperatives. The national fast of 1841 raised similar issues as the failed initiative in 1832. Outspoken Democrats dismissed it as a Whig political "pageant," "man-worship," and "sickening humbuggery"; Harrison's death merited celebratory feasting, not fasting.[25] These fast-day debates sharpened the partisan focus of the politics of religion, because people of faith identified with Democrats or Whigs in line with their fears of political "priestcraft" or welcome for religious "statecraft" that promoted a righteous nation. The partisan matchup was not perfect, but it broadly followed the contours of the conflicting religious cultures.[26]

Democrats found natural allies among those of all denominations who honored private piety and Christ's endurance of Roman political oppression. Primitive Baptists and other rural predestinarian Calvinists were generally Jacksonians, averse to Whiggish elitism and "improvement." So, too, were most Dutch Reformed and German Lutherans. The mass of Catholic immigrants thronged the Democratic Party: in sharp contrast to its role at the heart of many European confessional states, the Roman Church allied itself in America with an anticlerical party hostile to Protestant influence in government.[27] Protestants saw it differently, of course. "What other denomination called christian, ever go to the polls in a body?" asked one outraged minister alarmed by the electoral control of Tammany Hall and the growing power of "this ecclesiastico-political machine."[28]

Whigs found their natural religious constituency among supporters of state action to promote virtuous and socially enterprising citizenship. They appealed particularly to Congregationalists, reform-minded New School Presbyterians, and Unitarians. Among the smaller denominations, the Quakers were overwhelmingly Whig. They did not share evangelicals' faith and revivalist forms of worship, but their moral activism and pacifist objections to Indian warfare made Jackson's party repellent.

Mostly, however, the conflicting religious cultures cut through, not between, denominations. True to their Jeffersonian heritage, most Baptists remained strong Democrats, but in New England and the band of Yankee settlements into the Midwest, Whigs of that faith grew steadily in number, a measure of their enhanced social status. Whigs also made headway among Methodists, though Democratic politicians continued to benefit from the MEC's memory of victimhood at the hands of the historic Congregationalist establishment in New England. Presbyterians, too, presented a mixed picture. Their churches had long been divided between the Scots and Scotch Irish majority, strong in the South and West, and the minority of English, Welsh, and New England origin. The former—tenacious strict Calvinists loyal to their Scotch Irish president, Jackson—scorned the

Pulling Apart: A Fracturing Nation 39

doctrinal innovations of the Whig Congregationalists and New School Presbyterians who colonized the New England diaspora.[29]

These contending forms of religious faith and culture—a conflict over the sort of nation churchgoers wanted to live in—would persist beyond the confrontation of Democratic and Whig Parties into the new alignments of the 1850s and beyond. They played a part in energizing the emerging political configuration that pitted a continuing but diminished Democratic Party against a crusading Republican coalition. Above all, this was fueled by the irrepressible politics of slavery and the force of the associated religious nationalisms that turned the political arena into a crusaders' cockpit.

THE FAULT LINE OF SLAVERY

The diversity of religious identities would not have hurtled the churches and nation toward fracture without the presence of racial bondage in the young republic. Slavery, however, and its future place in the United States, would shake the antebellum religious world to its foundations, shattering the unity of many churches and philanthropic bodies. Those schisms gave succor to irreconcilable forms of religious nationalism; their widely felt shock waves helped erode trust in the American Union and contributed to the breakup and realigning of political parties during the 1850s. The Republican campaigns for the presidency—John C. Frémont's in 1856 and Abraham Lincoln's in 1860—gave voice to an ardent antislavery nationalism that overcame the conservative Unionism of their opponents, captured the White House, and detonated the political crisis that resulted in civil war.

Widely recognized by most northern evangelicals as a social evil, and described as such by some white southerners, too, the "peculiar institution" was, even so, rarely treated as a matter of personal sin during the early years of the republic. The hundreds of thousands of enslaved African American members of Baptist and Methodist churches, most of whose individual voices the historian can only guess at, quite probably did hold a damning view of slave owners' guilt: few were likely to have quarreled with Frederick Douglass's judgment that some masters' "pretensions to piety" were a thin disguise for their cruelty and personal depravity.[30] But among most white critics of slavery, North and South, who put their faith in schemes of gradual, step-by-step reform, there was great reluctance to question the moral character of individual slave owners. When in 1833 Theodore Weld declared that his Christian work as an abolitionist organizer, writer, and speaker was "the cause of *changeless eternal right* . . . of humanity and justice and righteousness," he set a prescription for religious purity and follow-up action on which, at the time, only black activists and a radical minority of whites could agree.[31] Like other spiritually reborn men and women of this subset, who preached the duty of all men and women immediately to separate themselves from sin, Weld had a romantic vision of a redeemed nation where black and white would live in justice and Christian harmony.[32]

When that radical minority—many of them, like Weld, converts of the revivals of the 1820s and 1830s—made heroic efforts to organize and campaign for the immediate abolition of slavery, they attracted the fire of the more conservative majority. Mainstream white Christians took alarm at the launching of a national organization in 1833—the American Anti-slavery Society (AASS)—that demanded not only the immediate start of a process of unconditional and uncompensated freedom for all slaves but also their integration into the American nation as equal members. The presence within that movement of William Lloyd Garrison and his "Christian anarchist" followers only added to the mainstream's perception of the AASS as a "whole tribe of lunaticks."[33] Garrison's critique of human government, as well as his assaults on the scriptures, the Sabbath, and the orthodox ministry, alarmed conventional evangelicals both within and beyond the AASS. But abolitionists of every stripe came under fire for deeming slavery a sin in all circumstances and demanding the end of any church fellowship with the owners of slaves. "I do not believe that all slaveholders are sinners," one leading free-state Methodist explained. "I know that some of them are pious men, so far as human judgment can go, and I would not harm them, even in my thoughts, for the world. I pity them."[34] Abolitionists' critics protested that castigating Christian slaveholders would set brother and sister against sister and brother, threaten convulsions in the church, tighten the bonds of slavery by alienating mas-

Pulling Apart: A Fracturing Nation 41

ters from the work of missionaries among their slaves, and derail progress toward the millennium.

What, above all, angered the Christian majority in the free states was that the radical abolitionists' doctrine, and especially their methods of agitation, brought the goal of human emancipation into disrepute. That slavery was cruel and unjust was a widely held view among northern churchgoers. Even those who considered the institution sanctioned by scripture spoke out to censure several of its features as practiced south of the Mason-Dixon Line: the separation of slave families, the prohibition of legal marriage, sexual assault, and the restrictions on reading and religious instruction. Northern Protestants generally fused Enlightenment philosophy and a reading of the Bible to declare slavery a "dark spot upon our national character," one that violated the slave's natural rights and the equity of God's law.[35] But for these critics the remedy lay not in violent and sudden emancipation imposed on the South from outside. Rather, it lay in the voluntary freeing of slaves by slave masters through what they considered the benevolent work of the American Colonization Society, founded in 1816 to promote the voluntary migration of freeborn blacks and emancipated slaves to Africa. Settling freed men and women there would, it appeared, offer them the chance of self-government and self-improvement denied to them in the United States. Christianized "Liberia," as the West African settlements became known, might serve as a millennial beacon for the rest of the African continent. The multiple conflicting purposes and possibilities of colonization as a panacea for domestic slavery would continue to animate political discussion before and throughout the Civil War and held a special and contested appeal for Lincoln himself.

The fault line within northern Protestant evangelicalism between these two approaches to millennial progress—the reforming gradualism of the colonizationists and the radicalism of those who damned the emigration schemes as a delusional bromide— was revealed in microcosm at Cincinnati's newly established Lane Theological Seminary, where Lyman Beecher had been appointed its first president and professor of theology in 1832. The student leader there was the eloquent Weld, whose charismatic advocacy of immediate abolitionism during a series of "Lane Debates" in 1834 won over most of his fellow students from their support for gradual measures. Their radical stance, when combined with the seminary's religious, educational, and other welfare work with the local African American community, led Lane's trustees to yield to white Cincinnatians' outrage at the social mingling of the races and to order the students to disband their antislavery society. Beecher himself was a convinced supporter of the American Colonization Society. Fearing the divisive implications of abolitionist agitation for national unity and God's millennial mission for the United States, and concerned for the prosperity of a seminary that he judged essential to the religious well-being of the West, he sought a compromise. Unwilling to yield, Weld led a walkout of the majority of the students. Most of these "Lane Rebels" provided the nucleus for a new collegiate foundation at Oberlin, committed to abolition, radical reform, and revivals. Weld devoted himself to lecturing on abolition, facing down hostile mobs, and organizing the AASS's forces in the West. Beecher, however, remained committed to his alternative prescription for millennial glory and never gave up his support for colonization.

Divisive though it was within the North, the issue of the proper Christian relationship to slavery had even more powerful ramifications nationally, both for the churches and for their missionary societies. Early in the century, Christians, North and South, had widely understood that the institution was a necessary evil that would gradually die out and was—as a Charleston Presbyterian put it—"at least injudicious as far as the happiness of the master was concerned."[36] But the doubling, and then tripling, of the slave population and a booming economy in staples, particularly cotton, encouraged a sea change in southern attitudes. By mid-century white evangelicals in the slave states had come publicly to present something of a pro-slavery consensus that the peculiar institution was neither transient nor evil, but a positive good. In the construction of a usable *defense* of slavery, evangelical piety fused with southern ideas of honor, to produce a more "manly" reforming evangelicalism than was current in the North. It fused, too, with a form of republicanism more deferential and class stratified than that which prevailed in the North.[37]

Southerners knew exactly what they were doing in choosing to march to the new tune of pro-slavery millennialism. The Baptist Iveson L. Brookes, when a student at Chapel Hill from 1816 to 1819, spoke out against slavery as "a moral wrong to the African race, . . . justified only upon the ground of necessity," but later, during the 1840s, became convinced that it was "God's Institution." Slavery sustained republican peace and safety by uniting labor and capital, cultivating "the mutual good feeling" of master and servant, and preventing the strife inherent in a free labor system. In Brookes's view the non-slaveholding states, "ignorantly fighting against God & the Bible," contained the seeds of their own destruction, since only "a monarchical and military despotism can ultimately control the populace, and secure the rights of the property-holders, where slavery is not the basis of society." In contrast, southern slaves were "the most contented and happy people on earth," while whites enjoyed "equality of social and political intercourse" unique in the civilized world.[38]

In this intellectual refashioning and evolution there was no single watershed moment. But one way or another, by 1850 southern churches had come to champion slavery as a Christianizing agent that would continue to improve the condition of the enslaved as the millennium approached. The South's deepening economic stake in slavery and cotton, the threat of slave revolts, the complex interplay of white and black evangelical churchgoers, and a concern for social cohesion: all encouraged this reappraisal.[39] But an important catalyst, too, was the abolitionists' campaign against the South. "I do believe," John Adger mused, unconvincingly, "that if these mad fanatics had let us alone, in twenty years we should have made Virginia a free State. As it is, their unauthorized attempts to strike off the fetters of our slaves have but riveted them on the faster."[40] To prevent abolitionists from "infecting the consciences of weak minded good Christian people of the South," southern churchmen deployed scripture to show that slavery was not a sin before God.[41] The Old Testament told how the Almighty had sanctioned "negro slavery, or the bondage of the Canaanitish descendants of Ham."[42] Enslavement was similarly recognized under the new dispensation. Christ and his apostles, living and working where bondage existed under Roman law, fixed the duties of masters and enslaved as they did those of parents and children. Those who argued that the Golden Rule ("All things whatsoever ye would that men should do unto you, do ye even so to them") demanded the freeing of slaves misunderstood

44   RIGHTEOUS STRIFE

the text. It meant quite simply, a Georgia Baptist explained, "that it is our duty to do unto others as it would be *reasonable* for us to wish others to do unto us, were our situations reversed."[43] The slave owed obedience to his master, the master humanity to the slave.

Equipped with the intellectual architecture of a pro-slavery millennialism, southern evangelicals pursued their own course toward social reform. Thus, Alabama Baptists urged masters to recognize their responsibilities as Christians; they should correct "the most erroneous abuses" of the slave system and prepare "to give an account to their master in heaven."[44] Slaveholders had a responsibility for their blacks' physical welfare as well as their spiritual development: when properly acquitted, this put masters on the moral high ground that northern employers of free labor, driven solely by money and the market, could never occupy. Missions to the slaves burgeoned through the 1840s and 1850s as planters—even in South Carolina, where chronic white concern over the possibility of slave rebellion ran deepest—ceased to fear that missionaries were abolitionists in disguise. By the eve of the Civil War most of the slaves were under religious instruction, thanks to the vigorous leadership of such self-consciously benevolent slaveholding ministers as Charles Colcock Jones and William Capers.

Southern evangelicals' public agreement that slavery was benevolent, scriptural, and civilizing was not the full story. As John C. Calhoun learned in 1849, "many religious people at the South" had "strong misgivings" in private.[45] A handful of these were emancipationists, largely from the upper South, for whom slavery was a rank sin. Much more typical of evangelical unease, however, were expressions that deemed human bondage not a sin but a "curse" or a natural evil. What troubled these observers were slavery's day-to-day cruelties, its assault on the family, its crippling moral influence on white and black alike, and its blight on enterprise. And then there was the scriptural truth of the common humanity and unitary origins of the races: slaves, too, were created in the image of God; they had everlasting souls. An anguished Presbyterian minister, Benjamin Smith, unable or unwilling to escape from selling, hiring, and disciplining slaves, lamented, "O what trouble, running sore, constant pressing weight, perpetual wearing, dripping, is this patriarchal institution! What miserable folly for men to cling to it as something heaven-descended."[46] Divided over whether slavery was an absolute good, a relative benefit, or a tolerable evil, southern evangelicals were of one mind that their peculiar institution conformed to scripture and erected no barrier to church membership.

The early republic's broad national consensus over Christian slaveholding had collapsed. Both antislavery and pro-slavery millennialists rejected compromise, splitting the countrywide evangelical churches during the late 1830s and the 1840s.[47] The slavery issue was inextricably bound up in the theological dispute that split Presbyterianism into Old and New School churches after 1838, southerners regarding abolitionism as the heretical offspring of New School theology. Among Baptists the issue came to a head over the question of the employment of slaveholding ministers by the denomination's missionary bodies. In Augusta, Georgia, in May 1845, ministers joined governors, congressmen, and other leading public figures in forming the Southern Baptist Convention. Northern Baptists followed by reorganizing their own missionary bodies.

No schism, however, endangered national unity more than the split within the country's largest denomination, the Methodist Episcopal Church. More organizationally integrated than Baptists and Presbyterians, the MEC experienced more bitterness as the schism played out. One of the Church's bishops, James O. Andrew of Georgia, had married a slave-owning widow. A majority of delegates at the General Conference meeting in New York in 1844 called on him to "desist from the exercise of his office" for as long as he remained "connected with slavery": although the Church embraced thousands of slaveholders, to accept one of them as an officer exercising nationwide authority would concede that slavery was a national, not local, institution.[48] Rather than surrender to what they judged the false doctrine of the sinfulness of slaveholding, southerners moved toward schism. The conference overwhelmingly agreed upon a plan of separation that provided for an independent church in the slave states, to be organized as the Methodist Episcopal Church, South, in 1845.

Mistakenly, some on both sides of the Mason-Dixon Line expected these schisms to strengthen the Union, by shutting down forums where sectional champions could collide. Conservative evangelicals, however, North and South, took a less hopeful view. The

North Carolinian Thomas Meredith despaired that Baptist separatists, in "frittering away the bonds of national union," invited "the horrors of civil war."[49] The Richmond Presbyterian William Plumer predicted that church divisions would "rend the star-spangled banner in twain . . . and the Potomac will be dyed with blood."[50] Methodists like Nathan Bangs also saw rupture as a national disaster, by destroying a system of ministerial interchange that had a "natural tendency to do away with those prejudices which grow out of local circumstances and habits."[51] Many shrewdly understood that fracture would weaken the centrists: unity provided the best guarantee that northern moderates would defend southern interests. The split in the centralized MEC in particular offered a stark warning of what was in store for the country as a whole: its sheer size made Methodists more representative and typical of the population at large.

Separation introduced new sources of bitterness and mutual stereotyping that further eroded evangelicals' sense of belonging to a Union impelled by a single, shared millennial vision. Quarreling and abrasion continued to mark north-south relations within Baptist and Presbyterian ranks throughout the 1840s and 1850s, but nothing in the experience of these two denominational families matched the trauma that schism visited on the Methodists. The Methodists' Plan of Separation, instead of providing a basis for the harmonious coexistence of the two branches of a divided Church, gave rise to a chronic and ugly conflict that presaged the Civil War. The twelve-hundred-mile line through the border states from Maryland to Missouri produced split congregations, litigation over local property, vilification in the press, and vigilante action. Invective once reserved for the other section's radicals was directed at all departed members. Magistrates seized and burned Methodist newspapers, their actions sustained by statutes, grand juries, and vigilance committees. Physical violence, notably against antislavery preachers, scarred communities in Missouri, Kentucky, Virginia, and the Eastern Shore of Maryland. Each side was convinced of the righteousness of its own reforming impulse and the defective morality of the other.

During the 1850s, the grip of pro-slavery ideology tightened in the South. "The dogma that slavery is sinful, or always an evil to both parties, is completely exploded," declared the *North Carolina Presbyterian*. Aggressive defenders publicly trumpeted the institution as a positive good that delivered unimaginable blessings to the enslaved. Self-righteous abolitionists endangered national harmony, as enemies of the Bible and deluded victims of what a contributor to The *Southern Quarterly Review* branded "a foul exhalation out of . . . New England Theology."[52] Southern Christians who had once deemed the bonds of Union to be as sacred as marriage vows came reluctantly to see the scriptural imperative of political divorce.

For their part, legions of free-state evangelicals lamented what they saw as a great apostasy confounding the South's moral sense. "Thirty years ago scarcely a man in the South justified, but simply excused, slavery," the Methodist Leonidas Hamline reflected. "Now nobody there excuses but justifies it—and 'O tempora! O mores!'—by the Bible, perverted to that base end."[53] When the proslavery ideologue Frederick A. Ross and other Presbyterian seceders established a united synod specifically to sanction slavery, they confirmed in the northern mind an imminent and inevitable crisis: southern Christians, in league with the political planter class—the Slave Power—would demand northern approval of slavery as a blessing to both races. But faced with that clamor, moderate antislavery northerners like the Boston Congregationalist Edward Norris Kirk stiffened their resolve. Over time, Kirk traveled from an empathetic concern for all people of the South to a painful struggle of conscience over slaveholding practice. He was provoked beyond compromise and cautious dealing by the words of the influential southern Presbyterian Benjamin Morgan Palmer that (in Kirk's shocked précis) "the peculiar and glorious mission of the South was, to build up a church and a state whose corner-stone was the slavery of the African race."[54] A recreant South, false to the values of Christian republicanism, had to be confronted and dragged back into the morally enlightened English-speaking world.

MOBILIZING ANTISLAVERY NATIONALISM

Religious conflict over slavery's moral legitimacy eventually engulfed the American political arena.[55] Party leaders in Washington during the 1820s and 1830s aimed to keep slavery off the political agenda, fearing its effect on national unity. But as cotton culture expanded into the Southwest, further entrenching slavery, the more difficult it became to gag political debate about its future. From the outset, most members of the AASS called for political action to supplement moral suasion: petitioning Congress, questioning candidates for office, voting only for antislavery men. Jackson's Democrats—tailoring their appeal to the fervid race prejudice of northern poor whites, including Irish Catholics, and the cherished states' rights of pro-slavery southerners—exerted little pull on abolitionist Protestants. Whigs' sympathy for reform and benevolent action made them a more natural political home, although the party's socially conservative, paternalist view of the world made it an uneasy berth for the most radical campaigners. For those who saw the two major parties as mere "divisions of the pro-slavery party," there was a simple solution: a separate political organization, devoted to abolition.[56]

The political force that then emerged, the Liberty Party, put up an antislavery presidential candidate, the Presbyterian James G. Birney, in 1840 and 1844, and ran candidates for a raft of local and state offices. In its program, activities, and composition the new party was an expression of socially concerned, revivalist Protestantism. Its leaders ("ministers—not statesmen or politicians," one Liberty man noted) spoke for supporters who deemed slavery a moral corruption as well as a social evil. Acknowledging that Congress could not constitutionally interfere with slavery within individual states, they still insisted that the federal authorities treat it as a mere local institution and make the interests of equality and free labor the controlling consideration in government action. Liberty meetings took on a revivalist character. "The Liberty party," one of its members later maintained, "unlike any other in history, was founded on moral principles—on the Bible, originating a contest not only against slavery but against atheistic politics from which Divine law was excluded."[57]

As a one-idea movement of "reformer politicians," the Liberty Party acted chiefly as a pressure group on Whig politicians and siphoned off enough votes to deny the presidency to Henry Clay in 1844. Its successor, the Free-Soil Party of 1848, more effectively capitalized on the sharpening of northern Protestants' reform sensibilities. By the second half of the 1840s, according to the Methodist John McClintock, "the division of Northern men into abolitionists and anti-abolitionists exists no longer. . . . In a word . . . the CON-

SCIENCE of the great Northern race is aroused."[58] That arousal resulted from political developments judged to expose the cumulative power of what was increasingly called the "slavocracy": congressional laws that gagged discussion, the annexation of the Texas Republic, and territory seized by force from Mexico. President James K. Polk's war-making provoked the hostility of particular evangelical forces in the Northeast: Congregationalists, New School Presbyterians, and Free Will Baptists, together with a determined minority of Baptists, Methodists, and Old School Presbyterians. Never doubting the wickedness of the Mexican conflict's origins, they saw in its outcome the acquisition of a vast domain standing at the mercy of the Slave Power. Ministers called on their congregations to reverse the "regular and constant progression" of slavery. "God himself consecrated the Soil of earth to Freedom," an Indiana pastor declared, "to be tilled only by the Sons of Freedom."[59]

As the movement for free soil gathered pace, Liberty clergy joined with thousands of religious defectors from the two main parties, Democrats and Whigs, to form a new third force. The organizing political convention of that Free-Soil Party, at Buffalo in August 1848, had more the character of a protracted revival meeting than a secular gathering. Twenty thousand supporters—men and women, black and white—under the canvas of "the great Oberlin canopy," encouraged the official delegates with prayers and hymns, imploring God to forgive the nation's complicity in slavery and racial intolerance. Speakers saw God's hand at work in making their convention the founding event of "a real Republic, to diffuse its light and truth to all Nations, until every member of the great human family shall know and rejoice in this great Salvation." The joyous expressions of millennialist hope that ended the convention ("The day of Freedom dawns at length—The Lord's appointed day!") swept Protestant clergy and laypersons into the campaign. God, they knew, had called them to serve in the apocalyptic struggle between "the dark hellish principles of the past unholy war, and of slavery extended" and "the rights of man, the rights of God, and the claims of Jesus Christ on earth."[60]

A series of landmark episodes during the 1850s sharpened radical antislavery sensibilities in the North and fed the anger of proslavery southern loyalists. A new and controversial Fugitive Slave

Law, one of the measures that comprised the unstable sectional armistice of 1850, compelled the free states to comply with legal provisions they widely abhorred. By denying constitutional rights to those deemed by a slave owner's word alone to be runaways, the law meant a black man or woman, whether free or slave, could be hunted down and kidnapped by federal agents. Southerners in turn denounced the free states for erecting legal barriers to securing the owners' constitutionally guaranteed return of persons "held to service or labour." The fugitive slave issue poisoned intersectional relations for the rest of a decade in which newly organized trans-Mississippi territories became the site of guerrilla warfare between pro-slavery and free-soil settlers. The pacificism that had shaped abolitionism since its Quaker origins continued to be the dominant characteristic of antislavery Protestantism, but a growing if small minority sanctioned physical resistance to the "Slave Power aggression" that disfigured the settlements of Kansas and, by the caning of Senator Charles Sumner, the halls of Congress itself. The pursuit of violent redress by a subset of the most radical black and white Christians in the North, impelled by a righteous vision of an inter-racial republic, reached its apogee in John Brown's seizure of the federal armory at Harpers Ferry. A strict Calvinist who saw himself as the prophetic instrument of an angry Old Testament God, Brown intended retributive justice on behalf of the enslaved, though no slaves were stirred to rebel. Seized, tried, and hanged, Brown took on the semblance of a Christian martyr, and some acclaimed him as "a Cromwellian Puritan," but most antislavery ministers rebuked his project as—in the words of a Massachusetts Congregationalist—the mad scheme of a "wild, misguided, perverted conscience."[61]

As antislavery sentiment intensified during the 1850s, only a small minority turned to righteous violence. Authority lay with those who confidently championed political means of resisting Slave Power influence, which took on new salience through a watershed crisis in 1854. Senator Stephen Douglas's Nebraska Act, by voiding the terms of the 1820 Missouri Compromise, gave southern slave owners hope of expanding the realm of enslavement throughout the territory of the Louisiana Purchase. Broad in the chest and short of stature, the "Little Giant" Douglas removed the outright ban on slaveholding within the western domain by recourse to the doctrine

Pulling Apart: A Fracturing Nation 51

of "popular sovereignty": the people of the territory would exercise their "democratic" right to settle the issue for themselves, though questions of precisely when and how were shrouded in a fog of deliberate ambiguity. The maneuver strengthened the Democrats' political hold on the South, but the party hemorrhaged electoral support in the free states. Ministers bombarded Congress with memorials against the bill: more than 500 signatories from the Old Northwest, 25 from Chicago, 150 from New York City, and more than 3,000 from New England. The northern pulpit reviled the perfidious Douglas, variously likened to Pontius Pilate, Benedict Arnold, and Judas Iscariot. The churchwomen of Alliance, Ohio, sent him thirty pieces of silver (three-cent pieces) sewn in gauze.[62]

The Nebraska reversal propelled antislavery Protestants into a variety of fusion movements that cohered into the Republican Party. On a platform headlined as "Free Soil, Free Speech, Free Labor, Free Men," Republicans established themselves in the presidential election of 1856 as the chief opposition to the victorious Democrats, now seen as the best defenders of southern interests. Here was the chrysalis of the party that would, in full adulthood, triumph four years later. Lincoln was vexed by the national convention's nomination of a former Democrat, John C. Frémont, as presidential candidate, but took heart from learning that the delegates had seriously considered him as Frémont's running mate: on one account "from that time Lincoln trimmed his sails to catch the breeze which might waft him to the White House."[63] Much of the new party's impetus derived from the energies of zealous—principally Yankee—evangelical Protestants impelled by conscience and obedience to a higher law to overturn "a system of unrighteousness" and open the portals of the Kingdom of God.[64] This brew of intersectional struggle and millennial religion found earnest expression in the diary of a Methodist itinerant preacher during the 1856 campaign. "The Lord came in power among the people and our souls rejoiced in the Lord," he exulted after a Connecticut revival meeting. He would soon register another Christian responsibility: "Election. Today the battle is to be fought between right & wrong. I went to the polls and did my duty. . . . May God aid the right!"[65]

Democrats branded Republicans "sectional" and "disunionist" enemies of American national integrity. Abolitionists had long debated the moral and religious integrity of a Union founded on a compromise with enslavers, which damned the Constitution as "a covenant with Hell." A small but vociferous minority continued to advocate separation from a leprous South. Republicans, however, rebutted the charge, adopting a determinedly nationalist position: their target was not the whole South but the "slavocrats," a minority within the white population whose authority kept in thrall not only the enslaved blacks but also their fellow whites, the majority of them non-slave-owning yeoman farmers and the "mud-sill" poor. Slave Power control of the South prevented advocates of antislavery—who balked at the murderous assaults on reformers south of the Mason-Dixon Line—from exercising there the free speech essential to American civic and democratic well-being. To those willing to hear, Republicans held out a vision of a nation of unfettered people profiting from the spread of free labor and free farms outside the South, whose archaic system would in time yield before a modernized economy, replacing human bondage with liberty and enterprise. Not they, but southern nationalist extremists with their empty threats of secession represented the real forces of disunion.

In 1860 the Republicans again offered themselves as the nation's conscience in an election whose key issues aroused Protestant evangelicals' moral concern, over the spread of slavery, the growing power of Catholicism, and proven corruption in the national administration. Lincoln, the party's presidential nominee, fully understood the mobilizing power of religious faith. As a Whig and then Republican organizer he well knew the cultural fault line in Illinois between settlers from slave states, who had located in the south and center of the state, and the later arrivals from New England and the wider Northeast, who settled to the north.[66] Addressing these mixed audiences, he had condemned slavery as a moral, social, and political evil. Beginning with his speeches in Springfield and Peoria in 1854, through his debates with the formidable Democratic champion Stephen Douglas—most powerfully at Galesburg, Quincy, and Alton—to his striking effort at New York's Cooper Union in 1860, he addressed the ethical dimension of the slave-bound labor and its inconsistency with the principles of natural rights given expression in the Declaration of Independence, principles inspired by "truth, and justice, and mercy, and all the humane and Christian virtues."[67]

Lincoln frequently insisted that there was "no reason in the world why the negro is not entitled to all the rights enumerated in the Declaration of Independence—the right of life, liberty and the pursuit of happiness. . . . [I]n the right to eat the bread without leave of anybody else which his own hand earns, he is my equal and . . . the equal of every other man." Jefferson's document "meant to set up a standard maxim for free society, which should be . . . revered by all; . . . constantly labored for, and even though never perfectly attained, constantly approximated, and thereby . . . augmenting the happiness and value of life to all people of all colors everywhere." In these political sermons Lincoln forcefully impressed on voters a stark choice between "the men who think slavery a wrong and those who do not think it wrong." No middle ground existed between slavery and freedom: "The real issue . . . is the eternal struggle between these two principles—right and wrong—throughout the world. They . . . have stood face to face from the beginning of time; and will ever continue to struggle. The one is the common right of humanity and the other the divine right of kings."[68]

Recognizing Protestant antislavery energy, but averse to abolitionists' moral absolutism, Lincoln fused Jeffersonian and scriptural precepts with a Whig-Republican ethic of self-improvement to minister to those who he knew found their inspiration as much from New Testament morality as Enlightenment ideals. His correspondents encouraged him to hold on to "high ground . . . up to the standard of the Christianity of the day." One believed the country was involved in a contest "for the advancement of the kingdom of Heaven or the kingdom of Satan . . . for an advance or a retrograde in civilisation."[69] Another, a Quaker, took delight in seeing Lincoln "fairly mounted on the eternal invulnerable bulwark of *truth*" against those fighting in the legions of the devil.[70] A former legal associate and antislavery reformer, William Perkins of Cincinnati, told Lincoln he had switched careers, trained for the Presbyterian ministry, and taken on the editorship of the church's *Christian Leader*, in order to stiffen Republicans' radical Christian muscle against political expediency in "our great Battle of 1860."[71]

The Republicans' 1860 campaign, promising an end to slavery's further expansion, achieved its ideological force from its blend of the economic, the political, and the moral: free soil and free labor, under threat from an aggressive and unscrupulous Slave Power, were not only an economic good; they were essential means of moral advance. Crusading Republicans rallied millennialist Protestants by setting the antislavery battle in a gospel context: the irrepressible conflict between free and slave labor was "Christ's doctrine of righteousness conflicting with evil."[72] Though Lincoln remained publicly silent following his nomination, his published speeches provided a staple of the Republican propaganda diet. At the same time, parading as the party of true Christian values, Republicans presented their candidate as a figure of sound Protestant faith and firm piety. The *Galena Advertiser* declared unblushingly that the "Glory of God demanded the election of Abraham Lincoln."[73]

The assertion that Lincoln was a devout Protestant offered a hostage to fortune. True, Lincoln and his family were pew holders in Springfield's First Presbyterian Church, but he was not a church member by profession of faith, and his record of attendance was spotty. Nor had he wholly silenced stories of his infidelity dating from his youthful dalliance in New Salem when, freed from the hard-shell Calvinism of his Baptist parents, he warmed to the rationalism of Tom Paine and other Enlightenment deists. According to the postwar testimony of Lincoln's friend and political associate Jim Matheny, during the late 1830s Lincoln had talked dismissively of the miraculous conception. He heard him "call Christ a bastard" and ridicule the scriptures for their inherent or apparent contradictions. Lincoln's enthusiastic infidelity, he asserted, sometimes bordered on atheism and, to the concern of his friends, endangered his future as an aspiring politician. When Lincoln ran for Congress against the barnstorming Methodist Peter Cartwright in 1846, he rebutted the charge of infidelity, but still, Matheny noted, "many Religious—Christian whigs" hated voting for him. As a result, he grew more discreet with age and "didn't talk much before Strangers about his religion." After 1854, as a rising figure, he aimed to remove the taint of irreligion by discussions with Christian ministers, who believed he was "a seeker after Salvation." Matheny recalled that letters were written "more or less all over the land that Lincoln was soon to be a changed man." William Herndon, Lincoln's law partner, recorded Matheny's view that he "played a sharp game on the Christians in 1858 to 1860." Herndon concurred, impressed by

Lincoln's "very politic" modus operandi in dealing with the devout. "When he was talking to a Christian, he adapted himself to the Christian. When he spoke to or joked with one of his own kind, he was indecently vulgar . . . ; he was at moments, as it were, a Christian, through . . . courtesy or good breeding . . . and in two minutes after, in the absence of such men, and among his own kind, the same old unbeliever."[74]

Others, however, pushed back against this indictment of Lincoln's faith, observing that after taking on professional and family responsibilities in Springfield, and suffering the devastating loss of his young son Eddie, Lincoln encountered and ruminated on a deeper Protestant theology than the rough-hewn evangelicalism of rural revivalists. As an attender of James Smith's Old School Presbyterian ministry, he sought out the intellectual, not the experiential. Although he rarely mentioned—let alone invoked—Christ in public and could not be classed as a believing Christian, this did not make him faithless. Herndon's conclusion that Lincoln *"was in short an infidel, was a universalist, was a unitarian, a theist,"* does not sound like unbelief to the modern reader.[75] What Herndon sought to establish was that Lincoln was not by conviction a Trinitarian Christian. That he could characterize unbelief in this way was a measure of evangelical Protestants' religious hegemony in mid-nineteenth-century America. From the perspective of orthodox Christians, the denial of Christ's divinity merited the label of unbelief, but the term does not do justice to Lincoln's ongoing religious inquiry. He discussed with Herndon and others the Unitarianism of William E. Channing and Theodore Parker, whose works he admired for their liberalism and rationality. According to Jesse Fell, a Bloomington lawyer and liberal Christian, Lincoln's religious views were "summed up on these two propositions, 'the Fatherhood of God, and the Brotherhood of Man.'" None questioned Lincoln's description of himself as a lifelong fatalist. "What is to be will be," he told Congressman Isaac Arnold, "I have found all my life as Hamlet says: 'There's a divinity that shapes our ends, / Rough-hew them how we will.'"[76]

The legacy of Lincoln's 1846 contest with Cartwright inflected Democratic commentary in 1860. Lincoln's bugle call to Republicans early in the election year—"LET US HAVE FAITH THAT RIGHT MAKES MIGHT"—drew the admiration of the party's

Christian crusaders, many of whom wrote to him in a spirit of religious encouragement during the fall campaign.[77] But canny Democrats were not slow in contriving slanderous gossip. An ally in Boston reported that Lincoln faced attack as "a pro-slavery man, and an intemperate, though 'not one who could bear so much whiskey as the little giant (Stephen Douglas)'!" Further, he wanted the candidate to rebut "the accusation that you are a duelist [who] . . . once challenged a man to mortal combat, & have not since changed your views of the wickedness of so doing."[78] From Philadelphia, Lincoln learned that his enemies claimed that "in religious opinions you are an open & avowed Infidel."[79] Elsewhere the Democratic press made him the soulmate of heretical abolitionists such as Beecher and Garrison, and godless German revolutionaries like Carl Schurz and Friedrich Hassaurek.[80] Lincoln, however, found a ready defender in the pastor of Springfield's Second Presbyterian Church, Albert Hale, who—lacking the term "spin doctor"—described his role as "a sort of Campaign Committee." He answered preachers' inquiries from across the country, dismissing fears that the Republicans had nominated a skeptic, drunkard, and tobacco user; defending Lincoln as a true, honest, and Bible-reading churchgoer; and wishing only that he could say of the candidate "he is born of God."[81]

Lincoln's victory was widely judged the redeeming triumph of "the Lord's side." Although the Democrats had their own religious strongholds, among Catholics and anti-Yankee churches, enough northern Protestants stood as Republican candidates, acted as Republican local organizers, delivered pulpit speeches, marched with the paramilitary "Wide Awakes," and saw themselves as "the Christian party in politics" to warrant their claim of exerting "a most controlling power in electing Mr. Lincoln."[82]

"POLITICAL PRIESTCRAFT EXPOSED": WHITE CHRISTIAN NATIONALISM

Throughout the antebellum decades, the Democrats positioned themselves as the resolute guardians of the slaveholding South, its northern allies, and the two sections' common values and economic interests. The party's assertive defense of slavery, appetite for the United States' expansion into the Caribbean, and calculated exploitation of white racial fears ensured a continuing national reach under the successive presidencies during the 1850s of the northerners Franklin Pierce and James Buchanan, the weak and pliable, or "doughface," agents of southern interests. The party stiffened its posture as antislavery opinion hardened into a free-soil movement intent on liberating the Union from the controlling influence of the overmighty Slave Power. Democrats' political leaders and broadranging constituencies of religious conservatives characterized the antislavery insurgency as "an uprising of the clergy" reminiscent of the days when clerical forces had organized to prevent the carrying and delivery of mail on Sundays.[83] Heirs of Jackson, the party instinctively assumed the voice of white religious anti-abolitionism.

Pro-Nebraska Democrats raised the specter of theocratic government in language that resurrected Jeffersonian and Jacksonian venom against "priestcraft" and the subordination of the state to dictatorial churches. Their rebuke of "meddling priests" helped give the long session of the Thirty-Third Congress (1853–55), in the words of an observer, "the semblance of an ecclesiastical council more than that of a legislative assembly."[84] Douglas charged that "recreant clergy" like Henry Ward Beecher ("Rev. Dr. Schreecher"), notorious for raising money to arm the free-soil settlers of Kansas Territory, aimed to make the whole religious community "a great political sectional party for Abolition." Democrats' allies in the churches joined the chorus. The Indiana Methodist minister William C. Larrabee typified northern Democrats hostile to spouters on "matters concerning which they know not whereof they affirm." Conservative Whig clergy, too, fretted over the pulpit's complicity in social disturbance.[85] The minority of Episcopalian antislavery clergy faced the wrath of their Democratic vestries.[86] Above all, the hierarchy and organs of the Catholic Church, whose Irish immigrant congregations were muscular defenders of the nation's racial order, condemned all strands of antislavery as manifestations of "higher law" fanaticism and, even worse, atheistic republicanism. They generally supported Pierce's Kansas policy and blamed abolitionists for the territory's civil war. Southern churches, too, lambasted the free-state clergy's "phrenzied fanaticism" and "politico-religious" message.[87]

Democrats reasserted the conservative religious character of the national project during the presidential campaign of 1856, a three-way sectional contest in which their candidate, Buchanan, faced the Republicans' John C. Frémont in the free states and the American ("Know-Nothing") Party's Millard Fillmore in the slave South. Stigmatizing Republican clergy for introducing "the *Northern Puritan* Compass" into politics, Democrats encouraged immigrant and native-born citizens' fears that fanatical ultra-Protestants controlled both Republicans and Know-Nothings. Catholics were firm for Buchanan.[88] The Boston *Pilot* urged the South to secede should Frémont win. Cincinnati's *Catholic Telegraph* excoriated Republicans for their "savage animosity" toward Rome and cheerful reliance on "Protestant associations and Irish Orangemen."[89] Buchanan denounced political distinctions based on "religious opinions and accidental birth-place." His allies berated "Church and State men" and "pulpit schreechers" as "the most dangerous class . . . to the peace of society." Philadelphia Democrats launched a campaign paper, *Political Priestcraft Exposed*. Banners in New York displayed a minister wielding a rifle and revolver while trampling on a Bible with the caption: "Beecher's Command—kill each other with Sharp's Rifles." A slave-state Episcopalian, traveling through the free states, condemned a contest that more than any previous canvass was "one in which the religious portion of the North takes an active part."[90]

Similar themes, pressed with no less ferocity, marked the presidential race in 1860. By then, the casuistical skein of Douglas's "popular sovereignty"—as glossed in his Freeport Doctrine and designed to hold northern and southern Democrats together—had unraveled and left the divided party fighting the election under two banners. With the Douglas forces unyielding on the principle of popular sovereignty, states' rights southerners ran their own candidate, John C. Breckinridge, demanding a federal guarantee of slave owners' property rights in the territories. Still, the two factions of the party were united in damning the Republicans' antislavery program and its implications for white supremacy. Southern Democrats, playing on the trauma of John Brown's abortive plot to initiate a slave revolt, and viscerally alarmed by the threat to their way of life and investment in human property, brandished Bible and Constitution. They, and Douglas men, too, scoffed at the notion that God's law prohibited slavery. Consider the Almighty's blessings. "What nation on the globe," one asked, "has been so wonderfully and bountifully blest as this people under our Constitution?" According to the Pennsylvania Democrat John L. Dawson, an omnipotent God must be left to engineer slavery's eventual demise, "at the very moment when it shall be to the advantage of the negro."[91] Douglas men warned that Lincoln's party, driven by "blue-light puritans" and "fanatical Sabbatarians," would loosen the sacred ties of a Union guaranteeing civil and religious liberty. If the Republican Party "had not slavery for a hobby," they sneered, "it would be vexing us about some other questions of morals or of social arrangement." Its credo in New York, where it had pushed a strict Presbyterian and Sabbatarian agenda, read, "No music but psalms; and no drink but water." The Little Giant (lauded as the drinkers' companion) would stand by the Jeffersonian principle of government as the friend of "social and political equality among the varieties of religious faith."[92]

The Democrats' political creed spoke to the values of Catholics and non-Yankee Protestants, including southern and western Methodists and Baptists (especially of the Primitive strain) who saw in Breckinridge and Douglas the nation's defense against infidel Republicans and Puritan "priestcraft." *The New York Herald*, the Democratic voice of the maverick James Gordon Bennett, claimed to speak for orthodox conservatives of every faith—"Christians and Jews, Catholics and Protestants"—distressed by the plethora of Bible-denying creeds feeding malignant Black Republicanism: "Fourierism, Owenism, Fanny Wrightism, free farmism, free loveism, women's rightsism, Bloomerism, Sabbatarianism, Maine Liquor lawism, abolitionism, and the other isms imported from Europe."[93] Conservative Protestants also rallied to the Constitutional Union Party of Tennessee's John Bell, strongest in the lower North and border slave states. Here continuity Whigs, declaring that "all opinions, moral, religious and political, not in violation of the Constitution, must be free," found an ethical bulwark against the "frenzied" and exclusive higher-law sectarianism of the Republican Party.[94] Those of all faiths who believed that the proper province of the church was a private, "nonpolitical" devotionalism—formulations eloquently developed by James Henley Thornwell and fellow Old School Presbyterians—turned to one of the two Democratic parties, or the Constitutional Unionists, to uphold their religious brand of American nationality.

———

A Protestant chorus saw the hand of God in Lincoln's election triumph. Here was the apotheosis of Republican religion. William Sloane, minister of Elkhorn, Illinois, told him the Democrats' defeat revealed the Almighty at work, directing the people's mind and doing *"terrible things in righteousness."* At Illinois College, Julian M. Sturtevant took up his pen to similar purpose. Lincoln knew him well. A New England Congregationalist and early settler in central Illinois, Sturtevant regarded his friend as a minister of righteousness who had secured a moral revolution in politics during the 1850s. He relished above all Lincoln's radical "House Divided" speech and its premise that ultimate truth was not a matter of human opinion but embodied immutable principles that accorded with the law of God. In his ecstatic letter of congratulation to the president-elect he declared the Republican victory a triumph of Christian values, the means of national transformation, and an expression of uncompromising religious support for the incoming administration. Lincoln stood for principles by which "we . . . shall leave to our children a free and glorious country, and *without* which ours is the vilest of nations." The new president would enjoy the support of tens of thousands of religious patriots who would not "bow down and worship the image which Nebuchadnezzar has set up." The nation stood on the brink of a new heaven and a new earth. "I need not tell *you*," he continued, "that our politics have now reached a deep religious element, of which these compromisers have no more conception than a man blind from birth has of color. Let these weak hearted, feeble kneed gentlemen know, that they can no more bind those religious convictions . . . than they can bind old ocean's waves with bands of iron."[95]

In Sturtevant's rapture at the imminent arrival of a new republican order can be seen the climax of the political narrative by which one brand of religious nationalism—mission focused, "Puritan," and antislavery—triumphed electorally over the conservative, pietist, white-supremacist, and pro-slavery variants of faith-based patriotism. The interpenetration of religion and politics was nothing new in American electoral experience, but that chemistry charged the contest of 1860 with unique power and was to shape the crisis to come. Within weeks of his defeat, James Buchanan responded to the unfolding danger by calling a fast day that, as the next chapter reveals, gave those fused elements of religious faith and secular interests further scope not to heal but to amplify the political clamor.

Sturtevant was indeed right to see the Republican victory as a most profound national watershed; at the same time, however, his elation blinded him to the political earthquake that would follow. From his vantage point as president of Illinois College he would watch in distressed outrage as the righteous victory of 1860 occasioned an intractable crisis that was finally resolved only by the bloody battlefield carnage that the most perspicacious of white Americans dreaded.[96]

CHAPTER 3

FAST DAY, JANUARY 1861: NATIONALIST RIPTIDES

On Friday, January 4, 1861, as the national crisis deepened, Abraham Lincoln called in at a Springfield hotel, the Chenery House, to welcome a distinguished visitor, Salmon P. Chase of Ohio. The victory of the Republican Party's standard-bearer had impelled South Carolina's secession from a political Union its leaders no longer trusted to protect their vital interests. With compromise schemes stalled, further states seemed likely to follow where South Carolina's radicals led. The struggling lame-duck president, James Buchanan, commanded diminishing respect. Meanwhile, the president-elect maintained a delphic public silence in his hometown.

As this new year dawned, Lincoln's concerns included shaping a politically balanced cabinet, to be convened after his March 4 inauguration. Chase—once his rival for the 1860 Republican nomination and now U.S. senator-elect for Ohio—had traveled at Lincoln's invitation. "Take him all in all," Lincoln told the editor of the Republican *Chicago Tribune*, Charles H. Ray, "he is the foremost man in the party." Chase had barely time to recover from his journey before the president-elect called to raise the prospect of his appointment as secretary of the Treasury: Would he accept it, were it to be offered?[1]

Fast Day, January 1861: Nationalist Riptides 63

That same day, public events in two Springfield venues told of the country's political turmoil. A morning talk at the courthouse examined Lincoln's election "from a moral and religious stand point"; an evening sermon there called for "a religious political revival" to calm the national mood and prepare for the new administration. The speaker, J. S. Burt, a staunchly antislavery state educator, was a graduate of Julian Sturtevant's Illinois College and the Chicago Theological Seminary, where his Calvinist training had given him special insight—the organizers declared—into "the relation of *religion* and *politics*." The country's crisis demanded the combined wisdom of ministers and statesmen.[2]

Burt's "patriotic discourses" contributed to a torrent of rhetoric on the day Buchanan had called for national humiliation, fasting, and prayer. Springfield's various Christian traditions assembled at the First Presbyterian Church. Lacking a contemporary account, we must rely on the description written twenty years later by the Baptist minister Noyes Miner.[3] The meeting, he recalled, was well attended by the most respectable sort. They included his near neighbor, Lincoln, seated in his customary family pew. The president-elect, Miner recalled, though not "an experimental christian" (he had made no declaration of faith), listened to the fervent prayers "with tearful and thrilling interest." As Miner was leaving, Lincoln took him by the hand, saying, "while the tears were standing in his eyes, Mr. Miner, 'this has been a good meeting, I hardly see how it could have been made better. I feel grateful for the prayers offered up for our distracted country and on my behalf and I hope they may be answered.'"[4] Over-colored though it was, Miner's account suggests the inevitable weight of responsibility Lincoln felt as his term of office approached.

Two days later Lincoln, his wife, Mary, and Chase returned to the First Presbyterian Church for a Sunday sermon. The full scope of what the two men discussed over that weekend is unknown. If they reflected on the religious observances, they might have found an unhappy augury in the fractious countrywide response. Buchanan's fast day has attracted scant attention in studies of the secession crisis, but the forces then at work molded Lincoln's presidency at least as much as did Chase's formidable bolstering of the Union's finances. For the fast day, rather than rallying the country behind a common national purpose, exposed and aggravated irreconcilable religious versions of American destiny. With the political crisis forcing citizens to ask fundamental questions about their Union, ministerial voices crystallized contending ideas about the nature and purpose of American nationhood. Come the war, those elemental ideas drove the party political antagonists who fought for the soul and direction of the loyal Union.[5]

In fast-day preachers' sermons, it is possible to hear a host of distinctive individual voices and detect something of ministers' various and complex relationships—warm, tense, and uncertain—with their congregations. Collectively, however, they delivered three broad and diverging perspectives on the nation's trauma. Unyielding antislavery nationalists dominated the pulpits of New England and parts of the upper North, manifestly sympathetic to the Republican Party and its program of freezing slavery where it stood. In those southern pulpits that observed Buchanan's proclamation, pro-slavery ministers resolved to resist unscriptural Republican madness, the poison of Yankee "higher law," and the assault on the glorious constitutional values of the founders. The third and broadest range of voices urged compromise and concession to save the nation from radical elements, North and South: the issue of slavery, whatever its moral dimensions, must not be allowed to sunder God's chosen nation. The individual elements of those contending ideas were not new, but the winter's crisis forged them into steelier contending expressions of religious nationality. The following analysis explores the turbulent and meaningful rhetoric of the fast day. It concludes with a short coda: the turmoil within the religious tradition that claimed both Buchanan's and Lincoln's religious affiliation, Old School Presbyterianism, which was exposed and inflamed by the political intervention of the Church's most influential theologian, Charles Hodge.

BUCHANAN'S DAY OF FASTING, HUMILIATION, AND PRAYER

No longer a feature of life in the United States today, fast days were for some two hundred years, until the late nineteenth century, regular community events commanding broad popular support. They kept a cultural grip until secularism and a scientific sensibility eroded the providentialism that made them relevant and purposeful means of caring for the public. Days of public fasting, preaching, and prayer derived from sixteenth- and seventeenth-century British practice, and played a central ideological role during the English Civil War, when the fast sermons of Puritan parliamentarians identified their godly cause with ancient Israel's. American colonial fast days, dating from the late seventeenth century, were observed first in Massachusetts and then in other parts of New England, proclaimed by governors as acts of penitence to protect settlers against natural disasters, bad harvests, and disease. During the American Revolution, Continental and state authorities sanctioned days of fasting and prayer to implore God's blessing on their cause. Clergy on warring sides—both Britons and Patriots—delivered sermons on God's overruling Providence, though British preachers seemed less sure than their colonial counterparts that they enjoyed God's approval and protection.[6] Fast-day sermons explained the fledgling country's survival during the Napoleonic era. Consistent with his reading of the Constitution's First Amendment, Jefferson called no national fast days but recognized that the venerable custom of fasts called by state governors enjoyed popular support, even among Baptists and other staunch opponents of religious establishments.[7]

Jefferson could not have expected that a few decades after his death contending Civil War presidents—though deeply at odds in their philosophy of government—would proclaim multiple national fast days. Humiliation, prayer, and fasting took on special significance as anxious citizens sought the intervention of Providence to halt and reverse the harrowing challenge to the Union's existence. Presidential proclamations closed government offices, urged a halt to secular business, prescribed preaching and prayer, and encouraged citizens—aided by penitential abstinence from food—to reflect in church and private on their personal sins and the nation's shortcomings.

In his fast-day proclamation of December 14, Buchanan had attributed "the present distracted and dangerous condition of our country," and the prevailing financial and economic uncertainty, to the utter disregard for "the wisest counsels of our best and purest men." A thoroughgoing Old School Presbyterian himself, he had urged the American people, "according to their several forms of worship," to recognize their "ingratitude and guilt towards our Heavenly Father." Only by fervent prayer and confession of individual and national sins would an omnipotent Providence "save us from the horrors of civil war and 'blood-guiltiness.'" That "the God of our fathers" had not deserted American Patriots during the darkest days of the War of Independence gave every hope that he would now intervene to "preserve our Constitution and our Union . . . for ages yet to come."[8]

In his appeal to the "several forms" of religious worship, Buchanan sought not only to mobilize the conservative instincts of the Old School churches that he knew best but, more broadly, to summon to his aid the vast numbers and cultural power of the American religious machine. Calculating the historical dimensions of that power, however, is more an art than a science. Definitive measures of church membership and attendance in 1860 do not exist. The U.S. censuses reported denominational seating capacity, which is important as an index of churches' strength relative to each other and of how well they could accommodate most of the rapidly growing population, but seats are a poor guide to the number of regular worshippers. Another problem is that some denominations were more committed to record keeping than others. Methodists, Presbyterians, and Congregationalists systematically tallied those in full membership; Baptists, for example, were laxer. Again, lists of members did not include church "adherents," those who attended but had not yet met, or chose not to meet, the spiritual and emotional demands of conversion or a public profession of faith. These included children and young people. More commonly, adherents were men more loosely attached to the church than the women of the family, a pattern exemplified at Springfield's First Presbyterian Church, where Mary Lincoln was a full member but Abraham not. The ratio of adherents to members varied widely and was necessarily impressionistic.[9]

With these caveats in mind, the best starting point is to take the figures for Protestant church membership in 1860—some five million—as a baseline for countrywide strength among the non-enslaved population of twenty-six million.[10] Protestants' power lay in their unequivocally evangelical denominations, notably the northern and southern branches of Methodist and Regular Baptist

Churches, Old and New School Presbyterians, and Congregationalists.[11] Beyond these, evangelicalism energized Low Church Episcopalian, Lutheran, and Reformed ministers in their contests with conservative "confessionalists." On a realistic estimate of two "hearers" to every converted member, evangelical Christians made up at least four in ten of the free population and constituted the nation's most influential subculture. Roman Catholic churches had seating for 1.4 million of their mostly immigrant population, on various estimates reckoned to number more than three million. Taking these and non-evangelical Protestants into account, it is probable that in 1860 at least 75 percent of the American people placed themselves within the orbit of Christian churches.[12] Beyond this, as Lewis Saum's study of the unremembered common folk of antebellum America suggests, residual Puritan, Calvinist, or more attenuated evangelical convictions persisted even among non-churchgoers.[13]

The wise counsels of the "best and purest" to which Buchanan nodded with approval undoubtedly included the prescriptions of his own message to Congress of December 3. There he blamed the crisis on a quarter of a century of northern antislavery agitation: radical abolitionists had fostered a chronic fear of servile rebellions that threatened the domestic security of the South. Slaveholders' alarm at Lincoln's recent election was understandable. However, they had no "just cause" to break up the Union. Lincoln, legally elected, would be restrained by the branches of government beyond the Republican Party's control: "Sufficient unto the day is the evil thereof." Buchanan urged southerners to pause unless and until they met an overt act of aggression. The Union was perpetual. Secession was an act of revolution. But if separation was unconstitutional, so, too, was the federal government's coercion of a state. The Union could not be cemented by bloodshed. Instead, the president proposed an asymmetric "compromise": an explanatory constitutional amendment confirming slave owners' right to their property, both in states where the institution existed and "in all the common Territories," and nullifying the free states' legal measures designed to make the 1850 Fugitive Slave Law unenforceable.[14]

In the days between his congressional message and the fast-day proclamation, the president's spirits sank further. He wanted a national constitutional convention to devise an explanatory amendment that clearly spelled out masters' rights to holding property in slaves in both states and territories and to the restoration of their escaped slaves. But his hopes depended on the slim chances of Republican conservative conciliators prevailing over the party's radical non-compromisers. At the same time, he watched ominous developments in the South and feared that South Carolina would seize the federal forts around Charleston: Sumter, Moultrie, and Castle Pinckney. When Howell Cobb resigned from the cabinet on December 8, it signaled that Georgia, too, could not be counted on. Others broke with the president: Secretary of State Lewis Cass and Senator John Slidell, moderates on opposite sides of the question of reinforcing the forts. Buchanan on December 10 prophesied, "I am truly sorry to say that South Carolina will secede about the 20th & the other cotton states will, in all probability, speedily follow."[15]

In many quarters Buchanan's calling of a national fast day appeared a desperate measure signaling executive weakness. That perception grew sharper during the three weeks preceding the fast day itself. Many believed, wrongly, that Buchanan was winking at secession, and even in league with its plotters. Cass reported that a jittery president was spending half his time crying, half praying. When South Carolina did indeed secede on December 20, he lost control of his increasingly divided and dysfunctional cabinet. The fault line between the administration's secession sympathizers and hard-line Unionists cracked wide open when news came of Major Robert Anderson's dramatic removal of his Federal forces from the garrison at Fort Moultrie to a single center of command at Fort Sumter. Buchanan had had no advance warning of this daring initiative. He now had to deal with angry South Carolina commissioners and appeasers in the cabinet, on one side, who urged him to order Anderson's withdrawal, and cabinet hard-liners (Secretary of State Jeremiah S. Black, Attorney General Edwin Stanton, and Secretary of War Joseph Holt), on the other, ready to resign should he do just that. At the same time, he was pinning his hopes on conservative Republicans winning Lincoln's support for the comprehensive compromise plan formulated by John J. Crittenden and the House Committee of Thirteen: at its core was a guarantee, by irrevocable constitutional amendment, of slavery's permanence, and the prohibition of slavery north of the $36°30'$ parallel (the former Missouri

Compromise line). Should that scheme fail, Buchanan would fall back on his idea of a national constitutional convention. Lincoln, however, resisted the tug, and Buchanan's former southern friends turned angrily on him when—relying on Black's robust text—the president declared his intention "to defend Fort Sumter . . . against hostile attacks, from whichever quarter they may come." This stiffening of resolve took practical expression on January 2 in his order, encouraged by General Winfield Scott, that Anderson be sent reinforcements. Even then, he tried to stop the relief expedition, but it had already embarked. These stressful weeks left the president distraught, desperate, and buffeted, until "he resentfully complained that he had not time even to say his prayers."[16]

This sequence of events, when embroidered by inevitable half-truths and rumor, shaped the public's perception of their lame-duck president. "Mr. Buchanan has a faith so astounding as to be able to pray for the preservation of what he is doing all in his power to destroy," scoffed the *Chicago Tribune*.[17] Gideon Welles registered the fast day in his diary with blistering contempt for the president. "Wretched man! Most of our public troubles are to be attributed to his weakness and wilful perversity."[18] The president had referred to himself as "an old public functionary" in his 1859 message to Congress. Now a Republican chorus blended ridicule with contempt for "the Old Pub Func," characterized as a spineless and feeble old-timer.[19] Recourse to a day of prayer made Buchanan "the most imbecile specimen of senility" ever to hold the highest office.[20]

Senility itself might have been forgivable; unrighteousness, hypocrisy, and treason in a Calvinistic president who summoned the nation to prayer were not. The report on deep-seated corruption within the administration, produced by John Covode's House committee in the summer of 1860, had done nothing for Old Buck's moral authority. A Tennessee Whig sneered that the day of fasting would have been unnecessary had "the obese old pub. Func." not fed on the spoils of office. His cabinet's corruption merited the words "*Let us prey*." At New York's Broadway Tabernacle, Joseph Parrish Thompson laid out a furious charge sheet against the doughface agent of slave interests. He had penned a "pirate's creed," the Ostend Manifesto of 1854, urging the seizure of Cuba from Spain, as a bulwark for slavery in the Gulf states. He had connived in the

Supreme Court's *Dred Scott* decision approving the right of property in man and championed the pro-slavery Lecompton Constitution imposed on Kansas by fraud and violence. As free-state Kansans themselves put it, "If the 'old public func' had not so villainously administered public affairs during the last four years, there would have been no present need of a special interposition of divine providence." A charitable view might pronounce the president insane, but the evidence told of a treasonable disruption of government.[21]

Buchanan's Republican critics accused him of a further inconsistency. As we have seen, Democrats had for decades berated their opponents—Federalist, Whig, and Republican—for their "political preaching" on matters of faith and conscience. Now, as the *Chicago Tribune* wryly noted, all had changed. A Democratic president had conceded that "subjects for prayer and preaching may be found less remote in history than ancient Babylon and Judea, and nearer than Borrioboola Gha" (the fictional setting of the African improvement scheme that so obsessed Charles Dickens's satirical character Mrs. Jellyby). Critics recalled the reaction against the clerical petitions against Douglas's Nebraska Bill. "It *then* was out of order for the religious element of our country to interfere with the events of the day . . . but *now* the tune is changed."[22]

The about-face was interpreted as executive cowardice. Where was the steely Democratic determination of Andrew Jackson that "by the Eternal, the Union must and shall be preserved"?[23] Faith and prayer were second-order weapons in the fight against treachery. The president must abide by the scriptural precept that "faith without works is dead."[24] "We have no right to ask God to do our duty," a Cincinnatian jeered. "There is no degree of . . . wrestling in prayer that will re-enforce Major Anderson."[25] When a storm-tossed vessel foundered, or a child fell into a well, it was a mockery to fall on one's knees instead of standing tall against danger. "There is a time for prayer," a New Jerseyite conceded, "but don't leave the devil in your house when you go to church. The patriots of '76, did not content themselves with 'humiliation and prayer' when Arnold betrayed their cause."[26]

Some Republicans disdainfully shunned the day's religious services, blaming their opponents for the gathering political crisis. "It is for . . . Democratic leaders and Democratic Clergymen (queer animals!) to get on their knees today and hourly confess before God that they have grievously lied," a Minnesota editor snorted.[27] It was "Saint Buchanan," as a fellow Presbyterian facetiously dubbed him, who should spend the day in personal humiliation, penitence, and remorse.[28] With characteristic flair, William G. Brownlow deemed the president no more qualified to lead the nation in prayer "than the Devil is to administer the Lord's Supper." In Massachusetts, the abolitionists William Lloyd Garrison and Charles Beecher wanted no part in "the traitor's fast."[29] Far better, it seemed to an Ohioan, to mark the day by slitting "the throat of a fat gobbler, . . . preying upon his carcass," and raising the toast "Confusion to all Compromises and Compromisers!"[30]

But these were the minority. In most places outside the lower South—where secessionist radicals considered Buchanan's call "a rebuke & censure of the seceding states, & of their cause"—churches attracted worshippers of all stripes, encouraged by a chorus of political and religious authorities.[31] Several state governors—in New England, New York, Ohio, and Maryland—formally endorsed the fast, one with a sharp Republican prayer that the president be given a backbone to maintain the government inviolate.[32] A small minority of churches denied the president's authority in matters of faith under a federal constitution "at war with God and his law."[33] But the ruling bodies and bishops of the Catholic and mainstream Protestant churches—particularly the Presbyterians, whose constitution of 1787 had made fasting a solemn duty—accepted Buchanan's summons. Whatever they thought of the outgoing and incoming administrations, ministers knew the nation's danger demanded patriotic communion.

In New York the city's banks, customhouse, public offices, and most shops remained shut, the day's legislative session was rescheduled, publishers suspended their evening newspapers, and special services took place in synagogues and all the churches except the Roman Catholics', who claimed that "prayers for the constitutional rulers of the nation are put up every day." Banks and stores closed in Boston. Reports from Baltimore, Boston, Richmond, Cincinnati, St. Louis, Portland, Philadelphia, and other towns and cities told of business suspended and churches crowded. In Chicago many stopped work, though "under the influences of good sleighing and a clear cold atmosphere a liberal use was made of livery and private establishments." Communities in Vermont patriotically fired thirty-three guns to mark the fast-day services, one for each state of the Union. Wisconsin fired a "national salute" to honor Major Anderson. On the Pacific coast, however, the last-minute arrival of the proclamation allowed only token observance; in Utah Territory it came too late for action.[34]

The day's biggest crowds gathered under dull skies in the nation's capital. With stores and government offices closed, denominational services drew vast numbers. At the New York Avenue Presbyterian Church, Buchanan listened to the consoling words of the pastor, Phineas Densmore Gurley, and prayers for the Union. At the Capitol, an unprecedented six thousand worshippers thronged the spacious Hall of the House of Representatives and its lobbies.[35] Here Gurley, as chaplain to the Senate, offered prayers, and Thomas H. Stockton, the House chaplain, delivered an ardent Unionist sermon.

Abstaining from food demanded a measure of self-denial that most failed to summon. Services for humiliation and prayer were one thing, daylong fasting quite another. An Ohio wit conjured up the image of a loyalist Democrat: "Soup—None. Fish—None. Boiled Dishes—None. Entries—None. Vegetables—None. Relishes—None. Pastry—None. Dessert—Hot Whisky and Lager Beer." George Templeton Strong, traveling by railroad to Baltimore, wryly noted that his good intentions were "strengthened by the absence of anything to eat. Except at Havre-de-Grace where something was tendered me called oysters, but in fact oyster shells softened by long boiling."[36] Henry Whitney Bellows made a principled case for eating. Humiliation and prayer, he agreed, were always in season, but fasting "never, and particularly not when all our bodily vigor and endurance may so shortly be required to meet the enemies of our national existence."[37] Claiming the moral high ground, the Boston *Pilot*—a Catholic and Democratic newspaper—sneered at Protestants' laxness in fasting and asserted that Roman churches, by contrast, culturally attuned to sackcloth and ashes, had been models of public penitence.[38]

It was not devotional laxity that threatened Buchanan's hopes for the day, however. Rather, it was the unbridgeable chasm between competing views of religious duty that gave it ominous significance.

The avalanche of stirring rhetoric on January 4 delivered some overarching themes that were common to all and deployed a common vocabulary of keywords: righteousness, patriotism, liberty, strength, will, conciliation, and sacrifice. In each instance, however, the meanings were plastic, shaped by context and the speaker's purpose. Open to conflicting interpretations, the words revealed that preachers and people, as they observed the president's request to confess "individual and national sins," disagreed profoundly over how a righteous country should address its existential crisis.

THEMES IN COMMON

Days of fasting, humiliation, and prayer had over time developed conventions and a familiar vocabulary. Allied to an anxious surge of patriotism during the present crisis, these well-established usages ensured that several common and uncontroversial, even formulaic, themes ran through the fast day's addresses: the scriptural sanction for fast days, their proven benefit in the country's past, the workings of Providence, God's punishment of personal and national sins, the power of prayer and repentance, the unique blessing of the American Union, and the millennial hope it inspired.

Few doubted the national peril, and most were in shock. The Philadelphia Presbyterian George Duffield Jr. recognized in the state secession conventions pending across the lower South the ominous portent of civil war.[39] In New York, William Adams took alarm at the radical change in national prospects since the state's recent day of thanksgiving. "A reversal so sudden, so entire, so unnecessary, so gratuitous, so unreasonable," he mourned, "brought upon us by no descent of fire or pestilence from heaven—by no invasion of a foreign foe—but altogether engendered within our own borders— is itself enough to afflict and mortify us." Charles Wadsworth lamented that, after a year of unsurpassed material advance, "the most prosperous and happy of all nations under heaven" should be facing a convulsion "unparalleled in our history."[40] The eras of blood and disorder following the breakups of the Macedonian, Roman, and Mogul Empires gave Otis H. Tiffany grisly precedents to chill the hearts of Chicago Methodists. His Episcopalian neighbor envisaged no less than "the flames of an earthly Hell."[41]

All knew that fasting had been the practice throughout the colonies' struggle for independence. But, as we have seen, during the early republic many questioned whether federally appointed fast days were consistent with the constitutional separation of church and state. Buchanan's invitation was a reminder to older worshippers of those concerns and of the limited reach of the national fasts called by Whigs in 1841 and 1849. Yet few now doubted that the ritual of fasting and humiliation, and the duty of self-examination, accorded with biblical precept and enjoyed God's approval in perilous times. As Wadsworth reminded his Philadelphia Presbyterians, the scriptures told of the necessary fasts of the Israelites, "when defeated by the men of Ai: of Ahab, when denounced by the prophet Elijah: of Jehoshaphat, when assaulted by the confederate forces of Ammon and Moab: of Nineveh, when visited by Jonah."[42]

It was a truism that God ruled over nations and furthered his purposes through them. Most conspicuously, the narrative of the Jews showed how the Almighty punished collective unrighteousness. Julius Foster, of Towanda, Pennsylvania, took the Israelites' experience from the time of Abraham to their final dispersion—their retreat into Egypt, captivity in Babylon, return to Judaea, and overthrow after the advent of Christ—to show how God dealt "with a *nation*—a much favored—a stiff-necked—a sorely punished nation." That Abraham's descendants remained scattered but distinct served as a lesson that "there is a God that *ruleth* over nations, and holds them accountable for their *national* as well as individual character and conduct."[43] Foster's sentiments typified the embedded Calvinist belief in the moral agency of the nation-state. In John B. Romeyn's classic statement, "national sins . . . must meet with national punishments" here and now. "Hereafter the judgment relates to men personally."[44]

What sins threatened national destruction? As will be seen, the question exposed deep religious fissures. But the preachers' formulaic jeremiads converged over hoary offenses against the Lord's commandments: worshipping false gods, or no god at all, under the thrall of Tom Paine and Revolutionary deists; violating the Lord's Day; sanctioning adultery, including Mormon polygamy; tolerating an epidemic of homicide, dueling, lynch law, and alcohol-fueled rioting. Collective and personal greed fetishized the dollar, repudiated debts, and compromised honesty, making the country a byword for crass materialism.[45] The nation's crisis sprang from the poison of false witness: the fake news and unfounded slurs of free-for-all electioneering. "What . . . slanderous falsehoods have the different political parties uttered of each other! How each has striven to degrade and blacken the character of his neighbor!" the Michigan Methodist James Smart mourned. "I think it not too much to say, that no man could have voted a straight party ticket in every case for the last ten years without sin."[46] The chicanery of elections had dulled the consciences even of godly men. Charles Wadsworth grieved that lies had been woven into "the woof of our social life, until our grand national boast of 'free speech,' and 'a free press' has become . . . infamous license."[47]

Skeptics asked what realistic hope of national salvation lay in a day of religious humiliation. Clinton Locke, pastor of Chicago's Grace Church, dismissed their sneers: "They say, 'what good is it going to do; is it going to put off secession, or tranquilize the country? We have brought this on ourselves and now we have got to bear the consequences.'" Such defeatism ignored how divine Providence had shaped the nation in the mold of the Protestant Reformation. When King Philip's great Spanish armada had borne down upon England, "whose hand was it that dashed that fleet upon the rocks and saved the Reformed Church from ruin?" Who, George Duffield asked, had reserved the land until it was ripe for civil and religious liberty? Who had prepared the thirteen colonies for nationhood, by their deliverance "in the Old French War; and in their various conflicts with fierce and merciless savages"? In the grueling struggle of the Revolution, who had endowed them with the wisdom, courage, and strength to make a permanent reality of the Declaration of Independence? Shower upon shower of spiritual awakenings before and since 1776 had confirmed God's special favor, doubly blessing the nation as the Land of Revivals and the Land of Liberty. Born as the child of Providence, it had been baptized as such by the Holy Spirit.[48]

Unshakably convinced of God's special purposes for the country, ministers insisted that the Lord would listen to His prayerful people. The crisis was His means of teaching the nation the value of its free institutions for the world at large. "God will bring us out of these trials gloriously," a Philadelphia Presbyterian declared. "Like the old Israelites, we have a great work to do for God, and He will strengthen us to do it." Brooklyn's Henry Ward Beecher agreed that the nation's great providential role lay ahead. Out of the current turbulence, God would deliver a "whole land, healed, restored to its right mind, and sitting at the feet of Jesus."[49] With epic certainty, and a hint of bravado, the leading Unitarian Henry Bellows—destined to inspire and lead the wartime U.S. Sanitary Commission—acknowledged that "the grandest political structure the providence of God ever allowed to be erected is to be finally tested by earthquake." But the national emergency would prove "that it rests on the rock of ages, and will endure while time shall last."[50]

ANTISLAVERY NATIONALISM

Feelings ran high during the national fast day, engulfing normally staid congregations. "The obsolete custom of applauding preachers was revived in several churches," the *Boston Transcript* reported. Cascades of appreciation interrupted Thomas Stockton's Unionist sermon in the Capitol.[51] Nowhere was fervor more intense than in the antislavery hubs of New England and the upper North, largely Republican in politics. Taking the fast day as a whip with which to chastise Buchanan and his cabinet, antislavery preachers used their pulpits and allied Republican Party newspaper presses to deliver an impassioned reading of the nation's righteous obligations and purposes. Rather than bewail sin in general, or dwell on secondary wrongdoing, they prioritized one particular biblical text, the words of the prophet Isaiah, to turn their fire on human bondage: "Is not this the fast that I have chosen? to loose the bands of wickedness, to undo the heavy burdens, and to let the oppressed go free, and that ye break every yoke?"[52]

Collectively, these champions of antislavery delivered a trenchant moral argument. By any reckoning, the enslavement of four million human beings was the nation's cardinal sin, a stupendous system of wickedness and the greatest of all the cruelties the country had more generally inflicted upon vulnerable people and races. This, they made clear, was not to underestimate the atroci-

Fast Day, January 1861: Nationalist Riptides 77

ties against the aboriginal people of North America, the "thousands of wronged and murdered red men," who had been provoked into hostility by broken treaties and forced removal and whose streaming blood "seemed like the incense of wrath ascending to the throne of God."[53] Nor was it a matter of pride that the nation, "the most boastfully religious people on the globe," had employed its gigantic strength in an impious war against Mexico "with almost no moral restriction."[54] Even so, the comparative iniquity was clear. "We have wronged the Indian, we have wronged the Mexican, but their united wrong is but as a drop in the bucket, or as the small dust in the balance, compared with the enormous wrong of which we have been guilty towards the African."[55] In this way the antislavery pulpit not only upheld the moral purport of Lincoln's victory, but crystallized a cogent and crusading nationalism to keep the country true to its godly fundamentals through the current and prospective political turmoil.

The pulpit's assault on the sin of slavery wove together God's law, Christian compassion, human rights, and economic justice. Few delivered a more comprehensive moral critique of southern slaveholding as "the embodiment of all oppression and crime" than the octogenarian Congregationalist minister and former president of Amherst College, Heman Humphrey. At the Methodist church in Pittsfield, addressing a congregation that included the former Massachusetts governor George N. Briggs, he leveled a familiar indictment of a ruinous system. He cataloged the evils: man stealing and human trading, reducing intelligent humans to mere plantation animals, denying them "the sacred ordinance of marriage," separating families, selling comely girls "to some lecherous keeper of a motley harem," branding flesh, starving four million minds of education, and denying them means of reading the Bible. Slavery corrupted the lives of white southerners, too, by its temptations to sin: it debauched planters and their sons, defiling "the holy sanctuary of household chastity, and bringing mixed blood into a thousand families." It developed a domineering, paranoid, and violent spirit in masters and a shiftless dependency among the white laboring class.[56]

By subjecting slaves to the owner's absolute control—denying them wages for labor, rights in property, freedom of speech and worship, and the right of resistance—the whole system of bondage became, in Henry Bellows's words, "a state of war upon its subjects." American slavery was a double outrage, upon God and man, and upon the spirit of Christianity and the political instincts of the nineteenth century. Under a republican government, "based on respect for human rights, political equality, universal representation, free speech, public discussion, general enlightenment, and progressive reform," enslavement contradicted every principle of the Declaration of Independence, the nation's political inspiration and conscience. That founding document had given a radical edge to the Republicans' Chicago platform on which Lincoln had run for office. Equally, the declaration assumed a righteous, talismanic role in preachers' fast-day narrative of the nation. God had smiled on its principles by protecting the American colonists during their Revolutionary struggle for freedom and leading them to a miraculous victory against herculean opponents.[57] The country's founding architects, embarrassed by the presence of slavery and their involvement in it, rose above their time to produce a visionary national prospectus designed to encourage their children to work for the equality of man in every sphere of life. It expressed the "Christian conviction of the nation's heart."[58] But tragic "paralysis and leprosy" had subsequently afflicted the declaration's doctrine of liberty. Henry Ward Beecher squarely blamed the corrupting influence of slavery. "The lives of the signers of the Declaration of Independence would not be worth one day's lease in Alabama, Louisiana, Carolina, or Florida," he declared, "if they were there to say the things plainly which they said when they framed this government, so utterly have the South vomited up their political views."[59]

These antislavery nationalists commonly recognized the moral ambiguities and legal constraints facing slaveholders. They conceded that the current owners had not imported the slaves. The historic trafficking in bodies and souls had been done by traders North and South. A lasting element of wrong had been cemented into the nation's constitutional architecture. "No perpetuity was intended or desired for it," Andrew Leete Stone of Boston's Park Street Church accepted, but it had still proceeded to corrupt "private life and character, patriotism, humanity, theology, Christianity, official honor and right."[60] State laws now prohibited masters, however humane and pious, from acts of emancipation. "What should we do were we placed in just such circumstances?" Heman Humphrey asked. "'Are we better than they? No, in no wise.' Our human nature is no better than their human nature; very unreliable at best." Nathaniel Hall, Unitarian minister of Dorchester, Massachusetts, had been raised amid slavery and taught to regard it as allowable, if not right. He understood why white southerners saw things differently: "God save us from too harshly judging them, as we would not ourselves be judged!"[61] Here were echoes of Lincoln's sentiments at Peoria in 1854: "I have no prejudice against the Southern people. They are just what we would be in their situation. If slavery did not now exist amongst them, they would not introduce it. . . . I surely will not blame them for not doing what I should not know how to do myself."[62]

Still, charitable empathy barely tempered the moral assault on an archaic slave system. Henry Bellows told southerners to recognize an irresistible tide of human progress and Christian civilization. Edwin Miller Wheelock, abolitionist and Unitarian, rebuked the South's ethical reversal from the days when slavery had been uneasily tolerated as "an inherited evil and sin, to be got rid of at the earliest possible moment and in all practicable ways." Sentimentalists who uncritically credited the warm generosity of the plantation South were chided for ignoring pro-slavery vigilantes' grievous tarring and feathering of emancipationists, or "the amiable impulse of inserting bowie-knives into our bodies, or of hanging us—good-naturedly, of course." Pro-slavery expansionists—"the jealous slave power"—who vilified devout antislavery Christians as fanatics and infidels had lost their ethical moorings.[63] In all its unrighteousness, slavery had provoked "lurid flashes of rebellion" against the Union and driven South Carolina into mad and revolutionary self-destruction.[64]

For all their emphasis on the *national* sin of human bondage, and the need for the whole nation to pray, antislavery evangelists conceded nothing to those, not least Buchanan, who blamed the current emergency on abolitionists. Opponents of expansionist slaveholders prayed on fast day not out of any personal guilt but because, as Michigan's James Smart explained, it was a righteous vanguard's duty: "Take Noah and his family out of the old world and it is overwhelmed. Take Lot out of Sodom and it sinks, though ten righteous men might have saved the city."[65] The greedy Slave Power had substituted narrow sectional advantage for the nation's greater good on issue after issue: nullification, internal improvements, protective tariffs, homestead bills, congressional gag rules, the annexation of Texas, the Mexican-American War, the repeal of the Missouri Compromise, and the settling of Kansas. Working to overthrow the dominion of slaveholders was no evil: it was, as the Congregationalist Homer Dunning put it, "God's wonderful work for the troubling of our Israel." Turbulence could be a purifying agent in national political life. Consider the lethargy of China, or the stagnant despotism of barbaric Russia, and contrast them with the rich history of political and religious agitation in England, which had made it a free, great, and powerful nation. God's method caused pain: the agitation over slavery was a thorn in the national flesh, but it served His providential purposes. It kept the nation up to the moral mark, a reminder that "man's chief end is to glorify God and do his will—to seek first his kingdom and righteousness."[66]

Lincoln's recent victory, a product of that moral turbulence, signaled the nation had nipped the worm in its bud by returning to the Christian principles of the New England Puritans, "that every man stands before God free and equal to his fellow-man." Their self-denying and painful pursuit of human rights—freedom of thought, religion, and person—had paved the way for the founding principles of 1776 and 1787. The wise intentions of the fathers had subsequently succumbed to degeneracy in public life, but Christians had now recovered public respect for "God's Higher Law." Elevating natural human rights above human slavery, they had confounded those "who scout the Declaration of Independence as a tissue of glaring falsehoods."[67] The country now saw that religion did, after all, have a proper place in political life. Radical abolitionist voices spoke of unique and hopeful omens for the nation's future.[68] Far from a sign of divine displeasure, the current perils told of awakened humanity in a people moved by the spirit of the gospel.[69] The election merited national rejoicing.

Nor was there reason to falter in the face of South Carolina's "insanity," whatever the political clamor for concessions. Lincoln's victory, denying slavery "another rood of free territory," must not be squandered by compromise. George Duffield spoke for those trusting that Lincoln, raised up by God to meet the crisis, would honor his words: "Only stand firm, and we will not fail!"[70] Transforming society came at necessary human cost. It would be craven folly to make "the price of peace *consent to wrong*" and "to cement the Union with the blood of our brother man." Scripture taught that Christ himself came to bring not peace to the earth but a sword. A fast-day poet sternly rhymed, "And *your* many compromises, / Fair and cunning though they be, / Shall not bar my wheels of justice, / For my children shall be free. / And the hour is waxing nearer / To the end that I have willed: / There shall be no peace forever / Till *my purpose* be fulfilled."[71]

Inflexible opposition to both compromise and secession drew strength from a sturdy millennial faith. Antislavery nationalists understood that honoring Isaiah's imperative "to let the oppressed go free" was, as the prophet declared, the distinguishing mark of "a nation that did righteousness."[72] America's foundation story and national narrative bore witness to its intended role as God's righteous instrument. In Albany, New York, the Baptist Justin Dewey Fulton insisted there was one acceptable compromise: an amendment to the Constitution "proclaiming the year of jubilee to every slave, according to the law laid down in the Bible." This national testing time would reveal how God would extend his special gift of liberty to the slave. Those of this sensibility shared Homer Dunning's elation at "the fiery ordeal through which the nation is now passing, though it may . . . revolutionize many cherished institutions." The hand of the Almighty was in it, "pushing on the wheels of his kingdom for the redemption of all the races of mankind." Preserving the Constitution and antislavery Union demanded but one course of action: "dare to do right, though the heavens fall!"[73] The millennial faith of antislavery nationalists, as trumpeted on January 4, took a frequent buffeting during the costly four years' conflict ahead. But an unyielding conviction in the righteousness of their political and social cause gave little room for doubt that God would be with them on their arduous journey to honor and realize His purposes. They more than most provided the magnetizing steel at the core of the Union's struggle and ultimate victory.

PRO-SLAVERY SOUTHERN NATIONALISM

The rhetorical drama of Buchanan's fast day was an instance of Hamlet without the Prince of Denmark. South Carolina's turbulent act of secession, to become a self-styled independent republic, had given the day its special urgency, but the ministerial voices of the departed state were notably absent from the national stage. They had spoken already, by taking to their pulpits on Wednesday, November 21, the day of statewide fasting and prayer set by Governor William H. Gist to prepare public sentiment for political separation. The governors of Alabama, Georgia, and Louisiana, too, scheduled similar fast days for late November.[74]

Deeply invested in the southern way of life, the region's preachers interrogated the moral meaning of the recent election. Lincoln's victory, the triumph of "ignorant demagogues," opened up the federal administration to malign crusaders determined to exterminate slavery.[75] These November sermons heralded the leading role ministers would shortly play in the surging secession movement that in February culminated in a separate southern Confederacy. Their religious justification for separatism provided an inspiring credo for the lower South and the basis for Confederate religious nationalism in wartime. Their words became a source for sympathetic preachers outside the region and, perhaps in even greater measure, evidence for the critics of southern extremism that the section's churches had fallen into a moral abyss.

Two addresses stood out, acclaimed throughout the seceding states: James Henley Thornwell's sermon on national sins, delivered in Columbia, South Carolina; and Benjamin Morgan Palmer's address to a packed New Orleans congregation, "The South: Her Peril and Her Duty," whose sixty thousand copies made it a publishing sensation. Palmer had studied under Thornwell at Columbia Theological Seminary and would become the first moderator of the Presbyterian Church in the Confederate States. The somewhat courtly and high-minded tone of Thornwell's elegant address befitted his reputation as an intellectual sophisticate, but it achieved an internally consistent defense of slavery only by skating over the institution's human abuses and miseries. Palmer, a brilliant orator and self-described "preacher of righteousness," offered more fiery fare, mixing a celebration of the slave South's providential moral order with a combative and fearmongering analysis of sectional politics and alleged northern aggression.[76]

Both ministers had long denounced "political preaching," and confessed how awkward they now felt in being driven to "intermeddle in politics." But faced with the South's existential crisis, they had a moral duty to champion separation. Their commitment to slavery, they insisted, was scripturally sound, principled, and disinterested. The institution uniquely and virtuously enfolded labor within capital, guaranteeing that workers would never go unemployed or unfed, as they did in the free states' perilous economy "with their labor and their capital grinding against each other like the upper and nether mill-stones." The South's providential trust was to conserve, perpetuate, and extend slavery, subject only to the limits imposed by God and nature. Guardianship imposed a "duty *to ourselves, to our slaves, to the world, and to almighty God.*" The South was morally obliged to find a refuge from the effects of a perverted republicanism that had "dethroned reason and justice, and . . . deified the people, making their will, as will, and not as reasonable and right, the supreme law." For a generation or more the erroneous "new divinity" of Charles Finney and his northern allies had led individual moral agents astray, unanchored from a literal reading of scripture that demanded their utter dependence on God in making moral choices. Consequently, and in parallel, the despotism of pure democracy had for a quarter of a century encouraged the aggression of atheist abolitionists, ideological clones of Marat and Robespierre. Their cry of "liberty, equality, fraternity" meant "bondage, confiscation and massacre." Fusing scriptural justification with the imperatives of the prevailing southern honor code, Thornwell and Palmer deemed the founding of a new nation, independent from a dishonorable North, the only redemptive course open to the slave states.[77]

Although they championed an ideology radically opposed to antislavery American nationalism, pro-slavery southern nationalists in the November and January fast days developed an argument that in key respects mirrored the interpretative framework of their critics. Each party lamented the other's betrayal of the principles and values of 1787. As abolitionists accused southerners of abandoning the principles of the founders, so their adversaries spoke bitterly of broken constitutional faith. The compact among the states had called for the mutual respect of all parties to it, but the southern states' equal rights in the Union had suffered "an enormity of treason equaled only by the treachery of a Judas." Reprobates had "for the wages of unrighteousness . . . undermined the foundations of the stateliest temple of liberty the world ever beheld."[78] Kidnapping slaves, repudiating the *Dred Scott* decision, sanctioning John Brown's bloody invasion, and opposing the extension of slavery: all were a fearful violation of the founding constitution and a betrayal of virtuous nationalism. An Alabama Methodist minister deemed any government that failed to protect its people's rights a tyranny, "whether it consist of the rule of Czar, or millions of Republicans."[79]

Likewise, antislavery voices that described the sectional struggle as an irrepressible conflict between irreconcilable civilizations found their counterpart in the pro-slavery nationalists' diagnosis of the Union's affliction as an irremediable disease—in Palmer's words, a "gathering imposthume." Configured into every social, political, and religious feature of the South, the scriptural blessing of slavery had rescued from the "barbarism" of Africa what George Henry Clark, rector of St. John's Church in Savannah, characterized as "a most degraded race in every way, physically, socially, intellectually and morally." "*American slavery*," Howard Henderson asserted, "*is the highest sphere of moral and social being that the negro ever enjoyed.*" Consequently, it was impossible simply to regard "the Irrepressible Conflict" as one between separate forms of civil polity. Rather, it represented an enduring contest between political madness and the higher law of God, between perverted human reason and the Bible. In this struggle, "Patriarch and Prophets, Christ and his Apostles, rise up and confront the enemies of our section and society, and denounce them as opposers of God's order and providence."[80] The fortunes of the world were at stake.

This meant, by inexorable logic, resisting surrender or compromise. Lincoln's election had ruptured whatever remaining confidence they had in northern fidelity to national interests. Whatever faith could be put in his political integrity, Lincoln was a powerless piece on a chessboard controlled by ideologues. The South would suffer the savagery of "a blood-hound that never bolts its track when it has once lapped blood." To wait for an overt act from the new president—until he had control of the armed forces, arsenals, forts, and treasury—would be "like Samson in the temple of Dagon, to pull down ruin upon herself." In this historic moment, conflict must be joined. Most pulpits of Richmond, Virginia, typified a broader intransigence. In the Gothic elegance of his Second Presbyterian Church, Moses Hoge interpreted Lincoln's victory and his plan for slavery's ultimate extinction as the prologue to northern coercion and full-scale civil war. Yet the ignominious surrender of inalienable rights and privileges would be far worse than war, horrible though that prospect was. The pastor of Broad Street Methodist Church, James Duncan, stirred up his congregation to a "righteous resolution to do or die."[81] A fellow Methodist at Centenary Church prayed for peace, but not at the sacrifice of right, even if maintaining it deluged the land in blood.[82] In Alabama, Henderson called on citizens to give up their political differences and "step forth under the common banner of Righteousness."[83]

Pro-slavery nationalists held out a millennial vision of the South separately prospering under God's protection. Its future leaders would be inspired by exhilarating godly examples: Moses, "at the lead of Israel *seceding* from Egypt"; or Daniel at the court of Darius; or Luther "bursting the chains of priestcraft and superstition"; or Cromwell, trusting in God but keeping his powder dry; or Washington, the model of a prayerful leader, during the War of Independence. Religious faith encouraged confidence that, should it come to a fight, the southern David would defeat the northern Goliath: "One can chase a 1,000 and two put 10,000 to flight." The South had to do no more than gracefully recognize this sublime historical moment, when it had the power to save not only itself but the whole country and the world. Taking the easy option would visit racial ruin on its children, but a strenuous defense of chartered rights promised a bright millennial future for the newly liberated southern nation. That bold step would invite temporary hardship and distress, but a permanent glory beckoned. "May the Lord God cover her head in this her day of battle!"[84]

CONSERVATIVE UNIONISM

Most January fast-day speakers inhabited a broad spectrum of opinion between the poles of northern antislavery radicalism and southern pro-slavery separatism. The integrity of the Union, not the future of slavery, drove these self-styled moderates to condemn those whose rhetoric and actions threatened a beloved nation. They might better be termed "conservatives" in view of their determined defense of the federal settlement of 1787 and subordination of the moral legitimacy and future of slavery, on which they held a broad range of positions, to what they saw as the more fundamental and certainly more urgent matter of saving the nation. Strongest in the lower North and the border slave states, with some outliers in the Deep South, they called for compromise and concession on behalf of congregations whose meshing of religious and political moderation had drawn them in 1860 into the orbit of conservative Republicans, the Constitutional Union Party, and Douglas Democrats.[85] Over the previous two decades they had discovered the alarming potential for church-related violence across the whole of the border region whenever antislavery crusaders contended with choleric and armed defenders of slave society. They were acutely aware, too, of the failure and unpopularity of antebellum schemes for gradual emancipation in the northern tier of slave states. And they were often embedded in communities whose economy meshed with northern interests, whose sympathies lay with the culture and society of the South, and whose ties of blood tugged in both directions.

Finding themselves tossed in a sea of troubles as 1861 dawned, on fast day these conservatives asked where, amid the tides of "insanity," was the enlightened statesmanship that had graced public life in the days of the founders? Theodore P. Bucher, Gettysburg's German Reformed pastor, searched for evidence of calm Christian judgment among the nation's political elite, but grieved that few had escaped the prevailing political madness. In Bath, Maine, John W. Fiske censured those who knew better but had deliberately stoked dangerous popular prejudices. At a joint meeting of the Orthodox and Baptist congregations of Canton, Massachusetts, George W. Hervey deplored how the constitutional privilege of free speech had licensed "fanatical ultraism . . . exercising lordship over the public mind." Perverting scripture and abandoning rationality, the extremists of each section—"the sturdy Puritan . . . and the gay Cavalier"—were riding blindly toward doom.[86]

Southern extremists—variously characterized as proud, headstrong, violent, wrathful, and vindictive—faced Unionists' contempt on two counts, as pro-slavery fanatics and as treasonous rebels. On the first charge, many conservatives shared antislavery nationalists' concerns over the South's reversal since the days when it had branded slavery an evil. Fiske, who had once resided in the South, blamed the poisonous profit motive: "While even despotic Russia, and Holland and France and other civilized nations are hastening to emancipate all their subjects from the thraldom of chattel slavery, in the southern part of our country the institution seems to be in full favor." Railing against the South's aim of extending human bondage, William Adams grieved over calls to reopen the African slave trade, stigmatized as piracy by the civilized world. Rabbi Morris Jacob Raphall, of the Greene Street Synagogue, New York, assailed southern fire-eaters and King Cotton: "King, indeed, and a most righteous and merciful one no doubt . . . since he only tars and feathers the wretches, who fall in his power, and whom he suspects of not being sufficiently loyal and obedient to his sovereignty."[87]

More frequent still was the Unionist assault on "the mad spirit" of secessionist treason: the armed rebellion of South Carolinians and the menacing mien of other southern states on the brink of separation.[88] Matters of political wisdom and morality fed the discussion. Joseph Trapnell of Keokuk, Iowa, voiced the widespread view that Lincoln's election gave no grounds for secession; the Republican Party merely echoed what Washington and Jefferson had sanctioned, the containment of slavery.[89] In the upper South, the Tennessee Methodist James Stringfield faced down grumbling congregants to damn "the noxious poison" of southern extremists, while Kentucky's Robert J. Breckinridge reviled South Carolina's fanatics for trampling government underfoot, annihilating American institutions, endangering its own citizens, preparing to treat with foreign nations, and exposing the country to armed invasion.[90] The Kentuckian exercised great influence representing the conservative center throughout the war. A slaveholder himself, he believed that both the Constitution and the Bible authorized slavery, though its American practice often fell short of the scriptural standard: in time it would die. He spoke for fellow Old School Presbyterians troubled by the Republicans' non-extension manifesto but more deeply alarmed by seceding traitors. His role as a mediator within the conservative Old School Presbyterian Church and more widely helped persuade many supporters of slavery in the border states that they were better protected within the Union than out of it.

Their argument fused politics and morality. Breckinridge called secession unrighteous because it trifled with sacred rights, solemn obligations, and the most vital interests of all concerned. Southern extremists defied the God whose wrath had once been visited on the Israelites for breaking their covenant with Him, and now invited disaster on this modern Israel. "A breach of covenant is *treason*," Julius Foster of Towanda, Pennsylvania, declared.[91] Otis Tiffany pointed to the moral damage of separation, by ending the American Revolution's role as a unifying common treasury. "Whose is to be the history of the Revolution after this threatened disunion?" he asked. "We cannot submit to lose it as a controlling and animating power of our future."[92] Historical memory was part of the glue of high-minded patriotism: pride in the shared splendors of the past sustained the nation in the present.

In censuring antislavery radicals, conservative religious Unionists focused on matters of both tone and substance. A chorus castigated what John W. Fiske called "the unscriptural heat of temper and harshness of judgment" toward southern brethren. Few were sterner than the Philadelphia Presbyterian Charles Wadsworth, who told antislavery agitators they had no more right to interfere with southern slavery than with Russian serfdom. Their wicked meddling, as busybodies in other men's concerns, equated—according to the apostle Peter's moral calculus—with murder, theft, and other moral outrages. In bearing false witness, they had launched against southern Christians "arrows poisoned with the venom of most malignant passions . . . taunt and vituperation." Fevered self-righteousness had become a controlling force in politics and religion, destroying parties, dividing churches, and bringing belligerent sections to the very verge of national destruction.[93]

This critique of "evil speaking" sprang from conservatives' belief in the legitimacy of slavery. No out-and-out apologists for southern slaveholders, they were still determined to uphold the South's legal rights and constitutional guarantees and thought they understood the section's fears. The deepest-dyed conservatives took the radicals' approval of John Brown's "wicked foray" into a slave state as an alarming portent of what would follow under a Lincoln administration. Republicans would "throw a cordon of fire" around slavery and utterly consume it. Instead of Christian persuasion, they would use the leviathan of mighty government. Hypocritically denying any responsibility for the bloody insurrection that must follow, they would self-righteously deplore the awful evils of slavery and say, "We told you so, and you ought long ago to have set your negroes free!"[94]

Conservative Unionists often empathized with the slave owners' dilemma. "We cannot ourselves tell what to do with the slaves," Fiske confessed. "Very few among us would dare to recommend that they all should be immediately and unconditionally emancipated." William Adams reflected, "Had we been born . . . in connexion with a system which sends its roots through the whole social structure, there is no reason to suppose that we should have been more humane, more kind, more wise than they." As we have seen, antislavery nationalists too were capable of empathy, but conservatives thought the radicals blind to the South's moral achievements. Sympathetic Unionists argued that the "wretched, impenitent *heathen*" inhabitants of Africa had been brought into Christian enslavement "*vastly* for their elevation and improvement." The sins of a small number of rogue slave owners had unfairly tainted the reputation of the kindly, paternalist majority. Conservatives rebuked radicals for their double standards: denouncing slave family separations but ignoring hundreds of sinful divorces closer to home; posturing as the friend of the enslaved while fearing the probable northern migration of ignorant and dependent freed people.[95]

Conservative Unionists forged their steely religious nationalism through a confident reading of the Bible. They picked a righteous middle way between southern pro-slavery triumphalism and what they called the corrupt religion, even infidelity, of antislavery radicals. Their unshakable central belief was that slavery, in and of itself, could not be judged a sin or a moral evil, even if the system was stained by the ill practice of the corrupt and decadent. Few pressed the scriptural case for its righteousness more powerfully on fast day than a cluster of religious leaders in New York City. They included the Episcopalian ministers of Broadway churches, Francis Vinton and Thomas House Taylor, a native of South Carolina; and Henry Van Dyke, Presbyterian minister of Brooklyn, a notoriously staunch champion of racial slavery and southern rights. Having recently delivered a blistering assault on abolitionists, Van Dyke now restricted himself to a simple confession of national sins, among which he identified antislavery Christianity—"the dishonoring of God's Holy Word"—as the chief evil. To this he added "the cries of the oppressed." These were the "hundreds and thousands of working girls" in northern factories and "the wife deserted by the husband." He studiously omitted the victims of biblically sanctioned bondage.[96]

No address, however, was richer in scriptural learning than that of Morris Jacob Raphall. Educated in Denmark, England, and Germany, and with a doctorate from the University of Erlangen, Rabbi Raphall was already a distinguished translator of Hebrew texts when in 1849, aged fifty, he left England for New York. His fast-day discourse, delivered to a congregation that included southerners and their sympathizers, centered on slavery's sinfulness. "How this question can at all arise in the mind of any man that has received a religious education," he said, "is a phenomenon I cannot explain to myself, and which fifty years ago no man dreamed of." The Old Testament, he insisted, manifestly sanctioned slavery: Noah's bitter curse condemned the descendants of his son Ham to enslavement (Genesis 9:25–27); the tenth commandment prohibited coveting a neighbor's male or female slave (Exodus 20:13); a thief unable to make restitution could be "sold for his theft" (Exodus 22:3); a miserably poor man could sell himself into slavery (Leviticus 25:39–46); runaway slaves had to be sent back to their owners (Deuteronomy 22:3); Abraham, Isaac, Jacob, and Job—"perfect, upright," and God-fearing patriarchs—were slaveholders (Job 1:8). Raphall, however, drew a distinction between the scriptural conception of the slave as "a person in whom the dignity of human nature is to be respected" (the Hebrew bondman was "fenced round with a protection against any abuse of power on the part of his employer") and heathen slavery, as practiced in ancient Rome. The American South had developed the Roman practice, reducing the slave to a thing with no rights. Its heathen slave code licensed "a few bad men to indulge in an abuse of power which throws a stigma . . . on the whole body of slaveholders." Still, the biblical sanction for slavery was clear. "My friends," Raphall ruefully reflected, "I am sorry to find, that I am delivering a pro-slavery discourse. I am no friend to slavery in the abstract, and still less friendly to the practical working of slavery. But I stand here as a teacher in Israel, not to place before you my own feelings and opinions, but to propound to you the Word of God, the Bible view of slavery."[97]

In this reading, antislavery preachers had invented a new sin not known to the Bible. Told that Henry Ward Beecher had said that the Old Testament had served its purpose and had been superseded "by the superior doctrines of the New," Raphall drew on Molière to liken the Brooklyn preacher to the physician "whose new theory removed the heart from the left side of the human body to the right." Many attributed such radicalism to the spirit of New England. Joseph Trapnell located the seeds of "*bastard*" Christianity in sixteenth-century Puritan bigotry.[98] Another wept over abolitionists' "insane ravings . . . in which the gibberish of falsehood is dressed up in the language of holy writ." Where in all this madness was the teaching of Christ? "We have subjected ourselves to the severe rebuke of our Lord . . . as 'hypocrites seeking to remove the mote in our brother's eye, with a beam in our own,'" lamented Charles Wadsworth. The self-righteous should heed the divine example of Christ: "Spending his whole earthly life in the midst of more despotic forms of slavery, [he] uttered against it no recorded word either of rebuke or denunciation."[99]

Over time, the glue of defensive Unionism would prove inadequate to hold this conservative coalition together. In January 1861 their immediate priority was to defend the nation against what they characterized as sectional extremism, North and South. That changed when the war began and another tier of slave states peeled away to join the southern Confederacy. The remaining loyal states of the upper South—Missouri, Kentucky, Maryland, and Delaware—had now to contend with internal conflicts fundamentally reducible to a single question: the Union or slavery? This simple question yielded complex and contested answers that would expose the fragil-

92 RIGHTEOUS STRIFE

ity and hidden factionalism of the fast-day coalition of conservative religious nationalists.

RIGHTEOUS CONTENTION

The firmer the expression of biblical support for slavery, the more earnest the riposte of antislavery radicals. These included Reform Jews and, above all, those Christian campaigners castigated by *The New York Herald* as spokesmen for the "Fanatico-Massachusetts" approach to national perils. Raphall came under attack from the Jewish biblical scholars Michael Heilprin and Rabbi David Einhorn, who noted tartly, "It has ever been a strategy of the advocate of a bad cause to take refuge from the spirit of the Bible to its letter."[100] Henry Van Dyke's notorious assault on abolitionism triggered a comprehensive demolition from the pastor of New York's Third Reformed Presbyterian Church, James R. W. Sloane. First delivered in his own church, Sloane's sermon enjoyed further oxygen during the fast-day weekend services in Union Square, at George B. Cheever's Church of the Puritans. By then thousands of copies of Van Dyke's reworked polemic were circulating in pamphlet form. Sloane linked it to Thornwell's and Palmer's pro-slavery gospel and dissected point by point their argument that abolitionism had no foundation in scripture. There were, he insisted, no words in the Hebrew language for slave or compulsory enslavement; the nearest was "servant," meaning service by voluntary contract. The Old Testament did not record any permitted sale by one person to another of an unwilling third party. Hebrew law protected the runaway servant against the tyranny of masters. In Judaea the law of the Jubilee rendered slavery impossible. God's covenant with Israel was intended to secure freedom and justice for all. American slavery could not have lasted a day in the Hebrew commonwealth. No rational reading of the New Testament could claim that Christ was *truly* silent over Roman slavery. His strictures against oppression and his use of the antislavery texts of the prophet Isaiah denied it all moral standing. That he did not address it by name could not be taken as approval: in all of his preaching, Christ "does not mention idolatry, did he therefore approve of idol worship? He does not once mention or allude to the [Roman] gladiatorial combats; are they, therefore, a divine institution?"[101]

Van Dyke was anathema to antislavery nationalists, who saw him as the extreme conservative embodiment of the Old School Presbyterian ministry and its mouthpieces, the *New-York Observer* and *The Princeton Review*. For at least some of his critics, Van Dyke served as a proxy for the denomination's most eminent but questionable representative, Buchanan himself; in this way, the president's integrity and churchmanship could be impugned without naming him. When Henry Ward Beecher condemned Van Dyke by name in his fast-day sermon, at least one of those present, the Methodist minister Albert S. Hunt, was startled by the congregation's open contempt, deeming it "most unbecoming in God's House." Even so, Hunt understood the concern that Buchanan was "too full of sympathy" for the secessionist insurgents and feared the White House cocooned a traitor.[102]

Buchanan's hopes of a healing countrywide fast thus foundered. Divergent religious nationalisms—contending expressions of American righteousness—drove wedges of rancor through and between congregations. Addressing the combined Presbyterians of Petersburg, Virginia, Theodorick Pryor delivered such a passionate disunion tirade—an "extemporaneous thunderblast" by one account—that the meeting broke up in disorder and the elders of the host church forbade him to speak again.[103] In Lewistown, Illinois, the abolitionist Methodist minister Milton L. Haney addressed a mixed congregation of Republicans and Democrats, several of southern descent. Holding out the promise of a slave-free nation, he watched his most influential church member storm out, coughing theatrically as he went; a female hearer urged some wild young bloods to avenge the "desecration" of the pulpit by riding the minister on a rail. Only cooled tempers and the marshaling of a strong Republican presence kept him safe at the subsequent "indignation meeting."[104] The halls of Congress were scarcely more immune to bitterness. Thomas Stockton's paean to the Union sought to unite free and slave states behind a vision of America's Christian purposes, "for the performance of the highest duties and the attainment of the highest destinies of our race." Insisting the conflict over slav-

94   RIGHTEOUS STRIFE

ery was repressible, he called on South Carolina to return to the fold. "O flag of stars!" he lamented, "superseded and dishonored by the pitiful palmetto!" This lapse from studied evenhandedness prompted hissing from the southern-rights contingent present and a scolding editorial from the Washington *Constitution*, incensed at what it called rampant partisanship and a *"vocabulary of contemptuous expletives."*[105]

CODA: THE FRACTURING *"STATE OF THE COUNTRY"*

Even when of one mind, individual churches felt keenly the contention within their wider denomination, as well as the dissonance between their own and other church traditions. The fast day served to aggravate existing sores. Not the least of these were the travails afflicting Buchanan's own church, the Old School Presbyterians. They, with the Catholic and Protestant Episcopal Churches, constituted a minority of denominations that could still boast a national presence. Centered philosophically on the conservative Calvinism of Princeton's theological seminary, the chief incubator of the Old School ministry, the denomination had trusted in that very conservatism as a glue. Many of its clergy, North and South, owed their training to the most influential theologian of mid-century Princeton, Charles Hodge, who as a teacher and the editor of *The Princeton Review* tried valiantly to counter the centrifugal forces at work. His efforts to hold the center ground would fail, but they merit attention both for their immediate import and because Hodge's influence, directly and by proxy, played a key role in shaping a powerful form of religious nationalism in the Civil War Union. It would seep into the religious rhetoric of the wartime president, Lincoln himself.[106]

When Sloane took a hatchet to Van Dyke's argument for slavery, he noted how much of it had drawn on Hodge, who in 1836 had published an influential defense of the institution in *The Princeton Review*. There and in later writings Hodge consistently argued that slavery, provided it conformed to the law of God, enjoyed scriptural sanction. That proviso was important. Hodge saw himself as a mediator between the "commotion" of intolerant abolitionism and slaveholders' blinkered defense of their peculiar institution's moral "abominations." Slaves' humanity entitled them to a policy of improving their moral, religious, and intellectual culture, as a route toward their eventual emancipation.[107] Hodge welcomed efforts to secure the manumission and voluntary emigration of slaves, and endorsed the abortive Kentucky plan of emancipation advanced by his Old School colleague Robert J. Breckinridge in 1849. Over the next decade he shed his conservative Whiggery, turning to the new, antislavery Republican Party. In 1856 he supported Frémont from a conviction that an expansionist Slave Power was diverting the Union from its true historic course. When the U.S. Supreme Court's *Dred Scott* decision ruled that Congress had no constitutional grounds for banning slavery from the federal territories, Hodge accused "extreme men of the Calhoun school" of effecting a revolution.[108] His dismay was compounded by the complicity of his Old School colleagues, notably Thornwell and Palmer, in this "reckless violation of historical truth," the product of "the new, unscriptural, and anti-Christian sentiment" that slavery was a positive good.[109] At the same time he also rebutted Thornwell's doctrine that the Church was "a spiritual body, clothed only with spiritual powers for spiritual ends, that all intermeddling with anything not directly bearing on the spiritual and eternal interests of men was foreign to its office." Thornwell had defined the term "spiritual" so narrowly, Hodge protested, that it pertained only to the method of salvation, as distinguished from the law of God. It denied the church the right to proscribe unjust slave laws and practices, "as well as . . . rebellion and disloyalty." Hodge later noted drily that Thornwell and his allies had subsequently found it impossible to stick to their doctrine when tempted, in the crisis over secession, to preach on slavery and to rally support for a new southern polity.[110]

Hodge venerated the American Union as a priceless treasure: estimating its material value was akin to monetizing parental love. A model to the world, the young nation fused political and religious liberties within a Protestant culture, free from the feudal rigidities and the "socialistic anarchy" that they bred in the Old World. As well as their political covenants, Americans were morally bound by kin, language, religion, geography, and history: they had spilled their blood in a common cause; "their ashes lay mingled in the same graves." Homogeneous and organic, the Union was more than "a mere association, such as binds together nations of different races, languages, and political institutions, as in the Austrian empire. . . . It cannot be permanently dissevered." Recourse to secession was no better a cure for national difficulties than "decapitation for the head-ache."[111]

These sentiments underpinned Hodge's celebrated article in *The Princeton Review*, "The State of the Country," which he composed as he watched South Carolina prepare to leave the Union, but which circulated in print only after the state had passed its secession ordinance. In every nation's history, he acknowledged, there were times when its destiny hung in the balance of the hour. There were occasions, too, "when political questions rise into the sphere of morals and religion; when the rule for political action is to be sought, not in considerations of state policy, but in the law of God."[112] With the interests of the nation, world, and Christ's kingdom at stake, he pursued two main lines of argument. First, southerners entirely misread northern opinion. Not one in a hundred was tainted by abolitionism. "We do not know of one clergyman among the Roman Catholics, or the Episcopalians, or the Dutch Reformed, belonging to the class of abolitionists. Of the three thousand Old-school Presbyterian clergymen in the country, we do not believe there are twelve who deserve to be so designated." The radical antislavery sentiments within the ranks of Baptists and Methodists were negated by a strong conservative element. His second theme was the unconstitutionality of secession, a criminal absurdity pursued by minds crazed through passion. The wrongs felt by the South were open to redress through compromise.[113]

Hodge saw his twelve-thousand-word essay as a call to moderation and justice in the face of southern extremism and "the poltroonery of Northern men" who "go down on their knees and call themselves the sole wrong-doers." This was possibly a dig at Buchanan and certainly a swipe at those Presbyterian colleagues who tried to block the article's publication, fearing it would set the church ablaze.[114] Hodge, however, took pride in his lifelong conservative role as a bridge builder in church and state. Born and bred in the lower North, a teacher of students recruited mainly from the middle states, and a lifelong friend of many from the upper South, he was most at ease with those who shared a vested interest in cultivating the center ground.[115] These were the people Hodge had most in mind in writing "The State of the Country": the moderates and conservatives of both sections. Believing he spoke for "the people of God in the North & West," and for nine out of every ten readers of *The Princeton Review*, he judged the article would temper "the *uncompromising* spirit" of Republican Party leaders and make them more amenable to John Crittenden's compromise proposals; equally, it would help reassure and strengthen the Unionist majority in the slave states and marginalize the disunionist hotheads.[116]

Reprinted as a pamphlet and carried in secular newspapers, the article reached well beyond the boundaries of Old School Presbyterianism.[117] It sent an electric charge through the Church itself, further animating its internal conflict over national righteousness. On one side, Hodge's appeal elicited warm support among northern and border-state moderates, and even some in the lower South. The ministers and distinguished laymen to whom Hodge sent advance copies reflected his social and political reach.[118] Their warm praise for the article's avoidance of extremes, admirable temper, and "christian conservatism of the North" was a herald of the cascade of tributes after publication. "You have spoken . . . as becomes a Christian and Patriot," said one; "your position is impregnable," wrote another.[119] Hodge's rebuke of southern secessionist "tomfoolery" and "the increasingly prevailing spirit of proslaveryism" was "eminently wise, just, candid, temperate and Christian." A New Orleans correspondent claimed that many ministers there, disturbed by Benjamin Palmer's extremism, fully endorsed the article.[120] Hodge could take encouragement from the support of Douglas Democrats and Constitutional Unionists, as well as conservative Republicans of his own stripe.[121]

That encouragement was countered by a gale of predictable reproach. A New York friend, South Carolinian by birth, had warned Hodge not to publish the article. It would be regarded in the South, he wrote, "as a specious & able" defense of a Republican Party that saw Lincoln's election as the first step toward overthrowing slavery. Southerners would not see "any essential difference between a *great deal* of what is called anti-slavery here & real abolitionism. They run into each other by insensible degrees."[122] He was right. Hodge had misread the temper of the South, overestimated the depth of Unionism within the cotton states, and lost friendships there.[123] Indignant southern Presbyterian presses bristled with recrimination.[124] Thornwell, Charles Colcock Jones, and other Old School ministers lamented that Hodge had condoned abolitionist infidelity and had "gone over to the enemy."[125] Others canceled their subscriptions to Hodge's *Princeton Review*. Grieving over the editor's political principles, a contemptuous Tennessean declared that if war came, "every man who voted for Lincoln will be guilty before heaven of Blood."[126]

Many northern Presbyterians, too—even those who acknowledged that Hodge had written "in the interests of Truth and Righteousness"—believed Hodge had dangerously underestimated antislavery sentiment. Lucius Elmer, a seasoned New Jersey Democrat alarmed by the power of Methodism, told Hodge that its ministers and people "have a vague idea, that slavery is a sin and have been controlled by this feeling in voting"; they had accepted, as he could not, the Republican doctrine that "all men are equal in reference to this very question of slavery" and the party's platform, opposing its westward spread.[127] He spoke for many Old School Presbyterians jittery over what appeared to be a stealthy abolitionist takeover through the Trojan horse of the Republican Party, and whose anxiety registered in the columns of the conservative *New-York Observer*. The moderator of the General Assembly told Hodge of their concern "that for aught they know you voted for Lincoln & are writing in the republican interest."[128] The stern anti-secessionist ministers Phineas Gurley and Robert Breckinridge both thought Hodge's intervention too political.[129]

Taken aback by the thrust of the criticism, Hodge insisted how evenhanded he had been in casting blame. It was not he but the southern radicals who had shifted their ground. "People rushing along on a railroad see the trees and fences flying in the opposite direction. So our brethren of the Gulf States who are hurrying from all their old positions, think that it is not they, but others who are in motion." "Abolitionist" and "Republican" were not interchangeable labels. He recognized the justice of the South's concern over fugitive slaves: the federal authorities had a duty to compensate all irrecoverable losses. Unlike hard-line free-soilers, he offered the restoration of the Missouri Compromise line as a solution to the territorial issue.[130]

Hodge, however, had underestimated the extent to which, as Robert J. Breckinridge told him, "force, and terror, and delusion" were pushing the southern revolution forward.[131] There was nothing unique in his misapprehension. Lincoln and most Republican leaders, too, overestimated the influence of southern Unionists. When, during the early weeks of 1861, it became ever clearer that neither the political Union nor the unity of the Old School was likely to survive the crisis, Presbyterians resigned themselves to the workings of Providence. True to their convictions as instinctive conservative Unionists, these religious nationalists trod a cautious path. As they looked to God, they apportioned blame evenhandedly. "The sins of slaveholders, and the almost equal sins of abolitionists in the north," Lucius Elmer told Hodge, "have provoked that righteous God, who punishes nations as well as individuals, and we must all suffer the consequences. He can & will bring light out of the darkness and good out of the evil; but the diseases afflicting us are too deep seated to be cured speedily." With little hope of man-made compromise, it seemed plain to ministers of this cloth and to their people that, circumspect though they were, their future path meant pain and suffering. They prayed the nation would be spared the convulsion of civil war, but their intercessions were increasingly more earnest than hopeful.[132]

Neither Buchanan's fast day nor Hodge's essay on the state of the country has won much attention in studies of the political drama of secession. It might well be asked, why should they? After all, January 4, 1861, was but a single day during a long, fevered winter and its preachers' rhetoric just a fraction of the millions of words generated by the crisis; Hodge's essay represented a mere fraction of that fraction. Yet the episode of the fast day merits serious attention, and the significance of Hodge's intervention deserves more than a footnote. They mattered because, as the political crisis forced individual citizens to ask fundamental questions about the Union, ministerial voices crystallized ideas about the nature and value of American nationhood. The individual elements of those ideas were not new, but the winter climacteric forged heightened, sterner expressions of religious nationalism. Hodge was the representative *American* citizen when he saw that the nation's "destiny for ages" would be "determined by the events of an hour." He was the representative *Christian* citizen when he declared that "the rule for political action" would be found "not in considerations of state policy, but in the law of God."

Through this crystallizing of nationalist thought, political postures were hardened into more resolute godliness. These would profoundly shape responses to armed conflict when eventually it arrived. To be sure, during the first few months of 1861 the increasing likelihood of a bloody war led some—Hodge included—to ponder the relative advantage of a peaceful separation, "by the common consent of the parties," provided that secession be repudiated and "the rights and essential interests" of both North and South be secured.[133] But with the outbreak of hostilities the full force of the religious nationalisms crystallized in January came powerfully into play.

At Lincoln's inauguration on March 4, 1861, an outgoing chief executive well disposed toward Old School Presbyterianism formally yielded office to an incoming president who worshipped in the same Church. The departing Buchanan had put his faith in the power of a countrywide fast to bridge the political divide, but his means of healing had served to expose an irreconcilable clash over what constituted a righteous nation. Indeed, it aggravated existing wounds. His successor, attending the New York Avenue Presbyterian Church, as Buchanan had done, would keep the presidential link with that Old School religious tradition. But time would reveal their profound differences in reading the Constitution and the Bible. The interplay of Buchanan's Calvinist theology and pro-slavery legalism so shaped his thinking about personal responsibility that it left him with little room for personal maneuver in preserving the nation. Lincoln's belief in the constitutional opportunities for freedom, by contrast, when allied to an evolving understanding of God and Calvinist moral accountability, would eventually nerve him to apply presidential power to radical new ends. That was for the future. Immediately he had to contend with a fractured nation in which religious understandings of its purposes ensured that its fissures would be destructive and profound.

CHAPTER 4

LINCOLN, NATIONALITY, AND PROVIDENCE

The Civil War affected every American. Military service and other calls on patriotism changed lives forever. Families faced cruel bereavements; communities suffered losses on a terrifying scale. Personal and collective responsibility for the common good demanded new ways of thinking about national well-being and citizens' duties to their fellow men and women. Notably, in its search for consolation, guidance, and certainty, an overwhelmingly Christian nation turned instinctively to God.

Lincoln himself felt the full force of the emotional and physical onslaught of the national struggle. All the evidence points to the four years of his wartime presidency broadening his humanity and deepening his inquiry into the spiritual and religious dimensions of humankind. It has been rightly said that no change in his attitudes during the Civil War was more evident, or mattered more, than his growing recognition of the capabilities of African Americans. The truth of that proposition lies at the heart of the story told in subsequent chapters. For the moment, however, the focus is the equally significant—though generally underappreciated—revolution in the ideas and impulses that shaped his defense of the American nation. He never lost sight of the secular political arguments in support of the national integrity of a historically unique republic. But he came to hold them alongside an equally powerful faith in superintending Providence: the Almighty God who intervened to shape human history and advance His own distinct purposes. Those religious ideas were encouraged by his conversations, extensive correspondence, and general immersion in the company of men and women whose encouraging faith in a higher power told of a nation under providential guidance and intervention. And, in time, Lincoln's continuing inquiry into a mysterious God's purposes for the nation would direct his approach to emancipation.

LINCOLN'S "NATIONALITY"

At the grand unveiling of Abraham Lincoln's statue in London's Parliament Square in 1920, David Lloyd George, the British prime minister, reflected that the American president was "one of those giant figures, of whom there are very few in history, who lose their nationality in death. They are no longer Greek or Hebrew, English or American; they belong to mankind."[1] He echoed a sentiment widely held in foreign circles ever since the president's death. "Abraham Lincoln was our brother," declared the French radical Léon Richer as news of his assassination reverberated around the world: he was one of those "true representatives of God upon earth."[2]

This legitimate reading of the sixteenth U.S. president's posthumous reach rather deflects from the reality that Lincoln had, in Lloyd George's parlance, a good deal of "nationality" to lose. He was proud and tenacious in his loyalty to the American nation—an "eternal fidelity," in his own words, to "the land of my life, my liberty and my love." Among the strands in the rope that bound him so resolutely to the Union was his awed appreciation of its unmatched material potential: the fertile land, natural bounty, physical grandeur, and economic advantages that set it apart from the world at large. Growing up in Kentucky and Indiana, and arriving as a young man in the infant Illinois, Lincoln shared the faith of the emerging Whig Party in the unique natural resources of the undeveloped country and its vast modernizing potential. He wrote of his adopted state: it "surpasses every other spot of equal extent upon the face of the globe, in fertility of soil, and in the proportionable amount of the same which is sufficiently level for actual cultivation; . . . she is endowed by nature with the capacity of sustaining a greater amount of agricultural wealth and population than any other equal extent of territory in the world." Lincoln the "improver" watched with pleasure the Union's galloping economic progress, to which his political career in the 1830s and 1840s had been chiefly devoted. Later he wrote with approval of the "aggregate grandeur" of the American experiment, as reflected in its industrious, burgeoning population.[3]

During the Civil War the London *Times* correspondent William Howard Russell noted Lincoln's "quaint reflections" on the potential might of his country: "He calculates . . . there are human beings now alive who may ere they die behold the United States peopled by 250 millions of souls. Talking of a high mound on the prairie, in Illinois, he remarked, 'that if all the nations of the earth were assembled there, a man standing on its top would see them all, for . . . the whole human race would fit on a space . . . about the extent of the plain.'"[4] On what would be the last full day of his life Lincoln told the Indiana congressman Schuyler Colfax, "I have very large ideas of the mineral wealth of our nation. I believe it practically inexhaustible. It abounds all over the western country from the Rocky Mountains to the Pacific, and its development has scarcely commenced." With the war ended, hundreds of thousands of immigrants would arrive annually "from overcrowded Europe. I intend to point them to the gold and silver that waits for them in the West. Tell the miners . . . I shall promote their interests . . . because their prosperity is the prosperity of the nation, and we shall prove in a very few years, that we are indeed the treasury of the world."[5] A celebration of America's vast natural resources, these remarks reflected an economic conception of the nation premised upon an autonomous and integrated market, secure from persistent British neocolonialism and untroubled by the indigenous inhabitants of the land.

Much more often, however, Lincoln's rhetoric addressed the ethical and political purpose of the Union: the physical and material grandeur of the United States was secondary to the moral magnificence of the nation's free institutions. Lincoln expressed his esteem for the nation's Revolutionary leaders and founding fathers in his unshakable respect for the cornerstones of the republic: the Declaration of Independence, a celebration of equality, and the federal constitution, the guarantor of freedom. Thanks to these legacies, the United States enjoyed a unique and unprecedented liberty, "far exceeding that of any other of the nations of the earth." Its distinctive features included self-government, or government by the consent of the governed, which he lauded as "absolutely and eternally right"; a bill of rights, which guaranteed a variety of religious and civil freedoms beyond those "which the history of former times tells us"; a legal system capped by a supreme court that he deemed "the most enlightened judicial tribunal in the world"; and a government whose chief purpose was to ensure that every citizen enjoyed an equal chance in life.[6] The American republican experiment was an exception, a historical outlier. "*Most governments*," he reflected, "have been based, practically, on the denial of equal rights of men . . . ; ours began, by *affirming* those rights." Skeptics claimed that "some men are too *ignorant*, and *vicious*, to share in government. Possibly so, said we; and, by your system, you would always keep them ignorant, and vicious. We proposed to give *all* a chance; and we expected the weak to grow stronger, the ignorant, wiser; and all better, and happier together."[7]

Lincoln never traveled abroad (unless, perhaps, he had crossed into Canada for a better view of Niagara Falls). His perspective on foreign states and governments was necessarily shaped by the authors he read, the many foreign-born visitors and citizens he met, and his more cosmopolitan associates. His early reading was limited to the Bible and the very few other books he could lay his hands on, but once he got to New Salem, according to Mentor Graham, "he devoted more time to reading the scripture, books on science and comments on law and to the acquisition of Knowledge of men and things" than any other he had known in his forty-five years as a teacher. From Mason L. Weems's *Life of George Washington*, and especially William Grimshaw's popular and Whiggish *History of the United States*, Lincoln acquired an understanding of the geopolitics that shaped the country's course to nationhood and its championing of Enlightenment principles. His reading of scripture, Edward Gibbon's *Decline and Fall of the Roman Empire*, and Plutarch's *Lives* delivered something of the sweep of history.[8]

Lincoln's reading gave him a keen sense of the United States' escape from the autocratic forces of the Old World. In this he was essentially a creature of his time: in the young republic the experience of the Revolutionary generation shaped a persisting, if fading, collective memory of the War of Independence from tyrannical rule. The stirring events of the American Revolution, he reflected in his Lyceum Address, "we hope . . . will be . . . recounted, so long as the bible shall be read;—but even . . . then, they cannot be so universally known, nor so vividly felt, as they were by the generation just gone to rest."[9] The ideological legacy of the Revolution would fuse with the defining foreign events of his own lifetime to give Lincoln an enhanced appreciation of his country's place in the world. Those events—above all, the independence movements within Spain's New World empire, the Greek war of independence, and the nationalist uprisings and movements of radical republican protest in Europe— were in part mediated for Lincoln through those of his political friends, acquaintances, and heroes whose travels or dealings gave them firsthand authority.[10] During his two-year congressional term he threw his support behind Irish famine relief and the European revolutions of 1848–49. He concurred in the Senate's congratulations to the French people on their "February revolution" to establish republican government; he would later, in 1851, share in the outrage over Louis Napoleon's "usurpation." In 1849 and again in 1852, he joined with other leading figures in Springfield to identify with the Hungarians in their bloody struggle for independence from the Habsburg Empire.[11] Springfield itself had a sizable community of Portuguese refugees, militant Protestants fleeing violent persecution in Catholic Madeira, the earliest of whom arrived in 1849; they were welcomed by a reception committee headed by Lincoln's close ally Simeon Francis, the editor of the *Sangamo Journal*.[12] Collectively, it is unlikely that any immigrant influence was greater than that of the Germans with whom Lincoln was involved after 1854 in bolstering the nascent Republican Party, several of them exiled revolutionaries of 1848, or—like George Schneider of Chicago and Gustave Koerner of Belleville—radicals who had fled Germany even earlier. As Koerner's memoirs reveal, these Germans remained deeply invested in the political future of the land they had fled. Lincoln clearly understood the common democratic-republican agenda they pursued on both sides of the Atlantic. His cultivation of the German vote in Illinois and beyond during the 1850s was driven by electoral arithmetic, but there was more to it than that. He knew that these European liberals and progressives would put mettle in the Republicans' ideological backbone.[13]

In this universal struggle between liberty and tyranny, and between social progress and lethargy, Lincoln conferred on the United States a global duty. His "Lecture on Discoveries and Inventions," delivered at Illinois College in February 1859, asserted the nation's advantage through its universal mission of freeing the human mind from the shackles of archaism:

> It is a curious fact that a new country is most favorable— almost necessary—to the immancipation [sic] of thought, and the consequent advancement of civilization and the arts. The human family originated as is thought, somewhere in Asia, and have worked their way princip[al]ly Westward. Just now, in civilization, and the arts, the people of Asia are entirely behind those of Europe; those of the East of Europe behind those of the West of it; while we, here in America, *think* we discover, and invent, and improve, faster than any of them. *They* may think this is arrogance; but they can not deny that Russia has called on us to show her how to build steam-boats and railroads—while in the older parts of Asia, they scarcely know that such things as S.Bs & RR.s. exist. In anciently inhabited countries, the dust of ages—a real downright old-fogyism—seems to settle upon, and smother the intellects and energies of man.[14]

Striking here is Lincoln's Enlightenment-inspired belief that progress depended above all on the intellectual ferment, human imagination, and cultural energy that would accompany the world's emancipation from stultifying social and political tradition. There was probably a racial element in his understanding of "civilization"— this was, after all, the common, Eurocentric perspective of the Enlightenment—but if so, it was surely of a piece with his cautious approach to issues of racial difference at home: a lack of dogmatism above all characterized his statements on the capabilities and potential of African Americans. Likewise, when it came to addressing policy toward the Mexican people or toward Native Ameri-

Lincoln, Nationality, and Providence   107

cans, Lincoln chose not to pursue racialized lines of argument. The weight of evidence—exiguous though it is—suggests that Lincoln, in measuring human behavior and capability, placed a higher value on social context and culturally shaped expectations than on racial or ethnic traits.

Throughout his pre-presidential public career, Lincoln's nationalism took an essentially secular character, marked by optimism and a rich sense of the country's moral purpose. He understood how progressive forces abroad commonly looked to the United States as an exemplar of republican liberty and an agent for the improvement of humankind. As a young man he had described his country as "that fair fabric, which for the last half century, has been the fondest hope, of the lovers of freedom, throughout the world." Later, as a congressman, he would invoke the Patriots of 1776 to assert the right of any people "to rise up, and shake off the existing government, and form a new one that suits them better. This is a most valuable,—a most sacred right—a right, which we hope and believe, is to liberate the world."[15] Such sentiments nourished Lincoln's hostility to nativist restrictions on the rights of immigrants, his scorn for Know-Nothing anti-Catholicism, and his determination to preserve America's western territories as "an outlet for *free white people everywhere,* the world over—in which Hans and Baptiste and Patrick, and all other men from all the world, may find new homes and better their conditions in life." Such social and economic opportunity— real enough, in his experience—reflected the ambitions of unfettered humankind. Declaring his faith in the American "system of labor where the laborer can strike if he wants to!" Lincoln added, "I would to God that such a system prevailed all over the world."[16]

Lincoln's faith in his country as a moral exemplar was not, he judged, fundamentally compromised by the existence of slavery. Unjust and wrong though the institution was, as he insisted in his most powerful prewar speeches, its confinement would slowly choke it to extinction. For as long as the federal government confined slavery to the South, using the powers constitutionally entrusted to the U.S. Congress to block its spread, the two sections could coexist despite their moral differences. In his eloquent address at New York's Cooper Union in February 1860, Lincoln perceptively noted that although the people of the South said they wanted to be left alone, what they craved was for the nation to be culturally cleansed of all antislavery sentiment. Since they judged slavery to be morally and socially good, southerners wanted it universally accepted as not only their legal right but a social blessing. Republicans' own moral, social, and political consciences stopped them from conceding that. He agreed that "we can yet afford to let it alone where it is, because that much is due to the necessity arising from its actual presence in the nation; but can we, while our votes will prevent it, allow it to spread into the National Territories, and to overrun us here in these Free States?"[17]

When, as president-elect, Lincoln made his railroad journey from Springfield to Washington, his speeches and brief remarks to patriotic gatherings echoed these familiar paeans to American democratic republicanism. In Cincinnati he lauded the benign influence of American free institutions. Popular devotion to those institutions and the liberties they protected, he told a cheering crowd in Poughkeepsie, made Americans "the most free, the most intelligent and the happiest people on the globe."[18] In addresses at Trenton—to the New Jersey Senate—and at Philadelphia's Independence Hall, he extolled the principled purposes of Washington and his self-sacrificing Revolutionary forces of 1776. What drove their noble struggle was more than mere separation from the mother country: it was the vision of freedom held out by the Declaration of Independence, "giving liberty, not alone to the people of this country, but hope to the world . . . that in due time the weights should be lifted from the shoulders of all men, and that *all* should have an equal chance." As he told an audience of Ohio German Americans, to laughter and cheers, "I esteem foreigners no better than other people, nor any worse. They are all of the great family of men, and if there is one shackle upon any of them, it would be far better to lift the load from them." If bettering their condition meant leaving for new homes, "I bid them all God speed."[19]

Equally, Lincoln called on his concerned audiences to hold fast to a dazzling future, the unfolding of a glorious national destiny. Addressing Governor Oliver Morton and other Indiana citizens, he reflected soberly that the loss of the Union and its liberties was "but little to any one man of fifty-two years of old age," but for the nation's thirty million inhabitants and their posterity "in all coming time" it was beyond price. He thanked the New York state legislature "in behalf of the civil and religious liberty for all time to come." And outside Independence Hall in Philadelphia, at the Union flag raising on Washington's birthday, he promised that the additional star representing Kansas, recently admitted as the thirty-fourth state, would be a permanent addition to American prosperity. Others, too, would be added, he declared, "until we shall number . . . five hundred millions of happy and prosperous people."[20]

LINCOLN'S PROVIDENTIALIST TURN

In these respects, the nationalist themes of Lincoln's addresses on his journey to Washington were entirely familiar to those who had followed his career. Strikingly new, however, was his repeated insistence that to survive its present extremity, the nation depended on God's guidance and support. Until then, throughout a career of almost thirty years, he had rarely spoken of Providence as the shaper of the Union's course, or of the Almighty as a judge of national righteousness and wrongdoing. James K. Polk's war with Mexico had prompted Congressman Lincoln's earnest assault on a national policy that demanded the guilty president see that "the blood of this war, like the blood of Abel, is crying to Heaven against him." During his political jousting with Douglas in the late 1850s he used the memorable words of Thomas Jefferson—"he trembled for his country when he remembered that God was just"—to contrast their moral purport with the Little Giant's morally slippery doctrine of popular sovereignty: a creed of racial enslavement that so "braved the arm of Jehovah" that the "nation had cause to dread His wrath."[21] Lincoln's providentialist rhetoric on these very few occasions was striking but did not define his nationalism. His drumbeat insistence during the 1850s that slavery was wrong was couched in the language of moral responsibility but barely of religious, or specifically Christian, faith.

However, in a sequence of key speeches along his route to the capital, he introduced with arresting and unprecedented regularity the notion of his own and the nation's dependence on God as the moral governor of the world. It was a chord he struck from the outset, in a poignant address at the Springfield railroad depot to those who came to bid him farewell. He faced a task, he told them, perhaps even more daunting than Washington's epic struggle for national independence. But with the support of "the same omniscient mind, and Almighty arm that directed and protected him," he was confident of success. He commended his audience to "the God of our fathers," urged them to pray for the nation, and requested that "with equal security and faith, you all will invoke His wisdom and guidance for me."[22] Spoken in the presence of many friends, neighbors, and acquaintances, these words cannot be dismissed as simply formulaic. They were, naturally, designed to give cheer and stiffen the public's confidence that he would depend on the Solomonic wisdom God alone could inspire. They no doubt evinced something of the emotion he felt at leaving the community where his family had nestled for a quarter of a century. It is likely that above all they bespoke the immeasurable burden of personal responsibility that, famously self-reliant though he was, Lincoln was bound to feel as he embarked on a political journey for which there were no navigational charts.

Variations on this theme marked his speeches in Ohio and New York, particularly the notion that the good sense and intelligence of the great American people would be the instrumentality through which the Providence of God—"the Almighty, the Maker of the Universe," "that Supreme Being who has never forsaken this favored land"—would rescue the nation and guide its leadership.[23] By the time he addressed the New Jersey Senate at Trenton, he had distilled the idea into memorable eloquence. "I am exceedingly anxious," he said, "that this Union, the Constitution, and the liberties of the people shall be perpetuated in accordance with the original idea" that inspired the sacrifices of the Revolution. "I shall be most happy indeed if I shall be an humble instrument in the hands of the Almighty, and of this, his almost chosen people, for perpetuating the object of that great struggle."[24] Lincoln's "almost" here carefully discouraged national self-righteousness even as he acknowledged the United States' special place in God's plan for His moral government of the world.

By the time Lincoln reached Washington, seven states of the Deep South had formed a de facto slaveholding confederacy. His inaugural address on March 4 ostensibly appealed to the rebel states, but its key purpose was to rally Unionist sentiment in the conditionally loyal upper South, to reach out to northern Democrats by affirming his peaceful intent and respect for the South's constitutional rights, and to reassure Republicans that he would not waver in faithfully executing the law in all the states. The speech dealt mostly with the constitutional and political aspects of the crisis. Lincoln once again repeated that it was not his purpose either to interfere with slavery in the states where it existed or to stymie its constitutional protections, including the return of fugitive slaves to their legal owners. Appealing to general principles and the history of the republic itself, he insisted that the Union of the states was perpetual, that he would defend and maintain it without bloodshed or violence, "unless it be forced upon the national authority," and that secession—the rejection of government by a constitutionally constrained majority—was a route to anarchy or despotism. The speech was short on patriotic rhetorical flourish, though naturally an appeal to nationalist sentiment was implicit in his discussion of the hard realities the country faced. Only in his concluding paragraphs—a refashioning of Seward's suggested improvements—did Lincoln echo the sentiments of his recent addresses, to invoke the unifying power of "intelligence, patriotism, Christianity, and a firm reliance upon Him, who has never yet forsaken this favored land." The president had taken an "oath registered in Heaven" to preserve and defend the government. The bonds of national affection, connected over the generations by the "mystic chords of memory," had the power to stop the course to civil war, "when again touched, as they surely will be, by the better angels of our nature."[25]

It was not until July 4, some twelve weeks after the Confederate assault on Fort Sumter, and with the Union under mass mobilization for war, that Lincoln again spoke at length to a people haunted by the likely cost in blood. Drawing on law, history, and the Constitution, he aimed to explain what was at stake, to rally the country behind a fight for the nation's existence, and to show that preserving popular and representative government, not slavery, was the fundamental issue. His message to the special session of Congress, universally circulated, laid out the aggressive, constitutionally indefensible course of "the seceded states, so-called." The founders had intended the Union to be perpetual. Its free institutions had "developed the powers, and improved the condition, of our whole people, beyond any example in the world." The world had to be shown that representative government was durable, "that those who can fairly carry an election, can also suppress a rebellion." The rebel slave owners had retreated from the high ground of republican freedom, "pressing out of view, the rights of men, and the authority of the people," by omitting the words "all men are created equal" from their adopted declarations of independence, and the phrase "We, the People" from their national constitution. This gave Lincoln his cue to distill the purpose of the war as "essentially a People's contest . . . a struggle for maintaining in the world, that form, and substance of government, whose leading object is, to elevate the condition of men—to lift artificial weights from all shoulders—to clear the paths of laudable pursuit for all—to afford all, an unfettered start, and a fair chance, in the race of life."

Lincoln ended his earnest address with a one-sentence paragraph: "And having thus chosen our course, without guile, and with pure purpose, let us renew our trust in God and go forward without fear, and with manly hearts." This was no desultory allusion to God-inspired courage. Its very brevity, and appeal to sacrificial courage and manliness against brother citizens, made it far more powerful than the overblown nationalist bravado typical of the time. Equally significant was Lincoln's invitation to trust in God. That this was more than a token, routine allusion to the divine is evident from an earlier draft, in which Lincoln urges "trust *in the justice* of God." Indisputably, the president believed in the justice of the Union cause. Why, then, did he cross out those three words? He might perhaps have considered the allusion unseemly. But it is possible that here is an early sign of what would become his preoccupation as the war proceeded: how to relate a human understanding of justice to the independent workings of a just God. More than simply aesthetic, Lincoln's deletion appears to offer a clue to his musing on Providence and the purposes of the Almighty.[26]

CHRISTIAN EXHORTATION

As we have seen, much is contested about Lincoln's religious faith before he became president. His invoking God and Providence in his public addresses during these critical months in 1861 could have been no more than self-protection. If he were simply adapting to the needs of a largely Christian public hungry for reassurance at a time of national crisis, his emphatic rhetorical embrace of Providence looks like political calculation. But without a window into a man's soul, we cannot say what really prompted this new language. Those who study Lincoln are commonly struck by his intellectual integrity and rigor. He did not usually take a new position that he could not in conscience defend. His providentialism *might* have been for show. But equally, it could have grown from an acute sense that the unprecedented national emergency would test his judgment, fortitude, and skill to their human limits—and possibly beyond. There need have been no shame in seeking and finding strength from a superintending higher power. What is certain is that later as war president Lincoln would express both privately and in public his belief in an interventionist and mysterious God. His appeal to Providence while president-elect foreshadowed that.

Whatever Lincoln's motivation, he could take pleasure in the public response. His words sparked widespread approval and acclaim. James A. Briggs, a Republican activist who had invited Lincoln to speak at New York's Cooper Union in 1860, extolled his eloquent farewell remarks at Springfield. "Thousands and tens of thousands read them with tearful eyes. There is a deep, strong, abiding, religious feeling in the minds of the American people, and your remarks so full of Christian faith, so trusting in Christian reliance, awakened that feeling & made it flow out from all hearts in response to your own."[27] Using a complex rhyme scheme, the poet Anna Bache celebrated the Christian essence of that address, evidence that Lincoln had taken to heart the scriptural text "The fear of the Lord is the beginning of Wisdom" (Proverbs 9:10). Assuming Lincoln's voice, she recalled Washington's Christian faith:

> *Like him, I seek for Aid Divine—*
> *His faith, his trust, his hope, are mine.*
> *Pray for me, friends, that God may make*
> *My judgment clear, my duty plain;*
> *For if the Lord no wardship take,*
> *The watchmen mount the towers, in vain.*[28]

These communications were representative of a cascade of letters and petitions to Lincoln seeking to praise, shape, and stiffen his resolve as he prepared for national leadership under God. They would continue after he entered office, and their pervasive religious tenor undoubtedly encouraged him to speak sympathetically in kind in his public role as president, whatever his personal understanding of the workings of Providence. Some of the incoming letters were surely drowned in the larger torrent of mail, but he had only to read and digest enough to see how far providentialist and specifically Christian ideas stirred the minds of his anxious public. We can be sure that Lincoln read Briggs's letter: he would soon reward him with a post in New York, one of the mountain of offices that by custom and practice an incoming president had at his disposal. It is probable, too, that he cast his eye over Bache's arresting tribute. John Nicolay estimated that, once in office, Lincoln saw only one item in fifty from the daily avalanche of correspondence. But it seems reasonable to assume that he read more copiously from his mailbag at this time as he prepared for his inauguration. He needed every gauge of public opinion at a moment of unprecedented political danger.

Unionists across the spectrum—from antislavery to conservative—encouraged Lincoln's providentialist nationalism. Joseph Butler of Bethlehem, Pennsylvania, was a stranger to Lincoln, but they had a mutual friend in the state's former governor James Pollock, a Princeton graduate and devout Presbyterian who had been one of Lincoln's Washington congressional messmates and was in the president's sights for a possible cabinet place. Pollock and Butler shared a firm faith in divine sovereignty and God's role in national affairs. As wartime director of the U.S. Mint, Pollock worked with Salmon Chase, the secretary of the Treasury, on the initiative that would see American coinage engraved with a declaration of the nation's trust in God.[29] For his part, Butler told Lincoln to be confident in the future of their beloved land. The history of the Revolution and the War of 1812 had shown its place "under the Auspices of the *Almighty*," who had directed Washington, Adams, Jackson, and Clay "to Contend *Successfully* for our Rights in the face of *Superior* foes." Now, in the turbulent present, "*Noble* [Major Robert] Anderson was under the supervision of that *Ever watchful* and

Lincoln, Nationality, and Providence 115

vigilant Eye that neither Sleeps nor Slumbers to Guard our National *Rights* and Honor."[30]

In similar vein, William Henry of Vermont, an 1860 Republican presidential elector who had served with Lincoln during the Thirtieth U.S. Congress, grieved that South Carolina's madness held the cotton states in thrall but urged the president-elect not to despair. "Providence will take care of us," he wrote. "Our Constitution must last more than 70 years." The Connecticut governor and staunch churchman William A. Buckingham sought to nerve Lincoln for the crisis under God's sure guidance. James R. Doolittle, Republican U.S. senator from Wisconsin, a devout Baptist, and the president's unbending wartime ally (he would tell a rally in 1864, "I believe in God. Under Him I believe in Abraham Lincoln"), wrote shortly after the forced evacuation of Fort Sumter to tell him that the God who had guided the nation's founders would stifle at birth "the most stupendous & insolent of all the Tyrannies of the world." Others who wrote to declare a firm faith in God's overruling Providence included George A. Pollard, an American missionary in Turkey, and David Smith, an uncompromising Reformed Presbyterian of Philadelphia, who—in thanking Lincoln for commissioning his brother-in-law—volunteered himself to serve against "the powers of darkness."[31]

In asking for the people's prayers, and recognizing his dependence on God's sovereignty, Lincoln struck a refreshing chord among those inured to the secularism of the political class. "It seems to be a popular opinion, that civil rulers are independent of the great Ruler of the universe," an Illinoisan told him. "Fatal mistake!" By contrast Lincoln's religious patriotism made him a special subject of prayer. "Thousands and tens of thousands of Christian men and women are praying for you," a Methodist acquaintance reported, "that you might have that wisdom in the present emergency that cometh only from God."[32] Joseph Butler, a Protestant to his boots, said he would pray, along with pious Mary Lincoln, that the president-elect would go to Washington "fully *anointed* with the Oil of *Gods Grace* as was King David with the Holy oil by Samuel (not Catholick oil)," and so be blessed "to Bring to nought the Schemes of Plotting Traitors."[33] Some prayed for a sign that Lincoln was more than a moral, upright, honest man, that by the influence of the Holy Spirit he had con-

116   RIGHTEOUS STRIFE

fessed Christ as his Savior. If he could not confirm he was a Christian, one woman wrote, "delay no longer, but hasten to the arms of redeeming love which have been so long extended to embrace you." Without God's grace and the Redeemer's blessed guidance, he would fail.[34]

At every stage of his progress from successful presidential candidate to the embattled executive of the late summer of 1861, Lincoln attracted stern reminders of his national duty under God. Antislavery voices demanded no backsliding. Writing from Bethlehem, Pennsylvania, an old-line Whig urged him to stand by "the Principles that God in Creation's morn flung forth as an Ensign to future Generations of Men, that all men were Created *free* and *Equal* in Respect to *Human Liberty*." The Illinois minister William Sloane told Lincoln to trust in the Lord and resist the menu of concessions to the South that for forty years had only "rendered her more insolent." A Rhode Islander assured him that one opinion prevailed, that "Old Abe will stand up," true to the cause of right and humanity. James S. Myers, a Pennsylvania delegate at the 1860 Chicago convention, declared that no greater calamity could befall the righteous cause than to pursue "a *timid, sickley, backing-out* course." God had called Lincoln to meet the crisis. Through grace and wisdom the Almighty would protect him from both external danger and the insidious poison of cowardice.[35]

A righteous nation required its leader to assemble a virtuous administration. An anonymous correspondent of "Mrs. President" sought to reach Lincoln's ear through his wife. She wanted a cabinet of wise, God-fearing secretaries, noting the stench of corruption attaching to Simon Cameron, widely expected to secure a cabinet position. Rather, she pressed the name of a good Republican lawyer, "unsofisticated in the art of Monouvering . . . in short . . . a liberal supporter of the Gosple and constant attenedant on the means of grace." Another, signing themselves "one who desires your good," told Lincoln to appoint only those who "Serve God and Hate Covetousness." William Sloane drew a moral lesson from Stephen Douglas's election defeat. Democratic leaders might appoint an efficient administration, but without divine assistance they would always fail. Douglas was talented, as was his able coterie of adherents, and enjoyed the benefit of electoral support from "the host of

Lincoln, Nationality, and Providence   117

Jesuits, by whom the nation is polluted." But by exposing the folly of impious Democrats, God had put it into voters' minds to do right.[36]

Beyond cabinet appointments there remained the hundreds of government offices waiting to be filled by each new administration. The Presbyterian Joshua Giddings, who had boarded with Lincoln as congressmen and admired his proven honesty, expected him to cleanse a government that he judged "at this time the most corrupt among all the Christian Nations of the earth." The Ohioan reminded him of the ease with which corruption could be hidden from presidential view, citing the case of John Quincy Adams, who had been unaware of the sharp practices under his own administration until he later served in the House. Buffeted by demands to honor promises of office that he had not personally made, Lincoln found the task of making appointments a demoralizing distraction. Some choices shook the confidence of those who had expected better. Amory Holbrook, a godly Republican member of the Oregon House of Representatives, told Lincoln how his supporters had expected a moral reversal after years of the Democracy's "wicked frauds and vile schemes." But, he complained, Lincoln's appointments, including his friend Anson G. Henry as surveyor general for Washington Territory, had spawned unprecedented corruption. He despaired of an administration whose head had "turned aside" from duty, honesty, and independence. Lincoln had written "Ichabod" on his own brow: his and his party's power was "utterly gone, its glory and its honor passed away."[37]

Holbrook's jaundiced protest was the exception. Broad Christian encouragement accompanied Lincoln as he entered office. "What a tower of strength is that man who can go to God and say 'Thou knowest it is my purpose to do just what is right in Thy sight,'" wrote Lincoln's acquaintance Joel Manning of Joliet. A prominent Methodist, and the former secretary of the board of the troubled Illinois and Michigan Canal, Manning rejoiced that in Lincoln's safe hands his administration would flourish and God's cause prevail.[38] The Milwaukee Republican editor Rufus King, later Lincoln's minister to the Papal States, looked to the president to serve as God's honored instrument in a national crisis that cried out for "the Christian and the patriot."[39] The elderly John G. Bergen, well known to Lincoln as Springfield's first Presbyterian minister and a founder of its Colonization Society, recalled the heartfelt "heavenward" sentiments of their parting words at the president-elect's farewell levee.[40]

As the fate of the Federal coastal defenses in the South assumed new urgency in late March, correspondents agreed that if Fort Sumter had to be evacuated, it would be the delinquent Buchanan's fault. Still, they called for audacious defense of every fort because, as to personal danger, "God rules—and man is immortal till his work of duty's done." The Illinoisan Joseph Blanchard entreated the commander in chief—in the spirit of Garibaldi and John Brown—to flex the Union's naval muscle. "Trust to Providence for the result, and all is well," he wrote. "To use a western expression . . . I am for 'standing up to the trough feed or no feed.'" In a fervent Easter Sunday appeal, Professor Jupiter Hesser of New York, a German immigrant composer, declared, "*Justice to all is the godlike conclusion after the Ressurexion day!*" Lincoln must defend the forts and punish southern capitulation to the devil and his spirits, the Confederate leaders. "Victory is ours, if we show to satan the allmighty sword of Justice, and act . . . without . . . giving up any thing of the property of the Union. . . . No more mercy, but Justice!" In a touching measure of loyalty to his adopted country, Hesser added, "If you want me, I will be Soldier to[o], I am only 61 years and 9 months of age."[41]

The steady stream of Christian encouragement reaching the new president's desk turned into a torrent after the Confederate assault on the Federal force at Fort Sumter on April 12. "I speak the mind of thousands of ministers of the Gospel, and of tens of thousands of Christian men and women, in Massachusetts and New England," the Congregationalist Alexander J. Sessions of Salem, Massachusetts, told Lincoln after the attack. "We have prayed for peace, we have prayed for disunionists and rebels. And now we pray to the God of battles to give right the victory. . . . Let the Government be strong."[42] During the spring and summer, the shock wave of war added institutional voices to those of pious individuals, the first expressions of what would be a continuing and varied denominational chorus of loyal advice throughout the war. An earnest statement of sympathy from the Welsh Congregational Church of New York and the loyal resolutions of Philadelphia's Reformed Presbyterian Church—the earliest declarations to reach the White House—would be followed by supportive petitions from, inter alia, the two hundred Methodist ministers of the New York Black River Conference and the Baptists of at least seven northern states.[43] From Lincoln's state of Illinois tumbled an avalanche of resolutions, from the General Assembly of the United Presbyterians, the General Association of Illinois Congregational Churches, the Illinois Conference of the Methodist Episcopal Church, and the Church of Christ.[44]

Representing the broad gamut of mainstream northern Protestantism, from radical antislavery nationalists to conservative Unionists, declarations of support glowed with incandescent rage at southern perfidy and without exception blamed the war on secessionists. Their shocking act of unprovoked and unrighteous rebellion against legitimate government—to extend and perpetuate "oppression, domestic corruption, barbarism and irreligion"—exceeded simple treason. Here was "a revolt against the Divine scheme for the world's advance in civilization and religion." Whatever the horrific cost—and few doubted a civil war's likely ferocity and loss of life— "heaven and earth" united in demanding the defense of law, persons, property, rights, and flag. The task of "our worthy President," wrote Welsh Congregationalists confident of his integrity, wisdom, and firmness, was never to forget that "the effectual fervent prayer of a righteous man availeth much." Lincoln, as a latter-day Elijah, would secure the triumph of liberty and Christianity: "*You* will gain the blessings of the present and future generations, and establish Righteousness for ever in our land."[45]

Lincoln's petitioners and correspondents interpreted the war as a rebuke for national sin and a compass for reading God's designs. Their sure faith in the Almighty's moral government of the world led to urgent requests for another day of national fasting and prayer. The U.S. Navy's paymaster, Thomas Looker, from his vessel off Fort Pickens, asked John Nicolay to place a confidential letter before Lincoln. Believing that his commander in chief "in these *dies irae* of the Country, . . . *trusts in God* . . . [and] *looks to & leans only on God, the Ruler of the Universe*," Looker hoped that "His Exc'y the President would now unite *the mighty Christian Element* in the Land—*the voice of God's own people*—and thereby obtain *the active, practical interposition, & blessing of the Almighty* on our Cause—by appointing a *Day of National humiliation, fasting & prayer!*"[46] Baptists made the case by practical example, reporting their own plans for a denominational day of humiliation and prayer in June. Old School Presbyterians invited their members to fast on July 4, earning the scorn of the United Presbyterians: How could a day of self-denial and abstinence be squared with the patriotic and celebratory ebullience of Independence Day? Rather, they asked Lincoln for a general fast to be observed soon after the special meeting of Congress on the nation's birthday.[47]

The desire for a fast day grew more palpable after July 21. On that day—a Sunday—the Union command prepared the public for victory in the first major battle of the war, at Bull Run. But the initial promise of success turned to ashes in the face of a powerful Confederate counterattack. The retreat became a disorderly rout as panic-stricken Federal troops ran back to Washington. The shock of defeat struck an almost tangible blow to Union pride, but of still greater consequence was the chilling reality that war would be long and bloody. Success would require more than enthusiasm. It would demand training, discipline, experience, and wise leadership. Above all, for many, it taught the lesson of God's sovereignty over national affairs. It did not go unnoticed that Jefferson Davis's proclaimed day of Confederate fasting on June 13, 1861, had resounded with voices declaring the new nation's unique Christian purpose and had been followed in no time by a stunning victory at Bull Run—confirmation according to a jubilant Richmond Episcopalian of its place "in the front rank" of world history. Davis's proclamation heralded many more civil fast days during the Confederate struggle. They flew in the face of the South's prevailing prewar doctrine of the spirituality of the church and its fierce condemnation of a "puritan political pulpit." The revolutionary new norm "Puritanized" the Confederacy, but not entirely to its comfort, as a later chapter will show.[48]

Aware that he would enjoy broad support, the U.S. senator James Harlan of Iowa, a significant mover in the Methodist establishment, introduced a resolution "requesting the President of the United States to recommend a day of public humiliation, fasting and prayer." Adopted by unanimous consent as a joint resolution of the House and the Senate on July 31, it was finally approved on August 5; it allowed Lincoln to proclaim a fast day with immensely more institutional standing than Buchanan had done nine months earlier by executive initiative alone.[49]

Lincoln, Nationality, and Providence 121

The following week, on August 12, Lincoln issued a recommendation of a national fast day to be held on the last Thursday of September. In the spirit of previous state and national proclamations of this kind, it began by acknowledging the supreme government of God, to whose frequent chastisements all people should contritely submit, by confessing their sins and praying fervently for the pardon of their offenses and for future blessings. In this "terrible visitation" of faction and civil war, it was "peculiarly fit for us to recognize the hand of God"; to remember "our own faults and crimes as a nation and as individuals"; and to pray "that we may be spared further punishment . . . that our arms may be blessed . . . for the re-establishment of law, order and peace . . . and that the inestimable boon of civil and religious liberty . . . may be restored in all its original excellence."[50]

Before turning, in the next chapter, to the events, consequences, and import of the September fast day, we should pause here to consider more immediate questions bearing on the proclamation's provenance and significance. Was it written by Lincoln himself? If so, did it express his personal convictions? Or was the text no more than recourse to the routine formulas of proclamations for special public worship, fashioned to honor the orthodox sentiments of the mainstream denominations to which it was chiefly addressed?

The document appeared over the signatures of the president and his secretary of state, William H. Seward. Because there is no definitive documentary evidence that Lincoln composed this or any of his later presidential recommendations of religious observance—days of either fasting or thanksgiving—some historians are hesitant about using them as a source for the development of his personal faith. Given Lincoln's record of consulting Seward in drafting or issuing other major texts—his first inaugural address and the preliminary emancipation proclamation—it seems only likely that the secretary of state would have had some hand in a document issued over his own name. The same could be said of Lincoln, of course. A forensic analyst of the proclamations attributes their authorship chiefly to Lincoln. Certainly, their deeper religious tone as the war progressed is consistent with what we know from other, more definitive sources about the phases in the development of Lincoln's faith during the war. The argument is not circular. To accept Lincoln as at least the co-author and over time the chief author of the procla-mations is more reasonable than not.[51]

The language of the August 1861 proclamation lacks the taut-ness and vigor that characterized Lincoln's prose at its best. "The numerous word pairs might be appropriate for a contract or a will," one commentator remarks, pointing to echoes of standard legal briefs familiar to both Lincoln and Seward, "but in this context they make the language hopelessly artificial: 'fit and becoming'; 'acknowl-edge and revere'; 'confess and deplore'; 'sins and transgressions'; 'fervency and contrition.'"[52] Compared with subsequent procla-mations, this one appears perfunctory and even commonplace. Yet there are two striking elements. First, in deeming by proclamation that the terrible visitation of war was the act of an interventionist God, Lincoln gave the providentialist turn in his language a more formal and explicit expression than ever. A document devoted solely to questions of divinity, prayer, and national salvation meant his reli-gious rhetoric achieved greater public impact than when, as previ-ously, it had been wrapped up with other concerns. Second, Lincoln now, as he had not done before, acknowledged that the Almighty as supreme moral governor had the power to chastise the people for their "faults and crimes as a nation" and, after repentance, to bestow "a blessing upon their present and prospective action." In articulating this understanding of justly deserved collective punish-ment, Lincoln signaled for the first time that the nation was itself a moral agent capable of "sins and transgressions." When in Febru-ary he had implicitly yoked the country with scriptural Israel—"this almost chosen people"—he had done so not to hint at punishment but to raise spirits and encourage faith that with God's help the nation would overcome its trials. Now, however, he allied himself with those for whom Israel was an admonitory example, a nation capable of sin and obliged to repent before it could be restored to divine favor.

Lincoln's proclamation did not state what the nation's sins and transgressions were. Notably, slavery goes unmentioned as one of its possible "faults and crimes." This failure specifically to identify the country's collective offenses could be taken to show the limits

Lincoln, Nationality, and Providence

of Lincoln's providentialist thinking. Was he simply repeating the hackneyed theme of generic national wrongdoing that preachers routinely lamented in their boilerplate sermons, failing to appreciate the reality or seriousness of sin? Perhaps so. But for the president to have encouraged nationwide contrition over slavery, by declaring it a heinous communal sin, risked alignment with the abolitionist minority in their pursuit of a war of emancipation. At this delicate juncture of the conflict, Lincoln's strategic priority was to maintain a broad coalition that encouraged the loyalty of the upper tier of border slave states. If theological conservatism restrained him from speaking out, so, too, did pragmatic politics. In the weeks between the proclamation's publication and the day of the national fast itself, events revealed just how well grounded was his caution on that score.

CHAPTER 5

LINCOLN'S FAST DAY AND ANTISLAVERY NATIONALISM, 1861

Lincoln's first fast day comfortably eclipsed Buchanan's. In January the country had remained riven by the party strife of the previous November. The hapless lame-duck president lacked authority. Numberless critics berated his administration. His call for national prayer, its sincerity widely questioned, evinced desperation. Conversely, Lincoln's September church gatherings enjoyed broad cross-party support. Even suspected Confederate sympathizers, including the maverick mayor of New York, Fernando Wood, paid formal lip service to the president's proclamation. In part, as the supportive *New York Times* noted, by working honestly for the good of the country, under unimaginable pressure, Lincoln enjoyed an authority few wanted to deny him. In larger part, public support for the September fast day grew naturally out of the desperate shock of war and widespread respect for the administration's assertion that "all exertions are vain unless they are blessed by a Higher Power."[1]

But what gave a powerful additional edge to the services of the day was the sharpening public debate over the future of slavery. It had assumed compelling urgency during the weeks between the publication of Lincoln's proclamation and the fast day itself, when events in Missouri starkly posed the question of a religious nation's proper

Lincoln's Fast Day and Antislavery Nationalism, 1861   125

plan for slavery. The commander of the Department of the West, John C. Frémont, acted to quell guerrilla activity and squeeze support for the Confederacy by putting Missouri under martial law. His electrifying proclamation of August 30 threatened to court-martial and execute civilians in arms against the government, to confiscate the property of those who aided the enemy, and to free the slaves of rebels. Considered dispassionately, the action indicated a general out of his depth in Missouri's turbulent waters. As a practical initiative, it threatened to undo Lincoln's border-state strategy by destabilizing the loyalist cause in the key state of Kentucky, where events were about to unfold to the Union's advantage following the Confederates' rash occupation of Columbus on September 2. Lincoln lost little time in writing confidentially to Frémont, asking him "in a spirit of caution" to reframe his military diktat by bringing it into line judicially with the Confiscation Act passed by Congress in early August; the act allowed the Union through court proceedings to confiscate and free slaves who assisted Confederate forces.[2] Lincoln's well-judged caution was soon endorsed by his Kentucky allies, notably his friend Joshua Speed, who told him that Frémont's foolish proclamation would "crush out every vestige of a union party in the state" were it not annulled. The general, however, indignantly refused the president's private request and asked that he publicly order a retraction, which Lincoln "very cheerfully" did.[3]

The episode sealed the gratitude of border-state loyalists, but elsewhere the president faced a tornado of criticism from euphoric supporters of Frémont's boldness. Throughout the early months of the conflict antislavery radicals were not alone in weighing the costs and benefits of taking the war to slavery itself. The defeat at Bull Run and the arrival of runaway slaves in military camps forced the question; the Confiscation Act showed that weighty members of the political class, including many Democrats, saw the logic of those events. In overturning Frémont's edict, the president could not doubt he was left politically injured. Schuyler Colfax, radical Republican congressman from Indiana, told him on September 7 that loyal men across parties approved Frémont's action, an assessment confirmed by the president's incoming mail.[4] A Springfield acquaintance, land agent, and abolitionist Republican, Erastus Wright, told Lincoln the proclamation was the key topic among the twenty-five thousand gathered at the Illinois State Fair in Chicago: "99 of every 100 said amen!"[5] In southern Illinois, wrote an ally, the president's action had destroyed confidence: "No disaster—not even the fearful one at Bull Run—has so dispirited and paralysed the friends of the Union as the course you have seen fit to take."[6] Lincoln's Chicago postmaster wrote that "the Northwest is, as near as such a thing is possible, an unit in support of Frémont's proclamation. It stirred the hearts of the people, as they had not been stirred before." Military enlistments were on the rise, as were subscriptions to the national loan. Even the most conservative of Democratic politicians professed themselves entirely satisfied with the general's bold initiative.[7]

The Frémont affair colored Lincoln's fast day and spurred antislavery nationalists to blaze against human bondage. At the same time the stern voices of conservative patriots, still upholding slaveholders' constitutional rights, denounced the treachery of the secessionist leaders. Despite their differences, religious nationalists of both stripes helped harness church congregations behind the Union. They gave Lincoln an encouraging gauge of the nation's appetite for military service and sacrifice in a just and righteous cause. And above all he learned that as the war made people's minds focus on what mattered most, some prewar conservatives had begun to think what once they thought unthinkable: to save the Union, slavery must be smashed.

LINCOLN'S FAST DAY, SEPTEMBER 26, 1861

As September 26 approached, religious communities across the Union prepared for Lincoln's day of fasting, humiliation, and prayer.[8] State and civic officials, calling on businesses to close, summoned a familiar language of God's overruling Providence to address the urgency of the moment. The newspaper press, Republican and Democratic alike, urged the claims of patriotism "upon every good citizen to render this fast acceptable to the Ruler of nations and armies," to secure a righteous peace and perpetual Union.[9] Customary Thursday routines gave way to Sunday solemnity. Banks, post offices, customhouses, navy yards, and departments of city governments stayed shut.[10] Courts and public schools closed, as did corn exchanges and most shops and stores. In Philadelphia, *The North American* reported, the scheduled high-profile sale of the captured Confederate prize ship *Amelia* was postponed, and the city's Chestnut Street "presented a continuous row of closed shutters, while in all the other promenades none but a very few of the 'one-horse' establishments disregarded the movement otherwise universal."[11] Newsboys' cries were stilled, with newspapers everywhere suspended.[12] Business at cattle markets dwindled as fast day approached; agricultural fairs ended early. The day's solemnity contrasted starkly with the routine shutdowns at Christmas and Thanksgiving. "Rarely if ever before was our city devoted to such outward compliance with the requirements of a Fast Day," the *Chicago Tribune* declared. "Not even the Sabbath has ever seen more quiet and order prevailing, nor places of business more universally closed."[13] Only the most profane communities ignored the day, notably the California gold miners and prospectors at Oroville who, putting panning before piety, "pursued their usual vocations."[14]

Amid the general observance, only a minority embraced full penitential self-denial. The Indianapolis banker and devout Methodist Calvin Fletcher—stirred "to bring my own weaknesses short coming & sins before the Lord also those of my nation"—spent the morning hours from six to ten in private devotion, attended crowded morning and afternoon church services for preaching and prayer, and abstained from usual meals during the day.[15] But total abstinence was not the norm. "Abstaining from food, save to a limited extent," one Ohio observer wrote, "does not in these latter days distinguish Fast from other days." This left Protestants open to Catholic gibes. "It was not a day of penance, but of indulgence in the best dress and the best of eating," the editor of the Boston *Pilot* sneered, noting "the consumption of as good chickens and turkeys as ever were carved on a Thanksgiving festival." Some noted how a holiday mood followed solemn worship. In Philadelphia, it was said that people poured in from the suburbs with all the high spirits of a peacetime Fourth of July and in the evening filled the places of amusement. Chicagoans caught excursion trains to the Wheaton county fair or stayed in the city for the afternoon prize trotting race

128 RIGHTEOUS STRIFE

between "the sorrel mare Kate" and "the roan horse Sam Roberts" at the Brighton track. "This is keeping fast day literally," the *Chicago Tribune* noted drily.[16]

In the main, solemnity ruled the day. Catholic authorities—wary of the Puritan aroma of fast-day preaching—ordered a High Mass, reading the collect for times of tribulation, and prayers for the civic authorities and the return of peace.[17] Protestant places of worship, Jewish synagogues, lyceums, and lecture theaters drew crowds of the devout—and the not so pious—for preaching, prayer, scripture reading, and orations.[18] Worshippers packed cross-denominational union meetings. At Chicago's Bryan Hall two thousand assembled under the auspices of the YMCA. Troops in the Federal camps, accompanied by marching bands playing "The Star-Spangled Banner," paraded in line of battle for the day's solemnities. At Camp Mather several thousand joined the men of the Thirty-Ninth Illinois Infantry, the "Yates Phalanx" (named after the Illinois governor), for religious exercises and the presentation of an embroidered regimental flag.[19] The U.S. Capitol played host to an afternoon lecture on the federal constitution by the professor of law and rhetoric Amasa McCoy. His audience included Lincoln, who had already attended church, members of his cabinet, and the diplomatic corps.[20]

Ministers painted the national trauma with a dark palette. Robert L. Stanton, an Ohio Presbyterian, saw the brutal plunge into war as a "world-astounding transition . . . that eclipses in its suddenness and magnitude all the extravagance of romance and fable." He stood aghast at the republic's tragic reversal. Its marks of high civilization—unmatched agricultural riches, burgeoning commerce and manufacturing, inventive genius, superior public education, universal religious vigor, popular representative government—had been inadequate to prevent catastrophic failure. With a million men in arms, half within forty miles of the nation's capital, the grim conflict engaged "larger armies than were ever led by Napoleon and Wellington, or Alexander and Xerxes, or Caesar and Hannibal, combined." Yet, a Boston Unitarian despaired, the rebels had not been crushed within the predicted three months. Despite the Union's vast resources, "the enemy . . . still mocks us."[21] In New York's Spring Street Church, Robert Davidson delivered a grim roll call of humiliations since the fall of Fort Sumter: the panic at Bull Run, Confederates' victories at Wilson's Creek and Lexington (Missouri), the invasion of Kentucky, privateers active, the national capital beleaguered, and foreign nations scenting weakness. "England withholds her sympathy. 'Aha! aha!' they say. . . . 'It is as we predicted. The model republic is dead. The bubble has burst!'" The return of bedraggled and leaderless troops drove home the grievous reality of war. A colossal struggle was shaking the nation to its core.[22]

Lincoln's day of *humiliation* satisfied the widespread emotional hunger. Thousands of ministerial voices formed a patriotic chorus of introspection. Much of their rhetoric might be dismissed as routine, even hackneyed, fast-day formulas that straitjacketed thought and expression. However, the profound threat to the life of the Union gave unfamiliar purchase and power to otherwise familiar, even hoary, oratorical conventions. The role of Providence, national and personal sin and righteousness, divine displeasure and punishment, God's purposes for the United States, and the country's special role in his wider plan for humankind: these well-rehearsed themes took on new and acute relevance after Lincoln dramatically overturned Frémont's audacious emancipation decree.

FRÉMONT'S PROCLAMATION AND ANTISLAVERY NATIONALISM: "THE LORD TRIETH THE RIGHTEOUS, BUT THE WICKED HIS SOUL HATETH"[23]

It was a commonplace of American political theology that God, as the creator of nations, kept them permanently on probation, educating and disciplining them in equal measure. The scriptural history of Israel had long been an American preachers' manual of lessons applicable to the nation the Almighty had chosen for a unique role in post-Reformation history.[24] Albert G. Palmer, Baptist minister of Stonington, Connecticut, offered a fast-day reminder of God's strenuous examination of the Israelites: "He leads them into the mazes of the wilderness, thrusts them into the desert, shuts them up between the mountains and the sea, or presses them into narrow passes of moral and religious conflict where principles must be tested."[25] The Union's descent into fratricidal bloodshed presented an equal trial of a religious people's righteous fiber. War was a just punishment for sins. Its coming had been irrepressible, a moral necessity. But it was also a route to national salvation.

Robert Stanton captured that prevailing theme when telling his fasting Presbyterian congregation that war, whatever its secondary causes, was always regarded in scripture "as a visitation of God upon nations for their offences" against His principles. With unsparing frankness, a New York Methodist minister told how the war, "the fruit of a wicked rebellion," was Almighty's rod to chastise "a *wicked nation*." Since, as the Baptist Francis Wayland reflected, the loyal Union could not be charged in justice with wronging the South, it could only be wrongs against God that had provoked the war. Quoting from Lincoln's "admirable" proclamation, Wayland invited humble prayer "in sorrowful remembrance of our own faults and crimes as a nation and individuals."[26] Reformed Presbyterians notably insisted that unless the U.S. Constitution was amended to acknowledge the Almighty, the Union would remain a flawed instrument of God's purposes. Confederates aggravated the wound by drafting the Almighty into the rebel constitution, an initiative Ezra Adams and others dismissed as a monstrous cover for lawless oppression. Adams called for God to be embraced by the U.S. Constitution—"the temple of national existence"—to house "a nationality . . . so pure as to become God's dwelling-place."[27]

As we have seen, the president's proclamation, and those of state governors and city mayors, followed custom by attributing God's wrath to generic, unspecified sin.[28] The northern pulpit's diversity in politics and theology can explain why Lincoln left the specifying of national wrongs to ministers themselves. But his prudence had a political price: the harsh criticism from antislavery radicals for a cowardly silence on the soul-convulsing issue of the time. In New York's Church of the Puritans, George Barrell Cheever could not believe that a proclamation demanding repentance of sin had been mute on the nation's comprehensive iniquity, "the most atrocious Slavery the world ever saw," sanctioned and maintained by government and people. Why, asked the *National Anti-slavery Standard*, the newspaper of the American Anti-slavery Society, did Lincoln not name the one gigantic crime that, if not speedily repented, would bring utter national destruction?[29]

In the months since Buchanan's fast day, unfolding secession

Lincoln's Fast Day and Antislavery Nationalism, 1861   131

and war had fanned antislavery fervor into an inferno of outrage. Much of the sympathy for the slaveholders' moral predicament melted as slavery propelled southerners onward. Cheever's assault on oppression typified the fury consuming the more radical pulpits of New York and beyond, particularly in New England and its diaspora.[30] At the Broadway Tabernacle, Joseph Thompson saw slavery "preying upon our vitals."[31] In a blistering sermon to a Dutch Reformed congregation on Staten Island, the Presbyterian Thomas Skinner condemned the malignant institution for its assault on "country, church, domestic institutions, law, order, honor, oaths, property, and freedom": at its bidding, "Repudiation, Treason, Rebellion, Revolution, spring forth, and armed hosts march against our Capitol." So much for southern honor and chivalry. A "slavocratic regency," encouraged by chameleon pro-slavery clergy, had upended republican government for diabolical ends.[32] They had, a Reformed Presbyterian told his Indiana congregation, adopted Satan's motto, "Evil, be thou my good."[33] Stanton pictured all the devils in hell's caverns relishing in wonder the upending of the best government known to humankind.[34]

The "demoniacal sophistries" of a pro-slavery doctrine had eviscerated the gospel of Christ, silenced the prophetic voice of Isaiah, scoffed at the notion of freeing the oppressed, exalted political necessity into moral principle, and undermined religion by palsying moral instinct.[35] No single declaration from the South drew more thunderous contempt than Alexander Stephens's infamous speech at the Savannah Athenaeum in March. There the Confederacy's vice president declared that the "cornerstone" of the new government rested, for the first time in the history of the world, upon "the great truth, that the negro is not equal to the white man; that slavery—subordination to the superior race—is his natural and normal condition."[36] Stephens's brutal words would remain a valuable weapon of the antislavery pulpit thereafter, quoted directly and by allusion until the Confederacy collapsed. Here, abolitionists declared, was the apotheosis of the heresy the southern pulpit had been cultivating for a generation, "to build up an empire whose foundations rest on slavery."[37] The South's tenacious grip on African slaves, Skinner protested, bore grim comparison with the Egyptians' oppression of the Israelites.[38]

Alert to the danger of northern self-righteousness—but not wholly escaping it—antislavery nationalists commonly pointed to countrywide complicity in embedding and spreading slavery since the republic's founding. For material gain the North had repeatedly "offered incense upon its bloody altar."[39] Greed had elected northern politicians allied to the South, reviled abolitionists, and blocked compensated emancipation.[40] The country had acquired territory through conquest and purchase to allow injustice to spread. An unrighteous war against Mexico, a stringent Fugitive Slave Law, the repeal of the Missouri Compromise line, and slavery's spread into western territories—although largely opposed by Republicans—testified to the North's moral vacuum.[41] The political system had repelled men of principle.[42] Elective positions had attracted "hungry adventurers" who contended "like savages fighting for scalps." Demagoguery, bribery, and "iron bound partyism" smothered ethical integrity.[43] In Haverhill, Massachusetts, Thomas Doggett sniped that "a disregard for the strict morality of the Bible has been one of the prime requisites . . . [in] a candidate for office." Was it any wonder, Robert Stanton asked, that such a bankrupt code of politics should have plunged the nation into civil war?[44]

Although many fast-day clergy dodged the question, the future of slavery loomed over all other issues. As the day approached, Lincoln could be in no doubt that some staunch Christian Unionists thought him too timid. Frémont had struck a chord by plainly exposing the hard underlying issue.[45] The general had recognized, a Connecticut minister told the president, that the national struggle "must issue either in a separate Southern Confederacy or in measures looking to a speedy abolishment of slavery. *There is no other alternative.*" He echoed Michigan church resolutions that "as the War is avowedly waged by traitors for slavery, common sense teaches that, in order to end the one, we have but to weaken or destroy the other."[46] The Methodist John Locke Scripps, the president's influential ally at the *Chicago Tribune*, reminded Lincoln of his maxim "This Nation cannot endure part slave and part free." He had not wanted war, but since the slaveholder had "forced it upon us, . . . I am for striking it wherever it is vulnerable." You need not be an abolitionist, explained John L. Williams of Chillicothe, Ohio, to see that the rebels must lose their slaves so they could never again make use of them. Another Ohioan, Virginia born and bred, told the president that he had "no prejudices against Slavry, as a local institution but when the question, is narrowd down to the existance of the Govement or Slavry, who will hesitate to make a choice?"[47]

By modifying what one admirer called Frémont's *"ritcheous proclamation,"* Lincoln punctured a mood of high elation and faced an emotional public, aggrieved, bewildered, and even furious. "You can heardly imagine the thrill of *pain* that you have sent through many Christian hearts," mourned a correspondent from Kalamazoo. In Lincoln's Springfield, according to another, it chilled the people "like a *snowstorm in June*" and would have "a very parallysing effect in all the Western Army." In upstate New York, one wrote, "only traitors applaud it."[48]

Suffusing these reprimands was disappointment that a president so widely admired as an honest agent of God had here defied scripture and Christian obligation. A critical "plain farmer" told him that his action had called to mind Christ's words: "In as much as you have done it unto one of the least of these that believe on me ye have done it unto me." By overturning Frémont, "did you think . . . that you had ordered Jesus Christ back into bondage. . . . [D]o not set yourself against God I beseach of you." True to his New England creed, Erastus Wright took on the role of Old Testament prophet: "If God has determined *freedom for the Slave* He will be very likely to do it—even to the Destruction of this wicked Nation." The South had enslaved and robbed the faultless black man, but the North had "served Old Satan for the honour of it." He begged "Friend Lincoln" to do right: " 'Let the oppressed go free' and save yourself and save the Nation from the wrath of God." These correspondents told the president personally what pious antislavery voices were telling others. "I pray God to forgive my vote" for Lincoln, a Cincinnati Unitarian wrote to Salmon Chase; the Unitarian minister Moncure Conway told Horace Greeley that Lincoln's name now elicited groans, not cheers.[49]

Those antislavery nationalists who scolded Lincoln, however, generally persisted in their Christian regard and prayers for a president who, they repeated, remained the channel of God's national purposes and was destined for historical greatness and global fame. "I firmly believe you are an instrument in the hands of Providence

134   RIGHTEOUS STRIFE

to preserve this glorious Govement, and may God endow you with Wisdom Prudence & courage to do it," wrote one from Greenville, Ohio.[50] A New Englander, H. W. Chafee, offered an unpunctuated stream of Christian encouragement "that you may look to god for wisdome and foresight and put your trust in our beloved lord who always blessed the children of Israel when they would follow him but when they forsook him only look at their defeats." What attention, if any, Lincoln paid to Chafee's prodding is unknown, but the arresting words of Scripps must have hit home. Through the rebellion God had handed Lincoln the means of wiping out an execrable stain, he wrote. "The destiny . . . of the great American people of all races and conditions, is committed to your keeping. *You must either make yourself the great central figure of our American history* for all time to come, or your name will go down to posterity as one who . . . proved himself unequal to the grand trust." Scripps prayed daily that God would nerve and guide his friend to meet these high responsibilities.[51]

During the weeks between Frémont's edict and Lincoln's fast day, the consequences of the proclamation heightened the sensibilities of both antislavery and conservative religious nationalists. Throughout, as Lincoln explained, he learned from disconsolate antislavery correspondents that Frémont's decree "was popular in some quarters, and would have been more so if it had been a general declaration of emancipation."[52] He would shortly find the fast day itself delivering a powerful antislavery nationalist coda to what had gone before. Pulpits and presses across the North, on September 26 and the days following, distilled the political and military lessons of the summer to defend Frémont's initiative. James Sloane equated the public grief that Lincoln's "grave mistake" had caused to the shock of the Bull Run disaster. A Chicago Congregational minister said it showed how much rulers needed to "clear the deck for action, throw overboard their pro-slavery piles of rubbish, and then see how freemen will work the guns." Ichabod Simmons was sure God's just purposes would overturn Lincoln's action.[53] Charles King Whipple, radical abolitionist, questioned if "a hundred *such* Fast-days [would] compensate for the harm the President has done in limiting Frémont's just and admirable Proclamation." Lincoln's transparent desire was "*not* that liberty should be proclaimed throughout this land, unto all the inhabitants thereof!" Unless he changed course, fast days would be meaningless, "though he should dispense with a dozen dinners, and go through the form of prayer in a dozen meeting-houses!"[54]

No event delivered greater or more relevant drama than the gathering in Siloam Presbyterian Church, Brooklyn. This was a mainly African American congregation led by James A. Gloucester, the son of a manumitted slave, who counted Frederick Douglass and John Brown as his associates. The congregation shared Douglass's belief that too many Union preachers lacked the courage to repent of the great national sin.[55] The minister's wife, Elizabeth, was a manumitted slave, too, and a talented businesswoman; her wealth had helped build Siloam into a center of radical antislavery influence and Underground Railroad activity. While Gloucester presided, a "large and respectable" meeting heard in thrilling detail an account of the rescue of a Virginia slave, William, as told by the fugitive himself and his white smuggler, "Mr. H. Jones." With emotions running high in the presence of a life traumatized and scarred, Jones lauded Frémont's proclamation: an inspiring, historic step toward the immediate emancipation for which all present yearned.[56]

More generally significant were the antislavery sentiments formalized in the fast-day resolutions of church bodies that collectively blended themes of national righteousness, justice, and strategic pragmatism. The urgent radical nationalists of the First Congregational Church of Williamsburg in Brooklyn, led by their pastor, Simeon S. Jocelyn, implored Lincoln to escape the righteous retribution of "the God of the oppressed" through universal emancipation.[57] The resolutions from Illinois churches made special claim on the president's attention. The combined Congregational, Baptist, and Methodist voices of Hamilton, Hancock County, begged him to use his war powers to reestablish Frémont's decree and press ahead to full abolition: "The God of justice will *take no part* with us in our present fearful conflict so long as the inhuman relation of human chattelhood is . . . sacredly protected by our national government." They, in common with the "faithful subjects of righteous government" at the Church of Christ in Stockton, Ford County, urged Lincoln to ponder the prophecies of Isaiah, as Frémont had done in "removing the yoke from the neck of the oppressed."[58] The resolutions from the First Congregational Church of Chicago bore the imprint of its emancipationist pastor, William Weston Patton. The war would be won only by a penitential antislavery policy "to enlist the sympathy of foreign nations, to suppress the rebellion, & to make the Union hereafter indissoluble."[59]

Together, the Frémont episode and the fast day served to crystallize thinking and reset the course of religious nationalism. Former defenders of the South's constitutional rights now questioned old certainties. Why should prosecuting a just war for national survival not sanction any and all necessary means? James Sloane, radical abolitionist, predicted that with the shock of rebellion "many lips long sealed upon the subject of Slavery, would be opened; there would be ten, perhaps a hundred, to speak out boldly to-day where there was one a year ago." Philadelphia's radical Unitarian William H. Furness proposed a new declaration of the principles of 1776 to abolish the "foaming fountain" of violence and blood demanded alike by natural justice, humanity, and national safety. Well before Lincoln embraced it, William Ford of Vermont presciently cited John Quincy Adams's argument that Congress had by right the power to abolish slavery in time of war. In Joseph Bittinger's graphic image, the hellhound of slavery had "broken his chain, come up from his infernal kennel, and clutched the master by the throat. . . . Let the *man* live—let the *beast* die; and let all the people say, Amen!"[60]

Evidence, as well as the wish, was father to these radicals' hopes. Pulpits around the country told of a sea change in sentiment. Writing to Lincoln as superintendent of the Wisconsin Institute for the Blind, Thomas H. Little confessed, "I have lived in the North & in the South, in the East & the West without contracting *abolition principles*; but in the midst this war, I believe that I am only one of thousands who have changed views very much."[61] In New York, Henry Bellows, putting government authority at the heart of his fast-day discourse, questioned the constitutionality and prudence of an act of immediate emancipation but admitted that events might force it.[62] Hartford's Joel Hawes saw how divisive it would be to make emancipation a war aim, but still hoped that God and the South's rashness would speed slavery's end. San Francisco's First Baptist Church heard their pastor, David B. Cheney, speak about slavery—

"the bottom cause of all our trouble"—for the very first time in his ministry. It appeared that God had listened at last to the cries of the oppressed. Should the Civil War free four million slaves, "we would most clearly see at last, 'God moves in a mysterious way.'"[63]

For radical abolitionist ministers such as Cheever, Channing, Gloucester, Jocelyn, and Whipple, the stupendous wrong of slavery could be resolved only by giving black people all the rights and freedoms of whites. Some foresaw a fully biracial society at home. William H. Furness was inspired by a "splendid" challenge: *"to convert four millions of Slaves into Free Laborers:* a problem, which there is no nation on the face of the earth so peculiarly qualified by native genius to solve, as this American people."[64] The less ambitious advocated black-run colonies abroad.[65] As antislavery nationalism widened its appeal, it attracted many who did not share the radicals' racial egalitarianism. "Blazing resentment" had inspired men to form the Republican Party and resist the Slave Power, but, Albert G. Palmer lamented, they "never meant to fight for the negro! no, indeed!" Shockingly, many of slavery's critics "cared as little for the negro as the negro cares for himself. And . . . there is, I fear, very little of humane or christian sympathy, and less of principle for the wrongs of bleeding Africa."[66] Palmer would have been unsurprised by what John L. Williams of Chillicothe had written to Lincoln a few days earlier. "Frémonts manifest has nothing to do with '*abolition*' in the Common Sense of that term," the Ohioan told the president. But when the rebels employed their slaves against the government, "they justly ought to be taken from them." If the country were to be kept "in an *eternal broil*" about racial slavery, "why object to Frémonts *right* way of getting clear of this *infernal pest.*"[67]

CONSERVATIVE RELIGIOUS NATIONALISM: "TO STRENGTHEN OUR NOBLE CONSTITUTION"

A barrage of conservative voices fought to stanch the swelling voice of antislavery religious nationalism. The churches' conservatives remained tenacious defenders of a Union whose southern secessionists—castigated as desperate, foolish, and treasonous—had done nothing to shake their confidence in its constitutional footings. Those foundations included a state's right to determine for itself, without external interference, the future of its domestic arrangements and its paramount institution, slavery.

Antislavery nationalists faced no more trenchant a conservative critic than the owner-editor of *The New York Herald*, James Gordon Bennett. One of the most influential newspapermen of the age, Bennett brought fierce independence and flamboyance to his three decades at the helm. Technologically savvy and often unpredictable, he was remarkably single-focused in his conservatism. Although hating Catholics and Jews, he leaned toward the Democrats, a natural political home for those like himself who championed white supremacy, sympathy for the South, and anti-abolitionism. Discussing the fast day, he blamed the war on the intrigues of British antislavery reformers and financiers, naive American abolition societies, and "the anti-slavery disunion doctrines preached from the pulpit, and reiterated by the fanatical press." With 400,000 Americans and brothers facing off across the Potomac, Lincoln had continued with the wise and conservative course that had won him "golden opinions." He had called a national fast, Bennett declared without evidence, hoping that those "led astray by the demagogues of the pulpit . . . would . . . return to the ancient landmarks of the constitution." Yet these fanatical clergy, in attacking slavery and the South, had missed the underlying cause of the nation's catastrophe, which Bennett captured in the editorial's title: "Treason and Mutiny in the Pulpit."[68]

The religious conservatives whose cause Bennett espoused were no less moved than others by the electric charge of patriotism pulsing through the North at the outbreak of war. During the spring and early summer of 1861, they aligned with political centrists and antislavery radicals across the broad spectrum of church bodies to declare allegiance to the political Union. The General Assembly of the New School Presbyterians, which unanimously approved the course of the federal government, sent loyal resolutions to the president. Diocesan and state-level conventions of Episcopalians stood firm for the Union. Similar declarations of dedication to the republic emerged from meetings of the American Baptist Union, Methodist conferences, the Old School Presbyterian General Assembly, Congregational associations, the Synod of the Moravian Church,

Evangelical Lutherans, United Presbyterians, and individual Roman Catholic dioceses.

Conservatives' declarations of loyalty were sincere but could not obscure underlying tensions. Those strains had little to do with the churches' small minority of Confederate sympathizers since, with public emotion surging against rebels, those fellow travelers prudently kept their mouths shut. More unsettling was the question of what the war's dislocations meant for slavery and its constitutional protections. Most immediately challenging for conservative religious nationalists was how best to honor the principle of the spirituality of the church. After years of attacking antislavery clergy for besmirching the pulpit by "political preaching," church conservatives now had to decide if institutional silence was proper when the nation's life hung in the balance. Throughout the turbulent party politics of the prewar era they had distinguished between the right of individuals to take political positions and the pulpit's duty to remain neutral on temporal issues. For ministers then to preach nothing but Christ the Savior might have been intellectually defensible, or at least a means of maintaining church unity. But was it sustainable in wartime?

The issue played out most arrestingly among Lincoln's Old School Presbyterians, the largest Protestant denomination with a national reach on the eve of the war. An early indication of the tensions within this naturally conservative denomination surfaced in North Church, Chicago. There, the deep pockets of the inventor of the reaper, the Virginia-born Cyrus Hall McCormick, had funded a conservative ministry, as well as editors and professors at the seminary, to repel the surging forces of northwestern antislavery they feared would cleave the Union. In 1857, McCormick installed in North Church the most celebrated antiabolitionist minister in the West, Nathan Rice. But four years later, in April 1861, Rice resigned, a victim of poor health and exhaustion from his battle against radicalism. Shortly afterward, McCormick's brother William described the congregational rift that his resignation and the onset of war had exposed. "Do you clap your Preachers on Sunday?" he asked a cousin in Missouri. "They do it here *loud* and *long*. I believe they pray substantially that every devil of you down south shall be *killed* (not die) in his sins. They don't pray that your eyes shall be opened to see the glorious light of the everlasting patron-*Saints* of the North, but rather that you may in your darkened understanding, plod along up to the cannon's mouth." He had no sympathy for secession, "but I fear the remedy is to be far worse than the disease."[69]

The mostly gray-headed and bespectacled representatives of the Old School gathered in Philadelphia for their annual General Assembly in May 1861. Priding themselves on their conservatism and immunity to the sectional antipathies that had fractured churches before the war, they wanted the impossible: to maintain institutional unity while also declaring devotion to the United States. The giants of southern Presbyterianism, Thornwell and Palmer, stayed away, as did most of the eligible commissioners from the Confederate states. It was seventy-six-year-old Gardiner Spring, pastor of the Brick Church in New York, who commanded the public's rapt attention. A deep-dyed conservative, hostile to abolitionism and sympathetic to the South, he was expected to sustain the policy of political silence. As a staunch nationalist, however, he introduced resolutions that— after several days' debate and modest revision by a committee led by Charles Hodge—won substantial majority support.[70]

The Spring resolutions summoned the Church to a day of prayer and declared the General Assembly's obligation "to strengthen, uphold, and encourage, the Federal Government in the exercise of all its powers under our noble Constitution." With this statement the Church in effect adopted a political loyalty test and took sides on the agitating question of whether citizens' allegiance was primarily to their state or the federal Union. To reach its decision, the Assembly had sounded out Lincoln's cabinet. The conservative Presbyterian Edward Bates put church unity ahead of a political declaration; conversely, the radical Episcopalian Chase saw "no valid objection to unequivocal expressions in favor of the Constitution, Union, and freedom."[71] Chase's position better reflected the grassroots Presbyterian nationalism that the Assembly could not ignore. The Spring resolutions having been adopted by a substantial majority, local presbyteries and synods voted on them over the summer and fall of 1861, exposing deep sectional divisions and the Church's fractured communities in the border states of Missouri and Kentucky. One by one, southern bodies chose to secede and, in early December, organized the Presbyterian Church in the Confederate States.

Lincoln's fast-day proclamation, by speaking generically of "our faults and crimes as a nation," licensed religious conservatives to focus not on slavery but on what exercised them most: national unity and southern treason. Old School Presbyterians had by then already observed their own day of humiliation, on July 1. Spring himself preached that morning to a large and fashionable congregation at the Brick Church, on the corner of Fifth Avenue and Thirty-Seventh Street. Like several other loyal clergy, he took as his text "Say ye not, A confederacy, to all them to whom this people shall say, A confederacy; neither fear ye their fear, nor be afraid. Sanctify the Lord of hosts himself, and let him be your fear" (Isaiah 8:12–13). The son of a Revolutionary officer, Spring delivered a patriotic history lesson. Rebellion against the federal government was a heinous crime. Unconstitutional, illegal, and mad, it was a sin before the Almighty. The nation's preeminent fault demanded national repentance. Spring's assault on treason—"a crime against God" and an "unholy conspiracy against our Union, our laws, and our liberties"—echoed throughout the church to become the major theme of conservative nationalist preaching on Lincoln's fast day.[72]

Conservative voices were loudest across the lower North and border states, above all in Catholic, Episcopal, and Old School Presbyterian churches. Ministers acknowledged that without slavery there could have been no war but refused to call it a sin. They resolutely trumpeted the institution's constitutional protections. An indignant New Jersey minister rebuked the hypocrisy of those who for months had been "most vehemently asseverating that the war we are waging is not waged against the social system of the South," but who now endorsed Frémont's action. Evidence of a growing appetite for emancipationist measures unnerved him and others. In a plaintive call for peace, the southern-born James Preston Fugitt, rector of Baltimore's Church of the Holy Innocents and a resolute champion of racial slavery, lambasted the "quack gospel" of maddened abolition preachers and their political allies. Mostly, however, conservatives' scriptural orthodoxy and awareness of divided congregations encouraged silence. Addressing New Jersey Episcopalians, Horatio Hastings Weld delivered a distinctly emollient lament over secession, likening the conspirators to Absalom, whose rebellion against his father, David, led to magnanimity in the face of deep hurt. Having "hurried the calamity of cruel and unbrotherly warfare upon us," the Confederates now faced a Union that, following David's example, would not "suffer the kingdom to pass to an usurper."[73] But they would not face vengeance on their loyal return. The future of slavery went unmentioned. It was evidently not at stake.

Similarly, against a backdrop of congregational drama, loyalty to the Union became the urgent issue at San Francisco's Calvary Presbyterian Church. Here the fast day arrived on the heels of the forced resignation of the southern-born pastor and Confederate sympathizer, William A. Scott. Reported to have said that Jefferson Davis was as much president as Abraham Lincoln, Scott had faced a storm of criticism, physical threats, and a symbolic hanging. His successor, Dr. George Burrowes, addressed an emotionally wrought congregation on the righteousness of loyalty under the Union flag, with no word about slavery.[74] Most of the churches in the District of Columbia, too, skirted the subject. The radical antislavery New York *Independent* scoffed that not a single orthodox clergyman in the capital dared treat slavery as the war's cause.[75] At the Union Prayer Meeting in Washington's E Street Baptist Church, a relative of Vice President Hannibal Hamlin tried to include slavery in the confession of national sins. The pastor, George Whitefield Samson, though no rebel sympathizer, blocked the attempt. As president of Columbian College, with its southern patrons, he would not admit a topic "forbidden by the rules of the meeting": recognized under the Constitution, slavery must not be discussed on this occasion—or, indeed, at all.[76]

Samson's example raises a question beyond a definitive answer: How many of these conservative fast-day preachers were southern sympathizers? Richard Fuller of Baltimore, renowned Baptist pastor, pro-slavery theologian, and president of the Southern Baptist Convention, exemplifies the difficulty. In May he had urged Lincoln during a private interview to accept the reality of the Confederacy in the interests of peace.[77] As ever, on fast day he eschewed, in his own words, "political utterances," telling his congregation that he was determined "not to know any thing among you save Jesus Christ and Him crucified." To keep the occasion politically sterile, Fuller urged them to follow Christ, "by rendering unto Caesar the things which are Caesars," and the apostle Paul, by "submitting to the powers that be." With these familiar texts he left some convinced that he sympathized with the Confederacy. But the desire for peaceful resolution in itself was not disloyalty. Fuller's prayers, rich in providentialist thought, were innocuously phrased, asking simply that "these calamities now pressing upon us may be overruled for the glory of God and the advancement of the gospel," and "that by his own righteous disposal of events war may cease, and tranquillity, prosperity, and happiness may be restored to this afflicted land."[78]

The slave state sympathizer Nehemiah Adams used the pulpit of Boston's Union Congregational Church to demand that the North "leave to the South all moral responsibility" for an institution that he warmly supported. Adams was notorious in antislavery circles for *A South-Side View of Slavery*, based on his travels through Georgia, South Carolina, and Virginia in 1854, which praised the religious benefits of enslavement. Likewise, Edward J. Stearns, a Maryland Episcopalian temporarily officiating in Newark, delivered a sermon shaped by Confederate sympathies and outrage at the use of the federal iron fist in his home state. "If I were preaching to Southern men . . . I should testify against the sins of the South," he announced, but "God forbid that I should preach to you, on an occasion like this, against another people's sins!" In the spirit of Bennett's *Herald*, he berated the "busybodyism-in-other-mens-matters" that Puritans had carried with them on the *Mayflower*, "leaving enough behind . . . to overthrow, in its madness, the Throne and the Church; and now, and here, it has overthrown the country." The fast day should focus on the North alone: here "the crying sin" of Pharisaism had filled the public sphere with claims of northern superiority "*intended* to set North and South by the ears; to exasperate the one, and to add to the self-righteousness of the other." Stearns boldly accused the "more than one, or two, or three" in the congregation whose "most comfortable consciousness of belonging to a *very* superior community" had provoked the unfolding national calamity. Several affronted members walked out, others hissed, and the district attorney was asked to parse the sermon for evidence of treason.[79]

Most conservatives, by contrast, turned their fury on southern rebels for violating the national covenant, while conceding that spiritual discipline demanded self-scrutiny, too. A New Hampshire editor asked, "Have we of the North no sins that provoke the wrath of Heaven and call forth its righteous indignation?" Those for whom slavery in itself could not be sinful drew on a tired litany of personal failings, including Sabbath breaking, swearing, and intemperance. The conservative Presbyterian *New-York Observer* lamented the ruinous shortcomings of the political class and the all-consuming passion for material gain.[80] These were protean concerns, of course. Conservative nationalists rebuked voters for electing corrupt public officials who lacked the disinterested patriotism of the founding generation, contending that wiser (conservative) heads would have prevented the national calamity. Antislavery nationalists, as already noted, lamented the spinelessness of those who had placated slaveholders. The sin of covetousness, too, was a concern equally for conservatives, who considered the love of money the beguiling sin of all Americans, and for antislavery nationalists, who attributed the moral ruin of the white South to the almighty dollar.[81]

Conservatives drew the contempt of antislavery nationalists for their fixation on secondary sins. These afflicted other nations, too, but had not catapulted them into civil war. The radical New York *Independent* scoffed at Washington preachers who blamed national troubles on some northern states' repeal of capital punishment laws or on the running of railway trains on the Sabbath. Robert Davidson rebuked those who mourned "Sabbath-breaking, or profanity, or licentiousness, or intemperance, or covetousness, or venality," but studiously ignored slavery. Were those sins any more prevalent than formerly? Was the country less pious than countries not at war with themselves? The American churchgoing community, thanks to the voluntary principle, compared well with others: revivals and prayer meetings had abounded of late; New York reformers had achieved the Sabbath closure of grogshops, theaters, and music halls; chaplains were active in the military camps; "soldiers have written home, not for provisions . . . but for hymn books." Moreover, "the love of money is no more peculiar to us than to the English, the Scotch, or the Germans. *The real and only cause of the present troubles is Slavery, nothing else.*"[82]

For the present, however, conservative religious nationalists strove to hold their ground against antislavery critics. What they did not foresee were the consequences of robust loyalty to the government. In trumpeting their determined stand for the Union, conservatives abandoned Christ-centered piety and opened wide their pulpits to a form of political preaching. To be sure, they eschewed conventional partisanship, which was easily done when prewar party loyalties were in flux and sensitive to the higher cause of patriotism. In making loyalty to political authority a measure of righteousness, conservatives would find themselves sorely tested when their government sanctioned emancipation.

UNIFYING RELIGIOUS PATRIOTISM

The first national wartime fast day in almost half a century highlighted the discord between religious nationalists determined to conserve the prewar Union and those on a mission to cut out the "gangrene in the body politic."[83] But a more potent patriotism bound them together in the common cause of saving the Union. In expressing their love of the nation, four powerful themes stood out: the unique historic role of a godly American nation and the global significance of its current crisis; the just resort to warfare in prosecuting a righteous cause; the Christian duty of sacrifice; and the millennial glory that would follow national purification.

First, fast-day speakers embroidered the familiar theme of America's place in history under God's special protection. As a Chicago Methodist put it, its claim to greatness lay less in its material splendor and preeminent power than in its role as an agent of Christian truth, humanity, and liberty. By divine plan, those eternal principles had shaped the nation's history since the Pilgrims landed, preparing the colonies for the Revolution and national independence.[84] Ichabod Simmons, cabinetmaker turned Methodist preacher, assured his Connecticut congregation that the American Revolution "never had its equal in profane history." God, sovereign over all human government, had instructed the new nation in the wisdom of the ages, to become the midwife in delivering His kingdom. The fallen republics of Greece, and Athens, and Rome had shown the framers of American government the key to glory. They had learned that the historic strength of a free nation was "religious and Christian." The Declaration of Independence shone with the brilliance of "the brightest political and social idea of the bible": the equality of men in their inalienable right to life, liberty, and the pursuit of happiness. In this way the American Christian republic—"the North star of nations"—was a vessel for the hopes of the world and the well-being of its future generations.[85] Francis Wayland spoke for the legions who feared what the war meant for the cause of universal liberty. If the benefits of republican freedom could not be maintained by a largely Protestant population, "with a Bible in every house, and education as free as air, and in the enjoyment of perfect liberty in religious concernments," then it was reasonable to conclude that they had no future anywhere.[86]

Second, the course of the crisis legitimized war. The Confederacy was making a bloody assault on "the best government for the largest happiness of man . . . upon which the sun has ever shone." It licensed a martial response. Thomas Skinner quoted Lincoln's assurance to the seceded states at his inauguration ("you can have no conflict without being yourselves the aggressors") to insist, "We have no choice . . . woe is unto us if we do not fight. The war is not of our seeking; it is forced upon us."[87] Disloyalty to one's country was disloyalty to God, a Dutch Reformed pastor explained: resisting the Confederates' high treason made it His righteous war. Robert Davidson captured the common conviction that, far from starting the war, the North had appeared paralyzed, as forts, arsenals, customhouses, and navy yards were surrendered "till it became a butt for ridicule on account of its forbearance and pusillanimity." It was the South that had "removed the ancient landmarks," proclaimed war for the maintenance and extension of slavery, and struck the first blow in an unnatural fratricidal contest.[88]

Pulpits and presses thundered against northerners ready to yield to the South. The Methodist editor Thomas Mears Eddy denounced those who colluded in "the vilest treason ever known since the great secession from heaven, with their dastard cry of 'peace at any price.'" There must be no peace until traitors had been subdued and hanged.[89] Physical force against the rebels and their covert sympathizers in the Union required no apology.[90] Better a war of extermination than a cowardly adjustment, declared the Unitarian Harvard professor Frederic Hedge. Those who urged peaceful separation to cleanse the Union ("What! kill a might[y] Protestant Nation for Ham! Slavery must come down, but not in this way") earned Wil-

Lincoln's Fast Day and Antislavery Nationalism, 1861 147

liam Wilson's scorn: "Why, war is holy for the subjugation of these rebels." The young Isaac Smith Kalloch, a devout New York Baptist and Republican, inquired of those who bewailed Lincoln's election and the ensuing war, "Is peace so great that it is to be purchased at the price of chains and slavery?" and answered, "No! . . . Cowards and fools alone are for peace."[91]

Third, war demanded martial duty and sacrifice. These themes took on special resonance at military fast-day meetings. William Henry Goodrich told the Forty-First Ohio Infantry Regiment, at Cleveland's First Presbyterian Church, that in years to come "men shall point to you and say, 'These, under God, were the saviors of the country in the great rebellion.'" Ichabod Simmons saw service for the nation as "the soul mounting above mere affection, into the atmosphere of heroic sacrifice." He delivered to Union troops an unvarnished truth: "It is yours to suffer, yours to die; but the church will enshroud you in her warmest memories. . . . Pray, oh pray *before* the battle, pray in the battle, and when you fire, take good aim and *fire for the glory of God!*" To repeated cheers from the men of the Yates Phalanx, Thomas Eddy proposed a compromise for those who attacked Lincoln's suspension of the writ of habeas corpus: "Henceforth each rebel shall have the full benefit of the *habeas* and we will *suspend his corpus!*" The regimental commander emboldened his men for duty and possible death with a patriotic hymn: "Then conquer we must, for our cause it is just, / And this be our motto—*In God is our trust.* / And the Star Spangled Banner in triumph shall wave, / O'er the land of the free and the home of the brave." The sacrificial, bloody struggle encouraged a creative reading of scripture. Searching for a model of Christ the "invincible and all conquering warrior," one ingenious preacher found him, long before his human birth at Bethlehem, in the guise of the Angel of the Lord who brought Moses victory over Pharaoh. The plan of campaign of this infinitely righteous and boundlessly powerful "Christ of battles" had been set from eternity. "He out-generals and overcomes all his foes. His wars are all defensive." This militant God merited Christian sacrifice.[92]

Finally, an exuberant millennialism—the promise of a sublime future—galvanized citizens for the battles to come and the peace that must surely follow. Inspired by Lincoln's message of July 4, and confident that God himself would "breathe into us an invincible strength," William H. Furness knew the result of war would be "transcendently glorious." One predicted that in six months the Federal armies would hold every major city and town in the South. Christ had designed Confederate successes at Fort Sumter and Bull Run to lull the enemy into a false sense of security. The Chicago Universalist James H. Tuttle kept the faith: "Dark clouds are around us now, but . . . the sun of revolutions never turns back. Progress is the law of nature and the law of nations. God reigns, and truth will reign by-and-by." The great moral forces of nineteenth-century civilization in its broadest Christian sense, declared the elderly Joel Hawes, were "hastening on the great plan of God to its final consummation." Ichabod Simmons presented a roll call of nations, the divisions of God's army advancing from barbarity toward a perfect civilization. Contrite Israel, the enlightened Italy of Garibaldi, emancipationist Russia, liberated France, wealth-yielding China and India, and progressive England made up a grand train led by "a giant of four score years." This American Samson marched under a banner inscribed "The Star-lighted flag of the Home of the Free! Purity and Righteousness are the secrets of strength! The Constitution is our safeguard, the Bible our law, and our War-cry, God and Humanity forever!" William Wilson deployed the future present tense to capture the joy after Christ's Union armies had destroyed the confederated powers of evil. "The way is now prepared for the full introduction of the millennium," he exulted. "Now 'the saints possess the kingdom.' Now universal liberty is established upon the basis of universal righteousness; and, as the result, 'the nations learn war no more.' "[93]

Collectively this cluster of powerful themes encouraged political and martial unity. Cross-party harmony in defense of the Union government became an objective that was, at this early stage of the war, widely achieved. Speaking to the Democrats of his Indiana Baptist congregation, Silas Bailey exonerated the "conservative" northern wing of the party. They had stood by the purposes of 1776 and the guarantees of 1787, as the South took radical new ground. "The conflict now progressing with us," Ichabod Simmons judged, had shed "political influences, and entered the domain of the religious." Thomas Doggett identified an apocalyptic contest between "light

Lincoln's Fast Day and Antislavery Nationalism, 1861 149

and darkness, good and evil, right and wrong, Christ and the devil, fought on a wider battlefield than has ever yet resounded with the noise of combat." In this cosmic struggle, Albert Palmer declared, the religious patriot's duty demanded "a patient, enduring, unflagging, unflinching, united loyalty to the government in this trial of its authority and strength."[94]

LESSONS

One element of Lincoln's capacious sense of humor was his notorious appetite for puns, an indulgence that encouraged groans as well as laughter. At the telegraph office on September 26, he joked with the busy employees, "Gentlemen, this is fast day and I am pleased to observe that you are working as fast as you can; the proclamation was mine, and that is my interpretation of its bearing upon you."[95] His buoyant tone was a striking counterpoint to the serious example he set at the morning's church service and afternoon's lecture. We do not know exactly what he learned from those solemn meetings. The day's wider observance, however, provided evidence from which he might draw instructive, even encouraging, lessons.

First, the fast day had achieved what James Harlan, Congress, and Lincoln had intended: the harnessing of communities of faith in the national cause. Compared with the fractured experience of Buchanan's fast day, it was an occasion of thunderous unity, one that forced most of the dissenting minority to stay prudently silent. Through personal contact and correspondence Lincoln was aware that a broad spectrum of opinion had clothed loyalty to the Union with the garments of a righteous crusade. Others, of course, not the president, had taken the initiative in proposing a proclamation, but he happily took ownership of it ("the proclamation was mine"). The pulpit's ability to go beyond national soul-searching, to administer an adrenaline boost to loyalty and patriotism, was a lesson that meant the proclamation would not be the president's last of its kind.

The public response to the fast day delivered a second lesson: the widespread regard for the president as a man of integrity and religious faith. Lincoln's proclaiming a fast day, "at the bidding of his own heart and conscience," betokened his administration's Christian honesty and wisdom.[96] Even many who questioned his policies and judgment conceded his honesty of intent. Few reached the exuberant heights of the admiring Orville H. Browning, who extolled him as "a President who was never surpassed by any man who ruled a people on earth, in all that constitutes patriotism, honor, integrity, and devotion to the great cause of human rights." But Albert Palmer spoke for many with the more modest view that "God has given us an honest President." Sidney Brooks, devout Christian and director of a Cape Cod seminary, would later recall "the thrilling events of '61" when "our Fast Day services were more solemn and fervent than usual" and "the heaven-directed acts of President Lincoln began to be admired and discussed and his noble qualities to shine forth."[97] Being seen as an honest man of God gave Lincoln a bank of moral capital on which he could draw as his course carried him toward an edict of emancipation.

Third, the fast day offered a broad gauge of the relative strength of the ideological ropes binding loyalty to the Union. It is unlikely that Lincoln gave much attention to even a fraction of the occasion's torrent of rhetoric, but his own mailbag delivered a sense of the growing force of Protestant antislavery nationalism. The Frémont affair had revealed that many who before the war had upheld the South's constitutional guarantees were now ready to take an ax to slavery as the price of saving the Union. Church petitions to the Executive Mansion gave Lincoln evidence of the nerve Frémont had struck among moderately conservative as well as more radical opinion, but probably nothing made the changing mood clearer to him, and more effectively, than the intervention of Orville Browning. Writing on September 17, the senator expressed his great regret that the president had modified a proclamation that to his knowledge had, without exception, won the support of "every true friend of the Government." Frémont's initiative might not have had express authority in law, he wrote, but traitors who warred on the Constitution had no right to expect its protection. Lincoln's response had greatly depressed staunch Unionists by seeking to satisfy those of doubtful loyalty in the border region. "There has been too much tenderness towards traitors and rebels," Browning asserted. "We must strike them terrible blows, and strike them hard and quick, or the government will go."[98]

Lincoln replied promptly. Browning was one of his staunchest allies: a Kentucky-born Illinois lawyer like himself, a Whig-Republican colleague since their days together in the state legislature, and a former rival who had become a trusted friend. Of the senator's letter he wrote, "Coming from you, I confess it astonishes me." He accused Browning of abandoning a conservative legal approach for a "reckless position" that surrendered constitutional government and tossed aside the prudent policy essential to holding Kentucky. He encouraged his friend to "give up your restlessness for new positions, and back me manfully." Browning, however, held firm. His fifteen-page reply laid out the established principles of international law that sanctioned the confiscation of rebel property, including slaves; at the same time, he reiterated his unwavering support and acknowledged that questions of political expediency were open to differences of opinion.[99]

In these exchanges Browning's focus on questions of law and public morale has diverted attention from the religious framework that shaped his ideas. His letters, he told Lincoln, were prompted by concern for the president's welfare, anxiety over the future of the Constitution and Union, and dedication to "the triumph of as holy a cause, in my judgment, as ever engaged men's feelings and enlisted their energies." This was not token piety but the faith-based nationalism of a devout Christian churchgoer. Browning's diary offers a record of assiduous Sunday worship, morning and evening, at the Old School Westminster Presbyterian Church in Quincy, his hometown. When away on business, he was a familiar figure at Presbyterian meetings in Chicago, Springfield, and elsewhere. Every New Year's Day he engaged in Christian self-examination, gave thanks for the "undeserved mercies" of Almighty God, and prayed for protection against sin.[100] He did not wear his religion on his sleeve, but he did believe the American nation to be answerable to an omnipotent Providence.

On July 18 this religious faith had undergirded Browning's first speech in the U.S. Senate, where he had been appointed to fill the Illinois seat left vacant by the death of Stephen A. Douglas. Without the aggressions of slavery, he said, there would be no "armed rebellion for so unholy a purpose." The conflict was "not a war for the extermination of slavery," but if the rebel South forced the issue by persisting in its mad course, "I am for . . . sweeping the last vestiges of barbarism from the face of the continent." Should it come to that, "let us . . . not shrink from the high and holy and sacred duties that are laid upon us, as the conservators not only of Government, but . . . of the eternal principles of justice and freedom for the whole human family." Speaking for the people of "the great Northwest," he declared that they, like him, would put the death of slavery before the demise of "the best and the most blessed Government that the world has ever known."[101] Previously regarded by the *New-York Tribune* as "one of those cautious conservatives, of ripe years and considerate speech," Browning now found himself lionized by several Republican radicals, including John P. Hale, Charles Sumner, Ben Wade, and Henry Wilson.[102] He repeated similar sentiments a week later, when voting with the majority to approve Andrew Johnson's resolution that the war's aim was not to overthrow slavery but to preserve the Union. That purpose was, he said, "the holiest cause that ever enlisted man's sympathies and energies," sustained by the right of self-defense, which was "as sacred and inalienable as any right with which the almighty Architect of the Universe ever endowed a creature of his creation." Before the closing of this special session of Congress in early August, Browning joined the majority in passing the first Confiscation Act, authorizing the federal seizure of rebel property, including slaves, used to support the rebellion.

Although Browning denied Lincoln's accusation of "restlessness for new positions," he had without doubt taken steps toward a more purposeful antislavery nationalism. By his willingness to embrace universal emancipation and arm black troops, if and when indispensable to the righteous cause, and by endorsing Frémont's military proclamation, he had taken more radical ground. Lincoln knew his friend's ideas were rooted in religious faith. When law and politics took him to Springfield during the 1850s, Browning often attended Lincoln's First Presbyterian Church.[103] In Washington, as senator, he customarily worshipped at Phineas Gurley's New York Avenue Presbyterian Church, as did the Lincolns, and they occasionally invited him to dinner. One Sunday afternoon, probably on July 28, the two men spent the whole time alone in the White House library. Lincoln was reading the Bible. Uniquely, in Browning's experience, their talk turned to religion. He later recalled saying, "Mr. Lincoln we can't hope for a blessing of God on the efforts of our armies,

Lincoln's Fast Day and Antislavery Nationalism, 1861   153

until we strike a decisive blow at the institution of slavery. This is the great curse of our land, and we must make an effort to remove it before we can hope to receive the help of the Almighty." The president's reply struck him forcibly: "Browning suppose God is against us in our view on the subject of slavery in this country, and our method of dealing with it?" This suggested that Lincoln "was thinking deeply of what a higher power than man sought to bring about by the great events then transpiring."[104] In return, Browning's statement gave Lincoln another example of how religious providentialism and pragmatic policy were combining to turn conservatives into antislavery nationalists. The September fast day subsequently helped crystallize those issues.

With his customary dry wit, Lincoln reputedly said during the war's early action, "I hope to have God on my side, but I must have Kentucky." Often cited as an example of his realpolitik, of a necessary trade-off between morality and hard pragmatism, the statement was more than that; equally, it was more than flippancy. It acknowledged that Providence had a role in shaping the Union's future, but that God's particular purposes were unclear and mysterious. Although Lincoln was not ready to join those willing to use emancipation as a tool of war, he knew that opinions were in flux and that among people of faith many attributed to the hand of God the conditions for a bold approach to emancipation. In his July 4 address to the special session of Congress, he had subtly indicated the war's potential to unsettle the political landscape. Speaking of his government's course toward the South once the rebellion had been put down, he said it would be "his purpose then, as ever, to be guided by the Constitution, and the laws; and . . . he *probably* will have no different understanding of the powers, and duties of the Federal government, relatively to the rights of the States, and the people, under the Constitution, than that expressed in the inaugural address."[105] On March 4 he had been at pains to emphasize the guarantees that the Constitution afforded slaveholders. Four months later that single word "probably" indicated a sotto voce recognition of the war's power to overturn peacetime certainties. That, too, was the message of Lincoln's fast day, one that would continue to resonate powerfully in the communities of faith who entered a dialogue with him over the next twelve months and more.

CHAPTER 6

LINCOLN, RELIGIOUS NATIONALISTS, AND EMANCIPATION, 1862

In signing his Proclamation of Emancipation on January 1, 1863, Lincoln took his most consequential strategic initiative of the war. He came to the decision by increments, taking account of the course of the fighting, the Confederates' tenacity in arms, and his reading of public opinion. Key to the president's political radar throughout the war was what he learned from his engagement with religious constituencies that ranged across the ideological spectrum from conservative Unionist to radical abolitionist. He knew the value of White House meetings with church leaders, and the avalanche of religious petitions and correspondence, as guides to mutual thinking. He would find that dialogue particularly productive between the September 1861 fast day and New Year's Day 1863.

Those fifteen months spanned three political phases. First, during the relative military calm of late 1861 and early 1862, and the productive spring offensive that followed, Lincoln encouraged schemes of voluntary gradual abolition, supported a measure freeing the enslaved population of the nation's capital, and kept his own counsel over more radical measures. However, hopes of a transformational military victory yielded to frustration and despair as McClellan's campaign to take Richmond stalled and then ended

Lincoln, Religious Nationalists, and Emancipation, 1862 155

in a humiliating withdrawal from the Virginia Peninsula. During the ensuing second phase, some conservative religious nationalists joined the growing chorus of demands from radical churches for an edict of emancipation as the only sure means of crushing the rebellion. Many other conservatives, however, resisted the tug—as Lincoln, engaged in a delicate balancing act between the two religious imperatives, understood only too well. The third phase began with Lincoln's preliminary emancipation proclamation on September 22, an acknowledgment that he had sided with the now-exultant religious forces of antislavery nationalism, who would thereafter work hard to keep the administration true to its declared purpose against a storm of conservative censure.

PETITIONERS

When Lincoln's cabinet met on Tuesday, October 29, 1861, he showed them radical church resolutions recently adopted by the Synod of the United Presbyterians. The familiar words of Proverbs—"righteousness exalteth a nation: but sin is a reproach to any people"—animated the document. The ministers saw the war as the punishment by "the righteous Ruler of the Universe" for the nation's sins, above all the "blighting curse" of slavery. They accepted that the conflict was not being waged explicitly against enslavement, but they wanted the president to accept that rebellious slave owners had "forfeited all claim to the protection of their peculiar institution." War would of necessity bring the government into contact with the iniquitous system. To end a wicked rebellion, the ministers advocated "the manumission by military proclamation of the slaves of all persons, who are found in arms against the Government, & the confiscation of their property." In this way would a defensive war fought "in accordance with the principles of righteousness" lead to slavery's extinction.[1]

It is not certain why, from the many church memorials he received during the first months of the war, Lincoln selected this one for cabinet consideration, nor do we know the nature of their discussion.[2] The petition had been delivered by the synod's senior members, led by the first moderator of the Church, the esteemed John Taylor Pressly. A South Carolinian by birth and for sixteen years a professor of theology in the Synod of the South, the elderly Pressly had since 1831 been an Allegheny pastor and professor at the city's seminary. This was the Pennsylvania heartland of the United Presbyterians. Conservative in theology but radical in its approach to slavery, the new Church was one of the smaller branches of Presbyterianism, though not a negligible force in western Pennsylvania and eastern Ohio. Pressly and his fellow commissioners told Lincoln they represented "some 444 ministers & 57513 communicants, scattered over not less than eighteen states of the Union." Whatever Lincoln's view of their denominational strength (United Presbyterians lacked the reach of his own Old School Presbyterian Church), he must have been struck by the unity with which the petitioners believed that a war for a restored Union could, and should, now become a war for emancipation.[3] That may well explain why he presented the resolutions to his cabinet.

There is no definitive total of the religious petitions and memorials that peppered the White House; the Lincoln Papers at the Library of Congress contain more than 120.[4] As this episode indicates, Lincoln took them seriously. Not least, they provided a means of reading opinion and identifying significant shifts in public attitudes. He later said that getting the timing of the Emancipation Proclamation right had been one of his chief concerns. "Many of my strongest supporters urged Emancipation before I thought it indispensable, and, I may say, before I thought the country ready for it," he told the artist Francis Bicknell Carpenter. "It is my conviction that, had the proclamation been issued even six months earlier than it was, public sentiment would not have sustained it."[5] The president's desire to take the public pulse kept his doors open to visitors of every kind and station. During the first eighteen months of the conflict the president welcomed committees and individual ministers across the Protestant spectrum: Methodists, Old and New School Presbyterians, Reformed Presbyterians, Baptists, Congregationalists, Evangelical Lutherans, and Progressive Friends. Beyond these, he had conversations with Catholics and Jews.[6] The political importance of the mainstream denominations was not lost on him. He remained in dialogue with the Union's devout and made himself accessible to their representatives, especially of churches command-

Lincoln, Religious Nationalists, and Emancipation, 1862   157

ing large and influential memberships. If it was an asymmetric relationship, the dialogue was still meaningful.

Similarly, religious memorials and petitions gave Lincoln insight into a broad range of church opinion. Between April 1861 and the end of September 1862 at least fifty-three sets of resolutions reached the White House; a further twelve arrived by the turn of 1863. Denominationally wide-ranging, they included submissions from bodies of Congregationalists (fifteen), Methodists (thirteen), Baptists (eight), New School, Reformed, and United Presbyterians (eleven), Wesleyan Methodists (two), Lutherans (two), Old School Presbyterians (one), Episcopalians (one), and Quakers (three). They came from across the North and were by no means skewed toward the antislavery heartland of New England. More than a third were the work of church bodies in the mid-Atlantic states of New York, Pennsylvania, and New Jersey. Another third emanated from the Northwest: Ohio, Indiana, Illinois, Iowa, Michigan, and Wisconsin. It is not necessary to assert—implausibly—that Lincoln pored over every word of the resolutions to suppose that he saw enough to get a feel for their balance of opinion.

After six months of the war, two broad religious visions of the postwar nation shaped conflicting political purposes within communities of faith. On the one hand, the prospect of a nation shorn of slavery slowly pulled together those who before the war had maintained only a divisive, fractious relationship: a spectrum of groups ranging from outright abolitionists to those whose deep dislike of slavery took grudging second place to the constitutional guarantees afforded the slaveholding South. These differences and their gradual yielding to a more unified demand for emancipation were evident in the bulk of the memorials addressed to the president. Barely half of them—47 percent between April 1861 and September 1862—specifically called on the administration to liberate the enslaved. Almost as many, however, blamed slavery for the war and prayed the conflict would bring about the demise of a national sin.

An almost equally powerful religious energy coursed through more conservative church communities, both Protestant and Catholic. For these forces, adopting emancipation as a war policy would betray the very constitution for whose preservation the conflict was being fought and fracture the unity of the North, so essential to victory. It would invite revolution and frightful bloodshed in the South, bring misery and suffering to the enslaved, end all hope of reconciliation between the contending parties, and make national reconstruction impossible. Conservative Presbyterians commended the pragmatically humane spirit of English antislavery reform. "Instead of driving like Jehu over constitution and laws, disregarding consequences and rushing madly to the conclusion, whatever horrors may be involved in the result," cautioned the *New-York Observer*, the true Christian example was to "take things as they are, and consider the smoothest and safest and most expedient plan to compass the end to be attained."[7] Most of the influential Catholic voices, though soundly loyal to the Union, were equally hostile to radical purposes and the "wretched spouters" of abolitionism.[8]

OCTOBER 1861–JUNE 1862

After the Union fiasco at Bull Run, Lincoln made George B. McClellan his general in chief and gave him command of the new Army of the Potomac. To the president's frustration, this did not bring about the desired fall offensive in the eastern theater. McClellan's overcautious inaction prompted concern that he was too close to conservative Democrats sympathetic to the rebels. However, the prospects for a successful Federal spring offensive in 1862 received a huge lift by dramatic developments in the West. General Henry W. Halleck's plans to drive Confederate forces out of Kentucky and Tennessee, and so control the waters of the Mississippi, were carried through by his subordinate, Ulysses S. Grant. The capture of Forts Henry and Donelson in February gave the Union a route into the South; in the same month Don Carlos Buell secured the fall of Nashville. After the war's bloodiest battle to date, at Shiloh in southwestern Tennessee on April 6 and 7, when Federal forces under Grant held their ground in the face of a powerful Confederate counteroffensive, the door to northern Mississippi was open. Elsewhere, Union field successes in modest engagements—at Pea Ridge, Arkansas, and Glorieta, New Mexico—added to a sense of Federal invincibility. Meanwhile, the Union navy was active on the coast of North Carolina, capturing Roanoke Island, New Bern, and Fort Macon. As McClellan's well-drilled, highly disciplined army prepared for its spring offensive against Richmond, the Confederate capital, the rebels appeared to be on the run.

Sharing the elation in Washington at these multiplying successes, Lincoln on April 10 issued a Proclamation of Thanksgiving for Victories that attributed the "signal" successes on land and sea to the pleasure of Almighty God and recommended public prayers to "render thanks to our Heavenly Father for these inestimable blessings."[9] The language of the proclamation developed the more routine providentialism with which he had closed his annual address to Congress a few months earlier, in December 1861, and which marked his formal response to a committee of Methodist ministers from the East Baltimore Conference in March.[10] It prefigured the similar sentiments in his reported remarks to an Indiana regiment the following month. Much more striking, however, was the expression of faith with which he concluded his arresting special message to Congress of March 6, in which he recommended that both chambers adopt a joint resolution committing financial support to any state that chose to adopt the "gradual abolishment of slavery." Lincoln had already urged the merits of gradual compensated emancipation with Delaware loyalists late in 1861, but this was a far more dramatic initiative. It would, he argued, shorten the conflict by ending the rebels' hopes of the upper South's defection and cost the country far less than the ever-swelling expense of war. His message, Lincoln knew, was historic: the first emancipationist proposal to which an American president had ever attached his name, one that assumed federal authority in promoting the gradual removal of slavery. Beyond that, it was striking for the personal expression of faith with which he ended his appeal. "In full view of my great responsibility to my God, and to my country, I earnestly beg the attention of Congress and the people to the subject." The Almighty had taken on the character of a personal God.

Religious nationalists, both radical and conservative, took heart from Lincoln's providentialism and evident respect for divine guidance during late 1861 and the first half of 1862. Equally striking, each party managed to accommodate his words to their starkly divergent visions of the nation's moral course.

It took time for emancipation-focused nationalists to modify their concerns over Lincoln's actions during the fall of 1861. They continued to lament Lincoln's handling of Frémont's proclamation; they questioned his action in telling Secretary of War Simon Cameron to withdraw a proposal to arm fugitive slaves; they were disappointed when the president's December message to Congress continued to propitiate loyal slaveholders and, instead of crippling the Slave Power with radical measures, simply proposed that those freed by the contingencies of war be removed to settle some remote territory. The editors of the influential New York *Independent* deemed the resettlement idea "thoroughly tinged with that colorphobia which has so long prevailed in Illinois, and was so strongly developed in the odious Black laws of that state . . . making color a basis of distinction in the rights and privileges of citizens."[11] These same emancipationists, however, continued to regard Lincoln as a leader of unimpeachable personal integrity and unquestioned patriotism, "a man of moderation and self-control, not driven by passionate impulses or stubborn resolves," but conscientious in his regard for the Constitution and the law.[12] Under Providence, the "logic of events" was building public support for emancipation.[13] Lacking the impetuous temper and imperious will of an Andrew Jackson, the president was praised for his steady republicanism and appetite for prayer: "Let none . . . forget that on the eve of assuming office, President Lincoln asked of his countrymen a remembrance in their prayers." Christians should beseech the Almighty to bless their president with the wisdom, courage, and firmness of purpose to deliver "the great decree of Providence in the cause of freedom and righteousness."[14]

Those earnest prayers blossomed into elation when on March 6 Lincoln proposed congressional support for gradual, compensated emancipation. Horace Greeley, the nationwide voice of the antislavery *New-York Tribune*, and a member and occasional preacher at Edwin H. Chapin's vast Universalist church on Broadway, hailed the special message as "the greatest public document issued since the American Declaration of Independence."[15] In the columns of *The Independent*, by some distance the most widely circulating religious newspaper of the day, Greeley rebuked those who considered Lincoln's policy timid and halting. The president faced substantial opposition to abolition from "besotted, degraded, worthless" white people, whose racial animus toward the black population was easily exploited by political demagogues. To have made emancipation a stated war aim at the outset would have alienated half the Democrats in the free states and nearly all the Unionists in the border region, including many officers and serving men. Admitting he had no private knowledge of the president's views, Greeley explained, "I judge him as he is entitled to be judged—by his public and official acts. I take his self-prompted and unique Special Message . . . as the best exposition of his secret thought, his animating purpose." *The Independent*'s editor, Henry Ward Beecher, similarly lauded the proposal as "one of the noblest deeds of a century."[16]

Joy over the March 6 message colored many sermons prompted by Lincoln's April proclamation of thanksgiving. English-born Robert Collyer, a former blacksmith whose abolitionist radicalism and liberal theology had cost him his Methodist license, soon rose to prominence ministering to Chicago Unitarians. He had cut his political teeth stumping for Frémont in 1856. Now he celebrated what he saw as the onward march of the providential cause under a "Western Country Lawyer . . . a man 'rich in saving common sense,' and as the great ones only are, in his simplicity, sublime."[17] Preaching in that city's Tabernacle Baptist Church, Nathaniel Colver heard in the recent victories against slaveholders the voice of God. Rebel masters had never had a moral right to their slaves; now, by rebellion, they had also lost their right in law. Loyal slaveholders, by constitutional protection, did have a continuing legal right to their property, but Colver welcomed Lincoln's principle: to remove the nation's curse, the nation itself should pay. Although he knew that "in justice the master ought to pay the slave," compensation was the practical means of removing the curse. "We have shared in the sin," he recognized. "Let us cheerfully bear our share of the burden which that sin has imposed."[18]

Likewise, the Evangelical Lutheran ministers who met Lincoln at the White House on May 13 extolled the compensation scheme. The committee represented their recent General Synod, where the only delegate from a rebel state had been a Tennessean "who had, in praying for the President, avoided arrest only in consequence of the fact that he conducted divine service in the German language." Henry N. Pohlman of Albany read out resolutions that avowed Lutherans' devotion to "the great interests of law and authority, of liberty and righteousness," deemed the war God's righteous judgment on the national sin, and hailed Lincoln's scheme to remunerate those slave states opting for constitutional emancipation.[19]

On April 16, after a few days' hesitation, Lincoln signed a measure abolishing slavery in Washington, D.C. Coming just six days after his proclamation of thanksgiving, it reinforced emancipationist ministers' jubilant accounts of a nation becoming ever more worthy before God. With this act, shaped by the Republican-controlled Congress, more than three thousand slaves were immediately freed, loyal owners promised compensation, and funds set aside to promote voluntary black emigration. Lincoln's own preference had been for gradual emancipation by popular vote, but he met the moment and signed into law an unprecedented federal statute. Previous measures had confiscated the individual slaves of rebel owners; this one abolished slavery as an institution, freeing the chattels of both loyal and disloyal slaveholders.[20] The Episcopalian John Crockar White of Dover, Delaware, celebrating, saw God's hand in "the cleansing of our national capital."[21] Chicago Baptists registered a historic watershed: "It is a *beginning*. The ice is broken."[22] Robert Collyer rejoiced in the purification of "the Mount Zion of our nation" and delivered a paean to Lincoln's leadership. Providence, not politics, had delivered a president of definitive common sense and perfect integrity, because "*God is for us.*"[23]

Nowhere, however, was there greater rapture than in the twelve churches that ministered to the fourteen thousand black residents of the District. After the bill had passed the House and Senate, but before Lincoln signed it into law, the Presbyterian, Methodist, and Baptist leaders organized a daylong Sabbath of prayer, preaching, and fasting in anticipation of the day of jubilee. A white observer, strikingly sensitive to the ingrained prejudices and facile condescension of his own race, found himself disarmed by the sheer joy of what he saw. Remarking on Presbyterians' well-regulated deportment, the more emotional and physical animation of the Methodists, and the evident "electricity of the African nature" among

Baptists, he was sure that "those who went to laugh departed wiser for the visit." Deeply affected himself, he reflected on experiencing "one of those spectacles which men need to witness occasionally to remind them of their humanity and the love they instinctively bear their fellows."[24] A correspondent of Jane Swisshelm's abolitionist newspaper described the scenes at the Methodists' Asbury Chapel, where the powerful "Amens" of a thousand hearers "seemed sufficient to unroof the church." The preacher encouraged their shouts, the loudest coming when he gloried that "they had reason to praise God that Jefferson lived and wrote the Declaration of Independence . . . and great reason to thank God that He had raised up a man from the common walks of life to sign the bill and make it a law. 'Yes,' said the speaker, 'praise God for ABRAHAM LINCOLN.'"[25] Ecstatic celebrations, allied to a near-universal rejection of offers of funded emigration, revealed the emerging force of a specifically African American religious nationalism. Writing pseudonymously for the New York *Examiner*, a Baptist weekly, Lincoln's secretary William O. Stoddard weighed the significance of emancipation from what he had "seen and heard among the blacks." A devout Baptist himself, Stoddard identified "the gradual entering of a new idea" in their liberated Christian minds: "They begin, the best of them, to feel and cherish the notion of their *nationality*." As a corollary they "refuse to regard themselves as Africans. . . . They insist that they are Americans."[26]

These steps toward emancipation, and the high hopes for McClellan's advance on Richmond, buoyed antislavery nationalists during May and June. When, on May 19, Lincoln publicly revoked the radical action of his abolitionist commander of the Department of the South, Major General David Hunter, antislavery critics reacted more temperately than they had when he rescinded Frémont's decree nine months earlier. Hunter had, on May 9, declared all the slaves under his control—close to one million men, women, and children, mostly in the South Carolina Sea Islands—"forever free." Lincoln voided the order, stating that he had not been consulted, nor had he authorized any commander "to make proclamations declaring the slaves of any State free." Two aspects of his explanation helped limit criticism. First, Lincoln made an unprecedented and pregnant claim of presidential authority, stating that as commander in chief he reserved to himself the power to decide whether and when a declaration freeing the slaves had "become a necessity indispensable to the maintenance of the government." Second, he implied that he was holding back that decision while he waited for the people of the border states to consider the plan of gradual, compensated emancipation that, on his recommendation, had passed both branches of Congress. He used his revocation of Hunter's order to appeal "earnestly" to border Unionists in words that encouraged a scriptural imperative to act. They should not be "blind to the signs of the times," by implication the upending of southern society and the growing public pressure to strike against slavery. His proposal, he wrote, "acts not the pharisee": it was not prompted by reproach, moral superiority, or self-righteous sanctity. Rather, here was an opportunity to take the smoother path to a better future. "So much good has not been done, by one effort, in all past time, as, in the providence of God, it is now your high previlege [*sic*] to do."[27] Through a close reading of Lincoln's text, some of his keenest antislavery supporters deemed it the word of a prophet. "It is the handwriting by the finger of the President on the wall, and can only he interpreted to mean, that the days of slavery are numbered," commented the *Chicago Tribune*. "It proclaims the great truth, that the morning of that glorious day will soon dawn, when the angel of the Union shall descend, and roll away the rock from the sepulchre, and then shall be found no arm, human or infernal, strong enough ever to roll it back."[28]

Many antislavery religious nationalists now concluded that the president was teetering on the brink of emancipation and needed only mobilized public opinion to nerve him into action. As William Lloyd Garrison put it, "If the sentiment existing at the North in favor of emancipation were only organized, concentrated and brought to bear upon the government through the legitimate channels, it would sweep everything before it." Besiege the Executive Mansion with visits of religious deputations and memorials from every locality, he urged, to show the president that "the mass of the honest-hearted people" would sustain him in an all-out antislavery policy.[29] It was to this end that a delegation of Progressive Friends had met Lincoln on June 20, an encounter probably arranged through the good offices of Senator David Wilmot and

Lincoln, Religious Nationalists, and Emancipation, 1862   165

three U.S. representatives, all of Pennsylvania, who accompanied the religious contingent and introduced them to the president. In keeping with Quaker principles of gender equality, the delegation comprised three men and three women. Their leader, Oliver Johnson, was Garrison's staunch disciple, an accomplished journalist, and currently editor of the *National Anti-slavery Standard.*[30] Eliza Agnew, Alice Eliza Hambleton, Dinah Mendenhall, and William Barnard represented a zealous Pennsylvania insurgency. The oldest member of the group, Thomas Garrett of Wilmington, Delaware, had devoted his adult life to protecting free blacks and escaped slaves. In fact, all six were involved either personally or indirectly in the work of the so-called Underground Railroad. Most were members of the separatist Longwood Progressive Meeting of Friends, housed among the scattered farms of Chester County and comprising those who had been "read out" of their orthodox Quaker meeting communities for political radicalism. Leading abolitionists, black and white, came to speak to the yearly meeting before and during the war. They included Frederick Douglass, Sojourner Truth, Harriet Beecher, and John Greenleaf Whittier.[31]

No regular visitor at Longwood was more welcome, visible, or active than Garrison himself. At the 1862 annual meeting, held over three days in early June, it was he who took the lead in preparing a fierce "testimony" on the government's duty to end the horrors of war by suppressing with all available force the slaveholding oligarchs' attack on the nation. The Society of Friends' support for military measures to end enslavement he deemed entirely compatible with their devotion to pacifism: a war for emancipation "conducted upon peace principles, is as paradoxical as a peace conducted upon war principles." Means had to be adapted to ends. Only immediate emancipation would cleanse the nation of its complicity in sin and end the trial that God had visited on both North and South. Garrison's statement, adopted by the meeting, gave shape to a discussion on the form of an entreaty to the president. Visiting radicals took the lead. They included Sella Martin, revered black Baptist minister of Boston; George Gordon, the Free Presbyterian president of Iberia College; and Theodore Tilton, assistant editor of *The Independent.*[32] A five-hundred-word memorial warned of "the infatuation as well as exceeding wickedness of endeavoring to secure peace, prosperity, and unity, while leaving millions to clank their chains in the house of bondage." Reminding Lincoln of his "House Divided" speech of 1858—which declared unsustainable the national division between freedom and slavery—the document pointed to his constitutional powers in time of war. He should seize this golden opportunity to decree "the entire abolition of Slavery throughout the land"; otherwise, "blood will continue to flow . . . until the work of national destruction is consummated beyond hope of recovery."[33]

Two weeks later Lincoln listened as Johnson read the memorial to him at the White House. The president set the tone of a good-tempered meeting with wry thanks for his visitors' assurance that they were not office seekers. His chief trouble, even more than slavery, he drily remarked, was from "that class of persons." He agreed with his Quaker visitors that slavery was detestable, but in quoting from his "House Divided" speech, they had omitted his words on the slave interests' formidable power. Without entrenched southern resistance, John Brown would have succeeded at Harpers Ferry. "Would a proclamation of freedom," he asked, "be any more effective" than the Constitution in securing the South's compliance? Johnson replied that, unenforceable though it was at present, that hard fact was not preventing federal efforts to impose it. Adopting Lincoln's familiar criterion of "indispensable necessity," the delegation believed abolition was now the only means of achieving the government's goals. When Johnson expressed sympathy with the president for the size of his task and hoped that he would be guided by God, Lincoln's reply left his visitors duly impressed. Confiding how "deeply sensible" he was of the need for divine assistance and revealing by implication that he had the power to issue an emancipation decree, he confessed "he had sometime thought that he might be an instrument in God's hands of accomplishing a great work and he certainly was not unwilling to be." Then, in words that echoed his previous year's conversation with Orville Browning on the Almighty's inscrutable nature, he reflected, "Perhaps God's way of accomplishing the end, which the memorialists have in view, is different from theirs." The meeting ended with the president repeating his "firm reliance upon the Divine arm" and his intent on "seeking light from above." Johnson and his party withdrew, gratified by how Lincoln had received them, aware that the nation's president was conscious of his duty under God, but no wiser about when he would act, if at all.[34]

Taking stock at the end of June, as the Peninsula campaign ground on, even some of the most radical antislavery nationalists found reason for hope. As Garrison explained, "the friends of impartial liberty" had grieved over the "shocking incongruities" of Lincoln and his administration: the annulling of Frémont's and Hunter's orders, the return of fugitives from Union camps, and—most recently—the suppression of schools for "contrabands" (escapees from enslavement) in North Carolina by its military ruler, Edward Stanly. But they also commended Lincoln for signal progress, including abolition in the District, the prohibition of slavery in the territories, and the recognition of the independence of Liberia and Haiti. Collectively these measures raised expectations that sooner or later they would be "gloriously crowned and consummated by one great comprehensive decree," through which *liberty is proclaimed to all the inhabitants of the land, without regard to race or complexion.*"[35]

Lincoln's strategic caution achieved a striking outcome: contending religious nationalists, across the spectrum from radical abolitionists to conservative Unionists, read his messages and actions as evidence of his essential sympathy with their own profoundly different convictions. What antislavery nationalists detected as emancipationist signals of intent took on a wholly different meaning for many religious conservatives, who saw an independent president untethered from his party and resisting its radical elements. At this period of the war only a small minority of the Union's religious conservatives were openly hostile to the administration's policies; their grounds of opposition are discussed in a later chapter. The majority tempered any unease by declaring patriotic loyalty to a government facing unlawful rebellion. Among the most powerful trumpets of conservative opinion were the resolutely Old School Presbyterian *New-York Observer* and most of the Catholic weekly press, including the official mouthpiece of the Archdiocese of Boston, *The Pilot*, and the New York *Metropolitan Record*, the organ of Archbishop John Hughes.[36]

These conservatives discovered signs of glory during the first year of war. Although it had originated in sin, and was taking incalculable toll of life, property, and enterprise, the resort to arms had "given splendid virtue to the North in all the features of exalted nationality."[37] God commanded submission to established political authority. Southern traitors led by Jefferson Davis—the "would-be murderer of his country"—had broken legally binding obligations to commit "the greatest crime against the freest country in the world."[38] The Union had met its religious duty to uphold lawful government and prevent the horrors of anarchy. There was "no race of men whom God hates more than covenant-breakers," declared the *New-York Observer*'s editor, Samuel Irenaeus Prime: "The rebellion is a breach of covenant, infinitely offensive to him who requireth truth in the soul."[39] The Catholic voice of *The Pilot* agreed. "Against rebellion to just and legal authority the face of Heaven is always turned," Patrick Donahoe wrote. "So speaks the infallible Church, so write the most learned men, so understand all human kind."[40] The war was not one of conquest, nor an abrogation of peace principles. Rather, it was only "right for Christians to uphold righteous government in righteous war" to secure the rebels' unconditional submission.[41] This was the essence of conservatism.

So, too, was conducting the conflict on the principles of the very constitution that the rebels had breached. It was morally right for the administration to avoid a war of subjugation by honoring "wisdom and prudence and a true conservatism"; equally, it was indispensable to maintaining the unity of free states and border slave states, of radicals and conservatives.[42] Without that unity there could be no victory or ultimate reconciliation. On pragmatic grounds alone, they reasoned, pursuing emancipation was strategic folly, the sure way of shattering the national consensus essential to suppressing the revolt. But more fundamental still, efforts to impose the emancipation of four million black slaves on six million southern whites would make the Union's leaders covenant breakers themselves, equally guilty before God.[43] In an unattributed editorial in the *Metropolitan Record*, Archbishop Hughes took aim at the small minority of emancipationists in Catholic ranks, above all their most articulate and radical spokesman, Orestes A. Brownson. The Church, Hughes agreed, condemned reducing free men to slavery and required masters to treat their slaves humanely. Interfering with slaveholders' property rights, however, was a wrong analogous to the expropriation of lands originally held by the Indian peoples: Catholics would not interfere with slavery where it already existed. Hughes's conservatism reflected Catholics' fears that a wartime decree of emancipation would trigger a slave insurrection of unimaginable savagery, akin to the Haitian Revolution of 1791. The lessons of the French Revolution taught that such terror would result in military despotism and national subjugation, North and South.[44] A less apocalyptic—but equally powerful—argument persuaded Irish workingmen in particular of the dire effect of emancipation on labor competition in the North. Competing with black freedmen for jobs would reduce white workers themselves to servitude.

These concerns rested on a conviction that the enslaved people of the South were unfit for freedom. Providence having decreed their physical and intellectual inferiority, they were better off under slavery than the rough-and-tumble of freedom. *The Pilot* voiced Boston Catholics' belief that black people were ignorant by nature: that "the gates of Heaven are open to all men" did not negate "one of the oldest established facts of nature . . . the *mental and physical fitness of the Negro for servility.*" The historical record revealed "that *the Negro race is happier in slavery than in freedom*" since, unless nurtured by whites, black people were "as stupid and as brutish as the beast."[45] Catholic tongues echoed the southern planters' claim that their slaves were better off than the working class of industrial Britain. The enslaved did not desire freedom and would not appreciate it. It was a fact of nature that "the negro is what the Creator made him—not a rudimentary Caucasian, not a human in the process of development, but a negro, and such he will be at the Last Day if the race is not extinct."[46] Conservatives who abhorred this extreme doctrine found other grounds for letting slavery alone, to run its course. Samuel Prime hated the idea that black people were inherently fit for slavery but looked to slaveholders themselves to modify their slave laws so that the "law of love" would regulate master-slave relations and effect the eventual disappearance of slavery. Like his Catholic counterparts he was adamant that the conservative religious element of the nation would be its salvation.[47]

This understanding of the nation's moral imperatives ensured that in conservatives' demonology abolitionists were no less wicked than the secessionists whose treachery had immediately caused the war: in advocating disunion for thirty years and more, antislavery extremists had fomented the current storm. "The career of Phillips, Garrison, Greeley, Beecher and Brownson is quite as treasonable as that of any of the public men of the South," declared *The Pilot*.[48] As abolitionists pressed ever more insistently for a war of emancipation, a conservative chorus berated them as archenemies of the Constitution pursuing "a delusion and a snare" to deprive white men of their republican freedom, as seditious allies of English power, hostile to Irish interests, and as anti-Catholic, Puritan champions of a crusading emancipationist army.[49] "The soldiers are not on the march for abolitionism," one protested. "They did not enlist for anything save the vindication of the Constitution."[50] Winning the war required the resources and self-sacrifice of the whole people, but lofty patriotism depended on national unity: thousands of families, Catholic and Protestant, suffered the absence of serving men who would not have enlisted if they thought abolition was the purpose of the war. They prayed on the April day of thanksgiving for the nation's leaders to disavow emancipation and be guided by "wisdom and prudence and a true conservatism."[51] Captured by the Democrats' political press, these antiabolitionist religious themes took on a coarser tone. The fanatics' "brutal and bloody dreams" would "send the Government and the Union to Tophet [Hell]," an Indiana editor declared. In language dripping with racial slurs, an inhabitant of Circleville, Ohio, jeered at the hundreds of "dirty scoundrels in this city . . . who go to church on the Sabbath, and offer up long hypocritical prayers! It is a pity that there is not a more tormenting hell than that kept by Beelzebub for such abolition fiends." William H. Jacoby berated the one-idea fanatic who preached like "the pot-house wrangler" on the necessity of every Christian becoming an abolitionist: "The Bible, the church, and the Constitution of the country must be made to bend to the visionary and impracticable theories of the *New York Tribune*, Henry Ward Beecher's sermons and Sumner's speech on the 'Barbarism of Slavery.' "[52]

In keeping his distance from the abolitionists, the president did more than avoid conservatives' venom: he enjoyed their broad approval. Lincoln's perceived moderation earned him an end-of-

Lincoln, Religious Nationalists, and Emancipation, 1862   171

year endorsement from Samuel Prime in December 1861. "The President of the United States, in all his utterances since his nomination and election, and emphatically since he came into power, has been conservative of the principles of the Constitution," the editor wrote. "Faction has raged around him, but he has been firm as the rock."[53] Six months later *The Pilot*, confident that the southern rebellion was about to be "utterly hacked to death," heaped praise on Lincoln for his leadership: "The greatness of his office has found corresponding greatness in his honesty and capacity."[54] These tributes reflected the political capital the president had built among conservatives during the second half of 1861. Modifying Frémont's proclamation, they said, had been "strictly CONSTITUTIONAL and eminently wise." In removing Cameron from office, following the secretary of war's "pestiferous" proposal to arm the slaves, he had acknowledged the inhumanity of a bloody-minded idea. His support for colonization revealed a commitment to gradual but not radical reform. Allowing commanders in the field to exclude fugitive slaves from military lines had testified to the army's sole purpose of crushing the rebellion, not ending slavery.[55]

The signs of Lincoln's backbone holding strong under radical pressure encouraged conservatives' acquiescence, even approval, when the president took modest steps toward emancipation during the first half of 1862. Welcoming his March proposals for gradual abolition in the border states, the *New-York Observer* declared, "Conservative men who for thirty years have resisted the revolutionary and disunion measures of radical abolitionists, hail with profound satisfaction the constitutional, statesmanlike, national and patriotic propositions" that were likely to be well received in the loyal states.[56] *The Pilot*, too, accepted that the proposal was bold and popular, even among Democrats. "There is not a tittle in it to which the strictest constitutionalist could object," though it was unlikely to find many takers among slaveholders. If any conservatives thought the proposal ill-timed, another wrote, they should think again: the need for state consent and the financial cost to the country would prevent its realization. In fact, he thought, the president's suggestions were designed to make abolitionists confront the impossible burdens and practical difficulties of emancipation.[57]

Conservatives' praise continued as Lincoln countermanded

Hunter's proclamation ("eminently Jacksonian" in its firm defense of slave owners' interests), appointed the conservative Unionists Andrew Johnson and Edward Stanly as military governors of, respectively, Tennessee and North Carolina, and chose not to intervene when Stanly shut contraband schools and returned fugitive slaves to their masters.[58] These actions colored their favorable interpretation of Lincoln's meeting with the Progressive Friends in June, noting his "guarded language."[59] James Gordon Bennett ridiculed the visiting committee of "broadbrims, long faces and shad bellied coats, . . . old women fanatics in breeches and would-be men in petticoats," and thought the president had delivered a palpable hit in musing that "perhaps God's way of accomplishing the end which the memorialists have in view was different from theirs." The *Herald*'s editor expressed his unalloyed admiration for the president's skilled handling of impertinent abolition committees, so different from Andrew Jackson's choleric explosions at unwanted visitors. Lincoln's equanimity was remarkable: "In his genial and kindly way he hears them, and then, in some amusing comparison, anecdote or expressive hint, gives them to understand that while he is grateful for their advice he will follow his own judgment."[60]

Lincoln even made political converts among conservative religious nationalists. "We ourselves firmly opposed Mr. Lincoln's election. This we did in view of his political character, which was a dangerous one; but he has now our support, because the Constitution is his guide," purred Patrick Donahoe, who hailed him as "one of the best Chief Magistrates the Republic ever had . . . and though his party has had much to do in provoking the rebellion which he is now so energetically putting down, history will vindicate himself as having been one of the most constitutional Presidents the country produced."[61] With the campaign for Richmond reaching its decisive climax, the *Metropolitan Record* took aim at "the wild, mad" schemes of emancipation and confiscation that would irrevocably shatter the Union if adopted, but Lincoln the "national man" would not fall into the trap.[62] A Fourth of July editorial listed his mistakes, notably in approving emancipation in the District, yet praised "his earnest purpose to restore the Union, and, under the Constitution, to preserve the rights of the sections."[63] Lincoln was not a party man but a true conservative patriot.

JULY–SEPTEMBER 1862

McClellan's spring campaign to take the Confederate capital, which had begun with hubristic confidence, concluded in ignominy. Robert E. Lee's dazzling generalship during the Seven Days' Battles saved Richmond and forced the Army of the Potomac to retreat in early July to the safety of Harrison's Landing on the James River. A psychological watershed accompanied this military turning point. When Lincoln visited McClellan on July 7, the general handed him a letter (which he made public) insisting that the war "be conducted upon the highest principles known to Christian Civilization": it should respect rights in private property and "the relations of servitude," and be open to the influences of a conservative Christianity that "would commend itself to the favor of the Almighty." This was McClellan's attempt to preempt what he feared would result from the traumatic effect of his failure: a demand from sections of an unnerved northern public for a more radical approach to war, including the confiscation of rebels' slave property, the use of black troops, and making emancipation an explicit war aim. *The Independent*, previously sympathetic, on July 10 questioned the president's military competence and the administration's attempt to hide "that we were within a hand-breadth of ruin." Visions of the Union army in Richmond by the Fourth of July had given way to newspaper spin, it noted sardonically, "to rejoice and acclaim—not at victory—but that we have just saved the army! McClellan is safe!—and Richmond too!" The heroic common people were desperate. "We have a sacred cause. . . . Let all good men pray that God would give us a Government!"[64]

A sequence of public and private developments soon confirmed the turning point. On July 12, Lincoln addressed a gathering of border-state congressmen, once more urging on them—again unavailingly—his scheme of compensated gradual emancipation, an offer they should accept, he said, before slavery was destroyed "by mere friction and abrasion." That same day the president received from Congress the newly approved Second Confiscation Act, whose provisions included the freeing of rebel-owned slaves who escaped across Union lines or lived in Confederate territory captured in future by Union troops. On July 13, while on a carriage ride, Lincoln startled his cabinet secretaries Seward and Welles by asking their views on the possibility of emancipation by presidential proclamation, since hard military reality now demanded the end of forbearance. Four days later Lincoln signed the Militia Act, which sanctioned the use of unarmed persons of African descent as military laborers, and the Confiscation Act. Then, on July 22, Lincoln read a draft order to a jolted cabinet. It included the declaration that "as a fit and necessary military measure," under his authority as commander in chief, "all persons held as slaves within any state or states" still under rebel control "shall then, thenceforward, and forever, be free."[65]

The cabinet, rarely of one mind, was unsurprisingly divided: Stanton wanted the order issued at once; Chase was stunned into silence by its radicalism; Montgomery Blair was opposed; Seward— who had been given time to ponder—counseled delay until after a battlefield victory that would prevent the appearance of desperation. Lincoln, uncertain, put his document to one side for what would grow into a two-month postponement. The historical narrative of that intermission takes two conflicting forms. One, set out forcefully by his private secretaries John Nicolay and John Hay in their ten-volume history of Lincoln and his administration, holds that the president maintained a "fixed purpose" throughout that period.[66] Lincoln took an irrevocable decision in July, but kept the draft proclamation in his desk drawer, waiting for military success. This, too, is the interpretative burden consensus of many classic biographies.[67] In this context, pressure from emancipationist public opinion made little or no difference to Lincoln's settled course. Greeley's celebrated public letter to the president in the *New-York Tribune* on August 20, headed "The Prayer of Twenty Millions," one of many abolitionist interventions, served only to force him into stressful concealment of his design that, according to Nicolay and Hay, made him "sensitive and even irritable" in his dealings with well-meaning petitioners.[68]

A contrasting line of argument holds that during these two summer months the die was not cast. Rather, the president continued to tussle with the issue as Federal forces suffered further humiliation at Second Bull Run under Major General John Pope, leading to Lincoln's recall of George McClellan to command in the east. According to a late-nineteenth-century biographer, "An incessant struggle against . . . emancipation went on in his mind through the whole period."[69] Some see the events of August and September working to invite a retreat from emancipation to a more limited war, forcing Lincoln—known for his reluctance to take a position from which he could not retreat—to reconsider his policy.[70] More problematic is the argument that Lincoln's overriding ambition throughout the summer of 1862 was to end the war with slavery still in place: having changed his mind about emancipation after the July cabinet meeting, he was waiting for a Union victory that, in destroying Lee's army, would eliminate the need for a proclamation.[71]

The question is not open to a definitive conclusion. Lincoln's account, as told to the painter Francis Bicknell Carpenter some eighteen months or so after the event, and later corroborated by Nicolay and Hay, supports the interpretation of a president who had set an irreversible course.[72] It is possible that in his conversation with the artist—then painting his celebratory portrayal of the first reading of the emancipation edict—Lincoln was either burnishing his reputation or succumbing to self-deception, but there is no compelling evidence that he had abandoned the policy that he had earlier declared. In fact, the case for emancipation was daily growing stronger: the Confederacy was resilient; Union recruitment had stalled; foreign recognition of southern independence seemed increasingly likely. And at the same time the bombardment of emancipationist petitions and advice from religious nationalists left him in no doubt of the sea change occasioned by the death of Union hopes on the Peninsula.

Lincoln's acute irritability and edginess shaped the fraught tone, if not the substance, of several episodes during August 1862. William Buckingham, the governor of Connecticut, visited him to present a petition from his state's antislavery activists, but before he uttered a word, Lincoln said "abruptly, and as if irritated by the subject: 'Governor, I suppose what your people want is more nigger.'"[73] Buckingham was taken aback by the president's coarseness. Lincoln quickly changed his tone. He knew that he had used a deeply offensive term, one he studiously avoided in his writing and public speeches. In prewar political exchanges he had made a point of taking the higher moral ground over Democrats like Stephen Douglas

176   RIGHTEOUS STRIFE

who frequently used the expression. His recourse to derogatory language in this meeting with the governor was uncharacteristic and a sign of his exasperation as—buffeted by pressure from all sides over the emancipation question—he had to keep quiet about an impending revolutionary act.

The president was no less brusque with a young cavalryman, Lucien Waters. The son of a preacher and a staunch Republican, Waters got a close view of plantations in Maryland while defending Washington and keeping watch on local southern sympathizers. The experience left him fearing God's judgment on the nation for its "*damnable stinky* curse of protecting the institution of Slavery!" Northerners, he told his parents, had "to awake from their supiness [*sic*] to save, what I hope in the future we may call 'great freedom's land,' but which at present does not answer to that name." Known by blacks as the "abolition Sergeant," he smuggled several of the enslaved to freedom aboard U.S. gunboats. He assumed his emancipationist mission enjoyed the blessing of his commander in chief, "Uncle Abe," whom his company escorted to and from his summer home, three miles from the White House. Writing to his parents, Lucien told how in early August he had waylaid the president. Seeking a furlough to go on a recruiting expedition in New York, he handed Lincoln his request for a temporary discharge. The president took the paper and sat informally on the floor of the White House portico, leaning back against a column, his knees drawn up "as high as his head." Before reading the sergeant's request, Lincoln looked up and snarled that the paper had "probably something to do with the damned or Eternal *niggar, niggar.*" The pious cavalryman was shocked by the president's sour outburst. "That spoke volumes to me," he remarked. Here was proof that the president was under the "insiduous & snaky influences" of Washington's southern sympathizers. The cavalryman was offended but kept "a close mouth," though he would have liked to give Lincoln "a 'right smart'" talking to. By way of mitigation, he added, "I pity the man from my heart for he is nearly worked to death. . . . Charity, Charity should be our watch word as well as the keen acumen of criticism."[74]

More public, and thus more controversial, was the candor of Lincoln's famous meeting with a delegation of free blacks invited to the White House on August 14 to discuss a topic that had been

Lincoln, Religious Nationalists, and Emancipation, 1862 177

simmering in the capital throughout the spring and summer: colonization.[75] The group of five were members of the capital's religious African American elite, selected at a meeting of representatives of Washington's numerous black churches at Union Bethel African Methodist Episcopal Church earlier that day. They were led by Edward Thomas, a respected cultural leader. His colleagues included the Oberlin-educated John F. Cook Jr., of the Fifteenth Street Presbyterian Church, and Benjamin McCoy, a co-founder of the all-black Asbury Methodist Church. Lincoln acknowledged their status, education, and independence when he addressed them in his remarks as "intelligent colored men."[76]

In the stenographer's record of Lincoln's address, his words were brutally frank. Noting the congressional appropriation of $100,000 in April to support schemes of voluntary emigration, he moved swiftly to the nub: "You and we are different races." The black race, he said, was through slavery suffering "the greatest wrong inflicted on any people." But because of race prejudice, "even when you cease to be slaves, you are yet far removed from being placed on an equality with the white race." He reminded them that the war—"white men cutting one another's throats"—was the consequence of racial slavery. "But for your race among us there could not be war, although many men engaged on either side do not care for you one way or the other." On this logic, he said, "it is better for us both, therefore, to be separated." His proposed remedy was voluntary removal to a colony in Central America, where climate, natural harbors, and opportunity for self-reliant employment in "very rich coal mines" made it an attractive place for settlement by "free colored people" wanting to live as "the equals of the best." In the interests of their race, he asked them as community leaders not to take "the extremely selfish view" that removal from the United States would invite hardship. Rather, they should "sacrifice something of your present comfort," after the fashion of George Washington, who had cheerfully endured great hardship in the Revolutionary struggle "because he was engaged in benefiting his race." He ended by urging them to reflect unhurriedly on what he had proposed and to take a very long view of "the good of mankind—not confined to the present generation."[77]

Widespread indignation and dismay followed the publication of Lincoln's words. His secretary of the Treasury, the Episcopalian

Salmon P. Chase, lamented the president's pragmatic tolerance of race prejudice instead of making "a manly protest" against it and asserting freemen's right to an American home.[78] Frederick Douglass lashed out, condemning Lincoln's "pride of race and blood," "contempt for Negroes," and "canting hypocrisy," and in later years never wholly forgot how the president's words had stained his reputation and, however unintentionally, encouraged northern racists.[79] The pages of *The Christian Recorder* blazed with furious contempt. The pious abolitionist, educator, and poet Frances Ellen Watkins Harper wrote from her AME-affiliated school in Ohio, "The country needs a leader, high and strong, and bold and brave: his heart the home of great and noble purposes," and not a president whose "dabbling with colonization just now suggests to my mind the idea of a man almost dying with a loathsome cancer, and busying himself about having his hair trimmed according to the latest fashion."[80] Indiana's T. Strother delivered the crispest dismissal: "I cannot conceive how the colored people have caused the war any more than I could conceive how slavery could be the author of its existence."[81]

Months earlier the AME's Henry McNeal Turner had estimated that the free black opponents of emigration schemes outnumbered supporters by some twenty to one. The abolitionist Strother spoke for that majority when he wrote, "I feel that this is my own native country. . . . I am contumaciously opposed to any scheme of colonization." Boiling with fury over the presumption of the delegation ("*this bogus party*") to act for "the *fifteen thousand* residents of color in this District" or "the *two hundred and twenty-five thousand Anglo-Africans in the District and in the States*," the pseudonymous "Cerebus" attacked the assumption that he and his black compatriots would voluntarily leave the land that "hath 'birthed and reared us,'" and "for which our ancestors fought, bled and died," to go to live "in the desolate wastes of Central America, or under the scorching rays of Liberia's sun, or with the bigoted and prejudiced Haytiens." He was not alone in fearing that voluntary emigration is "simply the stepping stone to *compulsory* expatriation."[82]

Black Christians' responses to the president's overtures were suffused with an emphatic providentialist faith. "God has wisely reserved to himself the distribution of the races of men, and he will have it as it pleases him, Abraham Lincoln to the contrary notwith-

Lincoln, Religious Nationalists, and Emancipation, 1862   179

standing," declared one. "It does not matter what any body may say, that which the Lord is going to do he will do," insisted another. Let the whites "give us but justice, and Providence and we will attend to the balance."[83] The greater the tumult of war, the greater the African Americans' faith in God's purposes for them and in their deliverance. At this juncture Henry McNeal Turner cast Lincoln as "the presidential Pharaoh" who, deaf to the pleas of the mystic Israelites (the enslaved), had been punished with a sequence of Egyptian plagues (the battlefield defeats since Bull Run). If he failed to comply with heaven's demand "the inexpressible tortures inflicted upon ancient Egypt" would be as nothing compared with the agony suffered by the American nation. In this apocalyptic conflict, another asserted, "the All-Wise, All-Powerful Jehovah, is the great Agitator." He had put asunder liberty and slavery. "There must be a war between them . . . for God hath decreed it, and His decrees are irrevocable. . . . Hear ye not God thundering in the moral and political heavens!"[84]

Lincoln's words to the August delegation have troubled later generations, just as they did contemporaries. As we shall see, they stand in stark contrast to the generous praise of African Americans in his public letter a year later, designed to rebuke those white voters in his hometown, Springfield, who harbored strong prejudices against blacks. The insensitivity of his language in August 1862, however, should not obscure key issues of substance. First, Lincoln knew that within the black community there were leaders receptive to the case for emigration. Notably, Henry McNeal Turner and many others in the AME Church refused to let abhorrent white motives—to rid the land of black people—obscure the benefits of colonial settlements.[85] "God has often made use of the devil and his instrumentalities, to work out for his people ineffable blessings," Turner wrote. Emigration had won freedom for many slaves who, he believed, would otherwise have died in chains; black colonies might in time come to be celebrated as evidence of the black man's capacity for self-government. Through this cadre of sympathetic black leaders, Lincoln thought, *voluntary* black settlements, taken on black initiatives, would spring and flourish. It was an essentially vain hope, but many free blacks responded positively to the Central America project, including Edward Thomas, the delegation's leader, and Douglass's son Lewis. Second, Lincoln called the meeting at the time that he did in order to prepare the ground for his preliminary emancipation proclamation. When it came, it would endorse the continuance of colonization schemes, partly to help sugarcoat a radical policy shift. The August 14 address, circulated Union-wide as he had planned, could perhaps mitigate conservative whites' hostility to a dramatic turn in the political direction of the war.

Six days after that White House meeting Greeley's self-important open letter called on the president—who would, he wrote, be accountable "at the bar of God"—to honor his Republican principles, enforce the Union army's compliance with the recent Confiscation Act, and protect the lives of the slaves brought under their care. His "prayer" on behalf of the whole northern population was no more preachy in tone than the chiding that Lincoln suffered from other radical antislavery voices. Orson Murray, an Owenite utopian socialist of Ohio, dismissed the president's "sham pretension of lacking the power to enforce emancipation." That argument was worthy only of "a small lawyer . . . a low, intriguing politician." In an hour of great peril, the commander in chief was conducting war policy "not patriotically—not righteously—not morally—nor manfully."[86] The *National Anti-slavery Standard* branded Lincoln "utterly ignorant," blinded by those who played on his idle fears that giving freedom to the slave was dangerous.[87] The president's candid friend, Beecher's *Independent*, begged for a more vigorous direction of affairs. "There never was a time when men's prayers so fervently asked God for a Leader!" Yet neither Lincoln nor his cabinet had risen to the challenge. Only military-led emancipation would suppress the rebellion, but the president had been "trying to put out a fire without wetting the house."[88]

More respectful language, naturally, characterized emancipationists' direct approaches to the president. A committee from the synod of the radical antislavery Reformed Presbyterians, accompanied by two Republican congressmen from Pennsylvania, Robert McKnight and James K. Moorhead, visited Lincoln on July 17 and urged him to take action. In a civil exchange, they stated their concern not to harass the president but "somewhat to strengthen his hands"; he agreed that slavery was morally abhorrent but could not painlessly be removed. Drawing on an analogy he often used—of the

Lincoln, Religious Nationalists, and Emancipation, 1862   181

cancerous wen whose surgical removal might kill the patient—he told them how deeply he felt his responsibility to God and country. "I assure you," he said, "I will try to do my best, and so may God help me." Struck by Lincoln's earnestness, simple manners, and careworn appearance, the deputation withdrew, encouraged to believe that their visit had done good.[89]

This encounter was prologue to a surge in religious pressure on the president over the next two months, above all through the resolutions of church bodies. Of the nineteen religious petitions in the Lincoln Papers dating from this period, from all regions of the North and every major Protestant denomination, all but two addressed the future of slavery.[90] Just one, from an association of Pennsylvania Baptists, expressed constitutional caution: "We see not how our Government can interfere directly with the system of Slavery in the revolted, more than in the Loyal Slave States; And are glad of its uniform and steadfast refusal so to do." Even then, however, they echoed the sentiment, universally expressed, that somehow God in his Providence would make the current angry debate "a great step toward the removal of a system which Washington deplored." Most petitions called on the administration, as the instrument of the divine hand, to uproot the prime national sin by a decree of universal emancipation and a vigorous execution of the Second Confiscation Act. The familiar themes of God's justice and His special purposes for an unrighteous nation shaped their argument. The United States had allowed slavery's victims to increase eightfold since independence, a chilling betrayal of duty that would "prove as disastrous to the American people now, as it . . . was, to . . . the State of Israel" when the prophet Jeremiah had rebuked the house of David.[91] The nation was at a historical crux. "God has now brought us in his providence to a point where we must destroy Slavery in this nation or Slavery will destroy what liberty it has not already destroyed," declared Wisconsin Methodists. "Never since the days of Moses did the voice of God more distinctly say 'Let my people go.'" Lincoln's responsibilities were awesome, but an emancipation proclamation would fill heaven and loyal hearts with joy, hell and rebel hearts with terror. "It would send the name of *Abraham Lincoln* down to posterity by the side of that of *George Washington:* forever honored: the one for freeing his country from the oppressions of Great Brittain [*sic*], and the other for freeing it from the infinitely greater curse of *Slavery*."[92]

THE CHICAGO INITIATIVE, SEPTEMBER 1862

Shortly after the Union's military disaster at the Second Battle of Bull Run, Confederate troops crossed the Potomac just twenty-five miles northwest of Washington. Commanding some forty thousand men, Robert E. Lee euphorically urged Maryland slaveholders to throw off their "foreign yoke."[93] If hindsight reveals that the Union capital faced no real threat of capture and that Marylanders were not going to rise up en masse, it remains the case that Lee's invasion acted as a hammer blow to northern morale after a summer of desperate military failure.

On the day Lee invaded Maryland—September 4—several hundred Chicago Christians gathered in the city's largest meeting place, Bryan Hall. A Methodist reporter emphasized the gathering's social and political mix: "men from the bench . . . from the counter . . . from hard daily toil . . . from the pulpit"; those "who had stood beside [Stephen] Douglas . . . men of old whig associations, men of the old free-soil party, men who voted the republican ticket." But, he purred, "party was out of sight," as all united to declare "that in this struggle God had been too much forgotten . . . that a great sin stood up against us, and that we must put it away or God's anger must burn against us."[94]

Although the military reversal at Second Bull Run cast its shadow over the Bryan Hall meeting, it was the cumulative setbacks of the summer that had prompted an appeal to "Christians of all denominations, who believe that the country is now suffering under divine judgments . . . and who favor the adoption of a memorial to the President of the United States urging him to issue a decree of Emancipation as a sign of national repentance, as well as military necessity."[95] The appeal's hundred or so signatories included laymen from Protestant churches across Chicago, together with all the Congregational clergy, and almost all the Baptist and Methodist ministers. (Presbyterian ministers, notoriously conservative, considered the call at their weekly meeting and voted not to sign it.)[96]

The driving force behind the Chicago initiative was a forty-year-old Congregationalist minister, William Weston Patton. The son of an eminent Presbyterian and trained at New York's Union Theological Seminary, Patton had accepted calls from Congregational churches in Boston and later Hartford, Connecticut. These pastorates gave him rein to preach the Oberlin doctrine of sanctification and champion the antislavery radicalism that it inspired. An admirer of the preeminent evangelist Charles G. Finney, Patton won a reputation as a successful revivalist and organizer. His achievements prompted a summons at the age of thirty-five to Chicago's First Congregational Church, a base from which he aimed to strengthen the hold of New England progressive theology and benevolent social action among the rapidly growing Yankee population of the Northwest. He quickly won admirers as an able and single-minded advocate of antislavery.[97]

Patton is a largely forgotten figure, but he merits attention. With the coming of war his antislavery radicalism translated into a principled Unionism. He encouraged enlistments and drilled new recruits. As the elected vice president of the Sanitary Commission of the Northwest, he inspected camps and hospitals in the western theater. Above all, he was concerned with the bearing of the war upon emancipation. Unhesitating in his admiration for John Brown, whose execution he had honored in the pulpit, he turned his hand to writing new, Christian lyrics to the song "John Brown's Body." In these, Brown emerges as a prophetic figure:

John Brown was John the Baptist of the Christ we are to see—
Christ who of the bondmen shall the Liberator be;
And soon throughout the sunny South the slaves shall all be free,
For his soul is marching on!

Patton characterized the Union forces as a Christian army of liberation, vindicators of what he deemed Brown's valor in Kansas and Virginia:

The conflict that he heralded he looks from heaven to view,
On the army of the Union with its flag red, white and blue.
And heaven shall ring with anthems o'er the deed they mean to do,
For his soul is marching on.

According to Patton's son, these words, which predated Julia Ward Howe's version by several months, circulated widely among the Union's fighting men.[98]

During the summer of 1862, Patton made an extended visit to the eastern theater of war. Within mainstream religious circles he found strong support for emancipation but regretted that it was not being effectively mobilized. Returning home, he set about organizing the Christian sentiment of the Northwest to lobby the Lincoln administration and drew up the call for the Bryan Hall event.[99] That meeting set up a committee to draft a memorial to the president and issued a call for a further mass meeting three days later.

A "mighty gathering" of professing Christians—their regular services canceled—met that Sunday evening. It was but the latest in a series of meetings of Union loyalists that had swelled the hall during the summer, each addressed by the city's combined political, business, and religious leaders.[100] The participants' overblown accounts of this event reveal an occasion buoyed by a sense of "sublime" historic purpose. After preliminaries that included prayer and a rousing rendition of "America," a rapt audience listened as Patton read out his memorial. Subsequent speakers included Thomas M. Eddy, the Methodist editor of the region's leading religious newspaper, and Lincoln's personal friend Julian Sturtevant, the president of Illinois College, whose address elicited "outbursts of applause, which not even the sanctity of a Sabbath evening could repress." After a collection, and a rousing solo of "The Star-Spangled Banner," the assembly rose as one to adopt the memorial and endorsed a set of resolutions prepared by the Baptist minister William W. Everts. Patton closed the meeting with the benediction.[101]

Of the ecumenical committee of four appointed to take the memorial to Washington, only two would make the journey: Patton himself, as chairman, and John Dempster, a sixty-eight-year-old professor at Evanston's Garrett Biblical Institute.[102] As a young man Dempster had been a stalwart of the Methodist itinerancy in his native New York. Never in robust health, however, he had withdrawn from the traveling ministry to pioneer ministerial education in New England and, more recently, in the Northwest. Dempster's passionate belief in the future of the United States and its capacity for progress made him a steely opponent of what he deemed slave-

Lincoln, Religious Nationalists, and Emancipation, 1862   185

holding Methodists' "vicious" reinterpretation of the antislavery tenets of their denomination's founding generation. As a delegate to the Methodist Episcopal Church's General Conference of 1856, he had helped lead the fight to stiffen the rule on slavery in the face of the "anathemas of border State men."[103]

The two ministers set out on the grueling rail journey to Washington concerned by the direction of military events. But reaching Baltimore "in safty & fateague," as he put it, Dempster took up his pen to reassure his wife. "We hear nothing new of the position or purpose of the Rebbles," he explained, though a major battle was undoubtedly imminent.[104] Arriving at the federal capital early on Thursday, they had no immediate access to the president. A sleepless Lincoln would remain preoccupied for the next two days with issues of military command and troop movements. But Patton asked a sympathetic Gideon Welles to arrange an introduction. "The President assented cheerfully," Welles recorded, and agreed to meet them on Saturday morning. Riding to the White House from the Soldiers' Home early in the day, Lincoln sprained his wrist in trying to restrain his runaway horse, but he received his two visitors affably enough, motioning them to seats near the end of his desk while he took the armchair behind it. The meeting opened with some formality as Patton spent ten minutes reading out the Chicagoans' memorial, and presented Everts's resolutions and a petition from the city's German citizens.[105]

The memorial began with a claim on Lincoln's special attention, as the voice of all Christian denominations of the city.[106] Its familiar premise was the interrelationship of the nation's rulers with the government and Providence of God, who in justice had acted with "exterminating thunder," as Thomas Jefferson had warned, to punish the crime of slavery.[107] Since God could not be expected to save a nation that clung to its sin, there could be no deliverance *till slavery ceases in the land.*" The war was daily more destructive, despite the Union's superior resources. Time was running out. National existence was imperiled. "While we speak the enemy thunders at the gates of the capital." God's Old Testament command to Pharaoh, through Moses, allowed no debate: "Let my people go!" Measures toward justice taken so far—abolishing slavery in the District of Columbia, prohibiting it in the territories, and encouraging emancipation in the border states—were inadequate. The president, the head of a Christian nation, must use his war powers to proclaim national emancipation. Action driven by mere political and military expediency lacked moral power:

> The rebels have brought slavery under your control by their desperate attack on the life of the Republic. . . . God and a waiting world demand that the opportunity be used. . . . [W]e will not conceal that gloom has filled our hearts at every indication that the war was regarded as simply an issue between the Federal authorities and the rebel states; and that therefore slavery was to be touched only to the extent that the pressure of rebel success might absolutely necessitate. Have we not reason to *expect* rebel success on that policy? . . . Has the fact no moral force, that the war has suddenly placed within the power of the President, the system that has provoked God's wrath? Is there not danger that while we are waiting till the last terrible exigency shall force us to liberate the slave, God may decide the contest against us?

Patton closed his reading with reference to the Old Testament narrative of Queen Esther, who had hesitated before intervening to protect the Jews in a time of their "national peril," only doing so after the solemn warning of her guardian Mordecai that she and her family would perish by delay. That episode was the prelude to the dramatic story of Haman, hanged on the high gallows he himself had erected for Mordecai. Lincoln's command of scripture—and the fact that Mordecai was, along with Abraham, the commonest name in his father's family—made it a story he knew well and had used more than once for political effect.[108] Esther's was a cautionary tale, designed to remind Lincoln of the inspiring truth that rulers worked under a God who gave them wide fields of opportunity. "In Divine Providence you have been called to the Presidency to speak the word of justice and authority which shall free the bondmen and save the nation," the memorialists declared. They prayed that Lincoln would go down to posterity yoked with George Washington, "as the second savior of our country."

Lincoln, Religious Nationalists, and Emancipation, 1862   187

Patton then extemporized, eager to remove any idea that, at a time of rebel invasion, they were attempting to dictate to the president. Rather, they were moved by "the fear, that our reverses might be made needful . . . to learn the moral lessons of the war." The president would surely see that "if military success was thought to render emancipation unnecessary, and defeat to make it unavailing, duty would become an idle word, and God's providence unmeaning."[109]

Thereafter the three men talked freely for about an hour. Lincoln left no record of the occasion, so we must rely on his visitors' account.[110] The president, Patton recalled, spoke "quite deliberately" and solemnly, though often "letting fall a half-humorous observation." As they talked, "he . . . warmed up towards us personally, as if we were true friends." Sitting stiffly at first, he gradually unbent, throwing a leg over the arm of his chair, "gesticulating freely, and looking us intently in the face." Such easy informality, Patton reflected, "would have shocked European ideas of official propriety," but it impressed on his visitors "the simplicity, frankness and sturdy honesty of his nature." Whatever signs of impatience might be read into Lincoln's reported words, the two Chicagoans felt they had been talking with a man who, mixing earnestness and lightness of touch, had given them a respectful, sympathetic hearing.

The discussion revolved around three issues: how to reach a right view of the question; the practical difficulties in the way of emancipation; and the possible benefits that it might yield. Lincoln raised the first of these at the outset. For months he had tussled with the question. "I am approached with the most opposite opinions and advice, and that by religious men, who are equally certain that they represent the Divine will." But one or other set of beliefs must be mistaken, possibly both. When the visitors remarked that "nevertheless *the truth was somewhere*," and that they appealed to the president's intelligence and his faith in divine Providence, Lincoln replied, "Unless I am more deceived in myself than I often am, it is my earnest desire to know the will of Providence in this matter. *And if I can learn what it is I will do it!*" But, he continued, "I hope it will not be irreverent for me to say that if it is probable that God would reveal his will to others, on a point so connected with my duty, it might be supposed he would reveal it directly to me."[111] Since these were no longer "the days of miracles . . . I suppose it will be granted that I am not to expect a direct revelation." Only from plain physical facts could a wise and right course be calculated. Patton and Dempster agreed that God worked by means, not miraculous revelation: this meant He might use humble instrumentalities like them, who represented Christian sentiment in the Northwest and beyond, to help make Lincoln's duty plainer. When Lincoln pointed to religious disagreement ("the rebel soldiers are praying with a great deal more earnestness, I fear, than our own troops, and expecting God to favor their side"), his visitors acknowledged this as a historical truism, but one that should not obstruct duty: "It was so in the war of our Revolution, and in the religious wars of Europe. Nevertheless, there was a right side, in each case. And we must pray, and must act, according to our own convictions of righteousness."

Lincoln moved to ponder the danger that an emancipation edict would remain toothless and unenforceable. "I do not," he remarked with rueful humor, "want to issue a document that the whole world will see must necessarily be inoperative, like the Pope's bull against the comet! Would *my word* free the slaves, when I cannot even enforce the Constitution in the rebel States?" The Second Confiscation Act, which he had signed earlier that summer, offered freedom to the slaves of rebel masters crossing into Union lines. Yet he knew of not a single slave prompted to move. When the delegation proposed that the advance of the Union armies would spread news of an emancipation decree to the slaves, so prompting their flight, Lincoln asked, *"What should we do with them? How can we feed and care for such a multitude?"* That was exactly the headache then afflicting Benjamin F. Butler, commander of Union forces in New Orleans. And what of the consequences when Federal troops had to shift ground and leave black people, free and slave, exposed to imprisonment by rebels, as had occurred recently in an incident on the Tennessee River? Patton replied that Butler's difficulties were the result of half measures and timidity: he should do more than merely receive and feed the slaves. "Paul's sound doctrine was, that those who eat must work." Slaves should be freed, made to labor, enlisted, and drilled, "to fight for their own liberty and for the Union which is to protect it." This was what the rebels most feared.

The two parties next discussed the likely benefits of a proclamation. If they were not of one mind, they reached a certain accord. Lincoln conceded that slavery was "the root of the rebellion, or at least its *sine qua non*." He accepted the delegation's argument that emancipation would be a help in foreign relations, by convincing the European powers "that we are incited by something more than ambition." When Patton and Dempster argued that a proclamation would inspire a more potent patriotism, Lincoln granted "that it would help *somewhat* at the North, though not so much, I fear, as you . . . imagine," adding, "I think you should admit that we already have an important principle to rally and unite the people in the fact that constitutional government is at stake. This is a fundamental idea, going down about as deep as any thing." Weighing the visitors' argument that the advance of Union armies would attract refugee slaves who could be deployed on the front line, the president conceded that this would weaken the enemy but doubted "we could do much with the blacks. If we were to arm them, I fear that in a few weeks the arms would be in the hands of the rebels; and indeed thus far we have not had arms enough to equip our white troops." The two visitors demurred: given the scarcity of weapons, wisdom suggested putting some in the hands of "those nearest the seat of the rebellion, having most at stake, and able to strike the heaviest blow."

In setting out the case against an emancipation edict, Lincoln raised a concern ("though it meet only your scorn and contempt") that had shaped his approach to slavery and freedom since the first summer of the war: the reaction of the loyal and Union-controlled areas of the upper South. "There are fifty thousand bayonets in the Union armies from the Border Slave States," he explained. "It would be a serious matter if, in consequence of a proclamation such as you desire, they should go over to the rebels." Lincoln judged that not all of them would, "not so many indeed as a year ago, or as six months ago—not so many to-day as yesterday." But the concern was real. For their part, Patton and Dempster—no political innocents, and fully alert to the issue's chronic influence on administration policy—seized on the president's admission that the danger was now much reduced. And whatever desertions might result would be more than offset by the animating effect of emancipation on the patriotic majority, who knew that "*nothing else has put constitutional government in danger but slavery.*" They restated their view that a proclamation of freedom would make "Union and Liberty" the inspirational watchwords of the war, "appealing alike to conscience, sentiment, and hope," and fanning nationalist ardor to a new intensity. When the visitors declared, "No one can tell the power of the right word from the right man to develop the latent fire and enthusiasm of the masses," Lincoln exclaimed with some earnestness, "I know it!"

The meeting ended with what Patton described as expressions of mutual cordiality and respect. The Chicagoans commended the president "to the gracious guidance of the All-Wise God" and left the White House buoyed by Lincoln's parting remarks. According to Patton, he alluded to the issue of timing. "Matters look dark just now. I fear that a proclamation, on the heels of defeat, would be interpreted as a cry of despair. It would come better, if at all, immediately after a victory."[112] He continued: "Do not misunderstand me, because I have mentioned these objections. . . . I have not decided against a proclamation of liberty to the slaves, but hold the matter under advisement. And I can assure you that the subject is on my mind, by day and night, more than any other." Then, more or less repeating what he had declared earlier, he added, "Whatever shall appear to be God's will, I will do." Comparing impressions afterward, Patton and Dempster took heart from their interview, convinced that Lincoln's rehearsing of outworn objections indicated that "they had lost to his mind most of the force which they might once have had," that he was in earnest in his scrutiny of divine Providence, and that a proclamation might be expected to follow a battlefield victory.[113]

———

Returning to Chicago, Patton and Dempster presented a written report to an immense meeting at Bryan Hall on September 19, two days after Federal forces had claimed a strategic victory at Antietam, driving Lee out of Maryland. The ministers' report appeared in the press on September 23, printed alongside the preliminary emancipation proclamation that Lincoln had issued the previous day.[114] This sequence of events prompted opponents of the measure to charge the Chicagoans with malign influence, just as emancipation-

Lincoln, Religious Nationalists, and Emancipation, 1862 191

ist Christians rejoiced at the lobbyists' success.[115] Illinois's governor, Richard Yates, thought their memorial "must have had great influence upon the President," but the timing of Lincoln's preliminary decree was determined by events on the Antietam battlefield, not White House meetings with clergy.[116] Even so, the Chicago ministers' visit was far from an irrelevant sideshow.

When he met the deputation, Lincoln knew that most of his religious petitioners blamed the conflict on slavery. The Chicago initiative confirmed the impression of those entreaties, that abolitionist voices had moved from the antebellum religious margins to command the wartime Protestant mainstream. The Massachusetts Republican George S. Boutwell—against the evidence—remarked of the White House meeting that Lincoln "stated the reasons against emancipation . . . so forcibly that the clergy were not prepared to answer them."[117] More plausibly, we should see Patton and Dempster's polite but firm responses to Lincoln's routine arguments helping to confirm the president's sense that mainstream opinion in the Union now stood reassuringly behind emancipation as a war measure.

The memorials to Lincoln served a further purpose, by collectively giving a meaning to the war that complemented his own attempts to fathom the workings of Providence. The president, "under God," had a duty to rescue the nation, a moral entity and the latter-day Israel, from complicity in covenant breaking. Lincoln did not share the millennialist evangelical faith of his pious petitioners, but his wartime responsibilities tugged him closer to the historic Calvinism that colored much of northern Protestantism.[118] He explained that "from the beginning" he had seen that "the issues of our great struggle depended on the Divine interposition and favor. If we had that, all would be well." In telling the Chicago deputation, "Whatever shall appear to be God's will, I will do," he spoke not simply as a leader burdened by secular duty but as one who felt responsible to an Almighty who ruled human actions. When his old Springfield neighbor the Baptist minister Noyes Miner visited him in the spring of 1862, Lincoln told him, "*It has pleased Almighty God to put me in my present position, and looking up to him for divine guidance, I must work out my destiny as best I can.*"[119] Alexander K. McClure, the Pennsylvania Republican political organizer, was sure

Lincoln's "Meditation on the Divine Will" [summer 1862?]

that his declaration to the Chicago ministers that he would seek and do God's will "tells the whole story of Lincoln's action in the abolition of slavery," reflecting as it did his "profound belief in God and in God's immutable justice": "He was one of the last men to believe in miracles ... but he did believe that God overruled all human actions; that all individuals charged with grave responsibility were but the means in the hands of the Great Ruler to accomplish the fulfillment of justice."[120]

Lincoln's discussion with Dempster and Patton revealed how

wartime events, and above all the increasingly urgent issue of emancipation, had borne him along to a new religious understanding, closer to the Calvinist tenor of much of northern Protestantism, that left him open to the idea of a God who actively intervened in history. The elements of this arresting change of outlook he set down in a private memorandum known as the "Meditation on the Divine Will," an undated document whose elements strongly suggest it was composed during the summer of 1862:

> The will of God prevails. In great contests each party claims to act in accordance with the will of God. Both *may* be, and one *must* be wrong. God can not be *for*, and *against* the same thing at the same time. In the present civil war it is quite possible that God's purpose is something different from the purpose of either party—and yet the human instrumentalities, working just as they do, are of the best adaptation to effect His purpose. I am almost ready to say this is probably true—that God wills this contest, and wills that it shall not end yet. By his mere quiet power, on the minds of the now contestants, He could have either *saved* or *destroyed* the Union without a human contest. Yet the contest began. And having begun He could give the final victory to either side any day. Yet the contest proceeds.[121]

The theology of this document distills key elements of the Westminster Confession of Faith, the Calvinist creed that shaped the Old School Presbyterian preaching Lincoln regularly attended at Gurley's New York Avenue church. In sum, they include God's sovereignty and Providence; His necessary grace ("mere quiet power") for human moral action; and His use of human means ("the best adaptation") to achieve His ends. Taken together, these amount to Lincoln's recognizing that it was his moral duty to act as a human agent in God's scheme. This did not mean that Lincoln "heard" a direct message from the Almighty. It has been rightly said he was not a moral narcissist who would claim to know God's will. But through his dialogue with religious delegations and his respected pastor Gurley, and with the growing evidence of a providential historical crisis over American slavery, he had concluded that a sovereign God, active in history, required human agency to further His intentions for humankind.

Lincoln startled his cabinet when he revealed on September 22 that his emancipation policy and interrogation of God's purposes were entwined. At that meeting, according to Gideon Welles, the president explained that "he had made a vow, a covenant, that if God gave us the victory in the approaching battle, he would consider it an indication of the Divine will, and that it was his duty to move forward in the cause of emancipation." Not he, but "God had decided this question in favor of the slaves." Now he would keep "the promise to myself, and"—here Secretary of the Treasury Salmon P. Chase spotted a hesitation—"to my Maker." As he weighed urgent military and political considerations, alongside the slaves' own active pursuit of freedom, Lincoln found intellectual inspiration in an expanded view of the Constitution and a theology that no longer, as in his younger days, viewed the Almighty as a remote figure disengaged from the daily round of human action. Now he was ready both to honor the mysterious and intrusive workings of Providence in human history and to acknowledge his responsibilities to a personal God.[122]

SEPTEMBER 1862–JANUARY 1863

Lincoln's encounter with the Chicago ministers highlighted a distinctive feature of his political decision making. According to Schuyler Colfax, the president put his searching questions and counterarguments to Patton and Dempster not because he was uncertain about his course but to elicit further arguments to support an emancipationist position already inflexibly held.[123] Whether or not the meeting served that purpose, it certainly encouraged the president to think the time was ripe for action and that he could rely on the mainstream Protestant churches as political engines of progressive nationalism. In the event, the Chicagoans' faith in the likely inspirational effect of an emancipation edict proved well grounded. The jubilant editorial comment in most of the religious press was channeled to the White House in a cascade of exultant church petitions and memorials.

Those messages, which represented the broad spectrum of anti-slavery Protestant church traditions, celebrated Lincoln's preliminary proclamation above all as an act of righteousness "founded upon the principles of eternal rectitude, justice and virtue as laid down in the Scriptures of Divine truth." By declaring that "all persons held as slave within any state" in rebellion on January 1, 1863, "shall be then, thenceforward, and forever free," the decree was hailed for satisfying both the prophet Isaiah's instruction to liberate the captive and the federal constitution's stated intent "to establish justice, ensure domestic tranquility, provide for the common defense, promote the general welfare, and secure the blessings of liberty to ourselves & our posterity." In opening the way to emancipating four million enslaved people and proclaiming "the first jubilee America has ever enjoyed," it was the most important presidential edict since the foundation of the republic. It honored the needs of the Christian citizen: "Now at last can the patriot feel he is on God's side, and in the hands of God for good. . . . He who carried his people from bondage through the wilderness, and established them in the promised land, can surely guide us!"[124]

Practical wisdom, too, empowered this righteous decree, which would deprive the enemy of a powerful resource, "strike dismay into the hearts & homes of the soldiers of the rebel army," and deliver a deathblow to rebellion.[125] At the same time, the Union's purification would impress foreign opinion. Universalists and Congregationalists exulted that it gave "the world the spectacle of a Great and Powerful Nation" fulfilling God's "manifest purpose in the formation of the Christian Republic on the basis of popular intelligence, of wholesome Liberty, and of Constitutional Self-Government."[126] Equally, it would unite the North by redefining the war as a simple contest between slavery and liberty. The previous seventeen months, Reformed Presbyterians asserted, had shown the signal failure of the conservative "rose-water" policy: now "the stern and thorough measures of radicalism" would save the country. Every Christian citizen must declare fealty to the government in this new-purposed war.[127] "There is no neutral ground for traitors to hide in," Beecher's *Independent* declared. "The . . . Proclamation will sift the North in this hour of its peril."[128]

Purists regretted that the proclamation would take neither

immediate nor universal effect. Unpersuaded by Lincoln's view of constitutional constraints, George B. Cheever told the president, "If you have the right to free any of the slaves, you have to free them all; and this right being given you, along with the opportunity by Divine Providence, it cannot be just to condemn any of them to continued slavery." He told Lincoln to reverse the exemption of those states returning to the Union before New Year's Day. Only a policy of absolute and unconditional emancipation throughout rebeldom would reinvigorate Republicans. Only a party inspired with enthusiasm and energy, he wrote, could stop "the proslavery democracy" riding over it roughshod.[129] Horace Greeley thought the plan more "cautious, limited, and temporizing" than he desired.[130] Although Lincoln considered the measure constitutionally defensible under his war powers, critics condemned his silence on the rights of the slave. "It cannot be a little thing to Christian men that the actions of a government are based upon principles, and not upon mere selfishness or expediency."[131]

"The world moves," exulted an African American missionary, marveling at the eighteen-month incremental advance toward revolutionary obedience to God's word. "We are living years in days, and centuries in years."[132] The preliminary proclamation energized and refashioned the agenda of antislavery Unionists. Labeling it a step toward national repentance, United Presbyterians urged Lincoln to crown it with a national fast day, a request echoed by the Episcopalian Alonzo Potter, on behalf of every Christian and Jewish communion of Philadelphia. "All have witnessed with delight the numerous proofs that you have given of faith in an overruling Power," the bishop wrote, "and that in this hour of our nation's sore trial you desire the prayers of the devout." The president, they knew, understood that for final success something higher than second causes and human instruments was needed. A repeat of the 1861 fast day would reveal to God and the wider world a religious people sacrificially enlisted in the nation's righteous crusade.[133] More radical still, Reformed Presbyterians called afresh for amendment of a federal constitution still silent on the ruling authority of Jehovah, a God "who will overturn & overturn until the kingdoms of this world become the kingdoms of our Lord & of his Christ."[134]

Lincoln's decree brought into sharp focus the rights and future

Lincoln, Religious Nationalists, and Emancipation, 1862 197

well-being of the four million people whose freedom would come at first piecemeal, with the advance of the Federal armies, but would embrace all the enslaved when the Confederate project ultimately collapsed. Consensus on the moral imperative of emancipation masked both uncertainty and the seeds of difference over the proper future place of those "brutalized by bondage." Some of Lincoln's petitioners pressed for the immediate enlistment of freedmen as a means of shortening the war.[135] Looking further ahead, others urged him to provide practical measures for the moral instruction of those cruelly denied the advantages of education. The wider debate took Lincoln's promotion of black colonization as a starting point for questions that included the likelihood of a black exodus from the South, the possibility of healthy race relations in a society where white prejudice consigned blacks to inferior status, and whether entitlement to the natural rights enumerated in the Declaration of Independence made freedmen equally eligible for full citizenship.[136]

When word of the preliminary proclamation eventually reached Southeast Asia in mid-December, exultant American missionaries wrote to "their beloved President" for his *"crowning act of States-manship."*[137] By then Lincoln had already garnered at home a harvest of praise as God's appointed man for the hour, his place in history secured "among the wisest rulers and noblest benefactors of the race."[138] Sylvanus Cobb, Universalist minister and editor, explained how he had consistently encouraged the public to understand "that Abraham Lincoln takes time & uses means to decide understandingly what is both right &, politic, &, when he has so determined, never backs down. I thank God that I am not to be disappointed."[139] Despite his regret at the exemptions, Horace Greeley still praised "a great, wise, and happy act," meriting thanks to heaven for Lincoln's stewardship of the nation.[140] In Rochester, Frederick Douglass exulted on behalf of the "long enslaved millions" at an act that lifted his hope in a president he had considered too cautious and hesitating. Although events greater than Lincoln had wrung the proclamation from him, Douglass wrote, he trusted that the president would not change his course once set.[141]

The weeks of apprehension between the preliminary and the final proclamations for Douglass and the army of antislavery nationalists have been vividly termed "a sleepless watch night that lasted three months." In the event, the "moral bombshell" of September led irreversibly to the New Year jubilee. In Boston's Tremont Temple, some three thousand gathered for a day of joyous speeches and song led by Douglass, William Wells Brown, and other black abolitionists. When, very late in the evening, the telegraph brought Lincoln's text, the baritone Douglass joined an old preacher in the anthem of freedom "Blow Ye the Trumpet, Blow." The celebrations continued until dawn at the Twelfth Baptist Church, sanctifying the war as a holy struggle for freedom.[142] Writing to Lincoln at the end of the jubilee day in Philadelphia—home to thirty thousand free blacks—the abolitionist Benjamin Rush Plumly rhapsodized over scenes of thanksgiving "like unto the solemn joy of an old Jewish Passover." Overflowing churches "sang and shouted and wept and prayed." Trusting deeply in Lincoln's devotion, justice, and honesty, they knew it was God's design that had given the name Abraham to "the 'Liberator' of a People." To be the nation's president was a great thing, Plumly reflected, but it was greater still "to be enshrined in the Religious sense of a People, yet in its plastic infancy, but destined to, a distant but grand maturity."[143] Equally heartfelt tributes reached Lincoln from the freed people at Beaufort, South Carolina, grateful that God had steeled the president's nerve to secure their deliverance, and poignantly realistic: "We never expect to meet your face on earth; but may we meet in a better world than this."[144]

The widespread celebration by the Protestant mainstream of the preliminary and final emancipation proclamations nourished the wider political response among loyalists. It encouraged Republican presses to present what was adopted as a weapon of war as evidence of the Union's righteousness. Appropriately, there was no more explicit blending of the secular and the religious than in Chicago, where the *Tribune* exulted that the New Year's Day decree would tighten the bond of Union and ensure "that until the last soldier of the righteous cause has offered up his life for the unity and indivisibility of the Republic," there would be no letting up in the labor of national preservation. What gave the edict its "fearful potency" was its closing sentence, in which the president—accommodating Salmon P. Chase's last-minute suggestion—had invoked "the gracious favor of Almighty God" upon an "act of justice, warranted by the Constitution, upon military necessity," and in so doing had

Lincoln, Religious Nationalists, and Emancipation, 1862   199

turned a legal document defensible under the president's war powers into one that also acknowledged his private faith. The *Tribune* cheered this tardy "recognition of the finger of God in the affairs of nations," since victory would only come if stamped with "the seal of the everlasting Right."[145]

Whatever pleasure Lincoln took from these accolades, he knew that the tough work of making emancipation a reality lay ahead. But he also knew that his proclamation, in fusing Christian emancipationist sentiment with loyalty to republican freedom, gave him a fighting chance of success. This was the burden of an editorial of November 1862 in Washington's *Daily Morning Chronicle*, very recently converted from a weekly newspaper by its editor and administration loyalist, John W. Forney. Lincoln had encouraged its daily publication and supplied occasional unattributed articles for the paper, which generally acted as an administration mouthpiece.[146] The editorial took stock of the profound social, commercial, and political changes of the first eighteen months of the war, to the point that it seemed "as if another race had been transplanted to these shores." It was, however, religion more than any other interest that had been most affected by, and influential in, the country's tumult. "Statesmen and politicians, merchants and lawyers, may have been comparatively slow to recognize the presence of a new instrumentality in the national crisis," Forney wrote, "but the Christian cannot hide from his heart the unanswerable Truth that in this struggle the right is with the Government; and that, inasmuch as the Rebellion is at once a revolt against God," there was only one side that conscience and duty could take. "Before . . . an agency which includes all the sincere believers in a righteous cause, of whatever church or denomination, nothing can stand."[147] Forney's was an understanding of religious instrumentality that the president could heartily endorse. It is likely he heard it from Lincoln himself.

———

Lincoln's adoption of an emancipation policy clearly energized the wartime purpose of antislavery religious nationalists: to that extent the Chicago delegates, Patton and Dempster, had been correct in predicting that a decree would inspire a more potent patriotism.

But when they and other religious emancipationists predicted the North would unite behind this redefinition of the war, they were desperately wide of the mark. It is true that, as the Republican senator Ira Harris reported, "men vastly more conservative than I" had yielded to the creed of the proclamation. But, as he recognized, it also catalyzed other conservative religious Unionists into a phalanx openly hostile to Lincoln's administration.[148]

Throughout the summer of 1862, after McClellan's retreat from the Peninsula, religious conservatives noted with concern the growing pressure on Lincoln to take a more radical approach to the Confederacy. The Old School Presbyterian minister and editor of the *New-York Observer,* Samuel Irenaeus Prime, urged Lincoln to stay loyal to the Constitution ("your buckler and shield") and to the conservative party of the North. These wisely recognized "the right of the humblest citizen in the farthest south to enjoy its protection, *if he wishes it*"; the president must not be bullied by the revolutionary party that sought to bring him down and whose words were ablaze with sedition. Guilelessly, he told Lincoln not to underestimate the strength of this faction: "Its numbers are in hundreds of thousands. Its leaders are in thousands of pulpits. Countless political and religious newspapers advocate a policy of war by which the constitution is virtually subverted, and REVOLUTION indirectly encouraged."[149] Lincoln responded noncommittally, with a short, polite note of thanks.[150] Prime addressed further letters to the president, in which he conceded that the desire to see slavery eradicated was universal in the North, but that the only legitimate means was a constitutional scheme of gradual emancipation and colonization.[151]

Catholic voices, above all, stiffened conservatives' defenses. Alarmed that labor competition would follow from emancipation, the Boston *Pilot* warned that the North was "becoming black with refugee negroes from the South. These wretches crowd our cities, and by overstocking the market of labor, do incalculable injury to white hands." State laws prohibiting black migration, modeled on those of Illinois, were the best solution. A contributor to *The Pilot,* willfully and racially blind to the reality of southern agricultural production, asserted, "To white toil this nation owes everything: but to black, nothing."[152] The *Metropolitan Record,* regarded as John Hughes's mouthpiece, also became more critical of the administration during July and August. It dismissed the president's gradual emancipation proposals for the border states as a diversion that divided the North and strengthened the Confederacy.[153] Lincoln had made grave mistakes: he must now "rise superior to the malign influences" working to prevent the restoration of the Union and "abandon all his predilections in favor of emancipation."[154] Some found reassurance in Lincoln's chilly interview with a deputation of black leaders to discuss colonization, as well as his response to Greeley's "Prayer," but remained unpersuaded by schemes to remove the black race: logistics and cost made such ideas impracticable, and besides, only slave labor could make the South productive. It would be better to colonize seditious abolitionists, not blacks. Why were Wendell Phillips and his ilk not subject to the laws of treason? "Is it a special privilege of abolitionists to ridicule the President, abuse the Cabinet, and sneer at the Union generals?"[155]

Conservatives, Catholic and Protestant, were stunned on September 22 by the president's "startling and extraordinary *pronunciamento*" and struggled to square the proclamation with what they had been sure was Lincoln's fundamental constitutional conservativism. Asserting that the patriotic masses of the North were aghast at a policy that would make the bloody horrors of the Santo Domingo massacres "mere child's play," Catholic voices repeated familiar arguments against emancipation: northern whites' prejudice against blacks, the impracticability of colonization, the stiffening effect on Confederate resolve, and the antipathy of slaves themselves to the idea of freedom.[156] Some conceded that Lincoln's honesty and patriotism were not in question, but he was, "in too many instances, the flexible tool of an unscrupulous party."[157] Perhaps, some surmised, Lincoln had taken the step to prove the fallacy of an emancipation policy, since only days before publishing his decree he had told the Chicago delegation that he did not want to issue a document that the whole world would see was unworkable.[158] Whatever his motives, he had made impossible any reconciliation or peace with an indomitable South that now faced a tyrannical foe, not an enemy pursuing evenhanded justice.

In making emancipation a weapon of war, Lincoln dramatically refocused the incentives and energies of contending religious nationalists. His preliminary proclamation exposed and deepened existing divisions in war-torn congregations. In Chicago's Old School Presbyterian North Church, most members favored the antislavery cause, but a minority of moneyed conservatives like Cyrus McCormick exerted some leverage by funding most of the minister's salary. When in a November 1862 thanksgiving address the recently installed pastor urged Lincoln to be more radical, McCormick's sister-in-law spat her fury at "the worst abolition sermon ever preached in the Church." The minister, she reported in dismay, thought the president's proclamation "did not go far enough and favored arming the negro or in any other way aid them to insurrection, and every other mean thing a *devilish heart* could devise." She found it intolerable to hear her own congregation applauding the preacher when he denounced the South: she thought about leaving the church.[159]

By placing himself on the side of the antislavery devout, Lincoln drove pious conservative Unionists to reassess their increasingly uneasy relationship with the government. "Is there any hope?" asked the editor of the Boston *Pilot*, seeing only the permanent estrangement of North and South resulting from the preliminary proclamation. He answered his own question: "Yes, the return to power of the Democratic Party."[160] He knew that the fall elections, as Lincoln's conservative cabinet secretary Montgomery Blair warned, would turn on the racial issues raised by an emancipation policy that made credible the charge of executive tyranny, especially when followed by the president's September proclamation suspending nationwide the writ of habeas corpus and by a spate of arbitrary arrests. The Democrats, who had been organizing confidently for the October 1862 polls, dealt their opponents punishing blows across the states of the middle and lower North. They captured thirty-five congressional seats from the Republicans, notably in Pennsylvania and the key western states of Illinois and Indiana, where narrow Republican majorities gave way to pro-peace Democratic control. They won the governorships of New Jersey and New York, where Horatio Seymour trumpeted his victory as a conservative triumph over abolitionists and secessionists that would pave the way to peaceful reunion. Conservative Republicans blamed government by unnecessary and overzealous proclamations, radicals the lack of energy and

Lincoln, Religious Nationalists, and Emancipation, 1862   203

ideological purity of the military command. The Illinois Methodist Leonard Smith despaired at the success of a corrupt Democracy: "They pretend to be Union persons when really they are traitors at heart. Secessionism is devilism."[161] Jubilant Democrats celebrated a bridgehead that augured well for the next presidential contest. But the margins of the party's victory were narrow; its advantage came chiefly from Republicans staying at home; and Lincoln's forces continued to control the House and the Senate.[162]

Shaken by the election outcome, Lincoln blamed it on "the ill-success of the war" more than his emancipation order, whose wisdom he did not question.[163] His annual message of December 1 struck a more conservative note in respect to slavery: he proposed constitutional amendments to secure gradual emancipation, federal compensation for loyal owners, and the colonizing of "the freed people . . . such as may consent."[164] The proposals, however, did not backtrack on his preliminary proclamation. Rather, they showed a president persisting in his conservative emancipatory course during the countdown to the New Year's Day deadline. At the same time, Lincoln attempted to bring greater military vigor to the Union cause, once more dismissing McClellan and replacing him with Ambrose E. Burnside. The disaster that followed the appointment, the military catastrophe on December 13 at Fredericksburg, plunged the Union into renewed despair and almost undid the delicate political balance within the president's cabinet.

As Lincoln navigated his troubled course toward January 1, critical religious conservatives did not spare the administration or the Republican Party ("the most iniquitous political faction this country ever had") but continued to temper their criticism of the president himself.[165] "It cannot be denied that Abraham Lincoln is an honest man," Patrick Donahoe wrote, "but he has yet to show . . . fine capacity; and in his Cabinet there are politicians that cannot be relied upon either for integrity or talent."[166] Honest patriot though he was, his lack of brilliance made him unfit for office.[167] However, as finally published on New Year's Day, Lincoln's proclamation outraged those who had believed his previous assurances that he would not interfere with slavery in the states. With all mention of colonization missing from the final text, and the arming of black soldiers now sanctioned, it was time to pray, "May the Lord save the nation from the able rebels and from the incompetent, fanatic, radical administration of Abraham Lincoln!"[168] From January 1, 1863, the battalions of conservative religious nationalists girded themselves for a cause they were desperate to win but destined to lose. How they defined and sustained their national project is a story in itself.

CHAPTER 7

CONSERVATIVE ATTACK AND LINCOLN'S REJOINDER, 1861–1863

Religious convictions inspired many of Lincoln's opponents. Conservative and anti-emancipationist, the Democratic Party comprised both a war-supporting loyalist majority and a substantial minority of increasingly vocal and animated Peace Democrats, or Copperheads, who took their name from the venomous snake and their cue above all from Ohio's Clement Vallandigham. That internal political dissension was frequently so bitter that it is easy to miss the common elements in the party's religious posture and motivation. Powerful pro- and antiwar conservative voices—Protestant and Catholic—gave religious authority to white-supremacist, pro-slavery, and anti-authoritarian political positions. Union politics took on the character of righteous strife between two parties, Democrats and Republicans, each convinced that in the scriptural integrity of their political faiths they commanded the moral high ground.

As we have already seen, the conservative opponents of the preliminary emancipation proclamation energized the Democrats in the fall 1862 state and congressional elections. This chapter delves into the character of that opposition and its increasing fierceness after the final emancipation edict of January 1863. The Democratic Party continued to score major electoral victories. The enlistment of African Americans and the introduction of conscription by the Enrollment Act foreshadowed the summer's bloody anti-draft riots in New York. Fervent religious champions of a conservative prosecution of the war developed an emotionally charged but coherent indictment of Union policies throughout 1863. Four major themes dominated the opposition's political platforms, pulpits, and presses: the moral iniquity and folly of emancipation policy; the feeding of bloodlust by conscription into an unholy "hard war"; the assault on precious individual rights and constitutional freedoms; and the imposition of political tests of faith.

We shall see how Lincoln held his nerve, encouraged by the midsummer military successes at Gettysburg and Vicksburg. Needing no lesson in the essential role of war-supporting Democrats in ultimate Union victory, he used his pen to address them directly and defend emancipation, black enlistments, and the draft. In key public letters, each shaped by characteristic reasoned coaxing, he spelled out the practical and moral imperatives behind those initiatives. Beyond his own interventions, and the more conventional fulminations of Republican editors, he found an unusual ally in a devastating satirical creation: the egregious Copperhead preacher and moral monstrosity, Petroleum V. Nasby. The work of a staunch Republican journalist, David Ross Locke, the widely read tirades of the fictional Nasby galvanized Union patriots. They gave Lincoln immense pleasure, serving as an essential therapy and source of resilience.

APOSTLES OF PEACE: THE COPPERHEAD VANGUARD, 1861–1862

The blaze of patriotic resolve that fired Unionist hearts in the spring and summer of 1861 helped thaw the customary frost between political parties. During the final days of his life, Stephen A. Douglas rallied his supporters to the common cause, insisting "that a man cannot be a true Democrat unless he is a loyal patriot."[1] Even southern sympathizers among Union Democrats felt the force of consolidating public sentiment. "There will now be but one party, one question, one issue, one purpose in the Northern States—that of sustaining the government," asserted James Gordon Bennett.[2] Appealing to a spirit of nonpartisanship, Lincoln appointed high-profile Democrats to positions of military command. Encouraged to sink party into patriotic duty, several local and state Democratic organizations chose not to run candidates in the fall 1861 elections; later they ran them on joint "Union party" tickets. By encouraging a "no-party" ethos, the Lincoln administration succeeded in containing, though not suppressing, the Democrats as an electoral force for the first year of the war.

From the war's outset, however, dissident voices challenged Lincoln's resort to arms and his use of expansive executive power to summon volunteers, suspend the writ of habeas corpus in designated areas, and set up a naval blockade of the Confederate states. Although most Democrats cited a precedent in Andrew Jackson's executive vigor, a peace-minded minority formed a nucleus of opposition. Clement Vallandigham of Ohio, rebuking Douglas, predicted that "sober second thought" would subdue the "surging sea of madness" and prevent unthinkable slaughter—sentiments that marked the start of the Ohioan's wartime career as an acknowledged and resolute leader of the anti-administration peace party.[3] He and several other voices of resistance, too fragmented at first to constitute a movement, fashioned religious and political imperatives that would give coherence to the growing ranks of Peace Democrats during 1863 and 1864. They included James McMaster, the Catholic editor of the *New-York Freeman's Journal and Catholic Register*; Edson B. Olds, an Ohio state congressman and Methodist lay preacher; Henry Clay Dean, Methodist preacher, barnstorming orator, and former chaplain to the U.S. House of Representatives; and the maverick Reverend Charles Chauncey Burr, a gifted editor. Each was tuned to Vallandigham's ethical and political wavelength. Their convictions revealed the dynamic interplay of earnest religious faith, deep-dyed constitutional conservatism, and a profound belief in the natural superiority of the white over the black race. All were masters of language. All were willing to suffer for their cause.

Vallandigham, born in 1820 of Flemish Huguenot ancestry, grew up in an Ohio household molded by the piety of his Scotch Irish mother and the rectitude of a strict Calvinist father. His elder brother James followed his father into the Presbyterian ministry. Clement, gifted and eloquent, chose law and politics instead, but the influence of a devout Christian upbringing persisted, as did his command of scripture. Under the ministry of James Hall Brookes at Dayton's First Presbyterian Church, he experienced in 1854 what he described to his mother as "*a peace and joy which the world never gave, and which, God be praised, I feel and am assured it cannot take away.*" Brookes, a superb communicator and biblical scholar, had found Vallandigham's sweet spot, ministering to his natural austerity with a high Calvinist doctrine of "the absolute sovereignty of God's electing love and the utter depravity and helplessness of man." This faith challenged the prevailing optimistic belief of evangelical reformers that society would be perfected before, not after, Christ's thousand-year reign. Vallandigham declared that Brookes's preaching "had been the means of leading him to see his ruin by nature and his need of Christ." He united with First Presbyterian, erected an altar at home, and told his mother that "morning and evening sacrifice shall daily be offered up so long as I do live. . . . I feel as if by *God's grace* I were at length a WHOLE MAN, made really in his image, and able now to do some good truly in the Church and the world . . . desiring in *all things* to serve the Lord." This was not a passing phase. His earnest wartime speeches quoted purposefully from the scriptures. Belief in his personal destiny under God's guidance made him resilient against attack. In January 1863, before leaving Congress, he defiantly repeated his credo: "*Do right; and trust to God, and the truth, and the people! Perish office! Perish honors! Perish life itself; but do the thing that is right, and do it like a man!*" A long-term political supporter attributed Vallandigham's moral courage when faced with the worst—notably his military arrest and subsequent banishment in 1863—to "a deep vein of actual piety and firmly seated religious conviction," maintaining that with incomparable firmness, "he believed that there was a *right side* and a *wrong side* to everything; that God ruled the world and provided for the ultimate triumph of *the right.*" This explained "the amazing energy and unswerving faith" with which he held steadfast to his political convictions.[4]

Those convictions were grounded in Vallandigham's strictest of strict readings of the states' rights doctrine of the Virginia and Kentucky Resolutions of 1798. Those views got him into youthful trouble at Jefferson College. Subsequently, his intellectual assault on consolidated power never ceased. He described himself as a "radical Democrat"—not, he said, "the *sans culottes* democracy of the faubourg," but the unique rational constitutional democracy of the United States, anchoring liberty in the individual and leaving "as much power with the people in their unorganised capacity as is compatible with the necessities and efficient existence of government." Preventing "pernicious and anti-democratic intermeddling" with private affairs and personal relations demanded the broadest possible diffusion of power: "that to the people of each particular State, county, township, city, and village, shall be committed . . . the exclusive regulation of their more immediate and local affairs." With the onset of war, he raised the alarm against federal consolidation and centralization. The rallying cry "Liberty and Union, now and forever," he read not as a call to arms, since war must end in their utter and final subversion, but as a duty to strive for a speedy and honorable peace.[5] The increasing intemperance of his criticism of the Union administration, in terms suggesting sympathy for the rebellion, would result in his military arrest, court-martial, imprisonment, and banishment as the war entered its third year.

In anchoring political rights and freedom in the individual citizen, Vallandigham honored white males alone. Political and personal liberty was "peculiarly an Anglo-Saxon right." Not for him the "negrophilism" that challenged slavery's racial hierarchy. He made himself the political voice of a white majority who believed "the subordination of the negro race to the white . . . as established in the South is far better every way, for the negro, than the hard servitude of poverty, degradation, and crime, to which he is subjected in the free states."[6] Speaking in the U.S. House before the war, he reveled in championing slavery. "This land . . . is of more value to us and to the world, for ages to come, than all the multiplied millions who have inhabited Africa from the creation to this day—if this is to be *pro-slavery*, then . . . I am all over and altogether a PRO-SLAVERY MAN." Slavery was nothing if not in accord with the scriptures.[7]

James McMaster was in some ways Vallandigham's clone. Also born in 1820, he, too, grew up within the tight bonds of strict Presbyterianism, showed precocious talent and command of scripture, chose law over the Christian ministry, and was noted for his disputatious and dogmatic spirit. Unlike Vallandigham—and to his family's alarm—he was converted to militant Catholicism in 1845 and entered the missionary Redemptorist order as a novice. Judging him over-frank and too impulsive for the priesthood, his teacher suggested a career in journalism. Encouraged, McMaster began writing for John Hughes's diocesan organ, the *New-York Freeman's Journal and Catholic Register*, which he bought in 1848. As its editor, he was fiery, fearless, and rash, and adamant that the constitutional protection of free speech extended to the "sacred authority" of the written word.[8] Casting himself as the "representative and defender of Catholic truth in a world of passion and corruption," he attacked all facets of social radicalism.[9] For a time Hughes valued McMaster's defense of Catholic rights, but he eventually found the weekly paper's vitriol and partisanship so distasteful that he discontinued it as his official organ.

McMaster fell into despondency after the shelling of Fort Sumter, certain that Lincoln had tricked Confederates into firing the first shots of war. He would soon fulminate against fanatical Union patriots whose actions endangered the rights of freemen: specifically, warmongering editors who were sabotaging the chances of reunion; military commissions that suspended habeas corpus; and a president who by his "infamous tricks" took executive authority to the brink of usurpation. Of the scores of northern newspapers sympathetic to appeasement, a small number of the most vociferous were suppressed in August 1861. They included two in Philadelphia, both religious: the *Christian Observer* and the *Catholic Herald*. A New York grand jury identified the *Freeman's Journal* and four other city papers as dangerous and seditious, leading to their suspension. Undaunted, McMaster published a new title, the *Freeman's Appeal*. An even more intemperate sheet, its appearance prompted his dramatic arrest, on the authority of Secretary of State Seward, and imprisonment at Fort Lafayette. His wife, Gertrude, wrote letters to Lincoln pleading for his release; they went unanswered. After a month's incarceration McMaster agreed under protest to take an oath of obedience to secure his release. When the *Freeman's Journal* began publication again in April 1862, he remained unrepentant: "We have no retraction to make—not a single word." His friendship with Confederate prisoners during his imprisonment in Fort

Conservative Attack and Lincoln's Rejoinder, 1861–1863   211

Lafayette had radicalized him further, he told his readers, making him "defiantly hostile to war" and increasingly sympathetic to the Confederacy.[10]

The Methodist minister Henry Clay Dean, son of a Pennsylvania stonemason, lacked Vallandigham's and McMaster's social advantages but was at least their equal in combative firepower. He matched in oratorical force the great Kentucky senator whose names he bore (Mark Twain wrote that Dean "used no notes, for a volcano does not need notes") but abandoned Clay's Whiggery under the influence of George W. Jones, the Catholic U.S. senator from Iowa, and became a staunch Democrat. Nicknamed Dirty Dean because of his dependably ragged and grubby clothes, he cultivated eccentricity. But his disheveled appearance belied the magnetic qualities that attracted admiring common folk in Iowa and other midwestern states, and served him equally well in the more refined setting of the U.S. Senate in 1855. They included a powerful mind formidably well stocked in scripture, theology, and the classics; a remarkably retentive memory; and uncommon eloquence.[11]

Dean gave up the regular pulpit before the war but did not abandon his Methodist faith or the emphatically Christian grounding of his politics. He opposed both secession and the resort to arms, convinced that coercion—unconstitutional and unholy—would make permanent separation inevitable. Denouncing the Union administration with no less venom than he directed at Jefferson Davis, Dean resorted to even more withering invective as Lincoln's initiatives on emancipation and conscription took effect. His meetings bristled with the possibility of violence, as peace partisans gathered under the menace of Union militias. As he prepared to speak in Mount Pleasant, his hometown, in February 1862, only "the ring of a score of sabres, drawn from their steel scabbards," persuaded Dean to take the oath of allegiance that Union officers, troubled by his influence among "Iowa secesh," demanded before letting the meeting proceed.[12] The following year at Keokuk a company of Union soldiers seized this "Great Mogul of the Copperhead fraternity" and marched him to the provost marshal. Arrested, he languished in a guardhouse for two weeks. Loyalists saw an arch-traitor held to account for "doing more injury to his country than he could by fighting against it," while his Democratic partisans lauded a Christian martyr suffering in the cause of "the magna charta of our liberties."[13]

More honored still in the Copperheads' pantheon of Christian martyrs was Edson Baldwin Olds. A former state legislator and a three-term U.S. representative from Ohio, the elderly Democrat was arrested by the military in August 1862 for allegedly discouraging enlistments. Olds was a devout Methodist, occasional lay preacher, and evangelist for peace, whose four-month imprisonment in Fort Lafayette provided a perfect narrative of "heathenish treatment" in a Christian land. Refused access to a Bible, held in solitary confinement without charge or trial, and in reduced health, the prisoner gave Peace Democrats a symbol of the Union's unrighteous and despotic rule. Eventually the commanding officer relented and sent him a copy of the scriptures, but by then the political damage was done. While he was still in his cell, Olds's allies ran him for the state legislature, to which he was triumphantly elected as the Christian model of a blessed peacemaker. Embarrassed Ohio Republicans successfully prevailed on the Union administration to authorize his release.[14]

These early pro-slavery critics of Lincoln's war policy and the Union's "bloodlust" found an ally in a master polemicist, Charles Chauncey Burr. A literary showman, political maverick, and professed minister of religion, Burr specialized in running to moral extremes.[15] *The Nineteenth Century*, a quarterly magazine he launched in 1848, served as a mouthpiece for the radical causes he shared with abolitionists, Free-Soilers, labor reformers, and women's rights advocates.[16] However, he soon disavowed his support of the free-soil movement and the Wilmot Proviso, which aimed to embargo slavery's expansion into the Mexican cession. In Whig caricature, he "thumped and bellowed" for Franklin Pierce in 1852 and, as a hardshell Democrat stalwart for southern rights, pledged to prevent the abolitionizing of the New York state party.[17] His conversion earned him a reputation as a "political prostitute" and "editorial 'confidence man.'"[18] Known, too, as a "notorious quack" (he was ready to lecture on any subject), he became during 1857 the traveling companion of Lola Montez, the infamous Irish Spanish dancer, courtesan, and former mistress of King Ludwig I of Bavaria.[19] Burr wrote her lectures and—probably—her autobiography. By then he had generally dropped the title "Reverend," though others continued to use it. His specific Protestant affiliation is unclear; spirit rappers and Catholics were among his targets.[20] By one unfriendly account he cast off his ministerial guise after his wife successfully obtained a divorce around 1850 "because he was a naughty Reverend—a wolf in sheep's clothing."[21]

Burr was in his mid-forties when war broke out. He belonged to a circle of New York editors and others sympathetic to the South, convinced that in time a strong peace party would emerge to halt Lincoln's rush to war. They included Gideon J. Tucker, Fernando Wood, and Wood's brother Benjamin, who edited the pro-secession *New York Daily News;* the editor of the equally conservative *Journal of Commerce*, Gerard Hallock; and John H. Van Evrie, publisher and editor of the *Day-Book*, a weekly trumpeting the superiority of the white race and the boon of slavery to black people.[22] Burr, the editor of the Bergen County *Democrat*, also contributed to the *Day-Book*. His incautious tongue invited several ugly public altercations and attempts at arrest. Soon after Fort Sumter, a New York Zouave officer heard him sympathizing with secessionists; in the ensuing quarrel, "the well-known *litterateur*" apologized and reportedly placated the crowd with champagne.[23] With troops mustering across the North, he was heard to say, "There's one of your d——d abolition Massachusetts regiments that went through New York this afternoon to fight the South. I hope every d——d one of them will have his throat cut before he gets through Baltimore." After the disaster at Bull Run, his name headed a New York peace petition suppressed by the police.[24]

Deemed dangerous and seditious by a grand jury, the *Day-Book*, the *Journal of Commerce*, and the *Daily News* joined McMaster's *Freeman's Journal* on the list of publications effectively shut down when from August 1861 they were denied use of the federal mail system. But they were not permanently suppressed. The city of New York remained, along with much of Ohio and other parts of the Midwest, nodes of acute hostility to the Lincoln administration. It was there above all that printing presses flourished by running on tanks of Copperhead ink.

THE DEMOCRATIC PARTY AND RELIGIOUS NATIONALISM, 1863

Vallandigham and his pro-peace Christian allies cast themselves during the early months of the conflict as prophetic nationalists grappling with Republican fanatics who turned "an eye of suspicion . . . upon every Democrat who does not bellow himself hoarse over this terrible war."[25] Confident that their day would come—once immeasurable gallons of blood and battlefield stalemate had brought the public to its senses—they saw the Democrats' fall election victories in 1862 as an essential first step toward restoring the old Union. "We have smitten the Philistines hip and thigh," Vallandigham exulted.[26] The polls left Lincoln's party in control of both the U.S. House and the Senate, but as we have seen, the combined forces of pro-peace insurgents and war-supporting, anti-emancipation conservatives delivered striking Democratic gains. The final weeks of 1862 and the early months of 1863 gave Democrats further hope that Republicans were digging their political grave by their irrational ideological fervor and mishandling of the war. Lincoln's second dismissal of McClellan, Burnside's catastrophic decisions at Fredericksburg, the final Emancipation Proclamation, an Enrollment Act introducing the first ever national draft, the ignominious defeat of Major General Joseph Hooker's forces at Chancellorsville, and the imposition by the military of loyalty oaths: collectively these fueled in equal measure the anger and political ambitions of conservative nationalists. Northern morale sank to one of its lowest points of the war.

In the event, both Republicans and Democrats found something to celebrate in the 1863 spring election results. Republicans rolled back some of the Democratic advances of the fall, but each of the Ohio cities where Vallandigham delivered his gospel of peace saw the triumph of the entire Democratic ticket. Enjoying his kudos, and with an eye on the coming fall elections, Vallandigham set about steering a path toward securing his party's nomination for governor. In April the commander of the Army of the Ohio, Ambrose Burnside, rashly threatened the use of military courts against any speaker or editor whose criticism gave comfort to the enemy. An order that empowered the military to identify the boundaries of legitimate dissent gave Vallandigham his cue. He engineered his arrest through a two-hour speech to a Democratic rally of defiant backcountry "Butternuts": settlers mostly originating from the South and so named after the tree dye that colored their clothes.[27] With military agents recording his words—a blend of contempt, insolence, and ridicule—Vallandigham called on his hearers, many wearing "Copperhead" pins, to abandon servility and topple "King Lincoln" from his throne. At 2:00 a.m. on May 5, a company of armed Union troops seized him after breaking into his Dayton home. A military commission found him guilty of disloyalty and sentenced him to imprisonment for the full term of the war.

Vallandigham's arrest, a key and compelling event in shaping the war's narrative, as told by conservative religious nationalists, gave Democrats a stunning propaganda coup. Here was incontrovertible proof that a tyrannical administration had replaced the Union's bonds of political affection with the chains of military rule. A violent backlash of protest rallies and assaults on Republican newspaper offices gave the Christian peace martyr precisely the outcome he had plotted. Although Lincoln shrewdly revised the sentence, freeing the prisoner and ordering his Federal escort into the Confederacy, by then Vallandigham's popularity had won him the Democrats' gubernatorial nomination. A month later he was in Canada, from where he conducted his campaign.[28]

"Valiant Val's" opponent in October, the man-mountain John Brough, had won the Unionist Party nomination through shrewd Republican management. As a former Democrat and staunch proponent of the war, and aligned with Lincoln's emancipation policy, Brough had the political talent to yoke enough war-supporting Democrats with loyal Lincolnites to secure a famous victory by 100,000 votes. Between the nominating conventions in June—when the momentum was firmly with Vallandigham—and the election itself, the decisive Federal victories at Gettysburg and Vicksburg had transformed the Republican-Union party's prospects. Vallandigham was also hurt by the deep animus against Peace Democrats in the Union army, whose Ohioans could vote in the field; he was probably damaged, too, by the false claims that he was behind New York's murderous anti-draft riots in July and had encouraged Lee's invasion of the North. Brough's victory came as euphoric relief to an anxious Lincoln. Ohio was part of a broader picture of Republican successes in the other midwestern gubernatorial races (Iowa, Minnesota, Wisconsin) and Pennsylvania.[29]

Vallandigham's fortunes in 1863 had a wider lesson. The Democratic Party was a fractious amalgam of purist peace advocates, who insisted (in the words of an Ohio editor) that "*he who supports the war is against the Union,*" and self-styled political realists, who believed that only by military force could the nation be saved.[30] Among these war-supporting Democrats were some willing to support Union tickets representing Republicans, too. The Ohio election was an example of the inevitable squeeze on the Democratic Party's electoral support when opposition to the administration and the Union party could be delegitimized as dalliance with treason, especially when, as in this case, the candidate was pro-peace. Yet the other, less immediately obvious feature of Vallandigham's October defeat was the sheer size of his vote, bigger than any previous count for a defeated or *successful* candidate in Ohio history. The 187,000 votes he secured suggested the power of party discipline and entrenched loyalties. They also testified to an ideological coherence among the base of loyal voters on whom Democrats could rely. War-supporting Democrats voted for Vallandigham despite his advocacy of peace at apparently any price. They berated him as divisive, but the mutual animosity of the two camps was over the means to the desired end of national reunion, not the character of the restored United States. A common religious dynamic—a shared conservative religious nationalism—informed the political and moral ambitions of both Peace and War Democrats.

The religious dimensions of the Democrats' nationalist faith were real enough but have been overshadowed in histories of the war by the Republicans' experience as the major political beneficiary of institutional Protestantism. In the 1863 Ohio race, for example, Brough won most of the Protestant vote. He was explicitly backed by Congregationalist, Methodist, and Mennonite authorities, as well as by the Catholic archbishop of Cincinnati, John Baptist Purcell, an antislavery thorn in the side of a predominantly anti-emancipationist Catholic Church. By contrast, Vallandigham's friends in the Old School Presbyterian ministry struggled to find pulpits from which to support him. Yet there is another side to the coin. The vast majority of Irish and German Catholics rallied to Vallandigham, as did many Protestants in Ohio's rural Butternut communities. Democrats throughout the lower Midwest enjoyed considerable minority support from churchgoers within most Protestant denominations; a similar pattern prevailed in the border states and other parts of the lower North, where Peace Democrats enjoyed their greatest support among anti-mission Baptists, Old School Presbyterians, and Disciples, churches whose members enjoyed strong cultural ties with the South.[31]

Sometimes the dissenters protested by simple reticence: ministers avoided taking the oath of allegiance or failed to pray for the nation and display the flag.[32] Some openly critical ministers were brought to trial and faced expulsion: Deacon Oliver H. McEuen of Pike County, Illinois, was expelled for allegedly preferring Democratic papers like *The Chicago Times* to the Methodists' *Central Christian Advocate* and advocating the exodus of every Democrat from the Methodist Episcopal Church into a new "conservative Church."[33] Church divisions were rife. "We are having some schism in the church," the young Illinois Methodist minister Leonard Smith recorded in May 1863, troubled by the strength of Copperhead sentiment. "Scratched the name of Thomas Austin off the Class Book. Has let the Devil & politics lead him from the right. Is an old rebel & slave admirer. Poor old sinner. Wants slavery perpetuated." A staunch antislavery member of the Union League who considered Democrats a "noisy dirty ignorant rabble," Smith found the going hard in parts of central Illinois, where clusters of southern sympathizers ("Dimmicrats") raised his blood pressure. He lamented that "politics are separating man & woman" within church communions, the effect of Copperheadism among those he described as "old hard shell Baptists" and anti-mission Methodists. More in hope than Christian charity he reflected, "It is some consolation that they are old and shortly may die & then better things will be accomplished."[34] Smith's experience exposed a common feature of church life in central and southern Illinois, where Baptist and Methodist ministers were more inclined than their congregations to favor abolition. John Van Buren Flack, a young United Brethren clergyman known to be a rare Democrat within the Illinois Conference, was on that account deluged with requests to preach by those who claimed not to have heeded any preaching for years, because "almost all the preachers were radical in politics." Flack became a favorite among poor rural congregations and believed his success in leading revivals and establishing new churches was because he avoided "questions gendering strife and dogmatic warfare, but preached the soul saving truth."[35]

The clergy and presses of the northern Catholic Church generally spoke with the Democratic voices of their congregations. From the perspective of Republican Protestants, those political loyalties bespoke the influence of deep border-state conservatism and anti–New England animus. The Chicago Methodist editor Thomas Eddy conceded that there were a few honorable exceptions to the general picture—Orestes Brownson, Archbishop John B. Purcell, and his brother Edward Purcell, the editor of the *Catholic Telegraph*—but he generally tarred Catholics as "intensely Southern in their character and sympathies, and bitterly hostile to . . . the 'Yankees'" on whom they blamed the war.[36] Protestant editors routinely played on suspicion of the Catholic faith and Vatican influence, stressing the Church's theologically and politically conservative instincts and ready acceptance of harsh social arrangements, including slavery, as necessary preparation for the afterlife.

This analysis bleached out the varieties of Catholic opinion, but it accurately identified the consistently Democratic orientation of most. The *New-York Freeman's Journal*, edited by the self-styled "Protestant-raised Democrat" James McMaster and reportedly read by a third of the country's priests, spoke with earnest Democratic outrage against the ongoing trauma of a war against southern brethren.[37] So, too, did John Mullaly's *Metropolitan Record*.[38] By contrast, Boston's Catholic newspaper *The Pilot*, owned and edited by the Irish-born Patrick Donahoe, accepted the necessity of bloodshed in the cause of reunion, but it, too, was staunchly Democratic. The chief organ of New England Catholicism, it loyally defended Archbishop Hughes's close relations with Seward and the administration, but warned against electoral coalitions with Republicans, which ran the risk of political obliteration. Donahoe insisted that reunion depended on following a pure Democratic road map: namely, nurturing loyal sentiment in the rebel South and removing abolitionist influence and maladministration from Washington.[39]

The Boston *Pilot*'s critique of Catholic antiwar campaigners was a dispute over means, not ends or the character of nationality. The paper defended Peace Democrats against charges of extremism: had their advice been heeded, there would have been no conflict. Fearless patriots, these antiwar Democrats had been incessantly at work to restore all the violated principles of the Constitution. Equally, they were right to assert that "from fighting, Union can never come." Yet, the editor insisted, in a contradiction that acknowledged the horns of his dilemma, there was no prospect of peace, surrender was impossible, and "the Republic must be preserved." One course alone remained: the coercion of the South. "This may be an inhuman proposition; but are we to let the Republic be severed, that is, destroyed? Never." The Lincoln administration had done unpardonable things but not enough to allow the nation to be perpetually subverted. "We are sorry to urge subjugation, but '*needs must*.'"[40]

The diverse religious voices of wartime conservative nationalism made a significant contribution to Democratic messaging and political mobilization, but their very diversity left their full potential unrealized. Democrats enjoyed nothing as powerful as the political benefit that mainstream Protestantism delivered to the Union-Republican party: a dynamic interdenominational mobilization in the name of national righteousness. Culturally embedded hostility to Romanism gave little hope that Catholics and anti-Lincoln dissenting Protestants would bond cooperatively as allies in the larger cause. Even so, and despite the abrasions between pro-peace and pro-war Democrats, the party's newspaper editors and politicians managed to weave the filaments of religious faith into a tapestry of conservative nationalism, using arguments that resonated with pious voters. *The Chicago Times*, the *New York Express*, the *Boston Courier*, the Philadelphia *Mercury*, and the *Cincinnati Enquirer* were typical of the urban presses that shared the explicit ambition of Samuel Medary's *Crisis:* to mobilize religious forces as effectively as did the Republican Party. To these prominent titles can be added many local newspapers whose Democratic editors ministered to their Christian readers' disgust at pulpit "fanaticism." Such, for example, was the role of the Episcopalian John W. Merritt's *Salem Advocate*, the Democrats' chief mouthpiece in Marion County, Illinois. Owners and editors of Democratic newspapers might be ministers themselves. The outspoken Illinois Methodist preacher Ira Norris bought *The*

Lacon Intelligencer in 1858 and made it into an out-and-out platform for Peace Democracy.[41]

EMANCIPATION

Religious conservatives met Lincoln's preliminary and final edicts of emancipation with a swirl of shock, anger, bewilderment, and disbelief. Their emotional outrage was palpable, fed and legitimized by preachers' and writers' rich polemic. After pledging to uphold the Constitution, they charged, the perfidious president had broken an essential bond of trust with his people and had launched a mad project to overthrow the historic Union of white men. The common humanity of black and white people did not make them equals, nor did it warrant an assault on slavery and the Bible that authorized the system. Here was the culmination—the climacteric—of that intrinsically despotic Puritanism that for generations had poisoned British and American life, and since the days of Jefferson had been the Democrats' nemesis.

Nothing better illustrates the interpenetration of conservative politics and religion than the strategic response to emancipation in New York, when in February 1863 prominent Democrats formed the Society for the Diffusion of Political Knowledge (SDPK). Over the next two years the organization would launch thousands of copies of polemical pamphlets, with each of its twenty or so titles embodying the conservative Calvinist and racial ideas of its septuagenarian president, Samuel F. B. Morse. Nationally eminent as a painter and inventor, Morse was the eldest son of the Massachusetts Congregational clergyman Jedidiah Morse and the brother of Sidney, the founder and pro-slavery editor of the conservative Old School Presbyterian *New-York Observer*. The SDPK's first meeting opened with Morse's statement of its purpose: to rescue stable government from the "widespread demoralization" of the public mind wrought by fanatics. Although they claimed the sanction of God's word, fanaticism was "a frenzy, a madness," that deceived simple folk by clothing "the spirit of the pit . . . in the garb of an angel of light." The new Democratic organization would uproot American infidelity in church and state by harnessing the thousands of "untainted theologians . . . who have not bowed the knee to the

Conservative Attack and Lincoln's Rejoinder, 1861–1863   221

abolition Baal." Morse's critics saw an irony in a New England Calvinist, former Whig, and staunch anti-Catholic acting as a Democratic cheerleader. But the Morse code in politics was consistently to fight on behalf of individual liberty and its conservative constitutional guarantees.[42]

Conservative nationalists, both Protestant and Roman Catholic, berated Lincoln the emancipating double-dealer. The New York Catholic and former U.S. congressman John McKeon, dismayed by the shocking treatment of constitutions as "simple parchments without any sanctity," attacked Lincoln's hypocrisy in telling Chicago ministers just before he issued the preliminary emancipation proclamation that an edict of freedom would be inexpedient and inoperative.[43] The *Metropolitan Record* chastised the president for going back on his pledges, abandoning the only moderate, conservative policy capable of rescuing the country, and rendering useless the vast resources "poured out for the *supposed* salvation of the Republic."[44] Boston Catholics grieved at the ugly truth behind this breach of trust: Republicans, after two years purporting to contend "for the Union, as it was, and as it ought to be," had all along aimed to prevent reconciliation, to launch an abolition war and its corollary, the "work of annihilation or ineffable disgrace on one side or the other."[45]

Whites' racial antipathies and ingrained belief in black inferiority, a mainstay of Democratic political ideology and rhetoric before the war, were essential drivers of the case against emancipation and the "design to overthrow the *White Man's Union*, formed by the glorious and immortal Washington," for a Union not worthy of the name, where "negroes should be amalgamated with the whites, and made equals."[46] No one expressed these convictions more assertively than Henry Clay Dean. "The negro race is tractable and capable of a superficial and limited improvement," he conceded, but "they have no capacity for the perpetuity of knowledge or the improvement of their offspring. An elephant may be taught the performance of the most extraordinary feats, but cannot teach them to its young; so may the negro receive knowledge from the white man, but will not impart it to his children." Jefferson and the founders had accepted that this made personal servitude essential when the races lived in proximity. Whites owed a duty of parental guardianship over the inferior race, with rules adapted to its dependent condition.[47] Candid James McMaster declared that the southern slave—"black as ink" and "marked by God Himself for inferiority in the social hierarchy"—would face destruction if ejected from "his Providential place."[48]

Religious conservatives accepted that the scriptures told of a single creation: all men and women, of whatever color, possessed souls. An Indianapolis Catholic acknowledged the Church placed "all humanity on an 'equality before God.'" Yet, he asked rhetorically, "who will assert, that the Church, as such, has ever attempted to place all men, without regard to races, on an equality, in social, political and civil positions?"[49] Similarly, the president of Dartmouth College and Congregational minister Nathan Lord, who had long recanted his former abolitionism, declared that there had been no voice in the course of God's Providence that "asserts the social and political equality of all the races; but the contrary is everywhere sounded out in tones that no reverent . . . believer can misunderstand."[50] The Episcopal bishop of Vermont, John Henry Hopkins, whose defense of slavery prioritized the evidence of primitive Christianity over modern moral sentiment, called the propositions of the Declaration of Independence fallacious dogma: God had given the races unequal capacities, decreeing that Africans should be childlike and dependent.[51] Black people themselves, it was claimed, recognized this reality. Contented in slavery, they had little interest in freedom or the chimera of equality. When planters quit their estates to avoid Union troops, the deserted black workforce would occasionally seek shelter in Federal camps, but "this is the full extent of their love of personal freedom." Slaves would either ignore the president's proclamation or soon "slink back" to their natural protectors.[52]

When a Democratic speaker pledged his life in the cause of peace and the old Union, "before the Great White Throne of my God," he could scarcely have been clearer about his racial prejudices.[53] The same held for a Pennsylvania protester charged with sedition for stating that God had "put a curse on negroes and Abe Lincoln had put himself above God by trying to remove that curse."[54] However, although racialized thinking was central to the assault on Lincoln's emancipation initiative, it was no more powerful a lever of persuasion and conservative mobilization than the scriptural case for slavery. As an arbiter of moral values and guide to right behavior, the Bible had no cultural rival in mid-nineteenth-century America.[55] Its precepts and example did more than merely decorate or rationalize firmly held beliefs about the character of the nation and its institutions. Rather, the scriptures had the power of a fundamental moral guide; they acted as a warranty and ethical guarantor in the ideological rough-and-tumble of political and cultural conflict. Vallandigham could say, without mental reservation, "I take the Bible and nothing but the Bible as my rule of faith and practice."[56] Drawing on the Bible as a pro-slavery handbook was, as we have seen, commonplace in the South before the war. In the free states, too, there was, as Lincoln put it, a squabble over its meaning. These inherited readings of Holy Writ gave razor-sharp edges to intemperate debates over emancipation. Biblical literalism authorized and sanctified racial prejudices and the social order built upon them.

The Catholic Church especially prided itself as a bastion of doctrinal traditionalism, political moderation, and social stability. It was the just boast of Catholic citizens, the *Louisville Democrat* purred, that "almost alone" among professed Christians, they had treated the slavery question with "marked conservatism." When dealing with the ills connected with enslavement, Catholics had followed the policy of the Holy Mother Church "by endeavoring to lessen these evils through means consecrated by God Himself in His revelation to man." McMaster gloried that the "Catholic Church, like her Divine Founder, seeks the eternal salvation of men. She wishes them, in this life, to be happy, or *otherwise*, according as the one, or the other, may best promote their *eternal* good. In things not in themselves a sin, as slavery is not, she leaves men to their own devices, and to their own arrangements." Neither canon law nor the Catholic commentators on civil law condemned slavery as sinful or contrary to natural justice. Their doctrines had not changed from the days "when our Lord commissioned his Apostles." Minority antislavery voices, like that of the *Catholic Telegraph*, disfigured their Church by linking it with "the infidel cradle" of the French Revolution.[57]

Although most northern Protestant churches, by contrast, scoffed at pro-slavery theology, a dissenting conservative minority took heart from sermons and tracts that defended human enslavement. Thousands of reprints of John Henry Hopkins's *Bible View of Slavery* were widely disseminated as an SDPK pamphlet; it won a greater audience still through the furious reaction it provoked within the Protestant mainstream, where a double-headed riposte circulated as a pamphlet of the Loyal Publication Society (the New York Unionists' answer to the SDPK).[58] A Philadelphia edition of *Bible View*—but with Hopkins's sympathy for secession deleted— took center stage in the Democrats' bid for the Pennsylvania governorship in 1863. Their candidate, Justice George W. Woodward of the state's supreme court, was an Episcopalian. By weaponizing the bishop of Vermont's pro-slavery tract, he alienated the vast majority of the Episcopal clergy of Pennsylvania, 160 of whom joined their bishop, Alonzo Potter, in vehement public protest against Hopkins's intrusion into their diocese to lend support to a partisan cause "unworthy of any servant of Jesus Christ." Only with great difficulty did the associates of an incensed Woodward prevent him from bringing a legal suit against Potter, "the cunning old fox who struts as Bishop."[59]

Nathan Lord's tract *A True Picture of Abolition* likewise argued the biblical case for slavery as a guarantor of social conservatism and moral government. It gave Democratic editors across the North a propaganda coup: here was the president of a distinguished New England college breaking ranks with the antislavery majority of the Congregational Church. Lord's political value was enhanced in the summer of 1863 when the Dartmouth Board of Trustees forced his resignation after he voted against giving Lincoln an honorary degree.[60] Democrats also actively promoted *Pulpit Politics*, the magisterial work of the Cincinnati journalist David Christy, which devoted six hundred pages to press the moral and scriptural case for letting slavery alone.[61] These themes surfaced regularly in Chauncey Burr's *Old Guard*. Although nearly every man that Christ encountered was either a slaveholder or one of the Roman Empire's sixty million slaves, the Savior never once denounced slavery as a sin. Yet, if he and his apostles were on earth now, "they would be denounced as 'traitors and sympathizers with rebellion.'"[62] With the punchy title "Why Christ Did Not Proclaim Emancipation," a *Quincy Her-*

ald article making a similar case was widely copied in the Democratic press.[63]

As self-assured scriptural purists, religious conservatives assailed the "wretched spouters" of fanatical abolitionism for their doctrinal perfidy. Having blamed antislavery insurgents for goading the South into rebellion and war, conservatives now castigated Lincoln's "Abolition despotism" for crushing slaveholders' constitutional rights.[64] At the heart of this madness they identified the ministers of antislavery churches and their editorial allies, unanchored and adrift from scripture and rationality. The prime culprits—notably Henry Ward Beecher, George B. Cheever, William Lloyd Garrison, Horace Greeley, Owen Lovejoy, Theodore Parker, Wendell Phillips, and Stephen H. Tyng—had succumbed to a "higher law" dogma lacking biblical authority and embraced the false religion of "negrophilism."[65] Nathan Lord grieved, "We have made God and man to exchange places: His institutes and His constitutions we have interpreted by the 'higher law' of our own conceits. We have converted the Sovereign Law Giver into a politician." Scripture told of God's judgment on the Israelites, whose commonwealth had been dismembered when its rulers rejected the divine law from "conceit of a higher wisdom."[66] Democratic presses capitalized "Valiant Val's" appeal to his party: "PATRIOTISM ABOVE MOCK PHILANTHROPY; THE CONSTITUTION BEFORE ANY MISCALLED HIGHER LAW OF MORALS OR RELIGION."[67] A Pittsburgh Democrat chided those who would appeal from the Constitution—the higher law in politics—to the higher law of religion, "for that is to appeal from the state to the church, from civil policy to ecclesiastical jurisdiction."[68]

It is hard to overstate wartime Democrats' bitterness at what they cast as Protestant Republicans' dictatorial temperament, galling assumption of superior morality, and self-righteous interference in the lives of others. They routinely deemed abolitionists the apotheosis of the "pestilential intermeddling with other people's business" that had characterized Puritan history. The nation, they grieved, had suffered from the chronic interference in the internal affairs of its separate states by "the six little busy, meddling, peddling and intolerant States of New England, and the pestiferous brood of

Puritan blood" that had emigrated westward.[69] Those antebellum animosities assumed more force and raised even greater alarm in wartime. The Philadelphia *Sunday Mercury* doubted if any confederation embracing New England could hold together: she was "too selfish . . . too intellectually conceited to subordinate her insane ideas of 'higher law' . . . and too meddling in other people's business." Catholic Democrats, with sharp memories of the antipapal violence and nativist political proscription during the 1840s and 1850s that had culminated in "the foul spirit" of the anti-immigrant Know-Nothing Party, saw in the Loyal and Union Leagues a continuation of the same Puritan ethos. James McMaster, flourishing a charge sheet of wartime outrages on Catholics, urged Archbishops John Hughes and John B. Purcell, "fast friends of Mr. Lincoln," to prevent a war against the people of the South becoming a war against the Catholic religion, too.[70]

Anti-Puritan emotions were no less intense among Protestant Democrats. Henry Clay Dean, a prewar Methodist campaigner against the Know-Nothings, blamed his arrest at Keokuk on squads of "Puritans and Roundheads," who "embraced the shouting Methodist and witch-burning Puritan, the Universalist and Unitarian, with every intervening class of Fanatics." Clement Vallandigham explained the war as a conflict of races, not of blood, but of mind, between the Liberalist and the Puritan, whose "narrow, presumptuous, intermeddling, and fanatical spirit" had spread its "chief fungus" of abolitionism across the North. No sustained philippic against Puritanism was more widely read than that of the Ohio congressman Samuel Sullivan Cox, whose New York speech to the Democratic Union Association in January 1863 served as an early call to arms for the 1864 presidential campaign. Sunset Cox—so called for his flamboyant description of the setting sun published in the *Ohio Statesman*—played to the gallery with a characteristically witty and entertaining address to fellow Peace Democrats. The Emancipation Proclamation, he declared, invited civil strife across the North. The "arrogant, selfish, narrow, and Puritan policy, now dominant in the Federal Government," would stoke resistance in the loyal central and western states, which would not bend to "the Constitution-breaking, law-defying, negro-loving, Phariseeism of New England!" Puritanism—the audience hissed at the name—was "bred in the bone. It is the same now . . . as the Tudors found it three hundred years ago, ever meddling for harm." Its character, he continued to applause, took "success for justice, egotism for greatness, cunning for wisdom, cupidity for enterprize, sedition for liberty, and cant for piety."[71]

Cox rejected the Puritans' "grand keynote" that slavery had caused the war and that "as men and Christians, we should extirpate it." Simply because "slavery was meddled with, and returned in violence what was given in wrath and malice," did not make slavery the *cause* of that violence. Among Democrats this was a familiar and comforting argument. Vallandigham made the same case the very next day in the House of Representatives, insisting that slavery was "only the *subject*, but Abolition the *cause* of this civil war."[72] Cox told his cheering audience that until dogmatic abolitionism arose, the Constitution and the Union had never been seriously menaced. Puritanism had introduced slavery into politics, and so Christianity "became a wrangler about human institutions. Churches were divided and pulpits desecrated. A certain class in a certain section were sinners and were damned forever." This new gospel had dissolved the glue binding civil society. Lincoln's edict had revealed how completely the poison of radical abolitionism had entered the bloodstream of the administration party. Those supporters of the president who contrasted necessity-driven wartime emancipation with Garrisonian radicalism fastened on a distinction without a difference: nothing really separated "the republicanism that sustains emancipation proclamations and the real old genuine Congo Abolitionism," he declared—and added, to thunderous applause and laughter, "They are two separate links of the same sausage made out of the same original dog."[73]

THE DRAFT FOR A "HARD WAR"

Under the terms of the Enrollment Act of March 1863 states unable to fill their assigned troop quotas with volunteers had the power to draft any shortfall. Conscription faced conservative opponents of the new emancipationist strategy with an unenviable choice: to accept the measure and take up arms for a cherished Union, but without endorsing the administration's change of purposes, or to resist the draft as declared pacifists. A devout German Lutheran of Wittenberg College wrote, "I may yet have to go into the ranks and fight against my will." He assured an abolitionist friend, a serving Ohio volunteer, "Don't think that I am a rebel. Oh! no! I am for the Union as it was, and the *Constitution as it is*." Not wishing "to do wrong," he was ready "in all my affairs to be Conscripted if I must be." In Christian resignation, he added, "Dear Friend! This is a wicked world and the great consolation we have that we do not need to stay here always. Let us then prepare for eternity and there enjoy endless bliss which is the highest thing that we aim after."[74]

Anti-conscription clergy were among the loudest champions of Peace Democracy. Making church ministers eligible for the draft—"to force priests to be bloodspillers"—they denounced as a gross violation of their faith.[75] Catholics complained that "Yankee cuteness," in exempting married men over thirty-five from the draft, gave Protestant ministers better chance of escaping service than their Roman counterparts, all celibates.[76] Political hostility to the war's radical purposes joined with personal self-interest to shape a sincere, if contingent, pacifism. William Paxson, an Illinois Methodist preacher and Douglas Democrat, a pro-war champion before the Emancipation Proclamation, changed course to join local Democratic leaders on the hustings in 1863. Charged by his conference with endorsing Copperheadism and defiance of the draft, he conceded only that he hated a radical policy that would unite the South and split the North: "Abolitionism and Secessionism" were equally destructive. The Lincoln administration, not he, had changed position. If Lincoln reverted to the original, limited war aims, Paxson declared he "would again take the stump for the same object."[77] He was acquitted.

The bloodiest resistance to the draft, the volcanic violence of the New York City riots during the week of July 12, 1863, left hundreds dead or injured and posed an unprecedented challenge to the authority of the Lincoln administration. The Conscription Act had hit New York's poor whites the hardest and subordinated the historic rights of city and state to unprecedented external power. Armed mobs blocked the enforcement of the draft, destroyed property, including an asylum for black orphans, and inflicted murderous assaults on the city's black population, the military, and the police.

To defuse this dangerous crisis, at the high tide of New York Copperheadism, Lincoln and Republican officials moved with shrewd caution. They avoided declaring martial law and worked with the city's conservative forces to press on with the draft. Lincoln's wise appointment to military command of John Adams Dix, highly respected by his fellow War Democrats and the city's elites, helped defuse the crisis.[78]

Orestes Brownson, a leading voice among the emancipationist Catholic minority, described "the immediate actors" in the bloody anti-draft riots as "almost exclusively Irishmen and Catholics."[79] In fact, the dominant narrative of Irish Americans during the first eighteen months of the war tells of their appetite to enlist. Joining brigades led by Thomas Meagher and other Irish nationalists gave them the chance to show how much they valued their American refuge; how wrong nativists had been to question their capacity for citizenship; and how keen they were to fight to uphold republican government. But the Emancipation Proclamation and the Conscription Act changed all that. Irish artisan craftsmen, industrial workers, and laborers alike in northern cities feared emancipation as a further threat to a competitive job market in which they were already locked with despised free blacks. And despite their reputation for valor, the Irish remained one of the most underrepresented groups in the Union army; the 1863 act fell on the Irish proportionately more than any other group.[80]

The powerful religious leaders of New York's Peace Democracy, chiefly Catholic, were tarred as key agents in provoking the terror. Through the *Metropolitan Record*, John Mullaly had in March encouraged opposition, armed if necessary, to the passing of the Conscription Act.[81] Troubled by his editor's incendiarism, John Hughes removed his own name from the newspaper's masthead, but many continued mistakenly to see the *Record* as the archbishop's mouthpiece. Chauncey Burr's *Old Guard* was just as inflammatory.[82] James McMaster, at a mass meeting of Peace Democrats in May, also invited violence, and in the midst of the riots Mullaly continued to incite resistance to "the most iniquitous measures ever devised by any Government."[83] The insurgents' profile gave force to abolitionists' assertions that Catholic priests had fostered among Irish workingmen "an infernal spirit in regard to the colored population." Equally, events prompted the conservative Episcopalian George Templeton Strong to lament that other cities had Irish, anti-conscription, and murderous mobs of the same type. "I would like to see war made on Irish scum, as in 1688," he raged. Taking the lines from a Catholic subversion of "Lillibullero," the Protestant march of the Glorious Revolution—"Now, now de [Yankee] Heretick all go down / By Christ and St. Patrick de Nation's our own!"—he delivered a fiery rejoinder: "Not altogether your own . . . my poor impulsive blundering misguided Keltic friend & brother! . . . You have done little good for yourself on your own national soil & we cannot trust you to rule us here in America."[84]

The shocking events in New York drove the Copperhead devout into a paroxysm of explanatory contradiction: condemning, excusing, and minimizing the racial violence. James McMaster proved an arch contortionist in argument. The violence, he agreed, was deplorable: "the unhappy negroes" had been the victims of misplaced wrath. But it had been preceded by a swelling number of outrages committed by the "semi-savage" black people of the free states, corrupted and fooled by New England abolitionist notions of freedom "to do whatever their brutal passions prompt them to do." What's more, armed black troops—"uniformed savages"—paraded insolently on northern city streets, encouraged by Frederick Douglass and other black recruiting agents, who demeaned the "All-wise Creator" with the blasphemy that "the negro and God had saved the country." At the same time, McMaster insisted, the violence was not the work of the respectable Catholic working class; he blamed a rabble of outsiders and regular Union troops who had fired on unarmed women and children. Besides, the force meted out by the excitable crowds was proportionate. They had "on their side the firm conviction of the most intelligent and the most law-abiding" that they resisted an unconstitutional conscription measure. Far more dangerous, by comparison, were "the lawless and revolutionary acts" of Lincoln and his agents. Playing on his readers' entrenched sectarianism, the editor condemned the resurgence of Know-Nothing Protestant contempt for the Irish and their religion. When first the war began, "Puritans and bigots drowned all other voices in lauding the Irish— 'the *dear* Irish! the *gallant* Irish' "—but now "the *Evangelist* gathers

Conservative Attack and Lincoln's Rejoinder, 1861–1863   231

up and distills the gall and venom of the *Post, Tribune, Times,* and other Abolition papers, against the 'Irish.' "[85]

The New York riots alarmed Copperheads but did nothing to dent their devotion to peace as a righteous cause. They pointed to the active role of clergy in restoring order once the initial violence against the draft officers—deemed a rightful expression of anger against dreadful injustice—had broadened into a general attack on life and property. Catholic priests persuaded rioters bent on destruction to attend meetings to discuss practical politico-legal means of challenging the draft and purchasing exemptions for the poor. The week ended with John Hughes's address to a massive crowd of five thousand workingmen. A phalanx of clergy at his side, the ailing archbishop declared his personal sympathy for the protesters. As a fellow Irish Catholic of humble origins, he called on them to pursue peaceful means and to end the destruction that tarnished their religion, their ethnicity, and the legitimacy of their cause. With the fury of the week now largely spent, Hughes's intervention proved well timed. The rioting came to a stop.[86]

The wartime Union harbored pockets of absolute pacifism. The principle that all war was incompatible with Christ's teachings led some Quakers, Mennonites, Moravians, and other religious minorities to refuse military service. Lincoln recognized the Friends' "very great trial" in having to contend with the irreconcilable imperatives of pacifism and fighting to free the enslaved.[87] The pacifism of most antiwar Democrats, by contrast, was contingent, not absolute.[88] Ministers known as enthusiasts for war with Mexico in 1846 were now horrified by "brethren imbruing their hands in each other's blood."[89] Still, pacifist biblical texts—frequently repeated in the Democratic press—gave ammunition to Christian dissenters against the "Holy War" of religious antislavery nationalists. Once freed from the "administration bastille" where he had been denied a Bible, Edson B. Olds told how he had been inspired by scriptural verses sanctifying peace: the prophet Isaiah's lauding of rulers for beating swords into plowshares and spears into pruning hooks, and Christ's blessing on peacemakers as the children of God.[90] He and his supporters did not so much renounce arms in general as eschew their use against southern brethren.[91] "Shall the churches heretofore consecrated to the God of Peace, henceforth ring with the cry of 'Extermination to every rebel'?" a Catholic asked, outraged that his Church be judged disloyal for preaching a pacific gospel to stem "the crimson tide which bedews the land."[92] At the June 1863 peace convention in New York, Fernando Wood lamented that beneath "the thousand spires . . . not one covers a pulpit devoted to the true principles of Christ."[93] The true glory of American nationality lay in peace.[94]

The conservatives' use of scriptural texts distilled a broader argument, that an "atheistic" spirit of revenge animated Lincoln's radical new strategy. The emancipation edict heralded an unchristian brand of warfare, a "hard war" waged to overthrow the Confederacy by targeting civilians and their property. McClellan, in his Harrison's Landing letter of July 1862, had offered the president a lesson in ethical conflict based on "the highest principles known to Christian Civilization." These sanctioned a war against armed forces and political organizations but not the general population; there must be no confiscation of property, political executions, or forcible abolition of slavery.[95] Pious Democrats lashed the administration and its pulpit supporters for bloodlust. "Instead of feeding your people with *the bread of life*,' you feed them with blood and gunpowder," scolded Chauncey Burr. "Your appetite for blood is not yet appeased. You are the leeches without bowels, that ever cry, *more!*"[96] The emancipation decree surely prefigured a bloody slave insurrection.[97] Scandalized by Francis Lieber's doctrine that belligerents forfeited municipal protection, James McMaster asserted that "Christian ethics have settled it that you cannot plunder the *private property*, of the *people* of States with which you go to war. Christian civilization has made the *people* of all Christian States brethren. Attack *governments*, attack *armed forces*, but the non-combatant *people* are not the spoil of any power."[98] David Quinn, a Chicago lawyer and spiritualist, thought diabolical forces alone explained the end of a Union founded on mutual assent and its replacement by a coercive military state.[99]

The sheer bellicosity of the Union pulpit and what Vallandigham called its "Gospel of Hate" confirmed Peace Democrats in their ethical superiority.[100] How could prayers for God's help in destroying "the rebellious race root and branch" and blotting them

Conservative Attack and Lincoln's Rejoinder, 1861–1863   233

"from the face of the earth" be squared with followers of the Prince of Peace?[101] William Gannaway Brownlow, Methodist polemicist second to none, shocked religious conservatives by his enthusiasm for unrestrained warfare and arming African Americans. "The true Union sentiment of the country calls for the putting down of this hell-bound rebellion at any cost of human life," Brownlow insisted. "And if we had the power . . . we would arm and uniform, in Federal habiliments, all the fowls of the air and the fishes of the sea—every wolf, panther, catamount, and bear in the mountains of America— every tiger, elephant and lion in Europe [natural history, manifestly, was not Brownlow's forte]—every rattle-snake and crocodile in the swamps of Florida and South Carolina—every negro in the Southern Confederacy, and every devil in hell. . . . We would convert hell itself into one great *torpedo*, and have it exploded under the very center of the Confederacy. Aye, we say put down the rebellion . . . if, in doing so, we have to exterminate from God's green earth every living human being south of Mason and Dixon's line." Aghast, one Democratic editor remarked, "The author . . . is confessed to be a minister of the gospel, and yet we are sending missionaries fifteen thousand miles to convert the heathen!"[102]

The administration's embrace of a hard war gave its pious critics a further line of ethical attack. By indefinitely extending a ruinous conflict, Lincoln had licensed what Sunset Cox called the "insatiate cupidity" of Yankee merchants, manufacturers, military contractors, and speculators, as well as the officers and men of plundering armies.[103] Material enrichment, not righteous purpose, explained the appetite for war. "There is no virtue of which such mercenary use is made as patriotism," Patrick Donahoe noted sardonically, as he watched Union Leagues spreading across the North during the early months of 1863. The stated purpose of these associations was to save the Union, but their real aim, he insisted, was "a continuation of power to those who now enjoy it, and of contracts to those who hold them."[104] James McMaster quoted Fernando Wood's charge that "New England favors the war, because, having lost a valuable customer in the South, she finds a profitable substitute in army contracts and government disbursements."[105] On the national fast day in April 1863 the Indiana Methodist minister and Democrat Samuel Chamberlain claimed that Union generals were fighting not for the country "but for the money they are making out of this war." John Van Buren Flack extended the charge to include opportunistic military chaplains who, he maintained, had confiscated southern civilians' treasures—silks, china, items of gold and silver—and sent them home for their loved ones.[106] Never a friend of understatement, Henry Clay Dean asserted that since the fall of Babylon "no such corruption, depravity and crime ever scandalized any city or country, as the gathered contractors, spies, pimps, thieves, office-hunters, office-holders, speculators, stock-gamblers, peculators and prostitutes of Washington city."[107]

William Krauss, Lutheran farmer and the chair of the board of education in Leipsic, Ohio, exemplified Copperheads' anguish over federal corruption. His letters to his son William directed a tirade against profiteers of all kinds. Scoundrel army contractors he berated as "dishonest scamps" who "prate like asses, union union"; but "union with them means offic[e], & money; they care nothing about the country . . . [and] rob even the dead." Union Leaguers had no wish for peace, for without war "who could steal the cotton & cheat the nation out of milions"? Army officers were "a set of unhung raskles, who . . . do the bid[d]ing of tyrants to be promoted & to gain greenbacks." Krauss grieved over his son's abolitionism but was at least sure a devout Lutheran upbringing had instilled correct principles: the young William could not become "the tool of men who have no other motive than to make money out of the misery and ruin of our country." As for himself, "if I . . . could obtain by dishonest means, money, honor & a great name in the world . . . I could not look an honest man strait in the face, but shame has fled from the American people & therefore we have so many who disregard everything honest, upright, respectable, & even sacrifice their peace of conscience, & their prospects of a future life."[108]

To the charge of the moral bankruptcy of conscription and a hard war, religious conservatives added its strategic folly. A strategy of destruction would bloodily protract an unwinnable struggle. In his defiant farewell speech to the House of Representatives on January 14, 1863, Vallandigham endeared himself to Peace Democrats countrywide by charging Lincoln with the certain failure of his "war for the negro." After six thousand years of human history (by scriptural calculation) that had exposed the folly of every form of government, "it was reserved to American statesmanship, in the nineteenth century of the Christian era, to try the grand experiment . . . of creating love by force, and developing fraternal affection by war!" History would record its utter, disastrous, and most bloody failure.[109] Patrick Donahoe could see only the indomitable spirit of the South: "While a Southern man remains, there will be a Southern will that cannot be conquered." Archbishop Hughes's outspoken support of conscription and reinvigorated warfare to end "this draggling of human blood" put him at odds with most of his bishops and clergy.[110] James McMaster found in the last monarch of the United Kingdom of Israel, the headstrong Roboam (Rehoboam), a damning scriptural lesson of a leader who would not compromise with those mistakenly branded traitors. The Hebrew king—like the occupant of the White House—had foolishly obeyed a "higher law" party by "putting his foot down firmly." Deaf to God's command to be reconciled with the separating Ten Tribes of Israel, Roboam had resorted to a hard war that simply cemented the national fissure.[111] A New Orleans correspondent of McMaster's *Freeman's Journal* told of a South undaunted by the Federal armies' trail of destruction. "Talk not of a reconstruction of the Union by subjugating the people of the South. . . . Destroying our plantations, stealing our negroes, and burning the dwellings and outhouses on the plantations does not tend to increase our desire to re-unite politically with a people who approve of so barbarous a mode of warfare." The best route to reunion lay in withdrawing Federal forces and leaving it to "the Almighty Ruler, who will do all things for the best."[112]

Collectively, these arguments from Christian principle gave a shield of righteousness to those who demanded an armistice or truce between the warring parties as the prelude to peace and reunion. Among them was the Illinois Methodist minister Ira Norris, an outspoken editor in Marshall County Democratic politics. When the state legislature's Copperhead majority passed an armistice proposal, he led demands for a national convention "to adjust the difficulties now pending." Norris's high political profile gave rise to a formal trial by the Methodist authorities. His acquittal prompted his friends to remark drily that it had been "considered possible for a Democrat to go to Heaven, and so Mr. Norris was not expelled from the church."[113]

RIGHTS OF THE CHRISTIAN CITIZEN

As mentioned earlier, Vallandigham and the scattering of other early religious critics of the war venerated as sacred the democratic rights of Christian freemen: only local political autonomy would protect personal liberty and private conscience against intrusive centralized power. The administration's adoption of an emancipatory "hard war" persuaded many of Vallandigham's previous critics to recast him as Christian prophet and fearless champion of individual rights. Swelling numbers of religious conservatives now augmented the vanguard of peace advocates who had suffered imprisonment during the first year of the war. Those like John Mullaly of the *Metropolitan Record*, previously willing to give Lincoln the grudging benefit of the doubt, spat their fury at measures that wrote into the history of the nation "the blackest record the world has ever seen." The president's pernicious course had defied "the great conservative majority of the North." No longer the servant of the people, the administration had become their military master. An autocrat in all but name, Lincoln had assumed no less power than "that which the Czar of all the Russias possesses."[114] Fulminating against a treasonous president, an Indiana Catholic cast him as "a Cromwell *minus* his craft; a Bonaparte, lacking his magnanimity; an Arnold, destitute of his bravery."[115] The Union's autocratic turn, an Ohio Lutheran shuddered, "foretold a 'reign of terror.'"[116] The soul of the nation was at stake.

Aghast at the diabolical constitutional subversion of emancipation, the *Metropolitan Record* turned its fire equally on the Conscription Act, "the most deadly blow that has yet been aimed at the liberties of the people." Overriding state sovereignty, and treating state governors as mere ciphers, the act's unconstitutional assault on citizens' rights would rend asunder "like so many cobwebs" the voluntary links that, by the wisdom of the founders, had bound the states into a "majestic aggregate of free federated republics."[117] A despairing Philadelphia Democrat asserted that all rational people knew that the war had become a mere abolition crusade, destroying the Union as a means to an end, and that "federalism has been beaten down and is dead."[118] A president contemptuous of individual liberties and a willing instrument of the abolitionists, Lincoln warranted impeachment. His administration had made the liberty of the white man "of secondary importance to that of the negro." He had put a choke on free speech, shut down newspapers, suspended the writ of habeas corpus, and quietly looked on when, by arbitrary arrest, citizens had been "dragged from their homes at the dead hour of night and flung into government bastiles."[119] William Krauss was sure that Lincoln—"King ape the great of N. America"—had authorized balloting in the field to manipulate the army vote and cling to power.[120]

"Personal liberty, in any sense of the word, is a peculiarly Christian idea," James McMaster declared. "It has its birth in the idea of the value of the individual man, of the worth of the human soul." The *Freeman's Journal* made contention over this fundamental right the crux of the war. The North had sided with the "pagan idea" that "the man was nothing; the Empire, the State, was all in all"; it had entered an ideological death struggle with the animating motives of the South and northern peace advocates, dedicated to "State rights, the rights of minorities, the rights of individuals, and the eternal principles of true liberty."[121] In similar vein, Henry Clay Dean asserted the primacy of "rights older than elections, for the protection of which elections are held, which they cannot destroy and dare not invade." More sacred than constitutions, these rights constituted the essential elements of manhood. Without them, citizens would be "idiots, lunatics and imbeciles, who tamely yield to the will of their keeper." They could be suspended only by the fiat of the Deity.[122]

Through their devotion to protecting citizens' rights through local autonomy, Peace Democrats ministered to conservative nationalists' religious faith. They saw local patterns of order and authority as divinely imposed constructs, to be reverenced and protected as expressions of God's will.[123] Threats to localism were threats to sacred order. Christianity had introduced into the world a new code of political life, one that made freely given consent the only foundation of lawful government. "It has created a *Christendom*— a Christian Republic, composed of all who accept and follow Christian teachings," McMaster explained. Here Christian freemen governed themselves; rulers served only as their agents. "Except for those that, by birth, or by consent, are slaves, there exists in no . . . set of men, the right to impose their will, or their rule, on any community of men." The editor delivered a Christian call to arms, one charged with characteristic racial prejudice: "Resolve, in your local organisations, to *die* sooner than permit your inherited rights and liberties to be taken from you! If not ready for this, spare the race of white men the disgrace of your tame surrender. Go, ink yourselves all over, and get up in the shambles and ask some one to buy you!" The Illinois coal miner Peter Mulvany, one of McMaster's many western subscribers, prayed for God's blessing on a newspaper he venerated as "the zealous advocate of His holy religion, and of the rights of man." In that spirit, Fernando Wood's peace meeting at Cooper Union in April 1863 asserted the right of the people to "the sacred and imprescriptible writ of *habeas corpus*"; Horatio Seymour, governor of New York, likewise declared the arrest of Vallandigham an offense against "our most sacred rights."[124]

These conservative nationalists yoked religious and civil freedom. Religious liberty, Henry Clay Dean explained, "with all of the hallowed rights of the conscience, draws its entire support from civil liberty."[125] Typically, Nathan Lord deemed the "organic law" synonymous with the law of God.[126] Consequently, the lay and ministerial loyalists of the Union-Republican party, by equating political platforms and absolutist religious belief, and imposing political tests of faith, imperiled the combined freedoms of a people providentially chosen to enjoy them. Vallandigham, the most prominent and eloquent among a grand army of critics of the political pulpit, insisted that partisan preaching injured both church and state; it meant "an end of all purity and usefulness in the ministry, and . . . of religion also." The minister's primary duty, he told his clergyman brother, lay in expounding "the *whole* Bible from Genesis to Revelation . . . to build a system of faith or rules of practice."[127] Pious Democrats commonly believed that antislavery concerns—together with temperance, Sabbath observance, and other questions of private morality—were matters unfit for legislation. Republicans were in grievous error in imposing their antislavery views "to determine by political legislation, questions that among a free people do not belong to politics."[128]

Protestant Republicans had faced this kind of censure ever since the party's emergence during the 1850s, but devout Democrats' resentment at the moral arrogance of a "political priesthood" assumed new intensity in the polarized climate of wartime. Demo-

Conservative Attack and Lincoln's Rejoinder, 1861–1863 239

cratic editors lamented how party allegiance and unquestioning loyalty to Lincoln's regime had become the only true measure of Christian faith. "Men do not go to Heaven by majorities," Samuel Medary scoffed, nor did Saint Peter "sit at the gate to count up election returns." Besides, the Republicans' faith evinced a terrible falling away from gospel truth into "babbling" politics. "In the apostolic day preachers were willing to suffer privation, toil and death for the sake of Christ." Now they "suffered" for greenbacks and the folly of abolition. Once preachers read the Bible, but now political newspapers. Once they preached peace, now war. Once they thanked God for a free country, now Lincoln for bastilles and dungeons.[129] Conservative religious nationalists' belief in their own righteousness, superiority, and innocence accompanied a sense of their role as victims of ungodly persecution.

Through disciplinary trials, proscription, and a predominant ethos of high-octane Union loyalism, mainstream Protestant churches subjected pious Democrats—especially those tinged with Copperheadism—to oppressive scrutiny. Democratic preachers faced an invidious choice: subtly to rebuke Republicans' political preaching by pulpit silence on all things political, or to speak out and invite the charge of hypocrisy, double standards, and disloyalty. "We could not remain silent and be in peace; we could not speak without censure and vile abuse following," one minister later explained. "If we used moderation, we showed treason; if we condemned unjust arrests in private, the same were published on the house tops." Disciplinary charges abounded across the Midwest. William Blundell, an Illinois Methodist preacher and Jackson Democrat, was tried for treason for consorting with a pro-Confederate rabble-rouser, John Powderhorn. Enos Errick of the North Indiana Methodist Conference, an unequivocal War Democrat at the outset, was by the spring of 1863 a furious critic of the Lincoln administration; following a church trial he joined the Evangelical Lutherans. Eleven Methodist preachers chose to leave the Central Ohio conference when faced with the charge of disloyalty by voting for Vallandigham. John Van Buren Flack, who kept in his pocket a likeness of "Valiant Val," rebuked Republican ministers for their diabolical gospel that "loyalty to the government atoned for all sin" and that "if bad men, with blackest stains and foulest oaths upon their lips, fell in the defence of the north, they would as certainly be saved as there was a God in heaven." After he was confronted by "the powder and smoke" of so-called vigilance committees and accused of muted patriotism by his mostly Republican congregations, Flack's health gave way. To preempt public humiliation by the church authorities, he resigned his ministry. Scores of similar disciplinary hearings, expulsions, and withdrawals affected the principal denominational families—Baptists, Methodists, and Presbyterians.[130]

In their rhetorical assault on the moral abomination of the Republicans' brand of nationalism, religious conservatives blended outrage and sheer incomprehension. Many saw the course of the wartime Union as a form of madness, a barely explicable delirium. Heads shaken in bewilderment partnered fists clenched in anger. The historic anchorages of the Union and the foundations of American republican power had yielded to the national nightmare of a militarized, tyrannical state driven by a self-righteous and demented religious sectarianism. When William Krauss's abolitionist son attempted to persuade his father of the bravery of the African American troops in battle, he was told that he had surrendered his power of reason: "You are certainly tinctured some with the notions of abolitionism you hear nothing else, you read nothing else your manhood is gone." No grounded, honest man could ally with antislavery insanity. "I would rather see you dead," Krauss senior wrote, "than sanction such damnable acts of these hellhounds of abolitionists, yet I have suffered enough by their acts, they killed your brothers & they will kill you too." Another reported his despair and mystification at the willful destruction of community cohesion in Ohio by the abolitionist provost marshals directed "to spy out the liberties of the people. . . . [M]y blood boils with indignation when I contemplate the state in which the once free people of America are placed." A Catholic writer treated the malign ideological force at work in the North as "a mental and moral epidemic" to which "weak minds and disordered imaginations fell an easy prey." This was the "hell-born plague" of abolitionism, which scrambled the sense of right and wrong, and led crazed victims into attempting "to rectify the work of the Omnipotent, and to abrogate the laws of nature as if they were those of the United States." These "plague-smitten monomaniacs" clung to their error as the drowning wretch did to a straw.[131] A Brooklyn physician, Gustav Braeunlich, told a peace gathering that there was an authenticated sickness "called political insanity, as was in the times of the Crusaders . . . , which must be treated like physical insanity. And the diseased patient must be deprived of dangerous weapons."[132]

"The nation is unquestionably mad," asserted David Quinn. A Chicago lawyer, Quinn attributed the country's bewilderment to the mesmerizing, or magnetic, effect of demons working on the minds of spiritualists and religious sectarians. The philosophy of these spirits, he maintained, "assumes as a fundamental ideality, that all things are intrinsically equal, and susceptible of continual and endless development, until they reach the standard of Deity." The mental infection caused by this harebrained political theory explained the nation's grotesque and self-destructive course, and "why the sun of American greatness is rapidly sinking in a sea of fraternal blood." A perverted president had been selected by diabolical spirits to achieve "the equalization of white men and negroes." He boasted conclusive evidence that the chief executive, members of his cabinet, and supportive editors held "spiritual circles" in the presidential mansion. "Mr. Lincoln is not only a spiritualist of the abolitionist school, but . . . has been, from the beginning of his term, directing the war under the direction of spirit rappings." In this, claimed Quinn, he was supported by, among others, Salmon Chase, Ben Wade—whose wife he took to be one of the best mediums in Ohio—and Joshua Giddings, all of whom had "for years been consulting the rappings." As if this were not enough, the president's demented administration had appointed a trance lecturer "ready at call to serve his excellency, as the witch of Endor served the Hebrew king, to bring forth the spirits of the dead."[133]

ARTISTIC AND SATIRICAL ATTACK

To the modern ear, Quinn's commentary has an element of comic satire. In his own era, however, such was the grip of spiritualist ideas that there is no reason to doubt they were his sincerely held beliefs. Nor need we question the earnestness of the more widespread conviction that frightful diabolical forces strove to shape human affairs. In the binary Christian cosmos of God and the devil, many believed Satan to be as active a presence in the world as the Almighty. In the words of a New York lawyer, John McCunn, "We have the great Jehovah of Peace on our side . . . our enemies are in league with the destroying angels of battle."[134] When conservative publicists used literary or graphic modes of political approval or attack, their work commonly sprang from, or at least acknowledged, these religious and cultural ideas.

The earnest Christian verses of aspiring political poets flavored the columns of the religious press. Typical of these was a submission to the *Freeman's Journal* by one Louisa Flanders of Malone, New York. Confident that Vallandigham's arrest was shameful in God's eyes, she took up her pen:

> *Vallandigham! the God whom thou dost serve,*
> *For every ill the tyrant heaps on thee,*
> *"His red right arm" with vengeance dire will serve*
> *To smite the foes of Right and Liberty.*
>
> *Vallandigham! wise, noble, brave and good!*
> *Honored of all whose hearts round Freedom twine;*
> *We'd sooner make thy garb, unstained by blood,*
> *Our God, than yield one nod at Lincoln's shrine.*

Poets encouraged Vallandigham's champions to occupy the moral high ground:

> *I'm not an Abolitionist! I am content to be*
> *Just what the ancient patriarchs were, And saints of high degree;*
> *To follow where our fathers led, To kneel where they have knelt,*
> *And ask that over all our land God's blessings may be felt.*
>
> *I'm not an Abolitionist! O, no! I only claim*
> *With Christians, men of every creed, To write my humble name*
> *With theirs who, by the Golden Rule, All men their brethren call,*
> *Nor judge, nor sneer, nor taunt, nor hate, For evils great or small.*[135]

Cruder in tone and language were many of the Democrats' campaign songs and poems. Notorious were those compiled by Feeks & Bancker, whose New York publications fed the appetite of their antiabolitionist white readers for choruses that demeaned the black race. Their *Copperhead Minstrel*, first published in 1863, ran through several editions. Songs to fit the meter of familiar tunes celebrated the "White Soldier" and denigrated "Massa Linkum" and the "Fight for the Nigger." Verses of "The Flag of Democracy" (set to "The Star-Spangled Banner") and "A Prayer for Liberty" (to the tune "America") called on God to "save our wretched land, From Lincoln's traitor band." They celebrated an idyllic past:

> *How peaceful and blest was America's soil,*
> *Till betrayed by the guile of the Puritan demon,*
> *Which lurks under Virtue, and springs from its coil*
> *To fasten its fangs in the life-blood of freemen.*[136]

No son of Puritanism was more vilified than the minister of Plymouth Church, Brooklyn:

> *There was a queer parson named Beecher,*
> *Not of Christ, but of bloodshed, a teacher;*
> *It was always a trifle*
> *Whether—Bible or rifle,*
> *Wrought the aim of this blasphemous preacher.*[137]

"The War-Demon's Song" cast the war as "Hell's carnival," whose feast of anguish, blood, and death fed a satanic appetite: "The Demon is happy today." In similar vein, the haunting tune of the popular Victorian ballad "Lord Lovell" provided the accompaniment to "Old Abe and Old Nick":

> *'Twas one wintry night, Abe Lincoln he lay,*
> *Resting his weary head,*
> *Strange stories to tell, the devil appeared,*
> *And unto Abe Lincoln he said—said—said,*
> *And unto Abe Lincoln he said—*

If you sell me your soul I'll make you king,
  And destroy your countaree.
"It's a go," said Old Abe, almost out of breath,
  A man of my word I will be—be—be.[138]

The theme of Lincoln's diabolical liaisons would be taken to a sulfurous extreme by Chauncey Burr, who saw the "criminal assaults" on liberty as proof that there were "legions of devils" in the dictatorial president and his party.[139] In an imaginative satire—"Cooking the Hell Broth"—Burr made Lincoln a satanic "wizzard," instructing three devil-possessed Shakespearean witches, the secretaries of Treasury, War, and State: Chase, Stanton, and Seward.[140]

Chase: *Double, double, toil and trouble,*
Fire burn and cauldron bubble;
Round about the cauldron go,
In the poison'd entrails throw
Copperhead that under stone
Of prison walls we've killed alone,
Heart of patriot, red and hot,
Boil thou in the charmed pot.

Seward: *The* Habeas Corpus *put it in,*
It is the charm by which we'll win . . .
Nor let free-press the cauldron 'scape,
Nor form of girl from negro's rape . . .
And freeman's tears and blood I'll get
From the dark cells of Lafayette . . .
Stir the fire and make it bubble,
Altars, Bibles, and such stubble,
Will make the cauldron fiercer bubble,
For a charm of powerful trouble
Must the hell-broth boil and bubble—
Our strength is in the people's trouble.

Lincoln: *O, well done, I commend your pains,*
And every one shall share your gains;
And now about the cauldron sing,

> *Like human devils in a ring,*
> *Accursing all that you put in . . .*
> *When shall the Cabinet meet again,*
> *In fraud, corruption, or for gain?*

> Stanton: *When the hurly-burly's done,*
> *And our battles* are not *won.*

> Seward: *When the country's lost and done—*
> *When sinks in blood its setting sun—*
> *And Time's decree its doom unrolls,*
> *And Satan's contract claims our souls.*

The core elements of the Democrats' brand of religious nationalism took graphic form in the work of the illustrator Adalbert John Volck. A German-born dentist of Baltimore, Volck produced dozens of etchings for Copperhead subscribers, published as *Sketches from the Civil War in North America*. In the best known of these, *Writing the Emancipation Proclamation*, Lincoln is portrayed as a diabolical agent. He sits at a table whose legs have satanic cloven feet and at whose corners are African heads with rams' horns. His pen dips into an inkwell held by a devil. On the wall is a satirical portrait of Saint Ossawatomie (John Brown, with halo), holding a palm of peace and a pike, and a picture of the massacres of Santo Domingo. The back of Lincoln's chair is carved as an ass's head; looking down at the president is a statue with a baboon's head. A drink decanter offers the gorilla emancipator courage in this act of constitution-trampling fanaticism.[141]

Volck gave prime place among his sketches to an elaborate image titled *Worship of the North*. It gave imaginative expression to the common Democratic inquiry, whether "our fellow-countrymen of the North are willing to erect an altar dedicated to the freedom of the black race, on the ruins of the only temple ever consecrated to the liberties of the white race."[142] Volck offers an apocalyptic representation of the Union's war as a diabolical betrayal of the Christian religion. Two shining lozenges, emblazoned "EGO," frame the top corners, to indicate that untrammeled and undisciplined individualism has led the Union disastrously astray. The North's political and

Adalbert John Volck's etching *Writing the Emancipation Proclamation*

Adalbert John Volck's etching *Worship of the North*

religious leaders idolize a black figure squatting on the Republican Party's antislavery Chicago platform of 1860. The cloven-footed altar is inscribed "The end sanctifies the means" and bears the head of a devilish Lincoln. Puritanism is the foundation stone of a sacrificial block whose upper tiers incorporate the fanatical creeds of the North that New England had spawned: atheism, rationalism, witch burning, socialism, spirit rapping, and free love. These mad corruptions of true religion are capped by the headstone, "Negro Worship." A slaughtered white man is offered up as a sacrifice. Henry Ward Beecher wields the knife, his action illuminated by a blazing torch held by Charles Sumner. A separate pedestal supports a revered statue of John Brown holding a pike. The emancipationist commanders John C. Frémont and David Hunter are among the worshippers. Other generals include Henry Halleck, who brandishes slave manacles in one hand and an emancipation ax in another; Winfield Scott, who holds a blunted spear and wears preposterous headgear (a nod to his nickname, Old Fuss and Feathers); and Benjamin F. Butler, who has belted to his waist a bag labeled "B F B 2,000,000," an allusion to his reputation as a war profiteer. A praying Harriet Beecher Stowe kneels on a copy of *Uncle Tom's Cabin*. Horace Greeley swings a censer emitting smoke, the product, it appears, not of purifying incense but of burning snakes. A reptile crawls through a skull. The figures of Secretaries Seward and Stanton denote the sanction of Lincoln's cabinet. A group of prosperous and well-fed loyalists cluster around an illiterate sign, "The holy armee of Contractors PRAISE THE[E]"; a banner demands "MORE BLOOD." In the distance a ruined church, with a vulture circling above, signals the willful destruction of orthodox Christianity. The ghostly image of an apocalyptic horseman rides across the sky.[143]

How influential was this extreme Democratic political and graphic abuse of the Union administration? There are no means of quantifying the public reception, though it is clear that some of the boldest expressions of Copperhead intransigence and fury—McMaster's *Freeman's Journal* and Burr's *Old Guard*—circulated widely beyond

New York, into the Midwest and lower North.[144] It is evident, too, that the New York publishers of the most scurrilous attacks on emancipationists and racial egalitarians found it commercially as well as politically profitable to minister to popular prejudice against African Americans and the mad "Puritanism" of their white allies. What was indisputably true was the force and breadth of the mainstream Democratic critique of the war's direction under Lincoln's leadership. Conservative nationalists' assault on the administration laid the groundwork during 1863 for the ultimate electoral test of Democrats' faith-driven politics in the following year's presidential contest. As we shall see in the next chapter, these themes would invigorate partisan critiques of the administration throughout 1863 and 1864 and encourage some to turn Lincoln's fast and thanksgiving days into a political jousting ground.

LINCOLN AND THE DEMOCRATS

Throughout 1863, Lincoln's course was buffeted by the violent political passions generated by the contending forces of religious nationalism. The dramatic upturn in the fortunes of the Federal armies from the midpoint of the year encouraged a degree of composure. He responded to the Democrats' assault through reasoned rejoinder in a series of public letters that addressed the key issues of civil liberties, emancipation, and race. At the same time, he sustained his well-being and equilibrium by recourse to a pertinent, if unusual, therapy: David Ross Locke's devastating satire at the expense of Copperheadism and its religious dynamic.

Public expressions of anger at Vallandigham's arrest in May included resolutions passed by Democrats meeting in Albany, New York. Sent to the president by Congressman Erastus Corning, they attacked the administration for suspending the writ of habeas corpus, suppressing free speech, and placing military orders above the processes of civil law. In a public letter of almost four thousand words dated June 12, Lincoln the lawyer delivered a point-by-point, uncompromising rebuttal. Since he privately disapproved of Vallandigham's arrest, the president broadened the issue to consider the question of civil liberties and the executive's constitutional power in time of rebellion. Later the same month, he responded in kind to the demands of a Democratic state convention in Columbus, Ohio, for the revocation of Vallandigham's banishment.[145] In both letters Lincoln asserted his constitutional right to suspend habeas corpus and sanction military detention in time of rebellion. His legal arguments were in some respects questionable, particularly the claim that anyone "who stands by and says nothing, when the peril of his government is discussed . . . is sure to help the enemy."[146] But his political touch was typically deft. He rebuked the Albany meeting for preferring "to designate themselves 'democrats' rather than 'American citizens.'" During a time of national peril, he wrote, "I would have preferred to meet you upon a level one step higher than any party platform." Regarding Vallandigham's arrest, he inquired, "Must I shoot a simple-minded soldier boy who deserts, while I must not touch a hair of a wiley agitator who induces him to de–sert?"[147] Answering his own rhetorical question, Lincoln wrote, "I think that in such a case, to silence the agitator, and save the boy, is not only constitutional, but, withal, a great mercy."[148]

The administration's supporters lavished praise on the Corning letter for its felicity of message and tone. An admiring Philadelphia lawyer claimed it had "utterly routed" the peace forces, "traitors in disguise."[149] The loyal editor John W. Forney boasted that he had almost committed it to memory: "God be praised the right word has at last been spoken by the right man, at the right time, and from the right place. It will thrill the whole land."[150] As head of the Loyal Publication Society, the jurist Francis Lieber proposed that it publish ten thousand copies of the "sterling" letter. It is probable that Lincoln's reply to Corning reached some ten million readers across the political spectrum.[151] The Indiana banker and comptroller of the currency, Hugh McCulloch, told Lincoln that the letter united all men "not on the side of The Rebels."[152]

Like McCulloch, the president understood that loyalty to the Union united both Republicans and the majority of Democrats. His aim in responding to the Albany resolutions had been to reach across party lines. His letter foregrounded points of shared purpose. Distilling the "propositions" of the petitioners, he noted their pledge "to support the administration in every constitutional, and lawful measure to suppress the rebellion." Although they had censured his administration over its military arrests, his critics' concerns showed they were "eminently patriotic." Between him and them there was agreement on fundamental purposes; they differed only over means. Lincoln gave thanks that "not all democrats" occupied the lower ground of party prejudice. Vallandigham had been arrested and tried by a Democrat (Burnside); the judge who refused to discharge him "on Habeas Corpus, is a democrat of better days than these, having received his judicial mantle at the hands of President Jackson." More telling still, "of all those democrats who are nobly exposing their lives and shedding their blood on the battle-field, I have learned that many approve the course taken with Mr. V. while I have not heard of a single one condemning it."[153]

To work its influence among the party's opinion formers, Lincoln's senior secretary John Nicolay sent the president's reply to several war-supporting Democrats. They included the U.S. congressman Edward Haight of New York, pleased that "the men of peace proclivities . . . squirmed under it and are prudently silent." Daniel S. Dickinson told Lincoln that his letter would be "admired for its clearness and good sense, until Martial Law shall be abolished by the ushering in of the Millennium." According to Hiram Barney, Democratic leaders in several midwestern cities made a lot of noise, but "the great majority are with the Administration and disposed to support the President in a vigorous enforcement of the laws against Copperheads."[154] Lincoln knew that, whatever their criticisms, most Democrats would continue to support the Union war effort. The Washington insider T. J. Barnett told his fellow Democrat Samuel Barlow in June 1863 he was sure "the President apprehends nothing from the Peace Party. He looks upon it as an amalgam of the elements of discontent in New York, and of folks apprehensive of the personal effect of the Conscription Act . . . and he thinks that 'it will give the Democrats far more trouble than it will anybody else.'" Barnett himself reviled Copperhead "partizans" for "carping and yelling about dead issues, or the secondary one of Constitutional law, which will keep well enough, till we have the power to settle it." With undisguised pleasure he reported Lincoln saying "he . . . will keep on 'having at the Rebels' [Peace Democrats], wholly satisfied that New York demonstrations are Pickwickian, and that his head will not be brought to the block. He thinks the Rebels the biggest fools in the world, as well as knaves. Says 'Mrs. Grundy will talk'—

Conservative Attack and Lincoln's Rejoinder, 1861–1863 251

but that, after all, she has more sense than to scald her own a[rs]e in her *own* pot."[155] This bawdy use of a social stereotype—the narrow-minded community tyrant—has the authentic stamp of Lincolnian earthiness and gives credibility to Barnett's account.

In defending the draft and the suspensions of the writ of habeas corpus, Lincoln's letters met his critics on their own ground of public safety and citizens' constitutional rights. His approach was above all lawyerly, careful, and earnest. Less narrowly so was the letter he wrote for a vast September meeting in his home city of Springfield, an event designed to reverse the 1863 surge in Illinois Copperheadism. The prospect of an Emancipation Proclamation had given a political blood transfusion to the state's Democrats before the fall elections of 1862: thus invigorated, they won control of both houses of the legislature. The New Year's Day edict produced a spike in desertions from Illinois regiments, a spate of peace resolutions intended to fan nationwide discontent, a choke on the state's war financing, and plans to neuter Governor Yates's military powers. When Yates responded by proroguing the "treasonous" legislature in June, Democrats organized a giant Springfield rally that achieved national reach through its out-of-state celebrity speakers, including Sunset Cox. To recapture the political initiative, Illinois Republicans planned a giant gathering that, by including some War Democrats, could be sold as a "Great Union Mass Meeting." Its organizers included the president's long-standing personal friend James C. Conkling, who, more in hope than expectation, invited Lincoln to attend. After giving the idea serious consideration, Lincoln decided, "I shall give them a letter instead; and it will be a rather good letter."[156]

Lincoln had for some time been pondering how to persuade doubtful Unionists to embrace emancipation and the use of black soldiers. When Frederick Douglass visited him in early August, he found the president impressively fluent in defending his policy toward "the whole slavery question and especially . . . to employing colored troops."[157] The Springfield rally on September 3 gave him a timely opportunity to reach a mass audience. He would ask Conkling to read his letter aloud at the meeting, before its national circulation. "You are one of the best public readers," Lincoln wrote. "I have but one suggestion. Read it very slowly. And now God bless you, and all good Union-men."[158] The tens of thousands who gathered in the state capital that day heard what stands as Lincoln's most sustained and eloquent defense of the policy and principle of emancipation, an unqualified answer to those who feared that he would renege on the proclamation in the face of costly political attack. What they heard was a cast-iron declaration that the edict "can not be retracted, any more than the dead can be brought to life."[159]

As in his Corning letter, Lincoln's text is shaped by a lawyer's pen. His primary target was not the loyal Unionists at the meeting but the Democrats who opposed emancipation and either were outright peace men or were vacillating in their support of a war of expanded aims. Peppering them with the forceful and aggressive questions that were his stock-in-trade in legal interrogation, Lincoln anticipated his critics' objections: "You desire peace; and you blame me that we do not have it. But how can we attain it? There are but three conceivable ways. First, to suppress the rebellion by force of arms. This, I am trying to do. Are you for it? If you are, so far we are agreed. If you are not for it, a second way is, to give up the Union. I am against this. Are you for it? If you are, you should say so plainly. If you are not for *force*, nor yet for *dissolution*, there only remains some imaginable *compromise*." But no compromise was possible that would maintain the Union. In this way, Lincoln repeated the key thrust of his Corning letter: that only by unity and doggedness in pursuit of military victory would the common aspiration of Democrats and Republicans be realized and the nation be again made whole.

At this point Lincoln's argument took a new direction. "But, to be plain," he said, "you are dissatisfied with me about the negro." Sharpening his practical reasoning with an ethical edge, Lincoln the lawyer pulled on a moralist's mantle. "Quite likely there is a difference of opinion between you and myself upon that subject. I certainly wish that all men could be free, while I suppose you do not." Yet he had neither proposed nor adopted "any measure, which is not consistent with even your view, provided you are for the Union." The proclamation, he insisted, was constitutional: slaves were property that a commander in chief could order taken in time of war to hurt the enemy. Military commanders in the field, including those neither abolitionist nor Republican in politics, believed that the use of black troops constituted "the heaviest blow yet dealt to the rebellion." Lincoln continued, unrelenting, "You say you will not fight to free negroes. Some of them seem willing to fight for you; but, no matter. Fight you, then, exclusively to save the Union." With deadpan dry humor he conceded that whenever they had "conquered all resistance to the Union, if I shall urge you to continue fighting"—this was preposterous, of course, once the emancipatory war had been won—"it will be an apt time, then, for you to declare you will not fight to free negroes." Securing the enlistment of "colored troops" depended on incentives: "Negroes, like other people, act upon motives." To ask them to "stake their lives for us, they must be prompted by the strongest motive—even the promise of freedom. And the promise being made, must be kept." The solemn, even sacred, pledge of emancipation could not be revoked.

Lincoln concluded with a passage that oozed contempt for those he had described in an early draft as dealers in "utter humbuggery, and falsehood," though he used more temperate language in his final text. Registering that peace appeared less distant than it had, he looked ahead to the likely postwar reckoning. Victory would have proved that in a democratic republic "there can be no successful appeal from the ballot to the bullet." Beyond that, "there will be some black men who can remember that, with silent tongue, and clenched teeth, and steady eye, and well-poised bayonet, they have helped mankind on to this great consummation." Yet, he continued, in fierce reproof, "I fear, there will be some white ones, unable to forget that, with malignant heart, and deceitful speech, they have strove to hinder it." Ministers of religion might here have spoken of righteous and unrighteous parties. Lincoln himself was more theologically circumspect but equally certain that in contention were right and wrong, justice and iniquity. In this same vein, invoking the power of justice, he drew to a close. An earlier version had invoked "a righteous God," but Lincoln altered his text to urge faith in "a just God, [who] in his own good time, will give us the rightful result."[160]

Conkling told the president his letter had sparked "the greatest enthusiasm" in Springfield. Read the same day in Syracuse, New York, it galvanized Unionists at their state Union convention.[161] The Union-Republican machine swiftly set to work. Printed in newspapers and pamphlets across the North, the document gave new vigor to antislavery religious nationalism. Emancipationists hailed its political force, Christian nobility, and moral severity. "Those who believe in Providential agencies will more than ever believe that Abraham Lincoln is a chosen instrumentality for this hour," an Ohio editor remarked, praising his "voice of salvation."[162] Indiana Methodists, devoted to an emancipationist president, resolved in conference that they had "more confidence in his practical wisdom and sagacity *now than ever before.*"[163] Maine Unionists told Lincoln his letter had swelled their majority in the September gubernatorial election.[164] The White House mailbag included tributes from Massachusetts. "May Almighty God bless you," Henry Wilson rejoiced. "Your noble, patriotic and christian letter will be on the lips and in the hearts of hundreds of thousands this day."[165] The veteran Josiah Quincy, recalling the founders' compromises over slavery, celebrated God's delivering the deathblow to human bondage through His instrument, Lincoln, "a subject of special glory, favor & felicity."[166] The collector of the port of Boston, John Z. Goodrich, told the president he heard "but one opinion expressed by the best men . . . 'it is Capital.'" Lincoln's severe words and sharp distinction—"the black man trying to save, & the white man trying to destroy his Country"—would fittingly punish race-baiting Copperheads, who "must feel that they are compared to the Negro quite to their disadvantage."[167] In fact Goodrich seriously underestimated the tenacity of Copperheads' white-supremacist dogma. Burr's *Old Guard* saw in Lincoln's naked Springfield address the climax to the wicked program he had pursued since his special message of July 1861, "*to elevate the condition of men,*" including black men.[168] At the same time, however, Goodrich's reaction exposed the unbridgeable chasm between the polar expressions of religious nationalism, emancipationist and conservative.

Those who promptly published the Springfield letter included David Ross Locke of Findlay, Ohio, the owner of *The Hancock Jeffersonian* and a journalist who held a special place in Lincoln's esteem. An upstate New Yorker by birth, Locke moved to Ohio in 1853, aged twenty, where he edited a succession of small-town papers before buying the *Jeffersonian* in 1861. He had been a Methodist class leader and exhorter, but in Findlay he joined the First Presbyterian Church, whose minister, James Meeks, preached an uncompromising Republican gospel. Locke was not deeply religious—over his life he moved from an evangelical to a more liberal Protestantism—but the influence of an antislavery father and equally devout mother left its mark. He found a natural berth among the minority of bold racial egalitarians within the young Republican Party. He was as good as his word: appalled by "infamous . . . prejudice against color," he refused to join the strike of white Cleveland printers unwilling to work on equal terms with a qualified African American. His first encounters with Lincoln—at the Quincy debate with Douglas in 1858 and in Columbus, Ohio, the following year—gave him easy access to a figure he enthusiastically supported for president. He was, though, no uncritical admirer. In one of their private conversations Locke expressed surprise that Lincoln had spoken out against black suffrage and racial intermarriage. Lincoln's explanation, that Republicans were electorally vulnerable on the issue of race, made sense to the purist Locke: "Hence his halting at all the half-way houses."[169]

The *Jeffersonian* under Locke's editorship took a hard-line Unionist stand on the war, acted as a candid and occasionally critical friend of the administration, and gave its enthusiastic support to Lincoln's emancipation policy. Hancock was a bellwether Ohio county. After a Democratic clean sweep in the fall elections of 1862, a fierce contest beckoned in the following October. As the absent Vallandigham wrestled with Brough for the governorship, and the campaign took an occasionally violent turn, Locke engaged in a constant war on "traitors" who talked of further secession to align West and South. He targeted Copperhead clergy and opened his columns to Ohio soldiers' red-hot anger at Butternut complicity in an "unholy rebellion." He summarized James Meeks's "masterly" campaign sermon on the incontrovertible Christian duty of ensuring that governments "accorded with Right." When Hancock played its part in Brough's stunning victory and reverted to complete Unionist control, Locke rejoiced, "Glory! Glory! We've met the Enemy and Scalped Him! The World, the Flesh and the Devil met in a square fight and whaled!" Vallandigham's crushing defeat, he wrote, marked a new era. "Let the friends of civil and religious liberty take fresh courage, and go on until the Republic is not only saved but purified."[170]

Lincoln reciprocated Locke's admiration. He appreciated the *Jeffersonian*'s firm Unionism, naturally, but it was not its editorial line that made him a huge fan. Locke's unique achievement lay in the powerful satirical weapon he fashioned to revile Copperheadism. His regular columns over the name Petroleum V. Nasby accompanied the newspaper's more orthodox political critique of Vallandigham and the Peace Democrats. The middle initial stood for "Vesuvius," a tribute to his insuppressible and caustic eruptions on the issues of the day. The fictional Nasby was a Copperhead loudmouth, the Christian pastor of "a strikly Dimekratic Church," founded in an imaginary Ohio village crossroads in June 1862, where for the rest of the war he preached an antiblack, proslavery gospel of peace. By the summer of 1863 it had been named the "Church uv St. Valandygum" (sometimes "Vandaldigum"), and later that year the "Church uv the Slawterd Innocents." It would reach its apotheosis in January 1864 as the "Church of the New [or "Noo"] Dispensashun."

Locke had firsthand experience of Copperheads' baleful religion. His church, First Presbyterian, split when Pastor James Meeks fell victim to the antiabolitionist Democrats who controlled his purse strings; Locke and other Republicans helped him set up a new, Congregationalist church. At the same time, Locke fashioned the egregious Nasby to embody the prevailing Unionist stereotypes of "yellow Butternut preachers" and their congregations of religious backsliders, typically branded as traitors "whose principal distinguishing characteristics are whisky-drinking, Sabbath-breaking, . . . and utter disregard for law from God or man."[171] In Locke's fertile imagination Nasby became the quintessence of the impregnable Copperhead villain, "a sort of nickel-plated son of a bitch"—dissolute, drunken, greedy, unprincipled, bigoted, hypocritical, dissembling, and sordid.[172] To present the pastor as the antithesis of the morally self-improving Protestant, Locke uses nonstandard spelling to indicate Nasby's vernacular usages and ill-educated speech—a frequent device in the comic writing of the era. Fundamentally feckless and lazy, Nasby rules that fast days require moderation in others but are "void in the case uv peepil over 35 and invalids, who may hev their sustainin floods ez usual." He plunders his congregation through coercion and outright cheating. He hankers after lucrative political jobs, above all the plum of a "post ori-fis."[173] The Trinity devoutly worshipped in his Copperhead citadel is a Confederate-sympathizing political trio: Fernando Wood of New York, Jesse Bright of Indiana—expelled from the U.S. Senate for acknowledging Jefferson Davis as president of the Confederacy—and the martyred Vallandigham, "who went to the stake with a kamness onparrallelled fer prinssipple." Nasby sanctifies resistance to both the draft and the arrest of southern sympathizers. Standing by the "rychusnis uv the Suthrin coz," he encourages the "mob-bin uv Methodis, Presbyterin, Luthrin, Brethrin and uther hetrodox churchis."[174]

The motors that drive Nasby's religion and politics are racial animus ("a holesum prejoodis agin evrything black") and pro-slavery fervor. Locke uses Nasby's scriptural illiteracy to mock the exegesis of Bible passages that pro-slavery theologians had pressed on audi-ences North and South: Noah's curse on Ham's son Canaan; Paul's instruction to the fugitive Onesimus; and the return of Hagar, the runaway Egyptian slave girl. Nasby's services begin by reading "one uv the follerin passages uv Skripter:—9th chapter uv Jennysis, wich relates the cussin uv Canaan, provin that niggers is Skriptoorally slaves, and the chapters about Hayger and Onesimus, wich proves the Fugitive Slave Law to be skriptooral." The preacher adds par-enthetically, "The rest uv the Bible we consider figgerative, and pay no attenshun to, whatever." Locke, the racial egalitarian, through-out uses Nasby's uninhibited recourse to the word "nigger" to ridi-cule its ubiquity in Democratic rhetoric and highlight the weight that racial issues carried in the Copperheads' appeal. Reflecting on how "Dimocrisy" could best keep the people "strung up the proper pitch," Nasby concludes, "Nigger is all the capital we hev left."[175]

Locke created Nasby in the belief, he explained, that he could "kill more error by exaggerating vice than by abusing it . . . until the people saw those errors and rose up against them." Locke's biting satire, by one verdict, etched the Civil War in sulfuric acid.[176] Nas-by's eruptions first appeared in the *Jeffersonian* in 1862 and through the system of newspaper exchange reached a huge and appreciative audience in New England, much of the Midwest, the West Coast, and even parts of the upper South. *The Nasby Papers*, a compila-tion of previously published letters and sermons, appeared in 1864.

Their subscribers ranged from conservative Unionists to the radical readership of *The Liberator.* The Philadelphia *North American* welcomed Nasby as an agent in crystallizing "right public sentiment."[177] Charles Sumner thought it "impossible to measure their value. Against the devices of slavery and its supporters, each letter was like a speech, or one of those songs which stir the people." The commissioner of internal revenue, George S. Boutwell, memorably ascribed the ultimate success of the Union cause to three forces: the army, the navy, and *The Nasby Papers.*[178]

Lincoln was an avid reader of Locke's alter ego. The editor visited the president twice during the war. Their first meeting followed Lincoln's invitation. "Why don't you come to Washington and see me? Is there no place you want? Come on and I will give you any place that you ask for," Lincoln wrote, prudently adding, *"that you are capable of filling—and fit to fill."*[179] Locke found the president "very much pleased" with the Nasby letters and kept a selection to hand "to read them on all occasions to his visitors, no matter who they might be, or what their business was. He seriously offended many of the great men of the Republican Party in this way."[180] Charles Sumner, who described Locke as Lincoln's "favorite humorist," recalled an occasion when the president took the pamphlet copy of Nasby from his desk and read it to him, "with infinite zest, while his melancholy features grew bright. It was a delight to see him surrender so completely to the fascination." The president repeated to Sumner the tribute he had expressed to Locke himself: "For the genius to write these things I would gladly give up my office."[181] Lincoln's personal copy of *The Nasby Papers* (held in the Library of Congress) is singed by candle flame, testifying to the nighttime comfort its reading brought him. Lincoln's good friend Leonard Swett believed the president read Nasby "as much as he did the Bible."[182]

Gentle humor at the expense of rustic religion and its ill-educated, enthusiastic practitioners had long been a staple of Lincoln's stories. The imaginary Nasby, however, offered him much more than scriptural bathos, absurdity, and simple jokes, though their delivery in the "shattered orthography" of what is known as eye dialect certainly appealed to his love of wordplay. What above all appealed to Lincoln, in Locke's judgment, was the savagery of the satire on pro-slavery religion. Lincoln admired the genre and had tried his hand at it. As an adolescent he had an aptitude for satiric bite.[183] Later Lincoln won admirers among his male acquaintances for a rough, obscene, and cutting satire—"The Chronicles of Reuben"—which dwelled on sexual inadequacy. Later still, sarcasm, anonymous scurrility in the newspaper press, and a sharp tongue— "the power to hurt"—punctuated his writing and political exchanges as a state legislator. In 1842 he contributed to a series in the *Sangamo Journal* at the expense of James Shields, the state auditor and a Democrat. In crossing the line from political satire to derogatory personal assault, Lincoln laid himself open to Shields's challenge to a duel, one avoided only by the good sense of the seconds and the ludicrous conditions Lincoln himself set. Deeply embarrassed, Lincoln never again essayed satirical writing, though his appetite for reading it remained as sharp as ever.[184]

As pro-slavery theologians grew in confidence during the 1850s, Lincoln turned not to satire but to scorn and dry wit. In a private memorandum he scoffed at those such as Frederick A. Ross, New School Presbyterian minister of Huntsville, Alabama, a former emancipationist who in *Slavery Ordained of God* had declared, "Slave-holding was one form of God's righteous government over men."[185] Lincoln provided a brutal summary of pro-slavery orthodoxy: "It is better for *some* people to be slaves; and, in such cases, it is the Will of God that they be such." The fact that the slave was never asked for his opinion, and that divining God's will was left to Ross, who "sits in the shade, with gloves on his hands, and subsists on the bread that Sambo is earning in the burning sun," invited the ironic question: Would he "be actuated by that perfect impartiality, which has ever been considered most favorable to correct decisions"? With rare exclamatory emphases, Lincoln continued, "But, slavery is good for some people!!! As a *good* thing, slavery is strikingly perculiar, in this, that it is the only good thing which no man ever seeks the good of, *for himself*. Nonsense!" Pro-slavery theology upended the prophet Isaiah's vision of universal harmony among all living creatures ("the wolf shall be the guest of the lamb"). "Wolves devouring lambs, not because it is good for their own greedy maws, but because it [is] good for the lambs!!!"[186]

Lincoln's relish of the satirical Nasby, Locke was sure, derived from his hatred of "horrible injustice. . . . Weakness he was never

Lincoln's "Fragment on Pro-slavery Theology" [October 1, 1858?]

ferocious with, but intentional wickedness he never spared."[187] One judgment stands out among the recollections of those who knew Lincoln best, that he made the polestar of justice his guide. Billy Herndon told of his law partner's "*will* that justice, strong and unyielding, shall be done, where he has got a right to act"; Joseph

Gillespie deemed his friend's "love of justice & fair play . . . his predominating trait"; David Davis was in no doubt that "Justice was Lincolns leading characteristic." In wartime, this feature fused with increasing reflection on the ways of the Almighty, an interventionist Providence, and divine justice. In the words of his friend Leonard Swett, "As he became involved in matters of the gravest importance, full of great responsibility and great doubt, a feeling of religious reverence, and belief in God—his justice and overruling power—increased upon him. He was full of natural religion. . . . He believed in the great laws of truth, the rigid discharge of duty, his accountability to God, the ultimate triumph of right, and the overthrow of wrong."[188] In concluding that Lincoln especially valued *The Nasby Papers* for their assault on injustice, Locke saw what others did and at the same time recognized a moral soulmate. Both men despised the unjust pro-slavery philosophy of Copperhead Democracy.

In part, Lincoln turned to Nasby for therapy. Humorous stories and jokes were, he acknowledged, "the vents" of his "moods and gloom," a means of temporarily lifting the heavy weight of responsibility under which he labored. But he also detected in Locke's abominable creation a powerful weapon. Like many others, he believed that satirical assault could crystallize support among those ambivalent toward the administration, as well as the already well disposed, even if it had little or no power to effect the conversion of souls resolute in their political perdition. As with his own letters to Corning and Conkling, Lincoln believed that Locke's written words had the capacity to change the course of public opinion for the better. The president's overtures to the forces of conservative religious nationalism would, however, do little to erode the underlying bedrock of the Democrats' political support. Indeed, the opposition party would remain confident about its election chances for much of the following year. An ongoing challenge to the embattled administration would be to sustain the zeal of antislavery religious nationalists while the Union armies, at deadly cost, ground down Confederate resistance in the field.

CHAPTER 8

LINCOLN IN THE TEMPEST OF RELIGIOUS NATIONALISMS, 1863–1864

As the toll of war mounted, Lincoln faced the daunting challenge of sustaining popular support for a conflict he had redefined as the cause of human freedom. We can now see that the Confederates' prospects of permanent separation never fully recovered from the severe reversals at Gettysburg and Vicksburg in July 1863 and the further setbacks at Chattanooga later in the year. It is also clear that the North's burgeoning war economy, industrial strength, and superior manpower were drivers of its ultimate victory. But these counted only as long as the public continued to accept the burdens of war. As the Union armies under Grant engaged in an attritional Virginia campaign during the summer of 1864, suffering fearful losses in their labored advance on Richmond, the Confederate command read into the desperation of northern voices the opening for a truce. The immeasurable gallons of blood that crimsoned the soils of the Wilderness, Spotsylvania, and Cold Harbor fueled an appetite in the North for a negotiated peace.

Naturally, Lincoln grasped that maintaining Union morale and inspiring the war weary, under a system of regular democratic elections that took the public pulse, were indispensable to ultimate victory. We shall see how, throughout the second half of the war, the

Lincoln in the Tempest of Religious Nationalisms, 1863–1864   263

president's multiple days of national worship for fasting or thanksgiving aimed to stiffen collective purpose. They made Lincoln's term of office unique in American presidential history, by his promoting an intersection of church and state that was unprecedented in its power and has not been repeated in that way since. At the same time, alongside Copperheads' clamor for peace, a countervailing nationalist resolve won over many key religious conservatives to the strategic value of emancipation. And, holding firm to his course, Lincoln could rely on one uniquely powerful force to help deliver an antislavery nation: the Federal army.

THE "HALF WAY CLERGYMAN":
THE PRESIDENT AS AN AGENT OF PROVIDENCE

Lincoln's allies as the champions of a renewed Union included legions who grounded their civic loyalty in religious faith. As president, Lincoln was peculiarly, even uniquely, privy to the rich complexity and ideological range of the nation's Judeo-Christian traditions. His formal meetings, informal encounters, and correspondence involved exchanges with men and women of all types and vocations. Among the myriad political and military leaders, ministers of religion, bankers, newspaper editors, writers, farmers, and plain working people whose communications swelled the White House mailbag, or who called in person, were hundreds whose religious convictions, forcefully expressed, gave meaning to the nation's battle for survival. They looked to a president who—they had good reason to believe, following the emancipation edict—recognized his role and duties as an agent of Providence. Throughout the final two or so years of the war Lincoln's faith in an omnipotent God became the common drumbeat of his well-publicized proclamations, public remarks, and private interviews. His religious convictions did not make him the born-again Christian that many believed he was or wished him to be. Like the majority of those who then attended Protestant worship, he was a church "adherent" but did not claim the experience of conversion that entitled those "blessed with the Holy Spirit" to enter into full church membership. Even so, the president was widely honored as a man of God whose faith made him the perfect instrument of the Almighty.

A scattering of those who contacted the president at various times throughout the war were eccentric religious visionaries, unwitting feeders of Lincoln's appetite for the absurd. Such was the letter purporting to be from God himself, through the hand of His medium Lydia Smith ("stopping at Mrs. Fitzgerald's 476 Pennsylvania Avenue"), that summoned the president to a divine seminar on how to end the war. Likewise, when Elias Gove, as the Almighty's self-appointed agent, audaciously told Lincoln to become king, summon a global congress of churches, and pay him $25,000 for his services, the president classified his letter "Foolery." A year later, when Gove raised his demand to $1 million, Lincoln correspondingly upped his verdict to "Crazy-man." A certain Samuel Cornell reported God's wish that Lincoln give him the reins of government, to let him take Richmond "with 2500 horsemen armed with Revolvers only," lure the rebel leaders to Washington, and confine Davis and his associates as lunatics in the U.S. Capitol. "Crazy," Lincoln wrote, an evident understatement. George F. Kelly cast himself as God's messenger: "The Angels, Showed me how God would destroy . . . [the enemy's] power and Save the Nation." Imploring the president to let him "render Service unto our Government *Without price*," he offered this prediction: "As the first Jesus was crucified as sure shall the Second (as Gods Servant) Save the 'world' through this Nation and with it go on to Glory." Lincoln read his correspondent's "wild" words with some bemusement, jotting on the envelope "a vision."[1]

These were fanciful and wholly untypical outliers. The scores of church conventions, synods, and annual meetings that peppered the president with memorials and resolutions from early 1863 to the end of the war delivered a more anchored orthodoxy. They represented every major Protestant tradition, evangelical to liberal, from all sections of the Union. Some expressed the certainties of a local congregation, but most spoke for their state, regional, or national communities. If no institution could match the boast of the Methodist Episcopal Church, the country's largest denomination, that it was the loyal voice of almost seven thousand ministers and a million members, other major religious bodies were equally determined to avow the breadth and depth of their patriotic resolve. The German

Lincoln in the Tempest of Religious Nationalisms, 1863–1864 265

Reformed Church clerk who sent Lincoln the memorials of its general meetings told him, with scant consistency, that the ministers valued actions, not "flaming resolutions and *buncombe* speeches." But in practice, like other denominations, German Reformed leaders fashioned declaratory statements of patriotic solidarity.[2]

As they had done from the outset, Lincoln's correspondents continued to clothe him in the mantle of Providence—an article of Calvinist faith—but now with that certainty cemented by the emancipationist turn of the war. His Chicago friend the lawyer J. Young Scammon exulted that by Almighty God "you have been raised up to accomplish so great an end. It is a great thing to be the Instrument in the hand of Providence, in regenerating our Country."[3] A female correspondent knit him a scarf emblazoned with the American eagle, a token of her faith in his providential destiny to pilot the ship of state through the tempest.[4] Officers of the African Civilization Society declared that "the living God" had raised him up "in the wisdom of Jehovah."[5] Even the less pious readily invoked Providence. The arch-fixer Simon Cameron knew that efforts to stop Lincoln's reelection would be fruitless: "You are in the hands of Providence—the people are His agents—and the Devil and all his imps cannot take Pennsylvania from you."[6] As Cameron implied, however, deference to Providence was no argument for passivity. During the prelude to the fall 1864 elections in Indiana, a state that prohibited balloting in the field, John Defrees nicely captured the unwisdom of human inaction. If Lincoln did not allow soldiers home to vote for Schuyler Colfax's reelection to Congress, Defrees told him, the candidate would lose, unless "there can be a special interference of Divine Providence—*for which I don't look.*"[7]

As president, Lincoln married qualified fatalist thought and political activism. His faith in the superintending role of Providence was fed by Phineas Gurley, his pastor at the New York Avenue Presbyterian Church. Preaching on the death of Willie Lincoln, for instance, the minister comforted the grieving family with a scriptural reading of God's Providence. "All those events which in any wise affect our condition and happiness are in his hands, and at his disposal," he gently explained. Every occurrence was part of God's good order; his mysterious dealing included suffering and affliction. "What we need in the hour of trial, and what we should seek by earnest prayer, is *confidence in Him who sees the end from the beginning and doeth all things well.*"[8] Classic providentialism, Thomas J. Sample assured Lincoln, taught "that a Divine power is controlling this war . . . to his own Glory." The Indiana judge, an occasional correspondent, reminded him of Gurley's proposition that "sense sees in history but confusion: faith beholds God in it, and the workings of redemption." Christian patriots scorned the "infidel" idea that God did not trouble himself with such affairs, "for if the very hairs of our heads are all numbered and a sparrow cannot fall to the ground without his notice, will he not take care for us?" Sample gloried in the sea change in providentialist sentiment over the course of the war. "Every where in the Executive—the Cabinet—the Councils—the Army & Navy—and amongst the people do we see a disposition powerfully manifested to refer the matter to God." But this did not mean embracing fatalist passivity. The president should see himself God's instrument "for some great purpose as much so as were Moses, Joshua, David, Cyrus, Titus and others."[9]

As we have seen in the "Meditation on the Divine Will," Lincoln accepted that he had some agency in prosecuting God's purposes. Behind the formality of his public words acknowledging "the overruling power of God," the "ever watchful providence of Almighty God," "the blessing of Divine Providence," and "the Great Disposer of events" lay a deepening personal theology, evident in his candid exchanges with Eliza Gurney and other Quakers. Responding to Mrs. Gurney's assertion that God's perfect purposes, though hard to perceive in advance, "must prevail," Lincoln acknowledged that as "a humble instrument in the hands of our Heavenly Father . . . as we all are," he had a duty to work out God's "great purposes."[10] To the head of the Christian Commission he wrote in similar vein: relying on "the Supreme Being, for the final triumph of the right, can not but be well for us all."[11]

Willing to be seen as a channel for God's overruling but mysterious power, Lincoln nurtured a mutually sustaining relationship with most of the Union's religious loyalists.[12] A staunch congressional ally, the former Illinois Congregational minister Owen Lovejoy was a common Sunday visitor; together they would read the Bible, particularly Psalms.[13] Correspondents assured him that for as long as he fulfilled his duties as "God's honored instrument," he would merit

Lincoln in the Tempest of Religious Nationalisms, 1863–1864 267

the loyal and reciprocal support of the devout.[14] "The delegated head of any nation," the Delaware Quaker John W. Tatum told Lincoln, "seems on the one hand, to be the . . . instrument of the Lord, for that People;—and on the other hand, the leader—Governor, and Judge of that People;—the responsibility is thus two-fold, and very great;—and so I believe thou feelest it to be—especially as all are required to 'Judge righteous Judgment.' "[15]

Lincoln continued to be bombarded with loyalist resolutions lamenting "God's *chastisement* for our manifold sins."[16] The curse of slavery headed the litany of evils, naturally, but the endless military struggle raised questions about the conduct of the Federal forces. "The Lord God of Battles" demanded action to stiffen the moral fiber of soldiers tempted by liquor, profanity, and other evils that all-too-many officers allegedly tolerated or even encouraged.[17] Upstate New York Presbyterians reminded Lincoln of George Washington's sentiment during the Revolutionary War: "We have but little hope of the blessing of God upon our arms, if we insult him, by our impiety & folly."[18] William E. Dixon, the clergyman brother of the Connecticut Republican senator and Lincoln political associate James Dixon, pressed the president to prescribe daily religious services, forbid profanity, and punish drunkenness.[19] Lincoln abstained from alcohol and was not much given to swearing, but he was too tolerant of human foibles to be tempted by an unworkable and counterproductive idea.

Less prosaic issues animated the Reformed Presbyterians, or Covenanters, fervent antislavery radicals, who pressed Lincoln to see that by emancipation he had acknowledged but one cause of the calamitous war: equally perilous was the nation's chronic neglect of God's law. A committee of the Washington Synod called on the president in February 1864. The people of the United States were indeed mostly Christian, they agreed, but because the country recognized "no God, no Bible, no Saviour" in its fundamental laws, it could not call itself a Christian *nation*. The pious patriot would search the Constitution in vain for any sign of Almighty God as the source of civil authority or of scripture as the supreme guide in civil affairs. For this, God's quarrel with the United States matched His anger over human bondage. Praising Lincoln for recognizing God's sovereignty, the committee asked his help in making an indisputably

Christian nation "by incorporating into its fundamental law a distinct recognition of the . . . providence of God, of the dominion of Jesus Christ, and of the divine law." Then would he lead the Union to victory. Giving a counter-spin to the scriptural text with which Alexander Stephens had described the pro-slavery Confederate constitution, the Covenanters demanded "such a re-construction of the national edifice as will make the Stone rejected of our builders the head stone of the corner."[20]

The Reformed Presbyterians assured Lincoln that, bound though they were to eschew voting, they stood defiant against rebel impiety. In reply he gave them no firm assurance but simply promised to "take the matter into serious consideration and give it such attention as his duty to our Maker and country seemed to demand."[21] Months later it proved a not entirely empty promise, for on the first Saturday in December, at a cabinet meeting to consider the text of his annual address to Congress, Lincoln startled his secretaries by reading out a paragraph proposing, as Gideon Welles reported, "an amendment to the constitution recognizing the Deity in that instrument." But before he did so, he expressed his own doubts about it, anticipating the unfavorable response it quickly elicited from around the table. He knew as well as his cabinet that the terms of the Covenanters' request breached the founding constitutional principle that the United States must be unaligned in religion. The separation of church and state did not outlaw indirect Christian or other religious influences on government, but Christianity could not be institutionally intertwined with government. The new nation had rejected a confessional state.

This concern probably influenced Lincoln's relations with the staunchly evangelical United States Christian Commission (USCC). Set up in 1861 to assist military chaplains' work with soldiers and sailors, the commission in time provided medical, recreational, and social support, too. Asked to bless its launch, Lincoln called it an enterprise "too obviously proper, and praise-worthy, to admit any difference of opinion." In 1863 its leaders invited Lincoln to chair the first annual meeting, in the House of Representatives. The high-profile event, planned for Washington's birthday, was the climax of a series of public meetings designed to counter disloyalty.[22] Lincoln consulted his departmental secretaries. Only two—Salmon Chase,

Lincoln in the Tempest of Religious Nationalisms, 1863–1864 269

the staunchest evangelical in the cabinet, and John P. Usher—encouraged him to go.[23] There is no record of their discussion. Lincoln coyly told the USCC's general superintendent, the Presbyterian Alexander Reed, that "for reasons which I deem sufficient, I must decline to preside."[24] He perhaps questioned the propriety of the nation's chief executive chairing a religious meeting. The political optics, too, were problematic. Was it advisable for the ecumenical president of citizens of every faith to serve as the sectoral leader of evangelical Protestantism?

Declining the USCC's request did Lincoln no harm. The commission continued to honor him as the nation's embodiment of faith. In January 1864 he attended its annual meeting and did so again the following year, when he was reportedly moved to tears by the hymn "Your Mission." Performed by the celebrated Philip Phillips of Cincinnati, the verses were second-rate poetry but unbeatably sentimental. Patriots, he sang, need not be blessed with wealth, special accomplishment, or fighting capacity. "If you cannot in the conflict prove yourself a soldier true, / If, where fire and smoke are thickest, there's no work for you to do; / When the battle-field is silent, you can go with careful tread, / You can bear away the wounded, you can cover up the dead." As a driven public servant, Lincoln surely felt the power of the concluding couplet: "Go and toil in any vineyard, do not fear to do or dare; / If you want a field of labor, you can find it any where."[25] He scribbled a discreet note to George H. Stuart, the USCC's president, "Near the close, let us have 'Your Mission' repeated by Mr. Philips. Dont say I called for it."[26] A Philadelphia merchant-philanthropist who never wavered in his respect for Lincoln, Stuart called on him in 1865 with several hundred commission members to register their thanks.[27]

Lincoln's personal journey in religious faith—a shadowy trail, allowing observers then and now more scope for speculation than certainty—indicated a growing belief in a God who intervened in the life of the nation for his own mysterious purposes. More than that we cannot say for sure. As we have seen, he dealt delicately with the Union's diverse faith communities and readily met every religious deputation that asked for an audience. He willingly acceded to requests to recommend—not order—days of prayer, fasting, and thanksgiving. Many welcomed them as evidence of his honesty, faithfulness, and spiritual authenticity. They pored over his words for signs of a Christian faith and yearned to hear him say that he had embraced Christ as his Savior. A certain Sarah Barnes wrote to her "Beloved President" sensing that only a true Christian could have written his proclamations.[28] "How much, I long to hear you Sir are the decided christian, openly espousing the dear Redeemers love," wrote a minister's widow. "Oh fail not to secure the everlasting crown alway[s] bright and without alloy."[29]

A striking quartet of evangelists individually encouraged the president to seek Christian conversion. Bishop Charles McIlvaine, an Episcopal ally, exulted when Lincoln's call for public thanks following military success used words "never uttered from that high seat of authority before, a solemn recognition of the being & influences of '*the Holy Spirit.*'" He prayed that future presidential proclamations would acknowledge "Christ as the Saviour of sinners. . . . May you, my dear Sir, have the full enjoyment of the precious hope of which He is the sure foundation!"[30] Eliza Gurney extolled the effects of vital faith: "a holy calm, a deep still undercurrent of soul-satisfying happiness which even the rudest storms of Time fail to disturb." To be able to say, "The Lord is my light and my salvation, whom shall I fear?" gave the Christian courage. "That this may be thy blessed experience is the fervent desire of my heart."[31] From Anna Maria Jenkins, for twenty years the intimate Christian correspondent of the Duke of Wellington, the president received a thousand-word letter rich in spiritual encouragement and fervent underlining. She rejoiced that Lincoln had spoken of "The *Saviour* of the world" when receiving a Bible from Baltimore African Americans. It confirmed "that your mind, if enlightened by *His* Grace, would become magnificently brilliant." An apostate Unitarian, she urged Lincoln to embrace the Trinity, seek Christ, and secure the promise of eternal life.[32] The Massachusetts industrialist Joseph Grinnell, Lincoln's former colleague in Congress, arranged for the president to meet Elizabeth Comstock, a Quaker minister, hoping to strengthen his faith. Alarmed by the manifest exhaustion of "the greatest man of his age," Mrs. Comstock urged Mary Lincoln to provide him with the wifely Christian encouragement he seemed desperately to need.[33]

Second- and thirdhand reports of Lincoln's Christian conver-

Lincoln in the Tempest of Religious Nationalisms, 1863–1864 271

sion circulated during the last months of his life, a case of the wish fathering the thought. In late 1864 the *American Messenger,* a New York publication of the American Tract Society, reported how a recent speaker at a Massachusetts Sabbath School convention had declared that "a friend of his" had asked the president during a private interview "if he loved Jesus." Lincoln allegedly "buried his face in his handkerchief and wept." On recovering his composure, he explained, "When I left home to take this chair of state, I requested my countrymen to pray for me. I was not then a Christian. When my son died—the severest trial of my life—I was not then a Christian. But when I went to Gettysburg, and looked upon the graves of our dead heroes who had fallen in defence of their country, I then and there consecrated myself to Christ. *I do love Jesus.*"[34] The story is touching but implausible. When William Herndon interviewed Mary Lincoln in 1866, she said her husband "had no hope & no faith in the usual acceptation of those words: he never joined a Church: he was a religious man always, as I think: he first thought . . . about this subject . . . when Willie died—never before. he felt religious More than Ever about the time he went to Gettysburg: he was not a technical Christian."[35] If Lincoln did uncharacteristically open his heart in private conversation, as the *American Messenger* reported, it is plausible that he did no more than praise the Christian sacrifice of Gettysburg's consecrated dead. His alleged conversion, however, led a rhapsodic correspondent to predict "the joy of every Christian heart throughout our land."[36]

Whatever the truth, Lincoln came to be seen, in the words of the radical Calvinist Jonathan Baldwin Turner, "a sort of half way clergyman."[37] Sundry church societies enrolled him for life, his subscriptions voluntarily paid by their members. The "spontaneous offering of infant patriots"—the children of Pennsylvania's Paschalville Methodist Episcopal Church—covered the president's and Mary Lincoln's life membership of the Philadelphia Conference Missionary Society; fundraising by the Sabbath school of the Harlem First Baptist Church ensured a formal tie with its Youth Missionary Society.[38] Enrollment certificates from Cincinnati's German Methodists and New York's Thirteenth Street Presbyterian Church likewise gave Lincoln signals of esteem.[39] The inspiration for these initiatives was probably the president's well-publicized life membership of the Young Men's Christian Association in Washington, D.C., paid for by his pastor, Phineas Gurley, and the Union naval commander Rear Admiral Andrew H. Foote.[40]

Christian loyalists cemented Lincoln's role as their faithful political anchor through the weight of prayer. "Have you dear Sir," one asked, "thought you are the subject of more ardent, heartfelt prayer than perhaps any one in our whole country, it may be the world?"[41] Lincoln's request for the people's supplications as he left Springfield won him continuing and wide acclaim. "I thank God for at last giving us a president who requests, recognizes, and appreciates, the prayers of Christians in his behalf," a female correspondent exulted.[42] On their day of jubilee, the celebrating black Baptists of Beaufort, South Carolina, told him of their pleas that God would "crown you with a crown of glory."[43] The commander of the Forty-Fourth New York, James C. Rice, alerted Lincoln to his regiment's thousand nightly intercessions to God to nerve the overtaxed president.[44] In similar vein, the elderly Jedidiah Burchard described the weekly prayer meetings in his village. For three years he had prayed for most of every morning asking God to guide the president's mind: the Almighty, he rejoiced, "has *heard* and *answered* my prayers."[45] A Boston minister, Augustus Thompson, described his awed encounters with American missionaries in Egypt, Palestine, Syria, Turkey, and Greece, who had made these sites of perceived tyranny "ring with anthems of freedom; and . . . fervent petitions for our government, our President, . . . and our righteous cause." He told how ("notwithstanding Mohammedan jealousy") he had plucked a sprig from a tree shading the site of the prophet Abraham's birth, as a prayerful token of respect for his presidential namesake.[46]

DAYS OF FASTING, PRAYER, AND THANKSGIVING

We shall see how, over a period of fifteen months from the spring of 1863 to the high summer of 1864, Lincoln proclaimed four separate days of national public prayer: two for thanksgiving and praise, two for humility and fasting. In addition, he twice responded to news of Union successes by asking for immediate prayers of thanks. This was, and remains, a striking record. No president had previously been so ready to use his authority to elevate religion in the public

Lincoln in the Tempest of Religious Nationalisms, 1863–1864 273

sphere. In doing so, he was responding to the requests of church bodies and of congressmen attuned to their constituents' wishes. But it also reflected the core providentialism of the "half way clergyman."

Lincoln's call to make April 30, 1863, a second day of humiliation, fasting, and prayer honored the key sentiments of a Senate request composed by James Harlan. As in the case of the Union fast day of September 1861, it took place soon after a Confederate day of fasting, but this was no slavish mimicry. Jefferson Davis's summons to national prayer on March 27, for God's "merciful protection," was the fifth such day that he had announced. His proclamations attracted Union scorn for their presumption that the Almighty would attend to the ungodly clamor of slaveholders. In New Orleans, Ben Butler forbade the observance of Davis's May 1862 fast day in the city's churches. The calls to fast also drew ridicule, in the light of reported food shortages in Richmond. A *Harper's* cartoon depicted a sanctimonious Davis—shortly after his baptism and confirmation in the Episcopal Church—with Satan's horns and fingering prayer beads, while dour and half-starved citizens peer at the proclamation of his third fast day posted at a street corner. A slave woman in a *Leslie's* cartoon tells her master, a Davis clone, that she had gone to the Richmond market and found no food, but by a "lucky coincidence" learned about the fast-day proclamation. "Ain't it real first-rate!" she says, grinning.

Receiving the Senate's request, the president took time to rewrite and swell its text. He amplified its Calvinistic, confessional acknowledgment of God's righteous justice toward national offenses while deleting the allusion to Jesus Christ's mediating role that Harlan, a Methodist Trinitarian, had instinctively included. The war, Lincoln sternly wrote, was a punishment for the whole people's presumptuous sins, deceitfulness, and deluded self-sufficiency: "We have forgotten God." Obligatory heart searching accompanied the launch of the Union's spring campaigns. In the east, the hubristic Joe Hooker was confident his army would avenge the December debacle at Fredericksburg; out west Grant plugged away, trying to find means of capturing Vicksburg, to control the Mississippi. A fast day uniting the people in humility and confession offered hope of securing "the pardon of our national sins, and the restoration of our . . . suffering Country, to its former happy condition of unity and peace."[47]

Within days of this outpouring of prayer, the Union suffered further anguish, when Lee exposed Hooker's incompetence with a stunning and brutal Confederate victory at Chancellorsville. Believers, however, kept faith: God would not be mocked. The first four days of July delivered to the Armies of the Tennessee and the Potomac, under Grant and George Meade, watershed triumphs at Vicksburg and Gettysburg. With the Confederacy split in two and Lee's incursion into Pennsylvania repelled, an ecstatic Union public saw the hand of Providence at work, interceding with divine prescience to honor the nation's day of independence.[48] Lincoln promptly made August 6 "a day for National Thanksgiving, Praise and Prayer," to recognize that God had listened to the people's supplications by delivering Federal victories "so signal" that sacrificial patriots could confidently expect the restoration of a permanent Union. "It is meet and right to . . . confess the presence of the Almighty Father and the power of His Hand equally in these triumphs and in these sorrows," the president wrote, and to "render the homage due to the Divine Majesty, for the wonderful things he has done in the Nation's behalf." He then turned to consider the rebels. With striking and unprecedented phrases he called for prayer to "invoke the influence of His Holy Spirit to subdue the anger, which has produced, and so long sustained a needless and cruel rebellion, to change the hearts of the insurgents" and "to lead the whole nation, through the paths of repentance and submission to the Divine Will, back to the perfect enjoyment of Union and fraternal peace."[49] Eliza Gurney rejoiced at Lincoln's recognition of a superintending Providence and especially the immediate influence of the Holy Spirit, "which perhaps never, in any previous State-paper, has been so fully recognized before."[50]

Barely four months later, another thanksgiving occasion—one that established the modern national holiday—encouraged loyalists to reaffirm faith in their prospects. The moving spirit behind Lincoln's invitation to "the whole American People" to make the last Thursday of November "a day of Thanksgiving and Praise" was the redoubtable and elderly Sarah Josepha Hale. Novelist, poet, Christian philanthropist, and forceful advocate of female education, Hale exerted immense cultural authority for forty years as editor

Lincoln in the Tempest of Religious Nationalisms, 1863–1864 275

of *Godey's Lady's Book*, a magazine unrivaled in influence and circulation. Writing to Lincoln in September, she set out the case for making "the *day of our annual Thanksgiving . . . a National and fixed Union Festival*." For years she had unsuccessfully pressed U.S. presidents and state governors to that end. Now she engaged her friend Secretary of State Seward to lobby the president for a national holiday, one that extended the New England thanksgiving tradition into states where it had yet found little purchase and encompassed federal territories, the District of Columbia, the Union army and navy, and communities of American citizens abroad. Within days, Lincoln issued the proclamation she requested. The handiwork of Seward, it reminded the loyal Union of its abundant blessings even in a time of "lamentable civil strife": agricultural abundance, commercial and industrial growth, an increasing population, respect for law and constitutional order, peace with foreign nations, and the advance of Federal forces. Those commonly blind to the workings of a watchful Providence were bound to recognize "the gracious gifts of the Most High God, who, while dealing with us in anger for our sins, hath nevertheless remembered mercy."[51]

Lincoln's Thanksgiving appeal, generally echoed by state governors, won wide acclaim.[52] Reports from his adopted Springfield, as elsewhere, told of churches filled beyond capacity.[53] News of a successful climax to the Union's Chattanooga campaign, arriving just too late for the day's meetings, gave a further boost to loyalists' optimism. Following the major Union setback at Chickamauga in September, Grant had taken vigorous command of Federal forces in the West. After hard fighting had driven the Confederates from their entrenchments on Lookout Mountain, George H. Thomas's men stunned their commanders by taking the apparently impregnable Missionary Ridge with a bold frontal assault. This spectacular rout of Braxton Bragg's Confederate army lifted the siege of Federal forces in Chattanooga, gave the Union control of Tennessee, and opened the way to Georgia and the lower South. When Grant additionally reported that General James Longstreet was retreating toward Virginia, an exultant Lincoln announced the news in a press release of December 7, recommending that all loyal people "informally assemble at their places of worship and tender special homage and gratitude to Almighty God."[54]

276   RIGHTEOUS STRIFE

Consequently, many expected the spring campaigns of 1864 to crush what remained of Confederate resistance. In March, Lincoln promoted Grant to the rank of lieutenant general and gave him overall command of the Union armies. At the start of active maneuvers, he told the commander that he was sure he, Grant, would avoid "any great disaster," praying that God would sustain "a brave army, and a just cause."[55] At the same time multiple voices urged Lincoln to launch military operations with a day of fasting and prayer, as he had in 1863. Jedidiah Burchard feared that since the great victory at Chattanooga joyful northerners who should have known better had "transferred their dependence . . . from God to the *creature*." Only a national fast to honor "the broad shield . . . of the *Almighty*" would ensure that Grant's "Western laurels" did not, by future griefs, become "Southern Willows."[56] Illinois Congregationalists in convention at Chicago made a similar request, communicated to Lincoln by his friend Julian Sturtevant.[57] To these and other demands for action the president responded with a press release on May 9 as Grant launched a new and brutal drive against Lee's army. By then the confusion of the Battle of the Wilderness had led to Federal casualties of more than seventeen thousand, which by any measure would have qualified as the "great disaster" that Lincoln had hoped to see avoided. But because Grant kept his promise to the president that there would be no turning back (and indeed, on May 8, ordered the Army of the Potomac to march south), Lincoln could put a positive gloss on events. "Enough is known of Army operations within the last five days to claim our especial gratitude to God," he wrote, "while what remains undone demands our most sincere prayers to, and reliance upon, Him, without whom, all human effort is vain." He called on "all patriots, at their homes, in their places of public worship, and wherever they may be," to unite not in fasting but in thanksgiving and prayer.[58]

Spring's early optimism withered as the Union losses in the Wilderness became the prelude to a summer of scorching carnage. Seventeen thousand Federal casualties at Spotsylvania Court House and some seven thousand killed at Cold Harbor were just the bloodiest punctuation points of Grant's elongated battle to crush Lee's forces, one that eventually stalled in a standoff before the Confederate earthworks at Petersburg. The accumulated Union deaths from

Lincoln in the Tempest of Religious Nationalisms, 1863–1864 277

this unremitting Virginia bloodletting of May and June, and Sherman's more modest losses in Georgia, reached a staggering 100,000 by August. This was the grievous context in which Lincoln, at the formal prompting of Congress, proclaimed on July 7 another day of national humiliation and prayer, set for the first Thursday of August. The House and the Senate cast their joint resolution in conventional terms: the duty to confess manifold sins and beseech the Almighty's favor, enlightenment, and blessing of fortitude, believing that it was "His will that our place should be maintained as a united people among the family of nations." Sharing their concern over the military stalemate, Lincoln aimed to make the day one of national political unification. Unlike previous religious proclamations, which took the form of a generic invitation to the "American People," this one specified those charged with the duty of observance: "the Heads of the Executive Departments of this Government, together with all Legislators, all Judges and Magistrates, and all other persons exercising authority in the land, whether civil, military or naval, and all soldiers, seamen and marines in the national service, and all the other loyal and law-abiding People of the United States."[59] The day would be a test of patriotism.

The frequency of national religious events naturally became a trial of public commitment. There can be no definitive measure of popular participation. Local newspapers and entries in private diaries commonly reported above-average attendance at the many different churches and the Sabbath-like suspension of business, through the closure of banks, stores, workshops, and public offices. The April 1863 fast day offers a case in point: a Washington correspondent claimed its observance exceeded previous similar occasions; Chicago's churches were described as "very generally" filled; New York, where the *Times* had "seldom known a holiday to be so generally kept," reported similarly.[60] But the evidence of even upbeat accounts suggests how attendance could be influenced, and limited, by considerations of social class, political loyalty, and religious conviction. Chicago's fast-day streets were said to be thronged with "the laboring classes . . . enjoying the day as one of recreation." In Evansville, Indiana—an Ohio River community in Copperhead country bordering Kentucky—the local *Journal* claimed services were "generally well observed as such days usually are" but criticized those who were absent "from want of sympathy with the cause or whose religious views were not in consonance with the President's recommendation."[61] A few months later, on the August thanksgiving day, Union loyalists berated southern Illinois Copperheads for paying "no more attention to the President's proclamation than if they had been residing in Richmond under the very nose of Jeff. Davis."[62]

As the war entered its fourth summer, the law of diminishing returns might have taken its toll on religious observance. Signs of a loss of pulling power marked the August 1864 fast day. The voice of New York Methodists, the *Christian Advocate*, feared that the fast would be virtually disregarded or only superficially observed. In his corner of Massachusetts the radical abolitionist Charles K. Whipple estimated only "a twentieth part (more or less)" attended church, "the remainder using the occasion as a holiday, for rest or recreation." The conservative *New-York Observer* regretted that the occasion there was "observed with less interest, and by fewer persons, than any similar day that was ever set apart by the President." Another noted that most of the city's Catholics ignored Lincoln's proclamation. A Romanist observer reported that most of "the stores and places of business 'down-town' are closed up, and our well-to-do citizens have gone out of town to—*feast*—not *fast*. . . . A few go to church; but the many go elsewhere."[63] Yet this was not a secular trend. A month later, congregations swelled once more for the national thanksgiving Lincoln called to honor the dramatic military triumphs of late summer.

Through his repeated religious initiatives Lincoln was taken to signal the Christian character of the United States and the churches' authentic political role.[64] An exultant Boston pastor typically acclaimed the government's unprecedented national recognition of God. Until this seismic change, a nation of millions of professed Christians had in its official face, he said, been "practically Godless."[65] Robert Curran, an Indiana local Methodist preacher, hailed Lincoln's proclamations as a rebuke to those who asserted "we are not a Christian nation." It was true, he conceded in a sermon he sent to the president, that many Americans were practically faithless. Yet, "if we are not a Christian nation, what are we? We are not Pagans; we are not Mahometans; we are not worshipers of Confucius; we know nothing about the sacred books of the Hindoos or

Chinese, except as matters of curiosity." For Curran, national days of worship proudly trumpeted that "the reformation and elevation of mankind rest alone upon the Bible and its Christianity."[66]

ANTISLAVERY RELIGIOUS NATIONALISTS AND THE CAUSE OF UNIVERSAL EMANCIPATION

The rhetorical tsunami released by Lincoln's sequence of proclamations channeled the turbulent currents of Union opinion.[67] A few speakers sheltered behind ritual phrases and tired formulas, but most endowed the days of fasting and thanksgiving with an urgent and inspiring patriotism. The Congregationalist Jeremiah Rankin's lapidary dictum captured the prevailing sentiment, that military prowess counted for nothing without a righteous cause: "The battle-field is the judgment-bar of nations."[68] According to the Methodist minister and radical abolitionist Gilbert Haven, "We trace our defeats and victories to no incompetent or competent generalship. A higher law regulates these matters." Federal military reverses occasioned anxious soul-searching; human suffering and the fear of hubristic celebration tempered the joy of victory.[69] In their sermons, and in their resolutions and memorials to Lincoln, the full range of voices from radical antislavery nationalists to ultraconservative loyalists contested the righteous national purposes of the war.

Common to all was the notion of providential justice and the testing of a Union endowed with unique resources and matchless potential. Most continued to characterize the war and its emotional switchback as the trial of God's special people. Widely shared themes of righteous sacrifice, national retribution and purification, and the global mission of the American republic accompanied scriptural precepts lauding loyalty to constitutional authority and resistance to treason.[70] The recurrent text—"Let every soul be subject unto the higher powers. For there is no power but of God: the powers that be are ordained of God"—demanded citizens' cheerful obedience to lawful authority.[71] As God's ministers, rulers had a righteous duty to "execute wrath" on the wicked.[72] To suppress a rebellion of barbarous fanaticism, religious patriots were duty-bound to bear arms and defy the siren calls for armistice and peace.[73] The mounting toll of the Union's slaughtered, wounded, and bereaved bore witness to the freely borne costs of Christian, self-sacrificing patriotism.[74] Inspired by a millennial vision of national cleansing and purification—the advent of a New Jerusalem, the *"grand consummation"* of God's hope for America—religious nationalists shared a determination that, in the words of Pennsylvania Episcopalians, "our now lacerated country may again be so united that from the lakes on the north to the Gulf on the south, and from the Atlantic to the Pacific, there shall be but one Union, one government, one flag, one Constitution, all converging to . . . that higher glory which shall make this nation Emanuel's land . . . a dwelling place of righteousness."[75] Confederate victory, Ohio United Brethren warned, would obliterate the American experiment in liberty: "The last best hope of mankind will have perished."[76] But by the grace of God, the nation would emerge purified from evil, "a beacon light to all the nations of the earth, demonstrating the . . . superiority of Republican government."[77]

There agreement ended. As the battlefield conflict continued into a third and then fourth year of grim slaughter, antislavery nationalists looked for a more fundamental emancipation than that prefigured in Lincoln's edict of January 1863. Progressive, and sometimes radical, their developing definitions of black racial freedom only widened the gulf between their own national vision and the religious nationalism of conservative white Unionists.

A cadre of the most zealous emancipationists, many from the ranks of prewar radical abolitionism, found little to relish in the terms of Lincoln's edict of freedom and its aura of political expediency.[78] It was unconscionable, a Michigan correspondent told him, to liberate the slaves of Confederates "as if slavery among union men would be less sinful or fatal to the Union than slavery among the rebels."[79] The proclamation was a mere cog in an engine of war and conquest, a Dutch Reformed preacher sighed, "as purely selfish an act as the slavery itself, which it proposes to destroy." Berating the administration for its moral cowardice, Charles K. Whipple despaired that at the outset the government had not invited all black people, slave and free, to help put down the rebellion in return for full citizenship and equality before the law.[80] Equally, the New York Methodist John P. Newman deemed the administration's course too lenient in its dalliance with the border states: the national imperative demanded a blazing sword. Eleven months into the working of

Lincoln in the Tempest of Religious Nationalisms, 1863–1864 281

the emancipation edict, when Lincoln issued a conciliatory Proclamation of Amnesty and Reconstruction to induce the rebels to return, he triggered a barrage of radical criticism. Furious Lowell abolitionists denounced terms that ignored "all the colored race," apparently gave back the traitors' immense estates, resurrected the former slave codes, dishonored the nation, and revealed a feeble president still faltering before the Slave Power.[81]

From this radical viewpoint, some derided Lincoln's days of humiliation and prayer as a hypocritical sop calculated to distract from the administration's neglect of the black race, its most powerful resource. Whipple scorned Lincoln's call for national fasting in August 1864: "To ask God to suppress this rebellion when the sufficient means for its suppression lie unused in our own hands is . . . a piece of presumptuous impertinence. . . . Surely this is not the fast that He has chosen."[82] Radical critics more commonly responded, however, not by dismissing national calls to prayer—they were in practice widely welcomed—but to rebuke the president for glossing over slavery as the nation's cardinal sin. Echoing the terms of congressional resolutions, Lincoln's proclamations used politic phrases to extend their reach. That of March 1863 spoke only of the duty of nations "to confess their sins and transgressions." In July a year later, when Lincoln confirmed the duty of government and people "to confess and to repent of their manifold sins," Gilbert Haven rebuked its timidity: "We bow the head, but not yet the knee." He conceded that the president had "come nearest to the demands of God," but still in no "single Executive summons to penitence is there a direct reference to our national transgression." Damningly, he concluded, "We are not honest before God. Our honest President here fails in honesty."[83]

Most antislavery nationalists, however, welcomed the edict of New Year's Day 1863 as the great ethical hinge of American history. "We have come to a swivel in the chain of our National life," a buoyant Thomas Richmond, a former antislavery member of the Illinois General Assembly, told the president. "A new history begins here. . . . We must have no more National sins to reproach us. . . . God grant us a true National life of right, Justice and peace."[84] By most estimates, however, Lincoln—though a man of moral conviction—was scarcely a radical crusader for racial freedom: rather, he was

282 RIGHTEOUS STRIFE

the secondary agent through whom the Almighty pursued His purposes. The Methodist minister Daniel Steele explained how it had required God's "eye-salve" to make the president see what some generals, notably Frémont and Hunter, had perceived much sooner, that the slave was their natural ally. A Michigan preacher, too, was sure only by "a Divine impulse" had Lincoln made his death strike at slavery.[85] James C. Rice likewise identified the hand of God at work. "He seems," he confessed to Henry Wilson, "to have as directly guided Abraham Lincoln in opening a path to freedom to every slave, as he did Moses in preparing the Red Sea as a transit to the oppressed Israelites."[86]

By antislavery Christian consensus, God's mysterious Providence had set the nation on its path to redemption by punitively prolonging the war. Lincoln's allies drew the lesson that too swift a Union victory would simply have reinstated the antebellum order.[87] "The *hand* of *God* is as perceptible in this war as it is in *conducting* the *seasons*," Jedidiah Burchard told him. "Had our arms been successful at Bull Run, and before Richmond, the rebellion might have terminated and a reconstruction of the Union followed with Slavery *entailed* upon us."[88] Instead, military necessity had become the instrument of justice.[89] God, Bishop McIlvaine wrote, had led the Union through "ways of darkness—of perilous straits & great fearfulness . . . all the while educating the people, taking away old ideas & prejudices that barred our path." The federal constitution, the prewar guarantor of slavery, could now be lawfully turned against it.[90]

By this logic, the war should continue until all were free. Earnest voices across the Protestant spectrum—Baptists, Methodists, Presbyterian, United Brethren, Unitarians, Quakers—urged the president to follow God's command "to break every yoke."[91] The hard-line Springfield abolitionist Erastus Wright, who shared a prickly relationship with the president, rebuked the administration's conservativism, including its dalliance with slaveholder compensation. "I do not wish to leave this world with blood on my skirts," he candidly confessed. "My old friend and Neighbor, May God have Mercy on you and forgive [you], and give you Wisdom to . . . Proclaim *Universal Emancipation* to all who are guilty of no crime. . . . The Nation *ought to*, and *will bleed* until this is done."[92]

This fervency yoked outrage about an embedded national sin

Lincoln in the Tempest of Religious Nationalisms, 1863–1864 283

with hardheaded realism over the Confederacy's political purpose. No manifesto for the rebel South did more damage to its moral branding than Alexander Stephens's "Cornerstone Speech" of March 1861. That address, establishing slavery as the Confederate bedrock, became a chronic and ubiquitous point of reference in the Union's political and religious assertion of the South's malignant intent.[93] The war could never yield a permanent peace by surrendering to "unprincipled demagogues . . . the most egotistic, haughty, proud, lazy, selfish, aristocratic, despotic and devilish the world has ever known," intent on erecting "a monster confederacy whose corner stone shall be human bondage."[94] As calls for a negotiated peace grew louder during the troubled summer months of 1864, a Massachusetts Episcopalian, A. St. John Chambré, typified loyalist resolve. As the root cause of the war, slavery must die: "When we are ready . . . to crush it out forever . . . then it will not be a peace for a day . . . but for all time. The nation will then be able to exist as a nation."[95]

Lincoln recognized the strength and political influence wielded by religious advocates of a slave-free nation. The letters, memorials, and ministerial visits of cheerleaders for emancipation did not in themselves determine the president's course. But they left him in no doubt that he enjoyed broad-based and growing support for the antislavery direction of his policy during 1863 and 1864. He famously declared that wartime emancipation was shaped by forces over which he had no influence. "Events have controlled me," he told the Kentucky editor Albert Hodges in April 1864. This "confession," as he termed it, was accurate insofar as political and military headwinds and the unpredictable contingencies of war shaped, set, and reset the administration's course. But it was scarcely the whole truth. Minimizing his personal agency in the decision on emancipation served Lincoln's electoral needs, but it did not do justice to his role as a calculating political activist alert to the contending force fields of public opinion and the strong religious character of antislavery nationalism.

Initially, Lincoln's emancipation edict polarized opinions and appeared to do little for the Union cause. But after the military triumphs of early July 1863 the president regularly stood by it as an irrevocable order, imperative to victory. "I think I shall not retract or repudiate" the proclamation, he wrote to General Stephen A. Hurlbut later that month. "Those who shall have tasted actual freedom I believe can never be slaves, or quasi slaves again." A few days later, on August 5, he told Nathaniel Banks, "I think I shall not . . . as executive, ever return to slavery any person who is free by the terms of that proclamation, or by any of the acts of Congress."[96] Shortly after that, at the White House, he rejected Frederick Douglass's accusation of "vacillation," telling the abolitionist he was unequivocally committed to emancipation: "No man can say that having once taken the position I have contradicted or retreated from it."[97] This conviction infused his address at the dedication of a military cemetery at Gettysburg in November. The "new birth of freedom" that he declared to be the war's goal avoided direct mention of slavery or the enslaved. But, for the avoidance of doubt, he repeated to Congress in December what he had written to Banks four months earlier, that as president he would not return to slavery any person freed by his edict of emancipation.[98]

Lincoln's proclamation left unresolved the place of slavery in the loyal border region and the exempted parts of the Confederacy, but he saw how it could become a step toward universal freedom. He repeatedly encouraged schemes of gradual emancipation, telling Hurlbut to urge this course on Unionist leaders in Arkansas and proposing similar terms for Louisiana and Texas.[99] Following military advance in Tennessee, he pressed Governor Andrew Johnson in September 1863 to get emancipation written into a new state constitution.[100] His Proclamation of Amnesty and Reconstruction of December 1863, though branded a sop to rebel slaveholders by a minority of radicals, in fact made abolition unequivocally a condition of a state's restoration and won the broad acclaim of antislavery forces. In his message to Congress introducing that document, Lincoln reiterated his support for gradual, compensated emancipation in the loyal border states and welcomed the steps several were taking toward freedom.[101] Kentucky and Delaware politics were dominated by conservatives who were unwilling to budge, but Missouri Unionists accepted a plan of emancipation in the summer of 1863;

when they split along radical and conservative lines, Lincoln failed to reconcile the "pestilent" quarreling factions and avoided openly taking sides, though in private he leaned toward those campaigning for immediate emancipation.[102] Nothing pleased Lincoln more than the advance of abolition sentiment in Maryland, where Unionists— with the president's approval—rewrote the state constitution to end slavery immediately and secured its approval by popular vote in October 1864.[103]

Extending emancipation beyond the scope of Lincoln's proclamation owed much to the edict's arresting and radical provision for freed people "of suitable condition" to serve in the Union's army. At first, recruitment encompassed only free blacks and the slaves of rebel owners in unarmed, noncombatant roles. That would change as slaves of compensated loyalists in the border states were recruited, too, and as Lincoln changed his mind about arming black troops. From the first, radical voices urged that they be given weapons. Lincoln was ready to listen to the Massachusetts minister Lewis C. Lockwood, the head of the American Missionary Association's work with contrabands at Fortress Monroe, who assured the president in early January that the intelligence and enthusiasm of refugees, when armed, would ensure the speedy suppression of the South.[104] A little later the Congregationalist Julian Sturtevant urged his old acquaintance to recognize that "three hundred thousand muskets each with a good lusty Negro at its breech" would speedily bring an end to the war and slavery. The prospect of conscription, he told Lincoln, had powerfully concentrated the minds of those white people previously horrified at the idea of arming black soldiers. Like the wife of James C. Conkling of Springfield, they now saw the value of hiring "a good able bodied negro" as a substitute for a drafted white son. That Conkling himself ("our excellent friend") felt the force of this argument would make him the natural mouthpiece for Lincoln's celebrated public letter to Illinois voters six months later.[105]

One particular voice encouraged the president's change of heart. The Chicagoan Thomas Richmond—abolitionist, former state legislator, shipping merchant, and Congregationalist turned spiritualist—wrote to him urgently in early March, certain that diminishing public faith in the Union war effort demanded recourse to "*every possible* instrumentality." With the supply of white recruits drying up and Federal forces stalled, he predicted the Confederates would push for victory by taking risks. Jeff Davis would free and arm the slaves, he warned: "The Negro race . . . fighting with the South for freedom, the Confederate States may well put the Govrmnt at defiance." Lincoln should preemptively promise arms and freedom to "the Mustle and Sinew of the slave population" in both rebel and loyal states. The amalgam of physical and moral power would sweep away all opposition and secure God's favor by recognizing "the manhood [and] the equality before the law of the Negro." Richmond's six-page letter won Lincoln's endorsement: "Good advice."[106]

These arguments resounded across the antislavery pulpit and beyond. Edmund Kelly, a black Baptist minister, sent Lincoln a copy of his speech calling on African Americans to enlist, to show their prowess and fitness for freedom. It was no vain hope. During the summer and fall of 1863 the heroism of "ebony soldiers," as "written in the trenches of Port Hudson, and on the parapet of Fort Wagner," encouraged a growing faith in African Americans' equal manhood and their capacity for freedom. James Rice saw God's hand at work: he would continue this war until "the African race in this country shall raise themselves to an honorable position by the valor of their arms."[107] By the end of the conflict 200,000 black soldiers and sailors had shown themselves to be not disempowered victims but agents of their own destiny. To be sure, white prejudice remained ingrained, resilient, and strong, but the war brought about a sea change in the racial attitudes of many whites.

Lincoln exemplified the open-minded spirit prompting a positive view of African American capabilities. In the racial culture of prewar Illinois, he had faced the contempt of race-baiting Democrats for what were, by the standards of the place and time, the progressive views he championed: claiming for both black and white people the rights enshrined in the Declaration of Independence. But he was at that stage of his life no racial egalitarian. His wartime experience, however, led him to associate with capable black men and women of outstanding talents. In Frederick Douglass, Martin R. Delany, Sojourner Truth, many black ministers, and others besides, figures of impressive ability and intelligence received a welcome at the White House. Lincoln's prewar appetite for the large-scale vol-

Lincoln in the Tempest of Religious Nationalisms, 1863–1864 287

untary colonization abroad of the free black population gave way to a reduced interest in schemes of that kind, and eventually to his giving up altogether the notion of separating the races. After all, black troops were establishing their own and their families' right to future citizenship in the country for which they were ready to lay down their lives.

Lincoln's correspondents piled on the pressure. Benjamin Rush Plumly, abolitionist and serving army officer, told him of the deep trust he enjoyed among churchgoing black Philadelphians, who were convinced he would not expatriate them: "Some one intimated, that You might be forced into some, form of Colinization. 'God wont let him,' shouted an old woman. 'God's in his *heart*,' said another, and the response of the Congregation was emphatic." Church meetings urged Lincoln to recognize the deep hunger of black people for education and equal citizenship and called for the scrapping of laws that made "odious distinctions on account of color" and "the annihilation of the spirit of caste-prejudice against the negro race." The president should acknowledge the truth that "God has made of one blood all nations of men."[108] The mettlesome wife of an officer in a black regiment, Carrie H. Purnell of Covington, Kentucky, in an exchange with the president, told of her ordeal among slaveholding rebels, including her own family, and the hope she drew from her Christian faith, the capability of brave colored troops, and the looming end to enslavement. She had been asked by a sneering "rebel woman" what would become of the black people. "Oh! I replied—If we will do our part I am more than sure the Lord will do His." Robert Curran, Methodist minister of Jeffersonville, Indiana, neatly reversed the question. Praising what free blacks had already achieved against all odds, he mused that the true question pertained to the master. How would he take care of himself when their forced partnership ended? "The master finds himself far the most helpless of the two, and here is where the shoe pinches," Curran crowed. "Oh, Christian! Oh, American!"[109]

Many of the speakers on Lincoln's days of national worship strove to make the case for black capabilities. Ministers became evangelists of racial progress, delivering a gospel of a nation redeemable only through black uplift and equality. God's purpose behind the war, a Vermont Congregationalist declared, was to "vindicate the claims of his sable children, to equal rights and peaceful citizenship." To that end, the New York *Evangelist* called for the North to repent of its sinful color bar by lifting the black race to "full manhood" and equal rights. Francis Zabriskie, Dutch Reformed minister of Coxsackie, New York, likened the nation's challenge to God's test of ancient Egypt regarding the Jews. How would the United States fare when measured by the treatment of "the poor, despised, degraded negro"? Had not the Almighty placed these people in North America to be a proxy for Christ himself? Implicitly the Savior posed the question, "Are you ready to give them . . . those rights and privileges . . . which I have freely given you?" Emancipation was but a start. To avoid the Almighty's chastening rod, the nation must follow its special mission to advance the race "whose destinies God has so mysteriously intertwined with our own."[110]

How in practice should the white American republic empower the crushed African race? The Methodist Daniel Steele offered a detailed prospectus for a black population that he calculated would swell to twelve million by 1900, "unless logarithms lie." Too numerous to be inhumanly shipped to Africa or Central America, and a proven national boon through their military service, they would find rich possibilities as free laborers in a burgeoning postwar industrial economy. As property holders and taxpayers, they would earn the vote and a citizen's education, "for taxation without representation America has repudiated from the beginning." But the right to vote involved the right of being voted for. "Do not be startled," Steele wryly mused, "if the day should come when Sambo will take the seat in the Senate vacated by Slidell. No punishment for the traitor can be found in all Dante's Inferno so severe as this." Loyal black hands, not those of lily-white rebels, would help pilot a nation that had annihilated political distinctions of color.[111]

Many antislavery religious nationalists balked at complete racial equality, but few doubted the toxicity of white racial prejudice. The examples of the New York City draft riots and the massacre of black Union troops at Fort Pillow in April 1864 showed how deeply that poison had seeped into the culture, North and South.[112] But in the vortex of war, it appeared that a new order was emerging, one that offered a real prospect of erasing the color line. The deep-rooted and venomous hatred of the black race encouraged by some north-

Lincoln in the Tempest of Religious Nationalisms, 1863–1864 289

ern presses had led the Unitarian Henry Bellows to despair at seeing any change in his lifetime, but now he judged (overoptimistically) that the prejudice was "swiftly melting away . . . under actual contact with the slave." Phillips Brooks, eloquent Episcopalian, asked his Philadelphia congregation, "If the negro is a man, and we have freed him in virtue of his manhood, what consistency . . . is it which still objects to his riding down the street in the same car with us if he is tired, or sitting in the same pew with us if he wants to worship God?"[113] The radical Gilbert Haven pressed the argument further still. "We must expunge the word 'colored' from our Minutes," he told his fellow Methodists. "Had we boldly taken the ground of Paul at the beginning, refused to know white or black, bond or free, in the Church . . . we should never have met with the difficulties we have."[114] With stinging logic, Haven asked his white audience how they could deny equal rights to their black friends and neighbors, "nine tenths of whom have English blood in their veins, and one half of whom have more of that blood than of their original African." On what possible grounds should black men be denied the role of officers or ministers in a church of mostly white members? Why should black troops be paid less than white? Equally unjustly, Lincoln denied lieutenancies to those "who, were they white and foreigners, would have been made major generals for their skill and valor."[115]

In conversation with Frederick Douglass, Lincoln defended black troops' inequality as "a necessary concession" to public feeling, but he was less cautious in navigating toward universal emancipation. During the early months of 1864 congressmen discussed proposals to amend the Constitution to guarantee full freedom throughout the United States. Lincoln initially held back, continuing to favor abolition through state-by-state action, by working quietly but energetically to encourage the drafting of antislavery constitutions in southern states under Reconstruction. The proposed Thirteenth Amendment passed in the Senate, but in the House it narrowly failed to muster the necessary two-thirds majority, stymied by opposition Democrats' fears that abolition would end all hope of reconciliation with the rebel states and lead inescapably to equal black citizenship and racial amalgamation.

Many radicals deemed Lincoln too moderate on racial issues—

black suffrage, soldiers' pay, freedmen's rights under Reconstruction—and looked to replace him as president. An internal struggle consumed the party during the first half of 1864. Some abolitionists stood with Garrison, who admired Lincoln's striking growth in moral stature since 1861 and urged his renomination; others joined Wendell Phillips in seeking a dependable radical leader who would embrace and fight for a racially just society.[116] Sensing an opportunity, Salmon P. Chase, the ambitious secretary of the Treasury, allowed Senator Samuel C. Pomeroy to launch a campaign on his behalf, but the movement soon collapsed. John C. Frémont, the darling of the abolitionists since his August 1861 edict of emancipation in Missouri, and no less ambitious than Chase, saw an opening. At Cleveland at the end of May an electoral coalition of radicals and War Democrats nominated him for president on a platform endorsing abolition and—at the behest of Wendell Phillips, Frederick Douglass, and other radicals—black suffrage and legal equality.[117]

Lincoln's popularity with rank-and-file Republicans ensured his renomination at the party's national convention in Baltimore a week later. In step with religious bodies' insistent requests to eliminate "this whole system of iniquity . . . root, branch and seed," Lincoln had instructed Edwin D. Morgan, the chair of his party's executive committee, to place an abolition amendment front and center of the convention's business.[118] Delegates gave an ecstatic welcome to the vote to "terminate and forever prohibit the existence of Slavery within the limits or the jurisdiction of the United States." Lincoln's letter accepting renomination extolled the plank as "a fitting, and necessary conclusion to the success of the Union cause." It alone could "meet and cover all cavils."[119] Now that the issue defined the president and symbolized his party, the House of Representatives became a campaign cockpit.[120]

Less radical than the Cleveland resolutions, the National Union platform divided opinion within the American Anti-slavery Society. Fresh from the Baltimore convention, a delighted William Lloyd Garrison, accompanied by Theodore Tilton, the brilliant editor of the New York *Independent*, paid a call on Lincoln to express their great satisfaction. The president, Garrison told his wife, unmistakably desired "to do all that he can . . . to uproot slavery, and give fair play to the emancipated."[121] But Wendell Phillips, George B.

Lincoln in the Tempest of Religious Nationalisms, 1863–1864 291

Cheever, Parker Pillsbury, William Goodell, and others continued to support the Frémont coalition. Tilton and Phillips played out their differences before *The Independent*'s seventy thousand subscribers, and beyond, with the lionized Boston orator extolling the Cleveland platform as "the high-water mark of American politics" and, in riposte, the politically savvy Tilton predicting that the unstable alliance of Democrats and abolitionists was a stalking horse for Peace Democrats, driven above all by antipathy to Lincoln. Tilton called the Cleveland equality plank a fraud and electoral liability, designed to wound the Republicans. "Now, we would be glad if a great political party could go before the country on the high issue of giving every black man a vote," he wrote. "But the country is not ready." Specifically, he added, "Let Mr. Phillips go to a Frémont ratification meeting and speak on the 'absolute equality' of negroes and Irishmen, and he will be rioted out of the house."[122] The two other leading abolitionist organs, the *National Anti-slavery Standard* and *The Liberator*, similarly insisted that a presidential campaign turning on full black equality would result in a Copperhead administration.

By this route Lincoln and his party won the support of most radical abolitionists. This added a sharp edge to the loyalty of the wider antislavery mainstream whose constancy the president had good reason to trust, in the light of his meetings shortly before the Baltimore convention with representatives of the Union's two largest denominations, the Methodists and the Baptists. These notable occasions captured the quintessence and power of antislavery religious nationalists, and their political import to the administration. The first, on the morning of May 18, saw a delegation of five ministers from the highest body of the Methodist Episcopal Church, its General Conference, ushered into Lincoln's angular presence at the White House. Bishop Edward R. Ames led the group, which comprised colleagues chosen for their scholarly distinction, cultivation, and—notably in the case of the Union army colonel Granville Moody—personal acquaintance with the president. Moody later described how Lincoln had requested an advance sight of the address they intended to deliver. He asked his friend about the Methodists' initiative. "Colonel Moody, how came you to do this? It is the very thing I would have asked you to do had I had your ear." Well prepared, Lincoln stage-managed the morning's event.

He stood at the center of a semicircle of his cabinet secretaries while Joseph Cummings—president of Wesleyan University in Middletown, Connecticut—read the address of the conference. A statement of Methodism's unbending loyalty to the nation, "the cause of God and humanity," it looked forward—as battles raged in the Wilderness—to the day when "this shall truly be a republican and free country," with slavery exterminated. Cummings had chaired the conference committee that had declared in favor of an abolition amendment to the Constitution. He ended his address with a prayer for a permanent peace "founded on the Word of God, and securing righteousness, liberty, and equal rights to all."[123]

At this point Lincoln made a bow and opened the drawer of his desk to extract the short reply he had already composed. "He stood before us straight as an arrow," George Peck recalled, and delivered a hearty tribute to Methodists' patriotism. It was short but in no way perfunctory. Lincoln was customarily circumspect, keen to recognize that every denomination had played its part in sustaining the government. He would utter nothing, he said, that "might in the least appear invidious to any." Yet through sheer numbers Methodists led in importance, sending "more soldiers to the field, more nurses to the hospitals, and more prayers to Heaven than any." With evident depth of feeling, he closed: "God bless the Methodist Church—bless all the Churches! And blessed be God who in this, our great trial, giveth us the Churches!" The tribute thrilled Moody and his colleagues: it was, he wrote, "an amaranthine wreath placed upon the brow of Methodism." After a brief conversation about public matters, the committee left.[124]

Lincoln fully recognized the Methodists' power and political value. In a conversation some weeks later with Moody and Samuel Galloway of Ohio—a Presbyterian elder and Lincoln's Republican appointee as a judge advocate—the president would praise the "controlling anti-slavery influence" of the MEC. In Moody's recollection, Lincoln had declared how the Church's bishops and ministers "leavened the whole lump" of public opinion. Even allowing for the rosy tint of Moody's memory, we must accept that Lincoln prized the remarkable reach of Methodist weekly newspapers and pulpits, and the MEC's antislavery course since the unfrocking of the slaveholder bishop James Andrew in 1844.[125] His May 1864 meeting

Lincoln in the Tempest of Religious Nationalisms, 1863–1864   293

> Gentlemen:
>
> In response to your address, allow me to attest the accuracy of its historical statements; indorse the sentiments it expresses; and thank you, in the nation's name, for the sure promise it gives.
>
> Nobly sustained as the government has been by all the churches, I would utter nothing which might, in the least, appear invidious against any. Yet without this, it may fairly be said, that the Methodist Episcopal Church, not less devoted than the best, is, by its greater numbers, the most important of all. It is no fault in others, that the Methodist Church sends more soldiers to the field, more nurses to the hospital, and more prayers to Heaven, than any. God bless the Methodist Church — bless all the churches — and blessed be God, who, in this our great trial, giveth us the churches.

Lincoln's response to a committee of the
Methodist Episcopal Church, May 18, 1864

with the Church's ministerial elite presented an unmissable political opportunity. In seizing it, he gave the deputation an arresting lesson in public relations. Peck and his colleagues returned by train to rejoin the General Conference in Philadelphia. The following morning, they prepared proudly to reveal the president's signed reply. They were, Peck recalled, "taken aback by discovering that it had been published in all the morning papers, and every body had read it." It had been telegraphed to Philadelphia and beyond, and was being typeset well before the deputation had left Washington. Lincoln's reply was directed at the more than one million members and adherents, and seven thousand ministers, of this "controlling public influence."[126]

Ten days later, on May 28, a hundred or so crammed into the White House for a meeting of the president with a delegation from the American Baptist Home Mission Society. The group was led by George B. Ide, pastor of the First Baptist Church of Springfield, Massachusetts; James R. Doolittle, U.S. senator from Wisconsin and a member of the First Baptist Church of Racine; and Alrick Hubbell, a New York Republican and former state senator. The occasion resembled the Methodists' encounter in the tone and substance of the loyal resolutions they presented. Rebellion and the creation of a slaveholders' confederacy they castigated as an assault on "civilization, humanity, freedom and God, unparalleled in all centuries." The president and Union authorities had won hearty assent for a policy of conquering disunion by uprooting slavery. Baptists would make every necessary sacrifice for "the final triumph of liberty and righteousness," and a "grander future for our country and the world."[127]

Lincoln offered a few words of thanks, acknowledging the political support "so unanimously given by all Christian denominations of the country," and asked for time to reply in writing. Two days later he penned two paragraphs in which he repeated with unusual severity a critique of pro-slavery theologians that he would fold with more emollience into his second inaugural address nine months later. It was hard to conceive how it was possible to read God's words "In the sweat of *thy* face shalt thou eat bread," and yet preach, "In the sweat of *other mans* faces shalt thou eat bread." Recognizing the judgment of a sovereign God, the argument then took a personal turn. "When brought to my final reckoning, may I have to answer for robbing no man of his goods" or, yet more intolerably, "for robbing one of himself, and all that was his." This was the crime of "those professedly holy men of the South" who upended the Golden Rule by asking the Christian world for help "in doing to a whole race of men, as they would have no man do unto themselves." In this, "they contemned and insulted God and His church, far more than did Satan when he tempted the Saviour with the Kingdoms of the earth. The devils attempt was no more false, and far less hypocritical." He concluded with a cautionary warning against self-righteousness, one that prefigured his second inaugural address: "Let me forbear, remembering it is also written 'Judge not, lest ye be judged.' "[128] In that spirit of restraint, he appears not to have issued the document.

When war came, Union radicals championed emancipation and a purified nation. In this 1861 Boston lithograph an American eagle carries aloft a freed slave and a white man who proclaims, "Break every Yoke; let the oppressed go free." A poem declares, "A man is a man howe'er dark his skin. . . . God regards not his color—and neither should we."

The words of this Confederate national anthem (1862) declare, "God make the right stronger than the might! . . . Let the proud spoiler know God's on our side."

In this savage Union cartoon, a grinning Satan greets Jefferson Davis and his Confederates, telling them their treason, murder, and other crimes make them "fit representatives of our Realm."

In writing the Emancipation Proclamation, Lincoln—the antithesis of diabolical rebels— is seen here to honor scripture and the Constitution. His hand rests on a Bible. A bust of the ineffectual president Buchanan hangs by a noose.

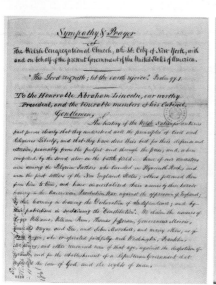

The loyal "memorial" of New York City's Welsh Congregationalists was one of the first wartime church messages to reach the president. Enemies of slavery, they declared that "the Welsh are Peaceable Christians, but they will fight like their forefathers for Civil and Religious Liberty." (April 16, 1861)

The radical resolutions of the Philadelphia Presbytery of the Reformed Presbyterian Church in North America deemed the war "a divine rebuke for the support which our government has given to Slavery," and a God-given opportunity for its extinction. (April 16, 1861)

As commander of the Department of the West, Major General John C. Frémont (1813–1890) ordered the emancipation of rebel Missourians' slaves in August 1861. By countermanding the proclamation, Lincoln stirred a political storm. Some radicals touted Frémont for president in 1864.

Orville Hickman Browning (1806–1881), U.S. senator from Illinois, 1861–63, and Old School Presbyterian. Lincoln enjoyed his company but was "astonished" by his conservative friend's support for Frémont's emancipation order.

far left: Charles Hodge (1797–1878), the influential conservative Calvinist principal of Princeton Theological Seminary. Although a defender of "scriptural" slavery, he came to support emancipation during the war.

left: Phineas Densmore Gurley (1816–1868) trained for the Old School Presbyterian ministry under Hodge at Princeton. A learned theologian and Lincoln's pastor in Washington, he won the president's trust and friendship.

far left: William Weston Patton (1821–1889), Congregationalist minister and abolitionist, led the September 1862 initiative that produced the Chicago churches' emancipation memorial to the president.

left: Edward R. Ames (1806–1879), Bishop of the Methodist Episcopal Church and the senior member of the MEC committee visiting Lincoln in May 1864.

The Pennsylvania Yearly Meeting of Progressive Friends at Longwood. A Quaker delegation of three women and three men met Lincoln in June 1862 to urge an immediate edict of emancipation.

left: William Lloyd Garrison (1805–1879), the embodiment of radical abolitionism, who grew in his admiration for Lincoln's steadfastness of moral purpose.

center: George Barrell Cheever (1807–1890), radical abolitionist and pastor of the Church of the Puritans, New York City. Doubting Lincoln's ability and integrity, he supported Frémont's candidacy in 1864.

right: Theodore Tilton (1835–1907), the gifted abolitionist editor of the nation's most influential religious-political weekly, the New York *Independent*.

left: Gilbert Haven (1821–1880), New England Methodist preacher, militant abolitionist, and uncompromising racial egalitarian who aimed to shape, not follow, public opinion.

center: Henry McNeal Turner (1834–1915), practical emancipationist, Republican activist, and AME minister in Washington, D.C. The organizer of a regiment of black troops, he served as its chaplain and as a reporter for his denomination's *Christian Recorder*.

right: Anna Elizabeth Dickinson (1842–1932), a sensational abolitionist lecturer and political campaigner ("with the tongue of twenty women, she combines the boldness of forty men"). Though no fan of Lincoln's, she campaigned hard for McClellan's defeat in 1864.

left: "Parson Brownlow's Quick Step"

bottom right: William Gannaway Brownlow (1805–1877), Methodist minister and editor of Knoxville. The prewar scourge of abolitionists, the Parson became a northern celebrity for his defiant Unionism. How many Union patriots danced his "Quick Step" is unknown, but he drew vast audiences for his scorching attacks on Confederate leaders. The "moral mania" of secession he blamed above all on southern clergy.

bottom left: "Scene in Richmond, VA" (*Harper's Weekly*, June 7, 1862). The caption reads, "The President stands in a Corner *telling his beads*, and proclaims A THIRD FAST . . . while . . . the sufferings endured by the people have never been parallelled in history."

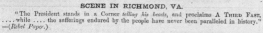

An 1860 anti-Republican cartoon portrays Lincoln's party as a ragbag of infidel radicals. Their perceived threat to conventional race relations prefigures the zealotry of The Miscegenation Ball.

top: Clement L. Vallandigham (1820–1871), U.S. congressman, 1858–63, and leader of the antiwar Democrats. Exiled, he ran for the Ohio governorship in 1863. The party's peace platform in 1864 bore his imprint.

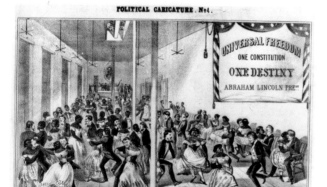

left: To exploit white race prejudice, a Democratic print of 1864—The Miscegenation Ball—shows white Republican men dancing with black women, "thus testifying to their faith by their works." Lincoln's portrait blesses the occasion.

left: Henry Clay Dean (1822–1887), Methodist minister, Peace Democrat, and a powerful speaker arrested and held in confinement for his withering antiwar diatribes.

right: Charles Chauncey Burr (1817–1883), sometime Universalist minister, fervent Peace Democrat, editor of the *Old Guard*, and a master of satire and invective.

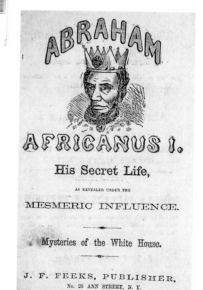

This satirical Copperhead tract portrays Lincoln as a hypocritical emancipationist artfully exploiting racial issues, in a pact with the devil to make him king.

Lincoln regarded *The Nasby Papers* (1864), a savage satire of Copperhead pro-slavery religion, as a work of genius.

Petroleum Vesuvius Nasby, as imagined by the gifted cartoonist Thomas Nast. Behind the preacher a halo adorns the portrait of "Saint Vandaldigum."

David Ross Locke (1833–1888), Ohio newspaper editor, creator of Nasby, and brilliant satirist of the Peace Democrats.

An 1864 election cartoon, "'Peace' Democracy on the Rampage—What We Want Be Jabers Is Peace and Liberty," plays on the reputation of Catholic Irish Americans after the 1863 New York draft riots as thieves, rioters, and murderers of free blacks.

A figure in Lincoln's likeness scythes through Copperhead snakes. He threatens the end of the slave labor system (right) and clears the way for free and fruitful black labor (left).

Among the 30,000 gathered for Lincoln's second inauguration was John Wilkes Booth, driven to murder the president six weeks later, raging against the notion of a new racial order in the South.

Alexander Gardner's photograph of Lincoln in February 1865 captures the war's physical toll on the president.

Lincoln's funeral car crawls through crowds of mourners in Philadelphia on Saturday, April 22, 1865. An estimated 300,000 people viewed his open coffin in Independence Hall.

Lincoln in the Tempest of Religious Nationalisms, 1863–1864 295

CROSSOVERS: BROWNLOW, HODGE, AND CONSERVATIVE CONVERTS TO EMANCIPATION

The turbulence of war challenged antebellum certainties about enslavement and emancipation. Most conservative Unionists stood firm under the tide of events, holding limpet-like to the prewar constitution, but significant figures sought and found new anchorages. Many learned to reassess African Americans' capabilities. "I must favorably mention the negro," an officer of the Third Minnesota Regiment wrote to Lincoln from Arkansas. An active Democrat in 1860, he boasted of subsequently swinging behind the Union administration. Although slaveholders delivered dire warnings of the diabolical consequences of emancipation, he protested, "it is a sublime fact that instead of committing excesses the only difference in the conduct of the colored people is that they are a little more vehement in their hallelujahs and seek to gain knowledge!" Likewise, another political convert, the Indiana Methodist preacher Robert Curran, sent Lincoln a copy of his recent fast-day sermon to show that "a large portion" of the state's "old democrats" had been won over to emancipation and slaves' capacity for freedom.[129]

More likely still to shift to new ground were conservative Whigs. None expressed a more practical theology than John Minor Botts, Virginia planter and lawyer and Lincoln's fellow Whig in the U.S. Congress of 1847–49. A devoted Unionist, Botts conceded that had Lincoln's emancipation edict preceded the war, it would have demanded his revolutionary resistance. But it had resulted from the secessionist treason of Davis and Confederate hotheads, "the most accuresed, the most flagitious, the most stupendious, and the most attrocious crime . . . committed since the day that Jesus Christ was crucified." Emancipation had cost him valuable property but, he wrote, "in the name of God let it go" if it would restore a Union on which "I religiously believe the happiness, welfare, and liberties of the people South as well as North depend." Botts took stern Calvinist comfort from the enforcement of God's law that "we are all, the good & the bad alike, made responsible for the original sin of that venerable old Lady, known as Madam Eve." By that doctrine of punishment and atonement, he would pay the price "of the original sin of those with whom it has been my fortune to be mixed up geographically." He had no quarrel with the president, he insisted, whose Emancipation Proclamation was above all vindicated by resting "upon precisely the same principle, as does the most important of all divine law."[130]

As a dissident in Confederate Virginia, Botts had less sway than did several former Whigs within the Union whose conservatism was catalyzed by war into a powerful force for change. The agency of one—Charles Hodge of Princeton—percolated quietly and without fanfare through the organs of Presbyterianism; in time, he was joined by a fellow leader of the Old School, Robert J. Breckinridge. The noisy, attention-seeking celebrity of another, a singular Methodist, extended far beyond the Appalachian boundaries where he had first made his name.

———

The Civil War marked a new stage in the emergence of modern celebrity culture. Mass circulation newspapers, the steam press, photography, and the telegraph fed a public appetite for stories and pictures of the famous, one sharpened by Americans' awareness that they were living through momentous events. In August 1864, the New York publishers Fowler & Wells advertised "Portraits of Leading Characters—Warriors, Clergymen, Poets, Canibals, Flatheads. . . . Generals Lee, Grant, Thomas, Foster, Hancock, Butler, McPherson, Napier, with . . . Brownlow, Dr. Tyng, Martin Luther." The presence of Union generals requires no explanation. More arresting, however, are the three religious figures. The father of modern Protestantism, Martin Luther, spoke to many Americans' self-perception as the authentic heirs of the Reformation now engaged in a holy contest. "Dr. Tyng" was Stephen Higginson Tyng, New York's leading evangelical Episcopalian and staunch emancipationist. But why did a Tennessee Methodist minister, William Gannaway Brownlow, feature in this exalted company? There was, after all, little in his prewar record—as a reckless controversialist, denominational chauvinist, incendiary newspaper editor, and apologist for slavery—to endear him to the northern mainstream public. The truth is that by 1864 he had become a commercially exploitable celebrity, transformed by war into a Lincoln loyalist and bellicose enemy of the Confederacy and its peculiar institution.

There were few more colorful public figures than Brownlow. Born in 1805 into a Scotch Irish family of slaveholder farmers, he was orphaned at the age of eleven. His conversion at a Methodist camp meeting propelled him into the itinerant ministry. An imposing stature, sharp mind, gift for language, and appetite for polemics gave him the edge in fighting the devil for souls in southern Appalachia. Subsequently settling as a local preacher in eastern Tennessee, he turned to journalism to champion his two loves, the Methodist movement and the Whig Party. The *Knoxville Whig* became the region's most influential political sheet, its ferocious, one-eyed partisanship earning it far-flung notoriety. When, he was asked, would he abandon the Whigs for the Democrats? "When the sun shines at midnight," he replied, "when the Pope of Rome will join the Methodist church . . . when proof is afforded, both clear and unquestionable, that there is no God."

A champion of slavery, Brownlow traveled north in 1858 to challenge abolitionist "freedom shriekers" to a public debate. He turned down a forum with Frederick Douglass (deeming it dishonorable to engage with a black man) and settled on meeting Abram Pryne, a Congregational minister and radical Garrisonian. Over five evenings in Philadelphia the two men traded abuse and substantive arguments. Brownlow drew on history, scripture, science, and the federal constitution to assert slavery's Christian purpose. *The New York Times* thought the polemical spectacle unedifying at best. "Of Brownlow, the kindest thing we can say is to hope he is insane," its editor remarked. Yet the "Fighting Parson" would soon be feted in the very same northern circles. By the logic of his staunch wartime Unionism, Brownlow the sectarian pro-slavery champion morphed into a loyalist hero. His combative and absolutist Appalachian temperament became a political and religious asset in time of war.

Brownlow cast the Confederacy as the self-serving project of the "nabobs of Cottonocracy," fiendishly working against the interests of the "honest yeomanry." His class rhetoric found a receptive audience in eastern Tennessee, with its high proportion of white landless households. When the state seceded, Brownlow used his

Knoxville Whig to rally Lincoln loyalists. However, fearing arrest, he shut his press and assumed the garb of a Christian martyr: better to be imprisoned than swear a sacrilegious oath conceding "the hand of God in the work of breaking up the American Government and the inauguration of the most wicked, unnatural, and uncalled-for war ever recorded in history." After fleeing into the mountains, he returned to military confinement and eventual banishment. "Glory to God in the highest, and on earth peace, good will toward men," he shouted as he crossed into the Union lines outside Nashville, "except a few hell-born and hell-bound rebels in Knoxville." There he would meet Lincoln's military governor of Tennessee, Andrew Johnson. For a quarter of a century the two men—Whig and Democrat—had been bitter antagonists, but now, united in loyalism, they "rushed into each other's arms, and wept like children."[131]

From there Brownlow launched himself at the North, to become a lionized champion of American nationhood. Feted by state governors—Oliver Morton, David Tod, Edwin Morgan, John Andrew—he reveled in his celebrity and by invitation visited the president at the Soldiers' Home.[132] Manner and matter set him apart from other speakers. Overflowing meetings, from Cincinnati and Chicago, to Philadelphia, New York, and Boston, discovered a tall, slender man, full of pent-up energy and looking older than his fifty-seven years. John Hay, Lincoln's secretary, described a figure with "long, black, straight hair, carelessly combed; sallow complexion, beardless cheeks, black sunken eyes, high cheek bones, and an unmistakable expression of fight on lip, cheek, and eyes." According to another of Lincoln's associates, David Davis, "He . . . never smiles. His nostrils are like a race horse. His face is iron and you can see by his eye that he does not fear the face of man." Brownlow's defining characteristic was linguistic versatility. "If I have any talent in the world," he declared, "it . . . consists of piling up one epithet upon another." He lashed with his tongue. "I never witnessed a race in my life, nor a fight, even a dog fight, but I took one side or another," he confessed with pride. A wordsmith himself, Hay warmed to the Parson's "demon of witty reminiscence" and "spicy remark." Though severe, he "was not blackguardly—though witty, was not scurrilous—though earnest, was not boisterous." Others were less charitable. "A more coarse-minded, vulgar, abusive, pugi-

Lincoln in the Tempest of Religious Nationalisms, 1863–1864 299

listic disputant it would be difficult to find," sneered William Lloyd Garrison's *Liberator.* That he resisted treason in Tennessee "makes him neither a gentleman nor a Christian."[133] Of Brownlow the stout Unionist, the English journalist George Sala commented, "The strongest, perchance, with whom it would be possible to meet out of the Bloomingdale Lunatic Asylum."[134]

For most, though, Brownlow was a heroic and beguiling figure. They saw more than showmanship and verbal acrobatics. Here was a southerner—a pro-slavery southerner, at that—who put the permanence of the nation above the interests of slave property, who risked martyrdom for his faith in the American Union as a vehicle of progress, who spoke with parsonical authority, who embodied the stubbornness of tough mountain folk, and who was determined to return to a cleansed eastern Tennessee, resurrect the *Knoxville Whig,* and play a part in the eventual downfall of the Confederacy. Brownlow presented as a man of integrity, of moral and religious scruple; a teetotaler who never smoked, swore, gambled, or went to the theater; a loyal Methodist minister bitter and vindictive toward his former associates who had conspired in secession.[135] "The worst class of men, so help me God, on Southern soil," the Parson declared, were the Methodist, Baptist, Presbyterian, and Episcopalian preachers, "unmitigated scoundrels . . . corrupt, treacherous and vile."

Over time, Brownlow became a political and religious voice for the forces of the Republican-Union party and the Lincoln administration. The anti Confederate absolutist worked to stiffen resolve, prodding generals and political leaders to abandon forbearance and crush the North's rebel sympathizers. Despite mistakenly believing the president was too casually neglectful of the Unionist pocket of eastern Tennessee, Brownlow extolled Lincoln's patriotism, honesty, and ability.

Brownlow, the pro-slavery voice of the 1858 debates, in wartime became a cheerleader for freedom. The enslaved labor force of the Confederacy released white men to fight. "I say confiscate everything they've got," he demanded. "Emancipate their negroes and drive the last scoundrel of the rebels down into the Gulf of Mexico, as the devil did the hogs into the sea." In the spirit of abolitionism he added, "Through the mercy of God, the firmness of Mr. Lincoln and the madness of the Southern Confederacy, we are all about to find a common level where we can at least boast that the Lord is the maker of us all." For Brownlow, along with other border-state nationalists, emancipation was tough but essential medicine. He was no sophisticated political theorist. His Unionism grew out of a Whig confidence in the economic beneficence of the federal government, a fear of the destructive potential of southern planter parochialism, and a powerful generalized patriotism. An enthusiast for enlisting black soldiers, he raged against their maltreatment. After the Confederates' massacre of black troops at Fort Pillow, he fashioned an image striking even by his standards: "Had we our wish, we would throw hell wide open, and place all such beast-like officers and men upon an inclined plane, at an angle of forty-five degrees, the plane with hog's lard six inches thick, with a wicket [gate] at the bottom, and send them, as one stream of traitors, robbers, and assassins, into the hottest part of the infernal regions."[136]

By the time Brownlow returned to Union-controlled middle Tennessee in 1863 to serve as a U.S. Treasury agent, he was a rich man. The 458 pages of *Parson Brownlow's Book*, which he churned out in record time, delivered his unique brand of belligerence to hundreds of thousands who had not heard him in person. Cheap pamphlet biographies and speeches, steel engravings and photographs, and even sheet music (the "Parson Brownlow Quick Step")—all were a measure of his fame as the Apostle of Freedom and swelled the funds to revive his newspaper when the way was clear. Federal troops took control of Knoxville in September 1863. Two months later Brownlow's *Knoxville Whig and Rebel Ventilator* resumed the job of verbally eviscerating the enemy, supporting Union candidates, sustaining the Lincoln administration, and working to reestablish civil government in Tennessee.

The Parson, then, was a uniquely compelling representative of a constituency essential to the Union's survival: the conservative loyalists radicalized by war to accept what they had once feared. No one was more extravagant than Brownlow in fusing righteousness and the Union as a potent weapon of war. With these words, he concluded his best-selling *Parson Brownlow's Book:*

> I have spoken plainly, vehemently. . . . I can spare no denunciation when I see . . . traitors deliberately plunging us into

Lincoln in the Tempest of Religious Nationalisms, 1863–1864 301

a fratricidal war fit only for the leadership of Cain. . . . God grant that the people may now raise their eyes and lift their hands . . . in fervent supplication that the Father of Mercies will compose the distractions of our suffering land, and eclipse the splendor of our annals in the past by the future renown, for ages to come, of the Re-United States![137]

In establishing the Civil War as a righteous and holy conflict, no minister did so with more combative force, sulfurous language, imaginative idiom, and immoderate appetite than the Fighting Parson of Knoxville.

———

Princeton's Charles Hodge, a naturally subtler theologian than Brownlow, and a more profound influence on religious minds, shared the Tennessean's Whiggery and his keen appetite for politics. Like Brownlow, he had been a fierce critic of abolitionists before the war and won the favor of southerners in presenting the scriptural case for slaveholding. His first justification, published in 1836, must be seen in the context of Princeton Theological Seminary's strong connections with the South and of the continuing presence of slavery in New Jersey long after the state's gradual emancipation act of 1804. Hodge was personally complicit in slaveholding through his purchase in 1828 of a black "servant," a teenage girl who by statute could not be freed until she was twenty-one. Equally significant, however, was his conviction that southern slavery should and would be a platform for the ultimate freedom of the enslaved, through the gradual elevation of the slaves through their moral, intellectual, and material improvement. He continued to assert that slaveholding in the abstract was not sinful, but that southerners' practice was profoundly corrupt, by withholding education and religious instruction from the enslaved and willfully denying them Christian marriage and family stability.[138]

For Hodge the wickedness of the Confederacy's ends—the exaltation of an unscriptural form of slavery—matched the iniquity of its means, a revolutionary assault on the Union. The apocalyptic strain and exotic millennialism of many Civil War evangelicals is absent in Hodge's writings, but he insisted on the righteousness and universal significance of the cause.[139] A bloody struggle for national existence, to subdue rebels who had sinned in disobeying the constituted authorities, was incontestably just and godly.[140] Surveying the battlefield failures in the summer of 1862, Hodge told his brother, "I still have full confidence that God is on our side, and that He will bring us safe, and I trust purified, out of all our troubles." Six months later, in the yet bleaker aftermath of Fredericksburg, he urged Unionists to be confident in the justice of the cause, though the outcome was not guaranteed: "We do not say that success will certainly attend the right. The wrong in this world, which for a time is the kingdom of Satan, often triumphs. But . . . it is a thousandfold better to be defeated with the right, than to be triumphant with the wrong."[141]

As editor of *The Princeton Review*, Hodge assumed the role of expositor, moral guide, and shaper of wartime Presbyterian opinion. Aiming to build the widest possible base of domestic support for the war, he reminded "all good men" of their duty to support an administration operating in the national interest.[142] His well-informed and lucid essays reveal a trenchant commentator on the war's political management and military strategy. Through his personal contacts, notably with his brother-in-law General David Hunter, and his immersion in the secular press, he kept abreast of developments in what he described as the Union's herculean task: managing extended lines of supply and communication against a well-resourced Confederacy.[143] His first intervention, the essay "England and America," lamented that in the crisis over the American seizure of the British steamer the *Trent* and its cargo of Confederate envoys, the British government had unwittingly sided with "an unrighteous effort to establish a government whose cornerstone is domestic slavery."[144]

Hodge provided a philosophical and practical defense of Lincoln's policies. In the month of the Emancipation Proclamation, he published an essay titled "The War." The government's only legitimate aim, in keeping with the terms of the Crittenden-Johnson resolutions of July 1861, was to preserve national existence under the Constitution, he insisted. Pursuing abolition would be morally wrong, for although slavery in the United States had become "a burden and curse," its violent removal would be the greater catas-

Lincoln in the Tempest of Religious Nationalisms, 1863–1864 303

trophe.[145] And it would be inexpedient. Victory depended on the unity of Republicans and Democrats, a brittle war coalition of conservatives and radicals never likely to cohere behind a policy of emancipation. That had been the lesson of the fall 1862 elections, when Democrats harnessed the opponents of Lincoln's preliminary emancipation proclamation. "We must keep right, and we must keep united," Hodge declared, "or we must be defeated."[146]

Hodge endorsed the administration's use of arbitrary arrest, press censorship, and conscription as indispensable to national survival and consistent with moral law. In keeping with republican ideals, the authorities had provided for the humane treatment of Confederate prisoners, respected rebels' private property, and refused to stir up servile rebellion. The real danger to American liberty, Hodge asserted, sprang not from federal action but from "the masses" and "State pride," the wellsprings of rebellion. A law-and-order Whig, fearful of Democratic populism, he saw no threat of presidential despotism. The citizen, he insisted, owed cheerful obedience. Subject to bouts of sleeplessness and tearful depression, he chastised himself, "We are bound not to despond." Grappling with Union calamities, human suffering, and the judgment of an inscrutable God, he offered his readers no false optimism. But his repeated message of obedience to the government, whatever the shortcomings and misjudgments of its leadership, helped sustain public loyalty to the Union cause over four bloody years.[147]

Most significant of all, Hodge embraced Lincoln's Emancipation Proclamation as a weapon of war that neither changed nor compromised the administration's primary purpose. The rebels having persistently refused terms that offered to protect slavery, the commander in chief had grasped a legitimate lever in the struggle for national existence. Emancipation was a means to an end, not an objective in itself. "If the abolition of slavery be made, either really or avowedly, the object of the war, we believe we shall utterly fail," Hodge declared.[148] Yet the reality of the proclamation, as he and Lincoln understood, would inevitably blur the line between means and ends. Preserving the Union was still the war's stated objective, but it would hardly be a Union for slaveholders. Hodge acknowledged that the end of slavery would follow "in a natural and healthful manner." The proclamation did no more than instruct military officers to treat slaves entering their lines as freemen, but it would secure radical change over time.

Hodge's journey toward an emancipationist nationalism encouraged and mirrored that of most, though far from all, of the Union's Old School Presbyterians. It is telling that *The Princeton Review*, as it embraced the administration's measures, lost no subscribers. The institutional Church, true to its conservative complexion, moved slowly. The annual Old School General Assembly avoided any mention of slavery in June 1862. But Lincoln's edict meant the issue could not be ducked in 1863. Meeting in Peoria, Illinois, the assembly's majority declared their support for the Union government and rebuked ministers who had sided with rebellion. Yet it failed to address the president's emancipation order head-on, merely noting their Church's testimony against slavery in 1818 and its later more qualified statements. Only in 1864 did the assembly take a frank and emphatic stand. A few local groups, notably in Ohio and other parts of the Midwest, had for years worked to secure what the majority now unequivocally declared, that the nation's trauma was a token of God's will that "*every vestige of human slavery among us should be effaced.*" As the root of "rebellion, war, and bloodshed," slavery had demonstrated its incompatibility with free Christian government. Here was justification for the president's emancipation policy, the proposals for emancipation measures in the loyal states, and the political initiatives for an emancipation amendment to the Constitution.[149]

Following in the footsteps of Hodge, and the most striking of the Old School converts of 1864, was the redoubtable leader of unwavering Kentucky Unionism and the guiding light of Danville Theological Seminary, Robert J. Breckinridge. As the influential editor of *The Danville Quarterly Review*, Breckinridge had never ducked the moral challenge of human bondage. An enslaver who was actively trying to reclaim his fugitive slaves during 1864, Breckinridge had long been the beacon light of gradual emancipation, but just as earnestly denounced abolitionists as law-defying anarchists. He held his ground against Lincoln's emancipation edict, an overreach of presidential authority he declared compatible with "neither *the Constitution as it is*, nor yet *the Union as it was*." Confident in the

Lincoln in the Tempest of Religious Nationalisms, 1863–1864 305

combined power of the Almighty and the Union, he called it "a folly, if not a sin, to attempt to frustrate the course of Providence."

But the slow grind of war worked a change of heart. In common with the Presbyterians of the Danville enclave and a few elsewhere, he epitomized the devoted Kentucky nationalist ready to put his love of Union above misgivings over Lincoln's incremental advance toward complete emancipation. In May 1864 he wrote to Reverdy Johnson to commend the senator's speech in support of an emancipation amendment to the Constitution. The following month, he nailed his colors to the mast of a slave-free nation at the National Union Party's opening session at Baltimore, where he presided pro tem after receiving three cheers as the "Old War Horse of Kentucky." To a convention comprising, in his words, "not only primitive Republicans and primitive Abolitionists . . . primitive Democrats and primitive Whigs," he defined their common purpose as "the destruction of this rebellion, root and branch," at whatever cost in blood. The folly and sin of secessionist treason had brought the nation to this moment of irrevocable choice. Returning human bondage to its prewar protection meant embracing pro-slavery principles that defied the Christian religion and universal natural rights. If emancipation were unconstitutional, as some alleged (and he, too, had believed), "We will change our constitution if it suits us to do so." Consequently, he declared to prolonged applause, "I fervently pray God that the day may come when, throughout the whole land every man may be free as you are, and as capable of enjoying regulated liberty." Joining Hodge and most of his fellow conservative Presbyterians, Breckinridge now stood on the very terrain that antislavery evangelicals had reached from another direction.[150]

RESOLUTE CONSERVATIVES

Most Presbyterians, but not *all.* The horrific bloodletting of early and high summer 1864 cemented Peace Democrats' conviction that only Union concessions could end the slaughter, gave the Democratic Party as a whole grounds for hope in the fall elections, and troubled the hearts of Republicans. So circumstanced, an ultraconservative Presbyterian minority deplored the decision of the Old School

Assembly—which met under the billowing Stars and Stripes—to align politically with the Union and its emancipation policy. In the divided heartland of the border states, the doctrine of the spirituality of the church had previously provided some defense against the intrusion of inflammatory political issues. That protective doctrine now yielded to what one critic scorned as the Church's "adulterous intercourse with the state." Dr. Stuart Robinson's *True Presbyterian*, published in Kentucky, shared the alarm. "What are Conservative men to do now?" the peppery controversialist asked. Robinson's supposedly apolitical editorship and contempt for "Spread Eagle" religion did nothing to inhibit his outspoken defense of slavery, nor his virulent assaults on abolitionists, whose "atheistic humanitarianism" he asserted would lead to the indiscriminate butchery of the families of southern Presbyterian brethren. With a readership across the border region, the lower North, and New York, the paper was suspected of disloyalty and links to Copperhead secret societies. Whatever the truth, Robinson grieved at the direction taken by the General Assembly. He urged fellow conservatives to stand aloof and "wait and watch for an opportunity to reconstruct our wasted temple out of the ruins of the old."[151] Prominent among these was the foremost Presbyterian layman of the day, Cyrus Hall McCormick. Unyielding Democrat, owner of *The Chicago Times*, and devout Old School Calvinist, McCormick prized his party and denomination as the two best hopes of a Union he believed irrecoverable by war.[152]

Robinson's and McCormick's dismay echoed the alarm in other churches over mainstream Protestants' surging support for emancipation. Most Catholics, many confessional Protestant churches, and evangelicals in the border states and lower North doubled down in demanding the return of the old Union. Speaking for its Irish Catholic readers, the Boston *Pilot* lamented the drive to abandon the war's original purposes and "make another Constitution," a development that slandered conservative patriots as traitorous fellow travelers of the secessionists. The republic's real enemies, the editor insisted, were "the members of the Government, the Congressmen, the ministers of religion, the presses, who have abused their position . . . to disturb the harmony of the North."[153] New York's weekly *Metropolitan Record*, boasting its role as "A Catholic Family Paper," continued its unswerving course of opposition to

Lincoln in the Tempest of Religious Nationalisms, 1863–1864 307

abolitionism, conscription, Washington despotism, and "fanaticism in every form," and bewailed an unholy war designed to reduce the southern people to "the most abject submission . . . almost as low as that of the negro."[154] The minority antislavery voices of American Catholicism—notably Orestes Brownson, Archbishop John Purcell, and the Cincinnati *Catholic Telegraph*, edited by the archbishop's brother Edward—struggled against the Church majority's cacophony of disdain. None was more caustic than James McMaster, whose *Freeman's Journal* routinely bracketed Catholic and Protestant abolitionists as crazed deviants from the immovable conservatism of Pius IX.[155]

Catholic churches mostly provided an institutional and ideological haven for their conservative majority, whether those willing to fight for the Union or peace advocates sure that the main obstacle to a negotiated reunion was the war itself. By contrast, many ultraconservative Protestants across the lower Midwest, Democrats in politics, faced such hostility from their churches' Republican majorities that they withdrew to form their own religious societies where their ministers could preach without restraint. These disaffected separatists set up a host of new churches, reactionary local responses to the emancipationist agenda of pro-administration Protestants. By 1864 there might have been some eighty new and independent Methodist churches in Illinois, led not by rural illiterates but by substantial farmers, magistrates, and political officeholders. Discontent among the United Brethren of northwestern Ohio prompted a similar new-church movement there, the Reformed United Brethren. Committed to "the Union as it was and the Constitution as it is, now and forever," it trumpeted such propositions as "The negro has no ability to enjoy liberty, consequently has no right to it." In February 1864 an Ohio statewide convention of dissident Methodists, Baptists, Presbyterians, Unitarians, Universalists, and United Brethren formed "the Christian Union" on an ecumenical platform, with its own religious newspaper. The handiwork of the Reverend James F. Given, Edson B. Olds, and other leading Democrats, the organization would absorb new churches throughout the Midwest. A kindred network of Democratic churches, the Illinois Christian Association, also gave a home to disgruntled Protestants who held that "a man may believe in the Westminster catechism and the

Apostles' creed, without at the same time subscribing to the tenets of abolitionism."[156]

These dissenting churches began life as reactive, spontaneous, and defensive movements, but in time they developed into calculated insurgency. Although they were sometimes described as networks of Copperhead Christians, the reality was more complex. A few leaders tried to maintain a genuinely apolitical stance. Others were out-and-out Peace Democrats dancing to the tune of Clement Vallandigham. But war-supporting Democrats, too, championed religious insurgency. The pulpit politics of Republican-leaning clergy drew Democrats of all stripes together in common affront.

The president's national days of thanksgiving, and of fasting and prayer, presented conservative Unionists with an increasing challenge as emancipation became the likely outcome of the war. Loyalist ministers of churches in the lower North and border states, some with congregations tied by family and culture to the South, trod carefully, even equivocally. Staunch Unionists eyed with suspicion the distinguished Baltimore Baptist pastor Richard Fuller for his prewar defense of slaveholding and, at the launch of the Confederacy, his initial support for peaceful separation. His fast-day sermon of April 1863 acknowledged the supremacy of the Washington government while lamenting the destruction of war; he rebuked specific sins and the neglect of God's sovereign Providence, but studiously avoided any mention of slavery. On the same day, the conservative ministers of Smyrna, Delaware, earned the contempt of administration loyalists for ignoring what they called the nation's greatest affliction, by dwelling instead on a hackneyed catalog of evils to explain God's sore displeasure: "Sabbath breaking, intemperance, idolatry of wealth, the cruelty to the Indians, profanity, speaking evil of our rulers, etc."[157] When in his national thanksgiving address of November 1863 an Illinois minister similarly kept a studied silence on the main issue of the day, a Republican editor called him out: "The onward march of the principles of freedom . . . cannot be stopped by efforts to anchor them to the fossilized idea of the 'Divine right of Slavery.'"[158]

Bold conservatives were more explicit. A Pittsburgh Catholic approved Lincoln's call for the national fast of April 1863, agreeing that the war was punishment for national sins, but denying that

Lincoln in the Tempest of Religious Nationalisms, 1863–1864 309

slavery was the nation's major evil. Neither section could be held responsible for the existence of human bondage, and while some slaveholders had sinned, others had exercised paternal care. As an evil, slavery was less heinous than the human failings of materialism, dishonesty, irreligion, and excessive national pride and vanity.[159] Lecturing on that day, Rabbi Raphall of New York stood firm for the Union while lambasting the "demagogues, fanatics and a party Press" that had brought on a needless sectional war over slavery.[160] This, too, was the Methodist Samuel Chamberlain's theme in the Universalist church at Manchester, Indiana. Chamberlain's reputation as a "real Butternut preacher," southern sympathizer, and antiabolitionist put his Unionism under the searching spotlight of Methodism's pro-administration partisans. By combining support for the Union with a lament over common suffering, North and South, he fell victim to a church trial and suspension for political disloyalty. A proxy for the fierce electoral conflicts raging between Democrats and Republicans in the Midwest, Chamberlain's case could not be separated from the high-temperature politics of 1863 and 1864. In reality, he loved the Union and yearned to see it healed, but only on terms that assured a white man's republic.[161]

As the war continued, hardened Democrats came to characterize national fasts and days of thanksgiving as partisan political weapons, functioning—perhaps even designed—to serve the "Satanic project" of Lincoln's administration. In a stinging critique of a Methodist's fast-day sermon in August 1864, an Ohio Copperhead told how the Republican minister—"wearing the livery of heaven to serve his master the devil"—had shattered his village's gathering for peace by extolling the war's "carnival of blood."[162] Several Democratic editors pushed back against "Abe Lincoln's ministers" on fast days. A paper in Kittanning, Pennsylvania, appeared with funereal borders to mourn the death of the Union, the Constitution, and freedom of speech. The *Illinois State Register* sarcastically welcomed "Massa Linkum's" call for fasting, humiliation, and prayer on the grounds that "the nation has ample reason for fasting, because Lincoln has made food so high; for humiliation at the disgraces his miserable, imbecile policies have brought upon us; and for prayer that God, in his goodness, will spare us a second term of *such* a president." *The Chicago Times* proposed its own prayer: "We know, oh our Father, that this wicked and devastating war was produced by unrighteous demagogues. . . . Make us to know that it is only by the retirement from power of such men as Mr. Lincoln and Mr. Davis, . . . that we can ever obtain that peace for which we are now supplicating. Amen!" James McMaster's *Freeman's Journal* lauded Cicero for putting peace above civil war. "He never split rails. He never destroyed his country. He never appointed a day of fasting and prayer, which his followers *improved* by a general neglect of business and a debauch." Those who wanted to hear the simple gospel on fast day, and find a respite from politics, should attend their local Catholic church.[163]

The explicit politicizing of fast days and national thanksgivings became inevitable once Lincoln, in embracing emancipation, followed a course that immeasurably aggravated the already sharp differences between conservative and antislavery religious nationalists. These contending convictions of righteousness would shape the fraught popular politics of the Union during the second half of 1864, from the battlefield stalemate of high summer to the fall elections and beyond. But by then, even in the darkest of days, the president had on his side a resolute and supreme agent of antislavery nationalism, the Union army.

RELIGIOUS NATIONALISTS IN ARMS

As antislavery nationalists strove to mold politics and policy on the home front, like-minded soldiers reshaped the political character of the Federal armies. At the war's outset Union volunteers, recruited from all parts of the loyal states, reflected the broad spectrum of opinion in their home communities. They included a minority of sincere abolitionists who saw the opportunity to crush slavery by force of arms. Most, however, signed up to defend the integrity of majoritarian republican government against what they saw as a vengeful assault by an undemocratic southern elite. During the first year of the conflict a majority fought to restore the prewar Union unchanged. In this they kept step with their commanding general, George McClellan, a Democrat in politics. Arrestingly, a few who

Lincoln in the Tempest of Religious Nationalisms, 1863–1864 311

had entered the army with the antiblack sentiment typical of white northerners advocated emancipation from the first, as a weapon of war.[164] Over time, Union soldiers' experience of hard combat, their firsthand encounter with the shocking realities of southern slavery, and their interactions with black regiments together tempered the steel of a more ambitious and determinedly antislavery nationalism. This was embedded in a providentialist Christian faith.

The notion that God took an active role in the world of His creation pervaded the Civil War armies, as it did the home front: the author of good, He permitted evil only for the ultimate betterment of His people.[165] But for soldiers, every element of their daily experience, above all exposure to death, setbacks, and horrific slaughter, prompted sharp questions about God's immediate purposes. Naturally, myriad individual soldiers prayed before battle to a superintending God who, as the infantryman Joseph Jones affirmed, "is our friend" and "dos nothing but what is right."[166] John Burrud of the 160th New York Regiment, in deeply religious and devoted letters to his wife, routinely urged her not to fear for him. "I think there is One With a strong arm that is protecting me and may I ever be thankfull for his Kind and bountiful mercies," he wrote when recuperating from wounds sustained during fierce fighting in Louisiana.[167] Falling to his knees to praise God for carrying him "through dangers both seen and unseen," he wrote, "tears of gratitude will start and blind my eyes so that I can hardly see to pen these few lines."[168] George Shane Phillips, the Methodist chaplain of the Forty-Ninth Ohio, had never seen such slaughter as the "terable" Union carnage at Chickamauga in 1863. When his field hospital was shelled, he thanked "my King and merciful Heavenly Father for His preserving care."[169]

Beyond personal protection, however, troops searched for a broader providential design. When Charlie Brewster of the Tenth Massachusetts pondered the gales disrupting a Union naval expedition in 1862, he told his sister, "I am not able to reconcile it with our ideas of the right side. We cannot believe that Providence can favor the wrong, and yet we cannot believe we are not right in this struggle both sides pray earnestly to the same god for each others destruction, and as far as the elements are concerned he seems to have answered Rebel prayers so far."[170] The Congregationalist

Joseph Hopkins Twichell, who had broken off his studies at Union Theological Seminary to enlist as chaplain of the Seventy-First New York Volunteers, grieved over the "palpable blunders" of Federal forces from the Peninsula in July 1862. Writing to his father from Harrison's Landing, the twenty-four-year-old was unwilling to blame his fellow abolitionists, the government, or the military command. "The course of Providence is often mysterious," he reflected, "but I think I can behold Divine Justice in this reverse," which had "rebuked a pride which needed crushing as much as the rebellion." God would not grant peace "till we are worthy of her abode with us."[171] Fifteen months later, Twichell's spirits soared. With the Third Corps, he had been in the thick of the slaughter at Gettysburg—"the most terrible battle field I ever beheld"—but recognized the blessings of victory. "I have . . . no doubt that we are in the way of saving the Union, feel certain that Providence guides the whole affair, and that is enough to keep me from small perplexities."[172]

The arresting triumphs at Gettysburg and Vicksburg on July 4, a day auspicious in the nation's providential history, struck Union forces as a message from God, broadcasting the justice of their war and its millennial purpose.[173] Private Silas Haven of the Twenty-Seventh Iowa Volunteers, a devout Baptist fighting to deliver slavery's deathblow and put the nation right with God, drew renewed faith from the summer's victories: "A kind providence has favored our army thus far. . . . God has had the ordering of all things pertaining to this war. . . . [W]e shall, through him, be victorious in the end and our nation become as in times past the admiration of all nations of the world."[174] Lincoln's August day of thanksgiving naturally ministered to this faith in divine superintendence. George Phillips, encamped at Tullahoma, Tennessee, evinced a keen appetite for "Father Abraham's" special services. "The first service is at four in the morning," he told his wife. "Quite early say you, yes it is. The second is at 10½ A.M. and 3rd at 6½ P.M."[175]

Union spirits again plummeted during July and August 1864. After appalling losses, Federal armies stalled outside Richmond and Atlanta. But a tenacious faith in God persisted. Even if the rebels "whip Grant and drive Sherman to the Ohio and burn the cities of Pa. I will still believe that they must finally be destroyed," a Pennsylvania soldier, John Harmer, declared. "I cannot believe that

Lincoln in the Tempest of Religious Nationalisms, 1863–1864 313

Providence intends to destroy this Nation."[176] The fall of Atlanta dispatched the gloom. A New Yorker rejoiced: the "cloud has passed away. Providence veiled his face and tried our faith. The country and the army trusted Him in the night time and since then He has blessed us with glorious victories"—surely evidence "that we are his people whom he will never forsake."[177]

The sheer ferocity of warfare during 1863 and 1864 raised troubling questions about the Almighty's intent. Chaplain George Shane Phillips told the men of his Ohio regiment to embrace their self-sacrificial fight for American republicanism and liberty as the fulfillment of biblical prophecy. Drawing on the history of ancient Israel, the book of Revelation, and the victory of the archangel Michael against the dragon, the minister cast the impending defeat of the Slave Power as the inauguration of the American republic's high destiny as the model of free government to the world.[178] Widely regarded by troops on both sides as God's chastisement for sin, the mounting bloodshed appeared to many serving northerners to mean only one thing: "Not till the last slave is freed need we expect peace." An English-born soldier described the Americans as "a sort of chosen people . . . who will ultimately lead the nations in their forward march toward a kind of millennium," but not until the liberation of all those in bondage. Union soldiers' concern with the moral dimensions of slavery grew ever more urgent after God's signal intervention at Gettysburg and Vicksburg. For Sergeant E. C. Hubbard of the Thirteenth Illinois Infantry, emancipation meant "the salvation of our country and in moral point the removal of an enormous sin."[179]

Hubbard typified those whose experience in arms had broadened their moral horizons. Before the war he had respected the South's peculiar institution, seeing in "a negro a parallel case of a dog," but after witnessing slavery up close he had, he said, been "*forced* to change" his opinion.[180] Amos Hostetter, a captain in the Thirty-Fourth Illinois Infantry, welcomed Lincoln's emancipation edict, assuring his skeptical family that men who had enlisted with no intention of interfering with slavery had become abolitionists: "We like the Negro no better now than we did then but we hate his master worse, and I tell you when Old Abe carries out his Proclamation he kills this Rebellion and not before." Like many others, they were repelled by the moral degradation of both the enslaved and the enslavers. Asked by his Illinois wife how slavery looked "to the naked Eye," the cavalry sergeant William Smith gave a disturbing account of enslavement in Alabama, which he found "*many* times worse than I ever imagined." He was shocked to see "*Pregnant Women* . . . at the hardest work, with only an excuse for a Shirt and short Petticoat on . . . when it would seem that they were on the very eve of confinement," and another tending acres of corn as she "suckled an infant that was born after she commenced to break the ground."[181]

As these first encounters with slavery were shaking some troops out of their ignorant complacency, the raw horrors of the slave system only fueled the righteous fury of informed abolitionist volunteers. "I thought I Hated Slavery before I came down heare but it has increased a hundred fold," John Burrud declared. Reviling "one of the most *damnibale* mean *degrading* soul killing God dishonering Institutions that ever was permited to exist on the face of the earth," he rejoiced he could "see its Death Struggle and here its Death Grones." Inspired by a Christian faith in the war's blessings for the downtrodden, he was sure "the Rebbels are the Ones that will suffer the most in this struggle." The North knew nothing of suffering compared with the South, "and that is just as it should be."[182]

Union soldiers saw that slave trading broke up families for profit and that some of those sold were the light-skinned offspring of the enslaved mothers and their owners. The widespread evidence of sexual mixing and the violation of enslaved women profoundly troubled the Christian sensibilities of northern troops. William Smith was struck by the close physical resemblance of a young wife and her slave. On inquiry, he learned the slave had been the father's wedding gift to his daughter: "The secret is out, they are half Sisters . . . the only difference is color—Great God! Who is Responsible for this sin—is it the Abolitionists of Illinois, or is it the Amalgamationists in Mississippi or Alabama?" With like contempt Amos Hostetter protested, "Any country that allows the curse of slavery and Amalgamation as this has done, should be cursed, and I believe in my soul that God allowed this war for the very purpose of cleaning out the evil and punishing us as a nation for allowing it."[183]

Troubled though they were by their experiences, Union soldiers

Lincoln in the Tempest of Religious Nationalisms, 1863–1864   315

did not easily shed the racial prejudices they had carried into the war. Yet many began to interrogate their sense of racial superiority and the North's complicity in slavery. In this they were encouraged, as Lysander Wheeler happily reported from Nashville, by Union army chaplains unafraid "to talk Politics . . . or AntiSlavery sentiments now that they have so good a chance in a slave state."[184] The young lieutenant Charlie Brewster had his own mind-broadening tutorial in racial capabilities when he acquired a seventeen-year-old runaway slave, David, as his personal assistant in January 1862. The fugitive was one of many "contrabands" seeking refuge with the Tenth Massachusetts outside Washington, D.C. Protecting his fellow man became a liberating project for Brewster, who resorted to accomplished deception to keep David out of the clutches of his pursuing master.[185] The character of the contrabands confiscated after the Union's capture of Baton Rouge impressed John Burrud. One fourteen-year-old, he told his wife, was "as smart as a whip. . . . He is learning to read. He has got a spelling book and very fast this war will educate thousands of slaves. . . . I was surprised to find those slaves so intelligent. I tell you the truth when I say they are the most intelligent portion of the inhabitance that are left."

What above all forced white soldiers to confront their racial certainties was the evidence of black soldiers' military manhood. "Fugitive slaves are nearly all enlisting in the army," Burrud wrote. "They make good soldiers they are tough hardy fellows."[186] Federal black volunteering— to save the principled Union, end slavery, secure equal rights for black Americans, and prove their equal humanity— fostered widespread and surging respect for the bravery, skill, and capacity of the African American regiments that made up the U.S. Colored Troops.[187]

Consequently, Union soldiers' ideas ran ahead of opinion on the home front. As antislavery Christian nationalists, they aimed to animate their families and civilian leaders with their appetite for racial freedom and, in some cases, equal justice. Their letters home might provoke sharp disagreement. The exchanges between William C. J. Krauss of the Eighty-Third Ohio Infantry and his Leipsic father revealed a stark generation gap. Nothing could span the cultural abyss between the son, willing to take a lieutenancy in a company of black troops, and his farmer parent, who angrily remonstrated that he hated "the idea of having these black cowardly rascles in our army."[188]

Krauss senior was horrified that his son had evidently abandoned his family's staunch Democratic convictions to side with the abolitionists, the naive pawns of those who had "no other motive than to make money out of the misery and ruin of our country." In truth, Krauss junior typified a growing number of loyal Democrats in the field who embraced emancipation as a national necessity and railed against the treachery of home-front Copperheads.[189] "Slavery is gone," the Democrat E. C. Hubbard declared in January 1864. "Peace propositions to Richmond won't save it." Those who had seen "the actual working of the Proclamation" knew the war could never be ended without destroying slavery. He rather overstated the case, since a border-state minority of Union troops remained opposed to emancipation, but the general direction of changing opinion in the ranks was clear enough.[190]

Federal forces, bonded by battlefield danger and the privations of war, largely subordinated their party-political loyalties in the common cause of national integrity. "Men that came here Strong Democrats are Democrats no longer," an infantry officer wrote from Tennessee in early 1863.[191] On Lincoln's August day of thanksgiving in 1863, the chaplain of the Fifty-Seventh Illinois, addressing his men at Corinth, exulted that "the cream" of "the old, time-honored Democratic party" had "come up . . . nobly" in the glorious struggle, leaving only "the skim-milk" of Copperheadism ("and very blue at that").[192] "If any man says that the North is divided, let faithful patriots point proudly to the *Arms* of the Republic," Joseph Twichell told his brother in March 1863. As an abolitionist New England Protestant who ministered to a regiment of mostly working-class New York Catholic Democrats, he earned their respect but had no illusions about the political gulf he had to bridge. "We are not all Republicans or antislavery men," he reported. Some hated "colored folk with all the intensity of depraved ignorance—who feel above *dying* on the same day with a negro." Some thought Lincoln "an imbecile." Many would rejoice to see Horace Greeley hanged, Henry Ward Beecher fired from a cannon, and "Massachusetts sunk in the Dead Sea." But none did not "deeply feel that the Copperhead-

Lincoln in the Tempest of Religious Nationalisms, 1863–1864 317

Peace Democratic party is a mighty mean set of fellows. They are a stench in all our nostrils." He and his men—"Abolitionist, Republican, Democrat, negro-hater, whatever we may be"—were all sworn to "the old Jacksonian creed" and loathed "the slime of a sneaking secessionism."[193] The staunch Protestant John Barnes approved of how the war mitigated party spirit and religious chauvinism. "We forgot that we were democrat or Republican—Protestant or Catholic. Our flag was one our country was one—our faith in a God of justice was one."[194]

Barnes plausibly identified a general tendency, but as Twichell's evidence suggests, he overstated his case. For none generated fiercer resentment among serving men than Peace Democrats. Silas Haven told his wife that there were some Copperheads in the Unionist army in Tennessee, "but they are Democrats that enlisted to escape the draft, . . . [and] have to keep their mouths shut." Men who had admired George McClellan regretted his playing the martyr after his removal from command, when he "at once fell into the hands of the Phillistines, who put out his eyes, and set him grinding their rotten copperhead politics." John Burrud steamed with fury at these "Accursed Copperheads" before the 1863 fall elections. He would leave it to loyal voters "to *Kill Them* with *Ballots*," though he would prefer "Killing Them with the Ball for that would put an end to the *Miserable Contemptable Supernal* God dishonerable & Rebelious Devels. I have not language to express My Supream lothing & utter Disgust for These Political *Miscreants* and every Soldier in the field have the same feelings towards Them." When the Republicans won that season's gubernatorial race in Iowa, Haven cheered his regiment's 5–1 vote for William Stone, a ratio that held good across the sum of the state's regiments. The Copperheads would prudently keep quiet, "if they could hear the curses of the soldiers from all the regiments that is launched at them." Only at the low point of Union morale during the brutal summer of 1864 did some troops openly welcome the Peace Democrats' surging appeal and the prospects of a deal with the South that would allow exhausted men to go home.[195]

As most soldiers became crusading Republicans, jeers at "Lincoln the imbecile" gave way to filial respect and even affection. Some critics, like the serving Copperhead William Standard, continued to rage at the "most despotic" government "found in the annals of

History," imposed by "one of the most Priest ridden people in the world."[196] But the tightening bond between the commander in chief and his men, which delivered 80 percent of the army vote for his reelection, spoke of his accessibility, visits to the field, lack of airs and graces, avuncular concern, and self-sacrificial exhaustion for the cause. The Presbyterian John Barnes recollected Lincoln's visit to his regimental camp: the president "spoke words so kind so fatherly and yet at times so humorously that they did us more good than all the medicine in the Surgeon General's department could have done, and after that it would have required more than a charge of bayonets to have any of us to quit the service."[197] Beyond that, however, and more potent still, Lincoln embodied and articulated the antislavery religious nationalism that energized so many troops, particularly during the final two years of the war.

By way of example, when the president visited Harrison's Landing in July 1862, the chaplain Twichell struggled to keep a straight face: he had seldom witnessed "a more ludicrous sight than our worthy Chief Magistrate presented on horseback. While I lifted my cap with real respect for the man raised up by God to rule our troubled time, I lowered it speedily to cover a smile that overmastered me." Would Lincoln's limbs, he wondered, become entangled with his horse's? The arm holding the rein "resembled the hind leg of a grasshopper—the hand before—the elbow away back over the horse's tail." His grip on the trotting horse as he raised his hat appeared laughably precarious. "But *the boys* liked him, in fact his popularity in the army is and has been universal." The following year he met "our good president" with the officers of the Third Corps. By then it was not Lincoln's amusing eccentricity that earned his affectionate respect but the president's moral navigation of national affairs. The chaplain now held his commander in chief in even higher religious esteem. "We all shook hands with him and I took occasion to thank him for the 'Day of Fasting and Prayer' lately appointed by him," the chaplain recorded. "He looked pale and careworn yet not dispirited."[198]

Equally, the pious evangelical Rufus Kinsley came to respect the religious inspiration of the president's initiatives. A radical white racial egalitarian, he believed from the first that Confederate treason would eventually destroy slavery: he enlisted in a Vermont regiment

Lincoln in the Tempest of Religious Nationalisms, 1863–1864 319

and in 1863 accepted a commission to command the black troops of the Corps d'Afrique (First Louisiana Native Guard). He had begun by thinking Lincoln "a little afraid to trust the People to follow the leadings of the 'Divinity that shapes our ends.'" But by the last year of the war that had radically changed. The devout officer thanked God for the president's reelection. "I have so much more confidence in the President's wisdom and honesty, than I have in my own, that I receive the news . . . with the deepest satisfaction."[199]

For high-minded radicals like Burrud, Kinsley, and Twichell, and antislavery Republicans of a more moderate mien, Lincoln's fast-day and thanksgiving proclamations, the Gettysburg Address, the second inaugural, and other compositions told increasingly of his godly and emancipationist seriousness of purpose. Many who had thought the president an overcautious, foot-dragging liberator saw compelling grounds for a generous reassessment. In referring to him as "Father Abraham," soldiers gave voice to their faith in him as a paternal ally in the cause of emancipation and racial justice. And in that same righteous cause most of the rank and file of the Union army stood prepared to slog it out to the end.

CHAPTER 9

THE ELECTION OF 1864

The National Union Party's Baltimore platform thrilled antislavery nationalists. The convention's unanimous support for a constitutional amendment to secure slavery's "utter and complete extirpation from the soil of the Republic" gave, in Theodore Tilton's words, "a great party" a manifesto on which it could wage "a great campaign." Its radical character, he declared in a jubilant editorial, went "beyond any point of anti-slavery commitment hitherto reached by any political convention known to American history."[1] In practice, however, the presidential campaign revealed the complex breadth of Lincoln's party, from the ideological purity of abolitionists to the pragmatism of staunch Unionists.

Democrats, too, told a similar story of internal divergence. Lincoln's insistence on emancipation as essential to peace negotiations and reunion alienated those Unionists who urged unconditional talks to stanch the summer's bloodletting. At the same time, at least some Democrats recognized that slavery's days were numbered. Likewise, Catholic-Protestant religious antipathies did nothing to promote harmony. For a brief period, however, until the Union's military successes in late summer, it seemed that—compromised though they were by internal acerbity—the Democrats were head-

The Election of 1864 321

ing for electoral triumph in November, beneficiaries of the fears they stoked over conscription, emancipation, wartime racial interactions, and the suppression of the civil rights of white Americans. A call for half a million men handed Democrats even more ammunition against a militarist administration.

In the event, the presidential ticket of Lincoln and Andrew Johnson triumphed. Their victory revealed the full flowering—the apotheosis—of the antislavery religious nationalism that had grown steadily since 1861. Lincoln's supporters sensed a unique historical moment, one that would determine the direction of the war and mold the nation's future. The moral imperatives, organizational power, and rhetorical color of the National Union Party revealed an interpenetration of religion and politics unprecedented in American electoral mobilization. The religious dynamic in Democratic politics was, by contrast, more defensive and reactive, more focused on racial fears, less inspirational, and less consistently expressed. But it was influential. If it could not animate the party with the same electric energy that distinguished Lincoln's Republicans, it served as an ideological bond that played an important part in holding together otherwise disparate elements.

Lincoln's victory illuminated the ensuing national thanksgiving. Loyal pulpits hailed the presidential contest as a moral triumph for republicanism and democracy, and a watershed event that meant no letup in the war until the South surrendered. Above all, when rescued, the nation would have shed its darkest sin. Thousands of sermons and addresses gave voice as never before to a triumphant antislavery religious nationalism that gloried in "the anti-slavery providence of God!"

DEMOCRATIC HIGH NOON: NOVEMBER 1864

The Overland Campaign of May and June 1864 in Virginia inflicted staggering losses on Grant's Union army. Of the total sixty-five thousand killed and wounded, eighteen thousand fell in Spotsylvania, and almost thirteen thousand in a disastrous single day at Cold Harbor. Democrats were sure the unprecedented carnage, the clamor for peace, the uncertain racial future, and the Frémonters' damage to Republican unity foretold the administration's electoral defeat. Successive drafts and drives for enlistment sharpened public resentment. The New Yorker Samuel Barlow, an ally of George McClellan's and a leading figure in the Democratic Party's inner circle, surveyed its political prospects from his position at the hub of an army of correspondents. The Ohio journalist Anthony Banning Norton told him with cheery certainty "that the miserable policy pursued by this administration has been of late multiplying anti-war men in the west and throughout the entire country."[2] The Boston lawyer Charles Levi Woodbury reported in similar terms from the East: "I have been about New England for two or three weeks past and have held more intercourse than usual with all classes of the people." In Massachusetts and beyond, "the signs indicate a great change in popular sentiment adverse to Mr. Lincoln. This is very manifest in the course and conduct of the Republican party themselves. They . . . think it will be a close thing in the election."[3]

Simultaneously, however, the attritional spring and summer of the war amplified the Democrats' chronic discord over how to reach the promised land of peace and reunion. The claim that an armistice and negotiations offered the only viable route to reunification drew the contempt of self-styled party realists, sure that superior military force alone could bring an unrepentant South back to its senses and the status quo ante.

The heat of these contending certainties scorched the pages of the Catholic press. James McMaster's *Freeman's Journal* and John Mullaly's *Metropolitan Record*, with a reach well beyond New York City and its Catholic churches, took the moral high ground in lamenting the "holocaust" of the war's "slaughter pens." McMaster grieved over the "hideous bed of death": "thrice damned, he be, that, urged by a wicked fanaticism, promotes the shedding of neighbor's blood by neighbor, in civil war, under any false pretext of a *moral*, or *religious* idea, such as Abolitionists plead. . . . May the God of heaven, who is the God of *peace* . . . send them quick to that region of eternal conflict."[4] Editors lauded the radical minority of Copperhead politicians. They particularly celebrated Ohio's Alexander Long, who had been censured by the House of Representatives for preferring Confederate independence over the South's "complete subjugation and extermination." Mullaly himself championed reunion but agreed with James Singleton of Illinois that the war had broken the sacred bond between North and South, leaving only the spirit of conciliation to bring a reunifying peace "honorable alike to the American character and Christian civilization." The editor convinced himself that the Confederates' "anxious desire for peace" implied a willingness to enter negotiations for it.[5]

In riposte, *The Pilot* of Boston, the main organ of Catholic opinion in New England, delivered a trenchantly patriotic defense of the war and the Irish volunteer regiments the paper's owner-editor, Patrick Donahoe, had helped recruit. The tone of truculent defiance from Richmond, he judged, and "the almost ferocious hatred" against the government of the United States across the South as a whole, showed a desperate resolve to render separation final and complete. Waiting for an armistice was a delusion that defined the northern friends of conciliation like McMaster and Mullaly as "impracticable dreamers, building their castle on a rope of sand." Only the complete overthrow of those southerners making superhuman efforts to destroy the Union could achieve a permanent settlement. Calls for peace reached a crescendo during July and August. Horace Greeley, as Lincoln's envoy, met unaccredited Confederate commissioners at Niagara Falls for talks that—as the president expected—proved fruitless. Keen though Donahoe was to find a route to peace, it would never do to recognize the southern Confederacy, he wrote, "for then the Union and Constitution alike, will be destroyed."[6]

The contending religious organs of the Democracy battled for advantage ahead of the party's nominating convention. John Mullaly derided all supporters of prolonging the war, whether Republican or Democrat, as enemies of popular freedom. "The Union which a war Democrat would give us," he snorted, "means nothing more nor less than a Union of force." Peace men, bound "by the holiest of ties" to defend their rights, felt themselves cresting a wave of electoral support swollen by the shocking carnage of war.[7] Clement Vallandigham's unauthorized return from political exile sent a thrill through their ranks, though Lincoln chose to ignore him. ("So long as he behaves himself decently," the president told Fernando Wood, "he is as effectually in disguise as a slovenly man who went to a masquerade party with a clean face."[8]) Both factions saw the political advantage in delaying the party's national convention. Leaving the choice of candidate and platform until late August would allow delegates to update their message in the light of the casualty lists and progress of Grant's Virginia offensive.[9]

Of that Chicago gathering, Lincoln shrewdly predicted that "it must put a war man on a peace platform, or a peace man on a war platform," adding, "I don't care much which."[10] McClellan, the "war man" and favored candidate of Sunset Cox and the financier August Belmont, secured the nomination, to the great relief of those who expected the coming election to turn on the soldiers' vote, but to the equal chagrin of Vallandigham's and Alexander Long's Peace legions, centered on Ohio, New York, and the border states. "Before God," Henry Clay Dean told the crowds beforehand, when asked about Little Mac, "we have one idiot in the Presidential chair, do not let us put another in it," and a fired-up McMaster warned, "A man who is in favor of this unnatural war insults the holy name of democracy. . . . He is a Judas, and should be cast out as an enemy to humanity and to God."[11] Through his place on the platform committee, however, Vallandigham had already secured—as Lincoln had foretold—the insertion of a purist clause declaring the war a failed experiment pursued by unconstitutional means; "justice, humanity, liberty, and public welfare" demanded immediate efforts for an armistice "with a view to an ultimate convention of the States." Bequeathed this millstone of a peace manifesto, a disgruntled McClellan considered his options. Vallandigham, who worried that the general's friends were advising him to repudiate the platform, wrote to warn him not "to *insinuate* even a little war" when accepting the nomination and implied that Peace Democrats might run a separate ticket if he did. Unmoved, Little Mac faced down the threat with a letter that sought to put some distance between him and his party's antiwar manifesto: he accepted the nomination while insisting that as a staunch nationalist he would put reunion first, to be followed by a peace that would honor the constitutional rights of the southern states.[12]

Mullaly and McMaster, ready at first to accept the rickety Chicago compromise in the interest of party unity, angrily withdrew their support over McClellan's "dishonorable" course. Added to his record of bellicose Unionism—his arrest of Maryland legislators, disregard of habeas corpus, support for conscription—the general's current perfidy raised the specter of a Democratic president "more dangerous to the liberties of the country than Lincoln is!"[13] Vallandigham, too, was furious. Personally affronted by the news, the strict Presbyterian gave vent to some un-Calvinist "tall cussing" and threatened to quit the party. Only the soothing words of Ohio insiders, including George H. Pendleton, the vice presidential nominee, led "Val" to accept that for the party's good he had to campaign publicly for McClellan. In an awkward speech outside his Dayton home, he extolled faithfulness to a party bearing "the Ark of the Covenant"—national purity—and for whose success he interceded with God.[14] Vallandigham's grudging change of heart led Mullaly also to backpedal, while warning McClellan of retribution should he not deliver on a peace plan. McMaster also fell sacrificially into line, disappointed by the near unanimity of the Democratic press behind the Chicago nominee but certain that the *majority* of those who will vote for McClellan, will vote for him as the *last hope for peace.*"[15]

In coalescing around a compromise ticket that straddled the internal party divide, Democrats honored the pragmatism that the religious presses of each faction had advocated throughout the year. The War Democrat Donahoe had urged them to sink their differences in the greater cause of defeating "the abolition party." To the same end, McMaster told the "simon-pure" peace party to proscribe no one "merely because he has been up to the elbows in blood, in a conflict we know to be unholy!"[16] Political expediency drove their coming together after the convention: Lincoln could be beaten only by a united party. But that pragmatic unity was just a single element in a richer story, one that told of shared religious values and a common constitutional doctrine. Donahoe saw no essential difference between the two sides as to principles or policy. "They are all friends of the Constitution and Union, all opponents of this wretched and wicked Administration." Mullaly conjured an imaginary, hardheaded, but constructive conversation between a Peace and a War Democrat to demonstrate an underlying unity around "identical" principles.[17]

Those principles centered on a die-hard attachment to states' rights. Democrats across the party spectrum honored a strict interpretation of national authority: as a compact between the states, they insisted, the U.S. Constitution and Bill of Rights gave only specified powers to the federal government. Fundamentalists like

McMaster and Chauncey Burr read these founding documents through the lens of Jefferson's and Madison's Virginia and Kentucky Resolutions, which protested against federal laws limiting civil liberties. Measured against these historic and legal benchmarks, the wartime federal government—with unprecedented military authority, conscription and emancipation measures, ballooning finances, and a choke on civil freedoms—had become the mortal enemy of free institutions, thundered the *Metropolitan Record*.[18] McMaster railed against Lincoln's efforts "to convert the Federal Union into a consolidated nationality." Lincoln had sought to substitute the arbitrary system of Russia, Austria, Prussia, and France "for our traditional system of a government—*weak intentionally*, except as strengthened by the affections, will, and sacrifices of the *people*," the sovereign authority.[19] The Boston *Pilot*'s Donahoe, no admirer of these New York papers' radical Copperheadism, took similar alarm at encroaching federal power but was buoyed by signs of popular yearning for the old Union and Constitution.[20]

Gallons of Democratic newspaper ink sanctified this reading of the Constitution. States' rights champions pored reverently over the debates and writings of the founding generation, no less determined to reinforce their case than theologians weighing scriptural texts. They invoked biblical sanction for the principle that in each state of the Union "*the supreme and complete sovereignty*, in temporal government, is vested in no one man, nor in any few, but in '*the whole organised community of freemen!*'" McMaster presented as an unchallengeable truth that God had offered his own chosen people of Israel—the "most enlightened community in primitive ages"—a constitution of judges who were answerable to those they led. It prefigured the handiwork of the American founders: "This form of government was singularly well adapted among the Israelitish Tribes, 'to form a more perfect *union*, establish *justice*, ensure *domestic tranquility*, provide for the *common defence*, promote the *general welfare*, and secure the blessings of liberty to themselves and their posterity!'" But the Israelites' growing power had made them ruinously ambitious. "They wanted to be as *other* nations, and to have a *king*, to lead them into *battle!*" Against the warnings of the prophet Samuel, they rejected God's system, to create a centralized government under Saul and his successors, David and Solomon. By repudiating Samuel, they had turned their back on God and paid the penalty: a split into northern and southern kingdoms.[21] These unhappy events prefigured the equally perverse, God-defying turn of the American Union.

Charges leveled at Lincoln's "monstrous despotism," erected on military power, gave added contemporary purchase to this Old Testament lesson about kingship. The Indiana Methodist minister Samuel Chamberlain delivered this charge from pulpit and Democratic platform both before and after his expulsion from the MEC ministry in September.[22] Hostile Catholic readers translated Lincoln's April letter to Albert Hodges into a confession that he had violated the Constitution.[23] They warned against "a *coup d'état* through which the perpetuation of supreme power can be secured in the hands of one man."[24] A Chicagoan feared that Lincoln's reelection would launch an era of terror in the North, while from Philadelphia an anxious Democrat warned of the president's conspiring to become king.[25] Issues of personal safety and freedom resonated keenly with editors who had been imprisoned (like McMaster) or the subject of arrest (Mullaly, on the eve of the Chicago convention).

The issue of the authorities' threat to liberty and freedom of speech had taken a spectacular turn in May. Two of New York's most rancorous opposition papers, *The World* and the *Journal of Commerce*, were duped into publishing a bogus presidential proclamation calling for 400,000 recruits, by inference a dire forecast of the likely casualties of Grant's grinding advance on Richmond. The forgers, in a scheme to manipulate gold prices, cunningly used a familiar stamp of authenticity: a presidential recommendation of a day "solemnly set apart" for "fasting, humiliation and prayer." Only a nation's willingness "to approach the throne of grace, and meekly implore forgiveness, wisdom and guidance," it read, would offset "the situation in Virginia, the disaster at Red River, the delay at Charleston, and general state of the country." Any discerning student of Lincoln's proclamations should have detected—as some did—suspiciously false notes, including the inelegant declaration of divine purposes: "For reasons known only to Him, it has been decreed that this country should be the scene of unparalleled outrage, and this nation, the monumental sufferer of the Nineteenth Century."[26]

Fearing that Confederates had conspired with New York sympathizers to corrupt the telegraph system, Lincoln—pressed by Seward—ordered the arrest of the newspapers' editors, proprietors, and publishers, the military seizure of their offices, and the imprisonment of the supposed culprits. This severe reaction prompted even administration loyalists, including the president's cabinet colleague Gideon Welles, to deem it "hasty, rash, inconsiderate, and wrong."[27] The affair encouraged Manton Marble, the opportunist young editor of *The World*, and other angry Democrats to damn the administration for a reckless assault on "the most sacred rights of men, communities and states."[28] Marble's three-thousand-word public letter to Lincoln combined insult and outrage to highlight the administration's double standards: newspapers loyal to the president, he complained, would not have been so treated had they, too, fallen for the scam. He seized the identity of the chief forger, Joseph Howard, for a thrust at the antislavery religious crusaders who comprised Lincoln's "zealous partizans." A gifted New York newspaperman who had worked for the *Times*, the *Tribune*, and *The Independent*, Howard relished practical jokes; he once stole a march on rival newsmen by monopolizing the telegraph wire to report the genealogy of Jesus Christ and donned clerical disguise to circumvent an order banning journalists from Brigadier General Philip Kearny's funeral.[29] With this forged proclamation the incurable hoaxer crossed the line into criminal roguery. As Marble was quick to observe, the crime ill-became the Republican son of a founder of Brooklyn's antislavery Plymouth Church. "Consider, sir," the incensed editor urged the president, "at whose feet he was taught his political education." Howard had been from childhood an intimate friend of the Republican clergyman Henry Ward Beecher and a member of his church. "He has listened year in and year out to the droppings of the Plymouth sanctuary." As a cheerleading reporter for Lincoln, he had given oxygen to Beecher's stump speeches, "which there follow prayer and precede the benediction."[30]

Howard's fabrication hit closer to home than he might have imagined. In a proclamation of July 18, Lincoln called for a further half a million volunteers for military service, some one hundred thousand more than the hoaxer had conjured up in May. It sparked howls of protest from the opposition for hitting hard those of lesser means—"a raid upon the North's orphans and widows, fathers of poor families, and clergy, for they are not excepted"—but above all for its likely effect on the election. If he got his full complement of 500,000 men, Mullaly declared, it was nonsense to talk about a presidential campaign: "We may have no election at all." In the troubled border slave state of Kentucky, "the Presidential joker" was allegedly planning the complete overthrow of the ballot.[31] There General Stephen G. Burbridge, an unconditional Unionist who authorized draconian measures to halt an alleged drift toward anarchy, arrested prominent Democrats for "treasonable" influence shortly before the election.[32] The Lutheran farmer William Krauss typified those sure that Lincoln's power depended on his "minions" in the military: in the coming campaign the "old imbecile" would have "the inside track by the bayonetts [sic] of the army."[33]

The fall election campaign acquired a new dynamic following Atlanta's surrender to Sherman's forces early in September and the advance of Sheridan's troops in the Shenandoah. Union military success, however, made little if any difference to the core themes of the Democratic religious nationalists' assault on the Lincoln administration. Why should news from the Union's front lines betoken more than yet another false dawn in "the alternating phases of this unhappy war"?[34] The Confederacy remained unconquered and, to all appearances, unquenchably determined. The government's policies and practice—castigated as foolhardy, incompetent, fanatical, and malign—invited lines of Democratic attack like those of the previous year, but now delivered with greater venom and desperation. In essence, critics accused the administration and its fanatical allies of wrenching the republic from its conservative Christian course to achieve a radical new constitutional and racial order, at incalculable human cost. A profound conviction of righteousness, rooted in religious orthodoxy, inspired these apostles of the old order to resist what they denounced as the zealots' bloodthirsty crusade. In the words of the War Democrat Henry L. Clinton, abolition fanaticism and vituperation must be faced down by "the judgment, the conscience, and the patriotism of the people."[35]

The pope himself, Catholic voices claimed, feared the effects on true religion and human progress by abolitionists' disruption of the Union through an accursed war.[36] The Protestant Vallandigham, however, became the epitome of the Christian purposes of the Democratic Party as the vehicle of national salvation. On his return to Dayton, "Valiant Val" became a regular attender at the new Evangelical Lutheran Church, where the interplay of his theological and political reasoning charmed his pastor, Daniel Steck.[37] Speaking at Sidney, Ohio, on September 24, Vallandigham insisted that "the true arts of statesmanship" could alone be found "inscribed on the pages of the blessed Gospel of Christ," which honored the "instrumentalities of peace." He celebrated his faithful upbringing by a Presbyterian father ("a true disciple of Him who was born in Bethlehem and died upon Calvary"). He had learned to revere "the Christian religion of the olden times," and to love its teaching of peace on earth and goodwill to men. Yet he had lived to see nearly every pulpit defile the Sabbath with coarse political passions, to make it "a day sacred, or desecrated, by the orgies of Mars; almost the bacchanalian revelries of Moloch." To the question "shall the old religion be restored?" he answered: only through the agency of the Democratic Party. Its teachings were "not only consummate human wisdom, but wisdom from above."[38]

The wisdom of the old religion outlawed the war's butchery. Such destruction of human life, Henry Clay Dean declared, had "never been known since the destruction of Sennacherib by the breath of the Almighty."[39] Ben Wood's *Daily News* warned that the North, like the Confederacy, would have to answer to the "Author of Peace and Lover of Concord" for their great "blood-guiltiness."[40] William Krauss rebuked his infantryman son: "You seem to think these barbarous deeds are only perpetrated by the south. . . . [W]ould to God they were but we are as guilty in some measures as they are."[41] These concerns struck a chord with War Democrats, too, who yearned for a leader "who loves his fellow-citizens too dearly to butcher them in order to destroy the local institution of Slavery and then to permit the poor negro, bereft of his only friend, to lapse into the barbarism in which he was found in his native jungles."[42]

Lincoln's emancipation policy, these conservatives argued, blocked the route to national reconciliation. His December 1863 Reconstruction plan for the rebel states had pivoted on loyalty oaths and new constitutions that put a permanent end to enslavement.

The Election of 1864

Then, during the summer slaughter, as the Niagara Falls peace initiative appeared to offer a gleam of hope, the president called the Confederate envoys' bluff with a public statement "To whom it may concern." He would meet with liberal terms any proposition that embraced peace, reunion, "and the abandonment of slavery."[43] The document brewed a storm of abuse from both Peace and War Democrats. Lincoln had gone too far. His mulish determination "to elevate the negro to a position in society which the God of nature never intended he should occupy," Ohio party loyalists fumed, was the sole obstacle to peace.[44] One claimed that "the old fool's declaration" had stunned even the friends of black people: "I'll vote for any man that goes for peace can be heard daily by radicals of the blackest kind."[45] Mullaly branded Lincoln's words a declaration of perpetual war, and the more temperate Donahoe rebuked the president for transforming the purposes of war with "new fangled notions."[46]

Pious Democrats invoked Christian moderation, scriptural orthodoxy, and racial "commonsense" in vilifying antislavery nationalists. John England's defense of slavery, a dense and stalwart Catholic text of 1840, gave episcopal assurance of "the compatibility of domestic slavery, as existing in this country, with the practice unto salvation of the Catholic Religion."[47] Playing not to the intellect but to the visceral prejudices of white workingmen, the *Copperhead Minstrel* fed Democratic political clubs the notion of the wise, contented enslaved "mammy" who knew her racial place and exalted spiritual over earthly freedom. In "A Southern Scene," she discusses with her young white charge God's purpose behind their physical differences and scoffs at Lincoln's emancipation project:

> *My chile, who made dis difference*
> *'Twixt mammy and 'twixt you?*
> *You reads de Lord's blessed book,*
> *And you kin tell me true.*
>
> *De Lord said it must be so,*
> *And, honey, I for one,*
> *Wid thankful heart will always say,*
> *His holy will be done.*

I tanks mas Linkum all de same,
But when I wants for free,
I'll ask de Lord ob glory,
Not poor buckra man like he.

. . .

De dear Lord Jesus soon will call
Old mammy home to him,
And he can wash my guilty soul
From ebery spot of sin.

And at his feet I shall lie down,
Who died and rose for me;
And den, and not till den, my chile,
Your mammy shall be free.

Come, little missus, say your prayers,
Let ole mas Linkum lone,
De debil knows who b'longs to him,
And he'll take care of his own.[48]

An Illinois delegate at Chicago blamed the national catastrophe on the riot of speculative madness that had fed the Christian churches of the North with a diet of "self-righteousness and Pharisaism."[49] They had merged Lincoln's forces with the intolerant Puritan party of New England.[50] Republican churches had submitted "to everything which Beecher, and Cheever, and Phillips, and Garrison *et hoc genus omne*" had set down as law.[51] The War Democrat editor of the *Wisconsin Patriot*, Stephen Decatur Carpenter, provided chapter and verse for the inspiration of this alleged insanity. His fast-selling *Logic of History: Five Hundred Political Texts: Being Concentrated Extracts of Abolitionism* circulated by the thousand in pamphlet and book form throughout the Midwest.[52] The *Copperhead Minstrel* put the case more crisply:

How peaceful and blest was America's soil
'Till betrayed by the guile of the Puritan demon,

Which lurks under Virtue, and springs from its coil
To fasten its fangs in the life-blood of freemen.[53]

Carpenter and others cast Puritanism as a threat to all Christian orthodoxy, but it was its history of anti-popery that gave extra bite to Democrats' polemics. When, during the Union occupation of Natchez, the Catholic bishop William Henry Elder declined to obey the military order requiring all clergy to pray for the president of the United States, he was imprisoned and his churches closed, until Secretary of War Stanton intervened to secure his release in August. The war on the Catholic Church had commenced in earnest, declared Mullaly: "Even loyal, unquestioning Abraham-fearing, Seward-trusting, Catholic Abolitionists . . . feel their gorge rise."[54] Paranoid though he was, a Philadelphia Catholic was not alone in believing that, bent on crushing slavery and popery, "Lincoln, Seward & Co. intend, so soon as they get through with the South, to go to war with the Pope, Maximilian [emperor of Mexico], and the Catholics of the United States."[55] Yet, Democrats fumed, it was loyal Irish Americans who bore the brunt of the fighting in the field.[56]

Some of the most artful, phony, and ugly attacks on the "insanity" of antislavery religion whipped up fears of the interracial consequences of the Republicans' emancipation policy: sexual amalgamation, or—in a new coining—"miscegenation." The term originated in a hoax publication fashioned by two journalists of the Democratic newspaper *The World.*[57] Their pseudoscientific pamphlet posed as a serious Republican manifesto for a multiracial America, to be achieved through social and genetic mixing. "All that is needed to make us the finest race on earth is to engraft upon our stock the negro element," they wrote, for "no race can long endure without commingling of its blood with that of other races."[58] Through a selective mix of Christianity, history, and faux science, they argued that the process would shape religious and human perfection, for "the ideal or type man of the future will blend in himself all that is passionate and emotional in the darker races, all that is imaginative and spiritual in the Asiatic races, and all that is intellectual and perceptive in the white races."[59] Published in January and widely reviewed, the pamphlet was mostly taken at face value, though the editor of *The Independent*, Theodore Tilton, sniffed out a Democratic hoax. He judged it "a burlesque . . . a snare to catch some good folk in, for a laugh at them afterward," and was determined that "the next Presidential election . . . should have nothing to do with Miscegenation."[60] The Republican satirist David Ross Locke scented a fellow joker and offered a backhanded compliment through the advice of his creation Petroleum V. Nasby to a "Dimekrat Missionary": "Preech agin amalgamashen at leest 4 Sundays per munth. . . . Lern to spell and pro-nownce Missenege-negenashun. It's a good word."[61]

Those who swallowed the bait included Sunset Cox. Seeing its campaign potential, the Ohio representative brandished the pamphlet during a February congressional debate on freedmen's affairs. Calling the idea "the millennial glory of abolition," and taking a dig at the House's "miscegenetic Chaplain" (the radical Unitarian William Henry Channing), he warned that Republicans would duly seek to impose interracial mixing in defiance of what he claimed was a truth, that "hybrid races, by a law of Providence, scarcely survive beyond one generation."[62] Cox's widely circulated speech established miscegenation as a salacious Democratic election issue.[63] "Boston will, we do not doubt, furnish forth a devoted band of zealous miscegenators," sneered the *Cincinnati Enquirer.* Clergymen who "see the movings of the divine spirit in the suggestion will not hesitate to put their hands to the miscegenation plow."[64] A series of lascivious and sexually suggestive lithographs by the firm Bromley and Company of New York included a cartoon of "The Miscegenation Ball" in which smartly dressed white men and black women, under the gaze of the president's portrait, enjoy "the rites of mazy dance and languishing glances." The print took its cue from a racially mixed event at the Lincoln Central Campaign Club on Broadway that *The World*, with more imagination than integrity, reported as a scene of debauchery.[65] Accredited Republican leaders, the image declared, willingly took part, in the spirit of religious reformers, "thus testifying their faith by their works." The millennium is "coming right along," Mullaly sarcastically remarked. "We must not stop at the *soirée dansante.* . . . By all means let us have a commingling of colors in the Cabinet. Let the revolution go on."[66]

Bromley and Company, along with the kindred publisher J. F.

Feeks, led in ministering to the coarse racial prejudices of Copperheads. Although not officially Democratic agencies, their graphic material and campaign songbooks exploited vulgar political appetites.[67] Tellingly, the firms enjoyed a close relationship with Mullaly's *Metropolitan Record*, which routinely inflamed the antiblack bias of Irish Catholic workers. Among its most provocative claims, the *Miscegenation* treatise asserted that the fusion between "the Irish and negroes . . . will be of infinite service to the Irish. They are a more brutal race and lower in civilization than the negro. . . . Of course we speak of the laboring Irish."[68] This gave Mullaly, and McMaster's like-minded *Freeman's Journal*, the excuse for spinning the remarks Lincoln made in March to a workingmen's group. Recalling the New York riots of 1863, the president warned against the evils of prejudice: "The strongest bond of human sympathy, outside of the family relation, should be one uniting all working people, of all nations, and tongues, and kindreds."[69] Mullaly promptly censured Lincoln's "official" embrace of "the new doctrine of 'miscegenation' . . . to reduce the white laboring classes of the country to negro equality and amalgamation." Sustained racist venom also poured from the *New York Day-Book Caucasian*, published by John H. Van Evrie and Rushmore G. Horton. The author of *Subgenation*, a riposte to the racial egalitarian thesis of *Miscegenation*, the monomaniac Van Evrie argued that subordination and enslavement by the "superior white man" was the natural condition of "the Negro race." No one worked harder to sustain until Election Day the attacks on "Republican" miscegenation. In their official pronouncements, Democrats steered shy of the scurrilous question, while Republicans kept largely, and wisely, silent. But as an issue of vernacular politics, it appears to have had real purchase and may explain why in the city of New York Lincoln's minority vote in November fell by several percentage points below his one-third share of 1860.[70]

At the Chicago convention, Sunset Cox described how the war had distorted Lincoln's ethical compass and blunted his sensibilities to bloodshed, death, and debt. A devout man "sang out, 'G——d d——n him.'" Cox demurred: "He did not agree with his pious friend. He hoped God would have mercy on Abraham Lincoln, but at the November election the people would damn him to immortal infamy." The exchange triggered immense cheering among the faithful, long primed to denigrate Lincoln's religious creed as a license for Republican fanaticism.[71]

In *The Lincoln Catechism, Wherein the Eccentricities & Beauties of Despotism Are Fully Set Forth*, the publisher Feeks took a satirical cudgel to the president's faith. The first lesson of this religious drill began: "I. What is the Constitution? A compact with hell—now obsolete. II. By whom hath the Constitution been made obsolete? By Abraham Africanus the First." Through a drumbeat of ridicule, the catechism summoned up an insulting and outrageous, yet coherent, critique of Lincoln's despotic assault on conservative racial, constitutional, and religious norms. His corruption of the Ten Commandments decreed, "Thou shalt have no other God but the negro. . . . Thou shalt fight thy battles on the Sabbath day. . . . Thou shalt not honor nor obey thy father and thy mother if they are Copperheads; but thou shalt serve, honor and obey Abraham Lincoln. . . . Thou shalt commit murder—of slaveholders. . . . Thou mayest commit adultery—with the contrabands." Lincoln's perverted Sermon on the Mount blessed government contractors ("theirs is the kingdom of greenbacks"), the unmerciful ("they shall obtain command"), and the vile in heart ("they shall be appointed judges"). A refashioned Lord's Prayer, addressed to "Father Abram," pleaded, "Thy kingdom come, and overthrow the republic." As for fast days, Lincoln advised, "Pretend to fast . . . but eat turkies, ducks, and especially roosters, that ye may crow over the Copperheads."[72]

Here and in a companion tract, *Abraham Africanus I: His Secret Life*, Feeks played on a popular supposition that Lincoln's swarthy complexion and unusual physique indicated a "taint" of African blood (the arresting cover of *The Lincoln Catechism* presented a gleeful, animated blackface). The pamphlets fed the notion that Lincoln's reelection, in the words of a "Native Catholic," would put administration policy under a despot "who has negro blood in his veins."[73] For William Krauss he was "old ape" and for Chauncey Burr "the gorilla tyrant."[74] Mullaly described "an uneducated boor . . . brutal in all his habits . . . filthy . . . obscene . . . vicious . . . an animal." An enemy of superfine civilization, coarse and foulmouthed in his humor, Lincoln was "the fittest scourge that the Almighty could have permitted, by Yankee and diabolic influences, to have been put over a falsely proud people."[75]

In his explanation of the springs of Lincoln's moral deformity Mullaly blamed two elements common to the Democrats' assault. Primarily, they cast him as the embodiment of New England intolerance and its dictatorial influence on politics, racial projects, and the military prosecution of the war. Henry Clay Dean vented the argument in a virulent Chicago lecture that compared Lincoln with Oliver Cromwell, as the quintessence of hard-line Puritanism. Dean's unstated historical method (such as it was) meant attributing to Cromwell the characteristics and methods he ascribed to Lincoln: putting his will above the law; rewarding his followers through plunder; seeking to be dubbed the nation's savior; ingratiating himself with the army; purporting to consult divine wisdom; playing the wicked joker; controlling elections by military force; removing defiant generals; exploiting a hireling press; suspending the writ of habeas corpus; and making "everything treason that opposed his will." By such accursed Puritan means, Dean concluded, the president had destroyed all religion and government. The parallel between Cromwell's acts and Lincoln's administration was so striking that no further elucidation was needed.[76]

The second theme, Lincoln's alleged openness to diabolical or satanic influence, appeared in a mix of Democratic polemical registers from imaginative satire to straight-faced assertions of fact. The reports of spiritualist proceedings in the White House, desired by Mary Lincoln, made it easy to allege—as did *The New York Herald*—that Lincoln himself, a pliant disciple of the mediums, had been mesmerized and captured by the occult.[77] His ready acceptance of stupefyingly irrational plans for an unworkable racial order, prosecuted through hellish warfare, showed him the prisoner of the darkest forces of evil. He was both subject to diabolical power and a fiend himself. The doggerel verses of "Old Abe and Old Nick" told of his Faustian pact with Satan.[78]

"Lincoln is an *infernal*," Chauncey Burr ranted, "a fiend. . . . His face is a faithful chart of his soul . . . that of a demon, cunning, obscene, treacherous, lying and devilish." For the *Daily News* the president was "the Abolition Mephistopheles."[79] In the final stanza of "The Walpurgis Dance at Washington," widely circulated in the party press, Lincoln took prime place in a witches' "revel and maniac rout too hideous for the sun." Circling a boiling cauldron of "hell-broth," a crowd of "Fierce war-zealots and preachers, Buffoons, contractors, thieves, Liars, blasphemers and parasites" clamored for blood. "Naked, obscene and cruel, / They screamed and jibed and roared, / They knew their God was the Devil, / Their King and Chief and Lord." While at prayer for a kingdom ruled by "drum-beat and flash of cannon,"

> One tall and bony and lank,
> Stood forward from the rest.
> And told a ribald story
> With a leer to give it zest,
> And said; "Our fire burns feebly,
> We must pile it up anew;
> Tell me the fuel to feed it with.
> Ye friend and comrades true!"
> And they shouted with mad rejoicing.
> "Blood! Blood! Blood!
> Let the witches' caldron boil
> With a nation's tears for water!
> Blood! Blood! Blood!
> Slabby and thick as mud,
> To sprinkle the hungry Baal
> For the carnival of slaughter!"

> He cut down the Constitution
> That grew so fair and well,
> And chopped the gracious tree to logs
> To feed his fire of hell.
> He threw in the crackling caldron
> With a satisfied "Ha! ha!"
> Reason, and Honor, and Justice,
> Liberty, Right and Law;
> While his greedy comrades shouted,
> "Blood! Blood! Blood!"[80]

The Election of 1864   339

As the Democratic alternative to Lincoln, George B. McClellan struggled to arouse full-throated enthusiasm. The general's commitment to what he called a "just and righteous" conflict against "the infinite evils of rebellion" naturally tempered the ardor of Peace Democrats drenched in antiwar and anti-Federalist ideology.[81] Still, even some of the most dedicated Copperheads found a way of accepting and championing Little Mac. On the eve of Election Day, Chauncey Burr perceived two candidates differing "as widely as heaven and hell . . . in their moral and military modes." He praised McClellan as a Christian gentleman who adhered to the rules of civilized warfare and—in contrast to the barbarian Lincoln—followed his humane instincts.[82] "McMaster was sure that as commander in chief he would conduct the war on the principles of "ameliorated Christian civilization."[83] McClellan's controversial Harrison's Landing letter of July 1862, haranguing Lincoln at the ignominious conclusion of his Peninsula campaign, provided the supporting text.[84]

McClellan's credentials as the epitome of a Christian warrior, devout and brave, peppered the Democratic press throughout the war. In April 1863 the New York *Journal of Commerce* glowed at news of his profession of faith at Dr. William Adams's Madison Square Presbyterian Church.[85] Newspapers told of his joining the American Bible Society, encouraging Sabbath observance in the army, attending religious services, and humbly sleeping on bare ground to give his bed to a visiting churchman.[86] "Go into his library," an Indianapolis editor noted, "and you will find strewn about the table military works, copies of valuable classics, and books on theological subjects. . . . The soldier, the statesman, the orator, the Christian such are the titles which history will award to George Brinton McClellan." In a striking analogy, Burr likened the general to John the Baptist, "who was not the Prince of Peace, but his 'forerunner,' preparing the way for him." So, in the journey to reestablish "the ancient peace and glory of Democracy," McClellan could not be accepted "as the true Messiah of Democracy, but we gladly receive him as its forerunner. He comes . . . to drive Satan out of Eden."[87]

The general's Christian integrity gave the cue to a campaign intervention from an unexpected source. At a Democratic convention in New York's Union Square in September, Robert Winthrop of Massachusetts, the former Speaker of the House and Whig senator, took the platform to expound the conservative vision of the Union that had shaped his lifelong career. Disclaiming ties to any political party, he spoke of his concern that a war for the restoration of the old Union had become a conflict to enroll Lincoln "as the great Liberator of the African race." He repeated the theme the following month at New London, Connecticut. Wading through seas of blood to reorganize the whole social structure of the South was, he declared, forbidden by Christianity and abhorrent "to every principle which I cherish as a statesman or as a Christian." Slavery was probably doomed by the wounds it had already suffered, he conceded, but the Constitution and laws must be honored. The Emancipation Proclamation had been one of history's most shocking exercises of "the one man power." Lincoln, the self-styled Moses, should clear the path for a patriotic Joshua to restore "the Union as it was, and the Constitution as it is." A gallant, brave, virtuous, and Christian leader stood in waiting.[88]

Democratic newspaper editors seized on Winthrop's speeches as propaganda manna. Hundreds of thousands of copies circulated as pamphlets under the auspices of the party's executive campaign committee. McClellan himself was jubilant at this endorsement, though Peace Democrats could not be, given Winthrop's insistence that military victory must be vigorously pursued. The question was, would Winthrop's ideological appeal to well-rooted cultural conservatism—the preserve of prewar supporters of the Constitutional Union Party and old-line Whigs, as much as Democrats—be enough for a Little Mac victory? Or would Lincoln's National Union Party succeed in coloring all its opponents with the distemper of Copperheadism?

"AMEN TO ABRAHAM LINCOLN!"

A remarkable intersection of church and political party, unique in its electoral power, delivered the presidency to Lincoln in November 1864. We shall see how Union party committees enlisted ministers as campaigners and, reciprocally, how religious leaders urged an army of Christ to embrace the glory of Republican politics in the name of justice, righteousness, and their Savior. Yet that dramatic

The Election of 1864   341

script would have appeared an implausible fiction at the height of the summer.

On August 23, six days before the Democrats' nominating convention, Lincoln wrote a short memorandum and asked his cabinet secretaries to endorse it without showing them the text. He considered it "exceedingly probable that this Administration will not be re-elected." He had reached this dispiriting conclusion after Thurlow Weed, Henry J. Raymond, and other candid party leaders reported that the public was "wild for Peace." If defeated, Lincoln pledged, he would dutifully cooperate with the president-elect to save the Union "between the election and the inauguration; as he will have secured his election on such ground that he can not possibly save it afterwards."[89] A day later, he drafted a letter to Raymond, who was chairman of the Republican National Committee and had proposed that the rebels be offered peace *"on the sole condition of acknowledging the supremacy of the constitution."* The letter gave Raymond authority to approach Jefferson Davis with the offer "that upon the restoration of the Union and the national authority, the war shall cease at once, all remaining questions to be left for adjustment by peaceful modes." But Lincoln then filed it, unwilling in conscience to abandon the emancipationist conditions of his July document "To Whom It May Concern." In the company of key cabinet colleagues, he met Raymond and his associates on August 25. All agreed that sending a commission to Richmond would be "worse than losing the Presidential contest—it would be ignominiously surrendering it in advance."[90]

Concurrently, antislavery nationalist voices matched Lincoln's sentiments to stiffen Union opinion through sermons and editorials and to steel the president himself. The mournful aspects of the war had done nothing to stifle its prime purpose, to crush rebellion, an Illinois preacher insisted. In fact, the casualties of war had strengthened the fibers of Unionism, now that thousands of patriotic soldiers "sleep the sleep of death on Southern soil."[91] William Grimes, AME pastor of New Haven, voiced sentiments universal among northern free blacks, urging "every laudable means" to support "our brave boys" in crushing the rebellion and wiping out slavery.[92] Thomas Eddy confidently predicted that recent drafts brought victory closer: instead of heeding "the malcontents, the treason-shriekers, the rebel-sympathizers," loyalists should trumpet the faith "that God *will hear* our nation and *help us. . . .* We are *cast down*, but we are *not destroyed;* we are perplexed but *not in* despair!"[93]

Trumpet it they did, immediately after the Democratic convention. A mass Union rally in Chicago's Metropolitan Hall and Court House Square chaired by the Lincoln admirer J. Young Scammon stirred loyal hearts for what he deemed the noblest moral battle ever waged, against the anathemas of Fernando Wood, Clement Vallandigham, and other cowardly worshippers of peace.[94] New York Methodists summoned up the spirit of the Revolution: in these latter-day "times that try men's souls," one wrote, surrender would be "politico morally" fatal to the country and its most sacred interests.[95] Simply to beat the Copperheads was not enough, the venerable Francis Wayland declared: they must be crushed.[96] The New Jersey lawyer Benjamin H. Brewster told the president to ignore the bogus "clamours & outcrys" for peace. "They are the inventions of the Devil. You are not & never were a politician." Almighty God had made Lincoln his instrument "to vindicate the cause of public liberty & human rights for the whole race." If he held his nerve, "the result will under Gods providence be the triumphant election of you as a terror to treason."[97]

The fall of Atlanta transformed Unionists' underlying nervousness into a Christian confidence as lustrous as Sherman's military achievement. Gauging Lincoln's reelection prospects as "brilliant," Theodore Tilton rejoiced that the "outrageous" Chicago platform, and "the sunshiny effect of our late victories by land and sea, have rekindled the old enthusiasm in loyal breasts."[98] Lincoln moved swiftly and astutely on September 3 to proclaim a national day of thanksgiving and prayer, to acknowledge "the Supreme Being in whose hands are the destinies of nations" and His role in the "glorious achievements" of the U.S. fleet and army. The day following, he set down some weighty private thoughts in a letter to Eliza Gurney. "The purposes of the Almighty are perfect, and must prevail, though we erring mortals may fail to accurately perceive them in advance," he wrote. "We hoped for a happy termination of this terrible war long before this; but God knows best, and has ruled otherwise."[99]

By calling a day of national thanksgiving for Sunday, September 11, Lincoln reset and reinvigorated his faltering political campaign. Confederates saw it as the cynical manipulation of the electorate; some Democrats openly sneered at this presidential "spasm of religionistic exultation." In riposte, a Lincoln loyalist jeered that the prayers of ministers not altogether enraptured by the success of Union arms fell "on closed ears" or the "desert air" of empty pews.[100] Far more churches than not, however, were packed with worshippers keen to pay tribute to martial courage, acknowledge the fearful cost of suffering and life, and sing their patriotism in a sacred cause. The stirring themes of the thanksgiving sermons set the tone for the next two months of National Union Party electioneering. Ministers' addresses ran the gamut from grounded reviews of the citizen's moral duty to millennialist readings of unfolding cosmic drama.

Collectively, the addresses echoed Lincoln's providentialist explanation of military success. Unlike those on the president's previous days of national worship, however, many mixed a providential message with the keen political urgency of reelecting Lincoln and driving on to military victory. Joseph Thompson's sermon at New York's Broadway Tabernacle, later published as a Union pamphlet by Francis Lieber's Loyal Publication Society, pointed to scripture's abundant evidence "that war and its issues"—implicitly the high electoral stakes—"are in the hands of God." Lieber sent John Nicolay a copy, believing "the President would not dislike to read some passages."[101] From his Pittsburgh New School Presbyterian pulpit Herrick Johnson graphically described a cosmic struggle between God and the powers of darkness, and sent the published sermon to Lincoln with his regards. The Lord pursued His purposes by "the shaking of the nations." The key to all history lay in these convulsions, preparing the way for the final "glorious dispensation . . . under the benignant and universal empireship of Christ." The Union's struggle for liberty, equality, and brotherhood in Christ Jesus, Johnson declared, presaged that great transformation, lifting the conflict far above petty party politics into a war of spiritual principalities and powers.[102]

Atlanta's fall encouraged much more than a sense that in the contest between praying Christians North and South, God had rewarded earnest pleas for the right. It meant, ministers declared, no negotiating with Confederates. A blessed morning of peace and liberty would succeed the long night of blood between two civilizations only by shunning compromise with the unrighteous.[103] Gilbert Haven took stock. With Tennessee, Arkansas, and Louisiana now under Union military governments, only eastern Virginia and the Carolinas retained any efficient hold upon their people, but slacken the Federal grip and traitors would "swarm from every hole in the South where they are now shut up."[104] Leonard Livermore, Massachusetts Unitarian, recognized the temptation to seek peace at any price but cautioned that ruthless tyrants would no more negotiate in honor than "a pack of famished and enraged wolves, eager to suck the blood of women and children." After so much sacrifice, a wretched peace would be a sin against God.[105] The president took note of the General Association of New York's unwavering support for "a peace untarnished by concession to treason or by compromise with wrong, and established in justice, in liberty, and in unity forever."[106]

Repelling southern overtures meant, a fortiori, rebuking the defeatism that had powered the Democrats' political insurgency during the summer and pushing back against those "baser than the rebels themselves," Copperheads clamoring for peace.[107] Those vipers, plotting "the dismemberment, the reënslavement of the nation," exceeded in perfidy the first great American traitor, Benedict Arnold.[108] Democrats' proposed armistice would give the rebels time to regroup, secure European recognition, and win permanent independence, "with the Potomac and the Ohio washing our southern shores."[109] The Chicago platform, "the spawn of hell itself," gave champions of the National Union Party exquisite moral clarity. *The Independent* distilled the stark dichotomies confronting voters: "patriotism and treason . . . Slavery and Liberty . . . a country and no country . . . Jefferson Davis and Abraham Lincoln. 'Choose ye this day whom ye will serve!'"[110]

McClellan's untenable position drew sustained Protestant scorn. A Methodist editor scoffed at the imbecile confusion of a War Democrat riding a Copperhead horse.[111] The convention's trickery in blending incompatible elements, a witty Kentucky Presbyterian remarked, reminded him of the newly invented binocular stereoscope: the eyes first saw the candidates and, by steady looking, ingeniously combined them into the platform. Tilton taunted McClellan for his puzzling course, which had all the strategic weakness, the editor joked, of his generalship in the field. The candidate's letter had been a desperate attempt to "arrest the quick-rot" of the Chicago platform, by half accepting and half rejecting it. "Not Catholic, not yet Protestant," he jeered, "he stands a Puseyite [High Church Episcopalian]," in politico-religious confusion.[112]

The quickened pulse of antislavery nationalism in print and pulpit after Atlanta echoed Lincoln's theme of the global reach of the Union's struggle. Even at his low point of near despair, in mid-August, he summoned stirring words to thank an Ohio regiment for their service in a momentous work. He echoed his sentiments at Gettysburg, remarking, "We have, as all will agree, a free Government, where every man has a right to be equal with every other man. In this great struggle, this form of Government and every form of human right is endangered if our enemies succeed." On their return home, he begged them "as citizens of this great Republic, not to let your minds be carried off from the great work we have before us." Hundreds of loyal religious presses repeated the message. By common agreement, only a peace honoring republican freedom and equality could sustain the hope of liberty in the Old World.[113]

Of course, Lincoln knew that in the nation as currently constituted, "every man" did not enjoy equal rights, but he did not mention the peculiar iniquity of enslavement in his short speech to the Ohio infantrymen. This was a wary tactical omission in deference to the likely political diversity of the men he addressed. But his concern for the moral shortcomings of the American polity, as embodied in human bondage, explains why he had demanded a constitutional amendment plank in the Baltimore platform, set abolition terms for any discussion of peace, and balked at releasing his draft letter of August 24 to Henry Raymond. For Lincoln and the forces of antislavery religious nationalism a peace "established in liberty" meant freedom for all, regardless of race.

The most radical among antislavery forces made that Baltimore pledge of an emancipation amendment and the freedom of all black people the lodestar of their fall campaign. Tilton, who had been opposed to Lincoln's nomination, urged unqualified support for a gloriously historic platform and drove himself to fainting exhaustion.[114] The Michigan Methodist minister James Smart accepted that the war had begun for the life of the nation, but now, he said, it had so completely fused with the issue of enslavement "that if slavery lives, the nation is ruined, and if the nation lives, slavery must die." Thanks to the emancipationist manifesto of the National Union convention "our country will at no distant day be not only *all one, but all free*. . . . Thus the genius of liberty is marching through the earth . . . proclaiming the brotherhood of man. . . . God speed the right!"[115] New York Congregationalists collectively acknowledged that complete emancipation depended, under God, on an unyielding government and a policy that looked to "the abandonment of slavery" (Lincoln's phrase) as the condition of permanent peace. "Slavery is gone down forever," Gilbert Haven predicted. "One more blow on his accursed brow by our soldiers, one more by every patriot arm at the ballot-box, and he lies dead forever."[116]

These resolute antislavery voices had to fight to be heard during the din of a Republican-Union campaign that prioritized the death of the rebellion. In a Brooklyn speech at the approach of polling day, Tilton protested that too many had made the war question their only topic, "burying the slavery question in silence . . . as if we ought, for prudential reasons, to thrust out of sight the nobler half of the Baltimore platform." Fears that it might frighten voters if "too freely handled" had pushed the glorious constitutional amendment from its proper headline place. He was correct on both counts. Republican managers had signaled their desire not to be identified, in Frederick Douglass's words, as the "N——r party" and consequently lost his services as a gifted orator, though the Union's African American pulpits and presses continued to work for Lincoln's victory.[117] Antislavery nationalists included those fearing that association with "the ultra Abolition Party" would become a roadblock to reunion. "You seem to be of the opinion that the war should continue until slavery is wholly abolished. But will not this be too destructive?" William Dixon asked Lincoln shortly before the Atlanta breakthrough. He urged the president to negotiate an end to the war, secure reelection, and—as the blessed instrument of "the Almighty & Beneficent Jehovah"—begin the entire removal of slavery over a period of ten years. While campaigning for Lincoln, the conservative Presbyterian William E. Dodge found his audiences worried by the president's "unfortunate" insistence on emancipation as a precondition of peace. He heard Democrats warn that Lincoln would "use all the Power of the Govt to continue the War till either the South is destroy'd or they consent to give up the Slaves." Was this so? he asked. Would it not be better to say, "lay down your arms, acknowledge the authority of the U S Govt. and come back to the enjoyment of its privledges under the *old Constitution* and leave Slavery to be disposd of by the States . . . under the full conviction that it has lost its Political Power."[118]

Lincoln's supporters in the border slave states navigated individual courses somewhere between enthusiasm for the complete removal of slavery, which animated very few, and unconditional loyalty to the Union, which all felt in their bones. In the key state of Kentucky, where a majority of religious loyalists favored the conservative Union Democrats, support for Lincoln and his emancipationist platform still reached 30 percent of the vote in November. The administration's most articulate religious champions ranged from John G. Fee, a luminous evangelical abolitionist outlier who lived and breathed interracial Christian equality, and the more conservative majority, who took their lead from Robert Breckinridge, who well understood that most Kentucky voters would heap "great odium" on him for fusing Unionism and emancipation. Some of Breckinridge's colleagues were ready to risk the same fate. They included J. A. Jacobs, nerved to pen a frank essay for *The Danville Quarterly Review*. "The Past Course and Present Duty of Kentucky" led readers through the Unionist logic of accepting the removal of slavery, even if done "somewhat forcibly and extra-constitutionally." He painted a post-emancipation scenario designed to reassure white Kentuckians fearful of political, civil, and social equality, and the amalgamation of the races, none of which, he maintained, was inevitable. In due course, "the black man . . . might be sent back to his native land" to be the pioneer of a large-scale Christian civilization, but while he lived free in Kentucky, the white majority should conquer their "unjust and inhuman prejudice, not against color merely, but against race—against condition and class." Besides, the black people could become valuable free laborers and, under the Providence of God, be raised to a higher level of civilization. Breckinridge and the Danville coterie would have defied electoral gravity to have captured Kentucky for Lincoln in November, but through their influence more voters rallied to his emancipation platform than could ever have been imagined in 1860.[119]

Conservative emancipationist arguments threw into stark relief the convictions of the party's crusading minority of racial egalitarians like Fee. Douglass, the ablest and most powerful of African American champions of racial justice, suffered frequent humiliation at the hands of fellow Republicans. He complained to his ally Tilton, "The Negro is the deformed child, put out of the room when company comes."[120] The strikingly progressive Gilbert Haven spoke with uncompromising clarity. True democracy—"the rights and fraternity of all men"—would not arrive until "there shall be no school to prepare white men to rule colored regiments, but such regiments shall be abolished, and men, without distinction of color, rule and serve in all the armies of the republic; when there shall be no white nor colored churches, but all in Christ shall be one in Christ." Haven had no illusions. "Fraternity, the oneness of man, is yet an unsolved problem in this land," he grieved. "Our hearts still hate our brothers—still we thrust them from our arms. . . . We must conquer our prejudices, or God will again cast us into weakness and agony." Haven's work for absolute racial equality meant working realistically with the grain of electoral politics, at odds with Wendell Phillips and George Cheever, uncompromising Christian patriot reformers who refused to support anyone falling short of their high standards.[121]

Consequently, a few out-and-out abolitionists refused to support Lincoln, even after their preferred candidate, Frémont, withdrew from the contest. But most, including Tilton, Gerrit Smith, and William Lloyd Garrison, beat the Union drum. Douglass, too, who had long accused Lincoln of excluding all moral feeling in pursuing "policy, policy, policy," was compelled to think again after a revelatory conversation in August, when the president asked him to form and lead a band of scouts behind enemy lines as emissaries of emancipation. By treating him "as a man," and seemingly blind "to the color of our skins," Lincoln, as Douglass saw it, displayed "a deeper moral conviction against slavery." The young Quaker lecturer and sensational star of Civil War platforms, Anna Dickin-

The Election of 1864 349

son, campaigned unstintingly against the Democrats. Lincoln fell short of the highest standards, but, she explained, this was "no personal contest." The party of national salvation required a sacrificial effort against an opposition subject only to "the will of their master, the Evil One." Then, after victory, the Republicans could lift their leader "to a higher plane, a broader and nobler work than any he has yet accomplished."[122]

A powerful chorus of supportive Christian voices rebutted the radical carping that Lincoln could not "pretend to any remarkable depth of mind or breadth of statesmanship." The president neither encouraged nor benefited from a cult of personality, but in their platform addresses, religious editorials, church resolutions, and election tracts administration supporters attested to the president's admirable moral qualities and political wisdom. Friendly partisan editors, well connected to the Executive Mansion, engaged in political spin, but the president's reputation for integrity was grounded in substance and burnished by the legions acquainted with him at first hand. "Mr. Lincoln is *always* approachable," a favorable insider wrote. "The people can get at him and impress upon him their views without difficulty." He had won many friends. "Men who were vexed at his course came . . . to complain—saw the President—and went home his ardent supporters." Eliza Gurney left their private meetings convinced he was "conscientiously endeavouring, according to his own convictions of right, to fulfil the important trust committed to him," and to perform his duties "not with eye service," as a man pleaser, but "in simpleness of heart, fearing God." In a widely read accolade that first appeared in *The Independent*, John Gulliver, Congregational minister of Norwich, Connecticut, extolled Lincoln's stern resolve, as *"true as steel!"* His church deacons included the Republican state governor and one of the president's staunchest supporters, William A. Buckingham. Gulliver explained to Lincoln that he had written his tribute in August to quell the doubts of fevered Republicans. Tilton published the article on the revival of Unionist spirits immediately after the Chicago Democratic convention.[123]

The Protestant opinion formers who lauded Lincoln's qualities included two of the most celebrated evangelical communicators of the age, the activist minister Henry Ward Beecher of Plymouth Church, Brooklyn, and his sister the acclaimed antislavery author Harriet Beecher Stowe. At the close of a regular Sunday evening service shortly before polling day, Beecher discussed at length the claims of the two presidential candidates. McClellan he dismissed as a decent man unable to influence the bad company holding him hostage. Always ready with a striking analogy, Beecher asked his congregation to imagine that he himself had signed up as a chaplain on a pirate ship. "If I should plead that I had enlisted in the hope of getting possession of the ship and converting all the officers and men to Christianity . . . I should be sent either to the gibbet or to the insane retreat." Lincoln, by contrast, led a party united on a nationalist platform he had helped shape. His perceived overcaution was no match for the fabled irresolution of a Union general lacking in boldness, decision, and dash. Beecher likewise rebuked those calling Lincoln a despotic usurper. Moderate and cautious, he had rescued the government from intestine war with proper measures; he could with justice have seized "ten times" more power. Rather, his was the tyranny of Christ, "the arch-tyrant that came to open prison-doors, and let forth the captives." The preacher reminded his Republican congregation of Lincoln's stunning record in office: ending slavery in the District; erasing the Fugitive Slave Law; making "free states" of Missouri, Arkansas, Louisiana, and West Virginia; and overseeing Maryland's adoption of a free constitution. Though lacking exterior polish and genius, he had—as "a common man, from the common people, with common sense"—acted so wisely that the republic faced the world "more strong, more dangerous, and more glorious, than ever before."[124]

Harriet Beecher Stowe's no less rousing appraisal of the president appeared earlier in the year in the Boston Baptist newspaper, the *Christian Watchman and Reflector*. It circulated widely as a campaign document. She anticipated her brother's rebuttal of Lincoln's alleged tyranny: his reverence for time-honored landmarks had made him "the *safest* leader a nation could have at a time when the *habeas corpus* must be suspended." Above all, she celebrated an instrument of God, a simple backwoodsman elevated to lead a great

The Election of 1864 351

people through a crisis of global significance. The Almighty had sent the Union no brilliant general, but He had seen Lincoln's "peculiar fitness." Another Moses, he had led his people empowered by God and "the awful lessons of His Providence." Cautious he might have been, but "we never doubted the good will of our pilot—only the clearness of his eyesight." The Lord, however, had guided him "to set his honest foot in that promised land of freedom which is to be the patrimony of all men, black and white—and from henceforth nations shall rise up to call him blessed."[125]

In comparing Lincoln to Moses, Mrs. Stowe followed a Calvinist tradition of mining lessons from scriptural Israel for the American national project.[126] Preachers of the Civil War Union regularly described the president as the latter-day embodiment of one or other of the Old Testament prophets. They included Ezra, esteemed for reuniting and rebuilding a nation, and Joshua, Moses's assistant and successor, charged with leading his people into the promised land. Herrick Johnson's September thanksgiving sermon described the nation's crisis as a struggle between "the reforming Joshua and the resisting Satan before the Angel of the Lord!" Later, on the threshold of the election, Tilton urged readers to support Joshua and his lieutenants, not a Democrat ready to make terms with "the idolatrous Canaanites."[127]

The Methodist George Peck made particularly striking use of the scriptural pattern book in a two-hour sermon, "A Compromise Rejected," a campaign assault on cowardly Peace Democrats. He took as his text a passage from the book of Nehemiah. Here King Nehemiah, leading the reconstruction of Jerusalem after the Babylonian captivity of the Jews, describes how his enemies—"the *confederate* parties" of the Ammonites of the South, and the Ashdodites and Arabs of the North—sought to stop the rebuilding by sending cunning messengers to request a meeting in the plain of Ono. Peck ingeniously turned Nehemiah into the president of a country beset by secessionist rebels who, failing to stop the reconstruction by open assault, sought an armistice to halt it. The congregation easily grasped the preacher's message, given the public pressure on Lincoln to accept Confederate peace overtures. As he put it, "The President was invited to an interview in the plain of Ono. Ono? he demanded, and answered O no! I wont!" Peck wanted his hearers to attach to Lincoln—unmentioned by name—the great qualities of incorruptible Nehemiah: executive ability, courage, prudence, determination, and psychological insight. As faithful man of God, whose "*puritan* rule" drew the contempt of profane "secessionists," Nehemiah the rebuilder of Jerusalem had in this account implicitly foreshadowed Lincoln's godly role in reconstructing a fractured Union.[128]

Campaign euphoria could turn measured praise into uncritical adoration. At the Illinois Republican nominating convention, an avowed "John Brown Abolitionist" declared, "Old Abe Lincoln is a special gift from God Almighty, and, if we reject him in this Convention, we reject God Almighty. He is God's annointed, and he has now got to hang on to the freedom of the slave or God Almighty: if he lets go of either, he is a goner!" To approving laughter he added, "Old Abe moves slow, and it is because God Almighty gave him such long legs . . . but he has an awful big foot . . . and when he puts it down, it *stays there*, and never slips backward." More reverential still, a New Jersey presidential elector confessed an admiration for Lincoln "as would be sinful to feel for any other man. . . . *My regard for him is almost the same as I feel for the Saviour of the world!*"[129]

Supercharged language overheated a Union campaign that both secular and religious crusaders defined as a sacred cause of transcendent historic importance. Previous presidential contests had won no prizes for restraint, but the extreme rhetoric of the 1864 canvass was not, on this occasion, an indulgence. It grew from an unshakable conviction that the nation faced a perilous fork in the road.[130] Frederick Douglass had laid out the issues earlier in the year, telling the Women's Loyal League, "The mission of this war is National regeneration": voters had to be made to see that a just peace meant entire emancipation, "for righteousness alone can permanently exalt a nation."[131] Addressing the National Union convention, the Indiana senator and renowned orator Henry S. Lane loftily declared, "Let a new era dawn upon the world—upon this great nation. Let the principles of the Declaration of Independence and of Christ's Sermon on the Mount, begin to have their first realization upon earth."[132] Ben-

The Election of 1864 353

jamin Crary spoke for a Methodist editorial corps whose souls were stirred by majestic moral considerations at an election that would mold history. This powerful sense of national destiny—"The Ides of November"—fed an almost total interpenetration of religious and political sensibilities in the Republican-Union campaign.[133] The pages of *The Christian Recorder* resounded with the voices of black Unionists trusting in a supreme ruler whose infinite power would resolve a crisis "pregnant with their weal or wo" and exulting that the few enfranchised blacks would uphold the manhood of African Americans against "low animal passions" of ignorant, foreign-born Democrats.[134]

Concerned for the very future of the nation, fierce Ellen Plattenburg, a Methodist of Canton, Illinois, embodied these fused sensibilities. "I never heard so much treason in my life," she wrote, after a rally of Vallandigham's supporters—"the ugliest big mouthed glaze eyed ignorant looking bushwhacking set of scamps that I ever saw." But she was sure Copperheads were losing ground. Shortly before polling day, she told her son, "Our M[ethodist] E[piscopal] Preacher Mr. Cumming preached to a crowded house on the state of our Country, his text 'Let every soul be subject unto the higher powers' . . . he said that the election of Mac would be the greatest calamity that had ever befallen us, but am sorry I was not there. I kept house to let others go and missed hearing it." Happily, she heard him repeat the "best speech" of the campaign a few days later.[135]

Through central direction and local initiatives, Union political committees enlisted clergy as campaign speakers for a cause that, as they saw it, transcended routine partisanship. In the guise of a patriotic national coalition, the renamed Republicans ministered to an embedded "antiparty" temper, an ethos attractive to those who, in Bishop Matthew Simpson's words, shared a cultural antipathy to "all party dialect."[136] In this spirit Gilbert Haven pleaded, "The Church should unite as one man," and secure Abraham Lincoln's reelection by every righteous means.[137] No patriot who put his country before party, the Boston minister Edward Norris Kirk declared in his stump speeches, could vote for the Democrats' Chicago platform, "the conspirator's text-book," when he could sustain the candidate of conscience, righteous government, magnanimous democracy, and the rights of blacks and whites.[138] During the campaign Simpson, dubbed "the evangelist of patriotism," came into his own, working for a president who had regularly consulted him since taking office, for Lincoln knew that grassroots Methodism reflected the range of public sentiment better than most. Crisscrossing the land, Simpson had spent two years honing his famed address on Providence and the "fiery ordeal" of the nation, whose climax—a paean to the war-torn, shot-riddled Union flag—reliably generated a tumult of excitement. On the Thursday before polling day the bishop delivered his signature two-hour speech to a packed and keyed-up audience of five thousand at the Academy of Music, nominally to the Young Men's Christian Association, but also to an intended national audience through the New York papers. "The demonstration, which was a purely political one, though disguised in the habiliments of religion," reported the *Herald*, elicited "round after round of applause" for the Union cause and the rail-splitting president.[139]

For Tilton "every righteous means" meant turning church societies into National Union clubs and marching in political processions. He flourished the model of a mid-October event in Woodstock, Connecticut, that drew a crowd of fifteen thousand, to demonstrate how to run a great campaign meeting. Besides the usual election paraphernalia of brass bands, flags, drums, fifes, banners, choirs, and glee clubs, the key attractions were Henry Ward Beecher and respected local clergy, as well as Senator Henry Wilson and Tilton himself. Come Election Day, *The Independent*'s editor urged, let the church once again, as in 1860, "march to the ballot-box, an army of Christ, with the banner of the cross, and deposit, as she can, almost a million votes for her true representative. Then will she give the last blow to the reeling fiend."[140]

When ministers implored God to move the hearts of voters to do "as becomes Christians and patriots in this perilous crisis," they knew to expect a roasting for "preaching politics." Democrat sympathizers like the Old School Presbyterian pastor Henry Van Dyke of Brooklyn used sophisticated theology and ecclesiology to insist that "the spirituality and independence of the church" demanded the pulpit steer clear of party-political issues, not to compromise its universal mission.[141] With less elegance, Democratic editors sneered at the hypocrisy of priests who turned their meetings into

The Election of 1864 355

campaign events. Visiting Maine during the canvass for the state election, James Brooks of the *New York Express* reported that while Democrats got ready for the Sunday religious meeting, "ninety out of every hundred Pulpits in this State, were *electioneering*, and about all day." Their excuse, he complained, was Lincoln's September thanksgiving, "purposely prearranged to be on the Sunday *preceding the Maine election*."[142]

Cruder still were the attacks of the sensationalist Copperhead press. "Would it not be well for some of the Satan serving, blatant skunks who continue to preach war, blood, thunder and robbery," asked *The Ashland Union*, "not to desecrate God's temples with their harangues about Copperheads?" The editor looked forward to the day "when it will be as disgraceful for a man to be known as having been an Abe Lincoln minister, as . . . to be known as a convict from the penitentiary." John Gulliver's widely reprinted panegyric to the president drew a low-level tirade from the *Dayton Daily Empire*. The minister boasted that his meeting with Lincoln had allowed him to see "into and through him" and—for all his faults—still to say, "*Amen to Abraham Lincoln!*" With crude sarcasm and faux sensibility, the editor exclaimed, "'Into and through him' Mr. Gulliver! What a privilege! . . . What sights you must have beheld! Clear into the stomach, and through the convolutions of the bowels, your eager gaze penetrated? . . . The next time you 'look into and through' old Abe, spare a suffering public the sickening details . . . ! It is so suggestive of such questions as 'where did you put your eye Mr. Gulliver; and what disposition did you make of your nose?'"[143]

Undeterred by Democrats' defensive taunts, antislavery ministers nerved their churches to march to the polls. Joseph Thompson stressed the moral weight of the ballot paper: it carried "the honor, the safety, the unity, the peace, the liberty of this nation." With that liberty duly established, Beecher declared, there would be no more wars: "The Apocalyptic vision will be fulfilled; Satan will be bound, and cast into the pit, and the stone will be rolled to its place, and the angel shall seal it for a thousand years, that he come out no more to torment the nations of the earth!"[144] On Election Day itself, one hundred Canadians wrote to Lincoln to acclaim his efforts to cleanse the nation of slavery and restore peace on the principles of "Religion, Truth and Honor." Trusting in a God who overruled all the tainted actions of men, they were sure He would return Lincoln—heroic and conscientious—to complete his great work. Perhaps unaware that in quoting from Shakespeare's *Henry VIII* they drew from one of Lincoln's favorite plays, they closed with the poignant words of the fallen cardinal Wolsey to his protégé Thomas Cromwell:

> *Be just and fear not.*
> *Let all the ends thou aim'st at be thy country's,*
> *Thy God's and truth's. Then if thou fall'st . . .*
> *Thou fall'st a blessed martyr.*[145]

"THE RESCUE OF THE REPUBLIC!"

Union party stalwarts mustered at New York's Cooper Union before the polls closed on Tuesday, November 8, and remained until the early hours to celebrate news of famous victories: unprecedented majorities in Massachusetts and Indiana, and assured success in every other state, except Kentucky, New Jersey, and Delaware. Rapture and relief marked a triumph already prefigured in the Republican majorities at the October state elections. Winning 55 percent of the popular vote, as finally tallied, Lincoln won a crushing 212 Electoral College votes to McClellan's 21. The result revealed that the National Union Party had mobilized support beyond the Republican vote of 1860, by drawing War Democrats and border-state Unionists into the coalition, as well as radical abolitionists. It showed, too, that a majority of the soldiers went for Lincoln, including former Democratic voters, though perhaps one in five Federal troops abstained and a similar proportion voted for McClellan.[146]

The Cooper Union meeting adjourned at two o'clock after a rousing rendition of the "Old Hundredth," or Doxology: "Praise God, from Whom all blessings flow." "Never before," *The Independent*'s Theodore Tilton exulted, "was such singing heard in a political meeting!" Returning to his desk, the editor worked until the gray light of dawn on Wednesday on an ecstatic editorial that acknowledged "an over-ruling Divine Hand outstretched to save the Republic." By this interposition of Providence, akin to His blessing of the

The Election of 1864

357

Revolutionary cause, God had shown "how faithfully the promises He made to the fathers are to be kept to the children!" The new dawn augured liberty and a speedy end to the nation's trials.[147]

Congratulatory messages assured Lincoln that God had opened the way for him to end the war and complete the great work of freedom.[148] The Chicago businessman and U.S. Christian Commission activist John V. Farwell gave him news of a huge Bryan Hall meeting that rejoiced, "God bless Abraham Lincoln." In his reelection, a Massachusetts merchant wrote, God had trumpeted His purpose: the president must proclaim liberty to the captives to avoid a fearful national retribution.[149] William Wilson, a plain, pious, and radical Ohioan, exulted over a victory that had left the Copperheads "Dum and Spachless." He sent Lincoln "a Barrel of Appels" to be shared at his second inauguration, "a treat for your faithfulness in watching over the interest of the American peple . . . and the nations of the Earth." No message would have surprised Lincoln more, however, than the words of his deceased friend Edward Baker, ethereally communicated through a New York spiritualist medium. "My much loved and dear friend I congratulate you in this realection," he rejoiced (the ether evidently an enemy of syntax and spelling). During "the mighty struggle . . . your heart went out in humble submission and said—not my will—but thine be done—O Lord. . . . Yes you will be permitted to see this national conflict end in a tryumphant victory—with freedom and liberty and our banner will yet wave in Justice with Mercy."[150]

Victory drew a celebratory serenade at the White House on reelection night and again two days later, when Lincoln spoke from a prepared text. The election had been a necessity, he explained. "We can not have free government without elections; and if the rebellion could force us to forego, or postpone a national election, it might fairly claim to have already conquered and ruined us." Although the contest had been full of the strife intrinsic to human nature, it had done good, too, by demonstrating what was previously uncertain, "that a people's government can sustain a national election, in the midst of a great civil war." Then, on a personal note, he added, "While I am deeply sensible to the high compliment of a re-election; and duly grateful, as I trust, to Almighty God for having directed my countrymen to a right conclusion, as I think, for their own good, it adds nothing to my satisfaction that any other man may be disappointed or pained by the result."[151]

Frederick Douglass echoed those sentiments a few days later, rejoicing that the nation had shown its fitness for self-government, striking a mortal blow against "King-craft and priest-craft" worldwide.[152] Unionists' conviction that God had directed the nation to a right conclusion naturally drew on Christian faith. But it also fed on the undeniable evidence that the Almighty's religious agencies had powered Lincoln to victory. "There probably never was an election in all history into which the religious element entered so largely, and so nearly all on one side," the editor of the nation's chief Methodist newspaper reflected: the Protestant pulpit and press had been, "under God, the agency of the nation's deliverance."[153] Democrats' sustained attacks on clergy who turned "from pulpit pounder to political expounder" merely confirmed devout Unionists' sense of their own weight of numbers. George Peck snorted at the double standards at play when peace politicians cherished those ministers who supported the Chicago platform; "thank Providence," he said, beaming, "there are not many of them."[154] Grieving at Lincoln's victory, James McMaster announced the arrival of the "Puritan Commonwealth," where most Protestant pulpits had become political rostrums.[155]

The major evangelical Protestant churches—Methodists, Baptists, New and Old School Presbyterians, Congregationalists—and their radical abolitionist offshoots rallied to Lincoln in ever greater numbers than in 1860. Friends, Unitarians, and other liberal Protestant denominations remained staunch supporters of a Republican Party now fully committed to emancipation.[156] Henry Ward Beecher saw "the old Cromwellian heroes voting over the prairies of the West, as they had done in New England."[157] However, some antiabolitionist ministers like the Presbyterian William B. Sprague of Albany, New York, a lifelong Democrat, switched parties less out of concern for emancipation than for the future of free institutions.[158] Significant pockets of Protestant conservatives remained loyal Democrats, including Episcopalians and Old School Presbyterians, and anti-mission Baptists, Disciples, and Methodists in the lower Midwest and the border states. Thomas Eddy grieved that the

Episcopal Church remained "a refuge for pro-slavery malcontents" and "the disloyal home-born." At the Old School Presbyterian Chicago Synod, a Methodist visitor recoiled when he heard that politics and Lincoln's platform were no business of that Church. Here was an echo of Henry Van Dyke's recent rebuke of the Old School General Assembly for "virtually" yoking the Church to Lincoln's platform.[159]

In general, the Catholic population, too, shared the conservative ground, the great majority loyal to one or other element of the Democratic coalition. For reflex anti-Catholics, like the New York *Christian Advocate*, this was the familiar story of foreign-born Romanists in the nation's cities voting "under the dictation of the priests of an essentially anti-American religion."[160] The Brooklyn correspondent of *The Christian Recorder* praised Ben Butler's military forces for protecting "the whole negro population" of New York against overwrought "young "Mic[k]s" eager for an Election Day fray.[161] Examining the returns in Indianapolis, the banker Calvin Fletcher concluded that all but "the catholic & Episcopalian churches were favorable to the union," noting that German Protestants had "gradually come to the sustaining of the union wheras the Irish French & German catholic people of foreign and native birth have grown more alien & unfavorable to the integrity of the U. states."[162] Horace Greeley's *Tribune* attributed the few instances of Democratic gains—chiefly in New York City and several mining counties of Pennsylvania—to the votes of newly naturalized or unnaturalized Irish Catholics. Unlike the patriotic, taxpaying native-born farmers, Greeley wrote, "Pat casts his vote (or votes) on the side which he is told is hostile to 'Naygurs,' and struggling to roll back a threatened inundation of free black labor from the South."[163]

Greeley's analysis, by its omissions, raised questions about the Church's wider demographic: namely, German and other non-Irish immigrant Catholics, and native-born and middle-class worshippers. Here the picture was more nuanced. "Gotham," the pseudonymous New York correspondent of Edward Purcell's *Catholic Telegraph*, did not deny the rampant Copperheadism of many "non-practicing, but always professing Catholics" among the Irish poor, which he blamed on the rabid journalism of McMaster and Mullaly and their monopoly of the New York Catholic press. He and others hankered for a religious press that would tell a more complex story. It would laud "true Catholics" like General William Rosecrans, who had banned the *Metropolitan Record* from his military department and knew the Church's "innate principles cannot teach disloyalty." It would recognize principled, liberty-loving German Catholics, some of whom he knew would vote for Lincoln. It would praise the Catholic priests of intellectual breadth and humane politics, like Cincinnati's antislavery archbishop, John Purcell. Their voting habits were often invisible to the public. Some Catholic abolitionists, like a Republican-voting priest of a Democratic congregation in Pennsylvania, kept silent about politics "from religious prudence."[164] A similar tactical concern shaped Edward Purcell's editorials. An authentic abolitionist, he kept his powder dry. Although his *Catholic Telegraph* castigated Peace Democrats as Union backstabbers, he treated War Democrats and Republicans as divisions of the same "great, resistless Union party." Purcell's evasion acknowledged his readers' political diversity.[165] Yet he did not disguise his unwavering abolitionism. Maryland's adoption of a free-state constitution prompted a jubilant eve-of-poll editorial that implicitly sided with a National Union Party promising emancipation: "We rejoice that . . . the cradle of the Catholic Faith in the United States, is now untarnished with slavery, that the 'Word made flesh' is no more dishonored by having His creatures in the same flesh sold as chattels in her markets."[166]

An estimated hundred thousand or so Jewish voters, the largest community of faith outside the dominant Christian churches, commanded the attention of both parties, although there was no consolidated vote to be won. During the campaign an ardent Jewish Republican, Henry Herman, warned the president that the Democrats were exploiting old sores.[167] Ulysses S. Grant's notorious General Order No. 11 of December 1862 had expelled "Jews as a class" from the Department of the Tennessee. Although his action sprang from complex issues involving the Union military, cotton traders, smugglers, and the general's own father, neither that mitigation nor Lincoln's reversal of the order lessened its value to opposition propagandists.[168] Democrats made similar use of the grievance of Jewish soldiers early in the war, when Edwin Stanton's rigorous application of the law denied them chaplains of their own faith. Only in

July 1862, on Lincoln's intervention, did Congress adopt amendments that sanctioned the ministry of Jewish rabbis. These episodes signaled a cultural anti-Semitism that was by no means confined to Republicans, but which surfaced in the party's rhetoric, often in reference to August Belmont and other Democratic financiers. Although not a major theme, Union speakers could win applause by accusing "the Hebrew money changers of Europe" with having the "once-noble" Democratic Party now in their pockets. When a Republican editor vilified "that accursed race who crucified the Saviour" as natural Democrats, and alleged they were "always opposed to the best interests of the Government in every land in which they roam," his words became a recruiting tool for the opposition.[169]

For their part, Republican leaders and Lincoln himself took steps to harness Jewish voters. The president renewed his connection with Issachar Zacharie (his chiropodist), Isidor Bush of St. Louis, and others who had worked for his campaign in 1860. These supporters again engaged in devoted electioneering. Samuel A. Lewis of New York, a wealthy Jewish communal leader, offered financial assistance. Two weeks before Election Day, Lincoln received a Jewish committee. The meeting gave rise to false rumors that he had sealed a deal with "mercenary and irresponsible men" who had come to solicit contributions in return for delivering the "Jewish vote." The precociously gifted twenty-four-year-old Myer Samuel Isaacs, eight years into an editorial role at his father's *Jewish Messenger* and secretary to the Board of Delegates of American Israelites, wrote in concern to Lincoln. "There is no 'Jewish vote,'" he explained, and even if there were, "it could not be bought. As a body of intelligent men, we are advocates of the cherished principles of liberty & justice." Unnecessarily, Isaacs tutored Lincoln on the political diversity of the Jewish community: "There are a large number of faithful Unionists among our prominent coreligionists—but there are also supporters of the opposition; and, indeed the Israelites are not, as a body, distinctively Union or democratic in their politics." *The Jewish Messenger*, he stressed, had supported the administration, but it had also consistently respected the Jews' disparate politics: "While we have earnestly counselled & implored attachment to the Union at whatever cost, we have refrained from interfering with the private political views of individual readers."[170]

NOVEMBER THANKSGIVING: TAKING STOCK

Antislavery religious nationalists of every faith, especially the Union's Protestant majority, delivered a faithful cascade of gratitude on Lincoln's proclaimed "day of Thanksgiving and Praise to Almighty God," the last Thursday of November. Signed after the Union party's success in the state elections, the president's proclamation exuded the confidence prompted by tokens of divine favor: signal victories, a buoyant economy, a free population augmented by emancipation and immigration, and such armed courage in "the cause of Freedom and Humanity" to promise a "happy deliverance from all our dangers."[171] When the day arrived, worshippers thronged to churches in New York, Boston, Chicago, Philadelphia, and other major cities, and filled a galaxy of meeting places in towns and villages, to celebrate a watershed in the nation's history. Lincoln attended the New York Avenue "President's Church" in Washington to listen to his favored minister, Phineas Gurley. Stores and offices closed. Hospitals held religious services. Federal garrisons served celebratory dinners: at Chicago's Camp Douglas two thousand Union soldiers sat down to devour some four hundred roast turkeys.[172] In Mississippi, the Christian abolitionist Rufus Kinsley feasted on roast coon, alligator stew, oysters, fish, crabs, and duck— suitably sumptuous fare, he wrote, for a day when slavery's death spiral meant "I never had so much to be thankful for."[173] More profane worshippers in New York, their devotions done, headed to the city's theaters and Barnum's for secular fun. In fiercely Republican Iowa the frozen Des Moines River hosted skaters after the church services. The least devout souls, a Pennsylvania minister scowled, contemptuously dubbed the day "Lincoln's holiday" and profaned it with dram drinking.[174] But observers generally remarked on the day's respectful good order and patriotic zeal.

Preachers took stock. They faced the task of squaring a day of thanksgiving with the continuing toll of a war that had already cost half a million lives. Henry Ward Beecher interpreted the nation's passage through its "Gethsemane" and "baptism of suffering" as the working out of the divine plan for national regeneration. Others spoke of lacerated hearts as due sacrifice for putting the nation back on the high road to a glorious future. Still, to rejoice was no

The Election of 1864 363

blasphemy. Out of the ruins of heretical state sovereignty, the war had established the nation of the United States and done so on the grave of slavery.[175] Taking his text from the book of Exodus ("I will sing unto the Lord, for he hath triumphed gloriously, the horse and the rider hath he thrown into the sea"), the pastor of Philadelphia's Union African Methodist Episcopal Church exulted over the evidence of God's just dominion, in burying General McClellan and the peace party "in the political sea." Lincoln's reelection, Alexander Vinton assured Bowery Episcopalians, marked a turning point in national destiny. Was there ever, he asked, anything more majestic than a people's decision "for principle, for conscience, for Christ, and for the blessing of the race for whom Christ died to liberate and to save"?[176]

Loyal religious nationalists echoed Lincoln's reading of the presidential contest as the moral triumph of republicanism and democratic government. New York's Samuel Corneille defined November 8 as the moment in human history when the elusive question—"Can man govern himself?"—had finally been met with a resounding "yes."[177] Electing a chief magistrate during the tumult of war—with factionalism raging, passions heightened, and guns everywhere—proved to Charles Wadsworth that intelligent self-government was the strongest of all political systems. None doubted the defeat it had inflicted on autocracy worldwide.[178] In the global struggle for freedom, Lavalette Perrin thanked God for using American immigrants from Europe and Asia as his agents: their "social telegrams" ran by "mystic wires" into the despotisms of the Old World, kindling a desire for liberty, "like the foxes and the firebrands of Samson in the corn-fields of the Philistines."[179]

The election won, a few partisan ministers sought to disavow their partisanship. The Congregational minister Homer Dunning exulted over the result of the election, not as a Republican, he protested, but because it meant the war would now be prosecuted vigorously to a triumphant close.[180] Others, more candid, addressed party allegiance head-on. The chaplain of the Eighth Connecticut Infantry relished the discomfort of Democrats who had wanted to close down the loyal churches to ensure a McClellan victory.[181] The Presbyterian who conceded that "Democrat and Republican, Protestant and Catholic, Native and Foreigner rally around one common standard, to do battle for the Union," did nothing to disguise his contempt for the defeated McClellanites: a "rattle-jointed" peace party appealing to "the ignorance, prejudice, cowardice and baseness of the unthinking masses." The antislavery Catholic archbishop John Purcell made a strikingly trenchant assault on those of his faith who had cursed Lincoln's administration, not the ruthless southern aggressor. Above all, he turned on the Copperhead editors and readers of the malignant *Freeman's Journal* and *Metropolitan Record* for their "evil words and deeds."[182]

Peace Democrats themselves assumed a sour, holier-than-thou defensiveness on the festive day. In Vallandigham's Dayton, the *Daily Empire* thought a day of humiliation and prayer, not thanksgiving, would have been better suited to purge blood spilling and political pandemonium.[183] The pulpit voices sympathetic to Copperheadism remained a minority: some, sotto voce grumblers; others, defiantly silent. One of them, the Presbyterian clergyman of Bedford, Pennsylvania, flouted convention by failing to read out the president's proclamation and compounded his disdain with a tart sermon that flailed everyone—people, rulers, clergy, religious and secular press—for their Unionist political fervor. It prompted the editor of the town's Republican newspaper, the Methodist minister Benjamin McNeil, who also spoke for his congregation, to deem the address "suited only to a nation of the vilest sinners."[184]

Antislavery religious nationalists, of course, exulted at Copperheads' dejection. They took equal pleasure at Confederates' dashed hopes of a Democratic victory that rebels had believed would consolidate southern independence. The antislavery Methodist John McClintock, delighted to find Jefferson Davis for the first time in the war emitting "a sharp cry of alarm and despair," predicted the end of hostilities within the year. After the military triumphs of late summer and early fall, preachers agreed, the election had cleared the way for final victory. The terms of peace now demanded attention. To create one nation in sentiment, Henry Boardman called for reunion without hatred or revenge. The Episcopalian Stephen Higginson Tyng yearned to see "humanity, religion and benevolence toward a repentant foe."[185]

Tyng insisted, however, that an honorable peace demanded the death of the nation's darkest sin: nothing less than "the universal prohibition of slavery a provision of our Constitution for the Government of the whole nation in all time to come." He spoke with a resolve common to the army of antislavery religious nationalists. Beecher located the model for national thanksgiving in the original Feast of Tabernacles, a political commemoration of the escape from Egyptian bondage of the children of Israel. Myer Isaacs chose a text for his sermon with a familiar antislavery subtext, "The stone which the builders refused is become the head stone of the corner."[186] Alexander Vinton read the people's vote for the Baltimore platform as a pledge to heaven to end the nation's greatest sin. With the ratification of an emancipation amendment, he rejoiced, "our Constitution shall echo the Gospel," and the nation "shall rise higher and higher, brighter and brighter to the millennium."[187]

On Lincoln's November day of thanksgiving the churches of Gloversville, in New York's Mohawk valley, met for worship led by the town's accomplished Congregationalist preacher, Homer Dunning. In a meditation on American slavery, war, and the workings of Providence—an explicit expression of antislavery nationalism—he led his hearers through the philosophical thickets surrounding divine authority and redemption. It was a sermon that typified his ministry in the small but growing glove-making town and equally characterized the far wider service of seminary-trained New Englanders in the Yankee diaspora. Dunning's mission, as declared early in his pastorate before the war, was inspired by the distinguishing characteristics of Puritan religion—"its *radicalism* and its *individualism.*" He had charged his people "*to found and improve society and its institutions,*" declaring, "It is as natural for New England men to institute and organize society as it is to breathe."[188] A prolific and respected preacher, he kept his wartime congregation up to the patriotic mark through his arresting sermons on national integrity and God's Providence. Several circulated in print. Like hundreds of ministers, he exerted strong local influence but without making a major impression nationwide.

Dunning's sermon of November 1864, "The Strangeness of God's Ways," explored the age-old puzzle: How was God's omnipotence to be squared with the disfiguring wrongs that plagued humankind? Since God's sovereignty was absolute, the evils of the world must exist only by His permission, the preacher concluded. The Garden of Eden revealed His moral design. The tree of the knowledge of good and evil, and the serpent of temptation, constituted the means of disciplining humankind. Those forces had been at work in the American nation from the first. The "Hand of Divine Providence" planted the tree of liberty in New England, but the very year of the Pilgrims' landing "brought the first cargo of African Slaves to Virginia." In this way, alongside the tree of life in this new Eden, God also planted the tree of slavery, "to be to our nation the tree of knowledge of good and evil." A beguiling serpent tempted the South, which ate the fruit and offered it to the North, whose "sons of liberty" fell for the lure of lucrative slave trading. "And so the whole nation ate of it, building up its magnificent temple of National Union and Constitutional Freedom . . . upon the black foundation of four millions of slaves!" In this way slavery—not by mere human agency, but by God's hand—became the grand instrument of national temptation and trial. So deeply embedded, it proved resistant to all moral influence and human wisdom.[189]

To heighten his dramatic moral narrative, Dunning switched to the historical present. "But now comes on the stage, the strange, wonder-working providence of God. War, God's red-handed messenger, with glittering sword, comes forth to cut the knot which man cannot untie. . . . And now the sharp questions strike home . . . shall the nation die that slavery may live, or shall slavery die that the nation may live?" God could have settled the war in a single campaign, but he chooses to extend the grueling conflict to raise His people's antislavery consciousness. Eventually they declare, "Let not only the rebellion be crushed, but let its very heart—slavery—be torn out and stamped under foot until its last vestige of life is trampled out forever!" The freedom that the nation's president proclaims has been achieved not through the organization of a moral society—Dunning's prewar prescription—but through the columns of mighty armies and their terrible and purifying baptism of fire. In sum, Dunning rejoiced, in words epitomizing the triumph of the now-dominant nationalist ideology, "the anti-slavery providence of God has made our nation an anti-slavery nation!"[190]

CHAPTER 10

EMANCIPATION
AND PROVIDENCE

Lincoln's reelection paved the way for congressional action to end all human enslavement in the United States. The president used his annual message in December to urge the lame-duck U.S. House of Representatives to pass the amendment it had previously rejected. Some congressional opponents continued to resist the administration's energetic lobbying, but on January 31, 1865, the historic measure passed with the support of Democratic vote switchers and border-state conservatives.

Meanwhile, Confederate preachers who had long professed that "God is with us" fell to anguished soul-searching over military failures. Among the lessons drawn by pious southerners, one increasingly stood out: when weighed in the balance, God's chosen people had not measured up to His test of slaveholding rectitude. Military need and scriptural doubts over southern practice encouraged pro-slavery nationalists to confront the possibility of a limited, tactical "emancipation."

In the supercharged climate of Confederate demoralization and the Union's faith in approaching victory, Lincoln gave the go-ahead for peace negotiations on the administration's terms. They came to nothing. But in the glow of the military endgame, and to mitigate the bone weariness of war, Lincoln at his second inauguration delivered an address of matchless profundity. The president's charitable spirit and unchallengeable political authority augured well for a healing reformist peace once the Confederate armies had demobilized.

Within days of Lee's surrender at Appomattox, however, Lincoln's assassination dislocated Union politics. Widely characterized as a Christian martyrdom, his shocking death sparked conservative and southern concern. Would vengeful emancipationists hijack Reconstruction policy and divert it from Lincoln's anticipated course of clemency and magnanimity?

"THE GREATEST ACT OF RIGHTEOUSNESS": THE THIRTEENTH AMENDMENT

Triumphant antislavery nationalists heralded Lincoln's reelection as an ideological watershed whose practical consequence would be an emancipation amendment to purify a desecrated country. Now that the people had spoken and endorsed the promise to end all human enslavement on national soil, there must be no delaying this act of national purification.

Throughout the war the Reverend Thomas Mears Eddy, the editor of Chicago's influential Methodist weekly the *Northwestern Christian Advocate*, had devoted his considerable talents to the cause of emancipation. When the partisan dust settled after the election, he reflected, as the Lincoln administration's loyal but candid friend, on the Union's future course. In the first of four weekly articles titled "New Issues," he reminded readers of Lincoln's characteristic sentiment that rescuing the Union lay not with any individual but with the people as a whole. Eddy agreed: God's preferred instrument was "the organic wisdom of the nation rather than the cunning of astute politicians." The stern common sense of the people, in championing emancipation and the use of black troops, had already proved "too strong for Presidential caution, Secretarial hesitation, and West Point abhorrence." The indomitable will of the American majority to "return to the old doctrine of the fathers of the Republic, and the ancient teachings of Christ" had empowered freedom's march into the District of Columbia, Louisiana, Maryland, Kentucky, West Virginia, Tennessee, and Missouri. It had shaped the

Emancipation and Providence 369

recent Republican victory. Very soon, "the Congress of 1864, if not, of 1865," would fulfill the demand of a righteous people and "set on foot the amendments which all the states will ratify, sweeping . . . [slavery] forever from the continent."[1]

While Eddy typeset his essay, the president submitted his annual message to Congress. Of the amendment, Lincoln noted that the question was not if but when. The recent Republican success meant the party would have the necessary numbers in the new House to send it to the states for ratification. "And as it is to so go, at all events, may we not agree that the sooner the better?" he asked. Like Eddy, he treated his election victory as a referendum: members of the current House might want to reconsider their opposition since "the voice of the people" was now, "for the first time, heard upon the question." Then, to reassure those who feared that the president's emancipationist left hand might be betrayed by a right hand of conciliatory peacemaking with "the insurgents," he repeated his striking declaration of the previous year: "While I remain in my present position I shall not attempt to retract or modify the emancipation proclamation, nor shall I return to slavery any person who is free by the terms of that proclamation, or by any of the Acts of Congress." To this he now added, "If the people should, by whatever mode or means, make it an Executive duty to re-enslave such persons, another, and not I, must be their instrument to perform it."[2]

Theodore Tilton, long a critic of what he judged Lincoln's moral equivocation, rushed to commend the president's iron resolve. "God bless Abraham Lincoln!" he exulted. The president's annual message, he told *The Independent*'s vast readership, such "sound sense, high-toned patriotism, fidelity to moral principle, [and] Christian courage in the Good Cause, has never come from his homely pen." Delighted by the pure gold and heroic dignity of Lincoln's irreversible personal stand on slavery, Tilton insisted that nothing now obstruct the emancipation amendment's passage. His high-watermark approval set the tone for widespread acclaim of the president's address in the Republican and abolitionist press. The Methodist editor Daniel Curry praised him as the agent of divine Providence in the most glorious work of modern times—the emancipation and preservation of a great nation. In Chester, Illinois, an AME church meeting of "colored citizens" pledged unstinting support for a president they trusted would labor faithfully until "the last vestige" of slavery should be destroyed.[3]

Laudatory and gratifying letters, some barely literate, swelled the White House mail. William Lloyd Garrison, proud to have defended the president against abolitionist critics, reiterated his faith in Lincoln's pursuit of black freedom "come what may." An approving New York Christian merchant offered to mobilize a thousand "most wealthy & influential Citizens" of his Union League Club against recalcitrant congressmen.[4] No message could have touched Lincoln more than that of Almira Adliza Knapp, a poor "Invalid Girl" of Saratoga County, New York, who had lost a brother at Antietam. In a two-thousand-word, unlettered torrent, she opened her Christian heart to "Our *second Washington* the *Second Father*" of the nation now drenched in blood by "the murdurer Cain, The Fratricidle Foe!" She had, she told the president, framed his treasured likeness with the Union flag and emblems of liberty: she knew it had to be a true photograph for he was "so calm & serene" in his "noble look." God alone had inspired him "to save this glorious land from despotic barbarity, and to free it from the Clanking Chan of—Slavery!"[5]

Beyond his high-minded radical purpose Lincoln saw probable political benefits from the amendment's passage. It would consolidate the Union party in the border region and, by putting the next stage of ratification in the hands of the states, negate the criticism that his personal antislavery purity blocked the route to peace. Since the support of three-fourths of the states was needed to ratify the amendment, at least two of the former rebel states would have to support it. This gave congressional radicals in Congress good reason to support Lincoln's contentious plan of Reconstruction, which allowed 10 percent of 1860 voters to form new state governments if they pledged loyalty to a Union of emancipation. Lincoln, Seward, and the radical Ohio congressman James Ashley lobbied and bargained with House Democrats to change their position; the secretary of state's agents probably supplemented the conventional enticements of patronage with more questionable methods.[6]

As they did so, George B. Cheever and other radical Christians petitioned Congress "to remove the great curse."[7] On Sunday evening, January 29, several hundred members of the Christian

Emancipation and Providence 371

Commission, whom Lincoln had previously received at the White House, thronged the floor and galleries of the Hall of Representatives. Accompanied by the president and other members of the cabinet, Seward presided. He encouraged the meeting to prepare for the Confederacy's military defeat and overthrow. "The cornerstone of the rebellion," he declared, had been "uplifted." That claim assumed new force when two days later the Thirteenth Amendment passed by a House vote of 119–56. By the slimmest of margins, and in the face of opposition from Sunset Cox and other scourges of "Puritanism," more than two-thirds approved the text that would instantly go to state legislatures: "Neither slavery nor involuntary servitude, except as a punishment for crime, where of the party shall have been duly convicted, shall exist within the United States, or any place subject to their jurisdiction." Enough lame-duck Democrats and border-state conservatives had switched to the antislavery cause for the chamber to explode into a five-minute tumult of celebration.[8]

None forgot those heady scenes, the climax of a quarter of a century's political striving. "We have wiped away the black spot from our bright shield and surely God will bless us for it," the exultant Republican congressman Martin Russell Thayer of Pennsylvania told Francis Lieber. "He seemed to smile from Heaven upon a regenerated people for as the great throng poured out . . . the Sun broke through . . . and lit up everything with his effulgence." Antislavery presses basked in the triumph. Edward Purcell, on behalf of abolitionist Catholics, attributed the sacred achievement to all, but especially to liberal-minded War Democrats who had defied their party caucus to cut loose from slavery's influences, in fidelity to the true principles of Democracy and the Church of God. Baptists declared that the nation born on the Fourth of July 1776 had been born again on January 31, 1865.[9] "Everywhere let the cannons roar, the bells ring," rejoiced the editor of *Zion's Herald*, the organ of New England Methodism. "Let the *Te Deum Laudamus* be sung with full heart and voice." The cruel war and the blood of patriot martyrs— "the gory baptism so profusely sprinkled upon the nation"—had given birth to a glorious political reformation that would inspire all the friends of liberty across Europe.[10] Tilton's *Independent* celebrated with John G. Whittier's ten-stanza poem "Laus Deo!"

> *It is done!*
> *Clang of bell and roar of gun*
> *Send the tidings up and down.*
> *How the belfries rock and reel,*
> *How the great guns, peal on peal,*
> *Fling the joy from town to town!*
>
> . . .
>
> *Let us kneel:*
> *God's own voice is in that peal,*
> *And this spot is holy ground.*
> *Lord, forgive us! What are we,*
> *That our eyes this glory see,*
> *That our ears have heard the sound!*[11]

More prosaically, Daniel Curry predicted the practical benefits that would follow. Slavery's de jure death, as he called it, would remove the danger of a dishonorable compromise with the rebels in future peace negotiations; extracting its poison would result in a visible purification of national politics; and the amendment must paralyze Confederate hopes of securing foreign intervention. Above all, the nation itself would soar to "a new consciousness of moral and of an invincible destiny," and Christian citizens would exult that the "Lord God Omnipotent Reigneth."[12]

Conservative religious nationalists' response to the new political reality ranged from outrage and repugnance to resigned acceptance. The choleric John Mullaly jeered at the "so-called amendment" and pilloried the list of all 119 supporters in the House. The Catholic editor concluded, after "cool deliberation" (irony was not his strong suit), that the spirit of anarchy, discord, and fanaticism had violated the Constitution's protection of property rights and the several states' sovereign power respecting slavery: Congress had supplanted the founders' confederated "Union" with a consolidated "nation." Besides, it was a mockery to think the freedman could master his new condition; experience had confirmed that social prejudice and his own inferiority would make him a still greater slave in the free states. To proclaim "freedom" was a double mockery, Mullaly spat, since he and other white men had suffered the tyranny of unlawful imprisonment for their outspoken dissent. An administration drunk on coercion, he feared, would equally impose ratification on the abolitionized legislatures of Tennessee, Arkansas, Louisiana, and recently fashioned ("bogus") West Virginia. But what if the Confederacy should prevail and "take its place in the family of nations" as an independent power? The amendment, the editor jeered, would then be not only a constitutional but a practical nullity.[13]

James McMaster, equally pugnacious, pushed back against the grating antislavery triumphalism of the "venomous Puritan Yankees" who edited much of the Republican press. He lashed out at his bête noir, Horace Greeley, "the poltroon of the *Tribune*," and conceded nothing to the champions of the amendment. These abolitionist critics of pro-slavery doctrine, he sniffed, misrepresented and misunderstood the ancient Christian framework of thought that undergirded human bondage. Catholic and Protestant theologians did not claim that slavery was instituted and ordained by God. To say so was "a piece of Puritan nonsense." But that it was instituted by human law for mutual advantage and that the institution was "*approved* and *sanctioned* by God" had been held by a great chain of authorities from the apostles' days to the present.[14]

More commonly, however, conservatives responded to Lincoln's reelection and the amendment campaign by accepting slavery's inevitable doom, their realism occasionally mixed with relief. In Boston, Patrick Donahoe drew on material from the minority abolitionist stream of American Catholicism to reposition the influential Boston *Pilot*. Catholic countries, the paper asserted, had the best record of humanitarian legal protections of the slave, a signal the Church's teaching had always been against slavery. It dismissed as unproven Greeley's claim that Catholic priests had never been heard favoring human liberty. True, they shunned the pulpit politics that besmirched abolition churches, but "the negro was always treated *as a man* by them"; they never followed the Protestant practice of segregating worshippers by race; none had written books in favor of slavery. After the passage of the Thirteenth Amendment through Congress, Donahoe no longer stood by the Constitution "as it was given to us." He conceded that once the amendment was ratified by the states, its impact on the prospects of peace, the southern labor system, and international opinion would place it "among the most important events in the history of the world. It is a momentous epoch in the revolution; it makes an era in the history of mankind." This was more than grudging acceptance. But the religious conservatives' temperament and politics denied them the jubilation that one representative radical derived from "the greatest act of righteousness this nation could possibly achieve; the greatest it has ever achieved; the greatest, perhaps, that it can ever achieve. Let God be praised, and 'let all the people say, Amen!'"[15]

CONFEDERATE "EMANCIPATION" AND FASTING

During the late fall and the winter of 1865, antislavery religious nationalists seized on mounting evidence of the Confederacy's mortality. Southern desperation presented a stark photographic negative of the Union picture. As full and unconditional emancipation made its way through the federal Congress, the rebel authorities angrily wrestled over offering a limited measure of freedom to bondsmen in return for armed military service. And in contrast to the Union's jubilant national thanksgiving for unfolding political triumph, Jefferson Davis proclaimed a fast day in March 1865 widely regarded as the last throw of the penitential dice. While religious northerners moved incrementally toward a broad emancipationist consensus, southern Christianity had to contend with disabling division.

The Confederates' chronic shortage of fighting power grew acute during 1864. With shrunken reserves of able-bodied white males, the notion of enlisting and arming slaves in return for their freedom took on special force. After the setbacks at Atlanta and in the Shenandoah, the blow of Lincoln's reelection, and Sherman's scorching march through Georgia, Jefferson Davis reconsidered the idea that he and his cabinet had rejected twelve months earlier. Muffled private debate now burst out into heated public argument. For critics like John Moncure Daniel of the *Richmond Examiner*, arming slaves was "totally inconsistent . . . with our social as well as political system. . . . If a negro is fit to be a soldier, he is not fit to be a slave."[16] But others, including Robert E. Lee, saw in black

Emancipation and Providence 375

enlistment the only hope of sustaining Confederate independence. For him, as for others, the scheme should give freedom to a relative few, whose qualified emancipation would secure the South's victory and the continuing enslavement of the black majority. The initiative would have foundered had it been left to planters whose homes and property remained undisturbed by the Federal onslaught. They spoke of sacrifice and military triumph, one Confederate soldier remarked with a scowl, "and no doubt weary heaven with their prayers for peace and independence," but prayed with equal fervor "to get through with whole skins and full purses."[17] Further military setbacks, however, including the fall of Columbia and Charleston to Sherman's forces in South Carolina, encouraged the passage by the narrowest of margins of a weak congressional bill. Authorizing the enlistment of 300,000 black troops, it fell far short of compulsory manumission. By the toothless measure that Jefferson Davis signed into law on March 13, enlistments would depend on slave owners' "free-will offering" of their slaves and on the slave's reciprocal faith in his master's assurances. The profitless outcome—a mere handful of black soldiers signed up during the final days of the war—served to confirm those who from the first had identified the policy as a fool's errand.[18]

The prospect of 300,000 black soldiers energizing the South's war effort gave Union Democrats an unlikely campaign issue. With peace as remote as ever under the administration's policy, moaned the Boston *Pilot*, these new recruits meant the war would continue "to subjugation and annihilation." But more often the dramatic turn in Confederate policy looked like desperation. Homer Dunning credited the antislavery impact of Federal armies in undermining the rebels' cause.[19] Reflecting on the instinctive human desire for liberty, a Dutch minister remarked that even the president of the "so-called Confederacy" could see freedom's influence on those slaves "who shall bravely fight to rivet tighter the chains of their own kindred."[20] None surpassed the ferocity of Theodore Tilton's censure of the plan. How, he asked, could one avoid loathing the craven selfishness of those "with the death-rattle in their throats, scheming and plotting to make the negroes' bodies their defense against Union bullets," while also seeking to keep their slaves in lifelong bondage? They would perhaps free the actual fighters, "but leave their wives and children in eternal chattelhood ('for the negro,' says one Richmond oracle, 'don't care who is left in slavery, so that *he* is free!')." The hypocritical authors of the policy had been gripped by an insanity grounded in wickedness and heralding a righteous retribution.[21]

The Confederate Congress completed the passage of the black enlistment bill on the eve of the day of public fasting, humiliation, and prayer that Jefferson Davis had appointed by proclamation for Friday, March 10, 1865. In this season of trial and adversity, the president's invitation declared, the public had a duty to acknowledge their dependence on God, confess their sins, give Him thanks for His goodness in time of bloody trial and sacrifice, and pray "that the Lord of Hosts will be with our armies and fight for us against our enemies, and that He will graciously take our cause into His own hand, and mercifully establish for us a lasting, just and honorable peace and independence."[22] Since June 1861, Davis had summoned the Confederate churches on eight occasions to observe fast days; he had also proclaimed two days of thanksgiving. Frequent state fasts swelled the total. Just as striking as the number and frequency of these days of inclusive community worship was the fact that they took place at all. The prewar South, generally attached to the notion of the spirituality of the church, had rarely engaged in days of state or national fasting. They smelled too much of New England practice and political sermonizing to be welcome in a religious culture shaped by the constraints of a slave society and the prevailing doctrine of the churches. But from the launch of an independent Confederacy in February 1861, with a God-honoring constitution and *Deo vindice* (with God as our protector) as its motto, Davis and other southern leaders recognized the value of civic expressions of religion in shaping a plain understanding of Confederate nationhood. Through their fast-day sermons, imitative of Puritan jeremiads in ritual denunciation of the sins of a chosen people and in applying the lessons of scriptural history, southern clergy helped forge southern unity. Fast days reinforced Confederate citizens' self-perception as God's special people.[23] The innovative fast-day rituals, multiplied throughout the myriad towns and villages of the Confederacy, sought to establish the South's new identity as the Almighty's covenanted nation.

Emancipation and Providence   377

From the first fast day, in June 1861, southern preachers lauded the Confederacy's distinctive role as a uniquely Christian nation blessed with God-given liberties and rights. They proclaimed a shining faith to shame the "infidel" and "fanatical" North. The earliest Confederate fast days were widely observed by the armies and the predominantly female congregations of the home front. Theirs was a just and holy crusade: the South's relative military weakness would be offset by a benevolent God of battles ready to bless His people if they would walk in His ways.[24] This required self-examination and atoning for personal sins, whose timeworn roster included materialism, love of money, pride, drinking, swearing, card playing, Sabbath breaking, gossip, and general "worldliness." That God honored self-denial and prayers of Confederate fast days had been "proved," initially at First Bull Run and later at the encounters of the Seven Days', Chancellorsville, and Chickamauga.[25] (There were skeptics, of course. "The parsons tell us every Sunday that the Lord is on our side," Senator Robert M. T. Hunter remarked to Mary Chesnut. "I wish, however, he would show his preference for us a little more plainly than he has been doing lately.")[26]

The South's early confidence and broad consensus frayed as the war took its toll. Military defeat, shortages and privation, inflated currency, profiteering, class tensions, and riots placed an unendurable strain on Confederate social cohesion. The unanimity initially forged by ritual jeremiads gave way to reduced observance of fast days and, in parallel, a growing criticism of political religion. The *Richmond Examiner*, like newspaper presses generally, at first endorsed the innovation of the fast day. But during 1862 its editor, John Moncure Daniel, lost patience with religious humiliation and moral reformation as the key to victory. Davis's fast-day proclamations and personal religiosity evinced not muscular manhood but mental weakness, he complained. "When we find the President standing in a corner telling his beads, and relying on a miracle to save the country, instead of mounting his horse and putting forth every power of the government to defeat the enemy, . . . the effect is depressing in the extreme. When the ship springs a leak, the efficient captain does not order all hands to prayers, but to the pumps," he protested soon after the May 1862 fast day.[27] The following summer he made a coruscating attack on days of fasting and thanksgiving, whose "puritanical sound" had become "pre-eminently hateful" to the southern ear. "They smack of the Latter Day sanctity; savor of the nasal twang and recall disagreeable reminiscences of Praise-God-Barebones, the Pilgrim Fathers, and their Yankee descendants." Confederates were right to trust in divine aid but not in the repugnant terms of the Puritans. Factional political preachers had brought about the fall of the Union. That dangerous malady now threatened the South. Confederate clergy should expound the unchanging universal principles of Christianity and leave their application to the hearers' good sense. "Let not our preachers discourse of Lincoln, or Seward, of Davis, or of Lee. Let them fulminate against Pharoah and Holofernes, and exalt Gideon and David. We have broken asunder from Yankee statesmanship and government; let us eschew their morality and manners."[28]

The collapse of the Confederates' consensus over fast days was related to ministers' concern that slavery hindered the advance of national righteousness. Was the mounting toll of war the Almighty's scourge for the sins of the South's slaveholding regime? Had scriptural principles been heeded in the treatment of slaves? In their sermons and denominational forums critical preachers felt free to speak out once independence had put slaves beyond abolitionist meddling. Divine help, they insisted, depended on masters' reform of sinful practices, and meeting their Christian duties to slaves, a sacred trust. Using God's words to Moses, Bishop Stephen Elliott rebuked masters for an abuse of their authority that invited national "vexation" and "pricks in our eyes and thorns in our sides."[29] Marriage was a divine institution, but, a Baptist minister lamented, among slaves it was subject to "the passion, caprice or avarice" of profiteering owners.[30] Slave trading broke up families, including "married" couples, while masters' sexual exploitation of slaves—a sin as ubiquitous as it was "virtually tabooed"[31]—seared the emotionally precarious lives of enslaved families. Literacy laws came under fire for denying Christian slaves the means of reading the Bible for themselves. As Protestants who embraced a theology of individual responsibility, grounded in direct encounter with Holy Writ, masters had a duty to teach slaves to read the Book that demonstrably sanctioned their enslavement. Such critiques did not shake southern whites' certainty that slavery had providentially blessed "the African race," but they did persuade many of the need for reform. Mary Jones, strong-minded widow of the Georgia Presbyterian minister Charles Colcock Jones, took from the racial history of the West Indies and New England that emancipation was a one-way street leading to the "extermination" of a "starved and perished" people beyond self-government. "Not that we have done our duty to them here; far from it," she confessed. "I feel if ever we gain our independence there will be radical reforms in the system of slavery as it now exists. When once delivered from the interference of Northern abolitionism, we shall be free to make and enforce such rules and reformations as are just and right."[32]

Davis's fast day of March 10, 1865, then, came at a time when an exhausted Confederacy showed signs of diminished religious confidence: in ultimate victory, in the certain merits of civil religion, and in the righteousness of southern slaveholding practice. Buoyant numbers observed the day in Richmond churches. The *Whig* urged the people to eat little or nothing and avoid "light conversation and unbecoming amusement."[33] Loyal preachers repeated that God, the friend of the South, purposed "our ultimate independence."[34] But in several places poor turnout signaled devotional exhaustion. In Charlotte, North Carolina, the local paper reported that very few had attended church, with work continuing all day at the Confederate Navy Yard ("as on similar days heretofore appointed"). "Can we, as a people," the editor complained, "expect Providence to smile upon and bless us, when we will not devote one day in 365 to calling upon Him for help?"[35]

Unionists interpreted this fast day—as they did southern "emancipation"—as a Confederate death rattle. They had rarely shown Davis's days of fasting much respect, generally deeming them a measure of rebel weakness and desperation. Some had scoffed that in view of southern food shortages during 1863 and 1864 they differed little from any other day in the South.[36] Now, on March 10, it appeared the game was up. "It is not unusual to see the guilty criminal, after . . . a life of wickedness and crime, when he is at last caught by the strong hand of justice, become prayerful, if not religious," smirked the *American Citizen*, a voice of Pennsylvania Republican loyalists.[37] But only the Puritans' scriptural fast, "to undo the heavy burdens, and to let the oppressed go free," would satisfy the Almighty. Had the rebels understood this, the *Chicago Tribune* grimly reflected, "there would have been no slavery, no rebellion, no war, no bloodshed, no devastation and ruin of the South, no necessity for this fast."[38] How strange that professing Christians should fast for a cause whose success would destroy the freest government in the world and "make slavery—the sum of all wickedness and all villainy—perpetual, as the chief corner stone of their confederacy." Ministers who prostituted their holy profession should heed the Lord's warning: "Vengeance is mine, and I will re-pay!"[39]

LINCOLN'S SECOND INAUGURAL ADDRESS

On the morning of Saturday, March 4, 1865, Washingtonians and thousands of visitors lined Pennsylvania Avenue for Abraham Lincoln's second inauguration.[40] The dark clouds and the incessant rain that had turned the ground to glutinous mud did nothing to quell the excitement. Crowds cheered the presidential carriage that made its way from the White House to the Capitol, escorted for the first time by African American troops. The carriage bore Mrs. Lincoln and her youngest son, but not her husband. He was already at the Capitol, busy signing bills and attending the traditional Senate ceremonies. The indoor business completed, Lincoln and the other members of the presidential party—the cabinet secretaries, governors, ambassadors, and a sadly intoxicated vice president—stepped outside onto a huge platform to face an audience of thirty to forty thousand people on the eastern front. A foreign observer, inspired by the grandeur of it all, marveled that "thousands of colored folk, heretofore excluded from such reunions, were mingled for the first time with the white spectators."[41] To music and cheers, Lincoln took his place.

Four years earlier, at his first inauguration, aged fifty-two, Lincoln had appeared vigorous and energetic; now, as the first reelected president since Andrew Jackson in 1832, he had, as John Hay put it, the look of a man "on whom sorrow and care had done their worst."[42] Still, the careworn Lincoln had cause for high spirits. To all appearances, the war had entered its final phase. The Union's capture of Fort Fisher in mid-January had denied the Confederates their use of Wilmington, North Carolina, the rebels' last blockade-

Emancipation and Providence 381

running port. Sherman's troops were marching north through South Carolina, where—after the fall of Charleston—the Union flag again flew over Fort Sumter; his army would soon enter North Carolina to join with Grant, himself closing in on Lee's beleaguered army in Virginia. Electoral triumph, military progress, and the death spasms of slavery gave Lincoln a sense of presidential authority he had never previously enjoyed.

The president embarked on a speech whose character and brevity reflected his conviction that events were coursing in the right direction. Just a week earlier, according to the painter Francis Carpenter, he had pointed to the roll of paper in his hand and said, "Lots of wisdom in that document, I suspect. . . . [I]t is what will be called my 'second inaugural,' containing about six hundred words."[43] Lincoln was still working on his text but completed it in good time to be printed and pasted onto a reading copy. When delivered, it had grown to a fraction over seven hundred words, the shortest inaugural address in the history of the republic.

Lincoln began with a simple, matter-of-fact introduction: "At this second appearing to take the oath of the presidential office, there is less occasion for an extended address than there was at the first. . . . Now, at the expiration of four years, during which public declarations have been constantly called forth on every point and phase of the great contest . . . little that is new could be presented." This startling disclaimer no doubt disappointed those hoping to hear something of the new administration's postwar intentions. "The progress of our arms," he continued, "is as well known to the public as to myself; and it is, I trust, reasonably satisfactory and encouraging to all. With high hope for the future, no prediction in regard to it is ventured."[44]

Lincoln followed this matter-of-fact opening paragraph with just three more. By contrast each was rich in concentrated meaning and striking rhetoric. The first summarized the process by which the nation had fallen into war. "All dreaded" the prospect and had sought to avert it. His first inaugural address had been "devoted altogether to *saving* the Union without war." At the same time "insurgent agents" were "seeking to *destroy* it without war—seeking to dissolve the Union . . . by negotiation. Both parties deprecated war; but one of them would *make* war rather than let the nation survive;

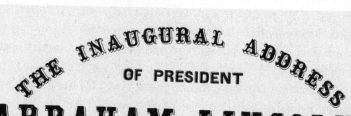

Lincoln's Second Inaugural Address, March 4, 1865

and the other would *accept* war rather than let it perish. And the war came." Lincoln's evenhandedness is striking. Although "destroy" is hardly a neutral term, Lincoln did not assign blame for the conflict.

The next paragraph, the longest, constituted more than half the speech and summarized the war's causes. The slaves of the southern part of the Union—"one eighth of the whole population"—"constituted a peculiar and powerful interest. All knew that this interest was, somehow, the cause of the war. To strengthen, perpetuate, and extend this interest was the object for which the insurgents would rend the Union, even by war; while the government claimed no right to do more than to restrict the territorial enlargement of it." The war, Lincoln reflected, had developed into a struggle whose dimensions and duration "neither party expected. . . . Each looked for an easier triumph, and a result less fundamental and astounding."

Lincoln was widely regarded as a man of faith, but few expected the next sentence, which took the speech in a direction unique among presidential inaugural addresses: "Both [parties] read the same Bible, and pray to the same God; and each invokes His aid against the other." This bold and striking religious turn has led subsequent generations to marvel at the distinctiveness and depth of what followed. In a speech that invoked God fourteen times, quoted or paraphrased four passages of scripture, and talked about prayer on three occasions, Lincoln reflected on the purposes of an Almighty God and His judgment on the American nation.[45] Yet none would have been surprised by his statement that throughout the struggle the two sides had implored the aid of the God of holy scripture. Davis's fast days and thanksgivings provided evidence enough for that. Lincoln personally understood the animating force of southern Christian faith: his wife's Confederate relations included his brother-in-law Benjamin Hardin Helm, who "fell at the head of his Brigade, honorably battling for the cause he thought Just, and righteous."[46] As was his wont, Lincoln's words avoided openly scoffing at "southern hypocrisy," much though his love of the satirical Nasby rested on his understanding of the power of self-deception and insincerity. Even so, some might have recalled how two years earlier he had declared that an embryo state committed to the perpetuation of human slavery had no place in "the family of Christian and civilized nations."[47]

Lincoln then drew on the book of Genesis and Jesus's Sermon on the Mount, distilling what he had written to loyal Baptists the previous year: "It may seem strange that any men should dare to ask a just God's assistance in wringing their bread from the sweat of other men's faces; but let us judge not that we be not judged." Lincoln resorted here to the rhetorical device of paralipsis, by which a speaker emphasizes something by purporting not to do so. The ploy may sometimes camouflage an insult, but this was hardly the president's purpose, though some of his audience might have concluded that hypocrisy alone explained the "strange" prayers of slave-holders. Lincoln here avoided the dry irony that he had sometimes brought to bear on what he considered contorted pro-slavery theology. Recall how before the war he had poured private scorn on the pro-slavery theologian Frederick Ross.

Lincoln's purpose in this section of the second inaugural was more profound than to score a sly point at the South's expense. He followed the advice to "judge not" with a statement that grounded the whole speech in his reading of God's providential purposes: "The prayers of both could not be answered; that of neither has been answered fully. The Almighty has His own purposes." This underlying theme of the second inaugural is related to one of the key elements of Lincoln's "Meditation on the Divine Will," which as we have seen was most probably conceived in the summer of 1862. The inaugural does not repeat the reflections of 1862 on God's use of human agents, but it is suffused with the meditation's providentialist ideas of a civil war willed by God and contested by parties whose purposes were quite possibly not His. Lincoln arrested his audience by attaching American national significance to Christ's words "Woe unto the world because of offences! for it must needs be that offences come; but woe to that man by whom the offence cometh!"[48] He saw no reason to doubt that "American Slavery"—not *southern* slavery—was "one of those offences which, in the providence of God, must needs come, but which, having continued through His appointed time, He now wills to remove, and that He gives to both North and South, this terrible war, as the woe due to those by whom the offence came." Lincoln made the whole nation complicit in a sin made durable by the North's political support and commercial involvement. "Fondly do we hope—fervently do we pray—that this mighty scourge of war may speedily pass away." But if God in his Providence willed "that it continue, until all the wealth piled by the bond-man's two hundred and fifty years of unrequited toil shall be sunk, and until every drop of blood drawn with the lash, shall be paid by another drawn with the sword, as was said three thousand years ago, so still it must be said 'the judgments of the Lord, are true and righteous altogether.' "[49]

Imputing the sin of slavery to *national* complicity opened the way for Lincoln's memorable concluding paragraph, which made

Emancipation and Providence 385

clear the core political intent of the address. Here he echoed the words of Malachi, invoking God's judgment against the oppressors of the widow and the fatherless:

> With malice toward none; with charity for all; with firmness in the right, as God gives us to see the right, let us strive on to finish the work we are in; to bind up the nation's wounds; to care for him who shall have borne the battle, and for his widow, and his orphan—to do all which may achieve and cherish a just, and a lasting peace, among ourselves, and with all nations.

Lincoln was a kindly man who sought to temper justice with mercy and by his own estimate probably had "too little" of the feeling of personal resentment. "A man has not time to spend half his life in quarrels," he reflected.[50] He saw the irony that as someone who did not bear a grudge, he had found himself at the center of so profound a conflict.

The speech delivered, Lincoln stepped forward to take the oath of office, administered by the new chief justice, Salmon P. Chase. The sunburst at that moment appeared to many a sign of divine approval and an omen of hope for the republic. Later that day Chase would send Mary Lincoln the Bible that Lincoln had kissed when taking the oath. It was, he remarked, a souvenir of a memorable day, and he prayed that the timely sunshine "may prove an auspicious omen of the dispersion of the clouds of war and the restoration . . . of prosperous peace under the wise & just administration of him who took it."[51]

Thousands thronged to enter the White House for the evening's inaugural reception. They included Frederick Douglass, who found his way blocked by policemen determined "to admit no one of color." Douglass managed to alert Lincoln, who greeted him as "my friend Douglass" and asked how he had liked the inaugural address, saying, "There is no man in the country whose opinion I value more than yours."[52] The nation's preeminent African American replied, "Mr. Lincoln, it was a sacred effort." Given his only-too-human appreciation of a compliment and his great respect for Douglass, Lincoln was undoubtedly pleased. But he was aware, too, of the risk he had run in delivering a speech that broke so completely with public expectations. The culmination of profound wartime reflection on God's historical purpose and the American republic's responsibilities under His Providence, the second inaugural address amounted to a call for national transformation. Several days later the president wrote with evident pride and realism to a fellow Republican that he expected the speech "to wear as well as—perhaps better than—any thing I have produced; but I believe it is not immediately popular. Men are not flattered by being shown that there has been a difference of purpose between the Almighty and them. To deny it, however, in this case, is to deny that there is a God governing the world. It is a truth which I thought needed to be told; and as whatever of humiliation there is in it, falls most directly on myself, I thought others might afford for me to tell it."[53]

In fact, Douglass's praise proved typical of emancipationists' welcome for a speech that surprised Lincoln's sometime radical critics by its depth and wisdom. No one exulted more than Theodore Tilton, once a thorn in the president's side, who now reached for superlatives. The president's inner sadness and "pleasing homeliness in gait and gesture," he wrote in *The Independent*, "gave a touch of undeniable majesty to this singular man." Lincoln's characteristically pithy words bespoke a heart mellowed by sorrow and a mind "greatened to the task which Providence has assigned him in the nation's struggle." The Almighty had anointed the president's moral vision, enabling him to discern the principles on which God exercised His rule over human government. Because he has lifted his face to the heavens, "the President's minor errors will be pardoned of God, and may therefore be pardoned of men." As he had done when praising the president's annual message in December, Tilton repeated "the people's prayer, 'God bless Abraham Lincoln!'"[54] The Republican Party press, too, lauded an "exceedingly Saxon" document, impressively direct and forceful, encompassing the whole contest, "without a word of boast for the past, or of pretended prophecy for the future," and in language that "the people of the United States, as a Christian nation will welcome from their Chief Magistrate and approve." Its depth was inversely proportionate to its brevity.[55]

Emancipation and Providence　　　　387

It was no surprise that the determined emollience and inclusivity of Lincoln's short speech did little to win the hearts of the many conservative religious nationalists who had opposed his reelection. Dyspeptic Democrats, especially the peace minority, made no concessions to the inaugural's spirit of reconciliation. Chauncey Burr read the day's "blackness truly terrible" as a signal of God's rebuke to Lincoln, "the perjured usurper": it was a daring mockery to take once again an oath to sustain a constitution he was striving to destroy. Critics scoffed at the brevity of the address, deeming it a mask for saying very little at all, and certainly nothing of substance. The maverick editor of *The New York Herald*, James Gordon Bennett, dismissed its "glittering generalities" as a way of dodging any discussion of peace terms; he inferred that the president sought the total extermination of slavery and the white race, which hardly conduced to charity for all. The acerbic John Mullaly thought the president's vagueness concealed alarming developments regarding potential European intervention.[56] Naturally, many found an easy target in Johnson's drunken behavior—hypocritically tolerated by an administration party that professed a monopoly of "loyalty, religion, humanity and morals."[57] Ohio Democrats frothed over Lincoln's evident commitment to continued butchery until slavery's demise brought spiritual damnation to the South and made the rest of the Union "heirs of eternal glory."[58]

These critics derided Lincoln's religious theme, sneering at his "vindictive theology" and "fanatical cant." In Vallandigham's Dayton, the chief Copperhead sheet ridiculed what it called the president's craven shifting of responsibility for events onto the Almighty. If that were the case, the editor jeered, to comment upon an inaugural, "inspired by Omniscience," would involve "a blasphemous audacity." The inaugural ball, he added sarcastically, "we presume was also of Divine origin, and the price of tickets fixed at ten dollars by suggestion from above!"[59] Manton Marble's New York *World* assailed a paralyzed president who had abandoned statesmanship for piety. He mocked Lincoln's speculation over the "praying match" between the warring sides. Prayer was all very well, but only to ask God to bless practical means: "We have no faith in staying the cholera by marching in procession with a black image of the Virgin; or the more terrible scourge of war by calling God's attention to the condition of the black race." The president's calumny that the bloodiest war in history had yet to balance the blood drawn by the slaveholders' lash was an "odious libel" inimical to the cause of peace. Not God but unhallowed sectional passions and personal ambition had brought on the war; "administrative incapacity on one side, and stiff necked obstinacy in rebellion on the other" had protracted it. More fundamentally, if the Bible demanded such bloody vengeance for the offense of slavery—universal throughout history—why was this "the only great war, in all the records of desolation, in which slavery has made such a figure"?[60] For one irate Catholic critic, unsurprisingly, the answer to the question "By whom did the 'offence' come?" was not, as Lincoln declared, the nation as a whole but the Puritan colony and state of Massachusetts that had pioneered the holding, selling, and stealing of slaves.[61]

Lincoln clearly intended his address to set a tone for the coming of peace and a postwar Reconstruction based on reconciliation. He had made slavery the responsibility of the whole nation. The institution seen as peculiar to the South owed its introduction and continued existence to the moral deficiencies of all. At no point did Lincoln call the South "the enemy," "rebels," or "Confederates." His language was inclusive. And he understood the moral absolutes that had been such a feature of patriotic Unionism would not serve the nation well in peacetime.

This did not mean that Lincoln was intent on a morally neutral solution to the challenges the nation now faced as it strove "to finish the work we are in" and secure "a just and lasting peace." The address makes explicit that it was the responsibility of *both* parties to seek God's help in understanding what was right and to pursue the answers with firmness in the right. How, then, did Lincoln define what he described as the right? His shocking assassination deprived the nation of a Lincolnian scheme of Reconstruction. Although we can only speculate about the course he would have pursued, and the attendant political bargaining, the remaining six weeks of Lincoln's life offered some clues.

Emancipation and Providence 389

On the day of his address, a new governor took office in Louisiana, where Lincoln had been pressing the Unionists for many months to advance Reconstruction schemes to secure education and civil rights for freedmen, some of whom he wanted to have the vote. The new governor was J. Madison Wells, a Unionist planter who had disguised his conservatism. Replacing a reformist governor, Wells promptly installed a new mayor of New Orleans, who in turn appointed many former rebels to the city's police force, judgeships, and other offices. Wells himself followed a similar approach at state level. Learning this, Lincoln sought to reverse the governor's course by sending General Nathaniel Banks back to New Orleans. And looking beyond Louisiana, where the program of wartime Reconstruction had depended on the loyalty of just 10 percent of those who voted in 1860, Lincoln recognized that with the arrival of peace that threshold was too low. But what proportion of the white population *could* be depended upon to secure a loyal government? The enfranchisement of blacks appeared to offer a means of achieving the necessary majority.

These matters lay heavily on Lincoln's mind when, at the White House on April 11, he addressed a crowd of well-wishers who had gathered to celebrate Lee's surrender at Appomattox. Lincoln told them he shared their joy and was preparing a call for a national thanksgiving. He then swiftly turned to the subject of reconstruction, which he noted was "fraught with great difficulty."

This speech should be seen as Lincoln's opening position in a debate with Congress and his own majority Republican Party. He declared his preference that the vote be conferred on two categories of African Americans: "the very intelligent, and . . . those who serve our cause as soldiers." He conceded that in Louisiana a mere twelve thousand voters had "sworn allegiance to the Union," but they had adopted a free-state constitution, opened public schools equally to black and white, and empowered the legislature to give African Americans the vote. To spurn this Louisiana initiative, he said, meant that to the freed people "we say 'This cup of liberty which these, your old masters, hold to your lips, we will dash from you.'" But sustaining the new government of Louisiana would encourage its work and "ripen it to a complete success." Grant that "the colored man . . . desires the elective franchise, will he not attain it sooner by saving the already advanced steps toward it, than by running backward over them?"

Lincoln ended this, the last public address of his life, with these words: "In the present '*situation*' . . . it may be my duty to make some new announcement to the people of the South. I am considering, and shall not fail to act, when satisfied that action will be proper." Was he moving in a more conservative direction, as Senator Charles Sumner feared, or in a more aggressively radical direction that would have put him on the side of the congressional minority who wanted full suffrage for freedmen and the confiscation of rebels' land? We cannot know for certain, since in the crowd there was one who, on hearing Lincoln's agenda, was determined the president should not have the opportunity to act. John Wilkes Booth took Lincoln's words to herald black citizenship and a world turned upside down. "Now, by God!" he declared. "I'll put him through."[62]

ASSASSINATION

Booth's Good Friday bullet plunged the Union into an Easter Sunday of gravest solemnity. Across the loyal states, mourning drapery replaced the usual emblems of festival joy. James Gordon Bennett's *Herald* told of every New York City thoroughfare festooned in black and white.[63] Civic and religious leaders in most communities scrambled to organize anguished rites of respect. Typically, in Evansville, Indiana—a heartland city of more than ten thousand people—most of the adults and children formed a vast procession comprising every rank: the mayor, common council, county officers, the Masonic Fraternity, Odd Fellows; circuit court judges and lawyers, officers on horseback, veterans and reservists, and convalescents from the hospital. An immense crowd thronged the central square for funeral exercises that began with fervent prayer and singing, "My country, 'tis of thee." From his position at the city bank's portico, the renowned Methodist preacher Benjamin Rawlins reminded his hearers how ancient Israel had often turned out spontaneously for the funeral of a good and great man "gathered to his fathers." Americans now did similar homage. The cannon's solemn boom, flags at half-staff, the tolling of bells, and altars draped in sable announced that Abraham Lincoln had "gone up to Abraham and Isaac and Jacob; to Washington and Jefferson and Adams, to take his place in the Kingdom of God." Angels had no doubt carried him "from yonder White House to our Father's House far in yonder heavens."[64]

Here was a wrenching reversal of the public euphoria of early April. Then, the Confederate army's retreat from Richmond had been likened to the fall of "Babylon the Great, Mother of Harlots." When that news reached New York, Tilton observed with twinkling irony that "Pentecost fell upon Wall street" as profane business-men "suddenly spake in unknown tongues—singing the doxology to the tune of 'Old Hundred.'" Gilbert Haven looked to an American future as a redeemed nation and likened Jefferson Davis to Pharaoh, "a homeless wanderer, through the regions he so lately ruled."[65] Following Lee's surrender, Henry Ward Beecher concluded a two-hour Good Friday address at Fort Sumter's flag-raising ceremony by congratulating the president for the "auspicious consummation of that national unity for which . . . he has laboured with such disinterested wisdom." But within hours he and a Union-wide multitude of distressed ministers were compelled to rewrite their Easter sermons and make sense of Booth's evil deed. "Never," Beecher grieved, "did two such orbs of experience meet in one hemisphere as the joy and the sorrow of the same week in this land."[66]

Victim of a fatal shot on Good Friday, Lincoln in death became for many a Christlike martyr, slain by the power of evil. Had he been allowed to utter a dying prayer for his assassin, Haven declared, it would surely have taken its cue from the words of the crucified Christ, "Father, forgive him, for he knows not what he does." More often, Lincoln took on the character of Moses. Both leaders had been called by God to save their nation: the deliverance of Israel from Egypt; the restoration of the United States. Yet neither, though within sight of their goal, had been allowed to enter the promised land alongside their people. Democrats joined Republicans in common lament over the loss of their martyred president.[67] Across the political and religious landscape, as the Catholic *Pilot* remarked, a unity in mourning left "all party feelings hushed."[68] With Lincoln now cold in his coffin, one editor reflected, "partizans who, blinded by their zeal, could see no good in Nazareth living, mourn Nazareth dead with an intensity and a fervor that augers most potently for our bleeding country."[69] Staunch Copperheads lamented—even in private—an inexcusable and frenzied act of madness, a national calamity.[70]

These were not crocodile tears. Citizens of all political persuasions took alarm at an act that struck at the very root of republican government and an ordered society. Alarmed Copperhead editors instinctively denounced a crime in which they feared they would be seen as complicit. But their blistering rhetoric drew, too, from a well of political values. James McMaster judged the murder of any political ruler a foul stain on civic virtue, forbidden by reason and Christianity. Resorting to cultural stereotypes, he urged true republicans to confound "the Asiatic system of 'despotism tempered by assassination.'"[71] Driven into hyperbole by a crime he declared unparalleled in the history of the world, a furious correspondent of the *Dayton Daily Empire*—the prime cheerleader for Vallandigham—protested that Lincoln, the electoral choice of the nation's twenty million, merited the respect of all who believed in majority rule. Democrats and Republicans agreed that the assassination of the humblest individual was a shock to honor, religion, and morality. But in the case of a chief magistrate it was "an infinitely deeper crime, for it affects not one man alone, but a Nation, and sets a precedent dangerous to all law and civil order." The Cleveland Presbyterian minister William Henry Goodrich concurred: assassination did violence to a whole nation.[72]

Ministers and editors collectively counseled citizens dazed by the shocking murder, explaining events through the common notion of a providential reckoning and pointing to Lincoln himself as their tutor in the ways of a mysterious Almighty who intervened in human history. As Evansville's Benjamin Rawlins noted, "God's providence with him was not a speculative theory, but a practical and abiding conviction."[73] The Congregationalist William Salter encouraged his Iowa congregation to recall that Lincoln acknowledged an inscrutable and all wise Providence whose judgments were "*true and righteous altogether.*" Only stark infidelity could fail to see the disposing hand of the Almighty in this national affliction. In almost every public address she heard, a New England woman

Emancipation and Providence 393

wrote, the speaker won universal approval by ascribing the death to God's intent.[74]

What lesson did the Almighty intend by this terrible stroke? Although, as a conservative Presbyterian put it, "God is his own interpreter, and he will make it plain," this did not stop a search for providential meaning.[75] Some, like the Methodist Bostwick Hawley, saw Lincoln's murder as a rebuke to idolatrous hero worship—trusting not in "the God of nations" but "in princes, in the arm of flesh, or in human wisdom."[76] At the capital's funeral rites, Lincoln's pastor Phineas Gurley acknowledged the role of the profane assassin but saw the more meaningful hand of a correctional divinity: "In the midst of our rejoicing, we needed this stroke, this discipline." Like many others, he read in the president's death a national punishment that would induce sanctified sorrow and hallow "the cause of truth, justice, law, order, liberty and good government, and pure and undefiled religion." The Catholic editor Patrick Donahoe also detected a fatherly hand raised to punish the nation for its mere lip service to God's role in saving it from destruction.[77]

The notion of a president whose great work had been completed offered a balm to much of the grieving public. God had sent Lincoln to save the Union and destroy the cancer of slavery. That done, William Salter explained, his whole mission in this world was complete. His glorious work was not to be "blurred by an appendix."[78] He had gone to his reward. "Mourn not for Lincoln," a New Haven speaker told a vast gathering on the Green. "He has fought the good fight, he has kept the faith, he has finished his course, and henceforth there is laid up for him—chief of the noble army of martyrs—a crown of glory." As Moses in death had continued to inspire his people, so Lincoln's enduring soul would ennoble the cleansed American nation.[79]

Frederick Douglass spoke for millions in calling Lincoln's death a "grand convulsion."[80] The four years' struggle had led him and other black leaders to a fundamental reappraisal of the president. They had been scathing when he overturned Frémont's and Hunter's orders of emancipation, encouraged black emigration to colonies abroad, and dragged his feet over enlisting "colored troops." But by 1865 they had been moved to admire his resolve as an emancipator and, inter alia, the wisdom of the second inaugural. Well before his death and apotheosis, Lincoln had come to be seen as the embodiment of a great national revolution. His image now adorned church pulpits. In March, a Long Island mass meeting of blacks lauded him as "the benefactor of our race, on whom we shall ever look with love and veneration, as God's appointed instrument to work out our salvation." The speaker confidently prayed, "May long life be added to his honesty, and prosperity to the purity of his statesmanship." But within weeks Booth's bullet turned hope into raw despair. An Illinois AME church meeting grieved that "we, as colored American citizens have lost a *tried friend*—A GREAT DELIVERER— A REAL BENEFACTOR."[81] Mourning southern blacks found a voice in Daniel Lynch. Freedmen, the Methodist bishop declared in Charleston, held for the divinely appointed president "a reverence next to that felt for the blessed Saviour." He had "led them through the red sea of blood to freedom . . . into the promised land of a redeemed South." In death he would continue to protect them, for his spilled blood had "sealed the covenant of the nation with the colored man, and henceforth, when his liberties are threatened, anywhere beneath the starry standard, the blood of Abraham Lincoln will speak."[82]

Behind the cross-party consensus of shock and grief lurked sharp differences—and a prospective conflict—between progressive and conservative religious voices. Republican editors and like-minded ministers refused to see the "rum-crazed play actor" Booth as the sole perpetrator of the crime. Whether or not there had been a wider conspiracy was immaterial. The rebellion had its origins in human enslavement, the Presbyterian Marvin R. Vincent told a multi-church meeting in upstate New York; the assassination was "the grand consummate expression of the spirit of slavery."[83] An echoing chorus blamed Lincoln's murder on the "essentially barbarous, heathenish, diabolic" interests of the slaveholders and their malign code of chivalry.[84] It was "secessionist work," surmised Leonard Smith. "They are dirty devils." The greatest villain, Gilbert Haven protested, was not Booth, a mere "babe in iniquity," but Robert E. Lee, who in trying "to assassinate the nation" had murdered multitudes in battle and imprisonment.[85]

Copperheads shared the blame. Leading his company in the

Shenandoah Valley, John Burrud burned with anger at the loss of God's "chosen Instrument . . . the Greatest Man that ever occupied the chair of state George Washington not excepted," and held Copperheadism to account for "the Hellish deed." So long as those "slimy reptiles" were allowed "to crall around and croak so long such crimes will be committed": "Jeff Davis with all His Black and Infernal Plotting is a Saint Compared with one of the Best Copperheads in the north," he fumed.[86] "Who are the men that have sometimes swung their hats and clapped their hands with joy at the successes of rebellion?" asked Leonard Bacon, pointing his finger at Booth's drinking companions who had persistently and foully denounced an illustrious patriot.[87]

On this logic, religious progressives read the assassination as God's way of questioning the spirit of conciliation Lincoln's inaugural had encouraged. Thoughtful abolitionists cautioned against making martyrs of rebels, but a widespread desire for stern retribution simmered beneath the surface and easily boiled over into Christian mourners' demand for the trial, conviction, and exile or death of guilty Confederates and the seizure of their estates.[88] The prospect of peace, Richard Edwards told his Peoria audience, had prompted talk of leniency and the full enjoyment of political rights by erring southern brothers, despite four years "of the foulest treason, of bloody perjury, and of the worst exhibition of bad faith ever made by beings in human form." From this idle and criminal dream, "God has aroused us by permitting this last crowning act of fiendish malignity." Lee and Davis would be held accountable, and slavery, for which their high crimes had been committed, would be swept away and the nation launched into a new and higher life. By such means were "the great purposes of Providence carried forward, human progress . . . promoted, and the ultimate triumph of truth and liberty secured."[89]

Providence, then, had permitted the assassination of a great man to alert the nation to its peril and, in Rawlins's words, "to tone us up to a more vigorous action and manhood."[90] God must have wanted an agent of postwar Reconstruction more fitting than the tenderhearted Lincoln. The New York Presbyterians William Adams and Samuel Spear warned against "senseless philanthropism" and "mawkish sentimentalism."[91] Robert Hamilton told the grieving black readers of the *Anglo-African* newspaper to see God's hand at work in the terrible event, but to say "Thy will be done" and take heart from knowing the rebel South would now get the full punishment it merited.[92] Alonzo Quint thought the prospect of unjust conciliation had angered the Almighty: southern barbarians should face the harshest penalties, including exile or death and the confiscation of their estates. And what would stop men like Vallandigham and other blatant traitors from dividing the North and comforting southern rebels? The consolation that Vice President Johnson—"not supposed to be over-lenient"—had escaped death told the purposes of a beneficent Providence.[93] Theodore Tilton knew that Lincoln would want mercy for his assassin, but without "the full measure of Christian retribution" his troubled ghost would wander "moaning at his wrongs unredressed." It was well that the new president (his drunkenness at the inauguration now forgiven) stood pledged to deal condign punishment to crimes against the republic.[94]

For their part, anti-administration forces agreed that the assassination had removed a magnanimous leader. Their alarm bordered on fright. "Great God! Have mercy upon us! This is the beginning of evils," groaned the jittery editor Thomas Hubbard, aghast at a murder he labeled the worst of all possible public calamities. Chauncey Burr, John Mullaly, James McMaster, and others of their Copperhead stripe earnestly concurred.[95] After years of demonizing the tyrant in Washington, they now engaged reverse gear. The hearts of even his earliest and strongest opponents had begun to warm toward Lincoln, Hubbard told his Dayton readers, citing the president's magnanimous signals in recent months. McMaster believed Grant's terms at Appomattox and Lincoln's disposition to conciliate his former enemies "without utter degradation" had given hope to the "wise and honest." The murdered president would surely have rejected the clamor of "the vile New England faction" for confiscation and extermination, and upheld the old rights of the southern people. For this reason, McMaster's instant reaction to the horrific news had been "some Puritan exterminationist must have done it!"[96] The editors of the Democratic *Ohio Statesman* recognized the calamitous loss of a president uniquely empowered to fashion a just peace, given his unequivocal electoral majority, the affection of

Emancipation and Providence 397

the army, and the growing respect of political opponents. Lincoln would have wielded an authority in bringing peace to the country that Andrew Johnson could not, "even were his character and intentions the best."[97]

In practice, few Democrats thought they *were* the best. Most found none of the consolation that radical Republicans took from the vice president's elevation. Johnson, having declared that the proper punishment for treason was death, evidently held views "infinitely more exacting" than Lincoln's. Conservatives chafed at the supposition of Republican clergy that God had removed Lincoln to derail a policy of perilous leniency toward the South. God could have changed Lincoln's heart without being so exacting. "Was it not, as easy for Him to have done this . . . by a natural death?" a querulous Hubbard asked. That would have been sufficient to startle the country: "To intimate that God works through assassination, we hold to be blasphemous."[98] A flawed theology gave no authority or sanction to a punitive policy of expropriating and executing guilty rebels.

Southerners took equal, if not greater, alarm at the prospect of a Johnson presidency. From prudence and political realism, Confederates publicly lamented Lincoln's murder, widely described as both a shocking deed and a mortal blow against the South's best hopes.[99] Self-interest surely prompted the sentiments of General Richard S. Ewell and other imprisoned Confederate officers at Fort Warren, who wrote at once to General Grant to deplore an appalling crime.[100] Circumspection certainly played its part in the outward show of horror in those parts of the rebel South under Federal occupation. But a good measure of political sincerity was at play, too, in the not unreasonable fear of vengeful punishment at the hands of Lincoln's successor. Naturally, after four years of unrelenting warfare, many white southerners shared the private jubilation of Georgia's Caroline Jones at Booth's act of "righteous retribution" upon Lincoln. "One sweet drop among so much that is painful," she wrote from Augusta to her mother-in-law, Mary, "is that he at least cannot raise his howl of diabolical triumph over us."[101] In public, however, Confederate responses voiced a wise appreciation of what the South had lost through the disaster of Lincoln's assassination.

MILLENNIAL PROMISE AND QUINT ESSENTIALS

The tide of conservative alarm that followed Lincoln's death swelled the political turbulence and bitterness that shaped postwar Reconstruction. But during the funereal time immediately after the assassination, when history appeared to be arrested, antislavery religious nationalists found comfort in believing they owned the future. In highly charged and eloquent sermons, editorials, and speeches they conjured a sublime vision of a nation blossoming on foundations built by the martyred president under the guidance of Providence. From the convulsive events preceding and surrounding the president's assassination, antislavery nationalists sculpted a triumphant providential narrative from their bedrock religious faith and cosmology.

As described by one narrator, Gilbert Haven, those crowning events had begun weeks before, in the early days of Lent, with the words of Lincoln's inaugural, "the most truthful, humble, and Christian" ever delivered by a ruler to his people. In this, his own requiem, he had sung a sacred swan song, one that "Jeremiah could not wish more penitential, Ezekiel more resolute, John more affectionate. . . . The voice of the ages, from David to Christ, went wailing through the strain." Later, on Palm Sunday, Lincoln as the liberator of an enslaved race had entered Richmond. This was his jubilate—moment of exultation—when he shunned the conventional pomp of the conquering hero to enter the city in humility, accompanied by only a few marines, officers, and friends, to be greeted by unshackled and dancing slaves. They had seen a face that shone "like that of Moses when he descended from the mount." The chosen instrument of Jesus of Nazareth, Lincoln had followed the same sacrificial path. As Christ, lauded with hosannas on entering Jerusalem, had met his death through that quixotic city's hatred, so Lincoln, after his welcome in the Confederate capital, had been slain on *his* Good Friday by a Richmond sympathizer, to follow "his Divine Master . . . to . . . glorious eternity." Lincoln had prophesied his own fate in his inaugural. "His, too, must be of the blood which God requires from the sword to repay that drawn by the lash, for two hundred years, from the shrinking flesh of His innocent children."[102]

Lincoln as national savior, Haven continued, had fulfilled his divinely appointed purpose in the ongoing fight between good and evil. Since the country's first settlements, God had reproved American sins but stopped short of national destruction. Wheat and tares had grown together. "Raleigh and the slave-trade gave their contrary impress to Virginia; the Pilgrims and persecution to Massachusetts; Huguenots and slavery to South Carolina; the Dutch greed of gain and love of liberty to New York." But he had converted New England intolerance into firmness for the right, New York covetousness into rivers of beneficence, and Lincoln's vicarious sacrifice had finally swung the moral hinge of the nation's history. Now that Lincoln had physically departed, to join valiant souls in a higher sphere, William Salter visualized him "with Moses, the man of God, with Elijah, the prophet of fire, with Paul, the Apostle of the Gentiles, with Luther, the Reformer of the Church, with Washington, the Father of his Country, and with Jesus, the Great Captain of Salvation." But on earth his soul lived on, to march in God's great movement of human progress and of human redemption.[103]

Lincoln, then, perceived in life as the agent of the nation's glorious transformation, and in death as the emblem of its sanctification, inspired hope in America's ethical future. His eloquent posthumous influence, through the Providence of God, would "change the Virginia slave-trade into righteous traffic, and South Carolina slavery into the grandest liberty of this continent." In this way God would "build us up as a beacon of liberty so pure, that our rays will penetrate the darkest corners of the earth."[104] Religious conflicts would give way to general harmony. "The Huguenot of Carolina and the Puritan of New England, the Roman Catholic of Maryland and Episcopalian of Virginia, the Quaker of Pennsylvania and Dutch Protestant of New York, the Baptist of Rhode Island and Methodist of the prairies, shall yet form . . . the true Church of our Lord and Savior Jesus Christ, on whose divine foundation the nation shall stand in perpetual unity, holiness, and love."[105]

From the grief over Lincoln's murder emerged a reinvigorated millennialist vision for the redeemed nation: a people united in religious faith, republican liberty, prosperity, and civilizing influence. A New England Congregational minister understood the essential power of Lincoln's murder for the American future. For the Christian above all, he said, nationality was "a sublime, a solemn, a sacred thing," with its own special destiny, "always built upon solemn sacrifices; . . . a compact always sealed with blood."[106] This redeemed country would be *Lincoln's nation*. Grieving African Americans predicted that his brutal death would cement its transformation. "For as the blood of the martyrs was the seed of the Church," a black Baltimorean declared, "even so will the blood of Abraham Lincoln be the seed out of which will come tens and hundreds of thousands of righteous men, who are to Christianize . . . this guilty and perverse nation, and make it indeed the 'land of the free and the home of the brave.'"[107] George Dana Boardman told Philadelphia Baptists that without the president's death no nation would have been born but his bier foretold "the birth of an emancipated, united, triumphant, transfigured, immortal Republic."[108] In his second Easter sermon of the day, Alonzo Quint lamented that the martyred Lincoln would not enjoy the fruit of his harrowing labors, yet his death, on the festival of the risen Christ, foretold an auspicious national rebirth. The purified United States would become the asylum of the oppressed from every land, a great republic feared by despots "as no name has been since Oliver Cromwell," and a nation recognized as the people of God.[109]

Quint's optimistic Christian millennialism incorporated and drove a more concrete and fierce political agenda. A New England Congregational pastor, he had served for three years as chaplain of the Second Massachusetts Volunteer Infantry. In words delivered the day before Lincoln died, he argued for full civil and economic rights for black people. While serving in the South, he told his New Bedford congregation, he had soon discovered "that the average intellect and thrift of the blacks is superior to that of the whites," as were their personal integrity and religion. The former slave, he pleaded, should be treated as a man. In the reconstituted state governments of the former Confederacy no distinction of race must be allowed: "Manhood, not color, is the only just foundation for government." The nation should say to the white leaders of the South that by despising any man for his color "you do sin against that God who made of one blood all the nations of the earth," and you violate the truth that all men are created free and equal. The old elite of the South must embrace simple justice or be barred from the U.S. Congress. Practical politics demanded that if there were no

Emancipation and Providence   401

loyal southern whites, "the blacks are all you can re-organize States with." But simple justice alone, not political pragmatism, compelled racial equality. "These men are our friends. They have been true to the government. . . . Put the power in their hands. Make them governors, judges, generals." With arms and the ballot, the representatives of Wagner and Olustee—the sites of African Americans' sacrificial courage—could "hold the Carolinas against whipped Southerners."[110]

Quint's essentials comprised the key elements of the postwar Radical Reconstruction program. Shaped by the most progressive of the Union's antislavery nationalists, its fate would depend on the persistence of the emancipationist coalition assembled during the war. Lincoln and the challenge of the rebellion had glued it together. With those influences gone, the prospects for millennialist radicalism hung in the balance.

EPILOGUE

Wars end but the course of history continues. This book could have ended with the triumph of the congressional passage of the Thirteenth Amendment, the collapse of the slaveholding South, or the grievous death of the president. But an honest perspective demands a leap beyond the turmoil of the Civil War and the achievements of its antislavery religious nationalists. They and the drive for victory had dramatically reshaped Union politics, creating a wartime emancipationist coalition that drew in influential religious conservatives who recognized that national survival required that slavery die. But holding that diverse bloc of interests together depended on the electromagnetism of war and Lincoln. Once an emancipation of sorts had been achieved, and the unifying national sin of slavery had been expiated, reunion and Reconstruction exposed the unresolved gulfs among religious nationalists. The following summary of that story robs it of complexity but foregrounds the key features.

No straight line of descent runs from the political ideologies of mid-nineteenth-century America to those of today. But the breaking up of antislavery religious nationalists' wartime coalition began the serpentine historical journey that has given the modern United States a conservative white Christian nationalism politically aligned

with the Republican Party. As the world's most radical mass democratic political movement of its time, Lincoln's party flourished
through the combined energies of like-minded religious reformers, social modernizers, and economic improvers eager to use the
levers of the federal government for national and moral progress. It
is a commonplace that today's Republicans bear little institutional
resemblance to their forebears of the 1850s and 1860s. The first
steps in that transformation began with the post–Civil War splinter-
ing of antislavery nationalist unity.

That was neither immediate nor straightforward. Evangelicals
were pleased to hear Andrew Johnson recognizing that "an inscrutable Providence" had raised him to the presidency; he won their
applause by calling a day of humiliation and mourning to honor
the martyred Lincoln, that the bereavement "might be sanctified
to the nation." Two days after the assassination he met sixty ministers from the Washington area. Led by Phineas Gurley, they promised to pray for him and for a nation now founded on "liberty and
righteousness." Radical abolitionists like George Barrell Cheever,
minister of New York's Congregational Church of the Puritans
who had been a chronic thorn in Lincoln's side, acclaimed the new
president's declared severity of intent. In two proclamations of May
1865, Johnson established a general amnesty for all except high-
status former rebels and set out his ground rules for the restoration
of the Confederate states: they had to nullify their secession ordi-
nances and abolish slavery.[1]

But the events of summer and fall tested northern Protestant
unity. Religious radicals believed a too-lenient president was moving with undue haste. Johnson absolved thousands of rebel leaders whom he had initially intended to punish: during September
his pardons averaged a hundred a day. He refused to interfere with
southern states' regulatory "black codes," which came close to reim-
posing slavery in a new guise. His failure to deliver suffrage to the
freedmen drove several Methodist, Baptist, New School Presbyterian, and Congregationalist bodies, as well as Quakers and Unitarians, to demand respect for the "great doctrine of human rights."
Cheever now gave up on the president, as did Gilbert Haven, believing he had surrendered the ex-slaves "into the power of traitors." In
the same spirit of justice and retribution, William Lloyd Garrison,

on a six-week lecture tour that took him to Chicago and Lincoln's Springfield, demanded equal rights for freedmen and the exclusion of southern representatives when the Thirty-Ninth Congress met in December.[2]

Yet most northern evangelicals during 1865 kept faith with Johnson's program, swayed by a misconceived belief that the people of the South, if not its leaders, would embrace a purified Union in the spirit of reciprocity and repentance. In the glow of victory, a broad romantic nationalism shaped a desire to end Reconstruction as soon as possible by reinstating the fundamentals of American "normality": namely, the prewar nation forged by its Christian and republican history but shorn of slavery and the poison of secessionism. They wanted conciliation, kindness, and caution, not coercion. The South's embrace of free labor and exposure to northern republican and evangelical ideals would, they hoped and believed, uplift both races. Most northern Christians lacked the keen empathy felt by visionary radicals for the needs and rights of the formerly enslaved. Although many believed in a duty of care to the freedmen, the notion of civic and political inclusion remained largely abstract. Henry Ward Beecher, once the slaves' champion and scourge of the white South, now cautioned against federal overreach and declared his anxiety over "too much northern managing of the negro," who should, just like the white man, "be left, and obliged, to take care of himself."[3]

In the event, Johnson's controversial political course over the next two years acted to hold together this uneasy antislavery coalition, driving alienated moderate evangelicals to side with radicals in common disgust. The president vetoed an appropriations bill to sustain the funding of the Freedmen's Bureau in February 1866. He followed with a veto of the civil rights bill in March. No longer cast as Joshua to Lincoln's Moses, the president had, in the words of a heartsick Brooklyn Congregationalist, become "a perfect Judas" who would "meet the fate of him who betrayed his Lord." According to the Ohio state senator Warner Bateman, Johnson's vetoes had handed over the defenseless freedman "to the tender mercies of state legislation and his exasperated master." New England fast-day preachers in April thundered their fury. Michigan's governor Henry Crapo called a fast day explicitly to counteract the influence

Epilogue 405

of "the Johnson-Copperhead party" and keep the Republicans up to the mark. With evident relish, he likened his proclamation's effect on the Democrats to "firing a whole battery of grape into the bushes where a thousand rebels lay concealed." Unmoved by shocking violence against the black inhabitants of Memphis in May and New Orleans in July, Johnson appeared de facto the enabler of southern white intransigence.[4]

In the midterm congressional election campaign, the president's speeches throughout an infamous eighteen-day "swing around the circle" aligned him with mostly Democratic candidates who supported his lenient terms of Reconstruction. Instead of driving a wedge between moderate and radical Republicans, Johnson's vituperation and ill-considered remarks (he compared himself to Christ in pardoning repentant sinners) bound them together in a landslide victory. In this way, the wartime evangelical alliance helped shape public opinion ahead of the 1866 midterms, which became a northern referendum on Johnson's policy. Without the ensuing Republican victories there would have been no postwar constitutional revolution. The electoral convergence drew in those like the instinctively conservative Charles Hodge. The Princeton theologian had balked at the suffrage provisions of the emerging Fourteenth Amendment: he thought voting a privilege to be restricted to those with the moral and intellectual ability to act for the common good. But he deplored the alliance of Johnson Republicans and Democrats behind a Copperhead gubernatorial candidate in Pennsylvania and voted against a party "to a large extent disloyal" in wartime. In 1868, he was once more a minority dissenting voice, this time against the campaign to impeach the president, which enjoyed the support of most northern Protestant bodies and presses. By then, opinion had hardened into unforgiving desperation. In suspending and then dismissing Secretary of War Stanton, Johnson defied the congressional Republican majority and their program of Reconstruction.[5]

In nominating Ulysses S. Grant as their presidential candidate in May 1868, Republicans found a new Joshua to replace the presidential Judas. Euphoric evangelicals anticipated the election as chief executive of God's instrument in the nation's purification and rebirth. Even Cheever, the sharpest of Lincoln's and Johnson's critics, saw Grant as the means of the country's salvation, while Gilbert Haven identified God's hand at work in the uplift of black Americans. As the new president prepared for office, Congress sent the Fifteenth Amendment, protecting black suffrage, to the states for ratification. Some saw this as the completion of the divine plan for slavery, placing African Americans on the brink of equal citizenship. "We must no longer know [the ex-slave] as a negro, no longer help him . . . as a negro, nor even as a freedman, but only as a man merged in one commonwealth of equal laws," Joseph Parrish Thompson asserted. "Philanthropy must not perpetuate caste."[6]

At the same time, Protestants in general and evangelicals in particular warmed to the new Joshua's approach to the Indian population. Grant's "Peace Policy" aimed at a new start in the treatment of Native Americans, long subject to violence, broken treaties, and the corrupt administration of the Bureau of Indian Affairs. He replaced dishonest Indian agents with religious missionaries and filled the new, supervisory Board of Indian Commissioners exclusively with Protestants of mostly evangelical hue. Scores of evangelicals became Indian agents, animated by the spur to Christian evangelism and the prospect of achieving greater national cohesion. By the end of Grant's first term, reforming Protestants deemed the policy of Christianization a success. They minimized reports of continuing violence, to laud an approach that gave Christians a chance of redemption after their ill-treatment of "enslaved Africans."[7]

The single-minded nationalist focus of the emancipationists' wartime coalition blurred, and their unity frayed, as northern evangelicals confronted indomitable southern defiance. The continuing alienation of the white South from the national mainstream, evident at its most extreme in the violence and fearmongering theatrics of the white-supremacist Ku Klux Klan, split opinion. Most former abolitionists continued, at least until 1871, to support the armed enforcement of a Reconstruction program dedicated to equal rights. But some conservative evangelicals attributed white resistance to an overhasty imposition of black equality, especially by carpetbaggers who encouraged "impudence" in the ex-slaves. Many had concluded that only a shared evangelical Christianity and the reunion of sectionalized churches would deliver reconciliation on the North's terms. Charles Hodge typified those who deemed the reunion of the Presbyterian Church "almost indispensable" to a political resolution. But he, along with northern Methodist and Baptist advocates of ecclesiastical reunion, did not recognize how strong pro-slavery religion still was. In their continued plain reading of a Bible that sanctioned slavery, southerners found a faith that legitimized their churches' antipathy to black equality, "political" religion, and the persisting legacy of abolitionism.[8]

These tensions within northern Protestantism took formal political shape in the new Liberal Republican Party. Designed to prevent Grant's reelection in 1872, the movement was animated by alarm over the notorious scandals of his presidency and by fear of centralizing federal power. Horace Greeley, the party's presidential nominee, Charles Sumner, and other wartime radicals like Theodore Tilton and Asa Mahan believed that black rights were now secure in the South and so stood alongside those pragmatic "New Departure" Democrats who endorsed the Fourteenth and Fifteenth Amendments. Some 25 percent of former abolitionists, including evangelicals, supported the Liberal Republicans in the belief that Grant's forceful approach to Reconstruction had failed and should give way to a campaign of moral suasion.[9]

By 1877, after a disputed election that a partisan commission awarded to the Republican Rutherford B. Hayes, almost half of wartime evangelical abolitionists put reconciliation before enforcement. They supported, at least at first, the new president's withdrawal to barracks of Federal troops in the South. The radical abolitionist Oliver Johnson endorsed Hayes, arguing that previous measures had merely aggravated racial hostility in the South: it would be best to leave the two races "face to face, with the slightest possible interference, and trust to moral influences chiefly to secure peace and good-will." His old friend William Lloyd Garrison was shocked. What had really changed? "The Southern question stands at present essentially as it has stood from the beginning," he wrote in rejoinder. "It is still 'the irrepressible conflict' between right and wrong, freedom and oppression, Christ and Belial." In this Garrison was out of step with several black leaders, who were initially willing to give Hayes the benefit of the doubt. Frederick Douglass's interview with the president-elect—when Hayes mixed the oil of federal assertion with the water of southern conciliation—left him convinced that federal policy would be in the hands of a just man who lacked room for maneuver. He later claimed, however, that he had warned Hayes about recalcitrant white southerners, their hands soaked in blood, who needed "to be taught that there is a God in Israel."[10]

Republican Reconstruction perished in 1877. The antislavery forces so powerful in 1864 and 1865 had been ground between the upper and the nether millstones of reconciliation with the white South and the protection of freedmen's rights. During Hayes's presidency, many of those who had initially believed that time and education would solve the race issue turned angrily on the white South for failing to protect black citizens from violence, terrorism, and suppression of their rights. But once both houses of Congress fell under Democratic control in 1879, there would be no legislative action. Republicans "waved the bloody shirt" in the 1880 elections and beyond, to rally their party against the solidly Democratic South, and many backed federal enforcement of voting rights until the Lodge Force Bill of 1890 was defeated. Others, however, supported the prevailing approach to the former Confederacy centered on moral suasion and conciliation, joined to a faith in the illusory interracial benefits of economic growth in a New South. The assassination in 1881 of "the last Lincoln Republican," the religious racial egalitarian James A. Garfield, a few months into his presidency, can be seen in hindsight as a symbolic mark of the draining political force of radicalism.[11]

With federal political levers lost to them, Christian progressives and humanitarians were thrown back on voluntarism and private resources to further their ends. In a speech to the American Missionary Association published in 1878, the Congregationalist Joseph Cook recognized the new reality and embraced it with remarkable ideological enthusiasm. "We are thinking that the General Government can do everything," he scolded his audience, "and leaning on Congress in a manner not at all fit for an Anglo-Saxon race." It was the glory of the American people to do things for themselves. "We do not lean on paternal Congresses and Parliaments. That is the European plan. It is the American custom to carry through great benevolent enterprises by private subscription. We do not want the government to pay our taxes for us, and feed us, as your Communist

Epilogue 409

wishes it to do."[12] Cook's recipe for action offered reformist nation-alists the means of escaping capricious party politics.

While Reconstruction was testing the durability of antislavery religious nationalism, the northern architects of that wartime ide-ology faced distracting new challenges. The evangelical hegemony in the antebellum nation could no longer be taken for granted. Immigration made Catholics, Jews, and members of other non-Protestant faiths a more conspicuous and powerful northern pres-ence. Many evangelicals saw an existential threat. At the same time, biblical criticism and scientific thought encouraged the advance of liberal Christianity and secularism.[13] Cheever's support for freed-men's aid, education, and racial justice did not waver during the 1870s, but he devoted more effort to battling Democrats, Catholics, and secularist trends. As the Darwinian theory of biological evolu-tion grew in popularity and won the attention of social theorists, it drew some evangelicals toward more liberal beliefs. In the case of Theodore Tilton, his trajectory took him into a troubling loss of faith.[14] Others, while true to their evangelical creed, tussled with the application of Darwinism to racial progress. Some succumbed to the notion of black inferiority, explained by different rates of evolution within the same species, and drew the lesson that time and educa-tion offered a surer means of social progress than the legal fabric of Reconstruction.[15] But a substantial minority of radical dissent-ers held to Gilbert Haven's view that "predestination in science is quite as faulty as predestination in theology. Men are not created by races but by individuals." Second-generation abolitionist diehards like Charles E. Russell and Francis J. Garrison dominated the early years of the NAACP in Boston and New York.[16]

Questions of empire gave particular focus to these divisions over race, a sign of the demise of the Civil War's coalition of antislavery forces. Students at Union Theological Seminary were told that God had placed America, like Israel of old, in "the center of the nations."[17] Several former evangelical abolitionists saw in overseas missionary activity and colonial conquest the means of Christian civilization. They supported the acquisition of Puerto Rico and the Philippines by the United States, arguing that this would be a temporary pos-session only, while their peoples were prepared for self-rule. Others, however, saw in any imperialist venture a betrayal of the principle of self-government that animated the American colonists in 1776. Anti-imperialists with an abolitionist background condemned the racial spirit coursing through American expansionists' talk of "the white man's burden," converting the Spanish-American War into a missionary obligation and religious crusade. Their assault on imperialists' racism propelled them into late-nineteenth- and early-twentieth-century civil rights agitation at home.[18]

A growing spirit of national reconciliation suffused white American culture by the 1880s and 1890s.[19] It owed much to the sentiment of literary productions that recast and romanticized the war as a heroic fraternal struggle. This reading gave a berth to the South's redemption myth of the Lost Cause. In accepting an account of the war that told of a suffering white South, most white northerners by default blanked out slavery and black emancipation from the narrative. It was left to Frederick Douglass and other African American voices to protest at this rewriting of their past, which removed their agency in excising the cancer at the nation's core. Black Americans were not entirely on their own, however. Many white Union veterans clung to their memory of a sacrificial emancipationist and righteous struggle. Reconciliation, in other words, had its limits. No white veteran labored more valiantly in this campaign of resistance than Albion W. Tourgée. Twice badly injured in battle and held for months in a Confederate prison, he launched an insightful counterattack on the calculated amnesia of "oblivion" and the abandonment of racial equality and black rights. In 1884 he wrote that in remembering the war, Americans should not dwell on the battles, the courage, and the suffering, *but only the causes that underlay the struggle and the results that followed from it.*[20]

Even so, most powerful cultural and political forces encouraged national reconciliation. A key pivot in the transition came during the 1890s. While northern Democrats had long sought sectional healing, only then did the Republican leadership wholly embrace reconciliation and finally abandon the South's formerly enslaved people to fend for themselves. Campaigning for the White House in 1896, the Union veteran William McKinley spoke for northern economic interests eager for an integrated national market; as president, he oversaw the final embedding of reconciliation in the nationwide

Epilogue 411

patriotism of the Spanish-American War. Albion Tourgée felt a bitter sense of betrayal. "There was a time when the American people believed that Liberty and Justice were essential elements of republican freedom and prosperity. That time has passed away."[21]

By then, too, the liberal and radical evangelicalism that had driven Lincoln's antislavery nationalist coalition was being overtaken by a reconfigured American Protestantism. Its broad outlines remain recognizable and powerfully relevant today. After the war, most black Christians moved into their own African American churches, living out politically their reading of the Bible to fulfill emancipation's promise and inspired by a belief in their special place in God's national plan.[22] White evangelicalism gravitated toward a more conservative theology and social agenda. The approach to scripture that antislavery northerners had pursued to rebut proslavery biblicism had indeed drawn many Protestants toward a more liberal Christianity, the Social Gospel movement, and secularism. But, with human enslavement outlawed, scriptural literalism lost its taint as the creed of slavery's defenders: growing numbers of northern and western evangelicals joined with southern whites behind the scriptural "fundamentals" and the profoundly conservative religious movement that they encouraged. Unlike their evangelical antebellum predecessors, reformist, optimistic, and modernizing, these white fundamentalist Christians put personal piety before social change. Pessimism and the doctrine of the spirituality of the church reigned. The creed encouraged sectional reconciliation, silence on racial segregation and lynching, and distaste for civil rights activism. The twentieth-century white evangelical mold was fixed. When white evangelical churches came to engage in political action once again, during the final third of the last century and the early decades of the new millennium, their Bible-based faith and practice, and their studied whiteness, flowed in the cultural channels dug after the Civil War.

The Republican Party's radical nineteenth-century founders would not recognize today's party of that name as a direct descendant. The self-sacrificial religious nationalism of antislavery white and black Civil War Republicans took its cue from the mostly Protestant voices that sharpened the moral edge of the party. Aspirational and visionary—though sometimes self-righteous and sanctimonious—

these emancipationists strove to live according to the better angels of their Christian nature. In contrast to many modern-day evangelicals' professed distrust of government, they wanted to deploy the full force of federal power to deliver progressive social change. They acknowledged Lincoln's moral rebuke of the nation when he quoted the stern text of the psalmist, "The judgments of the Lord, are true and righteous altogether." They felt the national shame of complicity in racial enslavement. Most of them were white, but whiteness was not, as it was for the Democrats of that era, a defining characteristic of their nationalism. The persisting racial whiteness of conservative evangelical nationalism since the late nineteenth century, however, has literally colored what its believers bring to the Republican Party in the modern age.

Select Glossary of Terms

ABOLITIONISTS: Militant reformers who sought an immediate start to the nationwide removal of slavery. Commonly driven by a perfectionist Protestant religious impulse and a belief that slavery was a personal sin, these absolutists split during the later 1830s; some followed William Lloyd Garrison into "Christian anarchism" and the rejection of political activity, while others aimed to use the political system to influence the major parties. Abolitionists represented only a small proportion of the larger antislavery constituency in the United States before the Civil War, when the majority looked to quarantine slavery within the slave states, where it would gradually wither away. Many—in the face of abolitionists' vehement opposition—advocated the transfer of the free black population to colonies abroad.

ANTI-MISSION BAPTISTS: Doctrinally strict (hard-shell) believers in baptism by full immersion, found mostly in the rural Midwest and South, who "out-Calvined" the sixteenth-century theologian John Calvin. Building on Calvin's understanding of a sovereign God's foreordination of events, they fashioned a strict predestinarian theology and condemned evangelism and all other missionary activity, including organized benevolence, which they associated above all with New England religious reformers.

ARMINIANISM: The anti-Calvinist theological doctrine emphasizing human ability and Christ's atonement for all. It took its name from the sixteenth-century Dutch reformer Jacobus Arminius. This ideology of democratic inclusivity and activity fueled the power-ful Methodist organization, which grew into the largest Ameri-can religious movement of the Civil War era. It split into separate Methodist Episcopal Churches, North and South, after the General Conference of 1844 (MEC and MECS).

BAPTISTS: Together with Methodists, Baptist churches constituted the most influential evangelical movement in nineteenth-century America, ministering to both black and white congregations. Both denominations subscribed to the doctrine of salvation by faith alone, but unlike Methodists, most Baptists adhered to a Calvinist theology of a limited, not general, atonement. They were above all distinguished by baptizing only professing Christians, by the rite of complete immersion. Congregational autonomy formed the funda-mental basis of their church governance, but with some power exer-cised by regional associations. *See also* EVANGELICAL PROTESTANTS.

BORDER STATES: The northernmost tier of slave states (Missouri, Kentucky, Virginia, Maryland, and Delaware), linked economically and culturally to both North and South. Of these, only Virginia seceded when war broke out, and it would suffer its own fracture, with the secession of West Virginia to the Union.

CALVINISM: The Protestant theology associated with John Calvin and other Reformation theologians, and commonly called Reformed Christianity. Its key doctrines, as expressed in nineteenth-century America, centered on *salvation by God's grace* alone and uncondi-tional election, the belief that some people are chosen (or predes-tined) by God to be saved. Reformed theologians took the idea of a covenant to describe God's fellowship with humankind.

CATHOLIC CHURCH: From tiny numbers (in one estimate, thirty-five thousand in 1789), the Catholic population of the United States grew to more than four million in 1860, by acquiring territory pre-viously under Catholic rule (French and Spanish) but mostly by mass Catholic emigration from Europe during the 1840s and 1850s. In 1860 well over half of American Catholics were of Irish extrac-tion. Papal and episcopal control strengthened priestly authority, with a particular emphasis on hierarchy, social conservatism, ritual, confession, and the Mass.

Select Glossary of Terms

CONFISCATION ACTS: The first Confiscation Act, of August 6, 1861, allowed the Federal army to free any slaves being used by the Confederacy for military purposes. The Second Confiscation Act, of July 17, 1862, meeting demands for a harsher ("hard war") policy, empowered the military authorities to confiscate the property, including slaves, owned by those deemed active rebels.

CONGREGATIONALISTS: Congregational churches subscribed to a Calvinist, or Reformed, theology and in their form of governance prized the autonomy of individual congregations. Congregationalists in the United States traced their roots to the Puritans of New England, their geographic heartland. Some migrants planted Congregational churches in upstate New York and farther west; under the Plan of Union others joined with Presbyterians to found churches of that name. *See also* EVANGELICAL PROTESTANTS.

COPPERHEADS: The antiwar element of the wartime Democratic Party, so named by their opponents after the poisonous snake that strikes without warning. They were especially strong in parts of the Union with ties to the South: New York City and the southern counties of Ohio, Indiana, and Illinois.

DEMOCRATIC PARTY: The political coalition fostered in the 1820s on the bisectional foundations of Jefferson's Democratic-Republican Party. From 1828—when Andrew Jackson won the presidency—until 1860, the party dominated national politics, committed to states' rights and laissez-faire doctrines and championing territorial expansion. It suffered devastating losses in the North after the passage of the Kansas-Nebraska Act. It split in 1860 over the federal government's power and responsibilities for slavery. During wartime a minority offered robust support to the Lincoln administration, while a "legitimist" majority contended electorally against the Republican-Union party. An antiwar element faced charges of "treason" for pursuing peace and so offering comfort to the Confederacy.

EPISCOPAL CHURCH: The organization of the Protestant Episcopal Church (PEC) broadly followed that of its colonial predecessor, the Anglican Church. The elected lay vestries of each congregation shared—and sometimes contested—authority with the ordained clergy of priests and bishops, who met in diocesan and national conventions. The PEC embraced High Church, or Anglo-Catholic, doctrine and liturgical practice (shaped by the understanding of itself as fundamentally a branch of the historic Catholic Church) and a Low Church movement animated by a faith doctrinally similar to the evangelical convictions of American mainstream Protestantism.

EVANGELICAL PROTESTANTS: Evangelicals stressed God's sovereignty and the individual's need for God's grace in conversion ("new birth") and recognized the Bible as the sole authority for the rule of life. They formed the largest subculture in the United States during the Civil War era, the main denominational families being Methodists (who numbered 1,738,000 members nationwide by 1860), missionary Baptists (1,025,000 members), and Presbyterians (426,000 members). Membership figures understated the churches' cultural presence: for each member there were commonly two or three "adherents," who attended but had not made a profession of faith.

FREE-SOIL DOCTRINE: The creed deriving from the view that the founding fathers had never intended slavery to spread beyond the limits of 1787, and that the U.S. Constitution gave the federal government the power and responsibility to keep the territories free from contamination by slave labor. For some the doctrine was a means of preserving the territories exclusively for white labor; for others it was an essential means in bringing about an antislavery and eventually slave-free republic.

FREE-SOIL PARTY: A coalition of antislavery forces—abolitionists, "conscience" Whigs, and anti-administration Democrats—who sought to keep slave labor out of the federal territories acquired by the war with Mexico (1846–48). The party ran a presidential ticket in the elections of 1848 and 1852 ("free soil, free speech, free labor, free men"); its members provided much of the energy that went into creating the Republican Party during 1854 and 1855.

HABEAS CORPUS: The common-law writ, a protection of civil liberties, which directs that a detainee must be brought before a judge for a hearing (*habeas corpus:* "that you have the body"). The U.S. Constitution, under article 1, section 9, stipulates that the privilege can be set aside only in cases of invasion or rebellion, but it does not say who has the right to suspend the writ.

Select Glossary of Terms

KANSAS-NEBRASKA ACT (1854): Stephen A. Douglas's controversial measure that passed after a bitter congressional struggle. The act invoked "popular sovereignty" as the principle for allowing the settlers of these territories to decide whether to sanction slavery.

KNOW-NOTHING PARTY: An outgrowth of secret anti-immigrant organizations. Instructing its members to feign ignorance when asked, the party was officially known from 1854 as the American Party. Know-Nothings fed the anxieties of native-born citizens over mass arrivals from Catholic Ireland and Germany, and over the major parties' failure to address crime, corruption, alcohol, and other challenges to Protestant values. Many Know-Nothings were staunchly antislavery, and when the national council endorsed the Kansas-Nebraska Act, the party's northern support leeched away to the emerging Republican coalition.

METHODISTS: From a modest American presence before the Revolution, Methodism had sprung stunningly to national numerical dominance by 1830. The movement's power derived from its democratic and personally empowering theology (*see* ARMINIANISM) and an organization that made it locally nimble and responsive. Itinerant and stationed ministers ran class meetings for small groups within each congregation. At the same time, the institutional power of the Methodist Episcopal Church (MEC) was centralized through the authority of quarterly and yearly meetings of the region's ministers in an annual conference. Ultimate authority lay with the bishops and representative ministers meeting in a national general conference every four years. The issue of episcopal slaveholding split the MEC, resulting in the formation of the Methodist Episcopal Church, South in 1845. *See also* EVANGELICAL PROTESTANTS.

MILLENNIALISM: The optimistic conviction, shared by most evangelicals, that the nation had a signal role to play in bringing about the Kingdom of God on earth. For Americans of the time, the country's progress toward a new moral and social order heralded the arrival of the millennial age. The advent of Jesus Christ was not expected until after the millennium: technically most evangelicals of the era were, thus, "postmillennialists."

418 *Select Glossary of Terms*

NATIVISM: The antagonism of native-born Americans toward immigrants, commonly on the grounds of religion and labor competition.

NEW SCHOOL CALVINISM: The "modern" or "Arminianized" adaptation of traditional Calvinist beliefs during the early republic, prompted in part by the stunning advance of Methodism. The doctrine took hold particularly among New England Congregationalists and—in the Northeast and "Yankee" settlements beyond—Presbyterians. These two denominations numbered some 350,000 members by 1860.

PRESBYTERIANS: An important part of Reformed Protestantism, Presbyterian churches are so named after their form of church government and rejection of episcopal authority. Groups of local churches were governed by the presbytery, an assembly of elected elders. The top-down authority within the Presbyterian system differed from the independence of each individual congregation that characterizes Congregationalism, although in their Calvinist theology the two denominations were aligned in the antebellum and wartime North. In 1837, over theological issues and the question of slavery, the main Presbyterian Church split into a conservative old school and a modernizing NEW SCHOOL. *See also* EVANGELICAL PROTESTANTS.

PURITANS: Strictly speaking, Puritans were Protestant reformers of the sixteenth and seventeenth centuries who wanted to purify the Anglican Church from continuing "Roman" ceremonies and espoused Calvinist ideas, notably of justification by faith alone and covenant theology. Among their descendants were the Congregational churches of New England. The term "Puritan" was commonly used to criticize the perceived extremism of the self-styled "saints." In the Civil War era it became a political shorthand for any "moral intermeddling" in other people's lives.

REFORMED PROTESTANTS: *See* CALVINISM.

RELIGIOUS NATIONALISM: The fusion of religious convictions and nationalist vision, which delivered politically the mutual reinforcement of religious and national identities. During the Civil War, religious nationalists comprised three broad constituencies, whose composition continued to shift in line with Union fortunes:

Select Glossary of Terms 419

- RADICAL RELIGIOUS NATIONALISTS. Abolitionists, black and white, who from the outset saw the war as the opportunity and means of cleansing the nation of its most terrible sin. They included those inspired by a Christian vision of a redeemed postwar nation founded on racial freedom and equality.
- ANTISLAVERY RELIGIOUS NATIONALISTS. Those who before the war had subordinated their deep dislike of slavery to the political integrity of the Union and the interests of the South. They came—at varying speeds—to see and welcome the opportunity for wartime emancipation.
- CONSERVATIVE RELIGIOUS NATIONALISTS. Champions of an undying Union founded on the principles and compromise of 1787. As they saw it, the nation's hope lay not in an unconstitutional emancipation agenda, to which the South would never yield, but rather in a return to the "Union as it was," on the rock of the "Constitution as it is."

REPUBLICAN PARTY: The political convergence during the mid-1850s of several elements, after the passage of the Kansas-Nebraska Act and the spread of civil war to "Bleeding Kansas." Free-Soilers, anti-Nebraska Democrats, antislavery Know-Nothings, and "conscience" Whigs coalesced locally across the North, not always taking the name Republican. The party kept radical abolitionism at bay and, adopting the slogan of "free soil, free speech, free labor, free men," united in opposition to the extension of slavery and to the Democratic administrations of Franklin Pierce and James Buchanan. In 1856 the party ran John C. Frémont for president. During wartime the Republican coalition often took other names—such as People's party or Union party—as it sought to broaden support for the Lincoln administration. It ran as the National Union Party in the presidential election of 1864.

UNITARIANS: The American Unitarian Association, formed in 1825, developed out of liberal Congregationalism. Its adherents espoused a doctrine of universal salvation and the fatherhood of God, rejecting Calvinist predestination and the divinity of Christ. The Unitarians' heartland was New England, and Boston in particular.

420   *Select Glossary of Terms*

WHIG PARTY: Founded in 1834 by the opponents of the "executive tyranny" of "King" Andrew Jackson, the party was a coalition of states' rights southerners and proponents of Henry Clay's nationalist economic program (the "American System" of internal improvements, protective tariff, and national bank). The Whigs' sectional split over slavery need not have destroyed the party, but its ambivalence over nativist issues opened the door to the Know-Nothings. A remnant of conservative "Old Line Whigs" strongest in the lower North and border states rallied under the Constitutional Union banner in 1860.

YANKEES: A term used to describe the people of New England and its diaspora. "Greater New England" included those parts of the upper North into which New Englanders had migrated westward, including the northern counties of New York, Ohio, Indiana, Illinois, and Iowa. During the Civil War, Confederates used the label to refer contemptuously to all northerners.

Acknowledgments

—

Righteous Strife began life with the Birkbeck Lectures at Trinity College, University of Cambridge, in 2004, "'Shall a Nation Be Born at Once?': Evangelical Religion in the Construction of the United States, 1776–1865." I am grateful to the Master and Fellows of Trinity, especially the late Patrick Collinson, the then Regius Professor of History, for inviting me to give them. The project subsequently developed in directions I had not foreseen. Along the way I have benefited from the help of many friends, colleagues, and institutions. I am pleased for this opportunity to express my thanks to them all.

I have been warmly welcomed by fellow historians on my transatlantic visits to the United States. The various Lincoln associations and institutes, through the overtures of Harold Holzer, Thomas Schwartz, Jonathan White, Bob Willard, and Frank Williams, have been notably hospitable. In particular I am pleased to acknowledge the encouragement of Bryon Andreasen, Edward Beal, William Blair, David Blight, Gabor Boritt, Michael Burlingame, Vernon Burton, Bill Carrigan, Catherine Clinton, the late Rodney Davis, Peter Eisenstadt, Stephen Engle, Eric Foner, Matthew Gallman, Daniel Howe, Carol Johnston, Simon Lewis, James McPherson, Bill and Jane Moore, James Moorhead, Mark Noll, Peter Onuf, Carl Oxholm, Jerald Podair, the late Elizabeth Pryor, Danielle Sigler, John Stewart, Harry Stout,

Acknowledgments

Grant Wacker, Ronald White, and—alphabetically last but by no means least—Douglas Wilson, who is not only a superb scholar but deserves an accolade as a rare American friend who is a cricket and rugby enthusiast.

I have taken advantage of several opportunities to float ideas about Lincoln and his religious milieu. I am indebted to invitations from, inter alia, the Indiana Historical Society; the University of Tennessee, Knoxville; the Mormon History Association (Jan Shipps Lecture); the European Association for American Studies; the British Library (Watson Lecture); Rowan University (President's Day Lecture); College of Charleston (Wells Fargo Lecture); the Woodrow Wilson Center, Washington, D.C.; the Program in British Studies, University of Texas, Austin (particular thanks to W. Roger Louis); the Lincoln Studies Center, Knox College; the Center for American Studies, Heidelberg University (thanks to Jan Stievermann); and the Kinder Institute, University of Missouri, Columbia. I owe a huge debt to the co-conveners Gary Gallagher and Joan Waugh for involving me in three glorious Civil War conferences (2011–18) at the Huntington Library. As leader of a Gilder Lehrman "Age of Lincoln" seminar in Oxford annually from 2005 to 2019, I enjoyed lively exchanges with fine schoolteachers and National Park personnel.

The wonders of online resources have eased the historian's job, but they have not removed the necessity—or the pleasure—of visiting archives and libraries in person. I am keen to record the professional assistance I have experienced in the U.K. at the British Library, the University of Sheffield Library, and the Vere Harmsworth Library at Oxford University's Rothermere American Institute. My myriad debts to the archivists and librarians in the United States include especially the staff of the Abraham Lincoln Presidential Library, Springfield, Illinois (notably Kathryn Harris and James Cornelius); the Huntington Library, San Marino, California; Chicago History Museum Library; the Klingenstein Library at the New-York Historical Society; the New York Public Library; the Styberg Library at Garrett-Evangelical Theological Seminary, Evanston, Illinois; Northwestern University Library; the Firestone Memorial Library at Princeton University; the Wright Library at

Acknowledgments 423

Princeton Theological Seminary; the Southern Historical Collection at Wilson Library, University of North Carolina at Chapel Hill; Duke University Libraries; and the Bird Library at Syracuse University.

Those visits were made possible by several generous fellowships: from the Leverhulme Trust (twice), the Huntington Library (twice), and as Stewart Fellow at Princeton University. I have enjoyed so much hospitality on my travels that I fear I may fail to acknowledge everyone who gave this itinerant Welshman a charmed life. The invariably good company and sharp wit of a long-standing friend, Constance Rajala, made my frequent research visits to Illinois a special pleasure. Other splendid hosts on one side or other of the Atlantic have included Beverly Brown, Patty Cleary and Hugh Wilford, Dan Feller and Claudia Dean, David Hempton, Lesley and Richard Herrmann, Carol Johnston, Ralph and Julia Ketcham, John and Kelly Knapp, Lewis Lehrman, Denyse and the late Joe McCuistion, the late Don Meinig, Jörg and Eva Nagler, Jann Parry, Connie Schultz, Bart and Diane Shaw, Bob and Harriet Sutton, Brian Vick, and Jenny Weber.

During the long haul of this project I have benefited from the morale-boosting encouragement of my Oxford colleagues in History: Gareth Davies, Kenneth Morgan (Lord Morgan), the late John Walsh, and John Watts merit special mention. Most of the book's research I carried out under my own steam. But there are important exceptions who merit a fanfare of trumpets. The late Bill Gienapp, a fellow laborer in the field of religion in electoral politics, shared copious relevant materials from manuscript archives. Michael Vorenberg, with breathtaking liberality, gave me copies of all his notes on the Samuel L. M. Barlow Papers. Anyone looking for a definitive job description for the perfect historical research assistant should consult the three who helped me crank through miles of microfilm: Nichola Clayton, Steve Tuffnell, and Sally Wiseman. A mere thank-you is inadequate.

It is rare that an author can turn, as I have done, to a galaxy of historians willing to read a long manuscript in full. In doing so, my friends Nigel Bowles, Robert Cook, Dan Feller, Brian Harrison, Steve Maizlish, Jay Sexton, and Adam Smith went far beyond

424 *Acknowledgments*

normal collegiality. Their critiques and suggestions pushed me to reconsider, clarify, and expand elements of my argument. One reader, John O'Brien, had friendship recently thrust upon him. He gave me, with marked grace, a shrewd and expert commentary on Old School theological issues. Gwion Jones, embarking on a promising academic career, and Donald Ratcliffe, the established British authority on American nineteenth-century politics, kindly read and improved portions of the manuscript. Andrea Greengrass, generous friend, has once again lived up to her reputation as an unsurpassed indexer. A roll of drums and a fanfare of trumpets to honor these, too.

My first editor at Knopf, the late Carol Janeway, often reassured me that she was prepared to wait for my increasingly overdue manuscript. I much regret that she did not live to see her patience rewarded. But it is more than small consolation to have been in the hands of her successors, Andrew Miller and Todd Portnowitz. Todd's keen eye, shrewd judgment, probing questions, and general encouragement have improved the manuscript no end.

My career as a historian began in Oxford in the 1960s as an undergraduate at Corpus Christi College, to which I returned as president in 2010. The founding statutes of Corpus, the first Renaissance college in Oxford, stipulated that its members form an industrious and well-regulated beehive. I have been truly blessed by warm friendships with many of the college's History Bees, who prompt this book's affectionate dedication.

I shall end with a loving but inadequate acknowledgment of the multiple roles played by my wife, Linda Kirk. As a helpmeet, fellow historian, generous but clear-eyed critic, and warrior for no-nonsense English usage, she has without doubt helped make this a better book.

Richard Carwardine
Sheffield, November 2023

Notes

ABBREVIATIONS

ALP   Abraham Lincoln Papers at the Library of Congress

ALPL   Abraham Lincoln Presidential Library, Springfield, Ill.

BRPR   *Biblical Repertory and Princeton Review*

CAJ   *Christian Advocate and Journal* (New York)

CHMC Charles Hodge Manuscripts Collection, Princeton Theological Seminary Library

CHP   Charles Hodge Papers, Manuscripts Division, Department of Special Collections, Princeton University Library

CW   Roy P. Basler et al., eds., *The Collected Works of Abraham Lincoln*, 9 vols. (New Brunswick, N.J.: Rutgers University Press, 1953–55)

GETS   Garrett-Evangelical Theological Seminary Styberg Library, Evanston, Ill.

HL   Huntington Library, San Marino, Calif.

MEC   Methodist Episcopal Church

NWCA *Northwestern Christian Advocate* (Evanston, Ill.)

NYFJCR *New-York Freeman's Journal and Catholic Register*

SHC   Southern Historical Collection, University of North Carolina, Chapel Hill

UMA   United Methodist Archives and History Center, Drew University, Madison, N.J.

INTRODUCTION

1. Holzer, *Lincoln and the Power of the Press*, 488–97; Harper, *Lincoln and the Press*, 290. For a more extended discussion, see chapter 9 below.

426   *Notes for pages xiii–xxi*

2. For validation of this approach, see Smith, *Chosen Peoples;* Grzymala-Busse, "Religious Nationalism and Religious Influence."

3. For the classic, foundational statement of the thesis, see Bellah, "Civil Religion in America."

4. Hollinger, *Christianity's American Fate*, 4–5.

5. "Notably, over one-fifth of those Americans who agree the United States should be declared a 'Christian nation' are seculars or those of non-Christian faiths." Gorski and Perry, *The Flag and the Cross*, 106–8. See also Alberta, *The Kingdom, the Power, and the Glory*, an indispensable and authoritative study of contemporary white conservative evangelicals; and Stewart, *Power Worshippers*, 45.

6. On Lincoln's faith in wartime, see esp. Temple, *Abraham Lincoln from Skeptic to Prophet;* White, *A. Lincoln;* Meacham, *And There Was Light;* Carwardine, *Lincoln;* Zeitz, *Lincoln's God.*

7. Noll, *America's God;* Rable, *God's Almost Chosen Peoples;* Stout, *Upon the Altar of the Nation.* Key earlier studies include Dunham, *Attitude of the Northern Clergy Toward the South*, and esp. Moorhead, *American Apocalypse.* See also Miller, Stout, and Wilson, *Religion and the American Civil War*, a turning point in apprehending the rich and underexplored significance of their subject.

8. Byrd, *Holy Baptism of Fire and Blood;* Shalev, *American Zion;* Noll, *Civil War as a Theological Crisis;* Wright and Dresser, *Apocalypse and the Millennium in the American Civil War Era;* Oshatz, *Slavery and Sin;* Faust, *This Republic of Suffering;* Schantz, *Awaiting the Heavenly Country;* Guyatt, *Providence and the Invention of the United States;* Woodworth, *While God Is Marching On;* Aamodt, *Righteous Armies, Holy Cause;* Williams, *Tabernacles in the Wilderness;* Wirzbicki, *Fighting for the Higher Law;* Volkman, *Houses Divided;* Ford, *Bonds of Union;* Holm, *Kingdom Divided;* Dunn, *Civil War in Southern Appalachian Methodism;* Lehman and Nolt, *Mennonites, Amish, and the American Civil War;* Kashatus, *Abraham Lincoln, the Quakers, and the Civil War.*

9. Several recent works point toward the approach I have followed in writing this book. Elizabeth R. Varon, *Armies of Deliverance*, tells the war's story through the biblical theme of rescue. In his Pulitzer Prize–winning study of the leading African American abolitionist, David W. Blight, *Frederick Douglass*, shows how his subject embraced holy scripture, and apocalyptic and millennialist themes, to define the meaning of black Americans' exile and suffering under slavery, the carnage of war, black regiments' role in crushing a sinful rebellion, and the promise of renewal in a reconstructed nation. Phillip Shaw Paludan, *A People's Contest*, gives attention to religion in a separate

Notes for pages xxi–xxiv 427

chapter. Vernon Burton's *Age of Lincoln* tells how Americans' religious faith, with its contending millennial impulses, shaped their socioeconomic ideals and democratic practice. Important, too, are Scott, *A Visitation of God*, and Wesley, *The Politics of Faith During the Civil War.* I differ from Zeitz in seeing substantial continuity *before* and during the war in Protestant leaders' political activism and in their perception of slavery as a collective transgression that blighted the nation's relationship with God. Zeitz, *Lincoln's God*, xiv–xv. I have profited from many landmark political studies of the American Civil War. Some nod toward the role of religious figures or churches, but without exploring the interpenetration of faith and politics. Key works include Baker, *Affairs of Party*; Hess, *Liberty, Virtue, and Progress*; Neely, *Union Divided*; Neely, *Boundaries of American Political Culture in the Civil War Era*; Neely, *Lincoln and the Democrats*; Smith, *No Party Now*; Weber, *Copperheads*; Gallagher, *Union War*; Gallman, *Cacophony of Politics.*

10. Hess, *Liberty, Virtue, and Progress* ("Introduction to the Second Edition," 1997); Lawson, *Patriot Fires*; Cook, *Civil War Senator*; Donald, *Charles Sumner and the Rights of Man.*

11. McPherson, *Struggle for Equality*; Howard, *Religion and the Radical Republican Movement*; Harlow, *Religion, Race, and the Making of Confederate Kentucky*; Brodrecht, *Our Country*. Valuable, too, are Peter Wirzbicki's insights into the role of "Higher Law" Transcendentalists in delivering a powerful moral edge to popular politics in wartime through their ideas on slavery, democracy, and equality. Wirzbicki, *Fighting for the Higher Law*, 218–57.

12. See particularly Kleppner, *Cross of Culture*; Kleppner, *Third Electoral System*. Also Holt, *Forging a Majority*; Holt, *Rise and Fall of the American Whig Party*; Formisano, *Birth of Mass Political Parties*; Swierenga, *Beyond the Civil War Synthesis*; Hansen, *Making of the Third Party System*; Baum, *Civil War Party System*; Silbey, *Partisan Imperative*; Silbey, *Respectable Minority*; Gienapp, *Origins of the Republican Party*; Cook, *Baptism of Fire.*

13. Gallagher, *Union War*; Oakes, *Freedom National*; Oakes, *Scorpion's Sting*; Oakes, *Crooked Path to Abolition*; Smith, *Stormy Present*. For the thick seams of conservatism that ran through northern ideas relating to the sources of political loyalty and the bounds of emancipation, see Fredrickson, *Inner Civil War*, chaps. 8 and 9.

14. See, for example, Striner, *Father Abraham.*

15. Smith, *Stormy Present*, 283.

16. Kantrowitz, "Looking at Lincoln from the Effigy Mound," 184–201.

428   *Notes for pages 5–9*

CHAPTER I   HOLDING TOGETHER: A RIGHTEOUS NATION

1. West, *Politics of Revelation and Reason*, 11–78; Lambert, *Founding Fathers and the Place of Religion in America*; Holmes, *Faiths of the Founding Fathers*; Waldman, *Founding Faith*; Kidd, *God of Liberty*; Dreistbach and Hall, *Faith and the Founders of the American Republic*.
2. McLoughlin, *New England Dissent*; Pestana, *Quakers and Baptists in Colonial Massachusetts*.
3. Butler, *Becoming America*, 185–224.
4. Byrd, *Sacred Scripture, Sacred War*; Benham, "British Exodus, American Empire," 9–31.
5. Rev. Rozel Cook, quoted in Sassi, *Republic of Righteousness*, 35.
6. Quoted in Bloch, *Visionary Republic*, 94.
7. Conant, *Anniversary Sermon Preached at Plymouth, December 23, 1776*, 25, recognized that the passage (Isaiah 66:8) might be read "in a spiritual sense," but believed the current crisis assured "a more literal fulfilment." Seven years later George Duffield exulted, "A nation has indeed been born, as at once. It has not been Israel's forty years of tedious wilderness journey. . . . But almost as soon as our American Zion began to travail . . . she brought forth her children, more numerous than the tribes of Jacob, to possess the land." Duffield, *Sermon Preached in the Third Presbyterian Church in the City of Philadelphia*, 5.
8. Murrin, *Rethinking America*, 197. Mark Noll describes the early republic's national culture as "politically fragmented, culturally barren, floundering in . . . space, and nearly overwhelmed by fractious local allegiances." Noll, *America's God*, 195. For the anti-statist political culture of the early republic, see Balogh, *Government out of Sight*. The states created a federal government to augment, not constrain, their power. Edling, *Revolution in Favour of Government*; Edling, *Perfecting the Union*. For the channeling and containment of divergent regional differences, see Meinig, *The Shaping of America*, 1:338–70.
9. Howe, *What Hath God Wrought*; Appleby, *Inheriting the Revolution*; Hall, *Organization of American Culture*.
10. Church buildings multiplied more than elevenfold between 1790 and 1860, the U.S. population eightfold. Butler, *Awash in a Sea of Faith*, 270–72; Noll, *America's God*, 161–86. For the effect of revivals on Methodist numbers and the flattening of their strength, relative to the population, after their dramatic increases of 1838–44, see Carwardine, *Transatlantic Revivalism*, 28, 30–31, 46–49.
11. Asbury, *Journal and Letters of Francis Asbury*, 3:58; Noll, *America's*

Notes for pages 10–13 429

God, 330–45; Wigger, *Taking Heaven by Storm,* 42–46, 173–74; Wigger, *American Saint,* 3.

12. Bangs, *History of the Methodist Episcopal Church,* 2:148–49; James Sowden, quoted in Andrews, *Methodists and Revolutionary America,* 238.

13. Carwardine, *Transatlantic Revivalism,* 39–40; *CAJ,* Feb. 17, 1827.

14. *Arminian Magazine* (London), 2 (1790), 564.

15. The term is from Noll, *America's God,* 206.

16. Washington, *Washington's Farewell Address,* 9.

17. Noll, *America's God,* 202–8. Old School Presbyterians were an exception, continuing to assert absolute dependence on God's grace.

18. Ibid., 187–224. For typical examples, see "Instructive and Animating Truths," *Connecticut Evangelical Magazine,* June 1807; "The Fourth of July, 1821," *Evangelical and Literary Magazine and Missionary Chronicle,* July 1821; "National Anniversary," *Literary and Evangelical Magazine,* July 1824; "Religion and Politics," *Western Recorder,* July 19, Oct. 4, 1825; "President's Message," *Christian,* Dec. 16, 1825; "National Societies," *Western Luminary,* Aug. 30, 1826; Thomas Goodwillie, "A Sermon, Preached at Montpelier, Before the Legislature of the State of Vermont," *Religious Monitor and Evangelical Repository,* July 1828, 72–88; Thomas Dewitt, "Speech . . . Before the United Domestic Missionary Society, New York," *Religious Intelligencer,* June 24, 1826; "Perils and Safeguards of American Liberty: Address Pronounced July 4, 1828, in the Second Baptist Meeting-House in Boston," *Spirit of the Pilgrims,* Aug. 1828; W. S. Balch, "An Address . . . July 4, 1829," *Trumpet and Universalist Magazine,* Aug. 8, 1829; "Righteousness Exalteth a Nation," *Trumpet and Universalist Magazine,* Sept. 29, 1838; "Sunday Mails," *Gospel Messenger and Southern Episcopal Register,* Feb. 1830; "Advantages of Religion to Society," *Western Christian Advocate,* Aug. 1, 1834.

   As republicanism came to take a more democratic turn, and embrace concepts of personal liberty and individual rights, so some conservative Christian voices could be heard defending the more classical, deferential version of republican ideas, but this would be a minority stream in the nineteenth century (Noll, *America's God,* 218–20).

19. Andrews, *Methodists and Revolutionary America,* 200.

20. Bangs, *History of the Methodist Episcopal Church,* 1:270–71, 351–56, 2:218–20; Coles, *My First Seven Years in America,* 230; Andrews, *Methodists and Revolutionary America,* 202–5.

21. Early Methodists had access to Reformed notions of "America as

430 *Notes for pages 13–18*

God's chosen people, of a covenant between God and the nation, of eternal purposes being worked out through the American experiment, . . . of religion as requisite to national prosperity, . . . of the millennium as an American affair," but they made no use of these ideas and remained apolitical pietists. Richey, *Early American Methodism*, xii–xiii, xvii–xviii, 33, 35–44, 102.

22. Bangs, *History of the Methodist Episcopal Church*, 1:334.

23. Dow, *History of Cosmopolite.*

24. Bangs, *History of the Methodist Episcopal Church*, 2:285–86, 296–97; Coles, *My First Seven Years in America*, 223; Andrews, *Methodists and Revolutionary America*, 230.

25. Gribbin, *Churches Militant*, 89–96.

26. Dow, *Discourse, Delivered by Request, July 4, 1806, in the Methodist Church at Belleville.*

27. Gribbin, *Churches Militant*, 95 (Ruter); Noll, *America's God*, 340–41, 347.

28. Tefft, *Republican Influence of Christianity*, 1–15, 17–18.

29. Harris and Kidd, "Religion and the Continental Congress."

30. For the text of Jefferson's "original Rough draught" and the declaration as adopted by Congress, see jeffersonpapers.princeton.edu /selected-documents/declaration-independence.

31. Randolph, *Memoirs, Correspondence, and Private Papers of Thomas Jefferson*, 4:357–58.

32. Waldman, *Founding Faith*, 20–24, 33–39, 182–85; Holmes, *Faiths of the Founding Fathers*, 53–57, 73–78.

33. Miller, "Presbyterian Signers of the Declaration of Independence."

34. Guyatt, *Providence and the Invention of the United States*, 95–133.

35. Davis, *Religion and the Continental Congress*, 85; Waldstreicher, *In the Midst of Perpetual Fetes*, 34–35.

36. Lee, *Memoir of the Life of Richard Henry Lee, and His Correspondence*, 2:201–2.

37. Davis, *Religion and the Continental Congress*, 84.

38. Guyatt, *Providence and the Invention of the United States*, 161–68.

39. Abbott, *Sermon, Preached on the National Fast*, 18–19.

40. Upfold, *"Sins of the People,"* 32 (quotation); Boardman, *Death of William Henry Harrison*, 17; Bullard, *Sermon on the Death of William Henry Harrison*, 5–12; Breckinridge, *Submission to the Will of God*, 22–23; Duffield, *Death of Gen. William Henry Harrison*, 14–16; Dwight, *Great Man Fallen*, 17–18; Finney, *Principles of Consecration*, 138–42; Gurley, *Sermon, Preached in Shelby, Richland Co., Ohio, May 14, 1841*, 12–13; Riddle, *"Morning Cometh,"* 12–18.

Notes for pages 18–23 431

41. Bacon, *Discourse on the Death of William Henry Harrison*, 24; Goddard, *Address in Commemoration of the Death of William Henry Harrison*, 27; Porter, *Discourse Occasioned by the Death of Wm. Henry Harrison*, 15; Ramsey, *Sermon, Occasioned by the Death of William Henry Harrison*, 11; Smith, *Sermon Occasioned by the Death of William Henry Harrison*, 12–13; Vanarsdale, *Lessons of Wisdom for a Mourning People*, 16.

42. Bullard, *Sermon on the Death of William Henry Harrison*, 12–13; Riddle, "Morning Cometh," 19, 22 (the text is John 18:14); Hewit, *Discourse at the Funeral Solemnities*, 8; Reynolds, *Discourse Delivered at the Furman Theological Institution, Friday, May 14, 1841*, 6.

43. The text is Proverbs 14:34. Riddle, "Morning Cometh," 6, 22–23; Duncan, *Discourse Delivered on the Fast Day*, 14; Hall, *Sermon Preached May 14, 1841*, 10–13; Porter, *Discourse Occasioned by the Death of Wm. Henry Harrison*, 13–14, 18; Boardman, *Death of William Henry Harrison*, 14; Abbott, *Sermon, Preached on the National Fast*, 5; Bacon, *Discourse on the Death of William Henry Harrison*, 6; Edwards, *Address Delivered on the Day of the National Fast*, 26–27; Ramsey, *Sermon, Occasioned by the Death of William Henry Harrison*, 14; Smith, *Sermon Occasioned by the Death of William Henry Harrison*, 14–15; Watson, *Oration on the Death of William Henry Harrison*, 19–24.

44. Riddle, "Morning Cometh," 6, 23.

45. Benedict Anderson, *Imagined Communities*, rev. ed. (London: Verso, 2016).

46. Boynton, *Oration Delivered on the Fifth of July, 1847*.

47. Krebs, *Righteousness, the Foundation of National Prosperity*, 6–7; Boynton, *Oration Delivered on the Fifth of July, 1847*, 16; Doggett, *Sermon on the Occasion of the Death of General William Henry Harrison*, 13–15.

48. Bouton, *Good Land in Which We Live*, 9; Boynton, *Oration Delivered on the Fifth of July, 1847*, 16; Skinner, *Religion and Liberty*, 38.

49. "America was potentially as great a religious battleground as had existed in the course of Western Civilization." Moore, *Religious Outsiders*, 210.

50. Murrin, "Religion and Politics in America from the First Settlements to the Civil War," 30–32; Andrews, *Methodists and Revolutionary America*, 190; Bloch, *Visionary Republic*, 105–15.

51. Peck, *Early Methodism Within the Bounds of the Old Genesee Conference*, 402; Brunson, *Western Pioneer*, 1:354; Bangs, *History of the Methodist Episcopal Church*, 2:351.

52. Cartwright, *Autobiography*, 64–72, 133–34.

53. Beneke, *Beyond Toleration*, 157–201; Meinig, *The Shaping of America*, 1:442–43. The effect of religious pluralism on national cohesion is

432 *Notes for pages 23–25*

contested. Moore, *Religious Outsiders*, 3–21, identifies a persisting consensus view of broad mutual accommodation among the dominant Protestant churches. This reading takes its cue from Baird, *Religion in America*, the first comprehensive analysis of American religious thought and practice; and from the German Reformed theologian Philip Schaff, who saw in the diversity of nineteenth-century American sects the residue of European controversies that he thought would dissipate in time. William Warren Sweet's historical studies show "the great Protestant churches" cooperating in their civilizing mission to a westward-moving people (*Story of Religions in America*, 411); Winthrop S. Hudson identifies the voluntarism that encouraged benign competition and reduced sectarianism in *The Great Tradition of the American Churches*. Influential, too, has been Will Herberg's *Protestant, Catholic, Jew*. By contrast, Moore asserts the dynamism of "outsider" traditions—including Mormons, Catholics, and Jews—and points to the antagonisms fueled by religious pluralism. His approach echoes aspects of Niebuhr, *Social Sources of Denominationalism*. Recent decades have seen an efflorescence of studies on the diversity of American faiths and the cultural-political tensions within the nation's plural Christianities. See esp. Brekus and Gilpin, *American Christianities*.

54. *CAJ*, Sept. 25, 1829.
55. Spicer, *Autobiography of Rev. Tobias Spicer*, 101–2. One observer commented that Washington preachers during the 1820s introduced "all the habits and hymns, of the Methodists into our presbyterian churches, after the regular service is closed by the clergyman." Smith, *First Forty Years of Washington Society in the Family Letters of Margaret Bayard Smith*, 159.
56. Carwardine, *Transatlantic Revivalism*, 3–23.
57. Haven and Russell, *Father Taylor, the Sailor Preacher*, 74.
58. Coles, *My First Seven Years in America*, 71.
59. Roman Catholic churches numbered a mere 65 in 1790, a little over 1 percent of total church provision. By 1860 there were 2,550 (about 5 percent), a rate of increase greater than any other denomination, even the Methodists, and a visible and concentrated presence in the major cities. Noll, *America's God*, 166.
60. Billington, *Protestant Crusade*, 185.
61. *New-York Observer*, Aug. 5, 1858; Carwardine, *Evangelicals and Politics in Antebellum America*, 292–96.
62. Dixon, *Personal Narrative of a Tour Through a Part of the United States and Canada*, 148.

Notes for pages 26–34 433

63. Moore, *Religious Outsiders*, 25–47.
64. Tocqueville, *Democracy in America*, 1:391. For the protean character of "infidelity" and the role of deists in the process of making "religious conflict . . . safe for American politics," see Schlereth, *Age of Infidels*. The complex wrestling with faith and doubt in the early republic is the theme of Grasso, *Skepticism and American Faith*, 153–391. For the limited cultural purchase of atheism and agnosticism before the Civil War, see Turner, *Without God, Without Creed*, 73–113.

CHAPTER 2   PULLING APART: A FRACTURING NATION

1. Baird, *Religion in America*, 370.
2. Two essential studies are Sassi, *Republic of Righteousness*, and Haselby, *Origins of American Religious Nationalism*.
3. The phrases are Sassi's in *Republic of Righteousness*, 186–87.
4. *Zion's Herald* (Boston), Jan. 9, 1823.
5. Bangs, *History of the Methodist Episcopal Church*, 2:148.
6. Klay and Lunn, "Protestants and the American Economy in the Postcolonial Period," 41.
7. Foster, *Errand of Mercy*, 32, 202–3, 214, 239–44.
8. Beecher, *Memory of Our Fathers*, 5, 7.
9. The commonly used term follows Finke and Stark, "How the Upstart Sects Won America"; Finke and Stark, *Churching of America*.
10. Williamson, *Vermont in Quandary*, 256; Taylor, "'Wasty Ways,'" 291–94; Faragher, *Sugar Creek*, esp. 51–52, 130–31; Griffin, *American Leviathan*.
11. Hatch, *Democratization of American Christianity*, 97.
12. Edward Dumas (Ga.), Allen Ellis (Miss.), C. T. Echols (Tenn.), W. Hyman (N.C.), J. Mickle (S.C.) in *Primitive Baptist* 5 (1840): 26, 54, 98, 165–66, 233 (March 28, April 11, June 13, Aug. 25, Sept. 12). For the common—even shared—opposition to "priestcraft" of free inquirers and anti-evangelical Protestants, see Schlereth, *Age of Infidels*, 202–36.
13. Brunson, *Western Pioneer*, 1:172–74; Cartwright, *Autobiography*, 98; Gillespie, *Recollections of Early Illinois, and Her Noted Men*, 6.
14. Brunson, *Western Pioneer*, 1:173; Kelley, *Cultural Pattern in American Politics*, 128, 167; Marsden, *Evangelical Mind and the New School Presbyterian Experience*, 39–67.
15. Wisner, *Nations Amenable to God*, 7–8.
16. Carwardine, *Evangelicals and Politics in Antebellum America*, 99–111; Goodell, *The Rights and Wrongs of Rhode Island*, 3–4, 8, 92, 119–20;

434 *Notes for pages 35-39*

Hodge, *Life of Charles Hodge*, 233, 346; Tucker, *A Discourse Preached on Thanksgiving Day*, 16.

17. Bethune, *Truth the Strength of Freedom*, 27.

18. Osgood, *Life and Christian Experience of Jacob Osgood*, 114–15. For a brilliant exposition of the internal contradictions of Jackson's political coalition, see Wilentz, *Rise of American Democracy*, esp. 281–424.

19. Haselby, *Origins of American Religious Nationalism*, 310–15.

20. Jortner, "Cholera, Christ, and Jackson," 237, 243, 245, 258.

21. Fast and thanksgiving days called by state governors in New England, however, were widely regarded as vehicles for the federal politics of Congregationalist clergy. Waldstreicher, *In the Midst of Perpetual Fetes*, 145–52.

22. New England Historical Society, "Did Thanksgiving Cost John Adams His Presidency?," accessed Sept. 28, 2022, www.newengland historicalsociety.com/thanksgiving-cost-john-adams-presidency -thought/.

23. Jefferson to Samuel Miller, Jan. 23, 1808; Thomas Jefferson, July 27, 1821, Autobiography Draft Fragment, Jan. 6 through July 1827, Thomas Jefferson Papers, Library of Congress.

24. *Register of Debates*, House of Representatives, 22nd Cong., 1st Sess., 3885–86, July 9, 1832.

25. "National Fast," *Cleveland Advertiser*, quoted in *Ohio Statesman*, May 26, 1841; "The Proclamation—or Rather 'the Recommendation,'" *Richmond Enquirer*, May 18, 1841; "The National Fast," *Boston Atlas*, May 21, 1841 (rebuking the *Boston Post* for questioning the fast day's constitutionality); "Communications," *Daily Ohio Statesman*, June 2, 1841. See also "Great National Bereavement," *North-Carolina Standard*, May 26, 1841; *Hawk-Eye and Iowa Patriot*, May 27, 1841, 2.

26. The national fast days recommended by Whig administrations in 1841, on the death of President Harrison, and in 1849, on the return of cholera, cheered Whiggish preachers, delighted by the revival of a practice that had been in abeyance since 1814. Boardman, *Death of William Henry Harrison*, 21–22; Breckinridge, *Submission to the Will of God*, 27–29. More than 60 percent of the sermons published on Harrison's death were Congregationalist, Presbyterian, or Unitarian compositions; 80 percent of all published addresses emanated from the Northeast.

27. Hamburger, *Separation of Church and State*, 219–46.

28. Beman, *Claims of Our Country on Young Man*, 22–23.

29. Carwardine, *Evangelicals and Politics in Antebellum America*, 121–32. Influential Whig Baptists included the Massachusetts governor

George N. Briggs and Brown University's president Francis Wayland. In the South, the growing number of Whiggish missionary Baptists drew the scorn of anti-mission Primitives. An English visitor in 1848 identified most of the Methodist ministers on his extensive travels as staunch Whigs. Dixon, *Personal Narrative of a Tour Through a Part of the United States and Canada*, 62–63.

30. Douglass, *Narrative of the Life of Frederick Douglass*, 53–56.
31. Barnes and Dumond, *Letters of Theodore Dwight Weld, Angelina Grimké Weld, and Sarah Grimké*, 1:99–101.
32. The vast scholarship on abolitionism is too complex to anatomize here. But among the works essential to an understanding of the movement's religious and assertive radicalism in the pursuit of "immediate emancipation," and alert to the agency of free and enslaved African Americans, are Perry, *Radical Abolitionism*; Friedman, *Gregarious Saints*; Frey, *Water from the Rock*; Davis, *The Problem of Slavery in the Age of Revolution 1770–1823*; Newman, *The Transformation of American Abolitionism*; Sinha, *The Slave's Cause*; Jackson, *Force and Freedom*. James Brewer Stewart's mastery of the subject is distilled in *Holy Warriors: The Abolitionists and American Slavery*.
33. Cyrus L. Blanchard to Jonathan Blanchard, May 17, 1841, Blanchard Papers, Wheaton College.
34. John McClintock to Stephen Olin, Dec. 31, 1846, McClintock Papers, UMA.
35. Labaree, *Sermon on the Death of General Harrison*, 20; *African Repository and Colonial Journal*, Oct. 1839, 303.
36. Thompson, *Presbyterians in the South*, 1:535.
37. Heyrman, *Southern Cross*, esp. 206–52.
38. Brookes to "Bro Slade," March 20, 1849, Iveson L. Brookes Papers, SHC; Brookes, *Defence of the South Against the Reproaches and Incroachments of the North*, 45–47.
39. Irons, *Origins of Proslavery Christianity*, esp. 12–21.
40. Thompson, *Presbyterians in the South*, 1:535.
41. Burton, *In My Father's House Are Many Mansions*, 27.
42. Brookes, *Defence of Southern Slavery*, 5.
43. Mell, *Slavery*, 19.
44. *Christian Index* (Penfield, Ga.), May 23, 1850.
45. Sellers, *Southerner as American*, 48.
46. Flournoy, *Benjamin Mosby Smith*, 57–59.
47. Goen, *Broken Churches, Broken Nation*, esp. 65–107; Snay, *Gospel of Disunion*, 113–50; Carwardine, *Evangelicals and Politics in Antebellum America*, 159–74, 245–48.

Notes for pages 45–51

48. Mathews, *Slavery and Methodism*, 264.

49. *Biblical Recorder* (Raleigh, N.C.), Jan. 4, 1845.

50. Thompson, *Presbyterians in the South*, 1:393–94.

51. *Pittsburgh Christian Advocate*, April 30, 1840; *CAJ*, May 14, 1845.

52. *North Carolina Presbyterian*, Jan. 14, March 24, 1860; J. Tyler, Jr., quoted in Ryan, "The *Southern Quarterly Review*, 1842–1857," 359–60.

53. L. Hamline to B. Isbell, Nov. 10, 1856, in Palmer, *Life and Letters of Leonidas L. Hamline*, 402. See also Abel Stevens, "Slavery—The Times," *Methodist Quarterly Review* 17 (April 1857), 260–80.

54. Mears, *Life of Edward Norris Kirk*, 271. Kirk here summarized Palmer's New Orleans thanksgiving sermon of November 29, 1860, published both North and South.

55. Among the superabundance of studies on the shaping of prewar antislavery nationalism, its growing political power, and Lincoln's influential distillation of its themes, see Fehrenbacher, *Prelude to Greatness*; Foner, *Free Soil, Free Labor, Free Men*; Jaffa, *Crisis of the House Divided*; Potter, *Impending Crisis*; Sewell, *Ballots for Freedom*; Gienapp, *Origins of the Republican Party*; Winger, *Lincoln, Religion, and Romantic Cultural Politics*, 134–56, 199–208; Fornieri, *Abraham Lincoln's Political Faith*; Peck, *Making an Antislavery Nation*.

56. Lewis, *Biography of Samuel Lewis*, 327.

57. Willey, *History of the Antislavery Cause in State and Nation*, 236–39, 260.

58. McClintock to Stephen Olin, Dec. 31, 1846, McClintock Papers, UMA; T. M. Eddy, "God's Righteous Government," sermon, Jan. 14, 1850, Thomas Mears Eddy Papers, GETS.

59. Morris, *Our Country*, 26–29.

60. *New-York Tribune*, Sept. 7, 1848; *Oberlin Evangelist*, Aug. 16, Sept. 27, Oct. 25, 1848.

61. Salter, *Slavery and the Lessons of Recent Years*, 6; Foster, *Four Pastorates*, 72–74; Carwardine, *Evangelicals and Politics in Antebellum America*, 283–85.

62. For the northern pulpit's assault on the Democrats—and above all Douglas—as the abettors of the Slave Power, see, for example, Nelson, *Discourse on the Proposed Repeal of the Missouri Compromise*, 11; Humphrey, *Missouri Compromise*, 20–26; Leonard, *Discourse Delivered in the Second Evangelical Congregational Church, Milton*, 6–13; Bittinger, *Plea for Humanity*, 4; Thomson, *Pulpit and Politics*, 16; Bacon, *Leonard Bacon*, 385–95; Bushnell, *Northern Iron*, 25–26.

63. Burlingame, *Abraham Lincoln*, 1:422–23.

64. See, typically, Hall, *Righteousness and the Pulpit* (quotation p. 9).

65. Benjamin Adams, Diary, Oct. 17, Nov. 4, 1856, UMA.

Notes for pages 52–56   437

66. Gillespie, *Recollections of Early Illinois, and Her Noted Men*, 6; Ford, *History of Illinois from Its Commencement as a State in 1818 to 1847*, 105.

67. *CW*, 2:501, 546–47 (speeches in 1858 at Chicago, July 10, and Lewistown, Aug. 17).

68. *CW*, 2:545–47, 3:220–22, 234, 249, 254, 280, 301–4, 310–12, 315–16 (1858 speeches at Lewistown on Aug. 17, Galesburg on Oct. 7, Quincy on Oct. 13, and Alton on Oct. 15).

69. Wilson and Davis, *Herndon's Informants*, 259, 654; A. Smith to AL, July 20, 1858, J. H. Jordan to AL, July 25, 1858, ALP.

70. A. Smith to AL, July 20, 1858, ALP; Schurz, *Reminiscences of Carl Schurz*, 2:93–96; Wilson and Davis, *Herndon's Informants*, 4–5, 716, 728; Stevens, *Reporter's Lincoln*, 89, 229; Douthit, *Jasper Douthit's Story*, 47–48.

71. Perkins to AL, Nov. 1, 1859, ALP.

72. *Albany Argus*, Sept. 26, 1860; *New-York Tribune*, June 12, 1860; *Albany Evening Journal*, Sept. 22, 1860; *Ohio State Journal*, June 25, 1860.

73. "Slavery Agitation," *Galena Advertiser*, Aug. 11, 1860, quoted in "German Republican Meeting. At the St. Louis Garden," *Galena Daily Courier*, Aug. 27, 1860.

74. Wilson and Davis, *Herndon's Informants*, 431–32 (William H. Herndon interview, Nov. 1866), 576–77 (WHH interviews, March 2, 1870), 582–83 (WHH interview, Dec. 9, 1873). Also Herndon, *Lincoln's Religion*. For Lincoln's religious thought and practice, see in particular Barton, *Soul of Abraham Lincoln*; Wolf, *Almost Chosen People*; Hein, "Lincoln's Theology and Political Ethics"; Trueblood, *Abraham Lincoln*; Guelzo, *Abraham Lincoln*; Miller, *Lincoln's Virtues*; Winger, *Lincoln, Religion, and Romantic Cultural Politics*; Carwardine, *Lincoln*; Carwardine, "Lincoln's Religion," 223–48; White, *A. Lincoln*; Meacham, *And There Was Light*, xix–xx, xxxiv–xxxv, 122–24, 127, 226, 260–62, 367–69.

75. Hertz, *Hidden Lincoln*, 64. Herndon wrote in similar terms to Francis E. Abbot, editor of the free-thought journal *The Index:* "In one sense of the word, Mr. Lincoln was a Universalist, and in another sense he was a Unitarian; but he was a theist, as we now understand that word. . . . Mr. Lincoln . . . was . . . sometimes quite wholly dwelling in atheism. In his happier moments he would swing back to theism, and dwell lovingly there." Lamon, *Life of Abraham Lincoln*, 495.

76. Arnold, *Life of Abraham Lincoln*, 81. See also Guelzo, "Abraham Lincoln and the Doctrine of Necessity"; Wilson, "William H. Herndon on Lincoln's Fatalism."

77. See, for example, W. B. Orvis to AL, Oct. 6, 1860; Alfred B. Ely to

438   *Notes for pages 56–58*

AL, Nov. 5, 1860, ALP. The quotation marks the climax of Lincoln's speech at Cooper Union, New York City, on February 27, 1860. *CW,* 3:522–50.

78. John W. Sullivan to AL, May 26, 1860, ALP. For Lincoln's duel with James Shields, which left him permanently embarrassed, see Burlingame, *Abraham Lincoln,* 1:190–94.

79. T. Charlton Henry to AL, May 26, 1860. See also *Daily Intelligencer* (Wheeling, Va.), June 6, 1860, 2; *Burlington (Iowa) Weekly Hawk-Eye,* June 2, 1860, 2.

80. "His Abolitionism," *Democrat and Sentinel* (Ebensburg, Pa.), Aug. 1, 1860; *Democrat and Sentinel* (Ebensburg, Pa.), Oct. 10, 1860, 2; *Daily Democrat and News* (Davenport, Iowa), June 13, 1860, 2; "Multum in Parvo," *Weekly North Iowa Times* (McGregor, Iowa), Aug. 22, 1860.

81. Burlingame, *Oral History of Abraham Lincoln,* 95–99, 155–57.

82. W. Hamilton to M. Simpson, Feb. 23, 1861, Matthew Simpson Papers, UMA; W. Nast to M. Simpson, Feb. 23, March 4, 1861, R. Ricketts to M. Simpson, April 17, 1861, Matthew Simpson Papers, Library of Congress.

83. Rohrer, "Sunday Mails and the Church-State Theme in Jacksonian America."

84. Johnson, *Chaplains of the General Government with Objections to Their Employment Considered,* 5–6.

85. *NYFJCR,* Dec. 22, 1855; *Western Christian Advocate,* Feb. 20, 1856; E. Everett, Diary, Oct. 25, 1856, E. Everett Papers, Massachusetts Historical Society (transcript courtesy of William E. Gienapp). The Presbyterian James W. Alexander feared the effects on New England, where "Politics, Abstinence, and Slavery, usurp the sacred desk." Hall, *Forty Years' Familiar Letters of James W. Alexander,* 2:227.

86. Dudley A. Tyng resigned from the Church of the Epiphany, Philadelphia, after losing a congregational vote of confidence. Tyng, *A Statement of the Congregation of the Church of the Epiphany.*

87. Armstrong, *Politics and the Pulpit,* 9–34; *Southern Christian Advocate,* March 24, 1854.

88. See, for example, Brown and Key-Stone Club, *Address on the Parties and Issues of the Presidential Election,* 16–35; *Richmond Enquirer,* quoted in *Albany Evening Journal,* July 21, 1856; Johnson, *Speech on the Political Issues of the Day,* 4–24.

89. Boston *Pilot,* quoted in *Western Christian Advocate,* June 25, July 23, Oct. 1, 29, 1856; *Catholic Telegraph,* Aug. 9, 23, Sept. 6, 1856.

90. R. McMurdy to J. Buchanan, Oct. 15, 1856, James Buchanan Papers, Historical Society of Pennsylvania (transcript courtesy of William E.

Gienapp); J. Williams to L. Summers, Sept. 3, 1856, L. Summers Papers, Iowa State Department of History (transcript courtesy of William E. Gienapp); A. M. Roberts to S. Cary, Aug. 1, 1856, S. Cary Papers, Maine Historical Society (transcript courtesy of William E. Gienapp); *Conspiracy Disclosed!!*, 16–17; Cluskey, *Buchanan and Breckinridge*, 16–19; Hodgston and A Layman, *Review of a Political Sermon*, 3, 5; *New-York Tribune*, Aug. 15, 16, Sept. 10, 1856.

91. *Albany Argus*, Sept. 18, Oct. 16, 1860; Dawson, *Speech*, 8.

92. *NYFJCR*, Oct. 6, 1860; *Albany Argus*, Oct. 24, 1860; *Sunday Mercury*, quoted in *New-York Tribune*, June 12, 1860.

93. "The Infidel Convention. Black Republicanism in League with Atheism," *New York Herald*, Oct. 12, 1860.

94. *Albany Argus*, July 2, 16, Oct. 4, 1860; *Albany Evening Journal*, Sept. 20, 1856; Dawson, *Speech*.

95. Sloane to AL, Dec. 5, 1860, Sturtevant to AL, Dec. 2, 1860, ALP; Sturtevant, *Autobiography*, 284–96; *CW*, 6:160 (AL to Charles Francis Adams, April 13, 1863).

96. Sturtevant, *Autobiography*, 296–98; Phillips, *Looming Civil War*.

CHAPTER 3   FAST DAY, JANUARY 1861: NATIONALIST RIPTIDES

1. Niven, *Salmon P. Chase*, 222–26; Holzer, *Lincoln President-Elect*, 202–8; Fehrenbacher and Fehrenbacher, *Recollected Words of Abraham Lincoln*, 375.

2. *Illinois State Journal* (Springfield), Dec. 28, 1855, Jan. 4, 1861.

3. *Illinois State Journal* (Springfield), Dec. 29, 1860, sneered at Buchanan's proclamation and did not report the day's event.

4. N. W. Miner, "Personal Reminiscences of Abraham Lincoln" (1882), 37–40, ALPL.

5. Studies of the five-month political crisis between Lincoln's election and the onset of war include two essential older works: Potter, *Lincoln and His Party in the Secession Crisis*; and Stampp, *And the War Came*. For more recent studies, see Crofts, *Reluctant Confederates*; McClintock, *Lincoln and the Decision for War*; Cooper, *We Have the War Upon Us*; Harris, *Lincoln's Rise to the Presidency*; and Holzer, *Lincoln President-Elect*. These works, if they address Buchanan's January fast day at all, treat it briefly and see it as a mark of political weakness and even desperation—which it was—but do not consider its significance as a rhetorical tsunami of nationalist ideas that would have persisting political force.

6. Guyatt, *Providence and the Invention of the United States*, 116; Donna

440 *Notes for pages 65–69*

Gilbreth, "Rise and Fall of Fast Day," New Hampshire State Library, 1997, accessed July 18, 2023, web.archive.org/web/20110102115710 /http://www.nh.gov/nhinfo/fast.html.

7. Hamburger, *Separation of Church and State*, 159–61, 174, 177.

8. Morris, *Christian Life and Character*, 555–56.

9. Carwardine, *Evangelicals and Politics in Antebellum America*, 43–44, 343.

10. This figure represents an increase on the approximately four million that Robert Baird had estimated in 1855, before the turbocharge of the 1857–58 religious revival. Baird, *Religion in America*, 28.

11. In church seating capacity, as reported in the 1860 Census of the United States, Methodists led, with accommodation for 6.25 million people (3.47 million in the free states). Second came Baptists, with 4.04 million seats (1.63 million in the free states), then Presbyterians of all types, with 2.56 million (1.62 million in the free states). Andreasen, "'As Good a Right to Pray,'" xiv.

12. Baird calculated, and probably overstated, the combined strength of evangelical members and adherents—by using a generous ratio of one to three—at almost two-thirds of the total population. Baird, *Religion in America*, 19–29, 462, 487, 496, 543; Smith, *Revivalism and Social Reform*, 17–21; Long, *Revival of 1857–58*, 144–50; Noll, *America's God*, 165–70, 499; *Minutes of the Annual Conferences of the Methodist Episcopal Church; Minutes of the Annual Conferences of the Methodist Episcopal Church, South; Baptist Home Missions in North America*, 554–55; *Minutes of the General Assembly of the Presbyterian Church in the United States of America* . . . [Old School]; *Minutes of the General Assembly of the Presbyterian Church in the United States of America* . . . [New School].

13. A study of the unremembered common folk of antebellum America indicates that residual Puritan, Calvinist, or more attenuated evangelical convictions persisted even among non-churchgoers. Saum, *Popular Mood of Pre–Civil War America*, xxii, 3–104.

14. Buchanan, *Mr. Buchanan's Administration on the Eve of the Rebellion*, 115–28; Klein, *Buchanan*, 363–64.

15. Klein, *Buchanan*, 362–66, 370–72.

16. Ibid., 387.

17. *Chicago Tribune*, Dec. 24, 1860.

18. "From the day of his election he seems to have considered himself not the Chief Magistrate of the whole Country, but the selected leader of an illiberal and presumptive party." White and Forand, "Secession Crisis Diary of Gideon Welles," 4.

Notes for pages 69–71 441

19. For gibes at "a hoary dotard . . . driving the . . . chariot of state with a slack hand and wandering eye . . . toward the gulf of anarchy and ruin," see *Boston Journal Extra*, quoted in *Lamoille Newsdealer* (Hyde Park, Vt.), Jan. 11, 1861.

20. *Wabash Express* (Terre-Haute, Ind.), Dec. 26, 1860.

21. *Clarksville (Tenn.) Chronicle*, Dec. 21, 1860; *Daily Gate City* (Keokuk, Iowa), Jan. 7, 1861; *New York Times*, Jan. 5, 1861 ("Sermon of Rev. J. P. Thompson"); *Emporia (Kans.) News*, Jan. 5, 1861; *Weekly Butte Record* (Oroville, Calif.), Jan. 5, 1861.

22. *Chicago Tribune*, Jan. 5, 1861; *Watertown (Wis.) Republican*, Jan. 4, 1861.

23. *Daily Evening Bulletin* (San Francisco), Jan. 5, 1861.

24. *Wabash Express* (Terre-Haute, Ind.), Dec. 26, 1860; *Daily Evening Bulletin* (San Francisco), Jan. 5, 1861.

25. *Cincinnati Daily Press*, Jan. 4, 1861.

26. *West-Jersey Pioneer* (Bridgeton, N.J.), Dec. 29, 1860. A Louisiana anti-secessionist exploded, "Put thy *shoulders* to the wheel, man; praying from now to kingdom come will do no good." *Sugar Planter* (West Baton Rouge, La.), Dec. 22, 1860.

27. *Muscatine (Iowa) Weekly Journal*, Jan. 4, 1861; *St. Paul Weekly Minnesotian*, Jan. 11, 1861.

28. D. Lord to C. Hodge, Dec. 28, 1860, CHP. "We . . . trust that . . . Mr. Buchanan himself may repent, in sackcloth and ashes, of his past acts, and thereafter do 'works *meet* for repentance,' that the last days of his administration may be less guileful than they have thus far been." *Mineral Point (Wis.) Weekly Tribune*, Jan. 1, 1861.

29. *Knoxville Whig*, Jan. 5, 1861; *Liberator*, Dec. 31, 1860; *National Anti-slavery Standard* (New York), Jan. 5, 1861; *Daily Gate City* (Keokuk, Iowa), Jan. 5, 1861. Vermont's Covenanter Presbyterians saw no binding force in a proclamation that condemned as evil "those very things we rather rejoice in." *National Anti-slavery Standard* (New York), Jan. 19, 1861.

30. *Cleveland Morning Leader*, Dec. 29, 1860. Some draped the American flag in black crepe; others proposed a day's thanksgiving for Buchanan's approaching departure from office. *Daily Democrat and News* (Davenport, Iowa), Jan. 7, 1861; *Watertown (Wis.) Republican*, Jan. 4, 1861.

31. These were the sentiments of the Virginian Edmund Ruffin, in Tallahassee on January 4 for the imminent Florida secession convention. Snay, *Gospel of Disunion*, 162–63.

32. *Vermont Watchman and State Journal* (Montpelier, Vt.), Jan. 4, 1861. Governors withholding support included Samuel J. Kirkwood of

442 *Notes for pages 71–76*

Iowa, staunchly antislavery, and the Democrat John Letcher of Virginia, observing the principle that religious duty should answer to conviction, not civil power. *Daily Democrat and News* (Davenport, Iowa), Jan. 7, 1861; *Alexandria (D.C.) Gazette*, Dec. 17, 1860. Cf. *Daily Evening Bulletin* (San Francisco), Jan. 4, 1861.

33. *National Anti-slavery Standard* (New York), Jan. 19, 1861.

34. *New York Herald*, Jan. 4, 1861; *Chicago Tribune*, Jan. 5, 1861; *Vermont Patriot and State Gazette* (Montpelier), Jan. 12, 1861; *Deseret News* (Salt Lake City), Jan. 16, 1861; *Daily Evening Bulletin* (San Francisco), Jan. 4, 1861.

35. *New York Herald*, Jan. 5, 1861.

36. *Cleveland Daily Herald*, Jan. 8, 1861; "George Templeton Strong Diary, 1835–75," New-York Historical Society, 3:363.

37. Bellows, "Crisis of Our National Disease," 294.

38. Editorial on the National Day of Fasting, Boston *Pilot*, Jan. 1, 1861.

39. Duffield, *God of Our Fathers*, 35–37.

40. Adams, *Prayer for Rulers*, 8; Wadsworth, *Our Own Sins*, 9.

41. *Chicago Tribune*, Jan. 5, 1861.

42. Duffield, *God of Our Fathers*, 6–7; Wadsworth, *Our Own Sins*, 5.

43. *Bradford Reporter* (Towanda, Pa.), Jan. 17, 1861.

44. J. B. Romeyn, *Duty of America in the Present Crisis: Fast Day Sermon, January 12th, 1815*, quoted in Duffield, *God of Our Fathers*, 30. Cf. Breckinridge, *Discourse of Dr. Breckinridge, Delivered on the Day of National Humiliation, January 4, 1861, at Lexington, Ky.* (Baltimore, 1861), 1.

45. See, for example, Read, *National Fast*, 14–15; "Rev. Mr. Thatcher's Sermon," *Daily Gate City* (Keokuk, Iowa), Jan. 5, 1861; Bucher, *Union National Fast Day Sermon*, 9–12; McGill, *Sinful but Not Forsaken*, 5–12.

46. Smart, *National Fast*, 6–7.

47. Bucher, *Union National Fast Day Sermon*, 12–15; Wadsworth, *Our Own Sins*, 6–8.

48. *Chicago Tribune*, Jan. 5, 1861; Duffield, *God of Our Fathers*, 11–12.

49. Wadsworth, *Our Own Sins*, 20–21; Beecher, "Peace, Be Still," 291.

50. Bellows, "Crisis of Our National Disease," 310.

51. *Chicago Tribune*, Jan. 17, 1861; Stockton, *Address by Thomas H. Stockton*, 2.

52. *Muscatine (Iowa) Weekly Journal*, Jan. 4, 1861; *Highland Weekly News* (Hillsborough, Ohio), Jan. 3, 1861; *Daily Gate City* (Keokuk, Iowa), Jan. 5, 1861; *Western Reserve Chronicle* (Warren, Ohio), Jan. 9, 1861; *Randolph County Journal* (Winchester, Ind.), Jan. 3, 1861; *Chicago Tribune*, Jan. 5, 1861; *Independent* (New York), Jan. 3, 1861; Smart,

National Fast, 4; *National Anti-slavery Standard* (New York), Jan. 19, 1861.

53. Smart, *National Fast,* 9, 20; Duffield, *Our National Sins,* 23–32.

54. Beecher, "Peace, Be Still," 269, 275–76.

55. Duffield, *God of Our Fathers,* 22–26.

56. Humphrey, *Our Nation,* 19–27. Cf. "Rev. Mr. Thatcher's Sermon," *Daily Gate City* (Keokuk, Iowa), Jan. 5, 1861.

57. Bellows, "Crisis of Our National Disease," 295–99; Humphrey, *Our Nation,* 9–10.

58. "Fast Sermons," *Christian Inquirer,* March 9, 1961 (sermon of E. M. Wheelock, Dover, N.H.); Dunning, *Providential Design,* 12.

59. Beecher, "Peace, Be Still," 284–85.

60. *Lamoille Newsdealer* (Hyde Park, Vt.), Jan. 11, 1861 (from the *Boston Journal Extra:* "The President's Fast Day in Boston").

61. Humphrey, *Our Nation,* 16–17; "Fast Sermons," *Christian Inquirer,* March 9, 1861.

62. "Speech at Peoria, Illinois," Oct. 16, 1854, in *CW,* 2:255.

63. Bellows, "Crisis of Our National Disease," 296–98.

64. Ibid., 296–98, 301–2; "Fast Sermons," *Christian Inquirer,* March 9, 1961; *Bellows Falls (Vt.) Times,* Jan. 11, 1861; Humphrey, *Our Nation,* 26–29.

65. Smart, *National Fast,* 20.

66. Dunning, *Providential Design,* 6–9, echoing the Westminster Confession.

67. Ibid., 10, 12.

68. *National Anti-slavery Standard* (New York), Jan. 5, 1861.

69. Bellows, "Crisis of Our National Disease," 294–95.

70. Humphrey, *Our Nation,* 28; Duffield, *God of Our Fathers,* 44.

71. *Lamoille Newsdealer* (Hyde Park, Vt.), Jan. 11, 1861 (A. L. Stone); Dunning, *Providential Design,* 17; *Caledonian* (St. Johnsbury, Vt.), Jan. 4, 1861.

72. Isaiah 58:2, 58:8.

73. "The Fast in Albany," *National Anti-slavery Standard* (New York), Jan. 12, 1861; Dunning, *Providential Design,* 8–14, 18.

74. In one estimate, less than 15 percent of all the southern fast-day sermons delivered during these months were given on January 4. Snay, *Gospel of Disunion,* 163.

75. Clark, "Sermon," 55–56.

76. Palmer, *South,* 5; Haynes, *Noah's Curse,* 125–60.

77. Snay, *Gospel of Disunion,* 157–59; Thornwell, "Our National Sins," 31, 34–35, 41, 68; Palmer, *South,* 10–11, 15. Cf. Christopher P. Gads-

444 *Notes for pages 84–88*

den (Charleston, S.C.), "Duty to God," *Philadelphia Inquirer,* Nov. 16, 1860, fusing God's Providence and honor.

78. Thornwell, "Our National Sins," 33–34. Cf. Clark, "Sermon," 55–56.

79. Henderson, *The Religion and Politics of the Crisis,* 11.

80. Palmer, *South,* 11; Clark, "Sermon," 55; Henderson, *Religion and Politics of the Crisis,* 6, 9–10.

81. Palmer, *South,* 13; Henderson, *Religion and Politics of the Crisis,* 6, 13; *Daily Dispatch* (Richmond, Va.), Jan. 5, 1861.

82. *Daily Dispatch* (Richmond, Va.), Jan. 9, 1861; Read, *Fast Day Discourse,* drew heavily, and with approval, on Thornwell in defense of slavery, but took no overt political position.

83. Henderson, *Religion and Politics of the Crisis,* 13.

84. Ibid., 15–16; Palmer, *South,* 16.

85. Sterling Y. McMaster (Palmyra, Mo.) to unknown, Jan. 26, 1861, UMA; "Fast Sermons," *Christian Inquirer,* March 9, 1961 (sermon of "Rev. Dr. Watson, of Natchez, Miss."). McGill, *Sinful but Not Forsaken,* assumed a rare and deafening silence on the issue of slavery, while belaboring the fanatics on both sides.

86. Wadsworth, *Our Own Sins,* 16; Bucher, *Union National Fast Day Sermon,* 6–7, 16; Fiske, *Sermon on the Present National Troubles,* 10; Hervey, *Liberty, as a Cloak of Maliciousness,* 4, 16–19.

87. Fiske, *Sermon on the Present National Troubles,* 5; Adams, *Prayer for Rulers,* 27–29; *New York Herald,* Jan. 6, 1861.

88. *Philadelphia Inquirer,* Jan. 4, 1861. Cf. Wadsworth, *Our Own Sins,* 16; Overton Bernard (Portsmouth, Va.), Diary, Dec. 13, 1860, Jan. 4, 1861, SHC; Pastor [Walter W. Pharr of First Presbyterian Church?], Statesville, N.C., on Buchanan's fast day opposed unilateral secession, in line with majority opinion in Iredell County and western North Carolina. *North Carolina Presbyterian,* Jan. 12, 1861.

89. *Daily Gate City* (Keokuk, Iowa), Jan. 5, 1861.

90. James K. Stringfield, Diary, Aug. 12, 13, 1857, Dec. 24, 1860, Jan. 4, Feb. 1, 1861, SHC; Breckinridge, *Our Country,* 250–51. The Presbyterian J. M. Galloway feared each government would have its own armies and navies, imposing injurious taxation without guaranteeing peace. *Raftsman's Journal* (Clearfield, Pa.), Jan. 16, 1861.

91. Breckinridge, *Our Country,* 252; "Discourse . . . the Day of the National Fast," *Bradford Reporter* (Towanda, Pa.), Jan. 17, 1861. See also Hervey, *Liberty, as a Cloak of Maliciousness,* 5. In Buchanan's Presbyterian church in Washington, the Old School pastor and staunch Unionist Phineas Gurley had a few weeks earlier directed his thanksgiving sermon at the looming threat of secession. "It was a sad day

in the history of ancient Israel, when the tribes . . . as one people were rent and divided," losing their glory through "terrible strifes, invasions and disasters." And an equally sad day would it be "when this modern Israel shall finally divide." *National Intelligencer,* Dec. 1, 1860, 3. Buchanan pronounced it "a splendid discourse." *Chicago Tribune,* Nov. 26, 1860, 2; *Lowell (Mass.) Daily Citizen and News,* Nov. 24, 1860, 2.

92. *Chicago Tribune,* Jan. 5, 1861.

93. Fiske, *Sermon on the Present National Troubles,* 5; Wadsworth, *Our Own Sins,* 12–14.

94. Fiske, *Sermon on the Present National Troubles,* 5, 9.

95. Ibid., 7–8; Adams, *Prayer for Rulers,* 35. "Religious," *Cleveland Morning Leader,* Jan. 5, 1861 (sermon of William H. Goodrich).

96. Van Dyke, "Character and Influence of Abolitionism," 127–76; Vinton, "Irreligion, Corruption, and Fanaticism Rebuked," 247–64; *New York Herald,* Jan. 6, 1861.

97. Raphall, "Bible View of Slavery," 227–46.

98. *Daily Gate City* (Keokuk, Iowa), Jan. 5, 1861. Quoting Beecher on the sovereignty of the individual conscience, Bucher asked, "Is this biblical? Is it not blasphemy arrogating to poor sinful humanity that to which the angels in heaven dare not aspire!" Bucher, *Union National Fast Day Sermon,* 15, 22.

99. *New York Herald,* Jan. 5, 1861; Wadsworth, *Our Own Sins,* 12–13.

100. *New York Herald,* Jan. 6, 1861; Korn, *American Jewry and the Civil War,* 20.

101. Sloane, *Review of Rev. Henry J. Van Dyke's Discourse,* 9–22.

102. Albert S. Hunt, Diary, Jan. 2 and 5, 1861, UMA.

103. A. A. Hodge to Charles Hodge, Jan. 9, 1861, CHP. Cf. Griffis, *John Chambers,* 115–17.

104. Haney, *Story of My Life,* 134–35.

105. Stockton, *Address by Thomas H. Stockton,* 2, 10–16.

106. Gutjahr, *Charles Hodge,* offers a meticulous study of Hodge's influential conservative Calvinism, and discusses (299–317) his political allegiances and the crisis of 1860–61 for the nation and Old School Presbyterianism. See also Carwardine, "Politics of Charles Hodge," 247–97.

107. Hodge, "Slavery"; Hodge, "Abolitionism"; Hodge, "Princeton Review on the State of the Country and of the Church," 638–41; Hodge, "Emancipation"; Hodge, *Life of Charles Hodge,* 333–36.

108. C. Hodge to H. L. Hodge, n.d. (ca. 1860–61), CHMC; C. Hodge to J. C. Backus, Dec. 28, 1860, in Hodge, *Life of Charles Hodge,* 464–65.

446   *Notes for pages 95–97*

109. Hodge, "The Church and the Country," 348–75; C. Hodge to H. L. Hodge, Feb. 18, 1861, CHP; Charles Hodge, "Short Notices. *Thanksgiving Sermon* . . . by the Rev. B. M. Palmer, D.D.," *BRPR* 33, no. 1 (Jan. 1861): 167–71.

110. Hodge, "General Assembly [1859]"; Hodge, "Princeton Review on the State of the Country and of the Church," 645–47.

111. C. Hodge to A. Alexander, Nov. 2, Dec. 21, 1826; C. Hodge to S. Hodge, Jan. 10, 1827; C. Hodge to H. L. Hodge, Dec. 29, 1851, in Hodge, *Life of Charles Hodge*, 106–12, 115, 203, 352–55, 359–60, 394; Charles Hodge, "Anniversary Address," *Home Missionary* 2, no. 2 (June 1829): 17–18; Hodge, "State of the Country," 2–3, 33; Hodge, "Civil Government," 127.

112. Hodge, *Life of Charles Hodge*, 462; C. Hodge to H. L. Hodge, Nov. 22, 1860, C. Hodge to R. S. Field, Dec. 15, 1860, CHP; Hodge, "State of the Country," 1.

113. Hodge, "State of the Country," 3–4; C. Hodge to J. H. Thornwell, Jan. 3, 1861, in Hodge, *Life of Charles Hodge*, 462–63.

114. C. Hodge to H. L. Hodge, Dec. 13, 1860, CHP.

115. Hodge, *Life of Charles Hodge*, 34–35, 43–46, 52–53, 159–62, 253–54, 291–310, 445.

116. C. Hodge to J. Leighton Wilson, Jan. 3, 1861, CHMC; C. Hodge to H. A. Boardman, Dec. 18 and Dec. 28, 1860, Jan. 17, 1861, CHP; Hodge, *Life of Charles Hodge*, 465–66. Hodge was cheered by the endorsements and supportive letters he received from across the country, from Douglas and Breckinridge Democrats, Constitutional Union men, and Republicans: they provided ammunition against correspondents like John Miller, who judged that Hodge's article would "denationalize the seminary & confine it to the Northern States." Miller to Hodge, Jan. 7, 1861, CHMC; Hodge, "The Church and the Country," 330–31.

117. Hodge, "Princeton Review on the State of the Country and of the Church," 628–30.

118. They included the former New Jersey attorney general Richard S. Field, who would serve as a Republican U.S. senator during the war; William M. Dunn of Indiana, Republican member of the U.S. House of Representatives; John Chester Backus of Baltimore, a Princeton trustee and moderator of the Old School Presbyterian General Assembly in 1861; and Orange N. Stoddard, professor of natural sciences at Miami University, Ohio. Field to C. Hodge, Dec. 15, 1860; Dunn to C. Hodge, Dec. 28, 1860; Backus to C. Hodge, Dec. 25, 1860; Stoddard to C. Hodge, Dec. 26, 1860, CHP.

Notes for pages 97–98

119. L. B. Todd (Lexington, Ky.) to C. Hodge, Jan. 10, 1861; John Otto (Buffalo) to C. Hodge, Jan. 11, 1861, CHP. See also Cortlandt Van Rensselaer to C. Hodge, Jan. 1, 1861; Henry M. Field to C. Hodge, Jan. 10, 1861; William B. Sprague to C. Hodge, March 21, 1861; Samuel Breck to C. Hodge, Feb. 3, 1861, CHP.

120. H. Hunt (Wyoming, Pa.) to C. Hodge, Feb. 1, 1861; N. C. Burr (Cincinnati) to C. Hodge, Jan. 25, 1861; Randolph A. DeLancey (Presbyterian minister and New Orleans agent of the American Bible Society) to C. Hodge, March 2, 1861, CHP.

121. Frederick Brown (Cleveland Republican) to C. Hodge, Jan. 17, 1861; J. Dorrance (Wilkes-Barre, Pa.) to C. Hodge, Jan. 21, 1861; J. N. Campbell (Albany, N.Y.) to C. Hodge, Feb. 15, 1861, CHP.

122. John Leighton Wilson (New York City) to C. Hodge, Dec. 19, 1860, CHP.

123. Ibid. For the breach with John Leighton Wilson, see Stewart, "Mediating the Center," 92–93. "Perhaps you saw the paragraph quoted from a Southern paper stating that it was a great mistake that the Southern Christian had not prayed for my death as I had lived a long life & was now doing more harm than good." C. Hodge to H. L. Hodge, Sept. 6, 1861, CHP.

124. John C. Backus to C. Hodge, Jan. 25, 1861; Joseph Atkinson to C. Hodge, Jan. 22, 1861, CHP.

125. N. C. Burr to C. Hodge, Jan. 25, 1861; R. L. Dabney to C. Hodge, Feb. 13, 1861; James Roswell King to C. Hodge, Jan. 16, 1861, CHP; Hodge, "The Church and the Country," 328–32; Hodge, "Princeton Review on the State of the Country and of the Church," 627–57; Myers, *Children of Pride*, 645, 648–51. Samuel I. Prime, Nathan Rice, and other Old School northerners formerly esteemed in the slave states joined Hodge as targets of southern fire. Carwardine, *Evangelicals and Politics in Antebellum America*, 289.

126. Edmund Cater to C. Hodge, Jan. 29, 1861, CHP.

127. Elmer to C. Hodge, Jan. 15, 1861, CHP.

128. The *New-York Observer* carried a sharp riposte to Hodge, probably the handiwork of Judge George Sharswood, a Princeton trustee who considered state sovereignty "absolute & unqualified" and held that "slavery is destined to be perpetual & that, if it were not so, the scriptures could not be fulfilled which says (Rev. 6:15) 'Every bondman & every freeman hid themselves in the dens [and in the rocks of the mountains].'" John W. Yeomans (Danville, Pa.) to C. Hodge, Feb. 2, 1861, CHP.

129. Correspondence with John O'Brien.

448 *Notes for pages 98–104*

130. Hodge, "The Church and the Country," 329; C. Hodge to J. H. Thornwell, Jan. 3, 1861, C. Hodge to H. A. Boardman, Jan. 17, 1861, in Hodge, *Life of Charles Hodge*, 462–63, 465–66.
131. Breckinridge to C. Hodge, Jan. 19, 1861, CHMC.
132. Elmer to C. Hodge, Jan. 21, 1861, CHP.
133. C. Hodge to J. H. Thornwell, Jan. 3, 1861, in Hodge, *Life of Charles Hodge*, 463; Hodge, "The Church and the Country," 339; Hodge, "Princeton Review on the State of the Country and of the Church," 634–35. For other ministers who appeared open to a constitutionally negotiated breakup of the Union, see Dunham, *Attitude of the Northern Clergy Toward the South*, 71–76; Parish, "Instruments of Providence," 33–34.

CHAPTER 4 LINCOLN, NATIONALITY, AND PROVIDENCE

1. "Address of the Honorable David Lloyd George at the Unveiling of the Statue of Lincoln, July 28, 1920," *International Conciliation* 156 (Nov. 1920): 498–99.
2. U.S. Department of State, *The Assassination of Abraham Lincoln, Late President of the United States, and the Attempted Assassination of William H. Seward, Secretary of State, and Frederick W. Seward, Assistant Secretary, on the Evening of the 14th of April, 1865. Expressions of Condolence and Sympathy Inspired by These Events* (Washington, D.C.: Government Printing Office, 1867), 92.
3. *CW*, 1:135 (Report and Resolutions Introduced in Illinois Legislature in Relation to Purchase of Public Lands, Jan. 17, 1839); 2:222 (Fragment on Slavery, April 1, 1854?). Cf. *CW*, 1:108 (Address Before the Young Men's Lyceum of Springfield, Jan. 27, 1838).
4. Russell, *My Diary North and South*, 214.
5. Fehrenbacher and Fehrenbacher, *Recollected Words of Abraham Lincoln*, 113–14.
6. *CW*, 1:108 (Jan. 27, 1838); 1:277 (Temperance Address, Feb. 22, 1842); 1:312 (Campaign Circular from Whig Committee, March 4, 1843); 2:265 (Speech at Peoria, Oct. 16, 1854).
7. "Notes for a Speech on Slavery and American Government, c. 1857–58," in Wilson et al., eds., *Great Lincoln Documents: Historians Present Treasures from the Gilder Lehrman Collection*, 20–21. See also Baker, "Lincoln's Narrative of American Exceptionalism," 33–44.
8. Houser, *Lincoln's Education, and Other Essays*, 112; Kaplan, *Lincoln*, 25–27; Wilson and Davis, *Herndon's Informants*, 10; Bray, *Reading with Lincoln*, 48–79, 225.

Notes for pages 105–108 449

9. *CW,* 1:115 (Address Before the Young Men's Lyceum of Springfield, Jan. 27, 1838).

10. Henry Clay, Lincoln's inspiration in domestic matters, provided a manifesto on the United States' global role that Lincoln also embraced. His fellow Kentuckian, Lincoln reflected, "witnessed . . . the throes of the French Revolution . . . the rise and fall of Napoleon . . . [and] the contest with Great Britain. When Greece rose against the Turks . . . his name was mingled with the battle-cry of freedom. When South America threw off the thraldom of Spain, his speeches were read at the head of her armies by Bolivar. . . . He . . . burned with a zeal for [his country's] . . . advancement, prosperity and glory, because he saw in such, the advancement, prosperity and glory, of human liberty, human right and human nature." *CW,* 2:123–26, 129–30 (Eulogy on Henry Clay, July 6, 1852).

11. *CW,* 2:62 (Resolutions of Sympathy with the Cause of Hungarian Freedom, Sept. 6, 1849), 2:115–16 (Resolutions in Behalf of Hungarian Freedom, Jan. 9, 1852); *Lincoln Log,* April 10, 1848; *Sangamo Journal,* Sept. 12, 26, Oct. 10, 1849; *Illinois State Journal,* Jan. 14, 17, 19, 31, 1852.

12. Their numbers grew to 350 by 1855. Angle, *"Here I Have Lived,"* 142–43. During the 1850s, German and Irish immigrants made up the majority of Springfield's foreign-born inhabitants; they constituted 50 percent of the city's population by 1860. Winkle, *The Young Eagle: The Rise of Abraham Lincoln* (Dallas: Taylor, 2001), 272–73.

13. *Memoirs of Gustave Koerner,* esp. 2:33, 46–51, 56–69, 109–16; Herriott, *The Premises and Significance of Abraham Lincoln's Letter to Theodore Canisius;* Herriott, *The Conference of German-Republicans in the Deutsches Haus.*

14. *CW,* 3:363 (Second Lecture on Discoveries and Inventions, Feb. 11, 1859).

15. *CW,* 1:112 (Address Before the Young Men's Lyceum of Springfield, Jan. 27, 1838); 1:438 (Speech in United States House of Representatives: The War with Mexico, Jan. 12, 1848).

16. *CW,* 3:312 (Seventh Debate with Douglas, at Alton, Oct. 15, 1858); 4:7 (Speech at Hartford, March 5, 1860).

17. *CW,* 3:547–50 (Address at Cooper Institute, New York City, Feb. 27, 1860).

18. *CW,* 4:198 (Speech at Cincinnati, Feb. 12, 1861); 4:228 (Remarks at Poughkeepsie, N.Y., Feb. 19, 1861). Cf. *CW,* 4:220 (Speech at Buffalo), Feb. 16, 1861; 4:225–26 (Address to the Legislature at Albany, N.Y., Feb. 18, 1861).

450   *Notes for pages 108–115*

19. *CW,* 4:235–36 (Address to the New Jersey Senate at Trenton, Feb. 21, 1861); 4:240–41 (Speech in Independence Hall, Philadelphia, Feb. 22, 1861); 4:203 (Speech to Germans at Cincinnati, Feb. 12, 1861).

20. *CW,* 4:194 (Reply to Morton at Indianapolis, Feb. 11, 1861); 4:226 (Address to the Legislature at Albany, N.Y., Feb. 18, 1861); 4:241–42 (Speech at the Flag-Raising Before Independence Hall, Philadelphia, Feb. 22, 1861). Cf. *CW,* 4:205–6 (Speech from the Steps of the Capitol at Columbus, Ohio, Feb. 13, 1861); *CW,* 4:222 (Remarks at Syracuse, N.Y., Feb. 18, 1861).

21. *CW,* 1:439 (Speech in the United States House of Representatives: The War with Mexico, Jan. 12, 1848); 3:220 (Fifth Debate with Douglas, at Galesburg, Ill., Oct. 7, 1858).

22. *CW,* 4:191 (Farewell Address at Springfield, Ill., Feb. 11, 1861).

23. *CW,* 4:199, 204, 207, 220–21, 226 (Speeches at Cincinnati, Feb. 12, 1861; to the Ohio Legislature, Columbus, Feb. 13, 1861; at Steubenville, Ohio, Feb. 14, 1861; at Buffalo, Feb. 16, 1861; to the Legislature at Albany, N.Y., Feb. 18, 1861). Cf. Lincoln to Peter H. Sylvester, Dec. 22, 1860: "The political horizon looks dark and lowering; but the people, under Providence, will set all right." *CW,* 4:160.

24. *CW,* 4:235–36 (Address to the New Jersey Senate at Trenton, Feb. 21, 1861).

25. *CW,* 4:262–71 (First Inaugural Address—Final Text, March 4, 1861).

26. *CW,* 4:421–41 (Message to Congress in Special Session, July 4, 1861). My reading takes its cue from Douglas L. Wilson's superb analysis of Lincoln's craft as a writer, *Lincoln's Sword,* 100–101.

27. Briggs to AL, Feb. 16, 1861, ALP.

28. Anna Bache, Poem, 1861, ALP.

29. Burlingame, *Abraham Lincoln,* 1:260, 731, 733; R. Andrew Myers, blog, Log College Press, July 25, 2020, accessed Sept. 2023, www.logcollegepress.com.

30. Butler to AL, Jan. 10, 1861, ALP.

31. Henry to AL, Jan. 8, 1861; Buckingham to AL, Dec. 28, 1860; Doolittle to AL, April 18, 1861; Pollard to AL, March 4, 1861; Smith to AL, April 29, 1861, ALP.

32. William Sloane to AL, Dec. 5, 1860; Joel Manning to AL, Feb. 4, 1861, ALP.

33. Butler to AL, Jan. 10, 1861, ALP. Cf. Alfred B. Ely to AL, Jan. 16, 1861; Henry C. Bowen to AL, Feb. 5, 1861; Pollard to AL, March 4, 1861; William Sprague to AL, April 11, 1861, ALP.

34. Anonymous to Mary Todd Lincoln, Jan. 1, 1861; M. M. Gibbs to AL, Jan. 29, 1861. Cf. Anson G. Henry to AL, Feb. 16, 1859, ALP.

35. Joseph Butler to AL, Jan. 10, 1861; Sloane to AL, Dec. 5, 1860; Edward Harris to AL, Dec. 10, 1860; Myers to AL, Dec. 10, 1860, ALP.

36. Anonymous to Mary Todd Lincoln, Jan. 1, 1861; Anonymous, "One who desires your good," to AL, Jan. 1861; Sloane to AL, Dec. 5, 1860, ALP.

37. Giddings to AL, July 2, 1860; Holbrook to AL, July 11, 1861, ALP.

38. Manning to AL, Feb. 4, 1861, ALP; George H. Woodruff, *The History of Will County, Illinois* (Chicago, 1878).

39. King to AL, March 19, 1861, ALP; Charles King, "Rufus King: Soldier, Editor, and Statesman," *Wisconsin Magazine of History* 4, no. 4 (June 1921): 371–81.

40. Bergen to AL, March 30, 1861, ALP; Angle, *"Here I Have Lived,"* 28, 52, 197. He was the unidentified "old man Bergen" in James H. Matheny's interview with William H. Herndon in 1870. Wilson and Davis, *Herndon's Informants,* 577, 787.

41. Oliver B. Peirce to AL, March 31, 1861; Blanchard to AL, March 28, 1861; Hesser to AL, March 31, 1861, ALP.

42. Sessions to AL, April 16, 1861, ALP.

43. New York City Welsh Congregational Church to AL, April 16, 1861; Philadelphia Presbyterian Church to AL, April 16, 1861; J. B. Foote to AL, May 13, 1861; Brooklyn New York Baptist Church, May 29, 1861 (including a printed pamphlet, *The Baptists of the North on the State of the Country*), ALP.

44. James Prestley to AL, June 5, 1861 (General Assembly of the United Presbyterian Church of North America, Monmouth, Ill.); Association of Illinois Congregational Church to AL, Aug. 1, 1861; Illinois Conference of Methodist Episcopal Church to AL, Sept. 13, 1861; George M. Thompson to AL, Sept. 2, 1861 (Church of Christ, Stockton, Ill.), ALP.

45. Association of Illinois Congregational Church to AL, Aug. 1, 1861; New York City Welsh Congregational Church to AL, April 16, 1861, ALP.

46. Looker to Nicolay, May 9, 1861, ALP.

47. James Prestley to AL, June 5, 1861 (General Assembly of the United Presbyterian Church of North America, Monmouth, Ill.), ALP.

48. Harry S. Stout and Christopher Grasso, "Civil War, Religion, and Communications: The Case of Richmond," in Miller, Stout, and

452   *Notes for pages 120–126*

Wilson, *Religion and the American Civil War,* 323; Stout, *Upon the Altar of the Nation,* 48.

49. *Journal of the Senate,* July 31, 1861, 128. Educated at Indiana Asbury University, and married by the Methodist bishop Matthew Simpson, Harlan had been president of Iowa Wesleyan College for the two years before his election to the Senate in 1855.

50. *CW,* 4:482 (Proclamation of a National Fast Day, Aug. 12, 1861).

51. Parrillo, "Lincoln's Calvinist Transformation," 238–39. The sole certain exception to Lincoln's authorship of the proclamations was the recommendation of a national thanksgiving in November 1863, written by Seward.

52. Ibid., 239–40.

CHAPTER 5   LINCOLN'S FAST DAY AND
ANTISLAVERY NATIONALISM, 1861

1. *New York Times,* Sept. 26, 1861.

2. *CW,* 4:506 (AL to Frémont, Sept. 2, 1861). For this episode and Frémont's subsequent removal from command, see Burlingame, *Abraham Lincoln,* 2:200–211.

3. Speed to AL, Sept. 3, ALP; *CW,* 4:517–18 (AL to Frémont, Sept. 11, 1861).

4. Howard, *Religion and the Radical Republican Movement,* 224; James Allen to AL, Sept. 21, 1861, ALP.

5. Wright to AL, Sept. 20, 1861, ALP; Angle, *"Here I Have Lived,"* 27, 213.

6. J. G. Roberts to AL, Sept. 17, 1861, ALP.

7. John L. Scripps to AL, Sept. 23, 1861, ALP. Scott, *Visitation of God,* 39, documents the storm of criticism that Lincoln's decision provoked among northern abolitionist churchgoers.

8. The fast day clashed with Shemini Atzeret, a Jewish day of jubilation and feasting commanded by the Hebrew scriptures. New York synagogues denied intending any disrespect for Lincoln's proclamation. "Services at the Jewish Synagogues," *New York Herald,* Sept. 27, 1861. For brief discussions of the fast day, see Rable, *God's Almost Chosen Peoples,* 80–83; Stout, *Upon the Altar of the Nation,* 75–80; Guyatt, *Providence and the Invention of the United States,* 275–81; Scott, *Visitation from God,* 40–44.

9. *Illinois State Journal,* Sept. 26, 1861, quoting the *Philadelphia Inquirer; Ottawa Free Trader,* Sept. 21, 1861; *Chicago Tribune,* Sept. 26, 1861.

Notes for pages 127–129   453

10. See, for example, *National Republican* (Washington, D.C.), Sept. 26, 1861; *Illinois State Journal*, Sept. 26, 1861; "Naval," *Boston Daily Advertiser*, Sept. 25, 1861; "National Fast Day," *North American* (Philadelphia), Sept. 25, 1861; "The Observance of Fast Days," *Cleveland Daily Herald*, Sept. 27, 1861; *Daily Evening Bulletin* (San Francisco), Sept. 25, 1861.

11. *North American* (Philadelphia), Sept. 26, 27, 1861.

12. *Boston Daily Advertiser*, Sept. 28, 1861. See also, for example, *Pomeroy Weekly Telegraph* (Meigs County, Ohio), Sept. 27, 1861; *Bellows Falls (Vt.) Times*, Sept. 27, 1861; *Oxford Democrat* (Paris, Maine), Sept. 27, 1861; "Sacramento Correspondence," *Placer Herald* (Auburn, Calif.), Sept. 28, 1861.

13. *Macomb (Ill.) Journal*, Sept. 20, 1861; *Caledonian* (St. Johnsbury, Vt.), Sept. 27, 1861; *Chicago Tribune*, Sept. 27, 1861. Cf. *New York Times*, Sept. 27, 1861.

14. *Weekly Butte Record* (Oroville, Calif.), Sept. 28, 1861.

15. Thornbrough and Corpuz, *Diary of Calvin Fletcher*, 8:197–98; Scott, *Visitation from God*, 42.

16. *Cleveland Daily Herald*, Sept. 25, 1861; Boston *Pilot*, Oct. 12, 1861; *North American* (Philadelphia), Sept. 27, 1861; *Chicago Tribune*, Sept. 27, 1861.

17. *New York Times*, Sept. 22, 1861; "To the Clergy of Baltimore," Boston *Pilot*, Sept. 21, 1861.

18. See, for example, *North American*, Sept. 27, 1861; *Boston Daily Advertiser*, Sept. 28, 1861; "The National Fast," *New York Herald*, Sept. 28, 1861; *Chicago Tribune*, Sept. 28, 1861; *Cleveland Daily Herald*, Sept. 27, 1861; *Nevada Journal* (Nevada City, Calif.), Sept. 27, 1861.

19. "Exercises at Camp Mather," *Chicago Tribune*, Sept. 28, 1861. Cf. "Fast Day in the Camp of Gen. Banks, Darnestown," *National Intelligencer* (Washington, D.C.), Sept. 30, 1861; "Fast Day at the Barracks," *National Republican*, Sept. 28, 1861.

20. *National Republican*, Sept. 26, 1861; *Lincoln Log*, Sept. 26, 1861. "Ten or fifteen hours of McCoy upon the Constitution, taken on an empty stomach, ought to adequately mortify the flesh for us of Washington," mused the Washington *Evening Star*, Sept. 25, 1861.

21. Stanton, *Causes for National Humiliation*, 8–9; Hedge, *National Weakness*, 4, 6.

22. Davidson, *Nation's Discipline*, 20–21; *Chicago Tribune*, Sept. 27, 1861; Skinner, *Comfort in Tribulation*, 6.

23. Psalms 11:5. Quoted by Adams, *The Temple and the Throne*, 6.

454   *Notes for pages 129–131*

24. For a quintessential fast-day description of the American republic as the designated heir, under God's Providence, of the Old Testament "Jewish commonwealth," see Ford, *American Republicanism*, 5–13.

25. Palmer, *Crisis and Its Lessons*, 12; Doggett, *Sermon Preached on Fast Day*, 6.

26. Stanton, *Causes for National Humiliation*, 10–12; "The Eighteenth-Street M.E. Church," *New York Times*, Sept. 27, 1861; Wayland, *Appeal to the Disciples of Christ of Every Denomination*, 3.

27. Adams, *The Temple and the Throne*, 8–9.

28. "The National Fast Day," *New York Times*, Sept. 22, 1861.

29. *National Anti-slavery Standard* (New York), Aug. 17, 1861.

30. "Discourse by Rev. Dr. Cheever," *New York Times*, Sept. 27, 1861; "Voices of the Pulpit on Fast-Day," *National Anti-slavery Standard* (New York), Oct. 6, 1861; Ford, *American Republicanism*, 16–17, 19–20.

31. "The National Fast," *New York Herald*, Sept. 28, 1861. In other New York churches James R. W. Sloane wore as a badge of honor the charge that he made slavery "a hobby": like all Covenanters he demanded the nation repent the sin of oppression. "The Third Reformed Presbyterian Church," *New York Times*, Sept. 27, 1861. The Episcopalian Stephen H. Tyng castigated "the most tyrannous curse on earth." Tyng, *Record of the Life and Work of the Rev. Stephen Higginson Tyng*, 327–35; "Dr. Tyng's Church," *New York Herald*, Sept. 28, 1861.

32. Skinner, *Comfort in Tribulation*, 21; Simmons, *Our Duty in the Crisis*, 10–11, 32–33; Palmer, *Crisis and Its Lessons*, 7; Doggett, *Sermon Preached on Fast Day*, 14.

33. Wilson, *Curse of Meroz*, 12. A "monster, conceived in sin," the rebellion found a parallel "only where the arch fiend [Lucifer] seduced from their allegiance the angels of glory, of traitors animated by the spirit of Satanic ambition, which rather reign in hell than serve in heaven." Skinner, *Comfort in Tribulation*, 6; Davidson, *Nation's Discipline*, 4–5; Simmons, *Our Duty in the Crisis*, 5.

34. Stanton, *Causes for National Humiliation*, 25.

35. Skinner, *Comfort in Tribulation*, 21–22; Stanton, *Causes for National Humiliation*, 18.

36. "Speech Delivered on the 21st March 1861, in Savannah, Known as 'The Corner Stone Speech,' Reported in the Savannah Republican," in Cleveland, *Alexander H. Stephens in Public and Private*, 721–23.

37. Hawes, *North and South*, 17–18, 30.

38. Skinner, *Comfort in Tribulation*, 19, 23. Cf. Stanton, *Causes for National Humiliation*, 19, 22; Davidson, *Nation's Discipline*, 8–10; "The Tract Societies and the National Fast," *Vermont Chronicle* (Bellows Falls,

Notes for pages 132–133   455

Vt.), Sept. 17, 1861 (Francis Wayland); Bailey, *Moral Significance of War,* 14, 16–17.

39. Stanton, *Causes for National Humiliation,* 13, 18; Palmer, *Crisis and Its Lessons,* 16–17; Skinner, *Comfort in Tribulation,* 12–13; "Fast Day Sermons" (Dr. S. W. Adams, First Baptist), *Cleveland Morning Leader,* Sept. 28, 1861; Bittinger, *Sermon on the National Fast Day,* 13–20. See also Jenkins, *"Show My People Their Transgression,"* 31.

40. *New York Times,* Sept. 27, 1861, reporting the services at the city's Eighteenth Street Methodist Episcopal Church.

41. Doggett, *Sermon Preached on Fast Day,* 7–8; Skinner, *Comfort in Tribulation,* 12–16; Bittinger, *Sermon on the National Fast Day,* 15, 17–18; Furness, *Discourse,* 17.

42. Jenkins, *"Show My People Their Transgression,"* 24–26. "If, as our President says in his Proclamation, the fear of the Lord is the *beginning* of wisdom," one minister reflected, "most of our representatives have been far from *beginning to be wise.*" Doggett, *Sermon Preached on Fast Day,* 13.

43. Hedge, *National Weakness,* 12; "The Brooklyn Tabernacle" (Rev. William A. Bartlett), *New York Times,* Sept. 27, 1861; Palmer, *Crisis and Its Lessons,* 13; Stanton, *Causes for National Humiliation,* 15–16. Cf. Wayland, *Appeal to the Disciples of Christ of Every Denomination,* 5.

44. Doggett, *Sermon Preached on Fast Day,* 14; Stanton, *Causes for National Humiliation,* 15–16.

45. "The true Union men of the Country are becoming tired of '*timid measures*' with the rebels," an Ohio loyalist told the president. "We want '*decisive measures,*' . . . carried out '*promptly*' and '*effectively*' under . . . '*Martial law*' . . . [by] a 'Jackson' of a man." A. Harris to AL, Sept. 17, 1861, ALP.

46. S. Hine to AL, Sept. 20, 1861; O. B. Clark and John Root, Resolutions, Sept. 17, 1861, ALP.

47. Scripps to AL, Sept. 23, 1861; Williams to AL, Sept. 19, 1861; H. C. Garst to AL, Sept. 18, 1861, ALP. "I have believed from the first that, in the great plan of Providence, this war was . . . for the overthrow of Slavery; and I do not think that the efforts of the north will prove successful until they shall be in harmony with the great plan." Warren Laplin to Francis D. Hemenway, Aug. 26, 1861, Hemenway Papers, GETS. See also D. D. Love to D. P. Kidder, Aug. 8, 1861, Kidder Papers, GETS.

48. H. Montague to AL, Sept. 17, 1861; Erastus Wright to AL, Sept. 20, 1861; E. G. Cook to AL, Sept. 21, 1861, ALP.

49. H. Montague to AL, Sept. 17, 1861; Wright to AL, Sept. 20, 1861,

456 *Notes for pages 133–136*

ALP; Howard, *Religion and the Radical Republican Movement*, 14; Nevins, *War for the Union*, 1:340.

50. H. C. Garst to AL, Sept. 18, 1861, ALP. "Heaven give you & your Advisors the Wisdom for Our emergency, is the daily prayer of Millions," wrote another, from Fredonia, N.Y. E. G. Cook to AL, Sept. 21, 1861, ALP.

51. Chafee to AL, Sept. 20, 1861; Scripps to AL, Sept. 23, 1861, ALP.

52. *CW*, 4:532 (AL to O. H. Browning, Sept. 22, 1861).

53. "The Third Reformed Presbyterian Church. How to Crush Out the Rebellion," *New York Times*, Sept. 27, 1861; "The National Fast Day. First Congregational Church," *Chicago Tribune*, Sept. 27, 1861; Simmons, *Our Duty in the Crisis*, 20–22.

54. "The President's Fast," *Liberator*, Sept. 27, 1861.

55. "The fast is not a repentance of the National Sin but only the consequence of that sin." *Douglass's Monthly*, Oct. 1861, 531, quoted in Guyatt, *Providence and the Invention of the United States*, 278.

56. "Story of a Fugitive Slave," *New York Times*, Sept. 27, 1861.

57. Jocelyn to AL, Sept. 26, 1861, ALP.

58. Hamilton Illinois Ministers to AL, Oct. 1, 1861; George M. Thompson to AL, Sept. 1861, ALP. Both communications cited a favorite antislavery text, Isaiah 58:5–6. Thompson's letter is erroneously dated—in another hand—"Sept. 2, 1861." Lincoln had not by then modified the decree. The resolutions were passed on the fast day. See also Branch County Michigan Baptists to AL, Sept. 28, 1861; Central New Jersey Baptist Association (Resolutions), Oct. 16, 1861, ALP.

59. Patton to AL, Oct. 12, 1861, ALP. The Illinois Conference of the MEC, meeting at Carlinville two weeks before the fast day, had already pledged its loyal support to the government and "cordially" approved Frémont's proclamation. Illinois Conference of Methodist Episcopal Church to AL, Sept. 13, 1861, ALP.

60. "The Third Reformed Presbyterian Church," *New York Times*, Sept. 27, 1861; Wilson, *Curse of Meroz*, 40; Furness, *Discourse*, 12, 19–20; Ford, *American Republicanism*, 22–24 (app.); Bittinger, *Sermon on the National Fast Day*, 20–22.

61. Little to AL, Sept. 17, 1861, ALP. An Ohio Presbyterian minister could not deny "there is a growing consciousness against the monster evil of slavery, and we for years have been patching up a hollow truce against it." "Fast Day Sermons," *Cleveland Morning Leader*, Sept. 28, 1861.

62. "Dr. Bellows and Dr. Osgood at All Souls' Church," *New York Times*, Sept. 27, 1861.

Notes for pages 137–144 457

63. Hawes, *North and South;* "The National Fast," *Daily Evening Bulletin* (San Francisco), Sept. 26, 1861; Lawrence, *Life of Rev. Joel Hawes,* 342–47. See also Bailey, *Moral Significance of War,* 19.

64. Furness, *Discourse,* 20.

65. "New Jersey Baptist Association," *West-Jersey Pioneer* (Bridgeton, N.J.), Sept. 28, 1861; "The Eighteenth-Street M.E. Church," *New York Times,* Sept. 27, 1861. William Wilson advocated colonization: "The colored population ought to be by themselves. Their own interests demand it. They will never prosper nor be happy, in close proximity to, nor intermingled with, the white population." *Curse of Meroz,* 40.

66. Palmer, *Crisis and Its Lessons,* 17.

67. Williams to AL, Sept. 19, 1861, ALP.

68. "The Recent National Fast Day—Treason and Mutiny in the Pulpit," *New York Herald,* Sept. 28, 1861.

69. Hutchinson, *Cyrus Hall McCormick,* 2:23–34; Wallace, "'The Bond of Union': The Old School Presbyterian Church and the American Nation, 1837–1861," vol. 3.

70. Vander Velde, *Presbyterian Churches and the Federal Union,* 48–75.

71. Ibid., 61.

72. Resolutions of the Presbytery of Buffalo City, quoted in ibid., 90–91.

73. Stearns, *Sword of the Lord,* 40; Fugitt, *Plea for Peace,* 5–6, 9–10; "Absalom. A Sermon Preached on the National Fast Day, September 26, A.D. 1861, in Trinity Church, Moorestown, N.J., by Rev. H. Hastings Weld," *North American* (Philadelphia), Sept. 28, 1861.

74. Astles, "Rev. Dr. W. A. Scott, a Southern Sympathizer," 149–56; "The National Fast," *Daily Evening Bulletin* (San Francisco), Sept. 26, 1861.

75. "Notes from the Capital," *Independent,* Oct. 3, 1861.

76. *New York Times,* Oct. 3, 1861.

77. *Memphis Daily Avalanche,* May 8, 1861, transcribed: civilwarbaptists.com/thisdayinhistory/1861-april-23/.

78. "The National Fast," *National Intelligencer* (Washington, D.C.), Sept. 26, 1861.

79. "The National Fast Day," *Boston Daily Advertiser,* Sept. 28, 1861; Stearns, *Sword of the Lord,* 6–8, 11–12.

80. Reprinted in *Farmers Cabinet* (Amherst, N.H.), Sept. 20, 1861.

81. For example, Hitchcock, *Our National Sin,* 12–24; "The National Fast" (David B. Cheney, First Baptist Church, San Francisco), *Daily Evening Bulletin* (San Francisco), Sept. 26, 1861.

458   *Notes for pages 144–150*

82. "Notes from the Capital," *Independent*, Oct. 3, 1861; Davidson, *Nation's Discipline*, 5–8.

83. Ford, *American Republicanism*, 16, 20.

84. *Chicago Tribune*, Sept. 27, 1861 (Wabash Avenue M.E. Church); Simmons, *Our Duty in the Crisis*, 7–8. Cf. *Chicago Tribune*, Sept. 27, 1861 (sermons of Zephaniah M. Humphrey, First Presbyterian Church, Chicago; James Pratt, Trinity Church, Chicago; Thomas M. Eddy, Camp Mather); *New York Herald*, Sept. 27, 1861 (Joseph Thompson, Broadway Tabernacle, New York City).

85. Simmons, *Our Duty in the Crisis*, 8; Skinner, *Comfort in Tribulation*, 6; Hawes, *North and South*, 21.

86. Wayland, *Appeal to the Disciples of Christ of Every Denomination*, 2.

87. Skinner, *Comfort in Tribulation*, 16–17; Stanton, *Causes for National Humiliation*, 17. Cf. Wayland, *Appeal to the Disciples of Christ of Every Denomination*, 1.

88. Gordon, *Reliance on God*, 9–27; Davidson, *Nation's Discipline*, 8, 13–14. See also Hawes, *North and South*, 12–13, 21–22.

89. "Exercises at Camp Mather," *Chicago Tribune*, Sept. 27, 1861.

90. For an extended discussion of how in a righteous cause lovers of peace could ethically and aggressively take up arms, see Dewey, *Sermon, Preached on the National Fast Day*, 5–22.

91. Hedge, *National Weakness*, 16–17; Wilson, *Curse of Meroz*, 29; "Laight-Street Baptist Church," *New York Times*, Sept. 27, 1861.

92. "Fast Day Sermons," *Cleveland Morning Leader*, Sept. 28, 1861; Simmons, *Our Duty in the Crisis*, 15; "Exercises at Camp Mather," *Chicago Tribune*, Sept. 27, 1861; Wilson, *Curse of Meroz*, 6–7; Stanton, *Causes for National Humiliation*, 10.

93. Furness, *Discourse*, 18–19; Stanton, *Causes for National Humiliation*, 36; "Church of the Redeemer," *Chicago Tribune*, Sept. 27, 1861; Skinner, *Comfort in Tribulation*, 27; Hawes, *North and South*, 24; Simmons, *Our Duty in the Crisis*, 23–24; Wilson, *Curse of Meroz*, 9.

94. Bailey, *Moral Significance of War*, 13–15; Simmons, *Our Duty in the Crisis*, 8; Doggett, *Sermon Preached on Fast Day*, 4–5; Palmer, *Crisis and Its Lessons*, 16.

95. Bates, *Lincoln in the Telegraph Office*, 198–99.

96. Palmer, *Crisis and Its Lessons*, 17; Stanton, *Causes for National Humiliation*, 7; Skinner, *Comfort in Tribulation*, 5; Ford, *American Republicanism*, 5.

97. Davis, "Meeting Abraham Lincoln," 162.

98. Browning to AL, Sept. 17, 1861, ALP.

Notes for pages 151–155

99. *CW*, 4:532 (AL to Browning, Sept. 22, 1861); Browning to AL, Sept. 30, 1861, ALP.

100. Pease and Randall, *Diary of Orville Hickman Browning*, 52, 89, 123, 166, 220, 311, 346, 389, 447.

101. Cong. Globe, Senate, 37th Cong., 1st Sess., 187–89.

102. Pease and Randall, *Diary of Orville Hickman Browning*, 483.

103. Ibid., 123–25, 167–70, 200, 273–75, 313–15, 350–53, 393, 416, 453. Browning split his time between Sabbath services at First and Third Presbyterian Churches, commonly attending both on the same day.

104. Burlingame, *Oral History of Abraham Lincoln*, 5. Browning placed this conversation, recalled fourteen years later, during the summer or fall of 1861; his diary indicates only two possibilities, July 28 or December 1, but it does not mention the exchange. Pease and Randall, *Diary of Orville Hickman Browning*, 488–89, 512. John O'Brien notes that Browning until New Year's Eve 1862 urged Lincoln not to sign the Emancipation Proclamation and hazards that through his later interview with Nicolay he was putting himself on the right side of history. But Browning's recollection of his conversation with Lincoln is consistent with his endorsement of Frémont, which so shocked the president.

105. *CW*, 4:439 (Message to Congress in Special Session, July 4, 1861). My emphasis.

CHAPTER 6   LINCOLN, RELIGIOUS NATIONALISTS, AND EMANCIPATION, 1862

1. United Presbyterian Synod to AL [with endorsement by Lincoln], Oct. 28, 1861, ALP. The United Presbyterian Church had been formed in 1858 through a union of the Associate Reformed Presbyterian Church and the Associate Presbyterian Church.

2. Basler's edition of Lincoln's works confuses the United Presbyterians' resolutions with a submission from the Presbyterian Synod of New York and New Jersey, to which Secretary of State Seward replied on November 27, 1861. The ministers did not press the administration for a policy of emancipation. They simply acknowledged that slavery "lies at the foundation of all our present national troubles" and recommended "to all our people to pray more earnestly than ever for its removal, and that the time may speedily come when God, by his providence, shall . . . bring it to an end." In reply, Seward stressed Lincoln's faith in the favor of God and his "great satisfaction" with

460 *Notes for pages 156–159*

the synod's patriotism; tellingly, he ignored the matter of slavery. *CW,* 5:7 (Memorandum: Resolutions of United Presbyterian Synod, Oct. 28, 1861); "The Presbyterians and the War," *New York Herald,* Nov. 30, 1861.

3. The synod had not been entirely of one mind. The Reverend J. T. McClure of Wheeling, a self-consciously lone voice of opposition, feared the emancipationist resolution would alienate Missouri, Kentucky, and western Virginia: he hoped the committee would receive a reply from the president "amounting in substance to an invitation to mind their own business." *Wheeling Press,* quoted in "Sensible and Timely," *Newark (Ohio) Advocate,* Nov. 1, 1861.

4. MEC Annual Conference records show that by no means all of the Methodist resolutions and memorials sent to the president are captured in the Lincoln Papers. That probably holds for other denominations, too. *Minutes of the . . . Providence Annual Conference of the Methodist Episcopal Church . . . April 2–7, 1862,* 22; *Minutes of the Fifteenth Session of the New York East Annual Conference of the Methodist Episcopal Church . . . April 1863* (New York, 1863), 33; *Minutes of the . . . New-York Conference of the Methodist Episcopal Church . . . April 15, 1863,* 32.

5. Carpenter, *Six Months at the White House,* 77.

6. *Lincoln Log.* See entries for June 11, Oct. 29, Nov. 26, 27, Dec. 11, 1861; Jan. 10, 12, March 17, April 8, May 13, June 20, July 17, Aug. 22, 1862.

7. Editorial, *New-York Observer,* Oct. 4, 1861.

8. Editorial, Boston *Pilot,* Jan. 25, 1862, 4.

9. *CW,* 5:185–86 (Proclamation of Thanksgiving for Victories, April 10, 1862).

10. The East Baltimore Conference numbered more than two hundred itinerant ministers and thirty-seven thousand communicants. Its three representatives—A. Gere, A. A. Reese, Geo. D. Chenowith— met Lincoln on March 17, 1862, accompanied by the Methodist Joseph A. Wright, U.S. senator from Indiana; Waitman T. Willey, U.S. senator and Unionist slaveholder from embryonic West Virginia; and the Unionist Cornelius Leary, U.S. representative for Maryland's Third District. They delivered the conservative but loyal resolutions of a body whose work embraced much of the western shore of Maryland and central Pennsylvania. Lincoln's reply of March 18 is misdated in Basler: *CW,* 5:215–16 (to I. A. Gere [*sic*], A. A. Reese, and George D. Chenoweth [*sic*]," [May 15?] 1862).

Notes for pages 160–163   461

11. "A Model Ruler," *Independent*, Oct. 10, 1861; "The President's Message," *Independent*, Dec. 5, 1861; *Christian Times* (Chicago; Baptist), Jan. 29, 1862, 2.

12. "Prayer for the President," *Independent*, Nov. 14, 1861.

13. "The Logic of Events," *Christian Times* (Chicago), Oct. 9, 1861; "Emancipation," *Christian Times* (Chicago), Dec. 11, 1861.

14. "Prayer for the President," *Independent*, Nov. 14, 1861; "The Government Policy," *Independent*, Jan. 2, 1861.

15. *New-York Tribune*, March 8, 1862, 5; "An Editor in the Pulpit," *Vermont Phœnix* (Brattleboro), May 22, 1862.

16. "The President's Message" and "The President's Emancipation Message. By Horace Greeley," *Independent*, March 13, 1862. The newspaper boasted a circulation three times as large as any other weekly religious title in the world, with subscribers in New England, New York and the middle states, and the upper Midwest. *Independent*, May 1, 15, 1862. Cf. "Lincoln's Special Message," *Christian Times*, March 19, 1862.

17. "An Eloquent Sermon on the War," *Chicago Tribune*, May 9, 1862; Holmes, *Life and Letters of Robert Collyer*, 140–86.

18. "Sermon," *Christian Times*, April 23, 1862.

19. The Reverend Levi Sternberg, a Republican sympathizer and professor of theology at Hartwick Lutheran Seminary, headed the delegation. "The Lutheran Synod on the War," *National Intelligencer* (Washington, D.C.), May 14, 1862; *CW*, 5:212–13 (Response to Evangelical Lutherans, May 13, 1862). Lincoln's reply (that "this Government . . . placed its whole dependence upon the favor of God") was widely reprinted. See, for example, *New Hampshire Statesman* (Concord), May 24, 1862; *Daily Nashville Union*, May 23, 1862; *Delaware State Journal and Statesman* (Wilmington), May 20, 1862; *Hillsdale (Mich.) Standard*, May 27, 1862; *National Republican* (Washington, D.C.), May 16, 1862; *Delaware (Ohio) Gazette*, May 23, 1862.

20. Foner, *Fiery Trial*, 198–202; Guelzo, *Lincoln's Emancipation Proclamation*, 81–89.

21. "A Sermon. Preached in Christ Church, Dover, Del., April 13, 1862," *Delaware State Journal and Statesman* (Wilmington), April 22, 1862.

22. *Christian Times*, April 23, 1862, 3.

23. "An Eloquent Sermon on the War," *Chicago Tribune*, May 9, 1862.

24. "Abolishing Slavery in the District," *Western Reserve Chronicle* (Warren, Ohio), May 21, 1862.

25. *St. Cloud (Minn.) Democrat*, May 8, 1862.

26. Stoddard, *Dispatches from Lincoln's White House*, xix, 78.

27. *CW*, 5:222–24 (Proclamation Revoking General Hunter's Order of Military Emancipation of May 9, 1862).

28. "Emancipation Sure," *Chicago Tribune*, May 24, 1862.

29. "Interview with the President on Emancipation," *Liberator*, June 27, 1862.

30. John R. McKivigan, "Johnson, Oliver," in *American National Biography Online* (Oxford University Press, 2000), www.anb.org.

31. Kashatus, *Abraham Lincoln, the Quakers, and the Civil War*, 47–54. See also Kennett Underground Railroad Center: www.kennettunder groundrr.org; Longwood Progressive Friends Meetinghouse and Cemetery, ca. 1855: pocketsights.com.

32. "Tenth Yearly Meeting of Progressive Friends at Longwood, Pa.," *Liberator*, June 20, 1862.

33. "The President Memorialized," *Alleghanian* (Ebensburg, Pa.), July 3, 1862.

34. *CW*, 5:278–79 (Remarks to a Delegation of Progressive Friends, June 20, 1862; source *New-York Tribune*, June 21, 1862). This account, with variations or summarized, was widely reported. See, for example, *Boston Daily Advertiser*, June 23, 1862; *Lowell Daily Citizen*, June 23, 1862; *Chicago Tribune*, June 21, 25, 1862; *Fremont Journal* (Sandusky County, Ohio), July 4, 1862; *Weekly Pioneer and Democrat* (St. Paul), July 4, 1862.

35. "Tenth Yearly Meeting of Progressive Friends at Longwood, Pa.," *Liberator*, June 20, 1862.

36. The *Metropolitan Record*, Jan. 11, 1862, estimated that one in seven Catholic families patronized church journals, in a church population of between three and four million.

37. Boston *Pilot*, May 17, 1862, 4.

38. "Editorial," Boston *Pilot*, Dec. 7, 1861; "Prospectus for 1862," Boston *Pilot*, Dec. 14, 1861.

39. *New-York Observer*, Feb. 27, 1862, 2; *Metropolitan Record*, Feb. 22, 1862, 8.

40. Editorial, Boston *Pilot*, March 1, 1862, 4.

41. *New-York Observer*, April 24, 1862, 2.

42. *Metropolitan Record*, March 29, 1862, 8.

43. *Metropolitan Record*, June 14, 1862, 8.

44. "Brownson's Review," *Metropolitan Record*, Oct. 12, 1861; Hughes to William H. Seward, Oct. 10, 1861, William Henry Seward Papers, University of Rochester Library (microform ed.).

45. Boston *Pilot*, June 14, 1862, 4.

Notes for pages 169–174 463

46. *Metropolitan Record*, June 14, 1862, 8.

47. "Three Theories of Slavery," *New-York Observer*, March 13, 1862.

48. Boston *Pilot*, May 3, 1862, 4.

49. Editorial, *Metropolitan Record*, April 26, 1862, 8; *Metropolitan Record*, Jan. 18, 1862, 8; Boston *Pilot*, May 3, 1862, 4.

50. Boston *Pilot*, Dec. 14, 1861, 4.

51. *Metropolitan Record*, Oct. 19, 1861, 8; Dec. 14, 1861 ("An Abolition Wing for Our Army"); April 19, 1862, 9.

52. "From Washington—a Revelation of the Plans of the Abolitionists," *Indiana State Sentinel* (Indianapolis), April 28, 1862; "Small Politicians," *Star of the North* (Bloomsburg, Pa.), April 16, 1862.

53. *New-York Observer*, Dec. 26, 1861, 2.

54. "Gov. Stanley [*sic*] in North Carolina—the Administration," Boston *Pilot*, June 28, 1862.

55. *New-York Observer*, Nov. 8, 1861, 2; *New-York Observer*, Jan. 16, 1862, 2; Boston *Pilot*, Jan. 25, 1862, 4; *Metropolitan Record*, March 8, 1862, 8.

56. *New-York Observer*, March 13, 1862, 2 (President's Special Message).

57. "The President's Message," Boston *Pilot*, March 22, 1862; "The President on the Subject of Emancipation," *Metropolitan Record*, March 15, 1862.

58. "A New Recruiting General for the South," *Metropolitan Record*, May 24, 1862; *New-York Observer*, May 22, 1862; Boston *Pilot*, May 31, 1862, 4; "Gov. Stanley [*sic*] in North Carolina—the Administration," Boston *Pilot*, June 28, 1862.

59. "Delegation of Friends Visit the President," *Weekly Pioneer and Democrat* (St. Paul), June 27, 1862.

60. "President Lincoln Quietly Disposing of the Abolition Radicals," *New York Herald*, June 27, 1862.

61. Boston *Pilot*, May 31, 1862, 4.

62. "A New Recruiting General for the South," *Metropolitan Record*, May 24, 1862; editorial, *Metropolitan Record*, June 28, 1862.

63. Fourth of July editorial, *Metropolitan Record*, July 5, 1862.

64. "The Country's Need," *Independent*, July 10, 1862.

65. *CW*, 5:317–19 (Appeal to Border State Representatives to Favor Compensated Emancipation, July 12, 1862); 5:336–37 (Emancipation Proclamation—First Draft, July 22, 1862).

66. Nicolay and Hay, *Abraham Lincoln*, 6:147–58. For an early statement of this narrative, see Holland, *Life of Abraham Lincoln*, 391–95.

67. Lord Charnwood, *Abraham Lincoln*, 321–22; Randall, *Lincoln the President*, 2:156–57; Thomas, *Abraham Lincoln*, 342; Neely, *Last Best Hope of Earth*, 109–12; Guelzo, *Abraham Lincoln*, 338–42; Guelzo,

464 *Notes for pages 174–180*

Lincoln's Emancipation Proclamation, 160–61 (for Lincoln's irreversibility); Foner, *Fiery Trial,* 226. See also Paludan, *Presidency of Abraham Lincoln,* 149–52.

68. "The Prayer of Twenty Millions," *New-York Tribune,* Aug. 20, 1862; Nicolay and Hay, *Abraham Lincoln,* 6:154.

69. Tarbell, *Life of Abraham Lincoln,* 3:118–19.

70. Donald, *Lincoln,* 74.

71. Bennett, *Forced into Glory,* 468–508. The argument that Lincoln issued the proclamation for essentially political reasons, to wrong-foot Republican radicals and to delay emancipation, is set out (though not endorsed) in Current, *Lincoln Nobody Knows,* 226–28.

72. Carpenter, *Six Months in the White House,* 20–23.

73. Buckingham, *Life of William A. Buckingham,* 261–62; Pryor, *Six Encounters with Lincoln,* 142–45.

74. Pryor, *Six Encounters with Lincoln,* 119–50.

75. Foner, *Fiery Trial,* 221–26; Guelzo, *Lincoln's Emancipation Proclamation,* 141–44; Page, *Black Resettlement and the American Civil War,* 120–35.

76. Masur, "The African American Delegation to Abraham Lincoln," 130–31.

77. *CW,* 5:370–75 (Address on Colonization to a Deputation of Negroes, Aug. 14, 1862).

78. Niven, *Salmon P. Chase Papers,* 1:362.

79. Foner, *Fiery Trial,* 225.

80. "Mrs. Francis E. Watkins Harper on the War and the President's Colonization Scheme," *Christian Recorder,* Sept. 27, 1862.

81. Ibid.; T. Strother, "For the Christian Recorder," *Christian Recorder,* Sept. 27, 1862.

82. H. M. Turner, "For the Christian Recorder," *Christian Recorder,* Dec. 14, 1861; T. Strother, "For the Christian Recorder," *Christian Recorder,* Sept. 27, 1862; "Washington Correspondence," *Christian Recorder,* Aug. 30, 1862.

83. "For the Christian Recorder," *Christian Recorder,* Sept. 20, 1862; T. Strother, "For the Christian Recorder," *Christian Recorder,* Oct. 4, 1862.

84. "The Plagues of This Country," *Christian Recorder,* July 12, 1862; "The Law of Agitation. By George T. Watkins," *Christian Recorder,* Jan. 10, 1863.

85. Masur, "African American Delegation to Abraham Lincoln," 117–44.

86. "The President Insults the People," *Liberator,* July 25, 1862.

Notes for pages 180–184 465

87. "President Lincoln and the Cameronians," *National Anti-slavery Standard* (New York), Aug. 9, 1862.

88. "A Leader for the People," *Independent*, Aug. 7, 14, 1862.

89. "President Lincoln and the Cameronians," *National Anti-slavery Standard* (New York), Aug. 9, 1862; *CW*, 5:327 (Remarks to Committee of Reformed Presbyterian Synod, July 17, 1862).

90. Clarion Association of Baptist Churches to A. G. Curtin, Aug. 23; Benjamin H. West to AL, Aug. 27 (Boston Park Street Church); New Hampshire Association of Presbyterian and Congregational Ministers, Aug. 28; William A. Stearns to AL, Sept. 3; Milwaukee Wisconsin Congregational Church Resolutions, Sept. 5; J. W. Chaffin and William Froth to AL, Sept. 6 (Miami Conference of Wesleyan Methodist Connection); Cincinnati Ohio Methodist Church Conference to AL, Sept. 8; Indiana Methodist Convention to AL, Sept. 12; J. W. Wellman to AL, Sept. 12 (Massachusetts Congregational Churches); Millburn Illinois Congregation to AL, Sept. 14; North Illinois Conference of the Methodist Church to AL, Sept. 14; J. Durbin to AL, Sept. 15 (North Ohio Annual Methodist Conference); W. C. McCarthy and Thomas Pert to AL, Sept. 16 (churches of Waverley, N.Y.); J. Lester Williams et al. to AL, Sept. 18 (West Wisconsin Methodist Episcopal Church Annual Conference); Timothy Stillman to AL, Sept. 18 (Genesee, N.Y., Presbyterian Synod), ALP (all 1862).

91. J. W. Chaffin and William Froth to AL, Sept. 6, 1862.

92. J. Lester Williams to AL, Sept. 18, 1862 (*West Wisconsin MEC Annual Conference Report on the State of the Country*).

93. McPherson, *Battle Cry of Freedom*, 536.

94. Thomas Eddy, "Righteous Men and the War," *NWCA*, Sept. 10, 1862, 292.

95. "Appeal to the President by the Christian Community of Chicago," Joseph E. Roy Papers, Chicago Historical Society. See also *Chicago Tribune*, Sept. 4, 1862.

96. Patton, *President Lincoln and the Chicago Memorial of Emancipation*, 9–10.

97. Patton, *Honour Thy Father*, 14–23, 42–43.

98. Ibid., 23–25; Stauffer and Soskis, *Battle Hymn of the Republic*, 73–74.

99. Patton, *President Lincoln and the Chicago Memorial*, 9; "The Christian War Meeting," *Chicago Tribune*, Sept. 5, 1862. Almost a year earlier Patton had prompted his First Congregational Church to direct a series of antislavery resolutions to the president. Patton to AL, Oct. 12, 1861, ALP. The concept of a combined political initiative by

466 *Notes for pages 184–186*

churches in Chicago and the Northwest was by no means new. For the protest against Stephen A. Douglas's Nebraska Bill in 1854, see Carwardine, *Evangelicals and Politics in Antebellum America*, 236.

100. *Chicago Tribune*, July 7, 21, 28, Aug. 7, 1862.

101. "Religious War Meeting at Bryan Hall," *Chicago Tribune*, Sept. 8, 1862; "The Christian War Meeting," *Chicago Tribune*, Sept. 9, 1862; *NWCA*, Sept. 10, 1862. In a letter to Charles Francis Adams, Lincoln called Sturtevant "one of my most highly valued personal friends." We need not doubt that they were reasonably close, even though Lincoln referred to him as "John." AL to Adams, April 3, 1863, ALP. Cf. Sturtevant to AL, Dec. 2, 1860, ALP.

102. Two of Chicago's leading citizens had been chosen to accompany the ministerial pair. Judge Mark Skinner, a Presbyterian and leading Republican, and the first chairman of the U.S. Sanitary Commission in the Northwest, had built his civic reputation through the law and real estate. Charles H. Walker, grain merchant, railroad developer, and sometime president of the Chicago Board of Trade, enjoyed a similar reputation for energetic philanthropy and business enterprise. As a Democrat and leading Baptist, he extended the denominational reach of the four-man deputation and gave it a cross-party mien. *Chicago Tribune*, June 30, July 1, 1868; Dec. 14, 1887.

103. Dempster, *Lectures and Addresses*, 11–20, 63–70 (Otis H. Tiffany, "Dr. Dempster as a Man of Progress").

104. John Dempster to Lydia Dempster, Sept. 10, 1862, John Dempster Papers, GETS. Dempster's unorthodox spelling was the mark of an autodidact, an educationalist who—in Otis Tiffany's words—was "unblessed with early culture." Dempster, *Lectures and Addresses*, 66.

105. Miers, ed., *Lincoln Day by Day: A Chronology*, 138–39; Patton, *President Lincoln and the Chicago Memorial*, 11; Gienapp and Gienapp, *Civil War Diary of Gideon Welles*, 44; Patton, *Honour Thy Father*, 25.

106. Although there was no roll call of those who thronged Bryan Hall when the memorial was adopted, most were mainstream evangelical Protestant churchgoers: Baptists, Congregationalists, Methodists, and Presbyterians.

107. For the full text of the memorial, see "The Christian War Meeting," *Chicago Tribune*, Sept. 9, 1862, reprinted in Patton, *President Lincoln and the Chicago Memorial*, 11–16.

108. "It may do no harm to say that 'Abraham' and 'Mordecai' are common names in our family." *CW*, 1:456, 459–60 (to Solomon Lincoln, March 6, March 24, 1848). Lincoln's uncle Mordecai was the eldest of three brothers, his father, Thomas, being the youngest. As a boy of

Notes for pages 187–191 467

fourteen, Mordecai killed one of the Indians at whose hand Lincoln's grandfather Abraham died. Ibid., 2:217 (AL to Jesse Lincoln, April 1, 1854). Referring to the Democratic administration of President James K. Polk and the conflict with Mexico, Lincoln told William H. Herndon, "The war is now to them, the gallows of Haman, which they built for us, and on which they are doomed to be hanged themselves." Ibid., 1:477. Cf. ibid., 2:321 (AL to Joshua Speed, Aug. 24, 1855).

109. Patton, *President Lincoln and the Chicago Memorial*, 17.

110. After the meeting Patton and Dempster promptly recorded their account. *CW*, 5:421–25 (Reply to Emancipation Memorial Presented by Chicago Christians of All Denominations, Sept. 13, 1862). This purports both to quote Lincoln verbatim and to summarize their discussion. Patton's later account, as delivered to the Maryland Historical Society in 1887, better captures the give-and-take of the occasion, while mostly retaining the phraseology of the earlier version. Patton, *President Lincoln and the Chicago Memorial*, 17–33. The next four paragraphs draw on both accounts.

111. This elegant formulation is more drily humorous than the vulgarized version reported by Schuyler Colfax: "If it [the call for emancipation] is, as you say, a message from your Divine Master, is it not odd that the only channel he could send it by was that roundabout route by that awfully wicked city of Chicago?" Rice, *Reminiscences of Abraham Lincoln*, 335.

112. Patton, *President Lincoln and the Chicago Memorial*, 32. This particular passage is not in the contemporary newspaper report. It appears only in Patton's account of 1887, which raises a question of authenticity.

113. Ibid., 32–33.

114. *Chicago Tribune*, Sept. 23, 1862. The report appeared in the *National Intelligencer* on September 26, 1862.

115. Dempster, *Lectures and Addresses*, 68.

116. Randall, *Lincoln the President*, 2:157n.

117. Rice, *Reminiscences of Abraham Lincoln*, 125.

118. Guelzo, *Abraham Lincoln*, 325–29; Carwardine, *Lincoln*, 221–28.

119. N. W. Miner, "Personal Reminiscences of Abraham Lincoln" (1882), 47–48, ALPL. At other times during this year Lincoln spoke of his "firm reliance upon the 'Divine arm,'" of "seeking light from above," and of being "a humble instrument in the hands of our Heavenly Father." *CW*, 5:279 (Remarks to a Delegation of Progressive Friends, June 20, 1862), 5:478 (Reply to Eliza P. Gurney, Oct. 26, 1862, a document in an unidentified hand).

468   *Notes for pages 192–196*

120. McClure, *Abraham Lincoln and Men of War Times*, 90.
121. *CW*, 5:403–4 ("Meditation on the Divine Will"). Basler suggests September 2, 1862, as an approximate date. John O'Brien plausibly argues for composition sometime between July 19 and August 22. "On Lincoln's 'Instrumentality' to End Slavery: 'Meditation on the Divine Will' and the Emancipation Proclamation," 42–46.
122. Gienapp and Gienapp, *Civil War Diary of Gideon Welles*, 54; Niven, *Salmon P. Chase Papers*, 1:394; Wilson and Davis, *Herndon's Informants*, 167–68.
123. Rice, *Reminiscences of Abraham Lincoln*, 334–35.
124. W. B. Lowry, H. Catlin, and J. F. Downing to AL, Sept. 23, 1862, Pittsburgh [Reformed] Presbyterian Church to AL, Oct. 1, 1862, Robert Patterson to AL, Oct. 13, 1862 (Chicago Reformed Presbytery), Caleb Russell and Sallie A. Fenton to AL, Dec. 27, 1862 (Iowa Quakers), ALP; "A Proclamation by the President of the United States" and "The War," *Independent*, Sept. 25, 1862. Cf. Lynn, Massachusetts, Congregationalists to AL, 1862 (Sept.–Dec.); Marcellus Barman and E. W. Stevens to AL, Sept. 25, 1862 (Wisconsin Conference of Wesleyan Methodist Connection), ALP.
125. New York Association of Congregational Churches to AL, Sept. 25, 1862; J. K. W. Levane and A. M. Milligan to AL, [Sept.–Dec.] 1862 (Reformed Presbyterians); A. C. Hand and W. W. Satterlee to AL, Oct. 11, 1862 (West Wisconsin Annual Conference of the Wesleyan Methodist Connection); Robert Patterson to AL, Oct. 13, 1862 (Chicago Reformed Presbytery).
126. New York Association of Congregational Churches to AL, Sept. 25, 1862; Samuel Hersey, E. G. Brooks, and Abel C. Thomas to AL, Nov. 3, 1862 (General Convention of the Universalist Church).
127. Pittsburgh Presbyterian Church to AL, Oct. 1, 1862, ALP.
128. "A Proclamation by the President of the United States," *Independent*, Sept. 25, 1862.
129. Cheever to AL, Nov. 22, 1862, ALP. Cf. Chester County, Pennsylvania, Society of Progressive Friends to AL, Oct. 1862, ALP.
130. "The Proclamation of Freedom. By Horace Greeley," *Independent*, Oct. 2, 1862.
131. "A Proclamation by the President of the United States," *Independent*, Sept. 25, 1862.
132. "The Proclamation," *Christian Recorder*, Oct. 18, 1862.
133. Thomas C. Guthrie and D. G. Bradford to AL, Sept. 30, 1862 (First United Presbyterian Synod of the West); Potter to AL, Sept. 27, 1862, ALP.

Notes for pages 196–201 469

134. J. K. W. Levane and A. M. Milligan to AL, n.d. (Sept.–Dec. 1862), ALP.

135. Sylvanus Cobb to AL, Dec. 27, 1862, ALP.

136. "A Proclamation by the President of the United States," *Independent*, Sept. 25, 1862; *Christian Times*, Sept. 24, 1862, 2; "The New Exodus," *Christian Times*, Oct. 15, 1862.

137. American Missionary Association in Siam to AL, Dec. 18, 1862, ALP.

138. W. B. Lowry, H. Catlin, and J. F. Downing to AL, Sept. 23, 1862, ALP.

139. Cobb to AL, Dec. 27, 1862, ALP.

140. "The Proclamation of Freedom. By Horace Greeley," *Independent*, Oct. 2, 1862.

141. Blight, *Douglass*, 379, 381; *CW*, 5:434 (Preliminary Emancipation Proclamation, Sept. 22, 1862).

142. Blight, *Douglass*, 380–84.

143. Plumly to AL, Jan. 1, 1863, ALP.

144. S. Peck to AL, Jan. 1, 1863; Beaufort, South Carolina, Baptist Church to AL, Jan. 1, 1863, ALP. Cf. W. B. Raber to AL, Jan. 29, 1863 (Pennsylvania Annual Conference of the United Brethren), ALP.

145. *Chicago Tribune*, Jan. 3, 1863; *CW*, 6:28–30 (Emancipation Proclamation, Jan. 1, 1863); Guelzo, *Lincoln's Emancipation Proclamation*, 179–80.

146. Holzer, *Lincoln and the Power of the Press*, 308–11, 413.

147. *Daily Morning Chronicle*, Nov. 8, 1862.

148. Harris to AL, Oct. 2, 1862, ALP.

149. "Letter to the President," *New-York Observer*, Aug. 28, 1862; Prime to AL, Aug. 21, 1862, ALP.

150. The letter is in John Hay's hand but signed by Lincoln. *CW*, 5:391 (AL to Prime, Aug. 23, 1862).

151. *New-York Observer*, Aug. 28, 1862. See also *New-York Observer*, Sept. 4, 1862. Neither letter is in ALP.

152. "Editorial," Boston *Pilot*, Aug. 16, 1862.

153. "The President and Emancipation of Slavery in the Border States," *Metropolitan Record*, July 26, 1862.

154. *Metropolitan Record*, Aug. 2, 1862.

155. "The President on Colonization," *Metropolitan Record*, Aug. 23, 1862; "Letter of the President—Some Serious Reflections Thereon," *Metropolitan Record*, Aug. 30, 1862.

156. "The President's Proclamation—an Emancipation Crusade to Be Inaugurated," *Metropolitan Record*, Oct. 4, 1862.

470   *Notes for pages 201–212*

157. Boston *Pilot*, Oct. 25, 1862, 4.

158. "The President's Proclamation—an Emancipation Crusade to Be Inaugurated," *Metropolitan Record*, Oct. 4, 1862.

159. Hutchinson, *Cyrus Hall McCormick*, 2:32–33; Vander Velde, *Presbyterian Churches and the Federal Union*, 288–89.

160. "The President's Proclamation," Boston *Pilot*, Oct. 4, 1862.

161. Leonard Smith, Diary, Nov. 6, 1862, ALPL.

162. Silbey, *Respectable Minority*, 143–46; Varon, *Armies of Deliverance*, 160.

163. AL to Carl Schurz, Nov. 10, 1862, in *CW*, 5:494.

164. *CW*, 5:534 (Annual Message to Congress, Dec. 1, 1862).

165. Boston *Pilot*, Oct. 11, 1862, 4 (forthcoming elections).

166. Boston *Pilot*, Nov. 29, 1862, 2.

167. Boston *Pilot*, Dec. 3, 1862, 4 (president's annual message).

168. "The Emancipation Proclamation," Boston *Pilot*, Jan. 10, 1863; Boston *Pilot*, Jan. 17, 1863, 4 (emancipation).

CHAPTER 7   CONSERVATIVE ATTACK AND
LINCOLN'S REJOINDER, 1861–1863

1. Johannsen, *Stephen A. Douglas*, 868–69.

2. Fermer, *James Gordon Bennett and "The New York Herald,"* 187–91.

3. Klement, *Limits of Dissent*, 63.

4. Vallandigham, *Life of Clement L. Vallandigham*, 495–508.

5. Ibid., 56, 398.

6. Vallandigham, "Speech on the Great Civil War in America, Jan. 14, 1863," in *Speeches, Arguments, Addresses, and Letters*, 418–53 (quotation p. 437).

7. Vallandigham, *Record on Abolition, the Union, and the Civil War*, 37.

8. Kwitchen, *James Alphonsus McMaster*, 79.

9. Ibid., 86.

10. Ibid., 115–44; Longley, "Radicalization of James McMaster."

11. Beisel, "Henry Clay 'Dirty' Dean."

12. "A Rich Scene at Mt. Pleasant," *Iowa Transcript* (Toledo), Feb. 27, 1862; *Buchanan County Guardian* (Independence, Iowa), March 4, 1862, 2.

13. *Burlington (Iowa) Weekly Hawk-Eye*, May 23, 1863, 4; "The Game Still Goes On," *Sioux City Register*, May 30, 1863; *Chicago Tribune*, May 19, 1863, 2; *Chicago Tribune*, June 9, 1863, 3.

14. Andreasen, "'As Good a Right to Pray,'" 37–42, 71.

Notes for pages 212–217

15. Hubbell, "Charles Chauncey Burr," 833–34.

16. *The Nineteenth Century: A Quarterly Miscellany for the Free Discussion of Popular Subjects, Conducted by C. Chauncey Burr, Assisted by H. Greely and Others* 1, no. 1 (Jan. 1848).

17. *North American and United States Gazette* (Philadelphia), June 8, 1852; *Weekly Herald* (New York), Oct. 1, 1853.

18. *Liberator,* April 7, 1854; "The Democrats at Tammany," *New York Herald,* Nov. 5, 1856; "Miscellaneous News Items," *Frederick Douglass' Paper* (Rochester, N.Y.), Aug. 24, 1855.

19. *Lowell (Mass.) Daily Citizen and News,* July 28, 1857.

20. *Ohio Statesman* (Columbus), June 16, 1851; *Weekly Herald* (New York), Feb. 2, 1856.

21. "Things in General," *Boston Investigator,* Aug. 23, 1871.

22. "The Peace Party at the North," *Potter Journal* (Coudersport, Pa.), Aug. 21, 1861.

23. *Frank Leslie's Illustrated Newspaper,* May 11, 1861, 411.

24. "Letter from New York," *Daily Evening Bulletin* (San Francisco), July 16, 1861. Cf. "Excitement over C. Chauncey Burr," *Cleveland Herald,* June 23, 1862.

25. *Coles County Ledger* (Charleston, Ill.), Jan. 30, 1862, quoted in Andreasen, "'As Good a Right to Pray,'" 138.

26. Vallandigham, *Record on Abolition, the Union, and the Civil War,* 164. This collection of Vallandigham's major speeches appeared early in 1863 with the discreet purpose of aiding his bid for the Ohio governorship later in the year. It sold well. Klement, *Limits of Dissent,* 129, 138.

27. McPherson, *Battle Cry of Freedom,* 31; Phillips, *Rivers Ran Backward,* 99, 128–29, 280.

28. Klement, *Limits of Dissent,* 138–228.

29. Ibid., 229–56; Weber, *Copperheads,* 93–94; Burlingame, *Abraham Lincoln,* 2:558–66.

30. Klement, *Limits of Dissent,* 136.

31. Ibid., 235–37, 56; Andreasen, "'As Good a Right to Pray,'" esp. iii–iv, 77–110, 120–268, 384–406, 534–45. For the contested religious terrain of the border region—the extended Ohio River valley and Missouri—see Ford, *Bonds of Union;* Holm, *Kingdom Divided;* Volkman, *Houses Divided.* See also Phillips, *Rivers Ran Backward,* 163–68 (for the Shakers of Kentucky), 176–80.

32. Confederate sympathizers in the MEC Baltimore Conference triggered a furious newspaper war with their protest against Governor

472 *Notes for pages 217–222*

Augustus Bradford's 1862 order that the "National flag be put into all churches." Martin, *Minutes of the Sessions of the Baltimore Annual Conference,* 12–13.

33. Andreasen, "'As Good a Right to Pray,'" 143–46.

34. Leonard F. Smith, Diary, July 31, Aug. 4, 28, Sept. 29, 1862; Feb. 4, April 16, 23, 28, May 1, 2, 10, June 11, 24, July 12, Aug. 10, 26, 1863; April 19, 1865, ALPL. Smith was especially indignant at the "morally mean" and "infidel" McDaniels family of Buffalo, Sangamon County, "opposers to the government & the present administration," who "tried to prove the divinity of slavery. Pshaw!" Ibid., Jan. 9, 11, May 1, 1863.

35. Andreasen, "'As Good a Right to Pray,'" 280–85. The Unitarian missionary Jasper Douthit—labeled "a notorious blood-thirsty Abolitionist" by the local lodge of the Copperhead "Knights of the Golden Circle"—risked his life by taking the enrollment for the draft in Shelby County, southern Illinois, and drew the terrifying attentions of armed Peace Democrats by his prayers for the president and the enslaved. Douthit, *Jasper Douthit's Story,* 55–72.

36. *NWCA,* July 29, 1863.

37. See, for example, *NYFJCR,* May 9, 16, 23, 1863; Hennesey, *American Catholics,* 147.

38. [Mullaly], *Washington Despotism Dissected.*

39. Boston *Pilot,* editorials, July 13, Aug. 24, 1861; Aug. 9, Oct. 4, Nov. 29, 1862; April 18, July 4, 1863.

40. Boston *Pilot,* April 4, Nov. 7, 1863.

41. Andreasen, "'As Good a Right to Pray,'" 58–65, 108, 457–58, 492–95.

42. Gallman, *Cacophony of Politics,* 97–98; Morse, Curtis, and Tilden, *Constitution,* 2–3.

43. McKeon, *Administration Reviewed,* 14–15.

44. "The Effects of Abolitionism . . . April 4, 1863," in [Mullaly], *Washington Despotism Dissected,* 33–36.

45. "The Emancipation Proclamation," Boston *Pilot,* Jan. 10, 1863.

46. *Abolition Conspiracy to Destroy the Union,* 31.

47. Dean, *Crimes of the Civil War,* 29–34.

48. "The Church Never Abolitionist," *NYFJCR,* May 2, 1863; "Aboriginal Traditions of the Negro Race," *NYFJCR,* May 9, 1863.

49. "The Cincinnati Catholic Telegraph and Slavery," *NYFJCR,* May 9, 1863.

50. "The Sectional Fanatical Party," *Indiana State Sentinel* (Indianapolis), May 6, 1863 (the text of Lord's widely circulated letter to the *Boston*

Courier, first published in Nov. 1862, and reprinted as *True Picture of Abolition* in 1863).

51. Hopkins, *Bible View of Slavery*, 9, 12. For a penetrating explanation of how the Civil War broke the High Church Episcopal tradition of political noninvolvement to link religion and nationhood, and leave a minority like Hopkins intellectually and emotionally stranded, see Mullin, *Episcopal Vision/American Reality*, 200–211. For Samuel Morse's contempt for abolitionists' "blind and mad resistance to a physical condition which God has ordained," and his tribute to Alexander Stephens for upholding in his "corner-stone speech" the "great truth" of African racial inequality, see Morse, *Letter of a Republican, Edward N. Crosby*. See also Mason, *Election in Iowa*, 4.

52. "The President's Proclamation," Boston *Pilot*, Oct. 4, 1862; "The Emancipation Proclamation," Boston *Pilot*, Jan. 10, 1863.

53. *Proceedings of the Great Peace Convention*, 55. The speaker was the lawyer John J. Van Allen.

54. Shankman, "Draft Resistance in Civil War Pennsylvania," 198.

55. Hatch and Noll, *Bible in America*; Byrd, *Holy Baptism of Fire and Blood*.

56. Vallandigham, *Life of Clement L. Vallandigham*, 511.

57. *NYFJCR*, April 18, May 2, 9, 23, 1863.

58. Hopkins, *Bible View of Slavery*; Andreasen, "'As Good a Right to Pray,'" 46–52; Gallman, *Cacophony of Politics*, 98–100; Drisler, *Part 1. A Reply to the "Bible View of Slavery by J. H. Hopkins,"* Newman, *Part 2. The Bible View of Slavery Reconsidered*.

59. Wainwright, "Loyal Opposition in Civil War Philadelphia," 304–6.

60. Lord, *A True Picture of Abolition*; Samuel W. Lawhon et al., "A History of Opposition," *Dartmouth Review*, Oct. 10, 2021, web .archive.org/web/20170609102606/http://www.dartreview .com/a-history-of-opposition/#disqus_thread.

61. Christy, *Pulpit Politics*; Andreasen, "'As Good a Right to Pray,'" 55–58.

62. "Abolition Preachers *Versus* Christ and the Apostles," *Old Guard* 2 (1863): 7–12.

63. Andreasen, "'As Good a Right to Pray,'" 387.

64. Boston *Pilot*, Jan. 25, Dec. 13, 1862; *NYFJCR*, April 25, 1863.

65. "The Church the Only Emancipator," Boston *Pilot*, Sept. 19, 1863.

66. "The Sectional Fanatical Party," *NYFJCR*, April 25, 1863; Lord, *True Picture of Abolition*, 8.

67. Vallandigham, *Record on Abolition, the Union, and the Civil War*, 39.

68. Cornwell, *Rights and Duties of the American Citizen*, 7.

474 *Notes for pages 226–231*

69. *Louisville Guardian*, quoted in Boston *Pilot*, Feb. 16, 1861; *NYFJCR*, Aug. 22, 1863.
70. *NWCA*, Dec. 31, 1862; *NYFJCR*, April 25, May 23, 1863.
71. Cox, *Puritanism in Politics*, 3–5.
72. Vallandigham, *Record on Abolition, the Union, and the Civil War*, 188.
73. Cox, *Puritanism in Politics*, 5–6.
74. "SDRM" (Findlay, Ohio) to William C. J. Krauss, March 2, 1863, Krauss Papers, HL.
75. Boston *Pilot*, Aug. 8, 1863; *NYFJCR*, Sept. 5, 1863.
76. "The Catholic Clergy and the Draft," *NYFJCR*, Aug. 1, 1863.
77. Andreasen, "'As Good a Right to Pray,'" 155–62, 207–8, 222.
78. Bernstein, *New York City Draft Riots*, 60–65.
79. Brownson, *Works of Orestes A. Brownson*, 17:412.
80. Ural, *The Harp and the Eagle*, 42–135, 174–89; Ural, "'Ye Sons of Green Erin Assemble': Northern Irish American Catholics and the Union War Effort, 1861–1865," in Ural, *Civil War Citizens*, 99–113; Samito, *Becoming American Under Fire*, 29–35, 111–18, 125–33.
81. [Mullaly], *Washington Despotism Dissected*, 7–16.
82. *Old Guard* 1 (1863): 94–95.
83. Man, "Church and the New York Draft Riots of 1863," 42–44.
84. Strong, *Diary*, 4:30–31 (July 16, 1863).
85. "Bloodshed Begun in New York," *NYFJCR*, July 18, 1863; "The Negro Delusion," *NYFJCR*, July 18, 1863; "The Disturbances in New York," *NYFJCR*, July 25, 1863; "Who Most Guilty!," *NYFJCR*, July 25, 1863; "Stirring the Bitter Waters!," *NYFJCR*, Aug. 1, 1863; "Chicago Correspondence," *NYFJCR*, July 25, 1863.
86. Union propagandists of the Loyal Publication Society, seizing on evidence of Catholic dismay over the riots, circulated Father Joseph Fransioli's censure of violent resistance to lawfully constituted authority. Scripture, the Brooklyn priest explained, taught that the true Christian patriot made a cheerful sacrifice "before the altar of his country, his property and his life." Fransioli, *Patriotism, a Christian Virtue*, 3, 5–8.
87. Kashatus, *Abraham Lincoln, the Quakers, and the Civil War*, 3–6. "On principle, and faith, opposed to both war and oppression, they [the Friends] can only practically oppose oppression by war," Lincoln reflected to Elizabeth Gurney. "In this hard dilemma some have chosen one horn and some the other." Faced with appeals for military exemption, Lincoln granted several, but many young Friends suffered imprisonment for refusing to serve. *CW*, 7:535 (AL to Gurney, Sept. 4, 1864).

Notes for pages 231–235 475

88. In the Midwest the nonresistance principles of Mennonites and the Amish made Democratic voters of some, and nonvoters of others. But the Union-Republican party benefited in Pennsylvania, where in Lancaster County in the 1864 presidential and congressional elections both Lincoln and Thaddeus Stevens ran strongly. Lehman and Nolt, *Mennonites, Amish, and the American Civil War*, 112–14, 153–62, 173–74.

89. Griffis, *John Chambers*, 112.

90. Andreasen, "'As Good a Right to Pray,'" 37–42.

91. New York Quakers grieved at the hypocrisy of "unscrupulous men, assuming the name of Peace-Makers ... doing all they can ... to rivet the chains of slavery in this land." William Wood to Society of Friends, London, Sept. 2, 1863, ALP.

92. "Chicago Correspondence," *NYFJCR*, July 25, 1863.

93. *Proceedings of the Great Peace Convention*, 6 (F. C. Dinninny), 16 (Wood), 61 (Willard Saulsbury).

94. Quinn, *Interior Causes of the War*, 65.

95. Sears, *Civil War Papers of George B. McClellan*, 344–46; Sears, *George B. McClellan*, 227–79.

96. "Letter to the Clergy," *Old Guard* 1 (1863): 11.

97. Boston *Pilot*, March 28, 1863; McKeon, *Administration Reviewed*, 15.

98. *NYFJCR*, April 25, 1863.

99. Quinn, *Interior Causes of the War*, 5, 8–9, 24.

100. Vallandigham, *Record on Abolition, the Union, and the Civil War*, 162.

101. Andreasen, "Conflicting War Sentiments on the Decatur Methodist Circuit," 281–82.

102. *American Citizen* (Butler County, Pa.), Sept. 7, 1864, 2; *Gallipolis (Ohio) Journal*, Sept. 8, 1864 (from *Brownlow's Whig*).

103. Cox, *Puritanism in Politics*, 4. Cf. [Mullaly], *Washington Despotism Dissected*, 25, 27, 36–37, 40, 71.

104. "Union Leagues," Boston *Pilot*, April 11, 1863.

105. "A Democratic Demonstration in New York," *NYFJCR*, April 18, 1863.

106. Andreasen, "'As Good a Right to Pray,'" 207, 297.

107. Dean, *Crimes of the Civil War*, 164.

108. W. Krauss to W. C. J. Krauss, May 3, May 23, Oct. 27, Dec. 13, 1863, Krauss Papers, HL.

109. Vallandigham, *Record on Abolition, the Union, and the Civil War*, 179–83.

110. Editorial, Boston *Pilot*, Oct. 25, 1862; "Letter from Archbishop Hughes, to the Hon. Wm. H. Seward," Boston *Pilot*, Nov. 22, 1862; Man, "Church and the New York Draft Riots," 40–42.

476   *Notes for pages 235–243*

111. "Compromising with Traitors," *NYFJCR*, July 25, 1863.
112. "New Orleans Correspondence," *NYFJCR*, May 23, 1863.
113. Andreasen, "'As Good a Right to Pray,'" 307–10, 457–58.
114. [Mullaly], *Washington Despotism Dissected*, 7.
115. "Lincoln as a President," *NYFJCR*, July 18, 1863.
116. "SDRM" to William C. J. Krauss, March 2, 1863; N. H. McCracken to William C. J. Krauss, May 30, 1863, Krauss Papers, HL.
117. [Mullaly], *Washington Despotism Dissected*, 7–16, 77–80, 87–91.
118. S. M. Johnson to Samuel L. M. Barlow, June 26, 1863, Samuel L. M. Barlow Papers, HL.
119. [Mullaly], *Washington Despotism Dissected*, 14, 27, 105.
120. W. Krauss to W. C. J. Krauss, May 3, May 23, 1863, Krauss Papers, HL.
121. *NYFJCR*, endorsing the Montreal *True Witness*.
122. Dean, *Crimes of the Civil War*, 34.
123. Andreasen, "'As Good a Right to Pray,'" 107.
124. *NYFJCR*, April 18, 25, May 16, 23, 1863.
125. Dean, *Crimes of the Civil War*, 47. For the similar sentiments of the Chicago Democrat B. G. Caulfield, see *Suppression of "The Chicago Times,"* 9.
126. "The Sectional Fanatical Party," *NYFJCR*, April 25, 1863.
127. Vallandigham, *Life of Clement L. Vallandigham*, 59, 510.
128. Kwitchen, *James Alphonsus McMaster*, 119.
129. Andreasen, "'As Good a Right to Pray,'" 43–45, 99, 393; "Peace for the Sake of Re-union," *NYFJCR*, May 16, 1863.
130. Andreasen, "'As Good a Right to Pray,'" 140, 244–45, 248–51, 256, 261–62, 266, 284–94; Andreasen, "Proscribed Preachers, New Churches," 196–97. For an instance when the boot was on the other foot—a firebrand ultrapatriotic minister charged (and acquitted) for false accusation against a fellow preacher who had reproached him for a sanguinary sermon—see Andreasen, "Conflicting War Sentiments on the Decatur Methodist Circuit."
131. W. Krauss to W. C. J. Krauss, Nov. 28, 1863, N. H. M. McCracken to W. C. J. Krauss, May 30, 1863, Krauss Papers, HL; [Mullaly], *Washington Despotism Dissected*, 92–94.
132. *Proceedings of the Great Peace Convention*, 58.
133. Quinn, *Interior Causes of the War*, 6, 8–9, 26–29, 49, 95, 100.
134. *Proceedings of the Great Peace Convention*, 31.
135. *NYFJCR*, May 16, 1863; *Vallandigham Song Book*, 18–19.
136. *Copperhead Minstrel* (1863), 37–39, 47–49.
137. Ibid., 25.

Notes for pages 244–252

477

138. Ibid., 15, 24, 27–28, 39–40.

139. "The Fecundity of Devils," *Old Guard* 1 (1863): 70.

140. "Cooking the Hell Broth," *Old Guard*, June 1864, 140.

141. Volck, *Sketches from the Civil War in North America.*

142. McKeon, *Administration Reviewed,* 14. Cf. Stoddard, *Dispatches from Lincoln's White House,* 97.

143. Volck, *Sketches from the Civil War in North America.*

144. It grieved the Methodist minister Leonard Smith to find the "rank Copperhead" *New York Day-Book* and the *Old Guard* in homes he visited in central Illinois. Diary, Jan. 9, 11, 1863, Feb. 9, 1865, ALPL.

145. *CW,* 6:301–6 (AL to Matthew Birchard and Others, June 29, 1863).

146. Burlingame, *Abraham Lincoln,* 2:509–10.

147. Douglas L. Wilson has shown how Lincoln crafted this touching image, by revising an earlier draft, to create "the nineteenth-century equivalent of a sound bite." Wilson, *Lincoln's Sword,* 173.

148. *CW,* 6:261–69 (AL to Corning and Others, June 12, 1863).

149. D. P. Brown to AL, June 15, 1863, ALP.

150. Ibid.; Forney to AL, June 14, 1863, ALP. See also Senator Jacob M. Howard of Michigan to AL, July 8, 1863; E. D. Morgan to AL, June 15, 1863, ALP.

151. Lieber to AL, June 16, 1863, ALP. See also H. Greeley to J. G. Nicolay, June 14, 1863; J. C. Ten Eyck to AL, June 16, 1863; W. A. Hall to AL, June 15, 1863; B. H. Brewster to AL, June 18, 1863; M. Delahay to AL, June 19, 1863; R. Conkling to AL, June 16, 1863, ALP.

152. McCulloch to AL, June 16, 1863, ALP.

153. *CW,* 6:261, 268–69 (AL to Corning and Others, June 12, 1863).

154. Haight to Nicolay, June 17, 1863; Dickinson to AL, June 19, 1863, ALP; Burlingame, *Abraham Lincoln,* 2:510. Of Pennsylvania Democrats, Edgar Cowan reported that "no man except a madman could doubt their loyalty." Cowan to AL, June 17, 1863, ALP.

155. Barnett to Barlow, June 10, 1863, Barlow Papers, HL.

156. Wilson, *Lincoln's Sword,* 182–97.

157. Ibid., 183.

158. *CW,* 6:399, 406–11, 414, 423 (AL to Conkling, Aug. 20, 26, 27, 31, 1863).

159. In Allen C. Guelzo's crisp summary, "a straight line runs from the Proclamation through the Conkling letter to the Thirteenth Amendment and the final abolition of slavery." Guelzo, "Defending Emancipation," 314. For the significance of the Conkling letter in the evolution of Lincoln's "moral imagination," see Miller, *President Lincoln: The Duty of a Statesman,* 289–313.

478   *Notes for pages 253–258*

160. Abraham Lincoln, "Memorandum on Reunion" [Aug. 26, 1863?], ALP.
161. Benjamin Field to AL, Aug. 26, 1863, ALP.
162. "The President's Letter," *Cleveland Morning Leader,* Sept. 4, 1863.
163. "Resolutions of Indiana Conference," *Richmond (Ind.) Palladium,* Sept. 25, 1863.
164. Israel Washburn Jr. to AL, Sept. 15, 1863, ALP.
165. Wilson to AL, Sept. 3, 1863, ALP.
166. Quincy to AL, Sept. 7, 1863, ALP. See also Charles Sumner to AL, Sept. 7, 1863; John M. Forbes to AL, Sept. 8, 1863; Christopher C. Andrews to AL, Oct. 7, 1863, ALP.
167. Goodrich to AL, Sept. 3, 1863, ALP. See also Burlingame, *Abraham Lincoln,* 2:563.
168. "Does Mr. Lincoln Wish to Save the Union?," *Old Guard* 1 (1863): 276–78. For Democrats' contemptuous dismissal of the Conkling letter, on constitutional and racial grounds, and its skewering of chances for negotiated peace, see, for example, "The President's Springfield Letter—Attainment of Peace," *Ohio Statesman* (Columbus), Sept. 5, 1863; "The Wood and Lincoln Correspondence," *Indiana State Sentinel,* Sept. 14, 1863; "Food for Reflection—Opportunities for Peace Rejected," *Dayton Daily Empire,* Sept. 14, 1863; "Those Dissatisfied," *Dayton Daily Empire,* Sept. 26, 1863; "'Loyal' vs. 'Disloyal,'" *Star of the North* (Bloomsburg, Pa.), Oct. 7, 1863.
169. Harrison, *Man Who Made Nasby,* 52–55.
170. *Hancock Jeffersonian* (Findlay, Ohio), Sept. 18, 1863, 1; "Sermon," *Hancock Jeffersonian,* Oct. 2, 1863; "The Copperhead Vallandigham Platform," *Hancock Jeffersonian,* Oct. 9, 1863; "The Result in the County," *Hancock Jeffersonian,* Oct. 16, 1863; "The Lesson," *Hancock Jeffersonian,* Oct. 23, 1863.
171. Andreasen, "'As Good a Right to Pray,'" 205, 208.
172. Harrison, *Man Who Made Nasby,* 98.
173. [Locke], *Nasby Papers,* 12, 26, 33, 37–39.
174. Ibid., 1, 19, 27, 29–30.
175. Ibid., 3–4, 22–26, 41. Locke's purpose in peppering Nasby's language with the term "nigger" was manifestly moral. He meant to shock as well as amuse. A crude and derogatory term, it was generally considered by the northern social elite to degrade both user and subject.
176. Jones, introduction to *Struggles of Petroleum V. Nasby,* xi–xiv.
177. *North American and United States Gazette* (Philadelphia), Nov. 12, 1864. My thanks to Nichola Clayton for helping plot Nasby's geographic reach, 1863–65.

Notes for pages 258–259 479

178. [Locke], *Struggles (Social, Financial, and Political) of Petroleum V. Nasby*, 13–14. Akin to Locke's Copperhead satire—though directed chiefly at New York, not Ohio, Peace Democrats—was Richard Grant White's anonymous publication *The New Gospel of Peace According to St. Benjamin*, a pastiche scriptural text in the idiom of the King James translation. Within a year "Book Two" and "Book Three" followed. *Harper's Weekly* reported that the pamphlets sold well, were "intimately known to every circle in the country," and did "very great" service for the Union cause. See also Danielle Brune Sigler, "War in the Land of Unculpsalm," *New York Times*, Aug. 2, 2013, archive.nytimes.com. Cowan, "Menard County Blacksmith," in *Chronicles of the War with Jeff, King of Dixie*, delivered in a hundred King James–style verses a narrative of the triumph of Abraham and the army of the Lord over "the rattlesnakes of Dixie and the sneak peace serpents."

179. Rice, *Reminiscences of Abraham Lincoln*, 439–43, 446–47.

180. Ibid., 447–48. The unamused included the cabinet secretaries Stanton and Chase, and Senators William Pitt Fessenden and James Speed. Gienapp and Gienapp, *Civil War Diary of Gideon Welles*, 585. They included Charles Sumner, too, according to Harris, *Lincoln's Last Months*, 56. Sumner later took a more positive view when he wrote his introduction to *The Struggles of Petroleum V. Nasby* on (appropriately enough) April 1, 1872.

181. [Locke], *Struggles (Social, Financial, and Political) of Petroleum V. Nasby*, 15. Representative James Ashley recollected an occasion when he heard Lincoln talking to himself. Lincoln explained that he was "just repeating" one of Nasby's phrases, and added, "I must invite Nasby to come to Washington and make me a visit, and you may say to him that I should be willing to resign the Presidency if I could write such letters." Harrison, *Man Who Made Nasby*, 112–13.

182. Wilson and Davis, *Herndon's Informants*, 167.

183. Kaplan, *Lincoln*, 37–40, 105–6, 119–20, 137–40.

184. Lincoln used the phrase "the power to hurt" in a congressional speech in 1848. As Douglas Wilson suggests, his likely source was Shakespeare's Sonnet 94. Wilson, *Honor's Voice*, 303; *CW*, 1:509 (Speech in the House of Representatives on the Presidential Question). For Wilson's investigation of Lincoln's anonymous or pseudonymous "attack journalism" and satirical voice, see 175–78 (the "Sampson's Ghost" letters), 265–76 (the Lost Township letters), 298–304 (the assault on the Reverend Peter Cartwright).

185. Ross, *Slavery Ordained of God*, 146, 183.

480   *Notes for pages 259–265*

186. *CW*, 3:204–5 ("Fragment on Pro-slavery Theology," [Oct. 1, 1858?]). Basler retained the date assigned by Nicolay and Hay. Lincoln, however, could well have written this during 1857, when Ross's public lectures and *Slavery Ordained of God* earned caustic reviews in the *Illinois State Journal*, July 13, 1857 ("The Aggression of the Democracy"), July 28, 1857 ("Dr. Ross's Slave"), Sept. 7, 1857 ("Why a Preacher Left His Church"). See also Fornieri, *Abraham Lincoln's Political Faith*, 70–91; White, *Lincoln in Private*, 105–16.

187. Rice, *Reminiscences of Abraham Lincoln*, 442.

188. Wilson and Davis, *Herndon's Informants*, 166, 182–84, 350–51, 507. For similar reflections, see ibid., 4 (Horace White), 18–20 (William Graham Greene), 153 (Richard James Oglesby), 238 (Samuel C. Parks), 494 (George Eisenmeyer), 632 (Henry Clay Whitney). See also Herndon and Weik, *Herndon's Lincoln*, 356–63.

CHAPTER 8   LINCOLN IN THE TEMPEST OF
RELIGIOUS NATIONALISMS, 1863–1864

1. Smith to AL, Oct. 4, 1862; Gove to AL, Jan. 1, 1864, Jan. 2, 1865; Cornell to AL, Jan. 9, 1864; Kelly to AL, Feb. 25, 1863, ALP.

2. At least fifty-three church petitions and memorials peppered the White House between January 1863 and April 1865. Baptist (sixteen), Methodist (nine), Congregational (six), United Brethren (six), Universalist (five), and Presbyterian traditions (four) made up the majority; Episcopalians, Friends, German Reformed, and Unitarians were also represented. Nine came from New England, twenty-four from the mid-Atlantic states, fifteen from the Northwest, one from the Far West, and four from the border slave states.

3. Scammon to AL, Nov. 2, 1863, ALP.

4. Mrs. H. S. Crocker to AL, Jan. 11, 1864, ALP.

5. African Civilization Society to AL, Nov. 5, 1863, ALP. Cf. Henry B. Carrington to AL, Jan. 14, 1863; Elias Nason to AL, April 16, 1861; W. Holmes to AL, Jan. 22, 1863; La Porte Indiana Baptists to Schuyler M. Colfax, June 1864; Thomas Russell to AL, Dec. 8, 1863, ALP. The Mexican War veteran Rush C. Hawkins reminded Lincoln that neither he nor a West Point education could in themselves make a great general: "God Almighty alone holds that patent in his hands," and so far in world history he had "sent forth but a comparatively Small number." Hawkins to AL, Jan. 22, 1863, ALP. Cf. James R. Doolittle to AL, June 29, 1863, ALP. The staunch Republican Hannah M. Neilson defended Hiram Barney, collector of the port of

Notes for pages 265–267 481

New York, against alleged corruption, thankful that Providence had swapped Buchanan's plundering administration for Lincoln's, where "dishonesty is the exception, and a cause for scandal." Neilson to AL, Jan. 20 [1864], ALP.

6. Cameron to AL, Feb. 13, 1864, ALP. Cf. Charles Sumner to AL, Oct. 12, 1864, ALP.

7. Defrees to AL, Aug. 29, 1864, ALP. Cf. Edward S. Cleveland to AL, Jan. 20, 1864, ALP. The godly Chauncey Huntington of Watertown, New York, had faith in "the Triumph of the <u>Right</u>" but, like Cameron and DeFrees, knew it alone was not enough. "'Faith as a grain of mustard seed' is so far from removing a mountain, that the greatest Saint, <u>cant</u> move a <u>pin</u>! The <u>will</u> is more powerful than faith," he reflected. C. D. Huntington to D. B. Huntington, [1863?], Zina Baker Huntington Family Letter, HL.

8. "Sermon Delivered by Phineas Densmore Gurley at the Funeral of William Wallace Lincoln, Son of Abraham Lincoln, at the White House, Washington, D.C.," Phineas Densmore Gurley Papers, Presbyterian Historical Society, Philadelphia, digital.history.pcusa.org /islandora/object/islandora:82297#page/1/mode/1up.

   For Gurley's classic providentialism, of an American Israel under God, see Gurley, *Our Prosperity, Our Ingratitude, and Our Danger.*

9. Sample to AL, Oct. 21, Nov. 10, 1864, ALP.

10. Gurney interview with AL, Oct. 26, 1862, Gurney to AL, Aug. 18, 1863, ALP; *CW,* 5:478 (AL to Gurney, Oct. 26, 1862).

11. AL to Alexander Reed, Feb. 26, 1863, ALP.

12. Raymond, *Life and Public Services of Abraham Lincoln,* 616–18.

13. Hay, *Inside Lincoln's White House,* 121; John L. Elliott, "Owen Lovejoy," *Cornell Magazine* 2 (1889–90): 234; Moore and Moore, *Collaborators for Emancipation.*

14. James C. Rice to AL, Feb. 8, 1863, ALP. Cf. James Hunt to AL, Oct. 12, 1863; Five Points House of Industry to AL, Oct. 16, 1863; James E. Yeatman to AL, June 25, 1864; Rufus K. Williams to AL, Oct. 3, 1864; Zadok Street to AL, Nov. 9, 1864; H. C. Townley and George Clapp, Sept. 24, 1863; William W. Pickering to AL, Sept. 8, 1864, ALP.

15. John W. Tatum to AL, Jan. 18, 1864, ALP.

16. General Conference of the Congregational Church in Maine to AL, June 22, 1864, ALP. Cf. R. Z. Wilson to AL, June 3, 1864; Free Regular Baptist Church, White Creek, Wis., June 20, 1863; James Delany to AL, Oct. 1863 (Preamble and Resolutions of the Wisconsin Baptist State Convention); General Conference of Methodist Episcopal

482   *Notes for pages 267–271*

Church to AL [with endorsement by Lincoln], May 14, 1864; Frank M. Hobson to AL, March 15, 1865, ALP.

17. Trenton, New Jersey, Sons of Temperance to AL, Feb. 23, 1863, ALP.

18. A. A. Wood (Moderator of the Presbytery of Geneva, Ontario County, N.Y.) and B. B. Goldsmith to AL, Jan. 20, 1864, ALP.

19. William E. Dixon to AL, Aug. 29, 1864, ALP; Burr, "United States Senator James Dixon." Cf. D. A. Mack to AL, March 25, 1863, A. A. Guthrie et al. to AL, Dec. 4, 1863, ALP.

20. William Brown et al. to AL (Committee of Reformed Presbyterian Synod, Washington City), Feb. 11, 1864, ALP. In the Gospels of Mark and Luke, Jesus quotes the psalmist, "The stone the builders rejected has become the cornerstone." Psalms 118:22; Mark 12:10; Luke 20:17. Cf. Acts 4:11.

21. *Chicago Tribune*, Feb. 13, 1864, 1 (from *New-York Tribune*); Moore, *Founding Sins*, 118–22.

22. U.S. Christian Commission to AL, Feb. 12, 1863; Hiram Barney to AL, Feb. 9, 1863, ALP. Williams, *Tabernacles in the Wilderness*, is the essential study of the Christian Commission and the evangelical millennialist nationalism that impelled its ministry to the Union armies; see esp. 2–17, 60–94.

23. Gienapp and Gienapp, *Civil War Diary of Gideon Welles*, 139–40.

24. AL to Reed, Feb. 26, 1863, ALP.

25. Moss, *Annals of the United States Christian Commission*, 256–57.

26. *CW*, 8:245–46 (Stuart, [Jan. 29, 1865]).

27. Stuart to AL, March 25, 1863; Jan. 29, June 18, 1864; Jan. 24, Feb. 1, 1865, ALP; James M. Platt and A. S. Kedzie to AL, Dec. 10, 1864, ALP; *CW*, 8:241–42 (Reply to Delegation of Christian Commission). Stuart sent Lincoln a gold pen, studded with diamonds, in the form of a goose quill, the gift of the president's admirers, purchased at a U.S. Christian Commission Fair. Stuart to John Hay, Feb. 18, 1865, ALP.

28. Barnes to AL, Feb. 7, 1865, ALP.

29. Cornelia Fonda to AL, Jan. 28, 1864, ALP. Cf. James Mitchell to AL, Jan. 19, 1864, ALP.

30. McIlvaine to AL, July 27, 1863, ALP.

31. Gurney to AL [with endorsement by Lincoln], Sept. 8, 1864, ALP.

32. Jenkins to AL, Sept. 9, 1864, ALP.

33. Grinnell to AL, Oct. 25, 1864; Comstock to Mary Todd Lincoln, Nov. 26, 1864, ALP.

34. Sarah T. Barnes to AL, Feb. 7, 1865, ALP.

35. Wilson and Davis, *Herndon's Informants*, 360.

Notes for pages 271–275 483

36. Benjamin Talbot to AL, Dec. 21, 1864, ALP. Cf. Ezra D. Kinney to AL, Dec. 6, 1864, ALP.

37. Howard, *Religion and the Radical Republican Movement*, 71.

38. James Neill to AL, Feb. 8, 1864; Thomas F. Smith to AL, March 14, 1864, ALP.

39. Theodore Baur to AL, Nov. 25, 1863; Andrew Lester to AL, Jan. 4, 1865, ALP.

40. William Ballantyne to AL, April 27, 1863, ALP. The women of the Christian Commission sent Lincoln a Bible, to signal respect for his faith and their devotion to the nation's holy cause. Williams, *Tabernacles in the Wilderness*, 46.

41. Cornelia Fonda to AL, Jan. 28, 1864, ALP. See also General Conference of Methodist Episcopal Church to AL, May 14, 1864, ALP. Cf. Henry B. Carrington to AL, Jan. 14, 1863; Silas M. Hamilton to AL, Aug. 15, 1863; Hannah M. Neilson to AL, Jan. 20, 1864; J. J. Thomas to Isaac Newton, June 2, 1864; George D. Henderson to AL, June 3, 1864; Frank M. Hobson to AL, March 15, 1865, ALP.

42. Mrs. M. P. Knowlton to AL, Oct. 31, 1864, ALP. Cf. Hinton Lloyd to AL, July 1, 1863 (Hudson River Baptist Association North, Schenectady); A. A. Wood and B. B. Goldsmith to AL, Jan. 20, 1864, ALP.

43. Beaufort, South Carolina, Baptist Church to AL, Jan. 1, 1863, ALP.

44. Rice to AL, Feb. 8, 1863, ALP.

45. Burchard to AL, April 12, 1864, ALP.

46. Thompson to AL, Sept. 28, 1864, ALP.

47. *CW,* 6:155–56 (Proclamation Appointing a National Fast Day, March 30, 1863); "Day of Prayer and Humiliation," Cong. Globe (1863), 1501 (March 3).

48. "Thanksgiving Discourse . . . in the New Jerusalem Temple," *Chicago Tribune*, Aug. 14, 1863; "The National Thanksgiving," *New York Times*, Aug. 6, 1863.

49. *CW,* 6:332–33 (Proclamation of Thanksgiving, July 15, 1863).

50. Gurney to AL [with endorsement by Lincoln], Aug. 18, 1863.

51. Hale to AL, Sept. 28, 1863, ALP; *CW,* 6:497 (Proclamation of Thanksgiving, Oct. 3, 1863).

52. Nathaniel P. Banks to Hale, Sept. 28, 1863; James Delany to AL, Oct. 1863 (Preamble and Resolutions of the Wisconsin Baptist State Convention); Whitman Metcalf et al. to AL, Oct. 15, 1863 (New York Baptist State Missionary Convention); R. K. Rodgers to AL, Oct. 28, 1863 (Presbyterian Synod of New Jersey); James L. Scott et al. to AL, Nov. 26, 1863 (Board of Foreign Missions of the Presbyterian Church); S. Sutton to AL, Nov. 27, 1863 (Wisconsin Conference of

484 *Notes for page 275–278*

the United Brethren in Christ); J. M. Carpenter to AL, Dec. 8, 1863 (New Jersey Baptist State Convention); M. Taylor to AL, Dec. 27, 1863 (Pennsylvania Baptist Convention), ALP.

53. "National Thanksgiving: How It Was Observed in Springfield," *Illinois State Journal*, Nov. 28, 1863.

54. *CW*, 7:35 (Announcement of Union Success in Tennessee, Dec. 7, 1863).

55. *CW*, 7:324 (AL to Grant, April 30, 1864).

56. Burchard to AL, April 12, 1864, ALP.

57. Sturtevant et al. to AL [with endorsement by Lincoln], April 28, 1864, ALP. Cf. Abner L. Frazer to Salmon P. Chase, April 2, 1864 [endorsed by Chase and Lincoln]; J. H. Jenne to AL, April 26, 1864, ALP.

58. *CW*, 7:333 (AL to the Friends of Union and Liberty, May 9, 1864). See also Francis Wayland to AL, May 14, 1864, ALP.

59. *CW*, 7:431 (Proclamation of a Day of Prayer, July 7, 1864).

60. "The National Fast in Chicago," *Chicago Tribune*, May 1, 1863; "The National Fast: Its General Observance in New-York," *New-York Tribune*, May 1, 1863; "Thanksgiving and Its Fruits," *New York Times*, Aug. 7, 1863; "From Washington," *Indiana State Sentinel*, May 13, 1863. Cf. George Templeton Strong, Diary, 1835–1875, vol. 4, 1862–1875, entries for April 30, 1863, Aug. 8, 1863, 23, 33, New-York Historical Society digital collections, digitalcollections.nyhistory.org.

61. "The National Fast in Chicago," *Chicago Tribune*, May 1, 1863; "Fast Day in Evansville," *Daily Evansville Journal*, May 4, 1863.

62. "From Springfield," *Chicago Tribune*, Aug. 15, 1863. Ever alert to Copperhead dissent, Leonard Smith rebuked the "many ungrateful wretches" who ignored a "fit & proper" request to rejoice when "God has discomfited ones enemies." Diary, Aug. 6, 1863, ALPL.

63. "The Appointed Fast," *CAJ*, July 14, 1864; "Form Versus Substance," *Liberator*, Aug. 19, 1864; *New York Evangelist*, Aug. 18, 1864, citing *New-York Observer*; "The Fast Day and Roman Catholics," *New York Times*, Aug. 6, 1864; "New York Correspondence," *Catholic Telegraph*, Aug. 10, 1864.

64. For representative and affirming commentary across the spectrum of secular and religious opinion, see, for example, "A National Thanksgiving," *Chicago Tribune*, Aug. 6, 1863; "Second Presbyterian Church: Rev. F. W. Patterson, D.D., Pastor," *Chicago Tribune*, Nov. 28, 1863; "The National Fast," *New York Times*, Aug. 4, 1864; "Thanksgiving Day," *Milwaukee Sentinel*, Aug. 5, 1863; Tyng, *Christian Loyalty*, 71–80; Zabriskie, *Weighed in the Balance*, 3–4. The Union's congregations of Jewish Americans also engaged in the days of national observance.

Notes for page 278–279 485

See, for example, "Thanksgiving Among the Jews," *New York Herald*, Aug. 7, 1863, listing the twenty or so New York synagogues holding the day's services in English or German; "Fast Day in the City: Wooster-Street Synagogue," *New York Times*, Aug. 5, 1864; David Einhorn (rabbi of the Congregation Keneseth Israel, Philadelphia), *Sermon, Delivered on Thanksgiving Day, November 26th, 1863*.

65. Chambré, *Conditions and Prospects of the Nation*, 16. Cf. Smith, *God in the War*, 5–7; "The Covenanters upon the President's Fast," *National Anti-slavery Standard* (New York), May 2, 1863.

66. Curran, *Sermon Preached by Request of the Pastor*, 4–5.

67. Published sermons and addresses were legion. For extensive summaries of the days' preaching in the Union's largest cities, see "The National Fast in Chicago," *Chicago Tribune*, May 1, 1863; "Thanksgiving Day in the City," *Chicago Tribune*, Aug. 8, 1863; "Thanksgiving in Chicago," *Chicago Tribune*, Nov. 28, 1863; "Thanksgiving: The Observances Yesterday," *New York Times*, Nov. 27, 1863.

68. Rankin, *Battle Not Man's, but God's*, 11. Cf. "Calculation and Chance in War," *New York Times*, Nov. 26, 1863; Haven, *National Sermons*, 393–406 ("Why Grant Will Succeed," May 15, 1864).

69. For representative examples, see Brainerd, *Patriotism Aiding Piety*, 17, 24–25; Couch, *Sermon, Preached . . . in the First Congregational Church*; Jackson, *The Union, the Constitution, Peace*, 3–5, 23–25; Livermore, *What We Have to Be Thankful For*, 3–10, 15–16; McKenzie, *Sermon Delivered in the South Parish Church*, 11–12; Chambré, *Conditions and Prospects of the Nation*, 3–4; Hill, *Strength in the Time of Trial*.

70. Bumstead, *Principles of the Constitution the Test of Loyalty*, 1–16; Upfold, *God, the Help of the Nation*, 3–24; Clark, *Unity of the American Nationality*, 7–14, 40–42; Carey, *God Doing Wonderful Things in Behalf of the Nation*, 3–16; Little, *Mission of Our Government*, 4–6.

71. William Hurlin to AL, Sept. 5, 1863 (Damariscotta Baptist Association, Maine); J. F. Lovering to AL, July 10, 1863 (Maine Unitarian Societies), ALP. Cf. F. H. B. Beegle to AL, March 18, 1863 (New Jersey Conference, Methodist Episcopal Church); Presbyterian General Assembly to AL, May 27, 1863, ALP; Ferris, *Duties of the Times*, 4–9; Baker, *Discourse Delivered on the Annual Fast*, 8–9. Citations of the text (Romans 13:1) were ubiquitous throughout the Civil War Union. Byrd, *Holy Baptism of Fire and Blood*, 305.

72. The Congregationalist Adam Reid deemed resistance to unrighteous rule justifiable on four grounds only. "The evils complained of must not only be . . . beyond further endurance; there must be no means of peacefully and constitutionally effecting their removal; the good

486 *Notes for pages 279–281*

to be secured must be more than sufficient to counterbalance all the evils that are sure to attend rebellion; and there must be a reasonable chance of success." Meeting none of these conditions, the southern rebellion was "a gigantic crime, condemned alike by reason and by religion." Reid, *Government a Divine Ordinance*, 13.

73. Alvan Rose to AL, Oct. 10, 1863 (Sandusky Annual Conference, United Brethren); Protestant Episcopal Church, Diocese of Pennsylvania, May 26, 1864, ALP; Cleaveland, *Our Duty in Regard to the Rebellion*, 7–17; Stewart, *The Nation's Sins and the Nation's Duty*, 9–15; Porter, *Fast Implies a Duty*, 11–22 ("We must conquer or be conquered").

74. Melvin Jameson to AL, Oct. 19, 1863 (General Association of Illinois Baptists); George M. Rice to AL, Oct. 19, 1863 (Unitarian Convention, Mass.); S. Sutton to AL, Nov. 27, 1863 (Wisconsin Conference, United Brethren); General Conference of the Congregational Church in Maine to AL, June 22, 1864; D. L. Clarke and A. G. Kirk to AL, Sept. 2, 1864 (Beaver Baptist Association, Pa.), ALP.

75. Protestant Episcopal Church, Diocese of Pennsylvania, May 26, 1864; W. Y. Potter to AL, Oct. 3, 1863 (Chenango, N.Y., Baptist Association), ALP; Gierlow, *Discourse on the Times*, 8.

76. William McKee to AL, Oct. 5, 1863 (Northwest Ohio United Brethren); United Brethren, Erie Annual Conference, April 11, 1864, ALP.

77. Alvan Rose to AL, Oct. 10, 1863 (Sandusky Annual Conference, United Brethren), ALP. Cf. William Miller to AL, Sept. 25, 1863 (Massachusetts and Rhode Island Christian Conference); John Wheeler to AL, Sept. 7, 1863 (North Ohio Conference, Methodist Episcopal Church), ALP; Giles, *Problem of American Nationality and the Evils Which Hinder Its Solution*, 22–24; Ottman, *God Our Leader*, 15; Jackson, *The Union, the Constitution, Peace*, 33; Peck, *Our Country*, 88–89 ("Fiery Trials of Our Free Institutions," delivered in the Presbyterian Church, Scranton, Pa., on the national thanksgiving, Nov. 26, 1863); Street, *Sermon Preached in the Presbyterian Church, York, Pa.*, 20–22; Steele, *Thanksgiving by Faith*, 15–16.

78. Clarke, *Discourse on the Aspects of the War*, 30; Zabriskie, *Weighed in the Balance*, 22.

79. William M. Stewart to AL, March 20, 1864, ALP.

80. "Form Versus Substance," *Liberator*, Aug. 19, 1864; Edward D. Holton to AL, Aug. 4, 1864 (Spring Street Congregational Church, Milwaukee), ALP.

81. Middlesex County Massachusetts Anti-slavery Society to AL, Dec. 27, 1863, ALP.

82. "Form Versus Substance," *Liberator*, Aug. 19, 1864.

Notes for pages 281–283   487

83. *CW,* 6:155–56 (Proclamation Appointing a National Fast Day, March 30, 1863); *CW,* 7:431–32 (Proclamation of a Day of Prayer, July 7, 1864); Haven, *National Sermons* (Fast sermon, Boston, Aug. 4, 1864), 423–24, 429. Cf. John M. Bull, "A True National Fast, with Its Attendant Happy Consequence: Sermon on the Occasion of the National Fast, April 30th 1863," 38, John M. Bull Papers, Syracuse University Special Collections Center.

84. Richmond to AL, Nov. 15, 1863, ALP.

85. Steele, *Thanksgiving by Faith,* 9; Ottman, *God Our Leader,* 14.

86. Rice to Wilson, Nov. 11, 1863, ALP. Cf. Eliza P. Gurney to AL, Aug. 18, 1863, ALP.

87. Henry B. Carrington to AL, Jan. 14, 1863, ALP; Paddock, *God's Presence and Purpose in Our War,* 18–19; John M. Bull, "God for the Right; or, Praise for National Blessings: Thanksgiving Sermon," Nov. 26, 1863, 29–31, Bull Papers.

88. Burchard to AL, April 12, 1864, ALP.

89. Presbyterian General Assembly to AL, May 27, 1863, ALP.

90. McIlvaine to AL, Jan. 6, 1864, ALP.

91. W. B. Raber to AL, Jan. 29, 1863 (Pennsylvania Annual Conference of the United Brethren); John Wheeler to AL, Sept. 7, 1863 (North Ohio Conference of the Methodist Episcopal Church); James Delany to AL, Oct. 1863 (Wisconsin Baptist State Convention); Whitman Metcalf et al. to AL, Oct. 15, 1863 (New York Baptist State Missionary Convention); George M. Rice to AL, Oct. 19, 1863 (Unitarian Convention); Isaac Mendenhall and Sarah M. Barnard to AL, Nov. 1, 1863 (Religious Society of Progressive Friends, Longwood); S. Sutton to AL, Nov. 27, 1863 (Wisconsin Conference of the United Brethren); General Conference of Methodist Episcopal Church to AL, May 14, 1864; George Parker and Charles Dawson to AL, May 24, 1864 (Wisconsin Primitive Methodists); Rhode Island Congregational Conference to AL, June 1864, ALP. For example, New Jersey Congregationalists called for another presidential edict to liberate every one of the republic's enslaved people, "in the name of God, who made them; in the name of Christ, who died for them; in the name of the Declaration of Independence, which declares their right to Freedom." Congregational Church, Paterson, N.J., to AL, July 4, 1864, ALP.

92. Wright to AL [with endorsement by Lincoln], Feb. 29, 1864, ALP.

93. See, for example, *Minutes of the Fourteenth Session of the New York East Annual Conference of the Methodist Episcopal Church* (New York, 1862), 21; Presbyterian General Assembly to AL, May 27, 1863, ALP; Witherspoon, *Hand of God in the Present Conflict,* 2; Chaplain,

488   *Notes for pages 283–286*

True Fast, 11; Marshall, *Nation's Inquiry*, 13; Nadal, *War in the Light of Divine Providence*, 10–11; Steele, *Thanksgiving by Faith*, 14–15; Eddy, *Necessity for Religion in Politics*, 9–11; Coxe, *Unjust Reproaches, in Public Calamity, Viewed as Part of the Divine Discipline*, 9–11; Bull, "God for the Right; or, Praise for National Blessings: Thanksgiving Sermon," Nov. 26, 1863, 20, John M. Bull Papers, Syracuse University Special Collections Center; Bumstead, *Principles of the Constitution*, 10. Cf. "The British Lion," *Liberator*, Feb. 21, 1862; "The Great Address from French and English Clergymen," *New Hampshire Statesman*, Aug. 14, 1863; "Arming the Slaves v. Rebels," *Cleveland Morning Leader*, Oct. 27, 1863; "God with the North," *Vermont Chronicle*, Nov. 14, 1863; "Amendment of the Constitution," *Milwaukee Sentinel*, April 21, 1864; "The Sure Ground of Our Hope" (from *New York Times*), *Daily Intelligencer* (Wheeling, Va.), July 21, 1864.

94. William McKee to AL, Oct. 5, 1863, ALP; "Mr. Stephens and the Rebellion," *Alleghanian* (Ebensburg, Pa.), July 19, 1864.

95. Chambré, *Conditions and Prospects of the Nation*, 9. Cf. Brainerd, *Patriotism Aiding Piety*, 23, 27–28; Bellows, *War to End Only When the Rebellion Ceases*, 13, 15.

96. *CW*, 6:358 (AL to Hurlbut, July 31, 1863); 6:364 (AL to Banks, Aug. 5, 1863).

97. Blight, *Douglass*, 409.

98. *CW*, 7:51 (Annual Message to Congress, Dec. 8, 1863).

99. *CW*, 6:358 (AL to Hurlbut, July 31, 1863), 6:364 (AL to Banks, Aug. 5, 1863); Fehrenbacher and Fehrenbacher, *Recollected Words of Abraham Lincoln*, 146 (Thomas H. Duval).

100. *CW*, 6:440 (AL to Johnson, Sept. 11, 1863).

101. *CW*, 7:53–56 (Proclamation of Amnesty and Reconstruction, Dec. 8, 1863).

102. *CW*, 6:234 (AL to John M. Schofield, May 27, 1863).

103. Foner, *Fiery Trial*, 274–84.

104. Lockwood to AL, Stanton, and Halleck, Jan. 12, 1863, ALP.

105. Sturtevant to AL, March 10, 1863, ALP. For "the low motive of selfishness" behind growing public support for black troops, see Clarke, *Discourse on the Aspects of the War*, 31. See also, for example, Augustus W. Bradford to AL, Sept. 28, 1863, ALP.

106. Richmond to AL, March 2, 1863, ALP. See also Richmond to AL, Nov. 15, 1863, ALP.

107. Kelly to AL, Aug. 21, 1863, ALP ("The Colored Man's Interest in the Present War"); Steele, *Thanksgiving by Faith*, 11; Rice to Henry Wilson, Nov. 11, 1863, ALP.

Notes for pages 287–290 489

108. Plumly to AL, Jan. 1, 1863; R. Z. Wilson to AL, June 3, 1864; General Conference of the Congregational Church in Maine to AL, June 22, 1864, ALP.

109. Purnell to AL, Jan. 20, 1864, ALP; Curran, *Sermon Preached by Request of the Pastor,* 19–20. See also Chambré, *Conditions and Prospects of the Nation,* 9–10.

110. Witherspoon, *Hand of God in the Present Conflict,* 14; Zabriskie, *Weighed in the Balance,* 23–26; Little, *Mission of Our Government,* 10–13.

111. Steele, *Thanksgiving by Faith,* 11–12; Bellows, *War to End Only When the Rebellion Ceases,* 17. See also Clarke, *Discourse on the Aspects of the War,* 32.

112. William McKee to AL, Oct. 5, 1863; Sturtevant et al. to AL [with endorsement by Lincoln], April 28, 1864, ALP.

113. Brooks, *Our Mercies of Re-occupation,* 23.

114. Haven, *National Sermons,* 343–54 ("The State a Christian Brotherhood," April 1863).

115. Ibid., 429–31 ("The Crisis Hour," Aug. 4, 1864).

116. The radical U.S. congressman Owen Lovejoy, who spoke of having "a niche for Lincoln," his ally in the cause of emancipation, praised Garrison's stance: "If he is not the best conceivable President, he is the best possible. . . . I know that he has been just as radical as any of his Cabinet." Owen Lovejoy, *His Brother's Blood: Speeches and Writings,* 408–9; Magdol, *Owen Lovejoy, Abolitionist in Congress,* 329.

117. Vorenberg, *Final Freedom,* 116–21.

118. Arnold, *Life of Abraham Lincoln,* 357–58; *Minutes of the Seventy-Fifth Session of the New-York Conference of the Methodist Episcopal Church . . . Newburgh, April 13, 1864* (New York, 1864); Asahel Moore to AL, April 28, 1864 (Maine Conference of the Methodist Episcopal Church, April 14–19, 1864); Julian M. Sturtevant et al. to AL [with endorsement by Lincoln], April 28, 1864 (Triennial Congregational Convention); R. Z. Wilson to AL, June 3, 1864 (Synod of Reformed Presbyterians), ALP. For church bodies' continuing pressure, see James P. Root to AL, June 20, 1864 (Rhode Island Congregational Conference); General Conference of the Congregational Church in Maine to AL, June 22, 1864; Edward D. Holton to AL, Aug. 4, 1864 (Spring Street Congregational Church, Milwaukee), ALP.

119. *CW,* 7:380–82 (Reply to Committee Notifying Lincoln of His Renomination, June 9, 1864).

120. Vorenberg, *Final Freedom,* 127–36.

121. William Lloyd Garrison to Helen E. Garrison, June 8–11, 1864, in Merrill, *Letters of William Lloyd Garrison,* 5:207–12.

490 *Notes for pages 291–299*

122. *Independent,* June 30, 1864.

123. Moody, *Life's Retrospect,* 441–45; Harris, *Journal of the General Conference of the Methodist Episcopal Church* (1864), 383.

124. Moody, *Life's Retrospect,* 445; Peck, *Life and Times,* 380.

125. By 1864 the MEC was spread across the Union in more than fifty annual conferences, from Missouri, Arkansas, and Kentucky in its southern reaches, to Vermont, Michigan, Wisconsin, and California. In each case ministers usually adopted a yearly report on "the state of the country." Throughout the war many conferences resolved that a record of their *published* voices, staunchly loyalist and antislavery, be sent to the president. However, the formal record obscured the anti-administration sentiments of a dissenting (commonly lay) minority. Thus, the Southern Illinois Conference could formally deem slavery the "bantling of hell" while harboring supporters of colonization and sympathizers with the South. *Minutes of the Southern Illinois Conference of the Methodist Episcopal Church, for the Year 1862,* 36–39.

126. Moody, *Life's Retrospect,* 446–47; Peck, *Life and Times,* 381.

127. *The American Annual Cyclopedia and Register of Important Events for the Year 1864* (New York, 1870), 163; *Ohio Statesman* (Columbus), May 30, 1864.

128. *CW,* 7:368 (AL to Ide, Doolittle, and Hubbell, May 30, 1864). I have found no evidence that Lincoln's response—out of character in its severity and claim of ministerial hypocrisy—was sent.

129. Christopher C. Andrews to AL, Oct. 29, 1863, Curran to AL, Aug. 24, 1864, ALP; Curran, *Sermon Preached by Request of the Pastor,* 16–20.

130. Botts to John B. Fry, Jan. 22, 1864, ALP.

131. *Harper's Weekly,* Sept. 17, 1864; Brownlow, *Sketches of the Rise, Progress, and Decline of Secession,* 63–64, 252; Brownlow and Pryne, *Ought American Slavery to be Perpetuated?,* 67; Coulter, *Brownlow,* 84–234.

132. *Lincoln Log,* Sept. 4, 1862 ("Meets with Garrett Davis of Kentucky, and Horace Maynard and William Brownlow of Tennessee at the Soldier's Home. *Evening Star* [Washington, DC], Sept. 5, 1862, 2d ed., 2:1"). Brownlow had called at the White House in June and taken umbrage when the president was too busy, "holding a council of war," to see him. Coulter, *Brownlow,* 232–33.

133. Hay, *Lincoln's Journalist,* 277–78; Coulter, *Brownlow,* 234; Brownlow, *Sketches of the Rise, Progress and Decline of Secession,* 422; *Liberator,* April 18, 1862.

134. Sala, *My Diary in America in the Midst of the War,* 2:403.

135. See, for example, "Reception of Parson Brownlow at Cincinnati,"

Wooster (Ohio) Republican, April 3, 1862; "Rev. Wm. G. Brownlow," *Lowell Daily Citizen and News*, April 26, 1862.

136. Brownlow, *Sketch of Parson Brownlow*, 22–23; "Parson Brownlow's Speech," *Chicago Tribune*, Oct. 27, 1862; "Confederate Military Honor," *Knoxville Whig*, Jan. 30, 1864.

137. Brownlow, *Sketches of the Rise, Progress, and Decline of Secession*, 258. The work was advertised and popularly known as *Parson Brownlow's Book*.

138. Guelzo, "Charles Hodge's Antislavery Moment," 299–325.

139. Moorhead, *American Apocalypse*, 56–65; Stewart, *Mediating the Center*, 109.

140. Hodge, "General Assembly [1862]," 519–21. The issue of the just war, and the justification of the present struggle, was widely and energetically addressed, with few evangelical voices raised in opposition to the chorus to which Hodge so vigorously contributed. Parish, "Instruments of Providence," 298–307; Dunham, *Attitude of the Northern Clergy Toward the South*, 111–18.

141. C. Hodge to H. L. Hodge, July 15, 1862, in Hodge, *Life of Charles Hodge*, 475; Hodge, "War," 168–69; C. Hodge to H. L. Hodge, April 15, 1865, CHP.

142. Hodge, *Life of Charles Hodge*, 470–71; Hodge, "War," 141, 155, 168; Charles Hodge, "Retrospect of the History of the Princeton Review," in *"The Biblical Repertory and Princeton Review" Index Volume from 1825 to 1868* (Philadelphia, 1871), 35; Hodge, *Life of Charles Hodge*, 460–61.

143. See, for example, C. Hodge to H. L. Hodge, July 24, 1861, in Hodge, *Life of Charles Hodge*, 472–74; C. Hodge to H. L. Hodge, April 8, 1863, CHMC.

144. Hodge, "England and America"; Hodge, *Life of Charles Hodge*, 468–69.

145. "The difference between [emancipation] being a means and an end, is as great as the difference between blowing up a man's house as a means of arresting of a conflagration, and getting up a conflagration for blowing up his house." Hodge, "War," 152.

146. Ibid., 150–55.

147. Ibid., 142–47, 155–65; C. Hodge to H. L. Hodge, July 15, 1862, in Hodge, *Life of Charles Hodge*, 475; Hodge, "Princeton Review on the State of the Country and of the Church," 634–36; Stewart, *Mediating the Center*, 98, 100–101.

148. Hodge, "War," 150–51.

149. Ibid., 166–67; Hodge, "Princeton Review on the State of the Country and of the Church," 638–41; Hodge, "The General Assembly

492   *Notes for pages 305–311*

[1864]," 538–51; Vander Velde, *Presbyterian Churches and the Federal Union*, 126–27.

150. Vander Velde, *Presbyterian Churches and the Federal Union*, 141–44; Parish, "Instruments of Providence," 311. For radical voices, see Howard, *Religion and the Radical Republican Movement*, 1–89; Moorhead, *American Apocalypse*, 96–104; McKivigan, *War Against Proslavery Religion*, 183–201; McPherson, *Struggle for Equality*, 52–307.

151. Vander Velde, *Presbyterian Churches and the Federal Union*, 167–77.

152. McCormick and his brother later withdrew from North Church, Chicago, when the preacher's Presbyterianism "bent itself . . . to suit the prejudices, the fanaticism, and the bad temper of its votaries." Klement, *Copperheads in the Middle West*, 223; Vander Velde, *Presbyterian Churches and the Federal Union*, 288–89. For the ubiquity of Copperhead sentiment, see, for example, Lemuel Abell's discovery that even in Owasco, among the Yankee settlements of upstate New York, one congregation was "so Coppery" that they would not allow the Calvinist minister to pray for the president. "Will such people ever get to Heaven? If they do God will have to reconsider the sentence that sent Lucifer to the lower Regions & permit him to escort them in." Abell, Diary, March 6, 1864, Abell Family Papers, HL.

153. Boston *Pilot*, May 7, 1862, 4.

154. *Trial of Abraham Lincoln*, endpaper; *Metropolitan Record*, Feb. 13, 1864 ("Can We Conquer the South?"), Feb. 20, 1864 ("The Washington Despotism Dissected").

155. See, for example, "What Are We Fighting For?," *NYFJCR*, July 9, 1864; "An Issue Met" and "The New Religion," *NYFJCR*, July 16, 1864.

156. Andreasen, " 'As Good a Right to Pray,' " 384–487.

157. "The Sin Afflicting Us," *Smyrna Times*, May 7, 1863.

158. "National Thanksgiving: How It Was Observed in Springfield," *Illinois State Journal*, Nov. 28, 1863. Cf. Washburn, *Sermon Delivered on the Day of National Thanksgiving*.

159. "The Causes of the War," Boston *Pilot*, May 2, 1863.

160. "The Fast Day and the Jews," *New York Times*, May 1, 1863.

161. Andreasen, " 'As Good a Right to Pray,' " 198–238.

162. "Fast Day in Ashland," *Ashland Union* (Ashland County, Ohio), Aug. 17, 1864.

163. "Pagan Versus Abolitionist," *NYFJCR*, May 9, 1863.

164. Manning, *What This Cruel War Was Over*, 72–80.

165. McPherson, *For Cause and Comrades*, 62–76; Woodworth, *While God Is Marching On*, 27–39; Carmichael, *War for the Common Soldier*, 66–88.

Notes for pages 311–314 493

166. J. Jones to N. E. Jones, Nov. 10, 1862, March 21, 1863, Collection of Joseph Jones, 79th Regiment Illinois, GLC 2739, Gilder Lehrman Collection, New York. Preparing for the Peninsular campaign, the devout Elisha Hunt Rhodes confided, "I have no fear of the future. If I die upon the battlefield I hope to receive the reward of the righteous and feel resigned to God's will." Rhodes, *All for the Union*, 56 (March 6, 1862).

167. John B. Burrud to Ocena N. Burrud, Feb. 17, April 12, July 20, Aug. 1, 1864, John B. Burrud Papers, HL.

168. John B. Burrud to Ocena N. Burrud, Dec. 30, 1864–Jan. 1, 1865, Burrud Papers, HL.

169. George S. Phillips to Elizabeth K. Phillips, Sept. 29, 1863, June 20, 1864; George S. Phillips to Miriam Phillips, May 7–8, 1864, Phillips Papers, HL.

170. Brewster, *When This Cruel War Is Over*, 90.

171. Messent and Courtney, *Civil War Letters of Joseph Hopkins Twichell*, 163.

172. Ibid., 269.

173. Manning, *What This Cruel War Was Over*, 115.

174. [Haven], *"Punishment on the Nation,"* 10, 96.

175. George S. Phillips [Camp Reid] to Miriam E. Phillips, Aug. 5, 1863, Phillips Papers, HL.

176. Mitchell, *Civil War Soldiers*, 187.

177. Woodworth, *While God Is Marching On*, 265.

178. George S. Phillips to Elizabeth Kauffman Phillips, May 26, June 1, 2, 8, July 20, 1863, Phillips Papers, HL. For similar sentiments ("I consider this struggle of more importance than the Revolutionary War"; "A gigantic revolution is now taking place on this continent and its influence will be felt throughout the whole Civalized world"), see John B. Burrud to Ocena N. Burrud, Feb. 7, 1863, Jan. 30–Feb. 3, March 4, Nov. 4–6, Dec. 27–29, 1864, Burrud Papers, HL. Phillips's admirers urged him to publish his ideas. They appeared as George S. Phillips, *The American Republic and Human Liberty Foreshadowed in Scripture*. Phillips's combination of American nationalism and Christianity stood out for the way he made Israel a model polity that was *historically fulfilled* by the United States. Grasso, *Skepticism and American Faith*, 442–59.

179. Manning, *What This Cruel War Was Over*, 116, 119.

180. Ibid., 268n33.

181. Flotow, *In Their Letters, in Their Words*, 148–49, 161–62.

182. John B. Burrud to Ocena N. Burrud, Jan. 1, 10, 1863, Burrud Papers, HL.

494   *Notes for pages 314–323*

183. Flotow, *In Their Letters, in Their Words*, 148–49, 161–62.
184. Letter, Nov. 27, 1863, Collection of Lysander Wheeler, 105th Regiment Illinois, Gilder Lehrman Collection, New York.
185. Blight, introduction to *When This Cruel War Is Over*, by Brewster, 19–20. See Brewster letters of Jan. 15, 23, Feb. 9, 22, 26, 1862.
186. John B. Burrud to Ocena N. Burrud, Jan. 1, 10, Dec. 24–25, 1863, Burrud Papers, HL.
187. Manning, *What This Cruel War Was Over*, 119–25.
188. William Krauss to William C. J. Krauss, Oct. 27, 1863, Leipsic, Ohio, Krauss Papers, HL.
189. Ibid.
190. Manning, *What This Cruel War Was Over*, 150–52.
191. Flotow, *In Their Letters, in Their Words*, 161.
192. Collins, *Prospect*, 9.
193. Messent and Courtney, *Civil War Letters of Joseph Hopkins Twichell*, 221–22.
194. John D. Barnes, "My Army Life," 212, HL.
195. Ibid., 604; John B. Burrud to Ocena N. Burrud, Oct. 31, 1863, Burrud Papers, HL; [Haven], *"Punishment on the Nation,"* 43, 102, 106, 207; Manning, *What This Cruel War Was Over*, 150.
196. Roberts, *"This Infernal War,"* 172–73.
197. Barnes, "My Army Life," 165, HL.
198. Messent and Courtney, *Civil War Letters of Joseph Hopkins Twichell*, 221–22.
199. Kinsley, *Diary of a Christian Soldier*, 169.

CHAPTER 9   THE ELECTION OF 1864

1. "The Baltimore Platform," *Independent*, June 23, 1864.
2. Norton to Barlow, June 22, 1864, Barlow Papers, HL.
3. Woodbury to Barlow, Aug. 18, 1864, Barlow Papers, HL. See also William H. Clement to Barlow, Aug. 20, 1864, Barlow Papers, HL.
4. "The War and Its Fearful Waste of Life," *Metropolitan Record*, July 9, 1864; "The Atrocities of This War," *NYFJCR*, Aug. 6, 1864.
5. "The Peace Movement in New York," *Metropolitan Record*, Aug. 6, 1864; "The Manifesto of the Confederate States," *Metropolitan Record*, July 23, 1864.
6. "Attitude of Compromisers," Boston *Pilot*, May 7, 1864; "Peace—and How to Win It," Boston *Pilot*, July 23, 1864; "Peace and Reconstruction," Boston *Pilot*, Aug. 6, 1864.
7. "The Next Presidency," *Metropolitan Record*, May 14, 1864.

Notes for pages 323–328   495

8. Burlingame, *Lincoln Observed*, 131.

9. Gallman, *Cacophony of Politics*, 231–34.

10. Fehrenbacher and Fehrenbacher, *Recollected Words of Abraham Lincoln*, 48 (Noah Brooks).

11. "The Convention. Opening Day," *Chicago Tribune*, Aug. 30, 1864.

12. Klement, *Limits of Dissent*, 279–87; Gallman, *Cacophony of Politics*, 242–43, 247–48.

13. "Gen. M'Clellan's Letter" and "Meet the Issue," *NYFJCR*, Sept. 17, 1864.

14. "Mr. Pendleton Serenaded," *Dayton Daily Empire*, Sept. 16, 1864; Klement, *Limits of Dissent*, 288–90.

15. "No Peace Candidate to Be Nominated" and "McClellan Mass Meeting," *Metropolitan Record*, Sept. 24, 1864; "Duty, as We Understand It," *NYFJCR*, Sept. 24, 1864.

16. Editorial, Boston *Pilot*, March 3, 1864; "The Presidential Question" and "Compromise," *NYFJCR*, July 9, 1864.

17. "A Conversation That Concerns Everybody," *Metropolitan Record*, Sept. 24, 1864.

18. "The Next Presidency," *Metropolitan Record*, May 14, 1864.

19. "Hearken to Their Voice," *NYFJCR*, Sept. 24, 1864.

20. Editorial, Boston *Pilot*, March 3, 1864; "Peace—and How to Win It," Boston *Pilot*, July 23, 1864; Editorial, Boston *Pilot*, Aug. 27, 1864, 4. See also Carpenter, *Logic of History*, 23–39.

21. "Considerations for North and for South," *NYFJCR*, Oct. 22, 1864.

22. "Treason and Traitors in the Republican Ranks," *Metropolitan Record*, Aug. 13, 1864; Andreasen, "'As Good a Right to Pray,'" 231–34.

23. "Honest Old Abe on His Own Policy," *Metropolitan Record*, May 7, 1864.

24. Ibid.; "How the Union Is to Be Restored," *Metropolitan Record*, April 30, 1864.

25. "Chicago Correspondence," *NYFJCR*, Oct. 1, 1864; "The Lincoln Conspiracy," *Metropolitan Record*, Nov. 5, 1864.

26. Harper, *Lincoln and the Press*, 289–303; Holzer, *Lincoln and the Power of the Press*, 488–97.

27. Gallman, *Cacophony of Politics*, 222.

28. "Horatio Seymour," *Ohio Statesman*, May 25, 1864; "The Freedom of the Press" and "The War in the Republican Ranks," *Indiana State Sentinel*, May 30, 1864; "Great Outrage on the Liberty of the Press," *Metropolitan Record*, May 28, 1864.

29. Starr, *Bohemian Brigade*, 240, 315–20.

30. "The Freedom of the Press!," *Columbia Democrat and Bloomsburg*

(Pa.) General Advertiser, June 4, 1864 (subsequently published as a Democratic campaign pamphlet). As one of Beecher's parishioners, Howard secured early release from imprisonment at Fort Lafayette, on Lincoln's instruction to Edwin Stanton: "I wish very much to oblige Henry Ward Beecher, by releasing Howard." *CW,* 7:512–13 (AL to Stanton, Aug. 22, 1864).

31. "Another Conscription!," "The Administration Raids upon White Men" and "The Lincoln Policy in Kentucky," *Metropolitan Record,* July 23, 1863; "Five Hundred Thousand More Victims to Abolitionism," *Metropolitan Record,* July 30, 1864.

32. Harlow, *Religion, Race, and the Making of Confederate Kentucky,* 181; Smith, *No Party Now,* 100.

33. W. Krauss to W. C. J. Krauss, April 23, June 12, 1864, Krauss Papers, HL.

34. "Fortunes of the War," *NYFJCR,* Oct. 1, 1864.

35. Clinton, *Speech . . . at Patchogue, Long Island,* 1.

36. "An Issue Met," *NYFJCR,* July 16, 1864.

37. Vallandigham, *Life of Clement L. Vallandigham,* 503–6. Steck's support for Vallandigham proved too much for Dayton's First Lutheran Church, whose council dismissed him in 1864. He took a substantial minority of church members with him to found St. John's Lutheran Church there. *See* www.ohiolink.edu.

38. "Speech of the Hon. C. L. Vallandigham," *Metropolitan Record,* Oct. 8, 1864.

39. Republican Congressional Committee, *Chicago Copperhead Convention,* 12.

40. *NYFJCR,* Sept. 3, 1864, 2; "One Plain Question," *Metropolitan Record,* May 7, 1864.

41. W. Krauss to W. C. J. Krauss, April 23, 1864, Krauss Papers, HL. Another Copperhead predicted "the most outrageous acts in Indiana and Ohio—the polls being taken possession of by the military—and the greatest violence used." John S. Griffin to Cave Johnson Couts, Oct. 13, 1864, Cave Johnson Couts Papers, HL.

42. Editorial, Boston *Pilot,* March 3, 1864. The War Democrat governor of Kentucky protested, "To permit the question of the freedom or slavery of the negro to obstruct the restoration of national authority and unity is a blood-stained sin." T. E. Bramlette to AL, Sept. 3, 1864, in *The War of the Rebellion,* ser. 3, 4:689.

43. *CW,* 7:451 (To Whom It May Concern, July 18, 1864).

44. "An Indictment of President Lincoln," *NYFJCR,* Aug. 20, 1864.

45. W. Krauss to W. C. J. Krauss, Aug. 21, 1864, Krauss Papers, HL.

Notes for pages 331–335 497

46. "An Effort for Peace," *Metropolitan Record*, July 30, 1864; "Lincoln's Claims to Another Presidential Term," *Metropolitan Record*, Oct. 29, 1864; Boston *Pilot*, Aug. 13, 1864, 2; Clinton, *Speech . . . at Patchogue, Long Island*, 2–13.

47. "Abolitionism Refuted," *Metropolitan Record*, April 30, 1864.

48. *Copperhead Minstrel*, 3rd ed. (1864), 28–30.

49. Republican Congressional Committee, *Chicago Copperhead Convention*, 4, 12.

50. "The Chicago Nominees," *NYFJCR*, Oct. 1, 1864.

51. "How the Union Is to Be Restored," *Metropolitan Record*, April 30, 1864.

52. Carpenter, *Logic of History*. Kindred campaign propaganda included several works by the New Jersey minister William D. Potts, M.D., "written in the spirit of Christianity" and dedicated to "God, McClellan, and my Countrymen." Potts, *Our Country Vindicated, and Democracy Sustained*; Potts, *Campaign Songs for Christian Patriots and True Democrats*; Potts, *Freemen's Guide to the Polls, and a Solemn Appeal to American Patriots*, 4.

53. *Copperhead Minstrel*, 3rd ed. (1864), 48.

54. "Persecution of a Catholic Bishop," *Metropolitan Record*, Sept. 3, 1864; "Like Slavery, Popery Is Doomed!," *NYFJCR*, Aug. 20, 1864.

55. "Our Philadelphia Correspondence," *Metropolitan Record*, July 2, 1864; "When Slavery Is Disposed of, Catholicity Is to Be Looked Into," *Metropolitan Record*, Aug. 6, 1864.

56. *NYFJCR*, Oct. 1, 1864, 5.

57. Kaplan, "Miscegenation Issue"; Gallman, *Cacophony of Politics*, 204–5.

58. [Croly and Wakeman], *Miscegenation*, 11.

59. Ibid., 25.

60. Kaplan, "Miscegenation Issue," 300–301.

61. [Locke], *Struggles (Social, Financial, and Political) of Petroleum V. Nasby*, 116.

62. Cox, *Eight Years in Congress from 1857–1865*, 358.

63. "Loyal Leaguers and Their Clubs," *Metropolitan Record*, May 14, 1864.

64. Kaplan, "Miscegenation Issue," 312.

65. Gallman, *Cacophony of Politics*, 255–58.

66. "The Era of Miscegenation Commenced," *Metropolitan Record*, Oct. 1, 1864.

67. *Songs & Ballads of Freedom* included several songs also published in *Copperhead Minstrel*, 3rd ed. (1864).

68. [Croly and Wakeman], *Miscegenation*, 29–30.

498   *Notes for pages 335–339*

69. *CW*, 7:259–60 (AL to New York Workingmen's Democratic Republican Association, March 21, 1864).

70. Kaplan, "Miscegenation Issue," 313–19. Mark Neely offers evidence that Democratic leaders played down or avoided raw racial themes in their official materials and higher-level discourse. Neely, *Boundaries of American Political Culture in the Civil War Era*, 123; Neely, *Lincoln and the Democrats*, 130–32. However, ordinary working-class voters with strong antiblack prejudices would have associated the party with the abundant cartoons, songs, and other materials that exploited fears of racial amalgamation. Gallman, *Cacophony of Politics*, 260.

71. Republican Congressional Committee, *Chicago Copperhead Convention*, 7. For an example of Peace Democrats' withering religious sarcasm, drenched in disgust at Lincoln's promise of a new racial order, see *God Bless Abraham Lincoln!*, esp. 13–16: "Let Hell open wide its Jaws, and jubilant in the works of Abolitionism, and, in derision of the Most High, *Laugh out* . . . GOD BLESS ABRAHAM LINCOLN."

72. *Lincoln Catechism*, 12–16.

73. *NYFJCR*, Sept. 24, 1864, 4.

74. W. Krauss to W. C. J. Krauss, April 23, Aug. 21, 1864, Krauss Papers, HL; Republican Congressional Committee, *Chicago Copperhead Convention*, 11–12.

75. "To Whom It May Concern," *Metropolitan Record*, Oct. 10, 1864.

76. "Abe Lincoln and Oliver Cromwell Compared," *Metropolitan Record*, May 7, 1864.

77. "The President and the Witch of Georgetown," *Metropolitan Record*, April 2, 1864.

78. *Copperhead Minstrel*, 3rd ed. (1864), 39; *Songs & Ballads of Freedom*, 23.

79. "McClellan and Lincoln" (from the *Old Guard*), *Metropolitan Record*, Nov. 5, 1864; "One Plain Question," (from the *New York Daily News*), *Metropolitan Record*, May 7, 1864.

80. "The Walpurgis Dance at Washington (*New York News*)," *Spirit of Democracy* (Woodsfield, Ohio), Aug. 10, 1864; *Indiana State Sentinel* (Indianapolis), Aug. 25, 1864; *Star of the North* (Bloomsburg, Pa.), Aug. 10, 1864, 1.

81. "McClellan's Damaging Admission," *Chicago Tribune*, July 9, 1864. The New York Peace Democrats' dilemma expressed itself in the resolutions of the Anti-abolition State Rights Society, leaving members to follow the dictates of conscience in this "choice of evils." "The Anti-abolition State Rights Society," *Metropolitan Record*, Oct. 8, 1864.

Notes for pages 339–342 499

82. "McClellan and Lincoln" (from the *Old Guard*), *Metropolitan Record*, Nov. 5, 1864.
83. "The Chicago Nominees—Some Reasons Why We Urge Their Support," *NYFJCR*, Oct. 1, 1864.
84. "What McClellan Originally Tho't of the War," *Holmes County Farmer* (Millersburg, Ohio), Sept. 15, 1864.
85. *Cleveland Morning Leader*, April 11, 1863, 1 (*Journal of Commerce*). "Any advance he may make against Satan's Kingdom, will be hailed by us with surprise and gratification," scoffed a Maine Republican. *Union and Journal* (Biddeford, Maine), May 1, 1863, 2.
86. "Interesting Correspondence," *Dayton Daily Empire*, Oct. 11, 1864; "General McClellan and Bishop Whipple," *Urbana (Ohio) Union*, Oct. 26, 1864; Andreasen, "'As Good a Right to Pray,'" 93–94.
87. "The General in Retirement," *Indiana State Sentinel*, Sept. 16, 1864; "McClellan and Lincoln" (from the *Old Guard*), *Metropolitan Record*, Nov. 5, 1864. "McClellan, I say it with reverence," declared Henry Clinton, "is a sincere, prayerful Christian"; Lincoln, if he attempted to pray, would stray into telling the Lord a profane anecdote. Clinton, *Speech . . . at Patchogue, Long Island,* 22.
88. Winthrop, *Great Speech at New London, Conn.*, in Freidel, *Union Pamphlets of the Civil War*, 2:1076–107; Gallman, *Cacophony of Politics*, 250–55; Smith, *Stormy Present*, 82–83, 212; Silbey, *Respectable Minority*, 88, 168.
89. *CW*, 7:514–15 (Memorandum Concerning His Probable Failure of Reelection, Aug. 23, 1864).
90. *CW*, 7:517–18 (AL to Raymond, Aug. 24, 1864).
91. "The National Crisis," *Central Christian Advocate*, Aug. 10, 1864.
92. "New Haven Correspondence," *Christian Recorder*, Aug. 27, 1864.
93. "Plain Talk," *NWCA*, Aug. 10, 1864; "Will God Hear Our Prayer?," *NWCA*, Aug. 17, 1864; "Reinforcements," *NWCA*, Aug. 24, 1864.
94. "Grand Union Rally," *Chicago Tribune*, Sept. 1, 1864.
95. "The Situation—Religious Aspects," *CAJ*, Aug. 11, 1864; cf. "The Way to Peace," *CAJ*, Aug. 25, 1864.
96. Wayland to C. G. Loring, in Wayland and Wayland, *Memoir of the Life and Labors of Francis Wayland*, 2:272. "We have all the argument, the honesty, the character, the patriotism, and power of appeal to the American heart," Wayland continued. "God grant us success. All is in his hand."
97. Brewster to AL, Aug. 29, 1864, ALP. Pennsylvania Baptists, summoning "great moral courage," opposed any armistice that prevented the rebels being brought to justice. D. L. Clarke and A. G. Kirk to

Notes for pages 342–344

AL, Sept. 2, 1864 (loyal resolutions of the Beaver Baptist Association), ALP. Cf. William E. Dixon to AL, Aug. 29, 1864, ALP.

98. "An Appeal to the People," *Independent*, Sept. 8, 1864.

99. *CW*, 7:533–34 (Proclamation of Thanksgiving and Prayer, Sept. 3, 1864); *CW*, 7:535 (AL to Gurney, Sept. 4, 1864).

100. "The Loss of Atlanta," *Fayetteville (N.C.) Observer*, Sept. 12, 1864; "News of the Week," *Urbana (Ohio) Union*, Sept. 7, 1864; "New York To-Morrow," *Daily Gate City* (Keokuk, Iowa), Sept. 14, 1864. Referring to his thanksgiving address, an Episcopalian clergyman explained his mixed feelings as patriotic duty contended with an aversion to preaching politics: "Though not a kind of discourse that I like in the pulpit, yet the crisis that is upon us as a nation, requires that even the Christian ministry should, on occasions appointed by public authority, leave the beaten track, and come to the help of the State." Platt, *Conflict of Two Civilizations*, 3. See, in similar vein, Crosby, *God's View of Rebellion*, 3–5.

101. "Peace Through Victory," *New York Times*, Sept. 19, 1864; Lieber to Nicolay, Oct. 11, 1864, ALP. An Ohio versifier expressed the sentiment with more zeal than elegance: "Let grateful thanksgivings in triumph ascend, / To the great God of battles; our Father and Friend: / Whose arm hath upheld from the far-reaching heaven, / The *Truth*, and the *Right*, and the victory given." "Atlanta Is Taken," *Delaware (Ohio) Gazette*, Sept. 16, 1864. Also "Sermon by the Rev. Mr. Gillette," *Cleveland Morning Leader*, Sept. 17, 1864.

102. Johnson, *Shaking of the Nations*, 7–8, 17.

103. "God's View of Rebellion," *New York Times*, Sept. 20, 1864; "Report of Committee on the State of the Country," *NWCA*, Oct. 12, 1864; "November the Eighth," *NWCA*, Nov. 2, 1864; Hitchcock, *Thanksgiving for Victories*, 6–7; Platt, *Conflict of Two Civilizations*, 6–8.

104. Haven, "The End Near," in *National Sermons*, 474–75, 478.

105. Livermore, *Perseverance in the War the Interest and Duty of the Nation*, 4, 7, 11.

106. J. Leavitt and G. B. Bacon to AL [with endorsement by Lincoln], Sept. 20, 1864, ALP.

107. Livermore, *Perseverance in the War the Interest and Duty of the Nation*, 14; *Minutes of the . . . Central Illinois Annual Conference of the Methodist Episcopal Church . . . September 1864*, 30; *Minutes of the Cincinnati Annual Conference of the Methodist Episcopal Church, for the Year 1864*, 19.

108. Haven, "End Near," 474.

109. "Peace Through Victory," *New York Times*, Sept. 19, 1864; "An

Notes for pages 344–349 501

Armistice—What Does It Mean?," *CAJ*, Sept. 22, 1864; "'Now or Never: Now and Forever!,'" *CAJ*, Oct. 27, 1864; "Sheridan's Victory," *NWCA*, Sept. 28, 1864; "November the Eighth," *NWCA*, Nov. 2, 1864; "Chicago Platform," *Central Christian Advocate* (St. Louis), Oct. 5, 1864.

110. "Our Course," *CAJ*, Sept. 15, 1864; "An Appeal to the People," *Independent*, Sept. 8, 1864. Similar sentiments peppered the loyal resolutions Lincoln received from religious meetings, denouncing what a Baptist association called "the covert assaults and serpentine wrigglings of secret foes." H. A. Guild to AL, Sept. 19, 1864 (resolutions of the Stephentown, N.Y., Baptist Association), ALP. Guild was a Baptist pastor and staunch Republican. See H. A. Guild to AL, Sept. 15, 1863, ALP.

111. "Anticipations of Peace," *CAJ*, Sept. 8, 1864.

112. "The Peace Panic—Its Authors and Objects," *Danville Quarterly Review* 4, no. 3 (Sept. 1864): 448–49; "An Appeal to the People," *Independent*, Sept. 8, 1864.

113. *CW*, 7:504–5 (Speech to the 164th Ohio Regiment, Aug. 18, 1864); Thompson, *Peace Through Victory*, 14–15; "November the Eighth," *NWCA*, Nov. 2, 1864.

114. Tilton editorials, *Independent*, June 23, Oct. 27, 1864; McPherson, *Struggle for Equality*, 284.

115. "State of the Country," *NWCA*, Sept. 14, 1864; "November the Eighth," *NWCA*, Nov. 2, 1864.

116. J. Leavitt and G. B. Bacon to AL, Sept. 20, 1864, ALP; Haven, "End Near," 486–87. See also Tyng, *Record of the Life and Work of the Rev. Stephen Higginson Tyng*, 353–54.

117. "The Death of Slavery," *CAJ*, Oct. 20, 1864; Blight, *Douglass*, 439.

118. Dixon to AL, Aug. 29, 1864; Dodge to D. Davis, Sept. 30, 1864, ALP.

119. [J. A. Jacobs], "The Past Course and Present Duty of Kentucky," *Danville Quarterly Review* 4, no. 3 (Sept. 1864): 426–42.

120. Blight, *Douglass*, 439. Black ministers never bought the argument that "politics" were off-limits. All had a duty under God to speak out against "moral and political disintegration." "The Church—Her Danger and Duty," *Christian Recorder*, June 7, 1862.

121. Haven, "End Near," 483–86; Gravely, *Gilbert Haven, Methodist Abolitionist*, 110–20.

122. McPherson, *Struggle for Equality*, 283–84; Blight, *Douglass*, 436–38; "The Duty of the Hour," *Independent*, Sept. 8, 1864.

123. Gulliver characterized Lincoln as "slow, if you please, but *true*. Unimpassioned, if you please, but *true*. Jocose, trifling, if you please,

502 *Notes for pages 350–353*

but *true*. Reluctant to part with unworthy official advisers, but *true* himself—*true as steel!*" *Independent*, Sept. 1, 1864, 1. References to Lincoln's "frank manliness," "kind heart," "honesty of purpose," and "fairness and integrity" peppered the assessments of his Christian admirers. See, for example, *Independent*, Oct. 1, 1864, Nov. 3, 1864 (Beecher sermon); Richard Eddy to AL, Sept. 15, 1863 (resolutions of the General Convention of Universalists in the United States of America, Sept. 15, 1863), ALP; H. A. Guild to AL, Sept. 19, 1864 (resolutions of the Regular Baptist Churches of the N.Y. Baptist Association, Sept. 14–15, 1864), ALP.

124. "The Two Candidates," *Independent*, Nov. 3, 1864.

125. "Abraham Lincoln," *Delaware State Journal and Statesman* (Wilmington), Jan. 15, 1864. See also, for example, *Evansville (Ind.) Daily Journal*, Jan. 19, 1864; *Soldiers' Journal*, March 16, 1864; *Monmouth Herald and Inquirer* (Freehold, N.J.), May 26, 1864; *Fremont Journal* (Ohio), Aug. 19, 1864; *Central Christian Advocate*, Aug. 24, 1864; *Jeffersonian* (Stroudsburg, Pa.), Oct. 13, 1864.

126. See, typically, A. K. Merrill to AL, March 19, 1864, ALP ("I believe you were just as much raised up by God for this crisis in our country's history as ever Moses was for his or Washington for his").

127. "The Model Ruler," *Independent*, Oct. 10, 1861; "The Hour," *Independent*, Oct. 27, 1864; Johnson, *Shaking of the Nations*, 18.

128. Peck, *Our Country*, 169–86. See also L. Grant to Peck, Nov. 1, 1864, George Peck Papers, Special Collections Research Center, Syracuse University.

129. "A Speech for Mr. Lincoln," *Star of the North* (Bloomsburg, Pa.), June 29, 1864; "Comparing Mr. Lincoln to the Saviour of the World," *Ohio Statesman* (Columbus), Aug. 15, 1864.

130. "Our Ministers Outspoken," *Jeffersonian Democrat* (Chardon, Ohio), Sept. 16, 1864.

131. "The Mission of the War: An Address Delivered in New York, New York, on 13 January 1864," in Douglass, *Papers*, 4:21, 23.

132. *Grand Lincoln and Johnson Ratification Meeting, at Washington City, D.C., June 15, 1864*, 8. Cf. Thompson, *Peace Through Victory*, 14. An Ohio Baptist feared for the future of "law, morality, and all that is sacred or worth preserving." "Our Ministers Outspoken," *Jeffersonian Democrat* (Chardon, Ohio), Sept. 16, 1864.

133. "The Ides of November," *Central Christian Advocate* (St. Louis), Oct. 26, 1864.

134. "Washington Correspondence," *Christian Recorder*, July 9, 1864; "New Haven Correspondence," *Christian Recorder*, Aug. 27, 1864; "From

Our New England Corresponding Editor" and "Brooklyn Correspondence," *Christian Recorder*, Sept. 10, 1864; "The Election," *Christian Recorder*, Oct. 15, 1864; "Louisville Correspondence," *Christian Recorder*, Nov. 5, 1864.

135. E. Plattenburg to P. D. Plattenburg, Oct. 31–Nov. 6, 1864, Ellen Plattenburg Letters, ALPL.

136. Smith, *No Party Now*, 10–15, 67–72, 80–84, 135–38, 148; Brodrecht, *Our Country*, 55–62.

137. Haven, "End Near," 479–82.

138. Mears, *Life of Edward Norris Kirk*, 305–10.

139. Crooks, *Life of Bishop Matthew Simpson of the Methodist Episcopal Church*, 370–86; Clark, *Life of Matthew Simpson*, 221–44; "Young Men's Christian Association," *New York Herald*, Nov. 4, 1864. Only the *New-York Tribune* carried a full report, on November 7.

140. Haven, "End Near," 479–82; "How to Make a Great Campaign Meeting," *Independent*, Oct. 20, 1864; "The Hour," *Independent*, Oct. 27, 1864.

141. Van Dyke, *Spirituality and Independence of the Church*. For a High Church Episcopalian's bristling over "worshippers carrying their mass meetings straight through Sunday, and invading the very Sanctuary with their unhallowed applause," see Ewer, *Protest Against Political Preaching*, 22.

142. "Democratic Explanation of the Maine Election," *Boston Daily Advertiser*, Sept. 15, 1864.

143. *Ashland (Ohio) Union*, Aug. 17, 1864, 3; "A Talk with Abraham Lincoln," *Independent*, Sept. 8, 1864; *Bedford (Pa.) Inquirer*, Sept. 9, 1864; "Gulliver and Lincoln," *Dayton Daily Empire*, Sept. 8, 1864.

144. Thompson, *Peace Through Victory*, 14; "The Two Candidates," *Independent*, Nov. 3, 1864. "Preachers who boast that they never preach politics, are generally the pliant tools of the meanest, most unscrupulous, most traitorous class of politicians," sniffed Benjamin Crary. "Preaching Politics," *Central Christian Advocate*, July 13, 1864.

145. J. Wilson et al. to AL, Nov. 8, 1864, ALP.

146. Varon, *Armies of Deliverance*, 372–73; White, *Emancipation, the Union Army, and the Reelection of Abraham Lincoln*, 98–128; Frank, *With Ballot and Bayonet*, 84–118; Manning, *What This Cruel War Was Over*, 182–86.

147. "The Rescue of the Republic!," *Independent*, Nov. 10, 1864.

148. H. C. Bowen to AL, Nov. 10, 1864, ALP. See also Carlton Chase to AL, Nov. 11, 1864, ALP. With newfound confidence in the president, Tilton told him, "The people are with you now as never before." Tilton to AL, Nov. 12, 1864, ALP.

504 Notes for pages 357–361

149. Farwell to AL, Nov. 12, 1864; T. K. Earle (Worcester, Mass.) to AL, Nov. 10, 1864, ALP.

150. Wilson to AL, Nov. 14, 1864; R. A. Beck to AL, Nov.–Dec. 1864, ALP.

151. *CW*, 8:100–101 (Response to a Serenade, Nov. 10, 1864).

152. "The Final Test of Self-Government: An Address Delivered in Rochester, New York, on 13 November 1864," in Douglass, *Papers*, 4:33–35.

153. *CAJ*, Nov. 17, 1864.

154. "The Bellefonte Meeting and Its Apostles," *Clearfield (Pa.) Republican*, Nov. 2, 1864; "Our Ministers Outspoken," *Jeffersonian Democrat* (Chardon, Ohio), Sept. 16, 1864.

155. "Lincoln Endorsed by the 'Ballot Box,'" *NYFJCR*, Nov. 19, 1864.

156. For Lincoln's grounds for confidence in Friends' support, see Gurney to AL [with endorsement by Lincoln], Sept. 8, 1864; Benjamin Tatham to Isaac Newton [with endorsement by Lincoln], Oct. 28, 1864, ALP.

157. "Henry Ward Beecher's Thanksgiving Sermon," *Burlington (Iowa) Weekly Hawk-Eye*, Dec. 3, 1864.

158. Vorenberg, *Final Freedom*, 174–75.

159. "Chicago Synod—Old School Presbyterian," *NWCA*, Nov. 2, 1864; Van Dyke, *Spirituality and Independence of the Church*, 7.

160. "The Late Election—Its Lessons," *CAJ*, Nov. 24, 1864.

161. "Brooklyn Correspondence," *Christian Recorder*, Nov. 26, 1864.

162. Thornbrough and Corpuz, *Diary of Calvin Fletcher*, 8:471 (Nov. 12, 1864).

163. "The Farmer's Vote," *NWCA*, Nov. 23, 1864; "Reasons for Thanksgiving," *Independent*, Nov. 17, 1864. See also Thornbrough and Corpuz, *Diary of Calvin Fletcher*, 8:471.

164. "New York Correspondence," *Catholic Telegraph*, Aug. 17, 1864; "Catholicity Opposed to Disloyalty," *Catholic Telegraph*, Sept. 21, 1864; "Memphis Correspondence," *Catholic Telegraph*, Oct. 5, 1864; "New York Correspondence," *Catholic Telegraph*, Oct. 12, 1864.

165. Editorial, *Catholic Telegraph*, Sept. 21, 1864; "What Is a Copperhead," *Catholic Telegraph*, Sept. 28, 1864; "An Analytical Politician," *Catholic Telegraph*, Oct. 5, 1864.

166. "Maryland a Free State," *Catholic Telegraph*, Nov. 2, 1864.

167. Herman to AL, Sept. 22, 1864, ALP.

168. Sarna and Shapell, *Lincoln and the Jews*, 112–18.

169. "A Lincoln Organ Attacking Hebrews," *Dayton Daily Empire*, Sept. 17, 1864, quoting the *Newburg Journal*.

Notes for pages 361–365   505

170. Sarna and Shapell, *Lincoln and the Jews*, 178–82; Lewis to AL, Oct. 26, 1864, Isaacs to AL, Oct. 26, 1864, ALP.

171. *CW*, 8:56 (Proclamation of Thanksgiving, Oct. 20, 1864).

172. "Thanksgiving," *New York Times*, Nov. 25, 1864; "Letter from Washington," *Cleveland Morning Leader*, Nov. 29, 1864; "Thanksgiving in Chicago," *Chicago Tribune*, Nov. 26, 1864.

173. Kinsley, *Diary of a Christian Soldier*, 168.

174. "Thanksgiving Discourse," *Alleghanian* (Ebensburg, Pa.), Dec. 8, 1864.

175. Edgar, *God's Help, the Ground of Hope for Our Country*, 18; De Normandie, *Christian Peace*, 10–11; Gibson, *Revolt of Absalom*, 11–15; Vincent, *Lord of War and of Righteousness*; Stebbins, *The President, the People, and the War*; Little, *Relation of the Citizen to the Government*.

176. "Thanksgiving," *Christian Recorder*, Dec. 3, 1864 (Rev. Anthony L. Stanford); Vinton, *Cause for Thanksgiving*, 7–8, 22–23. In his own slant on Confederate "corner-stone theology," Connecticut's Lavalette Perrin rejoiced that a sovereign people had "lifted their hands to Heaven, and said before God and the nations: '*Liberty first; peace next; war if it must be; disunion never. We . . . will give everything for the defence and maintainance of that great and sacred principle, placed by our fathers as the chief corner stone in their temple of liberty.*'" Perrin, "*Our Part in the World's Struggle*," 23–24.

177. Corneille, *Thanksgiving Sermon*, 11–12.

178. Wadsworth, *War a Discipline*, 17; Wells, *Sacrifice of Continual Praise*, 11.

179. Perrin, "*Our Part in the World's Struggle*," 12.

180. Dunning, *Strangeness of God's Ways*, 12.

181. Smith, *Past Mercies, Present Gratitude, Future Duty*, 13.

182. "Thanksgiving Discourse," *Alleghanian* (Ebensburg, Pa.), Dec. 8, 1864; "A Patriotic Prelate," *Chicago Tribune*, Nov. 26, 1864.

183. "Thanksgiving Days," *Dayton Daily Empire*, Nov. 26, 1864.

184. "A 'Fast' Thanksgiving," *Bedford (Pa.) Inquirer*, Dec. 2, 1864.

185. "Thanksgiving," *New York Times*, Nov. 25, 1864.

186. Ibid.

187. Ibid.; Tyng, *Record of the Life and Work of the Rev. Stephen Higginson Tyng*, 355–63; Vinton, *Cause for Thanksgiving*, 22–24. See also Wells, *Sacrifice of Continual Praise*, 23–24. Thomas Stockton's sermon *Influence of the United States on Christendom* was not a thanksgiving address, but its theme—the accelerated triumph of Christianity worldwide—was anchored in the millennialism common to so much of the thanksgiving rhetoric.

506 *Notes for pages 365–375*

188. Dunning, *Manual of the Congregational Church at Gloversville, N.Y.*, 28–29.
189. Dunning, *Strangeness of God's Ways*, 5–8.
190. Ibid., 8–12.

CHAPTER 10   EMANCIPATION AND PROVIDENCE

1. "New Issues," *NWCA*, Dec. 7, 1864.
2. *CW*, 8:149, 152 (Annual Message to Congress, Dec. 6, 1864).
3. *Independent*, Dec. 8, 1864; "The President's Message," *CAJ*, Dec. 15, 1864; "Celebration of the Emancipation Proclamation, Chester, Illinois," *Christian Recorder*, Jan. 28, 1865.
4. Garrison to AL, Jan. 21, 1865, Robert H. McCurdy to AL, Dec. 12, 1864, ALP. "It has benn said that man proposes but God disposis, how true it was in your cases," an upstate abolitionist farmer wrote. "Our Heavenly Father has herd the Prayers of Holy Men and womin in Your behalf. . . . I Pray that the day may not be far distant when the Rebbel Prissions Shal be forced and our Prissioners Set free, and not a Slave be found in these United States." Leonard Crocker to AL, Jan. 1, 1865, ALP.
5. Knapp to AL, Dec. 15, 1864, ALP. She gave Congressman James M. Marvin her letter to deliver to Lincoln personally.
6. Varon, *Armies of Deliverance*, 392; Samito, *Lincoln and the Thirteenth Amendment*, 93–102; Vorenberg, *Final Freedom*, 180–85.
7. Howard, *Religion and the Radical Republican Movement*, 92.
8. Vorenberg, *Final Freedom*, 197–210.
9. Ibid., 207–8; "The Constitutional Amendment Abolishing Slavery Passed Congress," *Catholic Telegraph*, Feb. 8, 1865; Howard, *Religion and the Radical Republican Movement*, 92–93.
10. "The Constitutional Amendment," *Zion's Herald*, Feb. 8, 1865.
11. "Laus Deo!," *Independent*, Feb. 9, 1865.
12. "Freedom Triumphant," *CAJ*, Feb. 9, 1865.
13. "Anti-slavery Amendment to the Constitution," *Metropolitan Record*, Feb. 11, 1865.
14. "Barnum, Shoddy, and New York," *NYFJCR*, March 11, 1865.
15. Boston *Pilot*, Dec. 17, 1864, 4; Boston *Pilot*, Dec. 31, 1864, 4; Boston *Pilot*, Jan. 21, 1865, 2; Boston *Pilot*, Feb. 11, 1865, 4.
16. Daniel, *"Richmond Examiner" During the War*, 213 (Nov. 8, 1864).
17. Levine, *Fall of the House of Dixie*, 254–55.
18. Ibid., 250–59; Varon, *Armies of Deliverance*, 390–91.

Notes for pages 375–380   507

19. Dunning, *Strangeness of God's Ways*, 13.
20. Wells, *Sacrifice of Continual Praise*, 24–25.
21. "Slavery's Last Hours," *Independent*, March 2, 1865.
22. "Proclamation by the President," *Opelousas (La.) Courier*, March 4, 1865.
23. Stout and Grasso, "Civil War, Religion, and Communications," 318–21.
24. Rable, *God's Almost Chosen Peoples*, 82.
25. Silver, *Confederate Morale and Church Propaganda*, 65.
26. Woodward, *Mary Chesnut's Civil War*, 505.
27. Daniel, *"Richmond Examiner" During the War*, 54 (May 19, 1862).
28. Ibid., 114 (Aug. 24, 1863).
29. Genovese, *Consuming Fire*, 53 (Sept. 1862).
30. Ibid., 58 (Isaac Taylor Tichenor, 1863).
31. Ibid., 56 (*Southern Presbyterian Review*, 1863).
32. Myers, *Children of Pride*, 1244 (Jan. 11, 1865).
33. "From yesterday's Evening Edition," Richmond *Whig*, Feb. 23, 1865; "Fast Day," *Daily Confederate* (Raleigh, N.C.), March 10, 1865.
34. Stout and Grasso, "Civil War, Religion, and Communications," 345 (quoting the *Religious Herald*).
35. "Fast Day," *Western Democrat* (Charlotte, N.C.), March 14, 1865. During the final year of the war, the letters of Private Christian M. Epperly of the Fifty-Fourth Virginia Volunteers, a discontented and devout infantryman, testify to a belief that a righteous God was punishing a wicked South. "Ma[y] God show us our erro[r]s and put us in the rite way and Bring us Back [our] old union again." C. M. Epperly to Mary Epperly, Feb. 21, March 5, 25 (quotation), June 15, Oct. 16, Nov. 2, Dec. 4, 1864, Feb. 5, March 24, 1865, Epperly Correspondence, Gilder Lehrman Collection, New York.
36. See, for example, "Jeff Davis' Fast," *Daily Green Mountain Freeman* (Montpelier, Vt.), May 10, 1862; "The Situation," *New York Herald*, May 24, 1862; "Jeff Davis Appoints Another Fast Day," *Evansville (Ind.) Journal*, Sept. 11, 1862; "Jeff. Davis Orders Fasting and Prayer," *Cleveland Morning Leader*, March 4, 1863; "Jeff. Davis' 'Fast Day,'" *Morgantown (W. Va.) Monitor*, March 28, 1863.
37. "The Confederates in Trouble!," *American Citizen* (Butler, Pa.), March 8, 1865.
38. "The Richmond Whig on Fasting," *Chicago Tribune*, March 1, 1865.
39. "Rebels in Sackcloth," *Kenosha (Wis.) Telegraph*, March 2, 1865.
40. The day was celebrated by civic events throughout the Union, to

508 *Notes for pages 380–388*

mark both military success and the inauguration of Lincoln's second term. "The Fourth of March," *Vermont Transcript* (St. Albans), March 10, 1865.

41. Chambrun, *Impressions of Lincoln and the Civil War,* 39.

42. John Hay, "Life in the White House in the Time of Lincoln," *Century Magazine,* Nov. 1890, 37.

43. Carpenter, *Six Months at the White House,* 234.

44. *CW,* 8:332–33 (Second Inaugural Address, March 4, 1865).

45. White, *Lincoln's Greatest Speech,* 101–2, 119–20, 144, 158–59; Leidner, *Abraham Lincoln and the Bible,* 133–35.

46. E. M. Bruce to AL, Oct. 6, 1863, ALP.

47. AL, Resolution on Slavery (April 1863), ALP.

48. Matthew 18:7.

49. Psalm 19:9.

50. Fehrenbacher and Fehrenbacher, *Recollected Words of Abraham Lincoln,* 232 (John Hay).

51. Achorn, *Every Drop of Blood,* 239.

52. Blight, *Douglass,* 458–60.

53. *CW,* 8:356 (AL to Thurlow Weed, March 15, 1865).

54. "President Lincoln's Inaugural Address," *Independent,* March 9, 1865.

55. "The News," *Chicago Tribune,* March 6, 1865; "The Inaugural," *Jefferson Democrat* (Chardon, Ohio), March 10, 1865; "The Inaugural," *Ellsworth (Maine) American,* March 10, 1865; "The Inaugural," *Caledonian* (St. Johnsbury, Vt.), March 10, 1865; "The Inauguration of Mr. Lincoln," *Cleveland Morning Leader,* March 6, 1865.

56. "Editor's Table," *Old Guard,* April 1865, 134; "President Lincoln's Second Inaugural—the Negro Question," *New York Herald,* March 5, 1865; "President Lincoln's Inaugural—What Does It Mean?," *Metropolitan Record,* March 11, 1865.

57. "The Vice President of the United States," *Cadiz (Ohio) Sentinel,* March 15, 1865; "The Inauguration," *Urbana (Ill.) Union,* March 8, 1865; "Mr. Lincoln's Inaugural," *Weekly Pioneer and Democrat* (St. Paul), March 10, 1865.

58. "President Lincoln's Second Inaugural Address," *Ohio Statesman* (Columbus), March 6, 1865; *Cadiz (Ohio) Sentinel,* March 15, 1865. See also "Now and Then," *McArthur Democrat* (Vinton County, Ohio), March 16, 1865.

59. "Principal and Agent," *Dayton Daily Empire,* March 7, 1865. The editor later criticized the president for taking the name of God in vain. "Profanity," *Dayton Daily Empire,* March 7, 1865.

60. Marble's editorial circulated widely. See, for example, "Mr. Lincoln

Notes for pages 388–392 509

on Providence and the War," *North Branch Democrat* (Tunkhannock, Pa.), March 15, 1865; *Holmes County Farmer* (Millersburg, Ohio), March 16, 1865.

61. "Mr. Lincoln's Inaugural" and "Historical Analogy of the Malignancy of Puritan Legislation, or Resemblance between the Virulent Spirit of Puritan Law-making in England and America," *Metropolitan Record*, March 18, 1865.

62. Alford, *Fortune's Fool*, 257.

63. "The Situation" and "A Mourning City," *New York Herald*, April 17, 1865.

64. "Honors to the Illustrious Dead," *Evansville (Ind.) Journal*, April 21, 1865. For the unique, complex, and evolving reaction of the American public to Lincoln's assassination, see esp. Hodes, *Mourning Lincoln*. See also Harris, *Lincoln's Last Months*, 218–46; Chesebrough, *No Sorrow Like Our Sorrow*; Turner, *Beware the People Weeping*; Scott, *Visitation of God*, 245–64; Rable, *God's Almost Chosen Peoples*, 376–87; Stout, *Upon the Altar of the Nation*, 448–56.

65. "The Great Overthrow," *Independent*, April 6, 1865; Haven, "Jefferson Davis and Pharoah," in *National Sermons*, 550.

66. Beecher, *Oration*, 33, 46. Cf. "Abraham Lincoln Dead," *Fremont Journal* (Sandusky County, Ohio), April 21, 1865.

67. "Movements of the Funeral Train," *Ohio Statesman* (Columbus), April 25, 1865; "Abraham Lincoln," *Cleveland Morning Leader*, April 17, 1865; Quint, "What President Lincoln Did for His Country," in *Three Sermons*, 17–18; Beecher, *Oration*, 46; Joseph A. Seiss, *The Assassinated President; or, The Day of National Mourning for Abraham Lincoln* (Philadelphia, 1865), 11–43.

68. "Assassination of President Lincoln," Boston *Pilot*, April 22, 1865; "The Lesson of the Bereavement," Boston *Pilot*, April 29, 1865. See, likewise, Mullaly tribute, "The Assassination of President Lincoln," *Metropolitan Record*, April 22, 1865.

69. "The Nation Still Mourns," *Jeffersonian* (Stroudsburg, Pa.), April 27, 1865. Cf. "President Andrew Johnson," *New York Herald*, April 17, 1865.

70. "Assassination of the President," *NYFJCR*, April 22, 1865; W. Krauss to W. C. J. Krauss, April 16, 1865, Krauss Papers, HL.

71. "Assassination of the President," *NYFJCR*, April 22, 1865. See also "The Late Assassination," *Metropolitan Record*, April 29, 1865; "Death of the President," *Old Guard*, May 1865, 240.

72. "April Fourteenth and Fifteenth, 1865," *Dayton Daily Empire*, April 15, 1865; "The Assassination of the President," *Ohio Statesman*

510   *Notes for pages 392–394*

(Columbus), April 17, 1865; "The Churches," *Cleveland Daily Herald*, April 17, 1865.

73. "Honors to the Illustrious Dead," *Evansville (Ind.) Journal*, April 21, 1865. See also Mayo, *Nation's Sacrifice*; Simpson, *Funeral Address*, 16; Vincent, *Sermon on the Assassination of Abraham Lincoln*, 24–25. See also Guyatt, *Providence and the Invention of the United States*, 295–96.

74. "The Death of President Lincoln," *Burlington (Iowa) Weekly Hawk-Eye*, April 22, 1865; "Death of President Lincoln," *CAJ*, April 20, 1865; Hodes, *Mourning Lincoln*, 106.

75. "A Nation in Tears!," *Bangor (Maine) Daily Whig and Courier*, April 17, 1865; "Fiendish Assassination," *Presbyterian*, April 22, 1865.

76. Hawley, *Truth and Righteousness Triumphant*, 5, 7–8, 12–14. Cf. Babcock, *Discourse on the Death of President Lincoln*, 11.

77. "Obsequies of the Late President Lincoln," *Dayton Daily Empire*, April 19, 1865; "The Lesson of the Bereavement," Boston *Pilot*, April 29, 1865.

78. "The Death of President Lincoln," *Burlington (Iowa) Weekly Hawk-Eye*, April 22, 1865. Cf. Vincent, *Sermon on the Assassination of Abraham Lincoln*, 34; Chesebrough, *No Sorrow Like Our Sorrow*, 68–69.

79. "Public Meeting Held on the Green Saturday," *New Haven Palladium*, April 17, 1865; Hawley, *Truth and Righteousness Triumphant*, 15. Cf. Simpson, *Funeral Address*, 17–18.

80. Blight, *Douglass*, 460.

81. "Our Domestic Correspondence," *Christian Recorder*, April 22, 1865; "Letter from Bloomington," *Christian Recorder*, April 29, 1865.

82. "Meeting of the South Carolina Conference," *Christian Recorder*, June 3, 1865. See also Hodes, *Mourning Lincoln*, 65–66, 91; Wesley, *Politics of Faith*, 168–93.

83. Vincent, *Sermon on the Assassination of Abraham Lincoln*, 10–15. The seeds of slavery, a Maryland editor grieved, had yielded a bloody harvest: "Treason, Rebellion, Assassination! Lincoln is sleeping in his bloody shroud—the victim of Slavery—a Martyr for Freedom and free institutions." "The Lesson," *Cecil Whig* (Elkton, Md.), April 22, 1865. William Patton, minister at New Haven, asked, "Who did this deed? Who marshalled the large armies of rebellion? Who, with fiendish barbarity, sabered and bayoneted our soldiers after they had surrendered? Who, with unrelenting cruelty, murdered sixty thousand of our braves by the slow agonies of starvation? The same hand struck this foul blow." "Public Meeting Held on the Green Saturday," *New Haven Palladium*, April 17, 1865.

84. "The Death of President Lincoln," *Burlington (Iowa) Weekly Hawk-Eye*, April 22, 1865; Quint, "Southern Chivalry, and What the Nation Ought to Do with It," in *Three Sermons*, 34–37; "What Shall Be the Retribution?," *Independent*, April 27, 1865; Blight, *Douglass*, 460.

85. Leonard F. Smith, Diary, April 15, 1865, ALPL; Haven, "The Uniter and Liberator of America," in *National Sermons*, 572.

86. John B. Burrud to Ocena N. Burrud, April 19, May 5–8, 18, 1865, Burrud Papers, HL.

87. "Public Meeting Held on the Green Saturday," *New Haven Palladium*, April 17, 1865.

88. Hodes, *Mourning Lincoln*, 109, 128–36; Harris, *Lincoln's Last Months*, 230–31; Scott, *Visitation of God*, 250–52; McPherson, *Struggle for Equality*, 315–16.

89. Edwards, *Life and Character of Abraham Lincoln*, 7.

90. "Honors to the Illustrious Dead," *Evansville (Ind.) Journal*, April 21, 1865.

91. *Our Martyr President*, 298, 301, 336. See also Vincent, *Sermon on the Assassination of Abraham Lincoln*, 35–38; "The Death of Abraham Lincoln," *Zion's Herald*, April 26, 1865; Burgess, *Life and Character of Abraham Lincoln*, 9.

92. Robert Hamilton, "Thy Will Be Done," *Anglo-African* (New York), April 22, 1865, in Hord and Norman, *Knowing Him by Heart*, 160–62.

93. Edwards, *Life and Character of Abraham Lincoln*, 8; Quint, "Southern Chivalry, and What the Nation Ought to Do with It," 42–44. See also, among many examples, Loring, *Present Crisis*, 5; "The Death of Abraham Lincoln," *Zion's Herald*, April 26, 1865; Mayo, *Nation's Sacrifice*, 12; Chester, *Lesson of the Hour.*

94. "If we comprehend the ethics of the New Testament," Tilton ended a forceful editorial, "we believe that to the severest utterances which he has made since his Presidential oath, the voice of Christian charity answers, Amen." "What Shall Be the Retribution?," *Independent*, April 27, 1865.

95. "A Great Public Calamity," *Dayton Daily Empire*, April 15, 1865; "Death of the President," *Old Guard*, April 1865; "The Assassination of President Lincoln," *Metropolitan Record*, April 22, 1865.

96. "Assassination of the President," *NYFJCR*, April 22, 1865. The country had lost "the pilot from whose skill and faithfulness we had much to hope" as a brake on vindictive radicals; "he had been learning and all of our hearts were turning to him." "April Fourteenth and Fifteenth, 1865," *Dayton Daily Empire*, April 15, 1865.

512 *Notes for pages 397–405*

97. "The Assassination of the President," *Ohio Statesman* (Columbus), April 17, 1865.

98. "The Country's Calamity," *Ohio Statesman* (Columbus), April 22, 1865; "Our Washington Correspondence," *Metropolitan Record*, April 29, 1865.

99. Turner, *Beware the People Weeping*, 90–99.

100. *The War of the Rebellion*, ser. 1, vol. 46, pt. 3, Correspondence: Section 2, 787; "The Late Assassination," *Metropolitan Record*, April 29, 1865.

101. C. S. Jones to M. Jones, April 30, 1865, in Myers, *Children of Pride*, 1268.

102. Haven, "Uniter and Liberator of America," 573–79.

103. Ibid.; "The Death of President Lincoln," *Burlington (Iowa) Weekly Hawk-Eye*, April 22, 1865.

104. "The Nation Still Mourns," *Jeffersonian* (Stroudsburg, Pa.), April 27, 1865; Chester, *Lesson of the Hour*, 16.

105. Haven, "Uniter and Liberator of America," 574–75.

106. Chamberlain, *Assassination of President Lincoln*, 10.

107. *Anglo-American*, April 22, 1865, in Hord and Norman, *Knowing Him by Heart*, 164–66.

108. Boardman, *Addresses Delivered in the Meeting-House of the First Baptist Church of Philadelphia*, 44–45. Cf. Swain, *Nation's Sorrow*, 11; *Our Martyr President*, 246.

109. Quint, *Three Sermons*, 29–30; Chesebrough, *No Sorrow Like Our Sorrow*, 88; Wayland and Wayland, *Memoir of the Life and Labors of Francis Wayland*, 2:274.

110. Quint, *Three Sermons*, 32.

EPILOGUE

1. Brodrecht, *Our Country*, 94–95.

2. Gravely, *Gilbert Haven, Methodist Abolitionist*, 110–57; Brodrecht, *Our Country*, 104; Howard, *Religion and the Radical Republican Movement*, 104–5; McPherson, *Struggle for Equality*, 339.

3. Brodrecht, *Our Country*, 100; Hodge, "President Lincoln," *BRPR* 37, no. 3 (July 1865): 50–56.

4. Howard, *Religion and the Radical Republican Movement*, 117–18.

5. Trefousse, *Andrew Johnson*, 263; Hodge, "Diversity of Species in the Human Race"; Hodge, "President Lincoln," 456–57, 486; C. Hodge to H. L. Hodge, Oct. 3, 1866, May 12, 19, 1868, CHP; Howard, *Religion and the Radical Republican Movement*, 128–64.

Notes for pages 406–411 513

6. Brodrecht, *Our Country*, 150.

7. Ibid., 158–62.

8. Ibid., 150; Hodge, *Life of Charles Hodge*, 491–98; Hodge, "Princeton Review on the State of the Country and of the Church," 651–55; Charles Hodge, "The General Assembly [1865]," 496–514; J. C. Backus to C. Hodge, June 28, 1866, CHMC; Harlow, *Religion, Race, and the Making of Confederate Kentucky*, 193.

9. McPherson, *Abolitionist Legacy*, 33–34, 81–91.

10. Ibid., 87–91; Blight, *Douglass*, 582–83.

11. McPherson, *Abolitionist Legacy*, 95–106; Arrington, *The Last Lincoln Republican: The Presidential Election of 1880*.

12. Cook, *Three Despised Races in the United States*, 17–18.

13. Turner, *Without God, Without Creed*, 171–261.

14. McPherson, *Abolitionist Legacy*, 25, 28–29, 54–55, 67–80; Brodrecht, *Our Country*, 155–56, 162–68.

15. Quist, "Theodore Foster: A Liberty Party Abolitionist" tracks the evolution of an antebellum abolitionist's thinking, as scientific racism and anthropological writing on Africa and Africans encouraged doubts about the intellectual capacity of emancipated people. See also Foner, *Reconstruction*, 228–80, esp. 230–31.

16. Gravely, *Gilbert Haven, Methodist Abolitionist*, 173–76; McPherson, *Abolitionist Legacy*, 385–93.

17. Nagel, *This Sacred Trust*, 251–52.

18. McPherson, *Abolitionist Legacy*, 324–32; Ahlstrom, *Religious History of the American People*, 877–80; Hutchinson, *Errand to the World*, 91–124.

19. For an incisive analysis of the expansive historiography of Civil War memory, see Robert Cook, "The Quarrel Forgotten? Toward a Clearer Understanding of Sectional Reconciliation." See also Cook, *Civil War Memories: Contesting the Past in the United States Since 1865*.

20. Blight, *Race and Reunion*, 217–20.

21. Cook, "Quarrel Forgotten?," 426–31 (quotation p. 431).

22. Stowell, *Rebuilding Zion*, 65–99; Harper, *End of Days*, esp. 1–44, 163–68. Hildebrand, *Times Were Strange and Stirring*, contrasts the appetite for politics among the leaders of the African Methodist Episcopal Church and African Methodist Episcopal Church Zion with the more politically inactive Colored Methodist Episcopal Church.

Bibliography

PRIMARY SOURCES

Manuscripts

Abraham Lincoln Presidential Library, Springfield, Illinois

N. W. Miner Papers
Ellen Plattenburg Letters
Leonard F. Smith, Diary

United Methodist Archives and History Center, Drew University, Madison, N.J.

Albert S. Hunt Diary
John McClintock Papers
Sterling Y. McMaster Papers
Matthew Simpson Papers

Garrett-Evangelical Theological Seminary Styberg Library, Evanston, Illinois

John Dempster Papers
Thomas Mears Eddy Papers
Frances Dana Hemenway Papers
Daniel Parish Kidder Papers

Gilder Lehrman Collection, The Gilder Lehrman Institute of American History, New York

Collection of Christian Epperly

516   *Bibliography*

Collection of Joseph Jones
Collection of Lysander Wheeler

Historical Society of Pennsylvania

James Buchanan Papers

Huntington Library, San Marino, California

Abell Family Collection
Zina Baker Huntington Family Letters
Samuel L. M. Barlow Papers
John D. Barnes Memoir
John B. Burrud Papers
Cave Johnson Couts Papers
Krauss Papers
George S. Phillips Papers

Library of Congress

Thomas Jefferson Papers
Abraham Lincoln Papers
Matthew Simpson Papers

New-York Historical Society

George Templeton Strong Diary (online)

Presbyterian Historical Society, Philadelphia

Phineas Densmore Gurley Papers
   (online)

Princeton Theological Seminary Library

Charles Hodge Manuscript Collection

Princeton University Library, Manuscripts Division

Charles Hodge Papers

Bibliography

Southern Historical Collection, University of North Carolina, Chapel Hill

Iveson L. Brookes Papers
James K. Stringfield Diary

Syracuse University Special Collections Center

John Margetts Bull Papers
George Peck Papers

Wheaton College

Jonathan Blanchard Papers

CONTEMPORARY PERIODICALS

Arminian Magazine (London)
Biblical Recorder (Raleigh, N.C.)
Biblical Repertory and Princeton Review
Boston *Pilot*
Catholic Telegraph (Cincinnati)
Christian
Christian Advocate and Journal (New York)
Christian Index (Georgia)
Christian Inquirer (New York)
Christian Recorder (Philadelphia)
Christian Times (Chicago)
Connecticut Evangelical Magazine (Hartford)
Danville Quarterly Review
Evangelical and Literary Magazine and Missionary Chronicle
    (Richmond, Va.)
Frank Leslie's Illustrated Newspaper (New York)
Gospel Messenger and Southern Episcopal Register (Charleston, S.C.)
Harper's Weekly (New York)
Home Missionary (New York)
Independent (New York)
Liberator (Boston)
Literary and Evangelical Magazine (Richmond, Va.)
Metropolitan Record (New York)
National Anti-slavery Standard (New York)
New York Evangelist

518 *Bibliography*

New-York Freeman's Journal and Catholic Register
New-York Observer
North Carolina Presbyterian (Fayetteville, N.C.)
Northwestern Christian Advocate (Evanston, Ill.)
Oberlin Evangelist
Old Guard (New York)
Pittsburgh Christian Advocate
Presbyterian
Primitive Baptist (Tarborough, N.C.)
Religious Intelligencer (New Haven, Conn.)
Religious Monitor and Evangelical Repository (Philadelphia)
Southern Christian Advocate (Charleston, S.C.)
Spirit of the Pilgrims (Boston)
Trumpet and Universalist Magazine (Boston)
Western Christian Advocate (Cincinnati)
Western Luminary (Rochester, N.Y.)
Western Recorder (Utica, N.Y.)
Zion's Herald (Boston)

NEWSPAPERS

Albany Argus
Albany Evening Journal
Alleghanian (Ebensburg, Pa.)
American Citizen (Butler County, Pa.)
Bangor (Maine) Daily Whig and Courier
Bellows Falls (Vt.) Times
Boston Daily Advertiser
Boston Investigator
Bradford Reporter (Towanda, Pa.)
Buchanan County Guardian (Independence, Iowa)
Burlington (Iowa) Weekly Hawk-Eye
Cadiz (Ohio) Sentinel
Cecil Whig (Elkton, Md.)
Chicago Tribune
Cincinnati Daily Press
Clarksville (Tenn.) Chronicle
Cleveland Herald
Cleveland Morning Leader
Coles County (Ill.) Ledger
Davenport (Iowa) Democrat and News

Bibliography

Dayton Daily Empire
Delaware State Journal and Statesman (Wilmington)
Deseret News (Salt Lake City)
Ebensburg (Pa.) Democrat and Sentinel
Ellsworth (Maine) American
Emporia (Kans.) News
Evansville (Ind.) Journal
Farmers Cabinet (Amherst, N.H.)
Fremont (Ohio) Journal
Galena (Ill.) Daily Courier
Green Mountain Freeman (Montpelier, Vt.)
Hancock Jeffersonian (Findlay, Ohio)
Highland Weekly News (Hillsborough, Ohio)
Holmes County (Ohio) Farmer
Illinois State Journal (Springfield)
Indiana State Sentinel (Indianapolis)
Iowa Transcript (Toledo)
Jefferson (Ohio) Democrat
Kenosha (Wis.) Telegraph
Keokuk (Iowa) Daily Gate City
Knoxville Whig
Lamoille Newsdealer (Hyde Park, Vt.)
Lowell Daily Citizen and News
Macomb (Ill.) Journal
McArthur (Ohio) Democrat
Mineral Point Weekly Tribune (Wis.)
Morgantown (W. Va.) Monitor
Morning Chronicle (Washington, D.C.)
Muscatine (Iowa) Weekly Journal
Nashville Union
National Intelligencer (Washington, D.C.)
National Republican (Washington, D.C.)
Nevada (Calif.) Journal
Newark (Ohio) Advocate
New Hampshire Statesman (Concord)
New Haven Palladium
New York Herald
New York Times
New-York Tribune
North-Carolina Standard (Raleigh)
Ohio State Journal (Columbus)

520   *Bibliography*

Ohio Statesman (Columbus)
Opelousas (La.) Courier
Ottawa Free Trader (Ill.)
Oxford Democrat (Paris, Maine)
Philadelphia Inquirer
Philadelphia North American
Placer (Calif.) Herald
Pomeroy (Ohio) Weekly Telegraph
Potter Journal (Coudersport, Pa.)
Raftsman's Journal (Clearfield, Pa.)
Raleigh (N.C.) Confederate
Randolph County (Ind.) Journal
Richmond (Va.) Dispatch
Richmond (Va.) Enquirer
Richmond (Ind.) Palladium
San Francisco Evening Bulletin
Sioux City Register
Star of the North (Bloomsburg, Pa.)
St. Cloud (Minn.) Democrat
St. Johnsbury (Vt.) Caledonian
St. Paul Weekly Minnesotian
St. Paul Weekly Pioneer and Democrat
Sugar Planter (West Baton Rouge, La.)
Vermont Patriot and State Gazette (Montpelier)
Vermont Transcript (St. Albans)
Vermont Watchman and State Journal (Montpelier)
Wabash (Ind.) Express
Washington Evening Star
Watertown (Wis.) Republican
Weekly Butte Record (Oroville, Calif.)
Weekly North Iowa Times (McGregor)
Western Democrat (Charlotte, N.C.)
Western Reserve Chronicle (Warren, Ohio)
West-Jersey Pioneer (Bridgeton, N.J.)
Wheeling Daily Intelligencer

BOOKS, TRACTS, BROADSIDES, SERMONS, AND CHURCH MINUTES

Abbott, Jacob. *A Sermon, Preached on the National Fast, May 14, 1841: Occasioned by the Death of William Henry Harrison.* Salem, Mass., 1841.

Bibliography

The Abolition Conspiracy to Destroy the Union; or, A Ten Years' Record of the "Republican" Party: The Opinions of William Lloyd Garrison, Wendell Phillips, Abraham Lincoln, William H. Seward, Salmon P. Chase, Horace Greeley. New York, 1863.

Abraham Africanus I: His Secret Life, as Revealed Under the Mesmeric Influence. Mysteries of the White House. New York, 1864.

Adams, E. E. *The Temple and the Throne; or, The True Foundations: A Sermon Preached in the North Broad Street Presbyterian Church, September 26th, 1861.* Philadelphia, 1861.

Adams, William. *Prayer for Rulers; or, Duty of Christian Patriots: A Discourse Preached in the Madison Square Presbyterian Church, New York, on the Day of the National Fast, January 4, 1861.* New York, 1861.

Armstrong, George D. *Politics and the Pulpit: A Discourse.* Norfolk, Va., 1856.

Arnold, Isaac N. *The Life of Abraham Lincoln.* Chicago, 1884.

Asbury, Francis. *The Journal and Letters of Francis Asbury.* London: Epworth Press, 1958.

Babcock, Samuel B. *A Discourse on the Death of President Lincoln: Preached in the Orthodox Congregational Church, in Dedham.* Dedham, Mass., 1865.

Bacon, Leonard. *A Discourse on the Death of William Henry Harrison, President of the United States: Delivered Before the Citizens of New Haven, on the 17th of April, 1841.* New Haven, Conn., 1841.

———. *Leonard Bacon: Pastor of the First Church in New Haven.* New Haven, Conn., 1882.

Bailey, Silas. *The Moral Significance of War: A Discourse Delivered in the Baptist Meeting House, in Franklin, Indiana, on the Occasion of the National Fast, September 26, 1861.* Indianapolis, 1861.

Baird, Robert. *Religion in America; or, An Account of the Origin, Relation to the State, and Present Condition of the Evangelical Churches in the United States, with Notices of the Unevangelical Denominations.* New York, 1844; rev. ed., New York, 1856.

Baker, A. R. *A Discourse Delivered on the Annual Fast: Before the Associated Evangelical Churches of Ward Twelve in Boston.* Boston, 1864.

Bangs, Nathan. *A History of the Methodist Episcopal Church.* 4 vols. New York, 1840–42.

Baptist Home Missions in North America. New York, 1883.

Barnes, Gilbert H., and Dwight L. Dumond, eds. *Letters of Theodore Dwight Weld, Angelina Grimké Weld, and Sarah Grimké, 1822–1844.* 2 vols. New York: D. Appleton Century, 1934; repr., 1965.

Bates, David. *Lincoln in the Telegraph Office; Recollections of the United States Military Telegraph Corps During the Civil War.* New York: Century, 1907.

522   *Bibliography*

Beecher, Henry Ward. *Oration at the Raising of "The Old Flag" at Sumter; and Sermon on the Death of Abraham Lincoln, President of the United States.* Manchester [U.K.], 1865.

———. "Peace, Be Still: A Sermon Preached at Plymouth Church, Brooklyn, on the Day of the National Fast, January 4, 1861." In *Fast Day Sermons.*

Beecher, Lyman. *The Memory of Our Fathers: A Sermon Delivered at Plymouth, on the Twenty-Second of December, 1827.* Boston, 1828.

Bellows, Henry W. "The Crisis of Our National Disease: A Sermon Preached at All Souls Church, New York, on the Day of the National Fast, January 4, 1861." In *Fast Day Sermons.*

———. *The War to End Only When the Rebellion Ceases.* New York, [1863].

Beman, Nathan S. S. *The Claims of Our Country on Young Men: An Address.* Troy, N.Y., 1843.

Bethune, George W. *Truth the Strength of Freedom: A Discourse on the Duty of a Patriot with Some Allusions to the Life and Death of Andrew Jackson. Pronounced July 6, 1845.* Philadelphia, 1845.

Bittinger, J. B. *A Plea for Humanity: A Sermon Preached in the Euclid Street Presbyterian Church, Cleveland, Ohio.* Cleveland, 1854.

———. *A Sermon, Preached Before the Presbyterian Churches of Cleveland: On the National Fast Day, September 26, 1861.* Cleveland, 1861.

Boardman, George Dana. *Addresses Delivered in the Meeting-House of the First Baptist Church of Philadelphia.* Philadelphia, 1865.

Boardman, Henry A. *A Sermon Occasioned by the Death of William Henry Harrison, the Late President of the United States: Preached on Sunday Morning, April 11, 1841 . . . in the Walnut Street Presbyterian Church, Philadelphia.* Philadelphia, 1841.

Bouton, Nathaniel. *The Good Land in Which We Live: A Discourse Preached at Concord, N.H., on the Day of Public Thanksgiving, November 28, 1850.* Concord, N.H., 1850.

Boynton, Charles Brandon. *Oration Delivered on the Fifth of July, 1847, Before the Native Americans of Cincinnati.* Cincinnati, 1847.

Brainerd, Thomas. *Patriotism Aiding Piety: A Sermon Preached in the Third Presbyterian Church, Philadelphia, on the 30th of April, 1863, the Day Appointed by the President of the United States for Humiliation, Fasting, and Prayer.* Philadelphia, 1863.

Breckinridge, Robert J. *Discourse of Dr. Breckinridge, Delivered on the Day of National Humiliation, January 4, 1861, at Lexington, Ky.* Baltimore, 1861.

———. *Our Country, Its Peril and Its Deliverance: From Advance Sheets of "The Danville Quarterly Review" for March 1861.* Cincinnati, 1861.

Bibliography 523

Breckinridge, W. L. *Submission to the Will of God: A Fast Day Sermon Delivered in the First Presbyterian Church, Louisville, on Friday, May 14th, 1841.* Louisville, 1841.

Brewster, Charles Harvey. *When This Cruel War Is Over: The Civil War Letters of Charles Harvey Brewster.* Edited by David W. Blight. Amherst: University of Massachusetts Press, 1992.

Brookes, Iveson L. *A Defence of Southern Slavery: Against the Reproaches and Incroachments of the North in Which Slavery Is Shown to Be an Institution of God Intended to Form the Basis of the Best Social State and the Only Safeguard to the Permanence of a Republican Government.* Hamburg, S.C., 1851.

———. *A Defence of the South Against the Reproaches and Incroachments of the North: In Which Slavery Is Shown to Be an Institution of God Intended to Form the Basis of the Best Social State and the Only Safeguard to the Permanence of a Republican Government.* Hamburg, S.C., 1850.

———. *A Defence of Southern Slavery Against the Attacks of Henry Clay and Alex'r. Campbell: in which Much of the False Philanthropy and Mawkish Sentimentalism of the Abolitionists is Met and Refuted: in which it is Moreover Shown that the Association of the White and Black Races in the Relation of Master and Slave is the Appointed Order of God, as Set Forth in the Bible, and Constitutes the Best Social Condition of Both Races, and the Only True Principle of Republicanism.*

Brooks, Phillips. *Our Mercies of Re-occupation: A Thanksgiving Sermon, Preached at the Church of the Holy Trinity, Philadelphia, November 26, 1863.* Philadelphia, 1863.

Brown, Aaron V., and Key-Stone Club, Philadelphia. *An Address on the Parties and Issues of the Presidential Election.* Nashville, 1856.

Brownlow, W. G. *Sketches of the Rise, Progress, and Decline of Secession with a Narrative of Personal Adventures Among the Rebels.* Philadelphia, 1862.

———. *Sketch of Parson Brownlow, and His Speeches, at the Academy of Music and Cooper Institute, New York, May, 1862.* New York, 1862.

Brownlow, W. G., and Abram Pryne, *Ought American Slavery to be Perpetuated? A Debate between Rev. W. G. Brownlow and Rev. A. Pryne. Held at Philadelphia, September, 1858.* Philadelphia, 1858.

Brownson, Orestes. *The Works of Orestes A. Brownson: Collected and Arranged by Henry F. Brownson.* Vol. 17. Detroit, 1885.

Brunson, Alfred. *A Western Pioneer; or, Incidents in the Life and Times of Rev. Alfred Brunson, A.M., D.D., Embracing a Period of over Seventy Years.* 2 vols. Cincinnati, 1872.

Buchanan, James. *Mr. Buchanan's Administration on the Eve of the Rebellion.* New York, 1866.

Bucher, T. P. *Union National Fast Day Sermon: Delivered in the United Presbyterian Church, Gettysburg, Pa., Friday, January 4, A.D. 1861.* Gettysburg, Pa., 1861.

Buckingham, Samuel G. *The Life of William A. Buckingham: The War Governor of Connecticut, with a Review of His Public Acts, and Especially the Distinguished Services He Rendered His Country During the War of the Rebellion.* Springfield, Mass., 1894.

Bullard, Artemas. *A Sermon, Preached in the First Presbyterian Church, of Saint Louis, Missouri, on the Death of William Henry Harrison.* St. Louis, 1841.

Bumstead, Samuel A. *The Principles of the Constitution the Test of Loyalty: Discourse Delivered in the Reformed Dutch Church of Raritan, Illinois, November 26th, 1863.* Burlington, Iowa, 1864.

Burgess, Chalon. *The Life and Character of Abraham Lincoln, with Some Lessons from His Death . . . April 30, 1865.* Jamestown, N.Y., 1865.

Burlingame, Michael, ed. *Lincoln Observed: Civil War Dispatches of Noah Brooks.* Baltimore: Johns Hopkins University Press, 1998.

———. *An Oral History of Abraham Lincoln: John G. Nicolay's Interviews and Essays.* Carbondale: Southern Illinois University Press, 1996.

Bushnell, Horace. *The Northern Iron: A Discourse Delivered in the North Church, Hartford, on the Annual State Fast, April 14, 1854.* Hartford, Conn., 1854.

Carey, Isaac E. *God Doing Wonderful Things in Behalf of the Nation: A Discourse; Preached on the National Thanksgiving Day, November 26th, 1863, in the First Presbyterian Church of Freeport, Illinois.* Freeport, Ill., 1863.

Carpenter, F. B. *Six Months at the White House with Abraham Lincoln: The Story of a Picture.* New York, 1866.

Carpenter, S. D. *Logic of History: Five Hundred Political Texts: Being Concentrated Extracts of Abolitionism; Also, Results of Slavery Agitation and Emancipation; Together with Sundry Chapters on Despotism, Usurpations, and Frauds.* 2nd ed. Madison, Wis., 1864.

Cartwright, Peter. *Autobiography of Peter Cartwright: The Backwoods Preacher.* Edited by W. P. Strickland. New York, 1857.

Chamberlain, N. H. *The Assassination of President Lincoln: A Sermon Preached in St. James Church, Birmingham, Ct., April 19th, 1865.* New York, 1865.

Chambré, A. St. John. *The Conditions and Prospects of the Nation: A Sermon Preached in the Parish Church, Stoughton, Mass., on the National Fast Day, August 4, 1864.* Boston, 1864.

Chambrun, Adolphe de Pineton. *Impressions of Lincoln and the Civil War: A Foreigner's Account.* New York: Random House, 1952.

Bibliography

Chaplain, John Francis. *A True Fast: A Fast-Day Sermon, Preached in Wharton Street M.E. Church, Philadelphia, Thursday, April 30th, 1863*. Philadelphia, 1863.

Chester, John. *The Lesson of the Hour: Justice as Well as Mercy, a Discourse Preached on the Sabbath Following the Assassination of the President, in the Capitol Hill Presbyterian Church, Washington, D.C.* Washington, D.C., 1865.

Christy, David. *Pulpit Politics; or, Ecclesiastical Legislation on Slavery in Its Disturbing Influences on the American Union.* Cincinnati, 1863.

Clark, George H. "A Sermon, Delivered in St. John's Church, Savannah, on Fast Day, November 28, 1860." In *Southern Pamphlets on Secession, November 1860–April 1861*. Edited by Jon L. Wakelyn. Chapel Hill: University of North Carolina Press, 1996.

Clark, Rufus W. *The Unity of the American Nationality: A Discourse Delivered in the North Ref. Prot. Dutch Church of Albany, November 26th, 1863, the Day of the National Thanksgiving.* Albany, 1863.

Clarke, James Freeman. *Discourse on the Aspects of the War: Delivered in the Indiana-Place Chapel, Boston, on Fast Day, April 2, 1863.* Boston, 1863.

Cleaveland, Elisha Lord. *Our Duty in Regard to the Rebellion: A Fast Day Sermon Preached in the Third Congregational Church, New Haven, April 3, 1863.* New Haven, Conn., 1863.

Cleveland, Henry. *Alexander H. Stephens in Public and Private.* Philadelphia, 1866.

Clinton, Henry L. *Speech of Henry L. Clinton, of New York, at Patchogue, Long Island, October 1st, 1864.* New York State, 1864.

Cluskey, M. W. *Buchanan and Breckinridge: The Democratic Hand-Book.* Washington, D.C., 1856.

Coles, George. *My First Seven Years in America.* New York, 1852.

Collins, Nathan G. *The Prospect: The Speech of Rev. N. G. Collins, Chaplain of the 57th Illinois, at Corinth, Miss., on the Day of National Thanksgiving, Aug. 3, '63, to the Officers and Men of Col. Bane's Brigade.* Chicago, 1863.

Conant, Sylvanus. *An Anniversary Sermon Preached at Plymouth, December 23, 1776: In Grateful Memory of the First Landing of Our Worthy Ancestors in That Place, An. Dom. 1620.* Boston, 1777.

Conspiracy Disclosed!! Kansas Affairs. Read! Read!! Read!!! Washington, D.C., 1856.

Cook, Joseph. *The Three Despised Races in the United States; or, The Chinaman, the Indian, and the Freedman. An Address.* New York, 1878.

Copperhead Minstrel: A Choice Collection of Democratic Poems and Songs, for the Use of Political Clubs and the Social Circle. New York, 1863; 3rd ed., 1864.

526   *Bibliography*

Corneille, Samuel J. *A Thanksgiving Sermon: Preached in All Saints Church, New York, Thanksgiving Day.* N.p., 1864.

Cornwell, John M. *The Rights and Duties of the American Citizen: An Address Delivered Before the Manchester Democratic Club, July 16, 1863.* Pittsburgh, 1863.

Couch, Paul. *A Sermon, Preached . . . in the First Congregational Church of Stonington, Ct., August 6th, 1863, Being the Day Appointed . . . for National Thanksgiving.* New York, 1863.

Cowan, Thomas P. *Chronicles of the War with Jeff, King of Dixie.* Springfield, Ill., 1864.

Cox, Samuel S. *Eight Years in Congress from 1857–1865: Memoir and Speeches.* New York, 1865.

———. *Puritanism in Politics: Speech of Hon. S. S. Cox, of Ohio, Before the Democratic Union Association, January 13, 1863.* New York, 1863.

Coxe, Arthur Cleveland. *Unjust Reproaches, in Public Calamity, Viewed as Part of the Divine Discipline: A Sermon Preached in Calvary Church on the Day of National Thanksgiving, Nov. 26, 1863.* New York, 1863.

[Croly, David Goodman, and George Wakeman]. *Miscegenation: The Theory of the Blending of the Races, Applied to the American White Man and Negro.* New York, 1864.

Crooks, George R. *The Life of Bishop Matthew Simpson of the Methodist Episcopal Church.* New York, 1890.

Crosby, Howard. *God's View of Rebellion: A Sermon Preached in the Fourth Avenue Presbyterian Church, on the Occasion of the National Thanksgiving, Sunday, Sept. 11, 1864.* New York, 1864.

Curran, R. *A Sermon Preached by Request of the Pastor and Official Board of Wall Street Methodist Episcopal Church, Jeffersonville, Ind., Thursday, Fast Day. August 4, 1864.* Louisville, Ky., 1864.

Daniel, John Moncure, ed. *The "Richmond Examiner" During the War; or, The Writings of John M. Daniel.* New York, 1868.

Davidson, Robert. *A Nation's Discipline; or, Trials Not Judgments: A Discourse Delivered on the National Fast Day, September 26, 1861, in the Spring Street Church, New York.* New York, 1861.

Dawson, John L. *Speech of Hon. John L. Dawson, of Pennsylvania, Delivered at a Democratic Mass Meeting in New Geneva, Fayette County, Pennsylvania, September 1, 1860.* Washington, D.C., 1867.

Dean, Henry Clay. *Crimes of the Civil War and Curse of the Funding System.* Baltimore, 1868.

Dempster, John. *Lectures and Addresses.* Edited by D. W. Clark. Cincinnati, 1864.

De Normandie, James. *Christian Peace: A Discourse Delivered on the Occasion of the National and State Thanksgiving, November 24, 1864.* Portsmouth, N.H., 1864.

Dewey, Orville. *A Sermon, Preached on the National Fast Day, at Church Green, Boston.* Boston, 1864.

Dixon, James. *Personal Narrative of a Tour Through a Part of the United States and Canada: With Notices of the History and Institutions of Methodism in America.* New York, 1849.

Doggett, D. S. *A Sermon on the Occasion of the Death of General William Henry Harrison, Late President of the United States, Delivered in the Chapel of Randolph Macon College, April 18, 1841.* Richmond, 1841.

Doggett, Thomas. *A Sermon Preached on Fast Day, September 26, 1861.* Haverhill, Mass., 1861.

Douglass, Frederick. *Narrative of the Life of Frederick Douglass. Written by Himself.* Boston, 1849.

———. *Papers: Speeches, Debates, and Interviews.* Vol. 4, *1864–80.* Edited by John W. Blassingame. New Haven, Conn.: Yale University Press, 1991.

Douthit, Jasper Lewis. *Jasper Douthit's Story: The Autobiography of a Pioneer.* Boston, 1909.

Dow, John. *A Discourse, Delivered by Request, July 4, 1806, in the Methodist Church at Belleville.* Newark, N.J., 1806.

Dow, Lorenzo. *History of Cosmopolite . . . Containing His Experience & Travels from Childhood to 1814.* New York, 1814.

Drisler, Henry. *Part 1. A Reply to the "Bible View of Slavery by J. H. Hopkins, D.D., Bishop of the Diocese of Vermont."* Louis C. Newman, *Part 2. The Bible View of Slavery Reconsidered: Letter to Rt. Rev. Bishop Hopkins.* Loyal Publication Society Pamphlet No. 39. New York, 1863.

Duffield, George. *The Death of Gen. William Henry Harrison, President of the United States; or, The Divine Rebuke: Being a Discourse Preached in the Presbyterian Church on Sabbath the Eleventh of April.* Detroit, 1841.

———. *Our National Sins to Be Repented of, and the Grounds of Hope for the Preservation of Our Federal Constitution and Union: A Discourse Delivered Friday, January 4, 1861, on the Day of Fasting, Humiliation, and Prayer Appointed by the President of the United States.* Detroit, 1861.

Duffield, George. *The God of Our Fathers: An Historical Sermon Preached in the Coates' Street Presbyterian Church, Philadelphia, on Fast Day, January 4, 1861.* Philadelphia, 1861.

Duffield, George. *A Sermon Preached in the Third Presbyterian Church in the City of Philadelphia, on Thursday, December 11, 1783: The Day Appointed . . . to Be Observed as a Day of Thanksgiving, for the Restoration of Peace, and Establishment of Our Independence.* Boston, 1784.

Duncan, John M. *A Discourse Delivered on the Fast Day: Recommended by the President.* Baltimore, 1841.

Dunning, Homer N. *Manual of the Congregational Church at Gloversville, N.Y., with an Anniversary Sermon, on the History and Mission of the Church; Preached Aug. 3d, 1856.* New York, 1856.

———. *Providential Design of the Slavery Agitation: A Sermon Preached to the Congregational Church of Gloversville on the National Fast Day, January 4th, 1861.* Gloversville, N.Y., 1861.

———. *The Strangeness of God's Ways: A Sermon Preached Before the Churches of Gloversville on Thanksgiving Day, November 24th, 1864.* Gloversville, N.Y., 1865.

Dwight, William Theodore. *A Great Man Fallen: A Discourse on the Death of President Harrison Delivered in the Third Congregational Church of Portland on Sabbath Morning, April 18, and on Thursday Evening, April 22, 1841.* Portland, Maine, 1841.

Eddy, Richard. *The Necessity for Religion in Politics: A Sermon Preached to the United Congregation of Universalists, in Philadelphia, in the Second Church, Thanksgiving Morning, November 26th, 1863.* Philadelphia, 1863.

Edgar, Cornelius H. *God's Help, the Ground of Hope for Our Country: A Sermon Preached on the Day of National Thanksgiving, November 24, 1864, in the Reformed Dutch Church, Easton, Pa.* New York, 1864.

Edwards, B. B. *Address Delivered on the Day of the National Fast, May 14, 1841, at a United Meeting of the Religious Societies in Andover.* Andover, Mass., 1841.

Edwards, Richard. *Life and Character of Abraham Lincoln: An Address, Delivered at the Hall of the Normal University, April 19th, 1865.* Peoria, Ill., 1865.

Einhorn, David. *Sermon, Delivered on Thanksgiving Day, November 26th, 1863.* Philadelphia, 1863.

Ewer, Ferdinand C. *A Protest Against Political Preaching: Being a Rector's Reply to Sundry Requests and Demands for a Political Sermon.* New York, 1864.

Fast Day Sermons; or, The Pulpit on the State of the Country. New York, 1861.

Fehrenbacher, Don E., and Virginia Fehrenbacher, eds. *Recollected Words of Abraham Lincoln.* Stanford, Calif.: Stanford University Press, 1996.

Ferris, Isaac. *The Duties of the Times, Preached on the National Thanksgiving, August 6, 1863, in the University Place Presbyterian Church.* New York, 1863.

Finney, Charles G. *Principles of Consecration.* Minneapolis: Bethany House, 1990.

Fiske, John O. *A Sermon on the Present National Troubles, Delivered in the Winter Street Church, January 4, 1861, the Day of the National Fast.* Bath, Maine, 1861.

Bibliography

Ford, Thomas. *A History of Illinois from Its Commencement as a State in 1818 to 1847*. Chicago, 1854.

Ford, William. *American Republicanism—Its Success, Its Perils, and the Duty of Its Present Supporters: A Sermon Delivered Before the Citizens of Brandon, on the Occasion of the National Fast, September 26, 1861*. Rutland, [Vt.], 1861.

Foster, Eden B. *Four Pastorates: Glimpses of the Life and Thoughts of Eden B. Foster, D.D., Consisting of a Biographical Sketch, Eulogies, and Selections from His Writings*. Lowell, Mass., 1883.

Fransioli, Joseph. *Patriotism, a Christian Virtue: A Sermon Preached . . . at St. Peter's (Catholic) Church, Brooklyn, July 26th, 1863*. New York: Loyal Publication Society, 1863.

Freidel, Frank, ed. *Union Pamphlets of the Civil War, 1861–1865*. Cambridge, Mass.: Belknap Press of Harvard University Press, 1967.

Fugitt, James Preston. *A Plea for Peace: A Sermon Preached in the Church of Holy Innocents, Baltimore, September 26, 1861, the Day of National Fasting, Humiliation, and Prayer*. Baltimore, 1861.

Furness, W. H. *A Discourse Delivered on the Occasion of the National Fast, September 26th, 1861, in the First Congregational Unitarian Church in Philadelphia*. Philadelphia, 1861.

Gibson, William T. *The Revolt of Absalom: And the Necessary Triumph of Union: A Discourse Pronounced in Grace Church, Utica . . . Nov. 24th, 1864*. Utica, N.Y., 1864.

Gienapp, William E., and Erica L. Gienapp, eds. *The Civil War Diary of Gideon Welles, Lincoln's Secretary of the Navy*. Urbana: Knox College Lincoln Studies Center and the University of Illinois Press, 2014.

Gierlow, J. *A Discourse on the Times, Preached August 6, 1863, Being the Day . . . for National Thanksgiving*. Augusta, Maine, 1863.

Giles, Chauncey. *The Problem of American Nationality and the Evils Which Hinder Its Solution: A Discourse Delivered on the Day of the National Fast, April 30, 1863*. Cincinnati, 1863.

Gillespie, Joseph. *Recollections of Early Illinois, and Her Noted Men*. Chicago, 1880.

God Bless Abraham Lincoln! A Solemn Discourse by a Local Preacher. Dedicated to the Faithful. N.p., [ca. 1863–64].

Goddard, W. G. *An Address in Commemoration of the Death of William Henry Harrison, President of the United States: Delivered Before the City Council and Citizens of Providence, on the National Fast, May 14, 1841*. Providence, 1841.

Goodell, William. *The Rights and Wrongs of Rhode Island: Comprising Views of Liberty and Law, of Religion and Rights, as Exhibited in the Recent and Existing Difficulties in That State*. Whitesboro, N.Y., 1842.

530 Bibliography

Gordon, William R. *Reliance on God, Our Hope of Victory: A Sermon Preached on the Day of Fasting and Prayer, September 26th, 1861.* New York, 1861.

Grand Lincoln and Johnson Ratification Meeting, at Washington City, D.C., June 15, 1864: The National Union League of America, in the Field! [Washington, D.C.], 1864.

Griffis, William Elliot. *John Chambers, Servant of Christ and Master of Hearts, and His Ministry in Philadelphia.* Ithaca, N.Y.: Andrus & Church, 1903.

Gurley, L. B. *A Sermon, Preached in Shelby, Richland Co., Ohio, May 14, 1841, on the Occasion of the National Fast.* Norwalk, Ohio, 1841.

Gurley, P. D. *Our Prosperity, Our Ingratitude, and Our Danger: A Fast-Day Sermon, Preached in the F Street Presbyterian Church, Washington, D.C., September 26, 1855.* Washington, [D.C.], 1855.

Hall, Edward Brooks. *A Sermon Preached May 14, 1841, Being the National Fast Occasioned by the Death of President Harrison.* Providence, 1841.

Hall, John, ed. *Forty Years' Familiar Letters of James W. Alexander, D.D., Constituting, with the Notes, a Memoir of His Life.* New York, 1860.

Hall, Nathaniel. *Righteousness and the Pulpit: A Discourse Preached in the First Church, Dorchester, on Sunday, Sept. 30, 1855.* Boston, 1855.

Haney, M. L. *The Story of My Life: An Autobiography.* Normal, Ill., 1904.

Harris, William L., ed. *Journal of the General Conference of the Methodist Episcopal Church, Held in Philadelphia, Pa.* New York, 1864.

Harshman, Samuel Rufus. *Memoirs of Samuel Rufus Harshman: Comprising His Autobiography, Recollections of Men and Events, Camp-Meetings, and Other Meetings Held in Ohio, Indiana, and Illinois.* Sullivan, Ill., 1914.

Haven, Gilbert. *National Sermons: Sermons, Speeches, and Letters on Slavery and Its War.* Boston, 1869.

Haven, Gilbert, and Thomas Russell. *Father Taylor, the Sailor Preacher: Incidents and Anecdotes of Rev. Edward T. Taylor, for over Forty Years Pastor of the Seaman's Bethel, Boston.* Boston, 1872.

[Haven, Silas]. *"A Punishment on the Nation": An Iowa Soldier Endures the Civil War.* Edited by Brian Craig Miller. Kent, Ohio: Kent State University Press, 2012.

Hawes, Joel. *North and South; or, Four Questions Considered: What Have We Done? What Have We to Do? What Have We to Hope? What Have We to Fear? A Sermon Preached in the First Church in Hartford, on the Day of the National Fast, Sept. 26th, 1861.* Hartford, Conn., 1861.

Hawley, Bostwick. *Truth and Righteousness Triumphant: A Discourse Commemorative of the Death of President Lincoln, Preached in the Washington Avenue M.E. Church, April 20, 1865.* Albany, N.Y., 1865.

Bibliography

Hay, John. *Lincoln's Journalist: John Hay's Anonymous Writings for the Press, 1860–1864.* Edited by Michael Burlingame. Carbondale: Southern Illinois University Press, 1998.

———. *Inside Lincoln's White House: The Complete Civil War Diary of John Hay.* Edited by Michael Burlingame and John R. T. Ettlinger. Carbondale: Southern Illinois University Press, 1997.

Hedge, Frederic Henry. *The National Weakness: A Discourse Delivered in the First Church, Brookline, on Fast Day, Sept. 26, 1861.* Boston, 1861.

Henderson, Howard A. M. *The Religion and Politics of the Crisis: A Fast Day Sermon.* Marion, Ala., 1860.

Herndon, W. H. *Lincoln's Religion.* Springfield: Illinois State Register, 1873.

Herndon, William Henry, and Jesse William Weik. *Herndon's Lincoln.* Edited by Douglas L. Wilson and Rodney O. Davis. Urbana: Knox College Lincoln Studies Center and the University of Illinois Press, 2006.

Hertz, Emanuel, ed. *The Hidden Lincoln: From the Letters and Papers of William H. Herndon.* New York: Blue Ribbon Books, 1940.

Hervey, George Winfred. *Liberty, as a Cloak of Maliciousness: A Discourse Before a Meeting of the Orthodox and Baptist Congregations in Canton, MA, on the Day of the National Fast, January 4, 1861.* New York, 1861.

Hewit, Nathaniel. *A Discourse at the Funeral Solemnities: Observed at Bridgeport Under the Direction of the City Authorities, April 19th, 1841: Commemorative of the Decease of William Henry Harrison, President of the U. States.* Bridgeport, Conn., 1841.

Hill, George. *Strength in the Time of Trial: A Sermon Preached in the Presbyterian Church of Blairsville, Pa., on . . . August 4, 1864, the Day Appointed . . . as a Day of Humiliation and Prayer.* Pittsburgh, 1864.

Hitchcock, Roswell D. *Our National Sin: A Sermon, Preached on the Day of the National Fast, September 26, 1861, in the South Reformed Dutch Church, New York City.* New York, 1861.

———. *Thanksgiving for Victories: Discourse of Rev. R. D. Hitchcock, D.D.: Delivered in Plymouth Church, Brooklyn, September 11th, 1864.* New York, 1864.

Hodge, A. A. *The Life of Charles Hodge, D.D., LL.D.* New York, 1880.

Hodge, Charles. "Abolitionism." *Biblical Repertory and Princeton Review* 16, no. 4 (Oct. 1844): 545–81.

———. "The Church and the Country." *Biblical Repertory and Princeton Review* 33, no. 2 (April 1861): 322–76.

———. "Civil Government." *Biblical Repertory and Princeton Review* 23, no. 1 (Jan. 1851): 125–58.

———. "Diversity of Species in the Human Race." *Biblical Repertory and Princeton Review* 34, no. 3 (July 1862): 435–64.

———. "Emancipation." *Biblical Repertory and Princeton Review* 21, no. 4 (Oct. 1849): 582–607.

———. "England and America." *Biblical Repertory and Princeton Review* 34, no. 1 (Jan. 1862): 147–77.

———. "The General Assembly [1859]." *Biblical Repertory and Princeton Review* 31, no. 3 (July 1859): 607–18.

———. "The General Assembly [1862]." *Biblical Repertory and Princeton Review* 34, no. 3 (July 1862): 464–524.

———. "The General Assembly [1864]." *Biblical Repertory and Princeton Review* 36, no. 3 (July 1864): 506–74.

———. "The General Assembly [1865]." *Biblical Repertory and Princeton Review* 37, no. 3 (July 1865): 458–514.

———. "President Lincoln." *Biblical Repertory and Princeton Review* 37, no. 3 (July 1865): 435–58.

———. "The Princeton Review on the State of the Country and of the Church." *Biblical Repertory and Princeton Review* 37, no. 4 (Oct. 1865): 627–58.

———. "Slavery." *Biblical Repertory and Princeton Review* 8, no. 2 (April 1836): 268–305.

———. *The State of the Country.* New York, 1861.

———. "The State of the Country." *Biblical Repertory and Princeton Review* 33, no. 1 (Jan. 1861): 1–36.

———. "The War." *Biblical Repertory and Princeton Review* 35, no. 1 (Jan. 1863): 140–69.

Hodgston, John, and A Layman. *Review of a Political Sermon Delivered in Dubuque, Iowa, on Sabbath Evening, July 16, 1856, by Rev. John C. Holbrook, Pastor of the Congregational Church.* Dubuque, Iowa, 1856.

Holland, J. G. *The Life of Abraham Lincoln.* Springfield, Mass., 1866.

Holmes, John Haynes. *The Life and Letters of Robert Collyer, 1823–1912.* New York: Dodd, Mead, 1917.

Hopkins, John Henry. *Bible View of Slavery.* New York, 1863.

Humphrey, Heman. *The Missouri Compromise: An Address Delivered Before the Citizens of Pittsfield.* Pittsfield, Mass., 1854.

———. *Our Nation: A Discourse Delivered at Pittsfield, MA, July 4, 1861, on the Day of National Fast.* Pittsfield, Mass., 1861.

Jackson, John Walker. *The Union, the Constitution, Peace: A Thanksgiving Sermon Delivered in the Locust St. M.E. Church, Harrisburg, Pa.* Harrisburg, Pa., 1863.

Jenkins, John. *"Show My People Their Transgression": A Fast-Day Discourse,*

Preached in the Calvary Presbyterian Church of Philadelphia, on Thursday, September 26th, 1861. Philadelphia, 1861.

Johnson, Andrew. *Speech on the Political Issues of the Day; Delivered Before the Citizens of Nashville on the 15th of July, 1856.* Nashville, 1856.

Johnson, Herrick. *The Shaking of the Nations: A Sermon . . . Sunday, September 11th, 1864.* Pittsburgh, 1864.

Johnson, Lorenzo D. *Chaplains of the General Government with Objections to Their Employment Considered.* New York, 1856.

Kinsley, Rufus. *Diary of a Christian Soldier: Rufus Kinsley and the Civil War.* Edited by David C. Rankin. Cambridge, U.K.: Cambridge University Press, 2004.

Koerner, Gustave. *Memoirs of Gustave Koerner, 1809–1896: Life-Sketches Written at the Suggestion of His Children.* 2 vols. Cedar Rapids, Iowa: Torch Press, 1909.

Krebs, John M. *Righteousness, the Foundation of National Prosperity: A Sermon Delivered in the Rutgers-Street Church, on Thursday, Dec. 10th, 1835, the Day Appointed by the Governor of the State of New-York for the Annual Thanksgiving.* New York, 1835.

Labaree, Benjamin. *A Sermon on the Death of General Harrison: Delivered in Middlebury, Vermont, on the Day of the National Fast.* Middlebury, Vt., 1841.

Lamon, Ward H. *The Life of Abraham Lincoln from His Birth to His Inauguration as President.* Boston, 1872.

Lawrence, Edward A. *The Life of Rev. Joel Hawes, D.D., Tenth Pastor of the First Church, Hartford, Conn.* Hartford, Conn., 1871.

Lee, Richard H. *Memoir of the Life of Richard Henry Lee, and His Correspondence.* 2 vols. Philadelphia, 1825.

Leonard, Edwin. *A Discourse Delivered in the Second Evangelical Congregational Church, Milton, June 4, 1854.* Milton, Mass., 1854.

Lewis, William G. W. *Biography of Samuel Lewis.* Cincinnati, 1857.

The Lincoln Catechism, Wherein the Eccentricities & Beauties of Despotism Are Fully Set Forth: A Guide to the Presidential Election of 1864. New York, 1864.

Little, Charles. *Relation of the Citizen to the Government: A Discourse Delivered on the Day of National Thanksgiving, November 24th, 1864.* New Haven, Conn., 1864.

Little, George O. *The Mission of Our Government: A Fast-Day Sermon Delivered at the 2d Presbyterian Church, Fort Wayne, Aug. 4th, 1864.* Fort Wayne, Ind., 1864.

Livermore, Leonard J. *Perseverance in the War the Interest and Duty of the Nation.* Boston, 1864.

534 *Bibliography*

———. *What We Have to Be Thankful For: A Sermon, on Occasion of the National Thanksgiving, Preached at Lexington, Ms., August 6, 1863.* Boston, 1863.

[Locke, David Ross]. *The Nasby Papers.* Indianapolis, 1864.

Lord, Nathan. *A True Picture of Abolition.* Boston, 1863.

———. *The Struggles, Social, Financial, and Political, of Petroleum V. Nasby.* Boston, 1872.

Loring, George B. *The Present Crisis: A Speech Delivered by Dr. Geo. B. Loring, at Lyceum Hall, Salem, Wednesday Evening, April 26, 1865, on the Assassination of President Lincoln.* South Danvers, [Mass.], 1865.

Lovejoy, Owen. *His Brother's Blood: Speeches and Writings, 1838–64.* Edited by William F. Moore and Jane Ann Moore. Urbana: University of Illinois Press, 2004.

Marshall, James. *The Nation's Inquiry: A Discourse Delivered in the Chesapeake General Hospital near Fort Monroe, VA, on the Day of the National Fast, April 30th, 1863.* Philadelphia, 1863.

Martin, John S. *Minutes of the Sessions of the Baltimore Annual Conference, Held at Harrisonburg, Va., March 14, 1862. Churchville, Va., March 19, 1863. Bridgewater, Va., March 10, 1864. Salem, Va., March 9, 1865.* Staunton, Va., 1899.

Mason, Charles. *The Election in Iowa.* Papers from the Society for the Diffusion of Political Knowledge, no. 11. New York, 1863.

Mayo, A. D. *The Nation's Sacrifice: Abraham Lincoln. Two Discourses, Delivered on Sunday Morning, April 16, and Wednesday Morning, April 19, 1865, in the Church of the Redeemer, Cincinnati, Ohio.* Cincinnati, 1865.

McClure, A. K. *Abraham Lincoln and Men of War Times.* Philadelphia, 1892.

McGill, Alexander T. *Sinful but Not Forsaken: A Sermon Preached in the Presbyterian Church, Fifth Avenue and Nineteenth Street, New York, on the Day of National Fasting, January 4, 1861.* New York, 1861.

McKenzie, Alexander. *A Sermon Delivered in the South Parish Church, Augusta, on Thanksgiving Day, November 26, 1863.* Augusta, Maine, 1863.

McKeon, John. *The Administration Reviewed. Speech of the Hon. John McKeon Before the Democratic Union Association, at Their Headquarters . . . Wednesday, October 29, 1862.* New York, 1862.

Mears, David O. *Life of Edward Norris Kirk.* Boston, 1878.

Mell, Patrick H. *Slavery: A Treatise, Showing That Slavery Is Neither a Moral, Political, nor Social Evil.* Penfield, Ga., 1844.

Merrill, Walter M., ed. *The Letters of William Lloyd Garrison. Vol. 5, Let the Oppressed Go Free.* Cambridge, Mass.: Belknap Press of Harvard University Press, 1979.

Messent, Peter, and Steve Courtney, eds. *The Civil War Letters of Joseph*

Bibliography

Hopkins Twichell: A Chaplain's Story. Athens: University of Georgia Press, 2006.

Minutes of the Annual Conferences of the Methodist Episcopal Church. New York, 1860.

Minutes of the Annual Conferences of the Methodist Episcopal Church, South. Nashville, 1860.

Minutes of the . . . Central Illinois Annual Conference of the Methodist Episcopal Church . . . September 1864. Chicago, 1864.

Minutes of the Cincinnati Annual Conference of the Methodist Episcopal Church, for the Year 1864. Cincinnati, 1864.

Minutes of the General Assembly of the Presbyterian Church in the United States of America . . . [Old School]. Philadelphia, 1860.

Minutes of the General Assembly of the Presbyterian Church in the United States of America . . . [New School]. New York, 1860.

Minutes of the . . . New-York Conference of the Methodist Episcopal Church . . . April 15, 1863. New York, 1863.

Minutes of the . . . New York East Annual Conference of the Methodist Episcopal Church. New York, 1862, 1863.

Minutes of the . . . Providence Annual Conference of the Methodist Episcopal Church . . . April 2–7, 1862. Boston, 1862.

Minutes of the Southern Illinois Conference of the Methodist Episcopal Church, for the Year 1862. Cincinnati, 1862.

Moody, Granville. *A Life's Retrospect: Autobiography of Rev. Granville Moody*. Edited by Sylvester Weeks. Cincinnati, 1890.

Morris, B. F. *Christian Life and Character of the Civil Institutions of the United States Developed in the Official and Historical Annals of the Republic*. Philadelphia, 1861.

———. *Our Country: Three Discourses on National Subjects*. Lawrenceburgh, Ind., 1848.

Morse, Samuel Finley Breese. *The Letter of a Republican, Edward N. Crosby, Esq., of Poughkeepsie, to Prof. S. F. B. Morse, Feb. 25, 1863, and Prof. Morse's Reply, March 2d, 1863*. Papers from the Society for the Diffusion of Political Knowledge, no. 4. New York, 1863.

Morse, Samuel Finley Breese, George Ticknor Curtis, and Samuel J. Tilden. *The Constitution: Addresses of Prof. Morse, George Ticknor Curtis, and S. J. Tilden, at the Organization*. Papers from the Society for the Diffusion of Political Knowledge, no. 1. New York, 1863.

Moss, Lemuel. *Annals of the United States Christian Commission*. Philadelphia, 1868.

[Mullaly, J.]. *Washington Despotism Dissected in Articles from the "Metropolitan Record."* New York, 1863.

536   *Bibliography*

Myers, Robert Manson, ed. *The Children of Pride: A True Story of Georgia and the Civil War.* New Haven, Conn.: Yale University Press, 1972.

Nadal, B. H. *The War in the Light of Divine Providence: A Fast Day Sermon.* New Haven, Conn., 1863.

Nelson, John. *A Discourse on the Proposed Repeal of the Missouri Compromise; Delivered on Fast Day, April 6, 1854, in the First Congregational Church in Leicester, Mass.* Worcester, Mass., 1854.

Nicolay, John G., and John Hay. *Abraham Lincoln: A History.* 10 vols. New York, 1890.

Niven, John, ed. *The Salmon P. Chase Papers.* Vol. 1, *Journals, 1829–1872.* Kent, Ohio: Kent State University Press, 1993.

Osgood, Jacob. *The Life and Christian Experience of Jacob Osgood: With Hymns and Spiritual Songs.* Warner, N.H., 1873.

Ottman, S. *God Our Leader: A Discourse Delivered on the Occasion of Our National Thanksgiving, August 6th, 1863, to the United Congregations of Edwardsburgh, Michigan.* Niles, Mich., 1863.

Our Martyr President, Abraham Lincoln: Voices from the Pulpit of New York and Brooklyn. New York, [1865].

Paddock, Wilbur F. *God's Presence and Purpose in Our War: A Thanksgiving Discourse, Delivered in St. Andrew's Church, Philadelphia, Thursday, November 26, 1863.* Philadelphia, 1863.

Palmer, A. G. *The Crisis and Its Lessons: A Sermon Delivered in the Baptist Church, Stonington Borough, on the Occasion of the National Fast, September 26, 1861.* Norwich, Conn., 1861.

Palmer, Benjamin Morgan. *The South: Her Peril and Her Duty: A Discourse, Delivered in the First Presbyterian Church, New Orleans, on Thursday, November 29, 1860.* New Orleans, 1860.

Palmer, Walter C. *Life and Letters of Leonidas L. Hamline, D.D., Late One of the Bishops of the Methodist Episcopal Church.* New York, 1866.

Patton, Cornelius H. *Honour Thy Father: A Sermon in Memory of William Weston Patton by His Son, Rev. Cornelius H. Patton, Congregational Church of Christ, Westfield, N.J., April 13, MDCCCXC.* N.p., 1890.

Patton, William W. *President Lincoln and the Chicago Memorial of Emancipation: A Paper Read Before the Maryland Historical Society, December 12th, 1887.* Baltimore, 1888.

Peck, George. *Early Methodism Within the Bounds of the Old Genesee Conference.* New York, 1860.

———. *The Life and Times of Rev. George Peck, D.D.* New York, 1874.

———. *Our Country: Its Trial and Its Triumph.* New York, 1865.

Perrin, Lavalette. *"Our Part in the World's Struggle": A Sermon Preached in*

Bibliography

the Centre Church, New Britain, at a Union Service, November 24, 1864. Hartford, Conn., 1864.

Phillips, George S. *The American Republic and Human Liberty Foreshadowed in Scripture.* Cincinnati, 1864.

Platt, G. Lewis. *The Conflict of Two Civilizations: An Address Delivered in St. Paul's Church, Red Hook, September 11th, 1864, on Occasion of the National Thanksgiving for Recent Victories.* Poughkeepsie, N.Y., 1864.

Porter, C. S. *A Discourse Occasioned by the Death of Wm. Henry Harrison: Delivered April 18th, Repeated by Request, April 25th, 1841.* New York, 1841.

———. *A Fast Implies a Duty: Sermon, Preached April 30, 1863, National Fast Day, in the Arch Street Presbyterian Church.* Philadelphia, 1863.

Potts, William D. *Campaign Songs for Christian Patriots and True Democrats.* New York, 1864.

———. *Freemen's Guide to the Polls, and a Solemn Appeal to American Patriots.* New York, 1864.

———. *Our Country Vindicated, and Democracy Sustained: Being a Review of the Fallacies, Fanaticism, and Delusions of the Abolition Preachers and the Policy of the Republican Abolition Party.* New York, 1864.

Proceedings of the Great Peace Convention, Held in the City of New-York, June 3d, 1863 ... Abridged from ... the New-York "Daily News." New York, 1863.

Quinn, David. *Interior Causes of the War: The Nation Demonized and Its President a Spirit-Rapper.* New York, 1863.

Quint, Alonzo H. *Three Sermons Preached in the North Congregational Church, New Bedford, Mass., Fast Day, April 13, and Sunday, April 16, 1865.* New Bedford, Mass., 1865.

Ramsey, William. *A Sermon, Occasioned by the Death of William Henry Harrison, Late President of the United States, Delivered in the Cedar St. Presbyterian Church.* Philadelphia, 1841.

Randolph, Thomas Jefferson, ed. *Memoirs, Correspondence, and Private Papers of Thomas Jefferson.* Vol. 4. London, 1829.

Rankin, Jeremiah Eames. *The Battle Not Man's, but God's: A Discourse Delivered Before the United Congregational Churches in Lowell, on the Day of National Thanksgiving, August 6th, 1863.* Lowell, Mass., 1863.

Raphall, M. J. "Bible View of Slavery. A Discourse Delivered at the Jewish Synagogue, New York, on the Day of the National Fast, January 4, 1861." In *Fast Day Sermons.*

Raymond, Henry J. *The Life and Public Services of Abraham Lincoln, Together with His State Papers.* New York, 1865.

538 *Bibliography*

Read, C. H. *National Fast: A Discourse Delivered on the Day of Fasting, Humiliation, and Prayer Appointed by the President of the United States, January 4, 1861*. Richmond, 1861.

Reid, Adam. *Government a Divine Ordinance: A Discourse Delivered on the Day of the National Fast, April 30, 1863, in the Congregational Church, Salisbury, Ct.* Hartford, Conn., 1863.

Republican Congressional Committee. *The Chicago Copperhead Convention: The Treasonable and Revolutionary Utterances of the Men Who Composed It. Extracts from All the Notable Speeches Delivered in and out of the National "Democratic" Convention.* Washington, D.C., 1864.

Reynolds, James L. *A Discourse Delivered at the Furman Theological Institution, Friday, May 14, 1841: The Day Appointed by the President of the United States as a Day of Fasting, Humiliation, and Prayer, in Consequence of the Death of Gen. William Henry Harrison.* Winnsborough, S.C., 1841.

Rhodes, Elisha Hunt. *All for the Union: The Civil War Diary and Letters of Elisha Hunt Rhodes.* New York: Orion Books, 1991.

Rice, Allen Thorndike, ed. *Reminiscences of Abraham Lincoln by Distinguished Men of His Time.* New York, 1886.

Riddle, D. H. *"The Morning Cometh."* Pittsburgh, 1841.

Roberts, Timothy Mason, ed. *"This Infernal War": The Civil War Letters of William and Jane Standard.* Kent, Ohio: Kent State University Press, 2018.

Ross, Frederick A. *Slavery Ordained of God.* Philadelphia, 1857.

Russell, William Howard. *My Diary North and South.* New York, 1863.

Sala, George Augustus. *My Diary in America in the Midst of the War.* 2 vols. London, 1865.

Salter, William. *Slavery and the Lessons of Recent Years.* Burlington, Iowa, 1859.

Schurz, Carl. *The Reminiscences of Carl Schurz.* New York: McClure, 1907–8.

Sears, Stephen W., ed. *The Civil War Papers of George B. McClellan: Selected Correspondence, 1860–1865.* New York: Da Capo Press, 1992.

Simmons, Ichabod. *Our Duty in the Crisis: A Discourse Delivered on the Occasion of the National Fast, September 26, 1861, in the M.E. Church, Simsbury.* Hartford, Conn., 1861.

Simmons, James B. *The Cause and Cure of the Rebellion; or, How Far the People of the Loyal States Are Responsible for the War.* Indianapolis, 1861.

Simpson, Matthew. *Funeral Address Delivered at the Burial of President Lincoln, at Springfield, Illinois, May 4, 1865.* New York, 1865.

Skinner, Thomas H. *Comfort in Tribulation: An Address Delivered in the Reformed Dutch Church, Stapleton, S.I., September 26th, 1861, a Day Kept*

Bibliography

as a National Fast, by Appointment of the President of the United States. New York, 1861.

————. *Religion and Liberty: A Discourse Delivered Dec. 17, 1840, the Day Appointed for Public Thanksgiving by the Governor of New York.* New York, 1841.

Sloane, James Renwick Wilson. *Review of Rev. Henry J. Van Dyke's Discourse on "The Character and Influence of Abolitionism," a Sermon Preached in the Third Reformed Presbyterian Church, Twenty-Third Street, New York, on Sabbath Evening, December 23, 1860.* New York, 1861.

Smart, James S. *National Fast: A Fast Day Sermon Delivered in the City of Flint, January 4th, 1861.* Flint, Mich., 1861.

Smith, Henry. *God in the War: A Discourse Preached in Behalf of the U.S. Christian Commission on the Day of the National Thanksgiving, August 6th, 1863.* Buffalo, 1863.

Smith, Margaret Bayard. *The First Forty Years of Washington Society in the Family Letters of Margaret Bayard Smith.* Edited by Gaillard Hunt. New York: Scribner, 1906.

Smith, Moses. *Past Mercies, Present Gratitude, Future Duty: A Discourse Delivered at the Camp of the Eighth Regt. Conn. Vet. Vol. Infantry, near Ft. Harrison, Varginia [sic], on the Annual National Thanksgiving Day, November 24, 1864.* New Haven, Conn., 1865.

Smith, Samuel Francis. *A Sermon Occasioned by the Death of William Henry Harrison.* Hallowell, Maine, 1841.

Society for the Diffusion of Political Knowledge. *Papers from the Society for the Diffusion of Political Knowledge.* New York, 1863–64.

Songs & Ballads of Freedom: A Choice Collection, Inspired by the Incidents and Scenes of the Present War. New York, 1864.

Spicer, Tobias. *Autobiography of Rev. Tobias Spicer; Containing Incidents and Observations, Also Some Account of His Visit to England.* New York, 1852.

Stanton, R. L. *Causes for National Humiliation: A Discourse, Delivered on the Day of Fasting, Humiliation, and Prayer, Recommended by the President of the United States, September 26, 1861 . . . [at] the First Presbyterian Church, Chillicothe, Ohio.* Cincinnati, 1861.

Stearns, Edward J. *The Sword of the Lord: A Sermon Preached in the House of Prayer, Newark, New Jersey, on Thursday, September 26, 1861, Being the National Fast Day.* Baltimore, 1861.

Stebbins, Horatio. *The President, the People, and the War: A Thanksgiving Discourse.* San Francisco, 1864.

Steele, Daniel. *Thanksgiving by Faith for Our Country's Future: A National Thanksgiving Sermon, Delivered at the Methodist E. Church, Lima, August 6th, 1863, Before the United Congregations.* Rochester, N.Y., 1863.

Stevens, Walter B. *A Reporter's Lincoln*. Edited by Michael Burlingame. Lincoln: University of Nebraska Press, 1998.

Stewart, William B. *The Nation's Sins and the Nation's Duty: A Sermon Preached in the First Presbyterian Church, Pottstown, Pennsylvania, on National Fast Day, April 30, 1863*. Philadelphia, 1863.

Stockton, Thomas H. *Address by Thomas H. Stockton, Chaplain U.S.H.R., Delivered in the Hall of the House of Representatives on the Day of National Humiliation, Fasting, and Prayer, Friday, January 4, 1861*. Washington, D.C., 1861.

———. *Influence of the United States on Christendom: A Sermon Delivered at the Chapel Corner of Eleventh and Wood Streets, Philadelphia, on Sabbath Afternoon, November 29, 1864*. Philadelphia, 1864.

Stoddard, William O. *Dispatches from Lincoln's White House: The Anonymous Civil War Journalism of Presidential Secretary William O. Stoddard*. Edited by Michael Burlingame. Lincoln: University of Nebraska Press, 2002.

Street, Thomas. *A Sermon Preached in the Presbyterian Church, York, Pa., on the Day of National Thanksgiving, November 26, 1863*. Philadelphia, 1863.

Strong, George Templeton. *The Diary of George Templeton Strong*. Edited by Allan Nevins and Milton Halsey Thomas. 4 vols. New York: Octagon Books, 1974.

Sturtevant, Julian M. *An Autobiography*. Edited by J. M. Sturtevant Jr. New York, 1896.

The Suppression of "The Chicago Times." Chicago, 1863.

Swain, Leonard. *A Nation's Sorrow: A Sermon Preached on the Sabbath After the Assassination of President Lincoln, in the Central Congregational Church, Providence, April 15 [i.e., 16], 1865*. [Providence?], [1865?].

Tefft, B. F. *The Republican Influence of Christianity: A Discourse Delivered on Occasion of the Death of William Henry Harrison, at Bangor, April 22, and Re-delivered at Hallowell and Augusta, May 14, 1841; Being the Day of the National Fast*. Bangor, Maine, 1841.

Thompson, Joseph P. *Peace Through Victory: Sermon*. New York, 1864.

Thomson, Edward. *The Pulpit and Politics: A Discourse Preached in the College Chapel of the Ohio Wesleyan University, April 23, 1854*. Columbus, Ohio, 1854.

Thornbrough, Gayle, and Paula Corpuz, eds. *The Diary of Calvin Fletcher*. Vol. 8, *1863–1864*. Indianapolis: Indiana Historical Society, 1981.

Thornwell, J. H. "Our National Sins: A Sermon Preached in the Presbyterian Church, Columbia, S.C., on the Day of the State Fast, November 21, 1860." In *Fast Day Sermons*.

Bibliography

Tocqueville, Alexis de. *Democracy in America*. Translated by H. Reeve. Edited by Francis Bowen. Boston, 1882.

Tucker, Mark. *A Discourse Preached on Thanksgiving Day, in the Beneficent Congregational Meeting-House, Providence, July 21, 1842*. Providence, 1842.

Tyng, Charles Rockland, comp. *Record of the Life and Work of the Rev. Stephen Higginson Tyng, D.D., and History of St. George's Church, New York, to the Close of His Rectorship*. New York, 1890.

Tyng, Dudley A. *A Statement of the Congregation of the Church of the Epiphany, Philadelphia, of Facts Bearing on the Action of the Vestry in Requesting the Resignation of the Rector*. Philadelphia, 1856.

Tyng, Stephen H. *Christian Loyalty: A Discourse, Delivered in St. George's Church, New-York, April 30th, 1863, the Day of National Fast*. New York, 1863.

Upfold, George. *God, the Help of the Nation: A Sermon Delivered in Trinity Church, Pittsburgh, on the Day of National Thanksgiving, Appointed by the President of the United States, November 26, 1863*. Pittsburgh, 1864.

———. *"The Sins of the People": A Discourse Delivered in Trinity Church on Friday, May 14th, 1841, the Day of Fasting and Prayer Recommended by the President of the United States*. Pittsburgh, 1841.

Vallandigham, Clement L. *The Record of Hon. C. L. Vallandigham on Abolition, the Union, and the Civil War*. Cincinnati, 1863.

———. *Speeches, Arguments, Addresses, and Letters of Clement L. Vallandigham*. New York, 1864.

Vallandigham, James L. *A Life of Clement L. Vallandigham*. Baltimore, 1872.

The Vallandigham Song Book: Songs for the Times. Columbus, Ohio, 1863.

Vanarsdale, Cornelius C. *Lessons of Wisdom for a Mourning People: A Discourse on the Death of President Harrison, Pronounced on the Evening of April 20, 1841, the Day of Public Funeral Solemnities*. Philadelphia, 1841.

Van Dyke, Henry J. "The Character and Influence of Abolitionism: A Sermon Preached in the First Presbyterian Church, Brooklyn, December 9, 1860." In *Fast Day Sermons*.

———. *The Spirituality and Independence of the Church: A Speech Delivered in the Synod of New York, October 13, 1864*. New York, 1864.

Vincent, Marvin R. *The Lord of War and of Righteousness: A Thanksgiving Sermon Preached in the First Presbyterian Church, Troy, N.Y., Nov. 24, 1864*. Troy, N.Y., 1864.

———. *A Sermon on the Assassination of Abraham Lincoln: Delivered in the First Presbyterian Church, Troy, on Sunday Morning, April 23, 1865*. Troy, N.Y., 1865.

542 *Bibliography*

Vinton, Alexander H. *Cause for Thanksgiving: A Sermon, Preached on the National Thanksgiving Day, November 24th, 1864.* New York, 1864.

Vinton, Francis. "Irreligion, Corruption, and Fanaticism Rebuked: A Sermon Preached in Trinity Church, New York, on the Day of the National Fast, January 4, 1861." In *Fast Day Sermons.*

Volck, Adalbert John. *Sketches from the Civil War in North America, 1861, '62, '63.* London, 1863.

Wadsworth, Charles. *Our Own Sins: A Sermon Preached in the Arch Street Church, on the Day of Humiliation and Prayer, Appointed by the President of the United States, Friday, January 4th, 1861.* Philadelphia, 1861.

———. *War a Discipline: A Sermon Preached in Calvary Church, San Francisco, on Thanksgiving Day, November 24, 1864.* San Francisco, 1864.

The War of the Rebellion: A Compilation of the Official Records of the Union and Confederate Armies. Washington, D.C., 1880–1901.

Washburn, Daniel. *A Sermon Delivered on the Day of National Thanksgiving, November 26, 1863, in Trinity Church, Philadelphia.* Philadelphia, 1863.

Washington, George. *Washington's Farewell Address to the People of the United States of America: Published in September 1796.* Harrisburg, Pa., 1847.

Watson, James C. *An Oration on the Death of William Henry Harrison: Late President of the United States, Delivered in St. James' Church, Gettysburg, Pa., April 22, 1841.* Gettysburg, Pa., 1841.

Wayland, Francis. *An Appeal to the Disciples of Christ of Every Denomination in Reference to the Approaching Day of Prayer.* Boston, 1861.

Wayland, Francis, and Heman L. Wayland. *A Memoir of the Life and Labors of Francis Wayland, D.D., LL.D., Late President of Brown University. By His Sons.* 2 vols. New York, 1867.

Wells, Cornelius L. *The Sacrifice of Continual Praise: A Sermon Preached in the Reformed Dutch Church, Flatbush, L.I., on Thanksgiving Day, Nov. 24, 1864.* New York, 1864.

Willey, Austin. *The History of the Antislavery Cause in State and Nation.* Portland, Maine, 1886.

Williams, William Bender. *A Few Acts and Actors in the Tragedy of the Civil War in the United States.* Philadelphia, 1892.

Wilson, Douglas, et al., eds., *Great Lincoln Documents: Historians Present Treasures from the Gilder Lehrman Collection.* New York: Gilder Lehrman Institute of American History, 2009.

Wilson, Douglas L., and Rodney O. Davis, eds. *Herndon's Informants: Letters, Interviews, and Statements About Abraham Lincoln.* Urbana: University of Illinois Press, 1997.

Wilson, William. *The Curse of Meroz; or, The Curse of the Neutral or Hostile*

Bibliography

Toward the Complete Extirpation of the Great American Rebellion: Together with Slavery Which Is Its Cause and Its Source . . . a Sermon, Preached on the National Fast Day, Sep. 26, 1861, in the Reformed Presbyterian Church, Garrison Creek, Indiana. Garrison Creek, Ind., 1862.

Winthrop, Robert C. Great Speech at New London, Conn., October 18: The Principles and Interests of the Republican Party Against the Union. The Election of McClellan the Only Hope for Union and Peace. N.p., 1864.

Wisner, William. Nations Amenable to God: A Fast Sermon Preached in the First Presbyterian Church at Ithaca, on the 14th Day of May, 1841. Ithaca, N.Y., 1841.

Witherspoon, A. Hand of God in the Present Conflict: A Discourse, Delivered Before the Citizens of Brandon, Vermont, on the Occasion of the State Fast, April 9th, 1863. Rutland, Vt., 1863.

Woodward, C. Vann, ed. Mary Chesnut's Civil War. New Haven, Conn.: Yale University Press, 1981.

Zabriskie, Francis Nicoll. Weighed in the Balance: A Fast Day Sermon, Preached in the Second Reformed Dutch Church of Coxsackie, Thursday Morning, April 30th, 1863. Albany, 1863.

SECONDARY SOURCES

Aamodt, Terrie Dopp. Righteous Armies, Holy Cause: Apocalyptic Imagery and the Civil War. Macon, Ga.: Mercer University Press, 2002.

Achorn, Edward. Every Drop of Blood: The Momentous Second Inauguration of Abraham Lincoln. New York: Atlantic Monthly Press, 2020.

Ahlstrom, Sydney E. A Religious History of the American People. New Haven, Conn.: Yale University Press, 1972.

Alberta, Tim. The Kingdom, the Power, and the Glory: American Evangelicals in an Age of Extremism. New York: HarperCollins, 2023.

Alford, Terry. Fortune's Fool: The Life of John Wilkes Booth. Oxford: Oxford University Press, 2015.

Andreasen, Bryon C. "'As Good a Right to Pray': Copperhead Christians on the Northern Civil War." PhD diss., University of Illinois at Urbana-Champaign, 1998.

———. "Conflicting War Sentiments on the Decatur Methodist Circuit: The Civil War Church Trial of Reverend Arthur Bradshaw." Journal of Illinois History 2 (Winter 1999): 273–88.

———. "Proscribed Preachers, New Churches: Civil Wars in the Illinois Protestant Churches During the Civil War." Civil War History 44, no. 3 (Sept. 1998): 194–211.

544 *Bibliography*

Andrews, Dee E. *The Methodists and Revolutionary America, 1760–1800: The Shaping of an Evangelical Culture.* Princeton, N.J.: Princeton University Press, 2000.

Angle, Paul M. *"Here I Have Lived": A History of Lincoln's Springfield, 1821–1865.* New Brunswick, N.J.: Rutgers University Press, 1950.

Appleby, Joyce Oldham. *Inheriting the Revolution: The First Generation of Americans.* Cambridge, Mass.: Belknap Press of Harvard University Press, 2001.

Arrington, Benjamin T. *The Last Lincoln Republican: The Presidential Election of 1880.* Lawrence: University Press of Kansas, 2020.

Astles, John B. "Rev. Dr. W. A. Scott, a Southern Sympathizer." *California Historical Society Quarterly* 27, no. 2 (June 1948): 149–56.

Baker, Jean H. *Affairs of Party: The Political Culture of Northern Democrats in the Mid-nineteenth Century.* Ithaca, N.Y.: Cornell University Press, 1983.

———. "Lincoln's Narrative of American Exceptionalism." In *"We Cannot Escape History": Lincoln and the Last Best Hope of Earth.* Edited by James M. McPherson. Urbana: University of Illinois Press, 1995.

Balogh, Brian. *A Government out of Sight: The Mystery of National Authority in Nineteenth Century America.* Cambridge, U.K.: Cambridge University Press, 2009.

Barton, William E. *The Soul of Abraham Lincoln.* New York: George H. Doran, 1920.

Baum, Dale. *The Civil War Party System: The Case of Massachusetts, 1848–1876.* Chapel Hill: University of North Carolina Press, 1984.

Beisel, Suzanne. "Henry Clay 'Dirty' Dean." *Annals of Iowa* 36 (1963): 505–24.

Bellah, Robert N. "Civil Religion in America." *Journal of the American Academy of Arts and Sciences* 96, no. 1 (Winter 1967): 1–21.

Beneke, Chris. *Beyond Toleration: The Religious Origins of American Pluralism.* Oxford: Oxford University Press, 2006.

Benham, Kristina. "British Exodus, American Empire: Evangelical Preachers and the Biblicisms of Revolution." In *Every Leaf, Line, and Letter: Evangelicals and the Bible from the 1730s to the Present.* Edited by Timothy Larsen. Downers Grove, Ill.: InterVarsity Press, 2021.

Bennett, Lerone. *Forced into Glory: Abraham Lincoln's White Dream.* Chicago: Johnson, 2000.

Bernstein, Iver. *The New York City Draft Riots: Their Significance for American Society and Politics in the Age of the Civil War.* New York: Oxford University Press, 1990.

Bibliography

Billington, Ray Allen. *The Protestant Crusade, 1800–1860: A Study of the Origins of American Nativism*. New York: Macmillan, 1938.

Blight, David W. *Frederick Douglass: Prophet of Freedom*. New York: Simon & Schuster, 2018.

———. *Race and Reunion: The Civil War in American Memory*. Cambridge, Mass.: Belknap Press of Harvard University Press, 2001.

Bloch, Ruth H. *Visionary Republic: Millennial Themes in American Thought, 1756–1800*. New York: Cambridge University Press, 1985.

Bray, Robert. *Reading with Lincoln*. Carbondale: Southern Illinois University Press, 2010.

Brekus, Catherine A., and W. Clark Gilpin. *American Christianities: A History of Dominance and Diversity*. Chapel Hill: University of North Carolina Press, 2011.

Brodrecht, Grant R. *Our Country: Northern Evangelicals and the Union During the Civil War Era*. New York: Fordham University Press, 2018.

Burlingame, Michael. *Abraham Lincoln: A Life*. 2 vols. Baltimore: Johns Hopkins University Press, 2008.

Burr, Nelson R. "United States Senator James Dixon, 1814–1873: Episcopalian Anti-slavery Statesman." *Historical Magazine of the Protestant Episcopal Church* 50, no. 1 (March 1981): 29–72.

Burton, Orville Vernon. *The Age of Lincoln*. New York: Hill and Wang, 2007.

———. *In My Father's House Are Many Mansions: Family and Community in Edgefield, South Carolina*. Chapel Hill: University of North Carolina Press, 1985.

Butler, Jon. *Awash in a Sea of Faith: Christianizing the American People*. Cambridge, Mass.: Harvard University Press, 1990.

———. *Becoming America: The Revolution Before 1776*. Cambridge, Mass.: Harvard University Press, 2000.

Byrd, James P. *A Holy Baptism of Fire and Blood: The Bible and the American Civil War*. New York: Oxford University Press, 2021.

———. *Sacred Scripture, Sacred War: The Bible and the American Revolution*. New York: Oxford University Press, 2013.

Carmichael, Peter S. *The War for the Common Soldier: How Men Thought, Fought, and Survived in Civil War Armies*. Chapel Hill: University of North Carolina Press, 2018.

Carwardine, Richard. *Evangelicals and Politics in Antebellum America*. New Haven, Conn.: Yale University Press, 1993.

———. *Lincoln: A Life of Purpose and Power*. New York: Alfred A. Knopf, 2006.

Bibliography

———. "Lincoln's Religion." In *Our Lincoln: New Perspectives on Lincoln and His World.* Edited by Eric Foner. New York: W. W. Norton, 2008.

———. "The Politics of Charles Hodge." In *Charles Hodge Revisited: A Critical Appraisal of His Life and Work.* Edited by John W. Stewart and James H. Moorhead. Grand Rapids, Mich.: William B. Eerdmans, 2002.

———. *Transatlantic Revivalism: Popular Evangelicalism in Britain and America, 1790–1865.* Westport, Conn.: Greenwood Press, 1978.

Charnwood, Lord (Godfrey Rathbone Benson). *Abraham Lincoln.* London: Constable, 1916.

Chesebrough, David B. *No Sorrow Like Our Sorrow: Northern Protestant Ministers and the Assassination of Lincoln.* Kent, Ohio: Kent State University Press, 1994.

Clark, Robert D. *The Life of Matthew Simpson.* New York: Macmillan, 1956.

Cook, Robert J. *Baptism of Fire: The Republican Party in Iowa, 1838–1878.* Ames, Iowa: State University Press, 1994.

———. *Civil War Memories: Contesting the Past in the United States Since 1865.* Baltimore: Johns Hopkins University Press, 2017.

———. *Civil War Senator: William Pitt Fessenden and the Fight to Save the American Republic.* Baton Rouge: Louisiana State University Press, 2011.

———. "The Quarrel Forgotten? Toward a Clearer Understanding of Sectional Reconciliation." *Journal of the Civil War Era* 6, no. 3 (Sept. 2016): 413–36.

Cooper, William J. *We Have the War upon Us: The Onset of the Civil War, November 1860–April 1861.* New York: Alfred A. Knopf, 2012.

Coulter, E. Merton. *William G. Brownlow: Fighting Parson of the Southern Highlands.* Chapel Hill: University of North Carolina Press, 1937.

Crofts, Daniel W. *Reluctant Confederates: Upper South Unionists in the Secession Crisis.* Chapel Hill: University of North Carolina Press, 1989.

Current, Richard N. *The Lincoln Nobody Knows.* New York: McGraw-Hill, 1958.

Davis, David Brion. *The Problem of Slavery in the Age of Revolution 1770–1823.* New York: Oxford University Press, 1999.

Davis, Derek H. *Religion and the Continental Congress, 1774–1789: Contributions to Original Intent.* New York: Oxford University Press, 2000.

Davis, Lydia. "Meeting Abraham Lincoln." *Harvard Review* 31 (2006).

Donald, David Herbert. *Charles Sumner and the Rights of Man.* New York: Alfred A. Knopf, 1970.

———. *Lincoln.* New York: Simon & Schuster, 1995.

Bibliography

Dreistbach, Daniel L., and Mark David Hall, eds. *Faith and the Founders of the American Republic*. New York: Oxford University Press, 2014.

Dunham, Chester Forrester. *The Attitude of the Northern Clergy Toward the South, 1860–65.* Toledo: Gray, 1942.

Dunn, Durwood. *The Civil War in Southern Appalachian Methodism*. Knoxville: University of Tennessee Press, 2013.

Edling, Max. *Perfecting the Union: National and State Authority in the U.S. Constitution*. Oxford: Oxford University Press, 2021.

———. *A Revolution in Favour of Government: Origins of the U.S. Constitution and the Making of the American State*. Oxford: Oxford University Press, 2003.

Faragher, John Mack. *Sugar Creek: Life on the Illinois Prairie*. New Haven, Conn.: Yale University Press, 1986.

Faust, Drew Gilpin. *This Republic of Suffering: Death and the American Civil War*. New York: Vintage Books, 2009.

Fehrenbacher, Don E. *Prelude to Greatness: Lincoln in the 1850's*. Stanford, Calif.: Stanford University Press, 1962.

Fermer, Douglas. *James Gordon Bennett and "The New York Herald": A Study of Editorial Opinion in the Civil War Era, 1854–1867*. Woodbridge, U.K.: Boydell Press, 1986.

Finke, Roger, and Rodney Stark. *The Churching of America, 1776–1990: Winners and Losers in Our Religious Economy*. New Brunswick, N.J.: Rutgers University Press, 1992.

———. "How the Upstart Sects Won America, 1776–1850." *Journal for the Scientific Study of Religion* 28, no. 1 (1989): 27–44.

Flotow, Mark. *In Their Letters, in Their Words: Illinois Civil War Soldiers Write Home*. Carbondale: Southern Illinois University Press, 2019.

Flournoy, Francis Rosebro. *Benjamin Mosby Smith, 1811–1893*. Richmond: Richmond Press, 1947.

Foner, Eric. *The Fiery Trial: Abraham Lincoln and American Slavery*. New York: W. W. Norton, 2010.

———. *Free Soil, Free Labor, Free Men: The Ideology of the Republican Party Before the Civil War*. New York: Oxford University Press, 1970.

———. *Reconstruction*. New York: Harper & Row, 1988.

Ford, Bridget. *Bonds of Union: Religion, Race, and Politics in a Civil War Borderland*. Chapel Hill: University of North Carolina Press, 2016.

Formisano, Ronald P. *The Birth of Mass Political Parties: Michigan, 1827–1861*. Princeton, N.J.: Princeton University Press, 1971.

Fornieri, Joseph R. *Abraham Lincoln's Political Faith*. DeKalb: Northern Illinois University Press, 2005.

548   *Bibliography*

Foster, Charles I. *An Errand of Mercy: The Evangelical United Front, 1790–1837.* Chapel Hill: University of North Carolina Press, 1960.

Frank, Joseph Allan. *With Ballot and Bayonet: The Political Socialization of American Civil War Soldiers.* Athens: University of Georgia Press, 1998.

Fredrickson, George M. *The Inner Civil War: Northern Intellectuals and the Crisis of the Union.* New York: Harper & Row, 1965.

Frey, Sylvia R. *Water from the Rock: Black Resistance in a Revolutionary Age.* Princeton N.J: Princeton University Press, 1991.

Friedman, Lawrence J. *Gregarious Saints: Self and Community in American Abolitionism 1830–1870.* Cambridge U.K.: Cambridge University Press, 1982.

Gallagher, Gary W. *The Union War.* Cambridge, Mass.: Harvard University Press, 2011.

Gallman, J. Matthew. *The Cacophony of Politics: Northern Democrats and the American Civil War.* Charlottesville: University of Virginia Press, 2021.

Genovese, Eugene D. *A Consuming Fire: The Fall of the Confederacy in the Mind of the White Christian South.* Athens: University of Georgia Press, 1998.

Gienapp, William E. *The Origins of the Republican Party, 1852–1856.* New York: Oxford University Press, 1987.

Goen, C. C. *Broken Churches, Broken Nation: Denominational Schisms and the Coming of the American Civil War.* Macon, Ga.: Mercer University Press, 1985.

Gorski, Philip S., and Samuel L. Perry. *The Flag and the Cross: White Christian Nationalism and the Threat to American Democracy.* New York: Oxford University Press, 2022.

Grasso, Christopher. *Skepticism and American Faith: From the Revolution to the Civil War.* New York: Oxford University Press, 2018.

Gravely, William. *Gilbert Haven, Methodist Abolitionist: A Study in Race, Religion, and Reform, 1850–1880.* Nashville: Abingdon Press, 1973.

Gribbin, William. *The Churches Militant: The War of 1812 and American Religion.* New Haven, Conn.: Yale University Press, 1973.

Griffin, Patrick. *American Leviathan: Empire, Nation, and Revolutionary Frontier.* New York: Hill and Wang, 2007.

Grzymala-Busse, Anna. "Religious Nationalism and Religious Influence." In *The Oxford Encyclopedia of Politics and Religion.* Edited by Paul A. Djupe, Mark J. Rozell, and Ted G. Jelen. Oxford: Oxford University Press, 2020.

Guelzo, Allen C. "Abraham Lincoln and the Doctrine of Necessity." *Journal of the Abraham Lincoln Association* 18, no. 1 (Winter 1997): 57–81.

———. *Abraham Lincoln: Redeemer President*. Grand Rapids, Mich.: William B. Eerdmans, 1999.

———. "Charles Hodge's Antislavery Moment." In *Charles Hodge Revisited: A Critical Appraisal of His Life and Work*. Edited by John W. Stewart and James H. Moorhead. Grand Rapids, Mich.: William B. Eerdmans, 2002.

———. "Defending Emancipation: Abraham Lincoln and the Conkling Letter, 1863." *Civil War History* 48, no. 4 (Dec. 2002): 313–37.

———. *Lincoln's Emancipation Proclamation: The End of Slavery in America*. New York: Simon & Schuster, 2004.

Gutjahr, Paul C. *Charles Hodge: Guardian of American Orthodoxy*. Oxford: Oxford University Press, 2011.

Guyatt, Nicholas. *Providence and the Invention of the United States, 1607–1876*. New York: Cambridge University Press, 2007.

Hall, Peter Dobkin. *The Organization of American Culture, 1700–1900: Private Institutions, Elites, and the Origins of American Nationality*. New York: New York University Press, 1982.

Hamburger, Philip. *Separation of Church and State*. Cambridge, Mass.: Harvard University Press, 2002.

Hansen, Stephen L. *The Making of the Third Party System: Voters and Parties in Illinois, 1850–1876*. Ann Arbor, Mich.: UMI Research Press, 1980.

Harlow, Luke E. *Religion, Race, and the Making of Confederate Kentucky, 1830–1880*. New York: Cambridge University Press, 2014.

Harper, Matthew. *The End of Days: African American Religion and Politics in the Age of Emancipation*. Chapel Hill: University of North Carolina Press, 2016.

Harper, Robert S. *Lincoln and the Press*. New York: McGraw-Hill, 1951.

Harris, Matthew L., and Thomas S. Kidd, eds. "Religion and the Continental Congress." In *The Founding Fathers and the Debate over Religion in Revolutionary America: A History in Documents*. Edited by Matthew Harris and Thomas Kidd. Online edition. Oxford Academic, 2011. doi.org/10.1093/acprof:oso/9780195326499.003.0001.

Harris, William C. *Lincoln's Last Months*. Cambridge, Mass.: Belknap Press of Harvard University Press, 2004.

———. *Lincoln's Rise to the Presidency*. Lawrence: University Press of Kansas, 2007.

Harrison, John M. *The Man Who Made Nasby, David Ross Locke*. Chapel Hill: University of North Carolina Press, 1969.

Haselby, Sam. *The Origins of American Religious Nationalism*. New York: Oxford University Press, 2015.

Hatch, Nathan O. *The Democratization of American Christianity*. New Haven, Conn.: Yale University Press, 1989.

Hatch, Nathan O., and Mark A. Noll. *The Bible in America: Essays in Cultural History*. New York: Oxford University Press, 1982.

Haynes, Stephen R. *Noah's Curse: The Biblical Justification of American Slavery*. Oxford: Oxford University Press, 2002.

Hein, David. "Lincoln's Theology and Political Ethics." In *Essays on Lincoln's Faith and Politics*. Edited by Kenneth W. Thompson. Lanham, Md.: University Press of America, 1983.

Hennesey, James. *American Catholics: A History of the Roman Catholic Community in the United States*. New York: Oxford University Press, 1981.

Herberg, Will. *Protestant, Catholic, Jew: An Essay in American Religious Sociology*. Garden City, N.Y.: Doubleday, 1955.

Herriott, F. I. *The Premises and Significance of Abraham Lincoln's Letter to Theodore Canisius*. Chicago, 1915.

———. *The Conference of German-Republicans in the Deutsches Haus, Chicago, May 14–15, 1860*. Danville, Ill., 1928.

Hess, Earl J. *Liberty, Virtue, and Progress: Northerners and Their War for the Union*. New York: New York University Press, 1988.

Heyrman, Christine Leigh. *Southern Cross: The Beginnings of the Bible Belt*. New York: Alfred A. Knopf, 1997.

Hildebrand, Reginald F. *The Times Were Strange and Stirring: Methodist Preachers and the Crisis of Emancipation*. Durham, N.C.: Duke University Press, 1995.

Hodes, Martha. *Mourning Lincoln*. New Haven, Conn.: Yale University Press, 2015.

Hollinger, David A. *Christianity's American Fate: How Religion Became More Conservative and Society More Secular*. Princeton, N.J.: Princeton University Press, 2022.

Holm, April. *A Kingdom Divided: Evangelicals, Loyalty, and Sectionalism in the Civil War Era*. Baton Rouge: Louisiana State University Press, 2017.

Holmes, David L. *The Faiths of the Founding Fathers*. New York: Oxford University Press, 2006.

Holt, Michael F. *Forging a Majority: The Formation of the Republican Party in Pittsburgh, 1848–1860*. New Haven, Conn.: Yale University Press, 1969.

———. *The Rise and Fall of the American Whig Party: Jacksonian Politics and the Onset of the Civil War*. New York: Oxford University Press, 1999.

Holzer, Harold. *Lincoln and the Power of the Press: The War for Public Opinion*. New York: Simon & Schuster, 2014.

———. *Lincoln President-Elect: Abraham Lincoln and the Great Secession Winter, 1860–1861*. New York: Simon & Schuster, 2008.

Bibliography

Hord, Fred L., and Matthew D. Norman. *Knowing Him by Heart: African Americans on Abraham Lincoln.* Urbana: University of Illinois Press, 2023.

Houser, M. L. *Lincoln's Education, and Other Essays.* New York: Bookman Associates, 1957.

Howard, Victor. *Religion and the Radical Republican Movement, 1860–1870.* Lexington: University Press of Kentucky, 1990.

Howe, Daniel Walker. *What Hath God Wrought: The Transformation of America, 1815–1848.* New York: Oxford University Press, 2007.

Hubbell, Jay B. "Charles Chauncey Burr: Friend of Poe." *Publications of the Modern Language Association* 69, no. 4 (Sept. 1954): 833–40.

Hudson, Winthrop S. *The Great Tradition of the American Churches.* New York: Harper, 1953.

Hutchinson, William R. *Errand to the World: American Protestant Thought and Foreign Missions.* Chicago: University of Chicago Press, 1987.

Hutchinson, William Thomas. *Cyrus Hall McCormick.* Vol. 2, *Harvest, 1856–1884.* New York: Century, 1935.

Irons, Charles F. *The Origins of Proslavery Christianity: White and Black Evangelicals in Colonial and Antebellum Virginia.* Chapel Hill: University of North Carolina Press, 2008.

Jackson, Kellie Carter. *Force and Freedom: Black Abolitionists and the Politics of Violence.* Philadelphia: University of Pennsylvania Press, 2019.

Jaffa, Harry V. *Crisis of the House Divided.* Reprint with new introduction by the author. Seattle: University of Washington Press, 1973.

Johannsen, Robert W. *Stephen A. Douglas.* New York: Oxford University Press, 1973.

Jones, Joseph. Introduction to *The Struggles of Petroleum V. Nasby*, by David Ross Locke. Edited by Joseph Jones. Abridged ed. Boston: Beacon Press, 1963.

Jortner, Adam. "Cholera, Christ, and Jackson: The Epidemic of 1832 and the Origins of Christian Politics in Antebellum America." *Journal of the Early Republic* 27, no. 2 (Sept. 2007): 233–64.

Kantrowitz, Stephen. "Looking at Lincoln from the Effigy Mound." In *Lincoln's Unfinished Work: The New Birth of Freedom from Generation to Generation.* Edited by Orville Vernon Burton and Peter R. Eisenstadt. Baton Rouge: Louisiana State University Press, 2022.

Kaplan, Fred. *Lincoln: The Biography of a Writer.* New York: Harper, 2008.

Kaplan, Sidney. "The Miscegenation Issue in the Election of 1864." *Journal of Negro History* 34, no. 3 (July 1949): 274–343.

Kashatus, William C. *Abraham Lincoln, the Quakers, and the Civil War: "A Trial of Principle and Faith."* Santa Barbara, Calif.: Praeger, 2014.

Kelley, Robert Lloyd. *The Cultural Pattern in American Politics: The First Century*. New York: Alfred A. Knopf, 1979.

Kidd, Thomas. *God of Liberty: A Religious History of the American Revolution*. New York: Basic Books, 2010.

Klay, Robin, and John Lunn. "Protestants and the American Economy in the Postcolonial Period: An Overview." In *God and Mammon: Protestants, Money, and the Market, 1790–1860*. Edited by Mark A. Noll. New York: Oxford University Press, 2001.

Klein, Philip Shriver. *President James Buchanan: A Biography*. University Park: Pennsylvania State University Press, 1962.

Klement, Frank L. *The Copperheads in the Middle West*. Chicago: University of Chicago Press, 1960.

———. *The Limits of Dissent: Clement L. Vallandigham and the Civil War*. Lexington: University Press of Kentucky, 1970.

Kleppner, Paul. *The Cross of Culture: A Social Analysis of Midwestern Politics, 1850–1900*. New York: Free Press, 1970.

———. *The Third Electoral System, 1853–1892: Parties, Voters, and Political Cultures*. Chapel Hill: University of North Carolina Press, 1979.

Korn, Benjamin Wallace. *American Jewry and the Civil War*. Cleveland: Meridian Books, 1951.

Kwitchen, Mary Augustine. *James Alphonsus McMaster: A Study in American Thought*. Washington, D.C.: Catholic University of America Press, 1949.

Lambert, Frank. *The Founding Fathers and the Place of Religion in America*. Princeton, N.J.: Princeton University Press, 2003.

Lawson, Melinda. *Patriot Fires: Forging a New American Nationalism in the Civil War North*. Lawrence: University Press of Kansas, 2002.

Leidner, Gordon. *Abraham Lincoln and the Bible: A Complete Compendium*. Carbondale: Southern Illinois University Press, 2023.

Lehman, James O., and Steven M. Nolt. *Mennonites, Amish, and the American Civil War*. Baltimore: Johns Hopkins University Press, 2007.

Levine, Bruce C. *The Fall of the House of Dixie: How the Civil War Remade the American South*. New York: Random House, 2013.

The Lincoln Log: A Daily Chronology of the Life of Abraham Lincoln. Illinois Historic Preservation Agency. www.thelincolnlog.org.

Long, Kathryn Teresa. *The Revival of 1857–58: Interpreting an American Religious Awakening*. New York: Oxford University Press, 1998.

Longley, Max. "The Radicalization of James McMaster: The 'Puritan' North as an Enemy of Peace, the Constitution, and the Catholic Church." *U.S. Catholic Historian* 36, no. 4 (Fall 2018): 25–50.

Magdol, Edward. *Owen Lovejoy, Abolitionist in Congress*. New Brunswick, N.J.: Rutgers University Press, 1967.

Man, Albon P., Jr. "The Church and the New York Draft Riots of 1863." *Records of the American Catholic Historical Society of Philadelphia* 62, no. 1 (March 1951): 33–50.

Manning, Chandra. *What This Cruel War Was Over: Soldiers, Slavery, and the Civil War*. New York: Vintage Civil War Library, 2008.

Marsden, George M. *The Evangelical Mind and the New School Presbyterian Experience: A Case Study of Thought and Theology in Nineteenth-Century America*. New Haven, Conn.: Yale University Press, 1970.

Masur, Kate. "The African American Delegation to Abraham Lincoln: A Reappraisal." *Civil War History* 56, no. 2 (June 2010): 117–44.

Mathews, Donald G. *Slavery and Methodism: A Chapter in American Morality*. Princeton, N.J.: Princeton University Press, 1965.

McClintock, Russell. *Lincoln and the Decision for War: The Northern Response to Secession*. Chapel Hill: University of North Carolina Press, 2010.

McKivigan, John R. *The War Against Proslavery Religion: Abolitionism and the Northern Churches, 1830–1865*. Ithaca, N.Y.: Cornell University Press, 1984.

McLoughlin, William G. *New England Dissent, 1630–1833: The Baptists and the Separation of Church and State*. 2 vols. Cambridge, Mass.: Harvard University Press, 1971.

McPherson, James M. *The Abolitionist Legacy: From Reconstruction to the NAACP*. Princeton, N.J.: Princeton University Press, 1975.

———. *Battle Cry of Freedom: The Civil War Era*. New York: Oxford University Press, 1988.

———. *For Cause and Comrades: Why Men Fought in the Civil War*. New York: Oxford University Press, 1997.

———. *The Struggle for Equality: Abolitionists and the Negro in the Civil War and Reconstruction*. Princeton, N.J.: Princeton University Press, 1964.

Meacham, Jon. *And There Was Light: Abraham Lincoln and the American Struggle*. New York: Random House, 2022.

Meinig, D. W. *The Shaping of America: A Geographical Perspective on 500 Years of History*. Vol. 1, *Atlantic America, 1492–1800* (New Haven, Conn.: Yale University Press, 1986).

Miers, Earl Schenck, ed. *Lincoln Day by Day: A Chronology, 1809–1865*. 3 vols. Washington, D.C.: Lincoln Sesquicentennial Commission, 1960.

Miller, Randall M., Harry S. Stout, and Charles Reagan Wilson, eds. *Religion and the American Civil War*. New York: Oxford University Press, 1998.

Miller, William B. "Presbyterian Signers of the Declaration of Indepen-

554   *Bibliography*

dence." *Journal of the Presbyterian Historical Society* 36 (Sept. 1958): 139–79. www.nps.gov/parkhistory/online_books/declaration/bio18 .htm.

Miller, William Lee. *Lincoln's Virtues: An Ethical Biography.* New York: Alfred A. Knopf, 2002.

———. *President Lincoln: The Duty of a Statesman.* New York: Alfred A. Knopf, 2008.

Mitchell, Reid. *Civil War Soldiers.* New York: Touchstone, 1989.

Moore, Joseph S. *Founding Sins: How a Group of Antislavery Radicals Fought to Put Christ into the Constitution.* New York: Oxford University Press, 2016.

Moore, Lawrence. *Religious Outsiders and the Making of Americans.* New York: Oxford University Press, 1986.

Moore, William F., and Jane Ann Moore. *Collaborators for Emancipation: Abraham Lincoln and Owen Lovejoy.* Urbana: University of Illinois Press, 2014.

Moorhead, James H. *American Apocalypse: Yankee Protestants and the Civil War, 1860–1869.* New Haven, Conn.: Yale University Press, 1978.

Mullin, Robert Bruce. *Episcopal Vision/American Reality: High Church Theology and Social Thought in Evangelical America.* New Haven, Conn.: Yale University Press, 1986.

Murrin, John M. "Religion and Politics in America from the First Settlements to the Civil War." In *Religion and American Politics: From the Colonial Period to the Present.* Edited by Mark A. Noll and Luke E. Harlow. 2nd ed. New York: Oxford University Press, 2007.

———. *Rethinking America: From Empire to Republic.* New York: Oxford University Press, 2018.

Nagel, Paul C. *This Sacred Trust: American Nationality, 1798–1898.* New York: Oxford University Press, 1971.

Neely, Mark E. *The Boundaries of American Political Culture in the Civil War Era.* Chapel Hill: University of North Carolina Press, 2005.

———. *The Last Best Hope of Earth: Abraham Lincoln and the Promise of America.* Cambridge, Mass.: Harvard University Press, 1993.

———. *Lincoln and the Democrats: The Politics of Opposition in the Civil War.* Cambridge, U.K.: Cambridge University Press, 2017.

———. *The Union Divided: Party Conflict in the Civil War North.* Cambridge, Mass.: Harvard University Press, 2002.

Nevins, Allan. *The War for the Union.* 4 vols. New York: Scribner, 1959–71.

Newman, Richard S. *The Transformation of American Abolitionism: Fighting Slavery in the Early Republic.* Chapel Hill: University of North Carolina Press, 2002.

Niebuhr, H. Richard. *The Social Sources of Denominationalism.* New York: Henry Holt, 1929.

Niven, John. *Salmon P. Chase: A Biography.* New York: Oxford University Press, 1995.

Noll, Mark A. *America's God: From Jonathan Edwards to Abraham Lincoln.* New York: Oxford University Press, 2002.

———. *The Civil War as a Theological Crisis.* Chapel Hill: University of North Carolina Press, 2006.

Oakes, James. *The Crooked Path to Abolition: Abraham Lincoln and the Antislavery Constitution.* New York: W. W. Norton, 2022.

———. *Freedom National: The Destruction of Slavery in the United States, 1861–1865.* New York: W. W. Norton, 2013.

———. *The Scorpion's Sting: Antislavery and the Coming of the Civil War.* New York: W. W. Norton, 2015.

O'Brien, John. "On Lincoln's 'Instrumentality' to End Slavery: 'Meditation on the Divine Will' and the Emancipation Proclamation," *Journal of the Abraham Lincoln Association* 45, no. 1 (Spring 2024): 17–49.

Oshatz, Molly. *Slavery and Sin: The Fight Against Slavery and the Rise of Liberal Protestantism.* New York: Oxford University Press, 2012.

Page, Sebastian N. *Black Resettlement and the American Civil War.* Cambridge, U.K.: Cambridge University Press, 2021.

Paludan, Phillip Shaw. *A People's Contest: The Union and Civil War, 1861–1865.* Lawrence: University Press of Kansas, 1990.

———. *The Presidency of Abraham Lincoln.* Lawrence: University Press of Kansas, 1994.

Parish, Peter J. "The Instruments of Providence: Slavery, Civil War, and the American Churches." In *Studies in Church History.* Vol. 20, *The Church and War.* Edited by W. J. Sheils. Oxford: Blackwell, 1983.

Parrillo, Nicholas. "Lincoln's Calvinist Transformation: Emancipation and War." *Civil War History* 46, no. 3 (Sept. 2000): 227–53.

Pease, Theodore Calvin, and James G. Randall, eds. *Diary of Orville Hickman Browning.* Springfield: Trustees of the Illinois State Historical Library, 1927–33.

Peck, Graham A. *Making an Antislavery Nation: Lincoln, Douglas, and the Battle over Freedom.* Urbana: University of Illinois Press, 2017.

Perry, Lewis. *Radical Abolitionism: Anarchy and the Government of God in Antislavery Thought.* Ithaca: Cornell University Press, 1973).

Pestana, Carla Gardina. *Quakers and Baptists in Colonial Massachusetts.* New York: Cambridge University Press, 1991.

Phillips, Christopher. *The Rivers Ran Backward: The Civil War and the*

556   *Bibliography*

Remaking of the American Middle Border. New York: Oxford University Press, 2016.

Phillips, Jason. *Looming Civil War: How Nineteenth-Century Americans Imagined the Future.* New York: Oxford University Press, 2018.

Potter, David M. *The Impending Crisis, 1848–1861.* New York: Harper Torchbooks, 1976.

———. *Lincoln and His Party in the Secession Crisis.* New Haven, Conn.: Yale University Press, 1942.

Pryor, Elizabeth Brown. *Six Encounters with Lincoln: A President Confronts Democracy and Its Demons.* New York: Viking, 2017.

Quist, John W. "Theodore Foster: A Liberty Party Abolitionist Confronts the Civil War and Emancipation." *Journal of the Civil War Era* 13, no. 2. (June 2023): 178–213.

Rable, George C. *God's Almost Chosen Peoples: A Religious History of the American Civil War.* Chapel Hill: University of North Carolina Press, 2010.

Randall, James G. *Lincoln the President.* 4 vols. New York: Dodd, Mead, 1945–55.

Richey, Russell E. *Early American Methodism.* Bloomington: Indiana University Press, 1991.

Rohrer, James R. "Sunday Mails and the Church-State Theme in Jacksonian America." *Journal of the Early Republic* 7, no. 1 (Spring 1987): 53–74.

Ryan, Frank W. "The *Southern Quarterly Review,* 1842–1857: A Study in Thought and Opinion in the Old South." PhD diss., University of North Carolina, 1956.

Samito, Christian G. *Becoming American Under Fire: Irish Americans, African Americans, and the Politics of Citizenship During the Civil War Era.* Ithaca, N.Y.: Cornell University Press, 2009.

———. *Lincoln and the Thirteenth Amendment.* Carbondale: Southern Illinois University Press, 2015.

Sarna, Jonathan D., and Benjamin Shapell. *Lincoln and the Jews: A History.* New York: Thomas Dunne Books/St. Martin's Press, 2015.

Sassi, Jonathan D. *A Republic of Righteousness: The Public Christianity of the Post-Revolutionary New England Clergy.* New York: Oxford University Press, 2001.

Saum, Lewis O. *The Popular Mood of Pre–Civil War America.* Westport, Conn.: Greenwood Press, 1980.

Schantz, Mark S. *Awaiting the Heavenly Country: The Civil War and America's Culture of Death.* Ithaca, N.Y.: Cornell University Press, 2008.

Schlereth, Eric R. *An Age of Infidels: The Politics of Religious Controversy in the Early United States*. Philadelphia: University of Pennsylvania Press, 2013.

Scott, Sean A. *A Visitation of God: Northern Civilians Interpret the Civil War*. Oxford: Oxford University Press, 2011.

Sears, Stephen W. *George B. McClellan: The Young Napoleon*. New York: Ticknor & Fields, 1988.

Sellers, Charles Grier, Jr., ed. *The Southerner as American*. Chapel Hill: University of North Carolina Press, 1960.

Sewell, Richard H. *Ballots for Freedom: Antislavery Politics in the United States, 1837–1860*. New York: W. W. Norton, 1976.

Shalev, Eran. *American Zion: The Old Testament as a Political Text from the Revolution to the Civil War*. New Haven, Conn.: Yale University Press, 2013.

Shankman, Arnold. "Draft Resistance in Civil War Pennsylvania." *Pennsylvania Magazine of History and Biography* 101, no. 2 (April 1977): 191–204.

Silbey, Joel H. *The Partisan Imperative: The Dynamics of American Politics Before the Civil War*. New York: Oxford University Press, 1985.

———. *A Respectable Minority: The Democratic Party in the Civil War Era, 1860–1868*. New York: W. W. Norton, 1977.

Silver, James W. *Confederate Morale and Church Propaganda*. New York: W. W. Norton, 1967.

Sinha, Manisha. *The Slave's Cause: A History of Abolition*. New Haven, Conn.: Yale University Press, 2016.

Smith, Adam I. P. *No Party Now: Politics in the Civil War North*. Oxford: Oxford University Press, 2006.

———. *The Stormy Present: Conservatism and the Problem of Slavery in Northern Politics, 1846–1865*. Chapel Hill: University of North Carolina Press, 2017.

Smith, Anthony D. *Chosen Peoples: Sacred Sources of National Identity*. Oxford: Oxford University Press, 2003.

Smith, Timothy L. *Revivalism and Social Reform: American Protestantism on the Eve of the Civil War*. New York: Harper & Row, 1965.

Snay, Mitchell. *Gospel of Disunion: Religion and Separatism in the Antebellum South*. Cambridge, U.K.: Cambridge University Press, 1993.

Stampp, Kenneth M. *And the War Came: The North and the Secession Crisis, 1860–61*. Chicago: University of Chicago Press, 1950.

Starr, Louis M. *Bohemian Brigade: Civil War Newsmen in Action*. New York: Alfred A. Knopf, 1954.

Stauffer, John, and Benjamin Soskis. *The Battle Hymn of the Republic: A Biography of the Song That Marches On*. New York: Oxford University Press, 2013.

Stewart, James Brewer. *Holy Warriors: The Abolitionists and American Slavery*, rev. ed. New York: Hill and Wang, 1996.

Stewart, John W. *Mediating the Center: Charles Hodge on American Science, Language, Literature, and Politics*. Princeton, N.J.: Princeton Theological Seminary, 1995.

Stewart, John W., and James H. Moorhead, eds. *Charles Hodge Revisited: A Critical Appraisal of His Life and Work*. Grand Rapids, Mich.: William B. Eerdmans, 2002.

Stewart, Katherine. *The Power Worshippers: Inside the Dangerous Rise of Religious Nationalism*. New York: Bloomsbury, 2019.

Stout, Harry S. *Upon the Altar of the Nation: A Moral History of the Civil War*. New York: Viking, 2006.

Stout, Harry S. and Christopher Grasso. "Civil War, Religion, and Communications: The Case of Richmond." In Miller, Stout, and Wilson, *Religion and the American Civil War*.

Stowell, Daniel W. *Rebuilding Zion: The Religious Reconstruction of the South, 1863–1877*. New York: Oxford University Press, 1998.

Striner, Richard. *Father Abraham: Lincoln's Relentless Struggle to End Slavery*. New York: Oxford University Press, 2006.

Sweet, William Warren. *The Story of Religion in America*. New York: Harper & Bros., 1950.

Swierenga, Robert P., ed. *Beyond the Civil War Synthesis: Political Essays of the Civil War Era*. Westport, Conn.: Greenwood Press, 1975.

Tarbell, Ida M. *The Life of Abraham Lincoln*. 4 vols. New York: Lincoln Memorial Association, 1895–99.

Taylor, Alan. "'Wasty Ways': Stories of American Settlement." *Environmental History* 3 (July 1998): 291–310.

Temple, Wayne C. *Abraham Lincoln from Skeptic to Prophet*. Mahomet, Ill.: Mayhaven, 1995.

Thomas, Benjamin P. *Abraham Lincoln: A Biography*. New York: Alfred A. Knopf, 1952.

Thompson, Ernest Trice. *Presbyterians in the South*. 3 vols. Richmond, Va.: John Knox Press, 1963–73.

Trefousse, Hans L. *Andrew Johnson: A Biography*. New York: W. W. Norton, 1989.

Trueblood, Elton. *Abraham Lincoln: A Spiritual Biography*. New York: Phoenix Press, 1986.

Turner, James. *Without God, Without Creed: The Origins of Unbelief in America*. Baltimore: Johns Hopkins University Press, 1985.

Turner, Thomas. *Beware the People Weeping: Public Opinion and the Assas-*

sination of Abraham Lincoln. Baton Rouge: Louisiana State University Press, 1982.

Ural, Susannah J., ed. *Civil War Citizens: Race, Ethnicity, and Identity in America's Bloodiest Conflict.* New York: New York University Press, 2010.

———. *The Harp and the Eagle: Irish-American Volunteers and the Union Army, 1861–1865.* New York: New York University Press, 2006.

Vander Velde, Lewis George. *The Presbyterian Churches and the Federal Union, 1861–1869.* Cambridge, Mass.: Harvard University Press, 1932.

Varon, Elizabeth R. *Armies of Deliverance: A New History of the Civil War.* New York: Oxford University Press, 2019.

Volkman, Lucas P. *Houses Divided: Evangelical Schisms and the Crisis of the Union in Missouri.* New York: Oxford University Press, 2018.

Vorenberg, Michael. *Final Freedom: The Civil War, the Abolition of Slavery, and the Thirteenth Amendment.* Cambridge, U.K.: Cambridge University Press, 2001.

Wainwright, Nicholas B. "The Loyal Opposition in Civil War Philadelphia." *Pennsylvania Magazine of History and Biography* 88, no. 3 (July 1964): 294–315.

Wakelyn, Jon L. *Southern Pamphlets on Secession, November 1860–April 1861.* Chapel Hill: University of North Carolina Press, 1996.

Waldman, Steven. *Founding Faith: Providence, Politics, and the Birth of Religious Freedom in America.* New York: Random House, 2008.

Waldstreicher, David. *In the Midst of Perpetual Fetes: The Making of American Nationalism, 1776–1820.* Chapel Hill: University of North Carolina Press, 1997.

Wallace, Peter J. "'The Bond of Union': The Old School Presbyterian Church and the American Nation, 1837–1861" PhD diss., University of Notre Dame, 2004.

Weber, Jennifer L. *Copperheads: The Rise and Fall of Lincoln's Opponents in the North.* Oxford: Oxford University Press, 2006.

Wesley, Timothy L. *The Politics of Faith During the Civil War.* Baton Rouge: Louisiana State University Press, 2013.

West, John G. *The Politics of Revelation and Reason: Religion and Civic Life in the New Nation.* Lawrence: University Press of Kansas, 1996.

White, Jonathan D. *Emancipation, the Union Army, and the Reelection of Abraham Lincoln.* Baton Rouge: Louisiana State University Press, 2014.

White, Jonathan W., and Danielle C. Forand, eds. "The Secession Crisis Diary of Gideon Welles." *Journal of the Abraham Lincoln Association* 41, no. 1 (Winter 2020): 1–23.

[White, Richard Grant.] *The New Gospel of Peace According to St. Benjamin.* New York, 1863.

White, Ronald C. *A. Lincoln: A Biography.* New York: Random House, 2009.

———. *Lincoln in Private.* New York: Random House, 2021.

———. *Lincoln's Greatest Speech: The Second Inaugural.* New York: Simon & Schuster, 2002.

Wigger, John H. *American Saint: Francis Asbury and the Methodists.* New York: Oxford University Press, 2012.

———. *Taking Heaven by Storm: Methodism and the Rise of Popular Christianity in America.* New York: Oxford University Press, 1998.

Wilentz, Sean, *The Rise of American Democracy: Jefferson to Lincoln.* New York: W. W. Norton, 2005.

Williams, Rachel. *Tabernacles in the Wilderness: The U.S. Christian Commission on the Civil War Battlefront.* Kent, Ohio: Kent State University Press, 2024.

Williamson, Chilton. *Vermont in Quandary, 1763–1825.* Montpelier: Vermont Historical Society, 1949.

Wilson, Douglas L. *Honor's Voice: The Transformation of Abraham Lincoln.* New York: Alfred A. Knopf, 1998.

———. *Lincoln's Sword: The Presidency and the Power of Words.* New York: Alfred A. Knopf, 2006.

———. "William H. Herndon on Lincoln's Fatalism." *Journal of the Abraham Lincoln Association* 35, no. 2 (Summer 2014): 1–17.

Winger, Stewart. *Lincoln, Religion, and Romantic Cultural Politics.* DeKalb: Northern Illinois University Press, 2003.

Winkle, Kenneth J. *The Young Eagle: The Rise of Abraham Lincoln.* Dallas: Taylor, 2001.

Wirzbicki, Peter. *Fighting for the Higher Law: Black and White Transcendentalists Against Slavery.* Philadelphia: University of Pennsylvania Press, 2021.

Wolf, William J. *The Almost Chosen People: A Study of the Religion of Abraham Lincoln.* Garden City, N.Y.: Doubleday, 1959.

Woodworth, Steven E. *While God Is Marching On: The Religious World of Civil War Soldiers.* Lawrence: University Press of Kansas, 2001.

Wright, Ben, and Zachary W. Dresser. *Apocalypse and the Millennium in the American Civil War Era.* Baton Rouge: Louisiana State University Press, 2013.

Zeitz, Joshua, *Lincoln's God: How Faith Transformed a President and a Nation.* New York: Viking, 2023.

Index

Page numbers in *italics* refer to illustrations.

Abbot, Francis E., 437n75
Abbott, Joseph, 18
Abell, Lemuel, 492n152
abolitionists, 50, 51–52, 84,
    93, 131, 136, 137, 165,
    198, 312, 403, 407, 409,
    413
  and anti-Catholic sentiment,
    229–30
  blamed for secession, 67, 79–80,
    99, 138
  denigrated in press, 306–7, 373
  and 1864 election, 290, 348
  and imperialism, 409–10
  and Liberal Republican Party,
    407
  and Lincoln, 80–81, 161, 174,
    280, 285, 287, 395
  opposition to, 41, 57, 139, 140,
    230, 240–41, 316, 329–30
  opposition to emigration
    schemes, 178
  responses to Frémont initiative,
    125–26, 134–35
  southern perceptions of, 40–41,

43, 47, 83–84, 403, 407. *See
  also* nationalism, religious:
  antislavery; conservative
Abraham Africanus, 336
Adams, Ezra, 130
Adams, John, 5, 16, 36–37
Adams, John Quincy, 117, 136
Adams, Nehemiah: *A South-Side
  View of Slavery*, 143
Adams, William, 73, 87, 89, 339,
  395
Adger, John, 43
Adventists, 26
African Americans
  black troops, 230, 285, 287, 380;
    arming of, 152, 233,
    285–86; bravery of, 240,
    286, 287–88, 315
  capabilities, perceptions of, 295,
    400–401
  on death of Lincoln, 400
  education, 197, 287, 389
  free blacks, 162–63, 198, 287,
    341, 407–8
  ministers, 165, 286, 501n120

562   *Index*

African Americans *(continued)*
  perceptions of Lincoln, 369–70,
    393–94
  and radical activism, 40, 135
  violence against, 228, 288, 405,
    407
African Civilization Society, 265
African Methodist Episcopal
    Church, 178, 179, 341,
    369–70, 394
Agnew, Eliza, 165
America
  as global model, 30, 133–34,
    146, 345, 449n10, 493n178
  national exceptionalism of, 7,
    102–4, 128, 145, 279
  shaped by Providence, 75–76,
    81, 109, 145–46, 288, 398,
    429n21
  worthy of God's special favor,
    129, 181, 279, 280, 362,
    409. *See also* Lincoln:
    speeches/writings, Second
    Inaugural
American and Foreign Christian
    Union, 25
American Anti-slavery Society
    (AASS), 40, 42, 48, 130,
    290
American Baptist Home
    Missionary Society, 294
American Baptist Union, 138
American Bible Society, 29, 339
American Board of Commissioners
    for Foreign Missions, 30
American Colonization Society, 41
American Education Society, 29
American Home Missionary
    Society, 29
American Missionary Association,
    285, 408

American Party. *See* Know-
    Nothing Party
American Protestant Society, 25
American Revolution, xvii, 3, 75,
    145–46
  Patriot clergy, role of in, 6–7
American Sunday School
    Union, 29
American Temperance Society, 29
American Tract Society, 29, 271
Ames, Edward R., 291
Amish, political allegiance, 475n88
Anderson, Robert, 68
Andrew, James O., 45, 292
Andrew, John, 298
Anglicans, 5, 9, 21
Anti-abolition State Rights Society,
    498n81
anti-Catholic sentiment, 22, 24–25,
    58, 117, 138, 219, 226, 333,
    359
anticlericalism, 26
anti-draft protests, 206, 215,
    228–31, 236–37, 250, 257,
    288, 322, 341–42, 472n35,
    474n86
Antietam, Battle of (1862), 190, 191
anti-Irish sentiment, 230–31
antisemitism, 138, 360–61
antislavery politics, prewar,
    47–56. *See* also nationalism,
    religious: antislavery
Appalachia, sectarianism in, 25,
    32–33, 297
Appomattox, Confederate
    surrender at, celebration of,
    389, 391
Arkansas, 158, 284, 344
Arminianism, 13, 21, 23–24,
    413–14
Army of the Ohio, 214

Index

Army of the Potomac, 158, 159, 173, 274, 276
Army of the Tennessee, 274
Arnold, Benedict, 344
Arnold, Isaac, 55
arrests, arbitrary, 202, 208–12, 214–15, 226, 236, 237, 238, 249, 327, 329, 333
Asbury, Francis, 9, 12–13, 13–14
Ashley, James, 370, 479n181
Atlanta, surrender of, 329, 342, 374

Bache, Anna, 113, 114
Backus, John Chester, 446n118
Bacon, Leonard, 395
Bailey, Silas, 148
Baird, Robert, 23
   Religion in America (1844), 28–29, 440n10
Baker, Edward, 357
Baltimore, 71, 141, 142
   Republican convention in (1864), 290
Bangs, Nathan, 10, 22, 30, 46
bank, national, 34, 36
Banks, Nathaniel, 284, 389
Baptists, 5, 9, 21, 23, 119–20, 130, 240, 414, 434n29, 440n11
   anti-mission, 32, 217, 358, 413
   as conservative Unionists, 86, 217
   Free Will, 49
   influence of Arminianism on, 24
   ministers, 31, 63, 118, 129, 142, 165, 184
   New Light, 5, 6, 31
   numbers, 66–67
   petitions to Lincoln, 119, 157
   political allegiance of, 38, 59
   Primitive, 22, 31–32, 434n29

and providentialism, 18
Regular, 28–29, 66–67
and religious divisions, 28–29
rivalry with Methodists, 21, 22, 25
and slavery, 42–43, 44, 45, 46, 49, 282, 371
suspicion of New England theology and influence, 26–27. *See also* fast days: denominational
Barlow, Samuel, 250, 322
Barnard, William, 165
Barnes, John, 317, 318
Barnett, Treffry J., 250–51
Barney, Hiram, 250, 480n5
Bateman, Warner, 404
Bates, Edward, 140
Beecher, Charles, 71
Beecher, Henry Ward, 42, 93, 328, 391, 404
   as antislavery nationalist, xix, 78, 161, 180; criticism of him as, 57, 91, 170, 225
   and 1864 election, 350, 354, 358
   and providentialism, 76, 362
   vilification of, 243, 247
Beecher, Lyman, 24, 30, 41, 42, 56
Bell, John, 59
Bellows, Henry Whitney, 72, 76, 78, 79, 136, 289
Belmont, August, 324, 361
Bennett, James Gordon, 59, 138, 172, 206, 387
Bergen, John G., 117–18, 451n40
Bible, the
   New Testament, 92, 142–43, 188, 383; Revelation, Book of, 313

564 *Index*

Bible, the *(continued)*
  Old Testament: Exodus, 363; Genesis, 383; Isaiah, 6–7, 76, 81, 92, 135, 141, 195, 231, 428n7; Nehemiah, 351–52; Proverbs, 113
  reading of, xii, 147
  use of scriptures, 208, 211, 232, 235, 351–52, 365; and equality, 222; to justify resistance to treason, 279; on secession as a sin, 41–42; in support of emancipation, 181, 185, 186, 282; in support of slavery, 43–44, 90–91, 257, 259, 297, 301, 407 (and claims against this, 92–93, 131); in support of states rights, 326–27
Birney, James G., 48
Bittinger, Joseph, 136
Black, Jeremiah S., 68, 69
"black codes," 160, 287, 403
Blair, Montgomery, 174, 202
Blanchard, Joseph, 118
Blundell, William, 239
Boardman, George Dana, 400
Boardman, Henry, 364
Board of Delegates of American Israelites, 361
Board of Indian Commissioners, 406
Booth, John Wilkes, 390
border states, 44, 87, 91, 111, 189, 257, 414
  conservative Unionists in, 86, 218, 306
  and 1864 election, 324, 347
  political allegiance in, 59, 217, 358
  religious division in, 46, 140

responses to secession, 141–42. *See also* Lincoln: as president, border states strategy
Boston, Mass., 22, 71, 78, 143, 362, 409
Boston *Pilot*, 167, 168, 375
  on days of fast, 72, 127
  as Democratic organ, 58, 218–19
  on Lincoln, 171, 391
  and opposition to emancipation, 170, 306
  and racism, 169, 200. *See also* Donahoe, Patrick
Botts, John Minor, 295–96
Boutwell, George S., 191, 258
Bradford, Augustus, 471n32
Braeunlich, Gustav, 241
Bragg, Braxton, 275
Breckinridge, John C., 58
Breckinridge, Robert J., xx
  and 1864 election, 347–48
  and emancipation, 95, 296, 304–5
  and secession, 88, 98, 99
Brewster, Benjamin H., 342
Brewster, Charlie, 311, 315
Briggs, "Daddy," 32
Briggs, George N., 77, 434n29
Briggs, James A., 113, 114
Bright, Jesse, 257
Brookes, Iveson L., 42–43
Brookes, James Hall, 208
Brooklyn, N.Y., 135
  Plymouth Church, 243, 328, 350
Brooks, James, 355
Brooks, Phillips, 289
Brooks, Sidney, 150
Brough, John, 215, 216

Index

Brown, John, 50, 245, 247
    raid on Harpers Ferry, 50, 89,
        183–84
Brown, William Wells, 198
Browning, Orville H., 150–53,
        459nn103,104
Brownlow, William Gannaway, xx,
        71, 233, 296–301, 490n132
    Parson Brownlow's Book,
        300–301
Brownson, Orestes A., 168, 218,
        229, 307
Bruce, Philip, 11
Brunson, Alfred, 33
Buchanan, James, 57, 58, 62, 68,
        444n91
    corruption in administration,
        69–70, 480n5
    critics of, 69–71, 93, 118, 124,
        440n18, 441nn26,28,29,30
    and secession, 67–69, 79. *See also*
        fast days: Union (Jan. 1861)
Bucher, Theodore P., 86,
        445n98
Buckingham, William A., 115,
        175–76, 349
Buell, Don Carlos, 158
Bullard, Artemas, 18
Bull Run, Battle of (1861), 120,
        125, 129, 377
Bull Run, Second, Battle of (1862),
        174, 182
Burbridge, Stephen G., 329
Burchard, Jedidiah, 272, 276,
        282
Bureau of Indian Affairs, 406
Burnside, Ambrose E., 203, 214
Burr, Charles Chauncey, 207,
        212–13, 224, 232, 244–45,
        326, 339
    on Lincoln, 336, 337, 387

Burrowes, George, 142
Burrud, John, 311, 314, 315, 317,
        319, 395
Burt, J. S., 63
Bush, Isidor, 361
Butler, Benjamin F., 188, 247, 273,
        296, 359
Butler, Joseph, 114–15
"Butternuts," 215, 217, 255, 256,
        309

Calhoun, John C., 44
Calvinism, 12, 13, 20, 23, 33, 38,
        50, 74, 193, 295, 414
    influence on Lincoln, 265, 273
    and religious division, 21, 22
Cameron, Simon, 116, 160, 171,
        265
Canada, 10, 355–56
Cape Cod, Seminary, 150
Capers, William, 44
Carpenter, Francis Bicknell, 156,
        175, 381
Carpenter, Stephen Decatur, 333
    Logic of History (1864), 332
carpetbaggers, 406
cartoons, political, 273, 334,
        498n70
Cartwright, Peter, 22, 32, 54
Cass, Lewis, 68
Catholicism, xix, 5, 26, 38, 94, 414,
        431n53, 432n59, 462n36
    abolitionist Catholics, 229, 307,
        360, 371, 373
    and antislavery, 57, 223, 329–30
    Catholic-Protestant antipathy,
        320
    and fast days, 72, 127, 128
    German Catholics, 359, 360
    growth of, 23, 24, 26, 67, 409
    Irish Catholics, 229, 231

Catholicism (*continued*)
political allegiance, 52, 56, 59, 216–17, 218–19, 359–60, 364
and religious conservative nationalism, 141, 223, 240; opposition to demands for emancipation, 157–58, 168–69, 201, 306
support for Union, 139. *See also* anti-Catholic sentiment; Hughes, John; Purcell, John Baptist
Catholic Telegraph, 58, 218, 223, 307, 359–60
celebrity, culture of, 296–97
Chafee, H. W., 134
Chamberlain, Samuel, 233-34, 309, 327
Chambré, A. St. John, 283
Chancellorsville, Battle of (1863), 214, 274, 377
Channing, William Henry, 55, 137, 334
Chapin, Edwin H., 160
Chase, Salmon P., 114, 133, 140, 241, 244–45, 268–69, 385, 405, 479n180
and 1864 election, 290
on Lincoln, 177–78, 194
response to preliminary emancipation proclamation, 174
Chattanooga Campaign (1863), 262, 275
Cheever, George Barrell, 92, 196, 403, 409
and antislavery nationalism, xix, 137, 370
and fast day (Sept. 1861), 130, 131

and Frémont initiative, 290–91
vilification of, 225
Cheney, David B., 136–37
Chenowith, George D., 460n10
Chesnut, Mary, 377
Chicago
Baptist response to abolition of slavery in Washington, D.C., 162
Bryan Hall, 128, 182, 190, 357
Congregationalist responses to Frémont initiative, 134
and fast days, 71–72, 127–28, 277
response to thanksgiving day (Nov. 1863), 362
Union rally (1864), 342
"Chicago Memorial," (1862) 184–91, 466nn102,106, 467n110
Chicago Times, 217, 219, 309–10
Chicago Tribune, 62, 380
on Buchanan, 69, 70
on fast day (Sept. 1861), 127–28
on Lincoln and emancipation, 132, 164, 198–99
Chickamauga, Battle of (1863), 275, 311, 377
Christian Advocate and Journal (New York), 10–11, 278, 359
Christian Recorder (Philadelphia), 178, 353, 359
"The Christian Union" (Ohio), 307
Christy, David: *Pulpit Politics*, 224
churches
buildings, 8–9, 428n10
dismissals and disciplinary hearings, 217, 228, 239, 240, 292, 309, 327, 438n86, 496n37

ecclesiastical reunion, postwar,
406–7
membership numbers, 66–67
postwar, 411
Cincinnati, 71, 108, 360
Lane Theological Seminary,
41–42
Cincinnati Enquirer, 219, 334
citizenship, perception of, xii,
14, 38
civil equality, 137, 197, 280, 287,
288, 289, 404, 406, 408
civil liberties, 238
habeas corpus, suspension of
writ of, 147, 202, 244. *See
also* Lincoln: as president,
and war powers
civil rights activism, xiv–xv, 410,
411
civil rights bill, veto of (1866), 404
Civil War
blamed on antislavery
movement, 138, 225
casualties, 276–77, 279–80, 305,
311, 312, 313, 321, 322,
341
effects on Confederacy, 374, 375,
377–78
foreign perceptions of, 129, 189,
195
global significance of, 313, 345,
351, 363
progress of, 120, 125, 129,
154–55, 158–59, 163, 172,
173, 174, 175, 182, 185,
190, 200, 203, 206, 214,
215, 248, 262, 273–74,
275–77, 312–13, 380–81
as punishment for national sin,
119, 129–30, 155, 176, 267,
273, 279, 308–9, 313

scriptural justification for, 279
seen as righteous conflict,
507n35
Clark, George Henry, 84
Clay, Henry, 36, 48, 449n10
"American System," 34
Clinton, Henry L., 329
Cobb, Howell, 68
Cobb, Sylvanus, 197
coinage, 7, 114
Coke, Thomas, 9, 13
Cold Harbor, Battle of (1864), 262,
276, 321
Colfax, Schuyler, 103, 125, 194,
265
collective punishment, concept
of, 73, 121, 122, 129,
144. *See also* Civil War, as
punishment for national sin
Collyer, Robert, 161, 162
colonization (black), 137, 200, 201
black responses to, 178–80
support for, 42, 457n65
Columbia, S.C., 82, 375
Columbus, Ky., 125, 249, 255
Columbus, Ohio, Democratic state
convention in (1863), 249
Colver, Nathaniel, 161
communications, 7–8, 296, 328
Comstock, Elizabeth, 270
Confederacy
and black enlistment, 373–76
clergy in, 376–77, 378–79;
support for, 134–35,
142–43
condemnation of, 146, 297–98
Confederate army, 275
Constitution, 112, 130
"cornerstone theology" in, 131,
283, 505n176
divisions in, 374–75

568   *Index*

Confederacy *(continued)*
  naval blockade of, 207
  Presbyterian Church in, 140;
    response to Lincoln's death,
    397
  and role of slavery within, 131,
    283
  southern unity, 376, 377–78. *See
    also* thanksgiving, days of
Confiscation Acts, 415
  first (1861), 125, 152
  Second (1862), 173, 174, 180,
    181, 188
Congregationalists, 5, 9, 12, 13, 23,
    67, 138, 297, 349, 392,
    399–400, 415, 434n21
  antislavery, 47, 49, 183
  Arminian influence on, 24
  ministers, 21, 77, 134, 183
  and moral improvement, 30
  numbers, 66
  petitions to Lincoln, 118–19,
    157
  Plan of Union, 415
  political allegiance, 38, 216
  and Providence, 6, 80
  and religious divisions, 28–29, 33
  response to Lincoln election
    (1860), 60
  response to preliminary
    emancipation proclamation,
    195
  Welsh, 118, 119
Conkling, James C., 251–52, 285
Connecticut, 21, 155, 175–76
  antislavery sentiment in, 132
conscription, 285, 322. *See also*
  Enrollment Act
Constitutional Union Party, 59,
  86, 97
Continental Congress, 16–17

Conway, Moncure, 133
Cook, John F., Jr., 177
Cook, Joseph, 408–9
Copperhead Minstrel, 243, 331–33
Copperheads. *See* Democratic
  Party: Peace Democrats
Corneille, Samuel, 363
Cornell, Samuel, 264
Corning, Erastus, 248
corruption, federal, 52, 69–70, 116,
  117, 132, 144, 233–34, 406
cotton culture, 42, 43, 47
Covenanters. *See* Presbyterians:
  Reformed
Covode, John, 69
Cowan, Edgar, 477n154
Cox, Samuel Sullivan ("Sunset"),
  226–27, 233, 251, 324, 334,
  335–36, 371
Crane, William C., 18
Crapo, Henry, 404–5
Crary, Benjamin, 352–53, 503n144
Crittenden, John J., 68–69, 97
Cromwell, Oliver, 20
Cuba, 69
Cummings, Joseph, 292
Curran, Robert, 278–79, 287, 295
Curry, Daniel, 369–72

Daniel, John Moncure, 374,
  377–78
Danville Quarterly Review, 304, 347
Danville Theological Seminary
  (Kentucky), 304
Dartmouth College, 222, 224
Darwinism, 409
Davidson, Robert, 128–29, 144,
  146
Davis, David, 261, 298
Davis, Jefferson, 364, 375, 391–92
  perceptions of, 168, 211, 395

Dawson, John L., 59
Dayton, Ohio
    Evangelical Lutheran Church,
      330
    First Presbyterian Church, 208
Dayton Daily Empire, 337, 355, 364,
      392, 508n59, 511n96
Dean, Henry Clay ("Dirty"), xx,
      234, 324, 330
    arrest of, 211–12, 226
    opposition to war powers, 207,
      237; defense of liberty, 237,
      238
    racism of, 221–22
Declaration of Independence, xvii,
      15–17, 52–53, 78, 145–46,
      163, 197, 222
Defrees, John, 265
deists, 4, 16, 22, 35, 54, 74
Delany, Martin R., 286
Delaware, 10, 91, 284, 356
Democratic Party, xxi, xxiv,
      116–17, 238–40, 412, 415
    campaign songs, 243–45
    Catholics in, 226, 228
    conservative religious support
      for, 358–59
    on death of Harrison, 18, 37
    on death of Lincoln, 392,
      396–97
    and defense of citizens' rights,
      236–38
    defense of slavery, 56–60
    Douglas Democrats, 86, 97
    and elections, 346–47; **(1856)**,
      57–58; **(1860)**, 55–56;
      (1862), 202–3; **(1863)**,
      214, 215, 216–17; **(1864)**,
      226–27, 261, 320–21, 339;
      Chicago platform, 344–45,
      353, 358–61

    and fast/thanksgiving days, 309
    and Frémont initiative, 125, 126
    New Departure, 407
    Peace Democrats
      (Copperheads), 205,
      212, 217, 219–20, 228,
      231–35, 255, 305, 322,
      415, 472n35, 492n152,
      496n41; and 1864 election,
      291, 324, 498n81; and
      Lincoln's Second Inaugural,
      387; opposed to federal
      centralization, 205, 209;
      opposition to, 351–52, 353,
      360, 364; and passage of
      Thirteenth Amendment,
      371; and religious
      division, 305–6, 308. *See
      also* McMaster, James;
      Olds, Edson Baldwin;
      Vallandigham, Clement L.
    political appeal of, 34–35, 38, 48,
      51, 58–60, 138
    political clubs, 331
    and proposals for gradual
      abolition, 171
    and prospect of southern use of
      black troops, 375–76
    pro-war, 205, 216, 219, 228, 229,
      290, 308, 325, 329, 330,
      332, 477n154, 496n42
    and racism, 48, 56–57, 221,
      222–23, 321, 331–32,
      498n70
    reactions to antislavery,
      57–60, 98
    and religious conservatives,
      220–27
    and religious diversity, 325
    and religious nationalism, xv,
      xvii, xix, 214–20, 245–47

570   *Index*

Democratic Party *(continued)*
  on Republicans, 51–52, 58
  and separation of politics and
    religion, 34–35, 70
  and thanksgiving day (1864), 364
  vilification of antislavery
    nationalists, 331–33
  wartime divisions within, xix,
    205, 216, 219–20, 322–27
  and white supremacy, 138, 205,
    207, 209, 221–22, 254. *See
    also* Petroleum Vesuvius
    Nasby
Democratic-Republican Party,
  33, 34
Dempster, John, 184–85, 190, 199,
  467n110
Dickinson, Anna, xix, 348–49
Dickinson, Daniel S., 250
Disciples of Christ, 217, 358
Dix, John Adams, 229
Dixon, James, 25, 267
Dixon, William E., 267, 346
Dodge, William E., 346–47
Doggett, Thomas, 132, 148–49
Donahoe, Patrick, 233, 323, 326
  and conservative religious
    nationalism, 168, 202, 235,
    236, 273–74
  and 1864 election, 325
  on Lincoln, 203, 393. *See also*
    Boston *Pilot*
Doolittle, James R., 115, 294
Douglas, Stephen A., xvii, 57, 70,
  206, 207
  Kansas-Nebraska Act, 50–51, 58
Douglass, Frederick, xix, 39–40,
  165, 178, 230, 286, 290,
  346, 410, 426n9
  and 1864 election, 347, 348, 352,
  358

and Hayes, 407–8
on Lincoln's death, 393–94
response to preliminary
  emancipation proclamation,
  197–98
response to Second Inaugural,
  385, 386
Douglass, Lewis, 179–80
Douthit, Jasper, 472n35
Dow, John, 14
Dow, Lorenzo, 13
draft, 206, 214, 227–28, 250–51,
  285, 317, 342. *See also*
  anti-draft protests
Duffield, George, 75, 81, 428n7
Duffield, George, Jr., 73
Duncan, James, 85
Dunn, William M., 446n118
Dunning, Homer, 80, 81, 363,
  365–66, 375
Dutch Reformed Church, 6, 13,
  36, 38, 131, 146, 280, 288

economy
  growth, 7–8, 103, 410
  southern, 42, 43, 408
  wartime, 262, 275, 362
editors, 216, 283, 304
  antislavery nationalist, 160, 161,
    165, 197, 199, 249
  arrests of, 327–28
  Catholic, 306–7, 322
  conservative, 138, 139, 143–44,
    168, 202
  Democratic, 170, 224, 233,
    238–39, 309, 332, 354–55,
    396; Copperhead, 355, 392
  and freedom of press, 214
  influence on Lincoln, 274–75
  Methodist, 24, 146, 184, 358, 369
  pro-South, 213, 220

Republican, 62, 117, 308, 394.
See also Beecher, Henry
Ward; Bennett, James
Gordon; Breckinridge,
Robert J.; Donahoe,
Patrick; Eddy, Thomas
Mears; McMaster, James;
Mulally, John; Prime,
Samuel Irenaeus; Tilton,
Theodore E.
Eddy, Thomas Mears, 146, 147,
184, 218, 341–42, 358–59
education, 8, 24–25, 34, 63, 184
Edwards, Richard, 395
Einhorn, David, 92
Elder, William Henry, 333
elections
campaign songbooks, 335
gubernatorial, 202, 215–16, 224,
254, 255, 317, 405
presidential: (1800), 36–37;
(1840), 33, 48; (1844),
48; (1856), 28, 39, 51, 58;
(1860), 3, 28, 39, 52, 53–54,
55–56, 58–59, 77; (1864),
226, 248, 289–94, 352–64,
475n88; (1868), 405;
(1872), 407; (1876), 407;
(1880), 408; (1896), 410
state and congressional, 265,
356, 362; (1846), 54,
55–56; (1861), 207, 214;
(1862), 202–3, 251, 255,
303; (1863), 214, 215–16,
228, 317; (1864), 475n88;
(1866), 405
Elliot, Stephen, 378
Elmer, Lucius, 98, 99
emancipation, xxiv, 41, 152, 460n3
compensated, 160, 161–62, 173,
200, 203

conservative opposition to calls
for, 157–58, 205–6
and fears of effects on white
labor, 169, 200, 229, 359
and fears of impact on
Confederate resolve, 201
and fears of slave revolt, 232
gradual, 40, 41–42, 86, 200,
304
growth in demand for, 141,
156–57, 184, 455n45,
456nn55,61
moral imperative of, 197,
487n91
perceived interracial
consequences of, 289, 295,
333, 347
voluntary black emigration, 95,
162, 163
as weapon of war, 198, 303–4;
caution about result of,
136. See also Lincoln: as
president
Emancipation Proclamation
(1863)
Catholic opposition to,
200–201
preliminary, responses to,
194–95, 199; critics of,
195–96. See also Lincoln: as
president
England, 65, 80, 138, 148, 158
England, John, 331
Enlightenment philosophy, 16,
30, 41
enlistment, 126, 183, 197, 205–6,
212, 253, 322, 375–76
Enrollment Act (1863), 206, 214,
227, 228, 229, 236–37, 250.
See also draft; anti-draft
protests

572 *Index*

Episcopal Church, 9, 21, 26, 67, 90, 94, 222, 230, 270, 415–16
   antislavery clergy, 57
   and conservative nationalism, 141
   and Democratic Party, 358, 359
   and Union, 138, 140
Epperly, Christian M., 507n35
Errick, Enos, 239
ethnicity, 5–6, 7, 8. *See also* immigration
European radicalism, influence on Lincoln, 105
evangelicalism, 66–67, 409, 411
   divisions within, 29–39, 40–42
   growth of, 9, 17–18, 23
   northern evangelicals and antislavery, 39–40
   and republicanism, 11–15
   and Slave Power, 49–50
   southern evangelicals and slavery, 43–45
Everts, William W., 184
Ewell, Richard S., 397

Farwell, John V., 357
fast days, xii, xvi, 10, 17, 36–37, 73–74, 434n26, 441n32
   colonial, 37, 64–65, 74
   Confederate, 120, 376
   denominational, 14 (Methodist); 119–20 (Baptist); 120, 141 (Old School Presbyterian)
   military observance of, 147
   politicization of, 309
   public calls for, 36, 119–21, 196, 276
   Union: **(1814)**, 37; **(1832)**, 37; **(1841)**, 18, 37, 74; **(1849)**,

74; **(Jan. 1861)**, 65–94, 99–100, 124, 439nn3,5; **(Sept. 1861)**, 119–53, 454n31; **(April 1863)**, 233–34, 273–74, 276–77; **(Aug. 1864)**, 278–81
Federalist Party, 17, 29, 33
Fee, John G., 347, 348
Fell, Jesse, 55
Fessenden, William Pitt, xxi, 479n180
Field, Richard S., 446n118
Fillmore, Millard, 58
Finney, Charles G., 23, 83, 183
Fiske, John W., 86, 87, 88, 89
Flack, John Van Buren, 217–18, 234, 239–40
Flanders, Louisa, 242
Fletcher, Calvin, 127, 359
Foote, Andrew H., 272
Ford, William, 136
Forney, John W., 199, 249
Fort Donelson, capture of, 158
Fort Fisher, capture of, 380
Fort Henry, capture of, 158
Fort Lafayette, 210–11, 212
Fort Moultrie, 68
Fort Pillow, massacre of black Union troops (1864), 288–300
Fortress Monroe, 285
forts, federal, 8, 68
Fort Sumter, 68, 117, 381, 391
Fort Wagner, Battle (1864), 286
Foster, Julius, 74, 88, 296
Founding Fathers, xvii, 3–5, 11–12, 23, 78, 221, 254
France, 148
Francis, Simeon, 105
Franklin, Benjamin, 5, 16
Fransioli, Joseph, 474n86

Index

Fredericksburg, Battle of (1862), 203, 214, 273
Freedmen's Bureau, 404
freedom of speech, 52, 86–87, 327–28
Freemasonry, 16, 32, 34
free-soil doctrine, 53–54, 57, 416
Free-Soil Party, 48–49, 416
Free Will Baptists. *See* Baptists
Frémont, John C., 51, 58, 247, 282
    and 1864 election, 290, 348
    emancipation edict in Missouri, 125, 126, 132, 134, 152. *See also* Lincoln: as president
French Revolution, 21, 169, 223
Fugitive Slave Law (1850), 49–50, 132
Fugitt, James Preston, 141
Fuller, Richard, xx, 142–43, 308
Fulton, Justin Dewey, 81
Furness, William H., 136, 148

Galloway, J. M., 444n90
Galloway, Samuel, 292
Garfield, James A., 408
Garrett, Thomas, 165
Garrison, Francis J., 409
Garrison, William Lloyd
    as abolitionist, 56, 71, 165, 167, 407
    and antislavery religious nationalism, xix, 40, 164
    and civic equality, 403–4
    critics of, 225
    on Lincoln, 290, 348, 370
Gere, A., 460n10
German Reformed Church, 86, 264–65
Gettysburg, Battle of (1863), 206, 215, 262, 274, 312, 313
Giddings, Joshua, 117, 241

Gillespie, Joseph, 260–61
Gist, William H., 82
Given, James F., 303
Gloucester, Elizabeth, 135
Gloucester, James A., 135, 137
Goodell, William, 291
Goodrich, John Z., 254
Goodrich, William Henry, 147, 392
Gordon, George, 165
Gove, Elias, 264
Graham, Mentor, 104
Grant, Ulysses S., 158, 296, 407
    as general, 262, 273, 274, 275, 276, 381; General Order No. 11 (1862), 360
    as presidential candidate, 405–6
Greeley, Horace, 133, 160–61, 174, 180, 225, 247, 373, 407
    and peace talks, 323
    response to preliminary emancipation proclamation, 196–97
Grimes, William, 341
Grimshaw, William, 104
Grinnell, Joseph, 270
Guild, H. A., 501n110
Gulliver, John, 349, 355
Gurley, Phineas Densmore, 72, 98, 193, 265–66, 272, 362, 393, 403, 444n91
Gurney, Eliza P., 266, 270, 274, 342, 349

habeas corpus, 416. *See also* civil liberties
Haight, Edward, 250
Haiti, 167, 169, 178
Hale, Albert, 56
Hale, John P., 152
Hale, Sarah Josepha, 274–75

574   *Index*

Hall, Nathaniel, 79
Halleck, Henry W., 158, 247
Hallock, Gerald, 213
Hambleton, Alice Eliza, 165
Hamilton, Alexander, 5
Hamilton, Robert, 395–96
Hamline, Leonidas, 47
Hancock Jeffersonian, 254, 255
Haney, Milton L., 93
Harlan, James, 120, 149, 273,
    452n49
Harmer, John, 212–13
Harper, Frances Ellen Watkins,
    178
Harpers Ferry, raid on. *See* Brown,
    John
Harris, Ira, 200
Harrison, William Henry,
    18–19, 33
Hassaurek, Friedrich, 56
Haven, Gilbert, 279, 344, 346, 391,
    403, 405–6, 409
  and civic equality, 289, 348
  and 1864 election, 353
  on Lincoln, 281, 394, 398–99
Haven, Silas, 312, 317
Haverhill, Mass., 132
Hawes, Joel, 136, 148
Hawkins, Rush C., 480n5
Hawley, Bostock, 393
Hay, John, 174, 175, 298, 380
Hayes, Rutherford B., 407–8
Hedge, Frederic, 146
Heilprin, Michael, 92
Helm, Benjamin Hardin, 383
Henderson, Howard, 84–85
Henry, Anson G., 117
Henry, William, 115
Herman, Henry, 360
Herndon, William, 54–55, 260,
    271, 437n75, 451n40

Hervey, George W., 86–87
Hesser, Jupiter, 118
Hodge, Charles, xx, 34, 64,
    94–100, 140, 301–4, 405,
    447n123, 491nn140,145
  on uniting Presbyterians, 406–7
  "The State of the Country,"
    96–98, 446nn116,118,
    447nn125,128
Hodges, Albert, 283, 327
Hoge, Moses, 85
Holbrook, Amory, 117
Holt, Joseph, 68
honor, southern ideal of, 42, 83
Hooker, Joseph, 214, 273, 274
Hopkins, John Henry, xx, 222, 224
Hostetter, Amos, 313, 314
Howard, Joseph, xi, xii, 328,
    495n30
Howe, Julia Ward, 184
Hubbard, E. C., 313, 316
Hubbard, Thomas, 396
Hubbell, Alrick, 294
Hughes, John, 167, 168–69, 200,
    218, 226, 229, 231, 235
Huguenots, 6
humiliation, requirement for, 65,
    72, 73, 74, 75. *See also* fast
    days: Union (Sept. 1861)
Humphrey, Heman, 77, 79
Hunt, Albert S., 93
Hunter, David, 163, 247, 282, 302
Hunter, Robert M. T., 377
Huntington, Chauncey, 481n7
Hurlbut, Stephen A., 284
hymns, patriotic, 147, 269

Ide, George B., 295
Illinois, 31, 157, 235, 281
  Christian Association, 307–8
  Church of Christ, 119

Congregational churches, 119
Copperheadism in, 251, 278
and death of Lincoln, 394
and elections, 52, 60, 202
Methodist churches in, 119, 307, 456n59
racism in, 160, 179, 200, 286
religious divisions in, 217–18
response to Frémont initiative, 126, 135
and thanksgiving days, 308
United Presbyterians, 199
Illinois College, 60, 63, 106, 184
immigration, 5–6, 30–31, 103, 105, 363, 409
and Democratic Party, 58
German, 24, 105–6, 118, 185, 449n12
Irish, 6, 24, 57, 449n12
political allegiance, 38–39, 216–17, 359
and religious affiliation, 67
Scottish, 6
imperialism, American, 409–10
Indiana, 31, 131, 157, 202, 265
anti-abolitionists in, 170
Democrats in, 148, 233
and 1864 election, 356
North Indiana Methodist Conference, 239
responses to Conkling letter in, 254
intemperance, 18, 29, 74, 144, 267, 308, 377
Iowa, 157, 317
and "Dirty" Dean, 211
in 1863 election, 216
and thanksgiving (1864), 362
Irish Americans, 333, 359
Catholic, 48, 216–17, 359
Isaacs, Myer, 365

Jackson, Andrew, xvii, 35, 172, 207
anticlericalism, 36
Indian policy, 34, 35, 77
and national identity, 35–36
opposition to, 36, 38
Jacobs, J. A., 347
Jacoby, William H., 170
Jay, John, 5
Jefferson, Thomas, xvii, 5, 16, 36, 87, 185, 221, 326
Bill for Establishing Religious Freedom, 4
quoted by Lincoln, 109. *See also* fast days: colonial
Jenkins, Anna Maria, 270
Jewish Americans, 6, 409, 431n53, 484n64
political allegiance, 360–61
Reform, 92
Jocelyn, Simon S., 135, 137
"John Brown's Body," lyrics, 183–84
Johnson, Andrew, 152, 172, 284, 298
and amnesty, 403
failure to deliver black suffrage, 403–4
impeachment of, 405
as vice president, 387, 396, 397
Johnson, Herrick, 343, 351
Johnson, Oliver, 165, 166, 407
Johnson, Reverdy, 305
Johnson, Richard M., 36
Jones, Caroline, 397
Jones, Charles Colcock, 44, 98, 379
Jones, George W., 211
Jones, H., 135
Jones, Joseph, 311
Jones, Mary, 379
journalists, 165, 206, 210, 224, 297, 299, 322, 333, 359. *See also* Locke, David Ross

Kalloch, Isaac Smith, 146
Kansas, 50, 70, 109, 183
Kansas-Nebraska Act (1854), 415,
    417, 419
Kearny, Philip, 328
Kelly, Edmund, 286
Kelly, George F., 264
Kentucky, 31, 46, 91, 125, 129
    conservative nationalists in,
        87–88, 284
    and 1864 election, 329, 347, 356
    religious divisions in, 140
    Unionism in, 304–5. *See also*
        Hodge, Charles
Kentucky Resolutions (1798), 208,
    326
King, Rufus S., 117
Kingsbury, Harmon, 33
Kinsley, Rufus, 318–19, 362
Kirk, Edward Norris, 47, 353
Kirkwood, Samuel J., 441n32
Knapp, Almira Adliza, 370
Know-Nothing Party, 58, 226,
    417
Knoxville Whig, 297–98, 300
Koerner, Gustav, 105
Krauss, William C. J., 234, 237,
    240, 316, 329, 330, 336
Krauss, William Jr., 234, 240,
    315–16
Krebs, John, 20
Ku Klux Klan, 406

labor, free, 52, 53–54. *See also*
    emancipation: and fears of
    effects on white labor
Lane, Henry S., 352
"Lane Debates," 41–42
Larrabee, William C., 57
Leary, Cornelius, 460n10
Lee, Richard Henry, 17

Lee, Robert E., 173, 182, 215, 274,
    296, 374–75, 381
    denigration of, 394, 395
Leland, John, 31
Letcher, John, 441n32
Lewis, David, 14
Lewis, Samuel A., 361
Lewistown, Ill., 93
Lexington, Mo., Battle of (1861),
    129
Liberal Republican Party, 407
Liberator, 258, 291, 299
Liberia, 41, 167, 178
liberty, xvi, 146, 148, 280, 429n18
    civil, threats to, 32
    defense of, 12, 209, 221
    personal, attack on, 327–28
Liberty Party, 48–49
Lieber, Francis, 232, 249, 371
Lincoln, Abraham
    background and character,
        xxiv, 466n108
    caution, 130, 167, 229, 255, 269,
        345, 350
    humor, 149, 153, 253, 259
    integrity, 113, 149–50, 160, 349,
        501n123
    as lawyer, 248, 251, 252
    love of justice, 260–61
    patriotism, 160, 201, 299
    perceived moderation of, 170–71
    perception of as honest, 150,
        201, 203, 269, 281, 299,
        501n123
    pragmatism, xxiv, 123, 153, 283,
        370
    pre-presidential career, 51, 54,
        102–3, 105–6, 107, 109,
        259, 286
    as president
        and abolitionists, 53, 174, 291

Index

and American Revolution,
105, 107, 108
and anti-Catholic sentiment,
107
appointment of Democrats in
military, 206–7, 229
on arming of black troops,
171, 203–4, 285, 286
assassination of, 368, 388,
390–97; blame for, 394–95,
510n83; responses to, 390,
398–401, 511nn94,96; seen
as national punishment, 393
and Beecher, Henry Ward,
495n30
and black colonization, 41,
171, 177–80, 197, 201, 203,
286–87
and black suffrage, 255,
389–90
and black troops, 289
border states strategy, 125,
164, 171, 173, 185–86, 189,
201, 280, 284–85
cabinet, 62, 116–17, 140, 155,
171, 174, 194, 203, 268–69,
341, 479n180
and Confederacy, 110–12
and Constitution, 103–4,
111–12, 153, 194, 268
correspondence with, 102,
125–26, 132–34, 136, 137,
149, 150, 154, 254, 263,
264, 266, 275, 287
critics of, 125–26, 130–37,
167, 236–37, 281, 289–90,
326, 327, 328, 335–38,
387–88. See also and war
powers, critics of
and Declaration of
Independence, 103, 108

and Democrats, 111, 248–61
and Frederick Douglass, 251,
284, 289, 385
election of (1860), responses
to, 60–61, 67, 80–85, 87
and emancipation, xiv, xxii,
153, 159, 160–62, 163–64,
171, 173–82, 206, 251,
283–85, 345, 369–70;
defense of, 252–53; gradual
compensated, 154, 161–62,
164, 171, 173, 203, 284;
as weapon of war, 201–2,
303–4. See also "Chicago
Memorial"
Emancipation Proclamation
(1863), 154, 156, 214, 220,
283–84, 296, 303–5, 313,
330, 340
and Frémont initiative,
125–26, 134–35, 150, 167,
171
and fugitive slaves, 111, 167,
171, 172
and his generals, 158, 163–64,
167, 172–73, 174, 203, 214,
276
"hard war," 206, 207, 227–35,
236, 302–3
influence of Clay on, 449n10
meeting with free blacks,
176–78, 201
and Native Americans, xxiv,
106–7
and postwar reconstruction,
289, 370, 388–90;
opposition to, 330–31
preliminary emancipation
proclamation (1862), 121,
155, 190–91, 194–98,
201–2, 203–4, 221–23

578 *Index*

Lincoln, Abraham
 as president (*continued*)
  and prewar nationalism,
   101–9, 111–12
  Proclamation of Amnesty and
   Reconstruction (1863), 281,
   284
  public letters of, 179, 206,
   248–55, 261, 285, 327
  and race, 101, 106–7, 177–78,
   179, 255, 286–87, 289–90
  and reconciliation, 382, 383,
   385, 395, 396–97
  reelection, responses to,
   356–58, 363, 368–70
  and religious nationalism,
   xvii–xviii, 4, 150–53,
   167–72, 266–72; antislavery,
   xviii, 125, 130–37, 155, 167,
   202, 253–54, 281–83,
   291–94, 349–52;
   conservative, xxiii–xxiv,
   167–72, 200–201, 220–21,
   222–23, 225, 248, 252–53,
   261, 291, 387–88
  religious petitions and
   memorials to, xiv, 114,
   165–66, 501n110; as means
   of judging public opinion,
   154, 157, 194, 264–65;
   calling for emancipation,
   155–56, 157–58, 164, 175,
   191, 283; and Frémont
   initiative, 150; numbers
   of, 156, 157, 181, 480n2;
   responses to Emancipation
   Proclamation, 194–95, 197.
   See also "Chicago Memorial"
  rhetorical skill, 159, 381–82,
   383–85; use of derogatory
   language, 175–76, 179, 259

  and satire, 248, 259–60, 261
  and slavery, xiv, 52–53, 107–8,
   109, 111, 154, 167, 177,
   180–81, 185–86, 203,
   382–83
  support for in second term,
   358–61
  and USCC, 266, 268–69,
   370–71
  and war powers, 101–2,
   163–64, 166, 167–68, 186,
   196, 202, 249, 251; critics
   of, 207–12, 213, 215, 219,
   233–34, 239, 326, 327–28;
   suppression of press, xi, 210,
   213, 328, 360; suspension of
   writ of habeas corpus, 147,
   202, 206, 207, 225, 236–37,
   248–49. *See also* fast days;
   thanksgiving, days of
 and religion
  and Baptists, 156, 181, 191,
   293–94, 358, 383, 451n43,
   499n97
  belief in Providence, xii, xiv,
   xvii, xxiii–iv, 102, 109–13,
   114, 122–23, 153, 159, 164,
   166, 186–87, 190, 191–92,
   253, 261, 263, 265–66, 273,
   274, 343, 384, 392, 450n23,
   467n119
  as Christian martyr, 368, 391
  and Congregationalists, 119,
   156, 157, 276, 358, 487n91
  evolving religious faith of,
   xii, xiii–xiv, xxiii, 54–55,
   112–13, 116, 121–22, 159,
   166, 191, 193–94, 263, 266,
   269–72, 437n75
  knowledge of scripture, 104,
   113, 266, 383–84, 412

Index

meetings with church leaders and religious deputations, xvii, 142, 154, 156–57, 159, 161–62, 164–67, 263, 269, 286, 290, 291

and Methodists, 156–57, 159, 181–82, 271, 282, 291–94, 354, 358

perceived as religious leader, 116–17, 271–72; as Moses, 266, 282, 340, 351, 391, 393, 398–99, 502n126

perceived irreligion of, 54–55, 56, 241, 243–45, 337–38

and prayer, 272, 274, 276

and Presbyterians, 54–55, 155–57, 180–81, 267–68, 271, 358, 459n2

and proslavery theologians, 259, 260, 294

and Quakers/Progressive Friends, 53, 164–67, 172, 231, 266, 267, 270, 474n87

speeches/writings, xiv, 54, 108, 109, 110, 113, 147–48

addresses to Congress, 111–12, 153, 159, 160, 203, 268, 284, 367, 369

Cooper Union, N.Y. (1860), 52, 107–8

debates with Douglas (1858), 52, 109, 175–76, 255

first inaugural address, 110–11, 121, 146, 381

"Fragment on Pro-slavery Theology," 259, 260, 480n186

Gettysburg Address, 319

"House Divided" (1858), 60, 166

"Lecture on Discoveries and Inventions," 106

Lyceum Address, 105

"Meditation on the Divine Will," *192*, *193*, 266, 384, 468n121

Peoria (1854), 52, 79

Response to a committee of the MEC (1864), 292–93, *293*

Second Inaugural Address, 294, 319, 368, 380–90, *382*, 394, 398

Trenton, N.J., 110

Lincoln, Mary Todd, 66, 115, 270, 271, 337, 385

Lincoln, William Wallace (Willie), 265

The Lincoln Catechism, 336

Little, Thomas H., 136

Livermore, Leonard, 344

Livingston, William, 17

Lloyd George, David, 102

localism, xvii, xix, 7, 237, 428n8

Locke, Clinton, 75

Locke, David Ross, xx, 206, 254–61, 334

Lockwood, Lewis C., 285

Lodge Force Bill, 408

Long, Alexander, 275, 322, 324

Longstreet, James, 275

Looker, Thomas, 119

Lord, Nathan, xx, 222, 224, 225, 238

Lost Cause ideology, 410

Louisiana, 82, 284

military government in, 344

state governor, 389–90

Lovejoy, Owen, 225, 266, 489n116

580   *Index*

lower North, 248
   conservative Unionists in, 86,
      141, 306, 308
   political allegiance in, 59, 217.
      See also "Butternuts"
Loyal Leagues, 226
Loyal Publication Society, 224,
   249, 343, 474n86
loyalty oaths. *See* oaths of
   allegiance
Luther, Martin, 296
Lutherans
   Evangelical, 67, 239; and
      compensated emancipation,
      161–62
   General Synod, 161–62
   German, 6, 38, 228
   petitions to Lincoln, 157
   support for Union, 139
Lynch, David, 394
lynching/lynch law, 74, 411

Madison, James, 5, 14, 22–23, 37,
   326
Mahan, Asa, 407
manliness, white, notion of, xix,
   112, 237, 240
Manning, Joel, 117
Marble, Manton, 328, 387–88
Martin, Sella, 165
Maryland, 10, 46, 91, 176, 190,
   460n10
   and emancipation, 285, 360
   and fast days, 71
   Lee's call to revolt, 182
Massachusetts, 18, 65, 388
   abolitionists in, 278
   and black migration, 200
   and 1864 election, 356
   sectarianism in, 21–22

materialism, condemnation of, 18,
   74–75, 144, 233, 308, 309,
   377
Matheny, James H., 54, 451n40
McClellan, George B.
   as general, 154–55, 158, 173,
      174, 203, 310, 317
   "Harrison's Landing Letter"
      (1862), 173, 232, 339
   as presidential candidate,
      324–25, 339–40, 344–45,
      350, 499n87
McClintock, John, 48–49, 364
McClure, Alexander K., 191–92
McClure, Rev. J. T., 460n3
McCormick, Cyrus Hall, 139, 202,
   306, 492n152
McCormick, William, 139–40,
   492n152
McCoy, Amasa, 128, 453n20
McCoy, Benjamin, 177
McCulloch, Hugh, 249
McCunn, John, 242
McEuen, Oliver H., 217
McIlvaine, Charles, 270, 282
McKendree, William, 14
McKeon, John, 221
McKinley, William, 410–11
McKnight, Robert, 180–81
McMaster, Gertrude, 210
McMaster, James, xx, 207, 209–11,
   226, 323
   and conservative religious
      nationalism, 218, 232, 233,
      235, 237–38, 324
   on death of Lincoln, 392, 396
   and 1864 election, 325, 326, 358
   incitement to violence, 229, 230
   racism of, 222, 238
   on slavery, 223, 307, 373

McNeil, Benjamin, 364
Meade, George, 274
Meagher, Thomas, 229
MEC (Methodist Episcopal Church). *See* Methodists
Medary, Samuel, 219, 239
Meeks, James, 254–55, 256
memory, historical, role of, 88, 410
Memphis, violence against blacks in, 405
Mendenhall, Dinah, 165
Mennonites, 6, 216, 231, 475n88
Meredith, Thomas, 46
Merrill, A. K., on Lincoln, 502n126
Merritt, John W., 219
Merritt, Timothy, 14
Methodist Bible and Tract Society, 30
Methodist Book Concern, 10
Methodists, 6, 10, 12–13, 14–15, 21, 23, 28–29, 49, 127, 240, 417, 429n21
  Annual Conferences (MEC), 119, 159, 460n10, 471n32
  and emancipation, 132, 184–85, 282, 291–93
  General Conferences (MEC), 9, 45, 185, 293
  growth of, 9–11, 13, 23, 66–67, 440n11
  ministers, 12, 31, 51, 57, 84, 93, 118, 130, 145, 163, 184, 207, 217, 278–79, 282, 327, 345–46, 390
  newspapers, 10–11, 368
  petitions to Lincoln, 157

  political allegiance, 38 (Whigs); 59, 117, 216, 358 (Republicans); 39, 217, 219–20, 307, 327, 490n125 (Democrats)
  and racial equality, 289
  rivalry with Baptists, 22, 25
  schism over slavery, 45–47, 217
  support for Union, 138, 264
  suspicion of New England theology, 26–27, 38
  as unifying national force, 10–11. *See also* African Methodist Episcopal Church
Mexican War (1846–48), 7, 49, 77, 132, 231, 466n108
Michigan, 132, 157, 280
Midwest, 239, 248, 257, 304, 307, 309, 332
  opposition to Lincoln administration, 213
  political allegiance, 38, 211, 217, 250, 358
migration, internal, 30–33, 52
military chaplains
  abolitionist, 315, 316
  and 1864 election, 363
  for Jewish troops, 360–61
  and Lincoln, 318
  and Providence, 311, 312
  and self-sacrifice, 147, 313. *See also* Quint, Alonzo; U.S. Christian Commission
military courts, use of, 214–15
military governors, 172, 273, 284, 298
Militia Act (1862), 174
militias, Union, 211
millennialism, 30, 399–400, 417, 426n9, 505n187

582   *Index*

millennialism *(continued)*
  and antislavery nationalists, 81
  and Civil War, 147–48, 280,
    301–2, 312
  in eighteenth-century America,
    xx, 11, 6, 21
  and pro-slavery nationalists,
    185
  and Republican Party, 51, 54
Miller, John, 446n116
Millet, Deborah, 24
Miner, Noyes, 63, 191
miscegenation, 333–35
"The Miscegenation Ball," 336
missionary activity, 29, 44, 409
  missionaries, 115, 197, 272
Missouri, 46, 91, 124–26, 140
  and emancipation, 284–85
  imposition of martial law in,
    125
Missouri Compromise (1820), 50
  repeal of, 132
mob violence, 34, 230. *See also* anti-
    draft riots
Montez, Lola, 212–13
Moody, Granville, 291, 292
Moorhead, James K., 180, 281
Moravian Church, 6, 37, 138, 231
Morgan, Edwin D., 290, 298
Mormonism, 22, 24, 26, 29,
    431n53
Morse, Jedidiah, 220
Morse, Samuel F. B., 220–21
Morse, Sidney, 220
Morton, Oliver, 108, 298
Mullaly, John, xx, 322–23, 359–60
  and draft, 229, 329
  and 1864 election, 324, 325
  on Lincoln, 331, 335, 336–37,
    387; death of, 396

opposition to "hard war"
    policies, 236
  and Thirteenth Amendment,
    372. *See also* New York
    Metropolitan Record
Mulvany, Peter, 238
Murray, Orson, 180
Murrin, John, 7
Myers, James S., 116

NAACP, 409
The Nasby Papers (1864), 257–58
Nashville, fall of, 158
Natchez, Miss., Union occupation
    of, 333
National Anti-slavery Standard, 130,
    165, 180, 291
National Union clubs, 354
National Union Party, 305, 321,
    344
  1864 campaign, 352–56
  Baltimore platform (1864),
    290–91, 320, 345–46,
    365. *See also* Republican
    Party
nationalism, religious, xiii,
    xvii–xviii, xxiv, 6–27, 39,
    99–100, 418–19
  antislavery, xviii–xix, xx, xxii,
    xxiii, xxiv, 39–40, 47–56,
    60–61, 64, 92, 408,
    411–12
  and 1864 election, 321, 346,
    363, 364–65, 366, 368–69
  and fast days, 64, 76–81,
    130–37, 138–42
  and Frémont initiative,
    124–26, 136, 152
  growth of, 3–6, 7–8, 13–14,
    19–20

millennial faith of, 80–81
and racial equality, 287–89
and Reconstruction, 403–9
responses to Lincoln's
emancipation policy,
159–67, 280–83, 290–91; to
preliminary emancipation
proclamation, 196
and Unionism, 183–84, 198,
199–200, 201–2, 253–54
views of Lincoln, 53, 180–82;
responses to death of,
398–401
conservative, xviii, xix, 56–60,
64, 86–92, 137–45,
216, 305–10. *See also*
Vallandigham, Clement L.
belief in legitimacy of slavery,
88–90, 141
divisions within, 86–92,
139–40, 201–2, 307–8
and emancipation, xviii, xix,
88–90, 126, 141–42, 155,
167–72, 263, 280
and fast days, 141–45, 308–10
on lack of statesmanship, 86
opposition to Lincoln
administration, 167,
200–204, 205
opposition to preliminary
emancipation proclamation,
205
on secession, 126, 143–44,
168
sympathy for Confederacy,
141–43, 211, 217, 257
and Thirteenth Amendment,
372–73
divisions within, xiii, 64, 91,
93–94, 170, 201–2, 254

converts from conservatism
to emancipation, 155,
295–305. *See also*
Breckinridge, Robert J.;
Brownlow, William
Gannaway; Hodge, Charles
proslavery nationalists, xiii, 82,
83–85, 367
Native Americans
Cherokee, 34, 35
Dakota, xxiv. *See also* Lincoln: as
president
nativism, 56, 226, 418. *See also*
Know-Nothing Party
Neilson, Hannah M., 480n5
New England, 5, 6, 8, 15, 19–20,
29, 38–39, 257
animus against, 143, 218,
225–27, 233–34, 248, 358,
378, 388; satirical attack on
Puritanism, 247, 332
antislavery nationalists in, 64, 76,
91, 92, 131, 400
fast days in, 65, 71, 434n21
perceived influence of, xvi–xvii,
26–27, 47, 92, 337, 365
progressive theology, 183
responses to death of Lincoln
in, 399
and spread of Methodism,
9–10, 12
New Jersey, 16–17, 108, 141, 157,
202, 301
conservative religious
nationalists in, 141
and 1864 election, 356
Newman, John P., 280
New Orleans, 82, 97, 188, 235,
273, 389
violence against blacks in, 405

584   *Index*

New York City, 12, 38, 87, 110,
    157, 183, 202, 213, 354
antislavery nationalists in, 131,
    133, 136, 147, 280, 296,
    342, 346
Broadway Tabernacle, 69, 131,
    343
Congregational Church of the
    Puritans, 92, 130, 403
Congregationalists in, 346, 403
conservative religious
    nationalists in, 89–90, 221,
    229, 250
and death of Lincoln, 394, 395
and elections: (1856), 58;
    (1864), 322, 324, 335, 359
and fast/thanksgiving days, 71,
    277, 278, 362
peace convention (1863), 232
Union Square, Democratic
    convention (1864), 339–40
Welsh Congregationalist
    Church, 118
New York Daily News, 213, 330,
    337–38
New York Day-Book Causasian, 213,
    335, 477n144
New York Express, 219, 355
New-York Freeman's Journal and
    Catholic Register, 207, 210,
    235, 237, 242, 247–88, 307,
    310, 322, 335, 364. *See also*
    Hughes, John; McMaster,
    James
New York General Association, 344
New York Herald, 59, 92, 138, 172,
    337, 354, 387, 390
New York *Independent*, 142, 144,
    160–61, 165, 180, 290, 291,
    334, 344, 349, 354, 356,
    368, 371–72, 386

circulation, 461n16
and preliminary emancipation
    proclamation, 195. *See also*
    Beecher, Henry Ward;
    Tilton, Theodore E.
New York *Journal of Commerce*,
    213, 327, 339
New York *Metropolitan Record*, 167,
    168–69, 172, 200–201, 218,
    221, 237, 322, 326, 335,
    360, 364
opposition to emancipation,
    306–7. *See also* Mulally, John
New-York Observer, 93, 98, 144,
    158, 167, 168, 171, 200,
    220, 278, 447n128
New York Times, 124, 277, 297
New-York Tribune, 152, 160, 174,
    359
New York *World*, 327, 328, 333,
    334, 387–88
Niagara Falls, peace initiative, 323,
    331
Nicolay, John G., 113, 119, 174,
    175, 250, 343
"nigger," use of term, 175, 243,
    257, 478n175
Norris, Ira, 219–20, 235
Norton, Anthony Banning, 322

oaths of allegiance, 206, 210, 211,
    214, 217, 238, 330
Oberlin College, 42, 49, 177, 183
Ohio, 31, 156, 157
antislavery religious nationalists
    in, 180, 304
conservative religious
    nationalists in, 280, 307
Democrats in, 325;
    Copperheads, 324, 387
in 1863 elections, 214, 215–16

and fast days, 71
Lincoln speeches in (1861), 110
Methodist disciplinary trials in,
239
opposition to Lincoln
administration, 213, 240
Republicans in, 212
Ohio Statesman, 226, 396
O'Kelly, James, 12–13
Old Guard, 224, 229, 247–48, 254,
477n144
Olds, Edson Baldwin, 207, 212,
231–32, 307
Ostend Manifesto (1854), 69
Overland Campaign (1864), 321
Owen, Robert Dale, 35

pacifism/pacifists, 14, 50, 228,
231–32, 474n87
Paine, Thomas, 74
Age of Reason (1794), 21
Palmer, Albert G., 129, 137, 149,
150
Palmer, Benjamin Morgan, 47,
82–83, 84, 92, 95, 97
pamphlets
antiabolitionist, 92, 332–34
and 1864 election, 336, 340, 343
religious, 10
Republican, 253–54, 479n178
on secession, 97. *See also*
Brownlow, William
Gannaway; Society for
the Diffusion of Political
Knowledge
Parker, Theodore, 55, 225
patriotism, xvii, 6–7, 29, 73, 88,
145–49, 233, 300, 411
fast days and, 126, 129, 277–78,
279–80. *See also* nationalism,
religious

Patton, William (father), 510n83
Patton, William Weston (son), 136,
183–90, 199, 465n99,
467n110
Paxson, William, 228
peace meetings, 238
calls for, 262, 283, 317, 322
peace petitions, 213, 341, 342, 344,
351, 367. *See also* Niagara
Falls, peace initiative
Pea Ridge, Battle of (1862), 158
Peck, George, 292, 351–52, 358
Pendleton, George H., 325
Peninsula Campaign (1862), 167
Pennsylvania, 157, 165, 202, 274,
460n10
antislavery radicals in, 180–81
in 1863 elections, 216, 224
and 1864 election results, 359,
475n88
Episcopalians in, 224, 280
and thanksgiving day (1864), 362
United Presbyterianism in,
156
Perkins, William, 53
Perrin, Lavalette, 363, 505n176
Petroleum Vesuvius Nasby, xx, 206,
256–58, 261, 334
Philadelphia
Baptists in, response to death of
Lincoln, 400
blacks in, 198, 287
conservative religious unionists
in, 88
Democrats in, 58, 236
fast days in, 127; Jan. 1861 fast
day, 71
Independence Hall, address by
Lincoln, 108, 109
Old School Presbyterian
Assembly in (1861), 140

586   *Index*

Philadelphia *(continued)*
   Reformed Presbyterian Church,
     115, 118
   response to Frémont's initiative
     in, 136
   sectarian violence in, 22
   suppression of press in, 210
   and thanksgiving day (1864),
     362
   United African Methodist
     Episcopal Church, 363,
     513n22
Philadelphia Conference
   Missionary Society, 271
Philadelphia *Mercury*, 219, 226
Philadelphia *North American*, 127,
   258
Philippines, acquisition of, 409
Phillips, George Shane, 311, 312,
   313, 493n178
Phillips, Philip, 269
Phillips, Wendell, 201, 225,
   290–91, 348
Pierce, Franklin, 57, 212
pietists, 60–61, 429n21
Pike County, Ill., 217
Pillsbury, Parker, 291
Plattenburg, Ellen, 353
Plumer, William, 46
Plumly, Benjamin Rush, 198, 287
pluralism, religious, 8, 21–27,
   43–31, 431n53
poets, 178, 242–43, 274, 371–72.
   See also Bache, Anna
Pohlman, Henry N., 162
political culture, American, 6–8
   electoral politics, seen as sin, 18
   political parties: growth of, 7, 8,
     33; and religion, 26, 32–39,
     58–60
Polk, James K., 49, 109, 466n108

Pollard, George A., 115
Pollock, James, 114
Pomeroy, Samuel C., 290
Pope, John, 174
popular sovereignty, doctrine of,
   50–51, 58, 109, 363
Potter, Alonzo, 196
Potts, William D., 497n52
Powderhorn, John, 239
prayer, 119, 140, 128
   as confession of sin, 130
   Lincoln calls for, 159, 160,
     275
   for peace, 292
   prayer meetings, 25, 142, 144,
     272
   for presidents, 14, 63, 115–16,
     133–34, 272, 333, 386, 390,
     403, 456n50, 472n35
   and Providence, 65, 143
   resistance to, 217. *See also* fast
     days; thanksgiving, days of
prejudice, white
   effect of Civil War on, 286, 287,
     288–89
   in Union Army, 311. *See also*
     African Americans: violence
     against; Democratic Party:
     and racism; Lincoln: as
     president, and race
Presbyterians, 5, 6, 9, 12, 13, 17,
   24, 29–30, 90, 113, 117,
   128, 165, 240, 302
   in the Confederacy, 140
   divisions within, 38–39, 45,
     139–40
   and emancipation, 196, 282, 304,
     305–6
   and fast days, 71, 120, 141
   General Assemblies, 9, 138, 140,
     304, 359

Index

New School, 22, 38–39, 45, 49, 67, 138, 156–57, 259, 343, 403, 418

numbers, 66, 156, 440n11

Old School, 22, 49, 59, 64, 65, 67, 88, 93, 94, 98, 99, 139–41, 193, 216, 217, 354, 429n17

Reformed, 115, 130, 131, 157, 180–88, 195, 196, 267–68, 454n31

United, 119–20, 139, 155–57, 196, 459nn1,2, 460n3

press, xvii, xxii, 8, 19, 97, 257, 296, 302

abolitionist, 163, 230–31, 291, 369

accused of antislavery sympathy, 138

African American, 346, 396

Baptist, 163

Catholic, 72, 167, 218, 223, 306–7, 322, 326, 360

and celebrity culture, 296

Democrat, 56, 72, 126, 170, 219–20, 225, 231, 325, 326, 333, 338, 339, 340; Copperhead, 213, 355

and fake news, xi–xii, 75, 215, 327–28, 333–34

freedom of, xi

Methodist, 10–11, 146, 182, 292, 358, 371

northern, and prejudice, 288–89

opposition to demands for emancipation, 158

Presbyterian, 82, 98, 167

and racism, 248, 255, 335

radical antislavery, 142, 144, 160

religious, xxiii, 134–35, 144, 184, 194, 210, 220, 242, 307, 325

Republican, 62, 117, 126, 198, 206, 215, 253–54, 264, 369, 373; response to Second Inaugural, 386

southern, defense of slavery, 47

suppression of, xi, 210, 213, 328, 360. *See also* editors

Pressly, John Taylor, 155–56

"priestcraft" (Puritan), opposition to, xix, 56–60, 120. *See also* New England: animus against

Prime, Samuel Irenaeus, xx, 168, 169, 171, 200, 447n125

Primitive Baptists. *See* Baptists

Princeton Review, 93, 94, 96–97, 98, 302, 304

Princeton Theological Seminary, 94, 301

prisoners of war, 397, 410

Progressive Friends, 144, 164–67, 267. *See also* Quakers

Protestantism

American fundamentalist, 411

conservative opposition to demands for emancipation, 157–58

divisions within, xvi–xvii; over slavery, 223–24

and growth of Catholicism, xv

Protestant churches and Copperheadism, 239–40

ultraconservative, 307–9

white evangelical, xiv–xv, 440nn10,11,12,13; confidence of, xv–xvi; numbers, 440nn10,11, 12; support for Lincoln's second term, 358–61. *See also* nationalism, religious

588 *Index*

Protestant Reformation Society, 25
Providence, belief in
  in antebellum America, xvi,
    14, 65
  antislavery nationalists and, xxii,
    6, 80, 133–34, 160, 161,
    181, 279, 354, 481n7
  black providential belief,
    178–79
  Catholics and, xix
  and Civil War progress, 120, 143
  conservative religious
    nationalists and, 308
  and emancipation, 282, 455n47
  and fast days, 73, 75–76, 126,
    129
  and Lincoln, 162, 186–87,
    281–82, 342, 356–57; death
    of, 392–93, 395–96, 398–99
  and national cohesion, 15–20
  and outbreak of Civil War, 118
  and redemption, 75–76
  and slavery, 169, 195, 288
  in Union army, 311, 313
Pryne, Abram, 297
Pryor, Theodorick, 93
publishers, 213, 243, 248, 296,
    334–35, 336
Puerto Rico, acquisition of, 409
punishment, divine, 129, 133,
    135–36, 181, 185, 282, 295,
    507n35
Purcell, Edward, 218, 307, 359–60,
    371
Purcell, John Baptist, 216, 218,
    226, 307, 360, 364
Puritanism, 19, 20, 365, 418
Purnell, Carrie H., 287

Quakers, 5, 6, 9, 21, 53, 165, 267,
    270, 348–49

and emancipation, 282, 475n91
and pacifism, 231
petitions to Lincoln, 157
political allegiance, 38. *See also*
    Lincoln: and religion;
    Progressive Friends
Quincy, Josiah, 254
Quinn, David, 232, 241
Quint, Alonzo, 396, 400–401

rabbis, 87, 90–91, 92, 309
racial equality
  calls for, xviii, 40, 137, 280, 286,
    287–88, 290–91, 348,
    400–401
  opposition to, xxiii, 137, 407
racism, 161, 169, 170, 178, 200,
    221–22, 243, 287, 408, 410
  racial amalgamation, fears of,
    289, 333, 335, 347, 498n70
  racial segregation, 411
  racial violence, 228–30
  and responses to emancipation,
    372–73. *See also* African
    Americans: violence against;
    Democratic Party: and
    racism; Illinois; Petroleum
    Vesuvius Nasby; press
Rankin, Jeremiah, 279
Raphall, Morris Jacob, 87, 90–91,
    92, 309
Rawlins, Benjamin, 390, 392, 395
Ray, Charles H., 62
Raymond, Henry J., 341
reconciliation, 404, 406, 407, 408,
    410–11. *See also* Lincoln: as
    president
Reconstruction, postwar, 398, 402,
    406, 407–8. *See also* Lincoln:
    as president
Redemptorists, 210

Reed, Alexander, 269
Reformed Presbyterians. *See*
　　Presbyterians
Reformed United Brethren, 67,
　　307
Reid, Adam, 485n72
religion
　　American civil, xiii, 426n5
　　American prewar, xiii, xvi–xvii
　　division between progressive and
　　　　conservative, 394–95, 397,
　　　　402–4, 406–7, 412
　　and growth of nationalism, 4–6,
　　　　11–12
　　institutional growth of, 8–9
　　and politics, linkage between,
　　　　xi–xii, xiii, xvi, xxii, 53–54,
　　　　60–61, 63, 145, 219, 220–21,
　　　　225, 238, 263, 305–6, 321,
　　　　340, 349–56, 365, 501n120;
　　　　opposition to, xxiii–xiv, 57,
　　　　471n32, 500n100. *See also*
　　　　fast days
　　and politics, separation from,
　　　　4–6, 36–37, 59–60, 74, 95,
　　　　120, 139–41, 142–43, 145,
　　　　196, 198–99, 238–39,
　　　　268–69, 278–79, 306,
　　　　354–55, 359, 360, 373, 376,
　　　　503n144
　　and prewar political parties,
　　　　33–38, 47–61
　　religious duty, differing
　　　　interpretations of, 72–73
　　religious pluralism, 4, 5–6, 21–27
　　religious violence, 22
　　revivals, 5, 9, 11, 17, 19, 23, 25,
　　　　30, 40, 51, 75, 144, 183, 218
　　republicanism, secular, xxi, 11–15,
　　　　42, 429n18
　　　　fear of tyranny, 12–13, 84

Republican Party, xv, xvi, xxi, xxii,
　　xxiv, 4, 70–71, 238, 253–54,
　　341, 410–11, 419
　　and antislavery sentiment, 51,
　　　　52–54, 87, 137, 176
　　conservative sentiment, 86, 97,
　　　　202–3
　　and elections: (**1860**), 53–54;
　　　　(**1862**), 202–3; (**1863**),
　　　　214; (**1864**), 289–94,
　　　　475n88
　　modern, xix–xv, 403, 411, 412
　　radical sentiment, 152, 202–3
　　and religious nationalism, xvi,
　　　　xviii–xiv, 219
　　support for, post 1864 election,
　　　　358–61. *See also* National
　　　　Union Party
revivals, religious. *See* religion:
　　revivals
Rhodes, Elisha Hunt, 493n166
Rice, James C., 272, 282, 286
Rice, Nathan, 139, 447n125
Richer, Leon, 102
Richmond, Thomas, 281,
　　285–86
Richmond, Va.
　　campaign to take, 173, 262
　　Confederate retreat from,
　　　　391
Riddle, David, 18–19
Roanoke Island, capture of, 159
Robinson, Stuart, 306
Romeyn, John B., 74
Rosecrans, William, 360
Ross, Frederick A., 47, 384
　　Slavery Ordained of God, 259,
　　　　480n186
Russell, Charles E., 409
Russell, William Howard, 103
Ruter, Martin, 15

590   *Index*

Sabbath, observance of, 34, 339.
    See also sin: personal,
    Sabbath-breaking
sacrifice, Christian duty of, 147,
    279–80, 313, 362, 411
Sala, George, 299
Salter, William, 392, 393, 399
Sample, Thomas J., 266
Samson, George Whitefield,
    142
Sangamo Journal, 105, 259
Sanitary Commission of the
    Northwest, 183
Santo Domingo massacres, 201,
    245
satire, 243–48. *See also* Petroleum
    Vesuvius Nasby
Saum, Lewis, 67
Scammon, J. Young, 265, 342
Schneider, George, 105
schools, 32, 33, 34
    Catholic, 24–25
Schurz, Carl, 56
Scott, William A., 142
Scott, Winfield, 69, 247
Scottish Common Sense
    philosophy, 17
Scripps, John Locke, 132, 134
secession, 62, 68, 82, 99–100, 213,
    224, 444nn88,90,91
    condemnation of, 80–82, 87–88,
        95–96, 119, 143–44, 211,
        305, 454n33, 485n72
    religious justification for, 82
    as result of perceived northern
        aggression, 49, 83–84,
        226–27
"Second Great Awakening," 9
sectarianism, 21–27, 28–33
secularism, growth of, 409, 411

sedition, 213, 222
self-discipline, and
    republicanism, 30
self-examination, duty of, 74,
    143–44, 151
self-improvement, 7, 30, 53
self-righteousness, as divisive force,
    88, 294, 332
Sessions, Alexander J., 118
Seven Days' Battles (1862), 173,
    377
Seward, William H., 121, 174, 210,
    244–45, 247, 275, 328, 370,
    371, 452n51, 459n2
Seymour, Horatio, 202, 238
Shakers, 6
Shakespeare, William
    Henry VIII, 356
    Sonnet 94, 479n184
Sharswood, George, 447n128
Sheridan, Philip Henry, 329
Sherman, William Tecumseh, 277,
    329, 342, 374, 375, 381
Shields, James, 259
Shiloh, Battle of (1862), 158
Simmons, Ichabod, 134, 145–46,
    147, 148
Simpson, Matthew, xix, 353, 354
sin, perceptions of, 18, 32, 74–75,
    121, 129, 130, 144, 377
    national, 90, 122–23, 129, 130,
        132; ill-treatment of Native
        Americans as, 308
    personal: adultery, 74; card
        playing, 377; covetousness,
        144; duelling, 74; greed,
        74–75, 377; murder, 74;
        polygamy, 74; pride, 377;
        profanity, 267, 308, 377;
        racial abuse, 18; rioting,

74; Sabbath-breaking, 18, 74, 144, 308, 377. *See also* Civil War: as punishment for national sin; fast days; intemperance; materialism; slavery, as a sin

Singleton, James, 322–33

Skinner, Mark, 466n102

Skinner, Thomas, 131, 146

Slave Power, 51
  perceptions of, 57, 95, 300
  responsibility for secession, 80

slavery
  African slave trade, 87
  biblical sanctioning of, 43–44, 84, 90–91, 223, 224, 257
  as cause of religious division, xvi, 27, 39, 407
  corrupting influence of, 77–79
  defense of, 42–47, 83, 84, 88–89, 131, 141, 143, 169, 205, 209, 213, 222, 224, 297, 306, 331, 373, 378–79
  expansion of, 50, 51, 132, 212
  fear of slave revolts, 43, 44, 58, 67, 169
  growth in slave population, 42, 181
  seen as cause of Civil War, 157, 189, 227, 283, 382–83
  seen as cause of Lincoln's death, 394, 510n83
  as a sin, 76–78, 79, 132, 135, 136–37, 181, 185, 281, 364–65, 378, 426n9. *See also* punishment, divine
  slaveholders, 39, 67, 78–79, 295–96, 304, 308; duties of, 44, 169, 378–79; perceptions of, 39–41

slaves: contrabands, 285, 315; fugitive, 50, 135; proposal to arm, 160; runaways, in military camps, 125

Slidell, John, 68

Sloane, James R. W., 92–93, 134, 136, 454n31

Sloane, William, 60, 116–17

Smart, James, 75, 79–80, 345–46

Smith, Benjamin, 44–45

Smith, David, 115

Smith, Gerrit, 348

Smith, Joseph, 22

Smith, Leonard F., 203, 217, 394, 472n34, 477n144, 484n62

Smith, Lydia, 264

Smith, Robert, 6

Smith, William, 314

Social Gospel movement, 411

social unrest, 57, 74. *See also* anti-draft riots

Society for the Diffusion of Political Knowledge, 220–21, 224

South, the, 34, 38
  culture, 42, 83

South Carolina, 44, 381
  Sea Islands, 163

Southern Baptist Convention, 45, 142

Spanish-American War (1898), 410, 411

Spear, Samuel, 395

Speed, James, 479n180

Speed, Joshua, 125

spiritualism, 232, 241–42, 285, 357

Spotsylvania Court House, Battle of (1864), 262, 321

Sprague, William B., 358

592   *Index*

Spring, Gardiner, 140, 141
Springfield, Ill., 105, 179, 275,
    449n12
  abolitionist sentiment in,
    125–26, 133, 282
  Colonization Society, 117–18
  First Presbyterian Church, 63,
    66, 152
  Lincoln's farewell speech in,
    109–10, 113
  Second Presbyterian Church, 56
Standard, William, 317–18
Stanly, Edward, 167, 172
Stanton, Edwin, 68, 174, 244–45,
    247, 333, 360, 405, 479n180
Stanton, Robert L., 128, 130, 131,
    132
state constitutions, antislavery, 330,
    389
state governors, 236, 238, 298
  and fast days, 65, 71, 82, 275,
    404–5, 434n21, 441–42n32.
    See also military governors
statesmanship, lack of, deplored,
    86, 132, 144
states rights, xix, 48, 58, 137–38,
    208, 237
  Democratic Party defense of,
    325–27
Stearns, Edward J., 143
Steck, Daniel, 330, 496n37
Steele, Daniel, 282, 288
Stephens, Alexander, 268
  "Cornerstone Speech"
    (Savannah), 131, 283
Sternberg, Levi, 461n19
Stevens, Thaddeus, 475n88
Stockton, Thomas H., 72, 93–94
Stoddard, Orange N., 446n118
Stoddard, William O., 163
Stone, Andrew Leete, 78

Stone, William, 317
Stowe, Harriet Beecher, 165, 247,
    350–51
Stringfield, James, 87
Strong, George Templeton, 72,
    230
Strother, T., 178
Stuart, George H., 269, 482n27
Sturtevant, Julian M., 60, 61, 184,
    276, 285, 466n101
suffrage, black, 405, 406, 408
Sumner, Charles, xxi, 50, 152, 170,
    247, 258, 390, 407, 479n180
Sunday Schools, 32, 271
Swett, Leonard, 258, 261
Swisshelm, Jane, 163
Syracuse, N.Y., state Union
    convention (1863), 253–54

Tatum, John W., 267
Taylor, Nathaniel W., 24
Taylor, Thomas House, 70
Tefft, Benjamin Franklin, 15
Tennessee, 31, 275, 284, 344
  and secession, 297–98
Tennessee, Department of, 172,
    360
territorial expansion, xxiv, 7, 8,
    49, 56–57, 132. *See also*
    imperialism, American
Texas, 284
  annexation of, 49
thanksgiving, days of, xii, xvi, 6, 10,
    14, 17, 36–37, 73, 202, 248,
    268–69, 272, 279, 319, 389,
    434n21, 436n54, 441n30
  Davis's, 376, 383
  Lincoln's: **(Apr. 1862)**, 159,
    161–62, 170; **(Aug.
    1863)**, 274, 278, 312, 316,
    484nn62,64; **(Nov. 1863)**,

274–75, 308, 452n51; **(May 1864)**, 276; **(Sept. 1864)**, 278, 342–44, 355, 500n100; **(Nov. 1864)**, 321, 362–66, 374

Thayer, Martin Russell, 371

Thomas, Edward, 177, 179

Thomas, George H., 275

Thompson, Augustus, 272

Thompson, Joseph Parrish, 69–70, 131, 343, 355, 406

Thornwell, James Henley, 59–60, 82, 83, 92, 95, 98, 140

Tiffany, Otis H., 73, 88

Tilton, Theodore E., 334, 348, 391, 409

  and antislavery nationalism, 165

  on Confederate black enlistment bill, 375

  and 1864 election, 320, 342, 346, 351, 354; on McClellan, 344–45

  and 1872 election, 407

  and Lincoln, 290, 369; on death of, 396, 511n94; on reelection of, 356–57, 503n148

  response to Second Inaugural, 386

Tocqueville, Alexis de, 26

Tod, David, 298

Tourgée, Albion W., 410, 411

Transcendentalism, xx, 427n11

transportation, improvements in, 8, 34

Trapnell, Joseph, 87, 91

treason, perceptions of, 216, 256, 397

  scriptural authority for resistance to, 279

secession seen as, 87–88, 141, 168, 295, 305

  trials for, 239

Trent, seizure of, 302

Trenton, N.J., 108

Truth, Sojourner, 165, 286

Tucker, Gideon J., 213

Tucker, Mark, 34

Turner, Henry McNeil, 178, 179

Turner, Jonathan Baldwin, 271

Tuttle, James H., 148

Twain, Mark, 211

Twichell, Joseph Hopkins, 312, 316–17, 318, 319

Tyler, John, 18

Tyng, Dudley A., 438n86

Tyng, Stephen Higgins, xix, 225, 296, 364–65, 454n31

Underground Railroad, 135, 165

Union army, 229, 230, 263, 310–19

  abolitionists in, 310, 312, 314, 316

  animosity toward Copperheads, 215, 316–17

  and antislavery nationalism, 311, 312, 313, 318–19

  conduct of, 267

  desertions, 251

  and fast day (Sept. 1861), 128

  Irish regiments, 323, 333

  opposition to emancipation in, 316

  and perceptions of slavery, 295, 313–16, 400

  political allegiance in, 316–17, 324, 356

  and racial prejudice, 315, 316

  views of Lincoln, 317–18, 319

Unionist Party, 215
Unionists
    conservative religious, 138–39
    opposition to Copperheads, 342,
        344
Union Leagues, 217, 226, 233,
    234, 370
Union Theological Seminary, 312,
    409
Unitarians, 4–5, 6, 22, 23, 38, 79,
    128, 133, 146, 282, 334,
    419
United Brethren, 217, 282
United Presbyterians. *See*
    Presbyterians
Universalists, 6, 148, 195, 197
U.S. censuses, 66
U.S. Christian Commission, 266,
    268–69, 357, 370–71,
    482nn22,27, 483n40
U.S. Congress, 149, 152, 162, 277,
    361, 370, 408
    33rd (1853–55), 57
    39th (1865–67), 404
    and slavery, 125, 136. *See also*
        Lincoln: speeches/writings,
        addresses to Congress
U.S. Constitution, xvii, 7, 130, 282,
    289, 292, 326
    Amendments: First, xxiii, 4, 5,
        23, 65; Thirteenth, 289,
        368–74; Fourteenth, 405,
        407; Fifteenth, 406, 407
    Bill of Rights, 325
U.S.-Dakota war (1862), xxiv
U.S. House of Representatives,
    120, 203, 277, 290, 322,
    367, 370–71
    House Committee of Thirteen,
        68–69

U.S. Navy, 119, 158–59
U.S. Senate, 120, 203, 257, 273,
    277
U.S. Supreme Court, *Dred Scott*
    decision, 70, 95
U.S. Treasury, 114
Usher, John P., 269

Vallandigham, Clement L., 205,
    207–9, 223, 225, 234–35,
    342, 471n26
    antiabolitionism of, 226, 227,
        232–33
    anti-centralization views,
        208–9
    arrest of, 209, 214–15, 242, 248
    critique of, 255, 256, 257
    and elections: (1863), 214;
        (1864), 323, 324, 325
    on Lincoln, 234–35
    and personal liberty, 209, 236
    on separation of religion and
        politics, 238, 329–30
Vallandigham, James, 207
Van Dyke, Henry, xx, 90, 92, 93,
    354, 359
Van Evrie, John H., 213
    Subgenation, 335
Verplanck, Gulian C., 37
veterans, white Union, 410
Vicksburg, Battle of (1863), 206,
    215, 262, 273, 274, 312,
    313
Vincent, Marvin R., 394
Vinton, Alexander, 363, 365
Vinton, Francis, 90
Virginia, 4, 5, 10, 11, 46, 183, 208,
    321, 381
Virginia Campaign (1864), 262
Virginia Resolutions (1798), 326

Volck, Adalbert John, 245–47
  *Sketches from the Civil War in
    North America*, 245
  Worship of the North, 245, 246,
    247
  *Writing the Emancipation
    Proclamation*, 245, 246
voluntarism, 408–9, 431n53
volunteers, calls for, 207, 321,
    328–29

Wade, Ben, 152, 241
Wadsworth, Charles, 73, 74, 75,
    88, 91, 363
Walker, Charles H., 466n102
"The Walpurgis Dance at
    Washington," 338
War of 1812, 7, 14, 17, 29
Washington, D.C.
  abolition of slavery in, 162,
    167, 172, 185–86; black
    responses to, 162–63
  black churches in, 177
  and fast days, 277
  New York Avenue Presbyterian
    Church, 72, 152, 193, 265,
    362
Washington, George, xxiii, 5, 6,
    11, 13, 14, 36, 87, 113, 177,
    186, 221, 267
Waters, Lucien, 176
Wayland, Francis, 34, 130, 146,
    342, 434n29, 499n96
Weed, Thurlow, 341
Weld, Horatio Hastings, 141–42
Weld, Theodore, 40, 41–2
Welles, Gideon, 69, 174, 185, 194,
    268, 328, 440n18
Wells, J. Madison, 389
Wesley, John, 12

Westminster Confession of Faith,
    193
Wheeler, Lysander, 315
Wheelock, Edwin Miller, 79
Whig Party, xvii, 4, 33–34, 35, 36,
    48, 57, 59, 116, 295, 296,
    300, 301, 303, 340, 420,
    434n29
Whipple, Charles King, 134–35,
    137, 278, 280, 281
White, John Crokar, 162
White, Richard Grant,
    479n178
white supremacy, 213, 348,
    372–73, 406. *See also*
    Democratic Party: and
    racism; racism
Whittier, John Greenleaf, 165, 371
  "Laus Deo!," 371
Wilderness Campaign (1864), 262,
    276
Wiley, Calvin, 34
Willey, Waitman T., 460n10
Williams, John L., 132–33, 137
Wilmot, David, 164
Wilmot Proviso, 212
Wilson, Edmund, xiv
Wilson, Henry, 152, 254, 282, 354
Wilson, James, 5
Wilson, William, 146–47, 148,
    357, 457n65
Wilson's Creek, Battle of (1861),
    129
Winthrop, Robert, 339–40
Wisconsin, 72, 136, 157, 216
Wisner, William, 33–34
Witherspoon, John, 5, 16–17
Wittenburg College, 228
Women's Loyal League, 352
Wood, Benjamin, 213, 330

Index

Wood, Fernando, 124, 213, 232, 233, 238, 257, 323, 342
Woodbury, Charles Levi, 322
Woodward, George W., 224
workingmen, 169, 229–30, 231, 331, 335
Wright, Erastus, 125–26, 133, 282
Wright, Fanny, 35
Wright, Joseph A., 460n10

"Yankee" culture and opposition to, 26–27, 28–29, 31–32, 34, 35, 64, 233, 373, 378, 420
Yates, Richard, 191, 251
YMCA, 128, 354

Zabriskie, Francis, 288
Zacharie, Isaachar, 361

ILLUSTRATION CREDITS

PAGES

192 John Hay Library, Brown University
246 (top) Library of Congress
246 (bottom) Library Company of Philadelphia
260 (top and bottom) Abraham Lincoln Presidential Library & Museum
293 Library of Congress
382 Broadside, Inaugural address of President Abraham Lincoln.
4 March 1865 (The Gilder Lehrman Institute of American History,
GLC06044)

PHOTO INSERT

PAGES

1 (top left) Library of Congress; (top right) Library of Congress;
(bottom left) Library of Congress; (bottom right) Library of Congress
2 (top left) Abraham Lincoln Papers, Library of Congress; (top right) Abraham
Lincoln Papers, Library of Congress; (bottom left) Photograph, John
Fremont as Major General (The Gilder Lehrman Institute of American
History, GLC05111.02.0378); (bottom right) Library of Congress
3 (top left) Library Company of Philadelphia; (top right) Presbyterian
Historical Society, Philadelphia; (center left) Chicago History Museum,
ICHi-059595; C. D. Mosher, photographer; (center right) Author's personal
copy (*Cyclopedia of Methodism*); (bottom) Haverford College Quaker &
Special Collections
4 (top left) Library Company of Philadelphia; (top center) Library Company of
Philadelphia; (top right) Library Company of Philadelphia;
(bottom left) Library of Congress; (bottom center) New York Public Library;
(bottom right) Library of Congress
5 (top) Henry E. Huntington Library, San Marino, California;
(center left) Library of Congress; (bottom left) Scene in Richmond, Virginia,
Albert and Shirley Small Special Collections Library, University of Virginia;
(bottom right) Photograph, William G Brownlow (The Gilder Lehrman
Institute of American History, GLC05111.02.0104)
6 (top left) Library of Congress; (top right) Library Company of Philadelphia;
(center) Library of Congress; (bottom left) Portrait of Henry Clay Dean, State
Historical Society of Iowa, Des Moines; (bottom center) C. Chauncey Burr,
by John Sartain, Philadelphia Academy of the Fine Arts. Bequest of Dr. Paul J.
Sartain; (bottom right) Houghton Library, Harvard University
7 (top left) Author's personal copy; (top center) Author's personal copy;
(top right) Library of Congress; (bottom left) Library of Congress;
(bottom right) Library of Congress
8 (top) Library of Congress; (bottom left) Library of Congress;
(bottom right) Photograph, Lincoln's funeral parade on Chestnut St.,
Philadelphia, 1865 (The Gilder Lehrman Institute of American History,
GLC05136.38)

A NOTE ABOUT THE AUTHOR

Richard Carwardine is the author of *Lincoln: A Life of Purpose and Power*, winner of the Lincoln Prize; *Lincoln's Sense of Humor*, winner of the Abraham Lincoln Institute Book Prize; and *Evangelicals and Politics in Antebellum America*. He received the Order of Lincoln, the state of Illinois's highest civilian honor, in 2009. In Queen Elizabeth's Birthday Honours of 2019 he was made CMG (Companion of St. Michael and St. George) for services to American History in the U.K. and U.S.A. He is Emeritus Rhodes Professor of American History and Distinguished Fellow of the Rothermere American Institute at Oxford University.

A NOTE ON THE TYPE

This book was set in Janson, a typeface long thought to have been made by the Dutchman Anton Janson, who was a practicing typefounder in Leipzig during the years 1668–1687. However, it has been conclusively demonstrated that these types are actually the work of Nicholas Kis (1650–1702), a Hungarian, who most probably learned his trade from the master Dutch typefounder Dirk Voskens. The type is an excellent example of the influential and sturdy Dutch types that prevailed in England up to the time William Caslon (1692–1766) developed his own incomparable designs from them.

Composed by North Market Street Graphics,
Lancaster, Pennsylvania

Printed and bound by Berryville Graphics,
Berryville, Virginia